AMERICAN NATIONAL
GOVERNMENT

Institutions, Policy, and Participation

FOURTH EDITION

AMERICAN NATIONAL
GOVERNMENT
Institutions, Policy, and Participation

FOURTH EDITION

Robert S. Ross
California State University, Chico

Study Guide by

Donald C. Williams
Western New England College

Brown & Benchmark
PUBLISHERS

Madison, WI Dubuque   Guilford, CT Chicago   Toronto London
Mexico City Caracas   Buenos Aires Madrid   Bogotá Sydney

Book Team

Sponsoring Editor *Scott Spoolman*
Managing Editor *John S. L. Holland*
Production Manager *Brenda S. Filley*
Managing Art Editor *Pamela Carley*
Editor/Art Editor *Catherine G. Leonard*
Designer *Charles Vitelli*
Permissions Coordinator *Janice M. Ward*
Typesetting Supervisor *Libra Ann Cusack*
Typesetter *Juliana Arbo*
Proofreader *Diane Barker*
Graphics *Lara M. Johnson*
Marketing Manager *Kirk Moen*

PUBLISHERS

Vice President of Production and Business Development *Vickie Putman*
Vice President of Sales and Marketing *Bob McLaughlin*
Director of Marketing *John Finn*

A Times Mirror Company

Cover Photo *Comstock Inc.*
Cover Design *Charles Vitelli*
Research by *Pamela Carley*

Library of Congress Catalog Card Number: 95-83215

ISBN 1-56134-409-5

Printed in the United States of America
by Times Mirror Higher Education Group, Inc.
2460 Kerper Boulevard, Dubuque, IA 52001

10 9 8 7 6 5 4 3 2 1

Preface

There could hardly be a more apt portrayal of American politics at the end of the twentieth century than the ancient Chinese curse, "May you live in interesting times." The election of President Bill Clinton in 1992 portended a major upheaval in "business as usual" in Washington. One personification of the change was poet Maya Angelou, who composed and read a poem at Clinton's inauguration ceremony: In 1961 the inaugural poet had been a white man; in 1993 it was a black woman. In later weeks, Clinton named four women, four African Americans, two Latinos, and an Asian American to his cabinet.

But within two years after his election, even more dramatic changes were in the making: Republicans had regained control of Congress after decades of Democratic rule, and they had promptly attempted to restructure the scope and direction of American government. In an atmosphere of such sharp and frequent redirection, we face the difficult task of separating the transient and ephemeral from the significant and long-lasting. Given the constant media attention to our nation's leaders, this is no easy task.

As an undergraduate, I remember coming across what seemed like one of the most ridiculous of political battles: The confrontation was between Carl Hayden, the 84-year-old senator from Arizona, and Clarence Cannon, the 83-year-old representative from Missouri. As Chairmen of the Appropriations Committees in their respective houses, they refused to meet during the summer of 1962 to arrive at a compromise spending plan for our national government. Hayden would not go over to the House side of the Capitol and Cannon would not go to the Senate side. The new fiscal year had begun without an adopted budget, prompting the *New York Times* to observe that the appropriations battle was really a "long-run comic opera starring two congressional octogenarians."

There was more to this struggle, as I was to learn later. At real issue was the relative power of the House and Senate in conference committee. For almost a year, the House had attacked the historical practice of the Senate to chair all conference committees and for all meetings to be held on the Senate side. The House wanted to alternate. Senator Hayden, speaking for the Senate, said they would agree to a compromise if half of the appropriations bills could originate in the Senate—by custom all appropriations had begun in the House. The House held fast, however, and eventually won. The chairs and locations for conferences now alternate between the House and Senate.

Much of what appears to be going on in government is not an accurate assessment at all, because we are distracted from the mundane by the dramatic; because we don't know what to look for; and because many of those in government do not want us to see things clearly. But fundamentally, our impressions of government are frequently inaccurate because of what we believe about how government functions. Consider the following:

- The Constitution provides that Congress is to make our laws, yet most scholars would agree that the executive branch has been the source of most of our laws in the last half-century. Now we face a Congress—the 104th—that has become the driving force behind new legislation. Is this a short-lived phenomenon, or has the fundamental balance shifted?

- A representative assembly from diverse geographic areas was intended by the Framers to filter parochial, local interests into a national interest, but Congress more often than not has focused on special interests to the exclusion of national concerns. Attempts by the new Republican majority to maintain a national agenda have been met by the same sidetracking interests that plagued the Democrats. Can any majority really provide national leadership?

- The public was to have an opportunity to assess the competence of their elected officials regularly, to allow for the easy replacement of those not measuring up, yet most incumbents are reelected. Even with the dramatic change in control of Congress in 1994, 90 percent of incumbents were returned to office.

- Reforms have been adopted to reduce the influence of money in elections, to increase the openness of the governmental process, yet money seems more important today than ever, and most decision making is done outside of public view. Republicans who campaigned on a promise of more open congressional dealings have nevertheless done most of their work behind closed doors.

The point is that although the study of American government can be confounding and confusing, it is necessary that we study it. In many cases it is easier to raise a question than to answer it, to describe a problem than to analyze or explain it. But then, what has one accomplished? This text, an introduction to the basic components of national government, will explore possible answers to the major questions posed. I believe that politics is concerned with making decisions that are binding on society as a whole and that individuals can and must participate in the making of these decisions. The emphasis here is on describing things as realistically as possible. Who gets to make what decisions and how those decisions affect other areas of decision making are discussed as an integral part of the structural components of the system. Students of American politics must understand the institutional framework within which policies are made, not only to fathom the complexities of how and why certain policies are adopted, but to find ways to alter policies with which they disagree. Therefore, institutions are presented in such a way as to show their contemporary functioning and their involvement in the formulation of public policy.

Contents and Organization

This book is organized into four sections, each logically deriving from and building on the previous one.

Part I: The Foundations of American Government

In chapter 1, I compare the 1992 presidential election with the 1994 congressional elections as a lead-in to the role of the individual in a participatory government, a theme that is developed throughout the book. Politics is defined. In chapter 2 the development of the Constitution and its basic principles are outlined, as is the role of the federal government in regional interactivity in chapter 3. Part I concludes with chapter 4, which discusses our civil rights and civil liberties found in the Constitution and their current interpretation by the Supreme Court.

Part II: The Structure of American Government

Congress is discussed in chapters 5 and 6. First its structure and legislative powers are outlined; then the individual member of Congress is considered—his or her salary, benefits, and committee selections. In chapter 7 the power and limitations of the presidential office are discussed. The organization and political impact of the federal bureaucracy are the focus of chapter 8, while chapter 9 covers the power of and political restraints on the Supreme Court.

Part III: The Process of American Government

Our major political parties are discussed in chapter 10—how they are organized and how they select and nominate a candidate for president. In chapter 11 the specific rules and regulations governing the selection of presidential candidates are detailed. In chapters 12 and 13 the focus is on the external influences on government policy making. In chapter 12 the influence of lobbyists and interest groups on bureaucratic decisions is discussed, and in chapter 13 we become aware of our political culture and discuss the impact the media and public opinion have on that culture.

Part IV: The Products of American Government

In chapter 14 a model of policy making is presented, focusing on agendas, processes, and conflict resolutions. Building on this framework for understanding how different policies are made, government economic policy is then outlined, using the savings and loan scandal as a thematic case study. The remainder of the chapter extends economic policy to the global arena, discussing U.S. participation in several international organizations.

Features

The analytical exercises at the end of the chapter have been expanded and revised in this edition. They call on students to be creative and thoughtful in offering solutions to practical and philosophical problems raised by the material. I have found that these exercises can stimulate learning through individual study or when used as the basis for class discussions or projects.

A new addition to this fourth edition is a complete, chapter-by-chapter Study Guide following the text. Each section contains a glossary defining the terms that were boldfaced in that chapter, along with highlights of the subjects covered and a thorough set of review questions. A selection of true-false, multiple-choice, and matching questions follows, with an answer key at the conclusion. I am indebted to Dr. Donald C. Williams of Western New England College for preparing this student aid.

Instructor's Resource Guide

The new edition of *Teaching and Testing with American National Government,* ably provided by Jack Waskey of Dalton College, contains the following teaching aids: a chapter outline, set of chapter objectives, glossary, chapter overview/teaching suggestions, an annotated list of supplementary readings, suggested uses for analytical exercises, and a set of suggested issues for classroom debate. Each debate topic includes a list of suggested readings, and one topic in each chapter is expanded into a fully outlined discussion.

Appended to each chapter is a comprehensive test bank containing more than 100 multiple-choice, true-false, and essay questions. The complete test bank is also available in computerized form for users of IBM-compatible and Macintosh computers on TestPak.

Final Note

I firmly believe that government is a participatory activity. I have served as an elected official for 12 years at the local level, a member of my party's State Central Committee for 6 years, and a campaign coordinator for state and national candidates. As a result, I have become aware of government's possibilities as well as its limitations. The strength of government lies in the knowledge of its members and their ability to act on that knowledge and their own beliefs. I hope that this textbook imbues students with a respect for government and a resolve to become active participants in it.

Robert S. Ross

Acknowledgments

I have accumulated a host of intellectual debts in writing this book. The sources of many theories and observations should be apparent from the citations in the text; for those ideas not credited to anyone, their originators may take consolation—albeit without fanfare—that their ideas have been accepted by another.

I am fortunate to have had a number of thoughtful scholars and friends share their insights into the workings of American government, often sending me off in new and productive directions: Danny Adkison, Louis Fisher, Conrad McBride, Bill and Joyce Mitchell, Ted Vestal, and my colleagues Ed Bronson, Chuck Price, John Sanzone, and Bob Stanley.

In preparing the fourth edition, I was informed by the thoughtful comments of instructors who have used the prior edition in the classroom. My thanks to Lydia Andrade and Constantine Danopoulos, San Jose State University; Donald Beahm, Doane Lincoln College; Carl Cavalli, North Georgia College; Paula Duda, Kutztown University; Greg Edwards, Reagan Hathcock, and Bill Stephens, Amarillo College; William Loiterman, Los Angeles Harbor College; Thomas Rhorer, American River College; David Roebuck, Bluefield State College; and Raymond Whiting, Augusta College, all of whom responded to the user survey conducted by Brown & Benchmark. Many of their suggestions are incorporated into this edition.

Getting from the planning stage to publication requires the considerable ability and tenacity of professionals. This book has profited greatly from the encouragement and guidance provided by my publishers. To Rick Connelly and Joe McGee I owe a debt of gratitude for believing that something worthwhile would come of this project. Editing the manuscript was acquitted with great skill and patience by Catherine G. Leonard, aided by the wise counsel of Managing Editor John S. L. Holland. I have tried to come up with someone to blame for any errors that remain, but, alas, they are wholly my responsibility.

This book is dedicated to

Nancy and Don Dayton,
for all the opportunities.

R.S.R.

Contents

Part II: The Structure of American Government

Study Guide

Chapter Outline

1

Politics, Participation, and Public Policy

Perhaps what characterizes political life is precisely the problem of continually creating unity, a public, in a context of diversity, rival claims, unequal power, and conflicting interests.

—Hanna Pitkin, *Wittgenstein and Justice*, 1972

Man's capacity for justice makes democracy possible, but man's inclination to injustice makes democracy necessary.

—Reinhold Niebuhr, *The Children of Light and the Children of Darkness*, 1944

Democracy is like blowing your nose—you may not do it well, but you ought do it yourself.

—G. K. Chesterton (1874–1936)

The two most recent elections have produced surprising winners; results no one would have predicted a year in advance. On November 3, 1992, William Jefferson (Bill) Clinton was elected our 42nd president. Seldom has a candidate overcome such odds to win major office. The popular vote showed Clinton with 43 percent, to 38 percent for George H. W. Bush and 19 percent for Independent H. Ross Perot. Clinton's electoral college victory was more sub-stantial—370 against 168 for Bush. Perot received no electoral votes. What is surprising in terms of presidential campaigns, which are usually launched years in advance, is that as late as August 1991, Clinton still had not decided whether to enter the race. Bob Woodward (1994), a *Washington Post* editor and well-known author, describes a conversation that took place at that time between Bill Clinton and his wife of 15 years, Hillary.

> "Well, you know," Clinton said, "a lot of people think this will be a dry run."
> "I don't," she said. "I think if you run, you win. And so you better be really careful about wanting to do this and making these changes in your life."

Not only did Clinton enter the race late, he faced significant obstacles. Hillary Clinton had indicated that he would need a high "pain threshold" if he ran (Woodward 1994, 18).

The euphoria of Democrats at having regained the White House after 12 years of Republican control turned, in 1994, to Republican euphoria as they gained control of Congress for the first time in 40 years. These dramatic swings in voter support suggest a turbulence, an unsettling of the political landscape. Taking a few pages to recount these recent elections provides some insight into our system of government. It also makes for some good stories—there is drama, heroic action, as well as bathos.

The 1992 Presidential Election

We elect our president in two stages, really: the first stage in which each party nominates a candidate from among a variety who seek their party's nomination; the second, a campaign for electoral votes to win the presidency. I will explore both of these in more detail in chapters 10 and 11. While the first step in the nomination process is in February of an election year, with delegates to a national convention chosen in Iowa and New Hampshire, candidates for president have usually been actively seeking the post for years. George Bush first ran in 1980, losing the nomination to Ronald W. Reagan, who had been campaigning aggressively since 1976.

The Democrats

Bill Clinton might have been unsure about 1992, but he had embarked on a political career early and probably intended to seek the presidency at some point. He had a distinguished academic career at Georgetown, was a Rhodes Scholar at Oxford, and then attended Yale Law School, where he graduated sixth in his class. He married Hillary Rodham, who graduated at the top of her class at Yale Law—you might say that he married up. After several years teaching law at the University of Arkansas, Clinton was elected Arkansas attorney general when he was only 30, and won the governorship in 1978, at age 32. Clinton brought in out-of-state specialists to assist him in government. The people of Arkansas were not impressed: they tossed Clinton and his carpetbaggers out two years later. This loss had a profound effect on Clinton. As one aide put it, "What he learned from the loss was that government officials, no matter how smart and idealistic they are, cannot decide what's best for the people and just do it" (Kolbert 1992, A10). He resolved to stay closer to the people, won back the statehouse in 1982, and held it until his election as president.

While Clinton was clearly one of the leading candidates for the Democratic nomination, there were other contenders, although none of the better-known Democrats, such as New York's governor, Mario M. Cuomo, chose to participate. One reason for the late start for Clinton and others was the anticipation of campaigns by Cuomo or other leading Democrats. The choice came down to Clinton; former senator Paul E. Tsongas of Massachusetts; Senator Joseph R. (Bob) Kerrey of Nebraska, a highly decorated war hero; Senator Thomas R. (Tom) Harkin of Iowa; and former governor Jerry Brown of California.

Clinton had moved to the front with superior organization and fund-raising, but he had to face serious charges of marital infidelity and draft evasion to avoid the Vietnam War. Nevertheless, he proved to be an aggressive campaigner and a tough one—he had, indeed, a high "pain threshold." He and Hillary appeared on CBS's "60 Minutes" to answer the marital infidelity questions. This broadcast was a harbinger of how TV was to be used in 1992: Get on free TV whenever and wherever you could.

After initial losses to Harkin in Iowa and Tsongas in New Hampshire, Clinton started to amass victories and delegates far in excess of the other candidates. One by one, the other candidates dropped from the race, to the point where it appeared over by mid-March. Jerry Brown staged a late rally, but by winning New York in May, Clinton had the nomination.

The Republicans

George Bush should have received a "free ride" in 1992: He had just concluded a successful war against Iraq; he was the incumbent president; his approval rating at one point had reached almost 90 percent. This is another reason, by the way, for the reluctance of some Democrats to mount a challenge. But, instead, Bush faced opposition from the right wing of his party. Many conservatives had never trusted Bush; indeed, he had spent much of his active political career trying to convince them of his allegiance. Patrick J. Buchanan, a former Nixon aide and political commentator, and, further to the right, David Duke, a past Grand Wizard of the Ku Klux Klan and state representative from Louisiana, entered the race. In 1988, Bush had made his infamous promise, "Read my lips: No new taxes." In the midst of the budget crises in 1990, Bush and Democratic congressional leaders had negotiated a solution that cut spending and raised taxes. Conservatives were furious. Combined with an economy in the midst of recession, the president had problems. Buchanan received an embarrassingly high 37.4 percent of the vote in New Hampshire, to the president's 53 percent. While Bush had forced both Duke and Buchanan from the race by mid-March, he had nevertheless taken significant "hits."

Enter Ross Perot

H. Ross Perot had made a fortune as a computer salesman. In the 1970s, he had gained notoriety by attempting to find MIAs in Vietnam and in securing freedom for several employees held captive by Iran. He had also headed a commission that studied and proposed changes in the Texas public schools. Appearing on "Larry King Live" two days after the New Hampshire primary, in which both Clinton and Bush had been bloodied, Perot said he would run for president if volunteers put his name on the ballot in all 50 states. The response was immediate: Several million Americans began carrying petitions and organizing on behalf of Perot. Free TV also boosted his candidacy. Brown had used a strategy of getting on every local talk show he could. Perot just carried this a step further. For the remainder of the campaign, candidates were clamoring to gain access to the King show, "Oprah," "Donahue," "Good Morning America," and even MTV. One reason these shows were appealing was a format that allowed candidates exposure to a segment of the electorate without having to answer the close, probing questions found on traditional news analysis shows, such as "Meet the Press" or "Face the Nation." Given the political weakness exhibited by the president, and the likelihood of the Democrats' selecting a wounded Bill Clinton, Perot was seen as an appealing alternative. Without running in a single primary or caucus, or even formally declaring his candidacy, Perot moved ahead of Clinton in the polls and at one point was ahead of the president!

The National Conventions

The Democratic convention in New York in June was well orchestrated and produced the expected "bounce" in the opinion polls. Candidates always get a lift from the continued exposure of a national convention. The polls after the Democratic convention showed Clinton up 20 points over the president—he had gone from third to first in one month. Much of that boost, though, came from the dramatic withdrawal of Ross Perot from the race during the convention.

The Republican convention in August was another story. Timing was off, so that major speeches did not come during prime time. What did show up on prime time were the spokespeople of the right wing of the Republican Party. In particular, Pat Robertson and Patrick Buchanan alienated many viewers with their harsh condemnations of those with dissimilar views. The Republican platform was also dominated by the themes of the most conservative wing of the party. (The platforms of the two major parties are compared on p. 238.) Bush did get some movement in the polls, but not enough to overcome Clinton's lead.

The Fall Campaign

The most significant variable in a presidential election is the state of the economy. President Bush had been assured by his economic advisers the pre-

Table 1.1

ECONOMIC CONDITIONS IN ELECTION YEARS

President	Term	Percentage Growth in Gross Domestic Product	Misery Index*
Nixon	1969–72	12.4	8.9
Nixon/Ford	1973–76	7.6	12.5
Carter	1977–80	11.5	18.2
Reagan	1981–84	10.1	11.4
Reagan	1985–88	14.0	9.7
Bush	1989–92	2.5	10.5

*Misery Index is the inflation rate plus unemployment at end of term.

vious year that the economy would be rebounding from recession by the middle of 1992. It didn't happen. Table 1.1 illustrates the growth in the gross domestic product and the "**Misery Index**" from 1969 to 1992. In 1980 and 1992, a weak economy was clearly a problem for the incumbent president. For Carter in 1980, massive inflation outpaced gross domestic product growth, and the crisis of Americans held hostage in Iran damaged his popularity as well.

Edward J. Rollins, who had directed Reagan's victory in 1984, called Bush's campaign the worst he had ever seen (speech at the Brookings Institution, November 5, 1992). Most serious political analysts would agree. The president seemed unfocused, and the campaign had no central theme: Attacks on Bill Clinton were its only message. Clinton, most would agree, ran an excellent campaign. With few exceptions, he was able to focus on a single theme of change, along with a corresponding attack on the administration for its economic failures.

But even an excellent campaign can be overrun by dramatic political events. Just when Clinton seemed to have things well in hand, Ross Perot reemerged as a candidate. Perot had kept his options open after dropping out, paying for "volunteers" to continue securing him a position on the ballot in each state. Perot's message was soon dominating the campaign. Focusing on the federal deficit, he claimed the other candidates were ducking the tough questions. Perot was invited to the presidential debates, which gave his message equal footing with the two major candidates.

The Election

Bush was not able to overcome the dominant criticism of his presidency: The economy was not responding and the president seemed to have no plan for dealing with it. Nor was Perot, who focused on this problem exclusively, able to articulate a clear plan of action. Clinton stuck to his original theme: Change. It worked.

Figure 1.1

REPUBLICAN STRENGTH IN THE ELECTORAL COLLEGE: 1968–1988

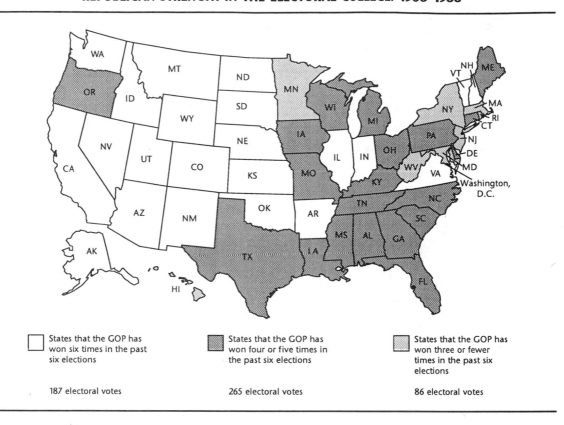

States that the GOP has won six times in the past six elections

187 electoral votes

States that the GOP has won four or five times in the past six elections

265 electoral votes

States that the GOP has won three or fewer times in the past six elections

86 electoral votes

The election broke the Republican Party's hold on the electoral college. James Carville, the leading Clinton strategist, said, "We just picked" the GOP's electoral lock (*USA Today* November 5, 1992, 1A). A look at Figure 1.1 shows the recent history of Republicans in the electoral college, with a solid base in the Rocky Mountain West and South.

Figure 1.2 gives the results in 1992. Clinton broke into both of these strongholds, taking five traditionally Republican states in the Rockies and six in the South. Combined with impressive wins in big states like California and New York, his electoral vote count soared.

Support for Clinton came from all segments of society. He won the overwhelming support of black and Latino voters, barely lost among whites, and also captured most of the votes of those making less than $50,000. Another important segment of Clinton's support came from younger voters. As in the past three elections, there was a gender gap: more women supported Clinton than did men.

Figure 1.2

ELECTORAL COLLEGE RESULTS FOR 1992

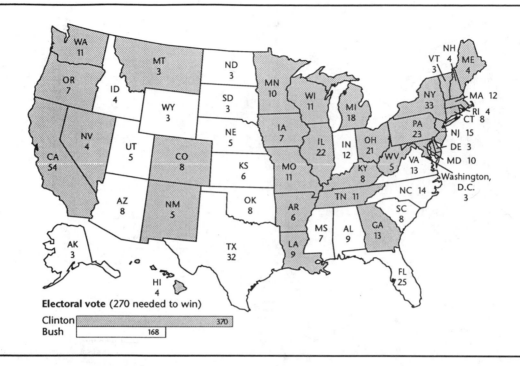

Electoral vote (270 needed to win)

Clinton	370
Bush	168

The 1994 Off-Year Election

While Clinton got high marks for the focus and organization of his election campaign, his presidency has been marked by a lack of both. Even an improving economy, along with the major accomplishments of his first two years—major deficit reduction, international trade agreements, and a major crime bill, among others—did not lead to increased popularity. Instead, the focus was on botched cabinet appointments, lingering stories of romantic liaisons, association with political scandal in Arkansas, and flip-flops in administration positions on major policy issues.

The party in power usually loses seats in Congress in **off-year elections.** Given Clinton's problems, losses for the Democrats seemed certain. Early predictions suggested that Democrats might lose 20 seats in the House and 3 or 4 Senate seats; instead, Republicans ended up winning control of both houses of Congress. Not since 1946 had the party in power lost more than 50 seats in the House! Not only did Republicans win control of Congress, they captured most of the governors' races and significantly increased the number of Republican legislators. If we look at Figure 1.3, we can see these changes. Republicans were especially strong in the South, winning a majority of House and Senate

Figure 1.3

1994 VOTE: THE STORY IN THE NUMBERS

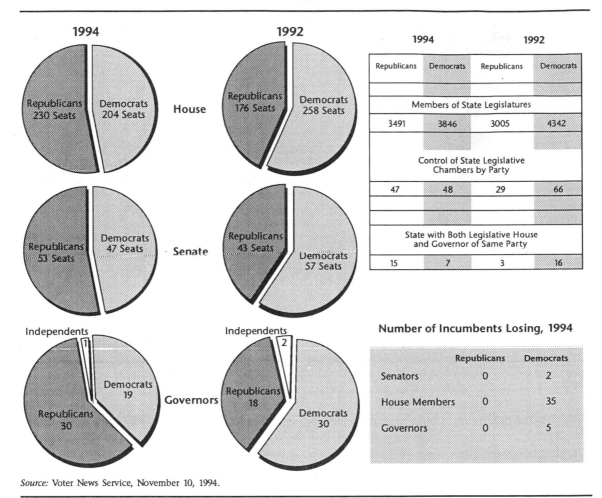

	1994		1992	
	Republicans	Democrats	Republicans	Democrats
Members of State Legislatures				
	3491	3846	3005	4342
Control of State Legislative Chambers by Party				
	47	48	29	66
State with Both Legislative House and Governor of Same Party				
	15	7	3	16

Number of Incumbents Losing, 1994

	Republicans	Democrats
Senators	0	2
House Members	0	35
Governors	0	5

Source: Voter News Service, November 10, 1994.

seats and governorships for the first time since Reconstruction. Later, in chapter 10, I will explore whether the Republican Party has become the new majority party in the United States.

Table 1.2 gives us some idea of the main strength of this Republican victory. There was still a gender gap—54 percent of women voted Democratic and 57 percent of men voted Republican. This is even more pronounced among younger voters: 60 percent of young men voted Republican, while 58 percent of young women voted Democratic. Minorities still supported Democrats, and for African Americans it was overwhelming: 92 percent. The major swing, then, between 1992 and 1994 was the result of more young white males voting Republican—63 percent in 1994. Of great importance also was the swing of Perot voters to the Republicans in 1994.

Table 1.2

EXIT POLLS

How Americans Voted in the 1994 Race for the House

	Republican	Democratic
All	51%	49%
Males	57%	43%
Females	46%	54%
Whites	58%	42%
Blacks	8%	92%
Non–high school graduates	40%	60%
High school graduates	52%	48%
College graduates	55%	45%
Postgraduate study	42%	58%
Talk-radio listeners	64%	36%
Gun owners	69%	31%
Crime victims	53%	47%
Contributors to Perot's "United We Stand"	69%	31%

Do You Want the President and the Congress to Be of the Same Party?
Same		54%
Different		34%

Source: Exit poll of 10,210 voters taken on Nov. 8, 1994, by Voter News Service. Margin of error is ±1.5%.

Republicans were able to unseat the Speaker of the House, Thomas S. Foley (D-WA), first elected to Congress in 1964; Dan Rostenkowski (D-IL), chairman of the House Ways and Means Committee, who had started service in 1959; Jack Brooks (D-TX), chairman of the Judiciary Committee, whose first election went back to 1952; and other prominent House Democrats, along with Senator Jim Sasser (D-TN), who was expected to become the new Majority Leader. While the prevailing wisdom has been that "all politics is local," as the former Speaker Thomas P. "Tip" O'Neill stated (1987), soon-to-be Speaker Newt Gingrich (R-GA) orchestrated a campaign that emphasized a referendum on Washington and the Clinton presidency. The campaign also went after the Perot voter with its emphasis on an anti-Washington, anti–big government message. Washington and Democrats, who are associated with big government, lost. Voters were upset with what had not been done during the two years since 1992. In most instances, voters base their decisions retrospectively, on what happened or did not happen; they usually don't vote prospectively, on the basis of what they think will happen. Democrats paid the price for not delivering on the promises made in 1992, on the accumulation of resentments for having dominated Congress for so long; Republicans benefited, though they were responsible in some cases for the lack of congressional action.

These dramatic changes were in the hands of those who chose to participate by voting. A surprising number of Americans didn't! Participation in 1992 was by about 104 million, or about 55 percent of those eligible to vote, the *highest* since 1972. It had fallen to just 50 percent in 1988. Participation in 1994 was at about 39 percent, slightly higher than the 37 percent in the 1990 off-year election. We will begin our investigation of the American political system with the problem of participation.

The Problem of Participation

If decisions are being made that affect our fundamental well-being, most of us would want to take part in their making, to be a participant. "**Participation** refers to *actions through which ordinary members of a political system influence or attempt to influence outcomes*" (Nagel 1987, 1). In some societies, Saudi Arabia, for example, we would have to be members of the royal family or at least closely connected to them to participate in the political system; in other societies, such as Turkey, we would have to be officers in the military; and in China we would have to be high-ranking members of the ruling party to have an effective say in collective decisions. One of the major differences between the United States and most other countries is our commitment to place political decision making in the hands of a large number of the country's citizens. We call this type of system a **democracy**. One analysis of democracy found few stable, long-term democracies (Burns, et al., 1992, p. 25).

A system in which all of those eligible to participate get together to make the policy decisions themselves is called a **direct democracy**. In a large, complex society such as ours, however, all of us cannot spend our time doing public business. We would have no time to earn a living. So we designate some to make decisions and others to enforce the decisions. We call such a system, where we choose others to make decisions for us, a **representative democracy** or a **republic**.

In the United States, most decision makers are chosen by popular election. Those of us who are over 18 years of age and are American citizens are, with only a few exceptions, eligible to vote. The ability of most of the adult population to choose those who will govern them, in elections held fairly frequently, is an important aspect of the modern meaning of democracy. Another is that the choices must be meaningful ones. For this to be true, we will usually want at least two candidates who have some chance of winning.

Democracy includes more than elections, however. In addition to voting and choosing decision makers, we are also able in this country to try to influence the decisions that are made. This can be done in a number of ways. The full range of political participation is depicted in Figure 1.4. Based on the work of Lester Milbrath (1982), Figure 1.4 ranks the various forms of political involvement along a hierarchical continuum. At the lowest level of the scale is merely "exposing oneself to political stimuli;" "holding public and party office" appears at the top; activities such as wearing a campaign button, attending a political rally, and making a campaign contribution fall between. Note that Milbrath ranks voting near the very bottom of his scale, where it is classified as a "spectator" activity.

Figure 1.4

HIERARCHY OF POLITICAL INVOLVEMENT

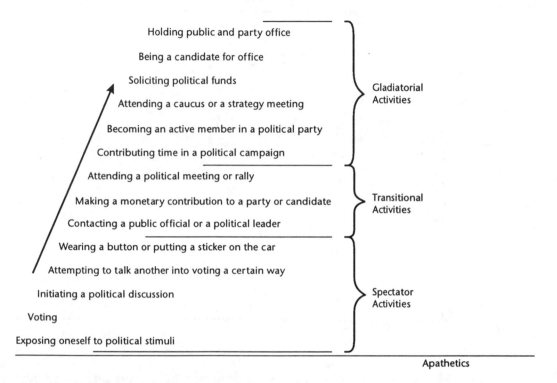

Source: Lester W. Milbrath, *Political Participation* (Lanham, MD: University Press of America, 1982).

According to Lester Milbrath, there are four distinct levels of political participation. At the lowest level are apathetics, who avoid all involvement with politics. At the highest level are gladiators, those who seek and hold public office. However, most people (approximately 61 percent) are political spectators whose most intense involvement with politics takes the form of wearing a campaign button or putting a political bumper sticker on their car.

Voting

Voting, then, is one of the least taxing forms of participation in the political arena. And voting data are readily available, easily analyzed, and can, if nothing else, help us see who does and does not participate in elections.

It becomes quickly obvious from an inspection of recent U.S. voting data that a limited number of Americans take the time to vote. As Table 1.3 indicates, only 38.7 percent of those eligible to vote in 1994 actually did so. The percentage voting in 1992, a presidential election year, is higher, just over 55 percent. (An election when the president is not being chosen, such as in 1994, is called an off-year election; participation rates in such elections are always lower than in presidential elections.) Still, the trend from 1960 to 1990 is clear. Fewer and fewer Americans have been voting. The increases in 1992

Table 1.3

**PARTICIPATION IN ELECTIONS FOR PRESIDENT AND U.S. HOUSE
OF REPRESENTATIVES, 1960–1994**

Year	Percentage Voting for President	Percentage Voting for U.S. House of Representatives
1960	62.8%	58.5%
1962		45.4
1964	61.9	57.8
1966		45.4
1968	60.9	55.1
1970		43.5
1972	55.2	50.7
1974		35.9
1976	53.5	48.9
1978		34.9
1980	52.6	47.4
1982		38.0
1984	53.1	47.7
1986		37.3
1988	50.2	44.8
1990		36.1
1992	55.2	50.9
1994		38.7

Source: U.S. Bureau of the Census, *Current Population Reports,* Series P-20, No. 440.

are explained by some as interest generated by a third candidate espousing
an antigovernment platform; the slight increase in 1994 over 1992 is probably
the result of the same antigovernment feeling. Even in the best years, participation was only about 60 percent of those eligible. This is a source of concern
to many analysts, citizens, and political leaders.

Because of extensive study, we know a great deal about the nature of
voters. First, a slightly higher proportion of women vote than do men. Second,
there are regional differences in voter participation. In 1994, participation was
slightly greater in the Midwest compared to the South, 49 percent to 41 percent. The East and West fell in between—45 percent and 46 percent respectively
(U.S. Census Bureau, *Current Population Studies* June 7, 1995). Age is a third
factor. Figure 1.5 compares the voter turnout across various age categories for
the 1990 and 1992 elections. As it indicates, participation increases as people
approach middle age, then remains high thereafter. This trend does reverse
itself after the age of 74—not shown in the graph—when participation falls,
although not to the level of the youngest voters.

Education is also associated with voting: the more educated a person is,
the more likely he or she will be to vote. Again using the 1994 figures, of
those with 8 years of school or less, only 23 percent reported voting, while
of those with four years or more of college, the figure was 63 percent. Employment is also a factor. The 1992 turnout among those who were employed

Figure 1.5

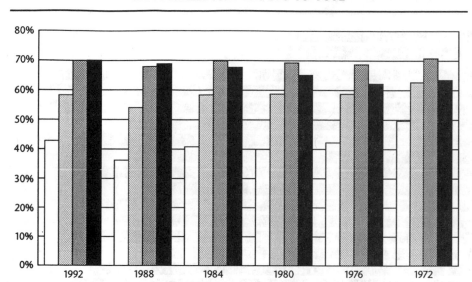

MOST LIKELY AGE GROUPS TO VOTE

Legend: 18–24, 25–44, 45–64, 65+

Source: U.S. Bureau of the Census, Current Population Reports, Series P-20, No. 440.

The percentage of eligible voters who actually turn out to vote is much higher among older groups of voters than among younger ones. Voters in the 18- to 20-year-old age group have the lowest participation rate of all. The highest participation rates are found among those aged 45 to 75.

was 64 percent; among those who were unemployed, it was only 46 percent (Stanley and Niemi 1994, 88).

The figures are rather depressing if one assumes that democracy requires full citizen participation. Indeed, there are some democratic countries that make voting mandatory—Australia, Belgium, the Netherlands, and parts of Austria and Switzerland. And even in those countries that do not require voting, the participation levels are much higher than in the United States, a problem that has perplexed political scientists for some time. A study of nonvoting persons in California (Ebeling 1988) provides some indication of why people don't vote. Respondents to a state-wide survey of 2,200 people gave the following reasons:

- 31.1% lacked interest in politics or the election
- 19.9% did not have enough time
- 16.8% were not registered
- 16.5% were traveling at time of election
- 8.4% gave a combination of other reasons
- 3.6% were new residents
- 3.6% had medical problems that prevented voting

Figure 1.6

VOTING TURNOUT WORLDWIDE: INDUSTRIAL DEMOCRACIES

UNITED STATES	1992	55.2%
UNITED STATES	1984	53.1%
AUSTRALIA*	1984	94.2%
AUSTRIA	1983	92.6%
BELGIUM*	1985	93.6%
CANADA	1984	75.7%
DENMARK	1984	88.4%
FINLAND	1983	75.7%
FRANCE	1981	85.8%
GREAT BRITAIN	1983	72.8%
GREECE	1983	80.2%
ISRAEL	1985	78.8%
ITALY*	1984	89.0%
JAPAN	1983	71.4%
NETHERLANDS	1986	85.7%
NEW ZEALAND	1986	88.5%
NORWAY	1981	81.2%
PORTUGAL	1985	78.2%
SPAIN	1986	70.7%
SWEDEN	1986	89.8%
SWITZERLAND	1985	48.9%
WEST GERMANY	1983	89.1%

Source: Congressional Research Service.

The United States has one of the lowest average voting turnout rates among modern industrial democracies. Only one-half of all eligible American voters have voted in recent national elections. In contrast, the turnout rate in most other Western nations is between 70 and 90 percent, as shown above.

When asked what might induce their participation, respondents cited registration just before the election (rather than the current 30 days used in most states), receiving help at the polls, lengthening the hours for voting, voting by mail, and placing fewer issues on the ballot (IV–25). Most of these structural changes have been proposed by reformers at one time or another.

There are several explanations for why people choose to participate in politics. One is that their participation increases as their stake in the community increases. Those with the most to gain or lose take the most active part in political decision making. The classic statement of this position is by E. E. Schattschneider (1960), whose study of politics, called appropriately *The Semisovereign People*, suggests that about 60 to 65 percent of the people have a vested interest in public business; the rest do not, and therefore do not take the time to participate. Lester Milbrath groups people into three basic cate-

Drawing by Ziegler; © 1995 The New Yorker Magazine, Inc.

"Don't ask, don't tell, don't give a crap—that's my contract with America."

gories: those who are nonvoters or apathetic (25 percent of the population); spectators (61 percent); and those active in politics (14 percent) (see Figure 1.4). In a more recent analysis of the American electorate, W. Russell Neuman (1986) divides us into three publics: those who do not monitor politics at all (about 20 percent); those who are active and attentive (about 5 percent); and the rest in the middle.

Over a period of time, different analysts have come to roughly the same conclusions. There is a small group that spends considerable time and energy on political matters, another that spends none at all, and a large middle group that spends a minimal amount of time. (When we analyze parties in chapter 10, I will note that the great challenge of political organizations is to mobilize or activate this group in the middle.)

Cases of Effective Participation

Aside from fulfilling a civic duty, why should we take the time to participate? What difference can our vote or political action make? We have been considering participation in the aggregate—large groups or categories of individuals acting or not acting in politics. However, groups do not act; people do. They may be acting on their own, or as representatives of a group, but the individuals are those who participate, decide questions, and attempt to mobilize others. The impact of an individual should not be underestimated. Let me sketch three cases to illustrate the point.

Massachusetts militiamen firing into the ranks of Shays's rebels. Engraving from Richard Devens, *Our First Century* (1878).

There are many stories of individuals who have an impact on our public life. They may choose to become politicians, hold elected office, gain appointment to the court or to positions in government service, or, by virtue of their positions, have an impact on public policy. Three individuals who have had such an impact despite *not* holding formal office are Daniel Shays, Rosa Parks, and Ralph Nader.

Daniel Shays: Revolutionary Hero and Rebel

Daniel Shays fought in the Revolutionary War and rose to the rank of captain in the 5th Massachusetts Regiment in 1777, when he was 30 years old. After the war he settled in Pelham, Massachusetts, and earned his living as a farmer.

Economic conditions deteriorated after the war, in part because the United States was no longer able to count on easy access to Great Britain's markets. One consequence was the inability of farmers to make enough money to pay for their supplies or to repay debts.

In the 1780s, the collection of debt in Massachusetts was handled by the Courts of Common Pleas. Merchants were able to use these courts to their advantage. In early 1784, Daniel Shays "was hauled into court by John Johnson for a twelve pound debt" (Szatmary 1980, 66). Later the same year another merchant prosecuted Shays for a three pound debt. The courts were thus seen by those in debt as a hostile institution. There was also a regional dimension to the conflict. Most of the debtors were from the western part of the state, with the merchants concentrated along the eastern seaboard.

When economic conditions became particularly difficult in 1786, farmers began organizing and attempting to shut down the courts. Their argument was that they were in the majority, and hadn't the Revolution been fought to give power to the people? This became what is known as Shays's Rebellion. Although Shays was a military leader, he never held a position other than being an influential member of Hampshire County's "committee of the people" (Szatmary 1980, 99). The merchants viewed the farmers' activities as a serious challenge. They also suspected that the British were supporting the rebellion. When it became apparent that Governor James Bowdoin was intent on crushing the uprising, the Regulators, as the rebels were called, decided upon an armed revolt. Thus, the action escalated from a nonviolent but forceful closing of the courts to prevent their use to collect debt, to a military action between the Regulators and the militia.

Shays, with a force of under 2,500 men, was defeated in several major battles by the state's militia, which at the time numbered 4,400: at the Springfield Armory on January 25, 1787; at Petersham on February 4; and at Sheffield on February 27. Shays and many supporters fled the state; except for isolated actions of intimidation against merchants, the rebellion was over by June of 1787. There are several reasons advanced for the collapse of the rebellion:

1. the election of the popular John Hancock to replace Bowdoin as governor;
2. the failure of the British to provide promised aid to the rebels;
3. the fact that many of the rebels left and resettled in western lands;
4. the improvement in the economy (Szatmary 1980).

Shays, now destitute, returned to Massachusetts in the 1790s to beg for a living. He played no further part in politics. But the revolt that bears his name was instrumental in the development of the Constitution. Political leaders from around the country were horrified at the prospect of a broader rebellion. This led many to favor a stronger national government, which was proposed at the Constitutional Convention in Philadelphia in 1787. There is some evidence, in fact, that the decision of many of the states to send delegates to Philadelphia was a direct consequence of Shays's Rebellion. Whereas only 5 states had been represented in Annapolis the year before Shays's Rebellion (see chapter 2, The Politics of the Constitution, p. 32), 12 states sent delegates to the 1787 convention in Philadelphia. In Massachusetts, Shaysites were in a majority at the convention held in Springfield in 1787, which was called to ratify the new Constitution, and which probably would not have been adopted had Massachusetts not ratified (Brown 1987). That it did, and the reasons why, are the topics of the next chapter.

Rosa Parks and the Civil Rights Movement

Rosa Parks rode the bus most days to get to her job in Montgomery, Alabama. So did about 17,000 other black people in the city, or about three-fourths of the riders. Parks would get on in the front, pay her 10-cent fare, and then often have to get off again and go to the back door before she could look for a seat in the colored section. That's because Montgomery's buses were segregated: the first 10 rows were for white passengers, the remainder for blacks. If there were blacks standing, and the white section was not full, blacks could not use those seats; but if the white section was full, blacks would have to vacate their seats to make room for white riders. That was the law. And it was enforced—by the white drivers, known for their disparaging treatment of black riders, and the police, if they were called.

On December 1, 1955, Rosa Parks finished work at the Montgomery Fair, the leading department store, where she was a tailor's assistant, did some shopping in the downtown area, and then waited for the Cleveland Ave. bus. When it came she got on, paid her fare, and sat in the first row of the colored section. In a short while the bus was full, blacks were standing in the back, and now a white man was also standing without a seat. The driver, James Blake, called for the four blacks in the first rear row to move—they could not even sit in the same row with a white! No one moved. Blake called out, "You all better make it light on yourselves and let me have those seats." Three moved, but not Rosa Parks. "Look, woman," said Blake, "I told you I wanted the seat. Are you going to stand up?" "No, I'm not," said Mrs. Parks (Siegel 1992, 13). Police were called; Parks was removed from the bus, arrested, and taken to jail. Word spread quickly through the black community. E. D. Nixon, a railroad porter and local head of the National Association for the Advancement of Colored People (NAACP), got a local attorney, Clifford Durr, a white opponent of segregation, to secure Parks's release on $100 bail.

This was not the first time a black had been arrested for failing to stand, but it was the time when a number of forces came together to make it a historic one; she "had been tracked down by the Zeitgeist—the spirit of the time," claimed Dr. Martin Luther King Jr. (*New York Times* September 1, 1994, 26). Local political activists, led by Mrs. Jo Ann Robinson, head of the Women's Political Council and a professor at Alabama State College, had been looking for a case to test the bus segregation law. Nixon and the NAACP were ready to challenge the status quo in Montgomery. And a cadre of young black ministers, headed by Ralph D. Abernathy of the Baptist Ministers Alliance, were ready to assume leadership. A meeting was held the next day at the church of a relatively new pastor in Montgomery, Martin Luther King Jr., where a boycott of the bus system was discussed. The Women's Political Council had already begun distributing leaflets calling for a boycott on Monday, the day of Mrs. Parks's trial. There was little choice for Montgomery's black leaders but to join in the plans for a boycott. It worked; few, if any, blacks rode the bus that day. Rosa Parks was tried, convicted, and assessed a fine of $10 and court costs of $4.

Rosa Parks had all the characteristics activists could ask for: She and her husband, Raymond, a barber, had worked hard all their lives. She was active in her church and in organizing youth groups in the community. And she and Raymond were committed to improving the lives of blacks, having become active in the NAACP. They were among the first blacks to be registered to vote in Montgomery, in 1945, after paying an $18 poll tax. In a recent editorial, the *New York Times* described her thus: "Seldom has such moral toughness come in a frailer-looking form. Seldom has physical courage spoken with a quieter voice or assumed a more modest manner" (September 1, 1994, 26). King wrote that "her character was impeccable and her dedication deep-rooted" (Holmstrom 1995, 14).

At a mass meeting on Monday night, the Montgomery improvement Association (MIA) was formed with King as president. King was already demonstrating the rhetorical leadership for which he became famous. Taking his themes from the Bible and calling for nonviolence, he said their work would not be finished "until justice rolls down like waters and righteousness like a mighty stream," words now engraved at the Civil Rights Monument in Montgomery. The boycott would continue. But people had to get to work each day and to school. Black-owned taxi cabs were used until forced to stop because they were charging only 10 cents, the same as a bus ride, and not the full taxi fare of 45 cents. The MIA organized volunteers into car pools, purchased their own cars when money was available, and coordinated getting people around the city. And people walked.

Montgomery's white establishment resisted fiercely: Parks and others were constantly threatened; she and others lost their jobs; homes and churches were bombed; cars from the car pool were cited for speeding; insurance was cancelled; every effort was made to prevent the boycott from succeeding. But succeed it did. In part, this was because an effective organization had evolved to move people around the city. In part, it was because blacks in Montgomery were ready to stand up to segregation, and in Rosa Parks they had an appealing symbol of a quiet, dignified, but adamant resister. And, in part, success was achieved because of the overreaction of the white establishment. I have mentioned the intimidations. On February 21, 1956, police arrested Parks, King, and 113 other leaders of the MIA for illegally organizing a boycott. What had been a local problem became a national one: The major media descended on Montgomery. Contributions now came from all over the country, even from abroad.

In April the U.S. Supreme Court ruled the segregated bus system in Columbia, South Carolina, unconstitutional. In June a federal district court in Alabama declared the Montgomery bus system unconstitutional. Still there was no willingness on the part of established leaders to end bus segregation; indeed, many joined the White Citizens Council, openly calling for suppression of the boycott. The Supreme Court upheld the district court decision; its order to desegregate the buses arrived in Montgomery on December 20, 1956. The next day, Rosa Parks got on a bus through the front door, paid her fare, and sat in the front seat of the bus. The boycott had lasted 381 days.

King and other leaders of the boycott went on to civil rights battles elsewhere, but Rosa Parks, now recognized as the mother of the civil rights movement, could not get her old job back. She and her husband moved to Detroit, where she did find work, eventually as an assistant to U.S. Representative John Conyers. She continued to speak publicly, and she continued to aid local young people. Numerous awards were conferred on her, including the Eleanor Roosevelt Woman of Courage Award in 1984, and streets were even renamed for Rosa Parks. Recalling that eventful day in 1955, she said, "I had made up my mind quickly." She would sit because "[I was] tired of being

Table 1.4

ORGANIZATIONS FOUNDED BY RALPH NADER AND HIS ASSOCIATES

Americans Concerned about Corporate
  Power
Aviation Consumer Action Project
Capitol Hill News Service
Center for Auto Safety Center for Public
Interest Law
Center for Science in the Public Interest
Center for Study of Responsive Law
    Bank Watch
    Freedom of Information Clearinghouse
    Harvard Watch
    Housing Research Group
Center for Women's Policy Studies
Citizens against Rate Hikes
Citizen Utility Boards
Clean Water Action Project
Clearinghouse on Professional
  Responsibility
Congress Probe
Congress Project
Connecticut Citizen Earth Action Group
Corporate Accountability Research Group
Disability Rights Center
Equal Justice Foundation
Essential Information
FairTest
FANS (Fight to Advance the
  Nation's Sports)
Multinational Monitor

National Coalition for Nursing Home
  Reform
National Coalition for Universities in the
  Public Interest
National Insurance Consumer
  Organization
Ohio Public Interest Action Group
Parents' Action Committee on Toys
Pension Rights Center
PROD
Professionals for Auto Safety
Public Citizen
  Buyers Up
  Citizen Action Group
  Critical Mass Energy Project
  Congress Watch
  Health Research Group
  Litigation Group
  Tax Reform Research Group
  Visitors' Center
Public Interest Research Group
Retired Professionals Action Group
Student Public Interest Research Groups
  nationwide
Telecommunications Research and Action
  Center
The Military Audit Project
Trial Lawyers for Public Justice
Voter Revolt

Source: D. Bollier, *Citizen Action and Other Big Ideas: A History of Ralph Nader and the Modern Consumer Movement*
(Washington, DC: Center for Responsive Law, 1989).

In the 30 years since Ralph Nader revitalized the consumer movement, he has almost single-handedly revised the concept of ethical and legal standards by which manufacturers, employers, and government itself should be accountable to the consumer, the employee, and the citizen. These organizations, founded by Nader, are the means by which proposals are made and legislation is effected.

pushed around, tired of the Jim Crow laws, tired of being oppressed. I was just plain tired" (Holmstrom 1995, 14).

Ralph Nader

In 1964 Ralph Nader was writing occasional pieces on automobile safety while attempting to practice what he called "public interest law" in Washington, D.C. Born to Lebanese parents, Nader grew up in Connecticut, went to Princeton University, where he was Phi Beta Kappa, graduating magna cum laude in 1955. He attended Harvard Law School, where he was an editor of the law journal and took an interest in Native Americans. He also wrote a senior paper on automobile safety. After 4 years of private practice, Nader went to Washington.

Nader volunteered his services to Daniel Patrick Moynihan, now a U.S. senator from New York, but then an adviser to New York's governor. Moynihan had also written about automobile safety. Nader also assisted a Senate subcommittee investigating automobile safety. This work led to a book on the topic, *Unsafe at Any Speed,* published in 1965, which became an instant success. It was critical of the automobile industry for paying more attention to the design features that looked good in the showroom than to auto safety. General Motors, for example, admitted to profits of $1.7 billion in 1964, while spending only $1 million on safety research for that year (Whitesides 1972).

Nader's major criticism was leveled at the Chevrolet division of General Motors and its Corvair models manufactured between 1960 and 1963. He thought that the Corvair, which had its engine in the rear, was unstable in turns and might roll over even when being driven under normal conditions. General Motors denied any design problems and initiated a public relations campaign to vindicate itself. In addition, the company hired private detectives to follow Nader to see if they could find anything to discredit him. Nader was subjected to subtle attempts to buy him off, to efforts to seduce him, and to harassing phone calls. The press joined in the fray and described the efforts aimed at getting Nader. In the end, the president of General Motors made a public apology before a Senate committee in 1965.

Supported by his book royalties and a half-million dollar settlement from General Motors, Nader created the Center for the Study of Responsive Law, a number of separate public interest law groups. Nader and his protégés, the so-called Nader's Raiders, have been directly credited with effecting a number of major pieces of legislation, including the Traffic and Motor Vehicle Safety Act of 1966 (because of this act, your car must come equipped with seat belts) and the Occupational Safety and Health Act of 1970. Much of the impetus for tax reforms enacted in 1986 came from the efforts of one of Nader's groups. Table 1.4 lists organizations founded by Nader and his associates.

Student activism in the late 1960s led Nader and his associates to help in the creation of Public Interest Research Groups based on campuses around the country. Beginning in Oregon, PIRGs now function in many states; student run and financed, they have been effective lobbyists for issues of interest to college-aged people.

Air bags provide an illustration of how Nader works. Air bags became the standard auto feature they are today because Nader got the General Services Administration (the agency that supplies and administers the national government's facilities) to require bids on government cars to include them. At first, no one wanted to bid; then Ford did, and since they were manufacturing them anyway, offered air bags as options on Tempo and Topaz models; Chrysler then did a one-upmanship and offered them on all cars.

Noteworthy recent actions have been stopping a proposed 50 percent pay raise for members of Congress and helping pass Proposition 103 in California to reform auto insurance. In battling the pay raise, he joined forces with the political right to mobilize talk-show hosts. This method of mobilizing popular opposition has, according to some political analysts, made talk-show hosts into significant political actors (Price 1989). Price's insight was made manifest in the 1992 presidential campaign, where candidates spent more time on such shows than on traditional news programs. And in 1994, talk radio became a significant player in the Republicans' gaining control of Congress.

Nader has not been without his critics, and not all of these are advocates of big business or corporate America. For example, liberals criticize his opposition to no-fault auto insurance. Nader and trial lawyers, the major advocates and beneficiaries of the current system, have joined forces over their concern for a citizen's access to court. A recent mailing from the American Trial Lawyers Association, for example, boasted, "From: Nader's Center for the Study of Responsive Law—Not a Trial Lawyer Document" (Spiro and Mirvish 1989, 28).

The Problem of Government

We have looked at participation, but in what are we participating and for what? So far we have looked at the choice of those who will make decisions for us, and at the influence of some in what those decisions will be. These decisions will be made by those in an institution we call government. What is government and why do we have it? James Madison, our third president and regarded by most as the principal author of the Constitution, stated, "If men were angels, no government would be necessary" (*The Federalist* No. 51). Government, then, arises out of man's imperfections. George Washington, our first president, is reported to have said, "Government is not reason, it is not eloquence, it is force; like fire, a troublesome servant and a fearful master" (Platt 1992, 147).

Aristotle, writing 2,500 years ago, saw a more positive side of government, or of the state, as he called it.

> When several villages are united in a single complete community, large enough to be nearly or quite self-sufficing, the state comes into existence, originating in the bare need of life, and continuing in existence for the sake of a good life. Hence it is evident that the state is a creation of nature, and that man is by nature a political animal. But justice is the bond of men in states, for the administration of justice, which is the determination of what is just, is the principle of order in political society. (McKeon 1947, 555–57)

Americans have harbored suspicions about government for some time. "I also believe," stated Henry David Thoreau, "that government is best which governs not at all" (*Civil Disobedience* 1849, 1). Even those in government are not immune to condemning it. "Government is like a big baby," Ronald Reagan stated in campaigning for governor of California, "an alimentary canal with a big appetite at one end and no sense of responsibility at the other" (*New York Times Magazine* November 14, 1965, 174). As president, Reagan was constantly frustrated by his inability to accomplish his objectives. "One of the hardest things is to know that down there, underneath, is a permanent structure that's resisting everything you're doing" (Rourke 1987).

While much of our attitude about government is negative, there are few areas of our lives for which we do not expect government support or protection. We depend on government for social, military, and consumer security, for safe water, protection in the workplace, a decent wage, and on and on.

With so many Americans viewing government as a necessary evil, how then can we explain the prevalence and continued importance of this institution? To explore this question, let's look at two rather simple stories.

The Tragedy of the Commons

Suppose that we live in a small village surrounded by a large meadow, and we make our living by raising sheep. We have no need for formal rules or organization. Each of us owns his or her own sheep, but the grazing land is held in common; that is, the land, or commons, belongs to and is available to all in the village.

Under such circumstances, each of us can maximize his or her own self-interest by adding to the flock. The cost of raising additional sheep is borne by the community, while the profit from the sheep accrues to the individual. The result is a rapid increase in the number of sheep in the village.

However, it does not take long for most of us to realize that allowing this process to continue unchecked will bring about disaster. Overgrazing will ruin the land; our commons will not be able to support any sheep! This is the tragedy of the commons: individuals acting in their own self-interest create a collective tragedy (Hardin 1971).

After a long day's work in the field, we all get together in the local pub and discuss the growing numbers of sheep and the potential hazard facing us. Helen, always one to speak her mind, castigates those who are letting their flocks grow and suggests we should all agree to limit our flocks. While this plan meets with the approval of most, Armand and Jill voice opposition. Armand is young and just beginning a flock. He sees no reason why he should be kept from adding sheep, since his flock is currently too small to provide an adequate living, and all indications are that he will be one of the better shepherds in the community. Jill's point is somewhat different. She has been tending sheep for some time and has been very successful; in fact, she has the largest flock in the village. Her point is that because of her skill she expects to be able to double her flock in the next few years. The discussion continues, with some finding merit in Jill and Armand's position, while others agree with Helen that the village needs to limit the size of its flocks. Finally, there is consensus that a limit must be placed; everyone leaves reasonably happy.

But a problem presents itself rather quickly. Virtually everyone, including Armand and Jill, has quit adding new sheep. Everyone, that is, but Jules, who is not abiding by the decision. Indeed, he has almost doubled the size of his flock since the villagers' agreement. Once again, the villagers gather at the pub, where considerable anger is expressed about Jules and his actions. Molly wants to build a jail and throw Jules in it; Bryan and Thomas want to run him out of town; Jennifer wants to confiscate his flock. Jules argues that while the others had agreed to the decision, he had not. And besides, he argues, there are no written rules and means of enforcement.

Jules's behavior highlights an important point. The village's system of voluntary compliance has created a situation where those who act morally, and limit their flocks, are at a disadvantage compared with those who act immorally, and increase their flocks. In other words, the system works to the benefit of those who break the voluntary agreement.

Interestingly, all of the solutions proposed by our angry neighbors would create a fundamentally different society from the one to which we villagers have been accustomed. Should we agree to impose rules and use force or sanctions to make sure that everyone abides by the community's decision, in formal terms, we will have created an **institution**, a formally established way of making and carrying out political decisions. This institution we call **government**.

As a voluntary association, our village has not needed a government. If, however, we wish to have a means of establishing and enforcing policies that will be binding on everyone, we must formalize the rules and regulations of our society. When citizens agree to this formalization, they give the government **legitimacy**, the belief that those making the laws have a right to do so. There are now two problems: what to do about the number of sheep we can raise, and how to handle those who violate our social decisions. What does our community do?

The Story of the Lighthouse

Now let's change the setting slightly. Once again we are residents of a small village, but this time we fish for a living. Indeed, we are located near one of the best fishing spots on the entire coast. Our harbor is quite adequate, but the entrance is narrow and treacherous, the coast frequently foggy, the currents tricky. All of us have had friends or relatives who have wrecked their boats on entering or leaving the harbor; some of them have died. One afternoon, as we all gather at the local pub, the topic of conversation turns to the problem of the gateway to the harbor. Andy suggests we build a lighthouse, which the rest of us find appealing. We agree to take several weeks off from fishing; contribute money, materials, and equipment from our own supplies; and build a lighthouse. And it helps! Indeed, it makes our location safe and attractive to others who fish the banks off our community's shore but who live farther down the coast where the harbor entrance is not as dangerous. Some of these people move to our village.

One afternoon, while we are again gathered at the pub, Rachel raises the complaint that those who have recently moved to our location did not contribute toward the lighthouse but take advantage of its usefulness. Josh, one of the newcomers, quickly volunteers a contribution that he suggests could be used for the light's upkeep. All of the other newcomers, except Homer, agree to make a similar contribution. Homer argues that while, for some, the light has made the harbor safer and the village more attractive, he had planned to come here anyway and, frankly, doesn't need a light to enter and leave the harbor safely. We decide to ignore Homer.

But the problem of Homer's failure to contribute while still enjoying the benefits of the light—we call him a **free rider**—soon grows: new people coming to our village side with Homer. Our voluntary system, like that in the story of the commons, breaks down. Soon none of those arriving want to contribute. What can we do? The light cannot be turned off and on at will, to be used only by those who paid. Matt suggests a tax on all boats using the entrance. Susan likes the tax but wants it to apply only to those who came after the lighthouse was built. The original villagers and those who have already paid agree to enforce a payment on all newcomers.

Collective or Public Goods

The problem posed by the lighthouse is a common one facing societies. There are some valuable goods and services that, like the lighthouse, cannot be bought and sold as individual items. These are called **indivisible goods**; if we have them, everyone can use them. Further, these goods and services can only be provided by the group; they are, as a general rule, too costly for individual ownership. The more commonly accepted indivisible goods include the following: defense against other societies; protection from violence within our own society; a monetary system; an economic infrastructure—that is, the basic things necessary for our economy to function, such as roads, safe harbors, and bridges; and, as Aristotle clearly saw, a system of justice.

The provision of such goods is one of the reasons why we have government at all. How we decide which of these goods to provide and how we go about providing them are questions each society answers in its own way by means of its own form of government. Some governments, of course, do much more than provide indivisible goods. Some operate on the premise that virtually all societal decisions are those the government will enforce. Taken together, what governments produce are known as **public goods** or **collective goods**. One of the most basic questions facing any society, then, is to decide just what are to be considered public and what are to be **private goods**. Where we in the United States draw the line between public and private action is central to a full understanding of the American system.

To illustrate the range of choices, let us return to the tragedy of the commons for a moment, which occurred because it was in an individual's self-interest to increase his or her flock at the expense of the larger society. Jamie proposes one way to solve the problem: turn the commons into private plots of land. There are numerous questions we would still have to resolve— how to distribute the land, how it could be transferred after the initial distribution, and so on. But notice one important consequence: It is now in the individual's self-interest to use his or her land productively. It no longer makes sense to add to the flock beyond the carrying capacity of the land. The individual's and society's interests are basically identical.

Another solution is offered by Carl. He suggests that we make the flocks a collective good, to be held in common like the land. We would face additional questions, of course. Are we to be compensated for the sheep we give up? If tending the flocks will no longer bring profit to us individually, how will we maintain our enthusiasm for the work? But notice that this, too, solves the tragedy. It would no longer be in any individual's self-interest to add to his or her flock and overgraze the land.

Both of these solutions raise the most difficult of political questions: How are society's decisions made, and by whom? How are people persuaded to accept them? Different societies have come up with different answers:

1. Birth: The assigning of the right to rule to particular families or racial groups.
2. Conquest and strength: The acceptance of armed force as the basis for leadership and enforcement.
3. Equity: The equal distribution of power and goods to all.
4. Leadership: Acceptance of the personal rule of a particular individual.
5. Merit: Acceptance of the principle that leadership should go to those with superior skill or talent.
6. Rational Choice: The notion that citizens can come together and decide on what is best for them.
7. Religion: The placement of decision making in the hands of a priest or prophet whose primary enforcement tool is the threat of excommunication or failure to attain heaven.

The Study of Politics

Political science is the study of how societies have answered these questions. It is also more. It is the study of government established on one of the principles above and the decisions made by that government. And as George Washington admonished us, governments are instruments of coercion: we follow decisions or we face **sanctions**. (A sanction is designed to prevent us from doing something or, if we have done it, to punish us.)

Political scientists have put forward a number of definitions to describe what they study. One definition that is popular was offered by Harold D. Lasswell. Lasswell saw politics as the study of influence and the influential, or, as his book is entitled, *Politics: Who Gets What, When, How* (1936). While this focuses our attention in the right area, some find it too broad in scope. My favorite definition is that of David Easton, who defines politics as the "authoritative allocation of values for a society" (Easton 1953, 129). **Authoritative** means that the decision is one people feel that they must obey. Values are items such as riches, fame, or positions of power that are in short supply and must be allocated or divided among people. So, let's get on with our study of how values are allocated in the American system.

Summary

Politics is basic to all societies. Once a society becomes large enough to require rules, and needs a way to enforce those rules, we have government. There is less need for compelling rule enforcement if citizens believe that those who make the rules have the right to do so. In this case we say the government has legitimacy.

The legitimacy of a democratic government such as we have in the United States rests heavily on citizen participation. Yet, as we have seen, not that many Americans actually participate in politics in an active way. This raises serious questions for our ability to govern ourselves and for the continued legitimacy of our political system.

Some argue that as long as the system is open to everyone, we still have democratic self-government. The vitality of competing groups keeps any one group from dominating and allows us freedom to participate in politics as issues of interest arise. Others suggest that those in power—that is, those who occupy key positions controlling the major institutions of American society—count on our lack of participation. If this is true, we are not so democratically governed as we imagined. I mention this now, but not because I intend to provide an answer. Rather, I challenge you to address this issue as you read on.

Analytical Exercises

1. Garret Hardin, the originator of the Tragedy of the Commons, has presented us with another morally ambiguous scenario, called the Ethic of the Lifeboat. Assume that there are about 200 of us on a ship that sinks. There is only one lifeboat, and it can accommodate only 50 people. The lifeboat is full, but there are 150 people in the water trying to get in. The water is so cold that those in it will not survive more than several hours, yet there is no likelihood of rescue for at least a day. You are in the lifeboat. What do you do?

- Attempt to get more people into the boat even though this might sink the lifeboat, with the loss of all lives.
- Now that the lifeboat is full, prevent others from getting in. It is better for at least 50 people to survive than for all to perish.
- Throw out those who are old, injured, or sick, making room for young, healthy survivors to come aboard. It is important to use valuable resources only for those with most of their lives still before them.

By the way, Hardin's choice is the second. He suggests that if you are bothered by this, then the appropriate ethic is for you to jump off the lifeboat, making room for someone else (Hardin 1974).

2. Games can be the source of considerable insight into political behavior. The advantages of living in a society under agreed-upon rules are portrayed in this rather simple game devised by Robin Farquharson. The rules are as follows: There are 5 players, each of whom is assigned to one of two groups in each round. One group is thus composed of three players (G3), the other of two

players (G2). Players are assigned to groups in a regular sequence; that is, a player would be in G3 for three rounds, then in G2 for two rounds. There are ten rounds, and in each round every player must nominate one group to win the round. The actual winning group is chosen by the banker, who manages the money, from among the nominated groups. The winning players each receive $10; the losers each have to pay $10. Assume that without any formal understanding among the players, they will always nominate the group they are in to win; the banker will always choose G2 to win. What are the results for each player after ten rounds?

Is there some way for the players to improve their performance? For example, notice what happens if the players make an agreement among themselves to nominate *only* the group with the majority of the votes. G3 is always the nominee; the bank must choose it in each round. Now calculate the return for each player after ten rounds (Farquharson 1969, 77–80).

2

The Politics of the Constitution

In these sentiments, sir, I agree to this Constitution, with all its faults, if they are such; because I think a General Government necessary for us, and there is no form of government, but what may be a blessing to the people if well administered; and believe further, that this is likely to be well administered for a course of years, and can only end in despotism as other forms have done before it, when the people shall become so corrupted as to need despotic government, being incapable of any other.

—Benjamin Franklin, in *Madison,* 1893

As the British Constitution is the most subtile organism which has proceeded from the womb and the long gestation of progressive history, so the American Constitution is, so far as I can see, the most wonderful work ever struck off at a given time by the brain and purpose of man.

—William Gladstone, 1878

The First Congress of the infant Republic of the United States was scheduled to convene in New York on March 4, 1789, but the first members of Congress faced obstacles to travel unimaginable today and had other occupations from which they had to extricate themselves. To be convened officially, Congress required that a **quorum** be present. A quorum consisted of an **absolute majority** in each house—50 percent plus one of the entire membership. The House of Representatives did not have enough members present to elect its speaker until April 1, and a quorum was finally reached in the Senate on April 6, when the ballots cast by the presidential electors were counted.

North Carolina and Rhode Island sent no representatives because they had yet to approve the new Constitution. For that matter, in several states only a very small majority supported the new Constitution: less than 55 percent of the delegates to conventions in Massachusetts, New Hampshire, New York, and Virginia voted for ratification. Clear anti-Constitution majorities at conventions in New Hampshire, New York, and Massachusetts were overcome only because of the strong leadership and effective strategy of those who supported ratification. These margins of passage were hardly overwhelming and have led some scholars to argue that a majority of the population was opposed to ratification (Bailey and Kennedy 1994, 178).

These were inauspicious beginnings for a government whose structure is basically the same today as it was then. Benjamin Franklin's cautious embrace of the new Constitution, which he had helped draft, reflects more than personal modesty. It reflects the mood of the times. In 1789 it was not at all clear that the new Constitution would work. There was not even complete agreement that it was needed.

How was the Constitution enacted? And how is it that it not only endured but became the object of such extravagant praise from so many sources, including the great British statesman, philosopher, and prime minister, William Gladstone?

Government before the Constitution

To answer such questions we must first examine the historical circumstances that led to the adoption of the Constitution. It was, after all, not the first governing document of the new American nation. It was the second. Some would say third, beginning their count with the Continental Congress even though no single organizing document was drawn up there. The first was the **Articles of Confederation**, adopted in 1781 by the newly independent American states just prior to the successful completion of the war with Great Britain.

The national government established by the Articles of Confederation was a very loose one described as a "league of friendship." Under the Articles, this league was governed by a Congress to which the states sent delegations. Each state had one vote, and decision making required the consent of 9 of the 13 state delegations. There was no independent executive or judiciary.

The government created by the Articles did have some notable accomplishments: it concluded a successful war with Great Britain, and it created a postal system. During the summer of 1787, even as the Constitutional Convention was meeting in Philadelphia, the Confederation Congress passed one of the most significant acts in all of American history: the Northwest Ordinance. Among other things, this far-reaching act provided for the equal treatment of new states from the territory northwest of the Ohio River, guaranteed government support of education in these states, contained a Bill of Rights, and forbade slavery.

Figure 2.1

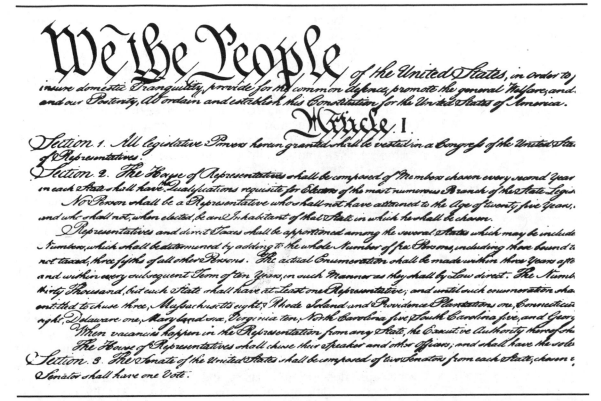

This is a portion of the original Preamble and opening articles of the Constitution. In the spring of 1952, Congress declared through the Joint Committee on the Library that the National Archives Exhibition Hall should have custody of the original documents of the Declaration of Independence, the Constitution, and the Bill of Rights. They are protected in filtered glass enclosures filled with helium and properly humidified. In addition, a vault of steel and reinforced concrete has been constructed under the floor of the Exhibition Hall, into which the three documents can be quickly lowered in case of emergency.

But overall, the new government proved extremely weak and generally inadequate to meet the challenges it faced. Among these were three particularly pressing problems that were to occupy the minds of the delegates at Philadelphia:

1. *Protection from foreign and domestic threats.* To present-day Americans, it may be "difficult to conceive of the international situation of the American states in the 1780s, when European aggression seemed both imminent and inevitable" (Riker 1964, 17). The British continued to occupy forts in the Northwest. They also controlled Canada, which they could use as a base of attack. Georgia felt the need for protection from Indian attacks and, along with South Carolina, felt the pressure of Spain waiting in Florida for the American experiment to fail. Commercial interests in various states wanted a navy to protect shipping.

Nor was foreign invasion the only military threat to the new nation. Domestic unrest was a continuing prospect as the nation's economic condition remained weak. Under the Articles of Confederation, such problems were the responsibility of the state governments. Many property and commercial interests, however, were skeptical of the states' ability to deal with threats of this sort. Their fears were greatly heightened by incidents such as Shays's Rebellion (see chapter 1, pp. 11–12).

In general, the national government under the Articles lacked the power to deal with military threats. Its only means of providing troops was to requisition them from the states, who had to provide them. If a given state chose not to do so, the Confederation Congress had no effective means to force the issue.

2. *Inability to raise revenues.* Just as the Confederation Congress lacked the power to provide troops, so it lacked the power to tax. It could levy "assessments" on the states but could not force them to pay. By the time of the convention, states were paying only about one-tenth of their assessments. The inability of the government to raise revenue was of particular importance, since debt owed to foreigners totaled over $11 million, while domestic federal debt amounted to about $42 million. In addition, the states themselves had an outstanding debt of more than $21 million (Bailey and Kennedy 1994, 187).

3. *Inability to regulate commerce.* Under the Articles, the states were allowed to enact their own commercial regulations. In practice, these tended to inhibit trade between states and favor states that had major ports such as New York. New York could impose a tariff on imported goods intended for New Jersey, and New Jersey had to accept the added cost or attempt smuggling. There was virtually no way to require that the two states cooperate. Further, states that shared a natural boundary had to agree to its use. George Washington, for example, was exasperated that his plan for a canal along the Potomac River was not supported by Maryland, which shared the river with Virginia.

The three preceding weaknesses in the Articles were a source of continuing problems. There was another. The Articles could not be amended unless all 13 states agreed. Thus, although many recognized the need for change, it was almost impossible to achieve.

The result was growing dissatisfaction with the existing government. An initial attempt to do something about the problem led to a call for a convention in Annapolis, Maryland, in 1786. The immediate impulse for this meeting came from the group of men—including Washington—who had been frustrated in their attempt to open up navigation on the Potomac. An insufficient number of states responded to this call, thus dooming the **Annapolis Convention** to failure. The delegates, however, resolved not to give up and, shortly thereafter, induced Congress to issue a call for a new meeting to be held the following summer in Philadelphia. Although expressly called for the purpose of "revising the Articles of Confederation," this meeting was to result in the drafting of an entirely new document, the Constitution.

The Constitutional Convention

Great political events such as the framing of the Constitution do not just happen. Even if people think something should be done, it takes a triggering mechanism, a catalytic action, to produce change. Shays's Rebellion was such an event. As Kenneth M. Dolbeare and Linda Metcalf describe it:

> Shays's Rebellion, that heroic and desperate act by a handful of farmers, is surely the dominant symbol of the period and in many ways the real source of the Constitution. It was the frightening, triggering event that caused a particular selection of delegates to be appointed by their legislature, induced them to spend a hot summer at an uncertain task in Philadelphia, and provided the context for their work and its later reception. For Hamilton and his cause, it was a godsend. (1987, 127)

And so the call for the Philadelphia Convention went out. Fifty-five delegates from 12 states responded. (Rhode Island chose not to participate.) For 16 weeks (from May 25 to September 17) they deliberated behind closed doors. This privacy was considered important, since the delegates were just as aware of public opinion and the influence of the media as we are today. In the words of George Washington, who admonished the delegates when a copy of the Virginia Plan was found outside the convention hall, "I must entreat Gentlemen to be more careful, lest our transactions get into the News Papers, and disturb the public repose by premature speculation" (Riker 1986, 91).

The Delegates

Historians often refer to the delegates as **Founding Fathers**; I prefer and will use the term "Framers" throughout this text. The reverence with which we speak of these men is testimony to their foresight in designing a successful instrument of government. Thomas Jefferson, who was in Paris at the time, called it "an assembly of demigods" in a letter to John Adams, then in London (Cappon 1988, 106). But they did not solve all of our problems, nor did some of their solutions work especially well. As noted political scientist John P. Roche reminds us, "Well over a million men had to die on the battlefields of the Civil War before certain constitutional principles could be defined—a baleful consideration which is somehow overlooked in our customary tribute to the genius of the framers" (1961, 819). Moreover, there is substantial evidence and a volume of literature to support the contention that the Framers represented a small minority of the population—an elite. Most were wealthy and had extensive land and commercial holdings, including 15 of the nation's largest planters and slaveholders (Dye and Zeigler 1993, 33). One noted political scientist called them "the well-bred, the well-fed, the well-read, and the well-wed" (Burns 1983, 33).

Undeniably, the delegates were wealthy and well-educated and certainly not common men. Most had been active in the Revolution; 39 of the 55 had served as representatives to the Confederation Congress; 2 were college presidents; and 31 had attended college in Britain or in the colonies, a rare privilege

Drawing by Bernard Schoenbaum. © 1991, The New Yorker Magazine, Inc.

"I may not know much about the Constitution, but I certainly know what I like. "

in those days. Most of these delegates were highly apprehensive about granting real power to the masses. Evidence of this attitude was the overwhelming rejection of the direct popular election of the president, a Supreme Court appointed for life, and the grant to state legislatures of the power to elect U.S. senators. And there seems little doubt that they perceived giving too much power to debtors and those without property as a threat to their economic well-being.

Nevertheless, delegates to the convention were more supportive of popular rule than the ruling elite in other countries were at this time. They chose, for example, to leave questions of **suffrage** almost entirely to the states, allowing them the freedom to retain their existing suffrage laws and placing no restraints on future changes. Most of the states had liberalized their voting requirements in the years prior to the convention. Georgia, Pennsylvania, and Vermont (soon to be a state) had granted the vote to all adult, male taxpayers. Under certain conditions, women could vote in New Jersey; when too many women began to exercise their franchise, New Jersey in 1807 repealed this right (Conlin 1993, 143). This flexibility in leaving the issue of suffrage open was recognized recently by Senator Bill Bradley (D-NJ) as the real genius of the American system. In a congressional hearing in 1991, Bradley stated, "The genius of the Founders was to construct a system in which participation could be broadened and each generation could create America anew" (*Congressional Record,* S15838).

In order to characterize the delegates to the convention it is important to understand several factors. Their high economic status was only one consideration; they were also revolutionaries, having fought in the Revolutionary War. Indeed, at the time of the Constitutional Convention, they were considered radicals by the leaders of most of the established governments of Europe. At the same time, they could be viewed as nationalists—men who were concerned with resolving the difficulties encountered with foreign adversaries under the Articles of Confederation. Furthermore, as Roche contends, they could be viewed primarily as good politicians, concerned more with providing a strong, workable national government than with securing personal economic advantage (Roche 1961).

The delegates were not, however, without differences of opinion. Some favored a strong central government (**Federalists**), and some opposed it (**Anti-Federalists**). The delegates' degree of political experience prior to the convention was of primary importance in shaping their attitudes in the dispute. Two noted students of American government have argued that for some of the delegates, the Revolution was a contest merely to establish a separate and independent colony, while for others, it was a *real* revolution, encompassing ideal as well as physical goals. "The Federalists were, on the average, 10 to 12 years younger than were the Anti-Federalists" (Elkins and McKitrick 1961, 203). The Revolution was the issue on which the Federalists had cut their political teeth and to which they owed their reputations. The Anti-Federalists, on the other hand, were older men who had begun their political lives in the colonies prior to the Revolution; they were interested primarily in retaining individual rights and preventing loss of state power to a national government. The Federalists were in the majority at the convention even if they did not represent a majority of the population.

The Proceedings

In issuing its call for the meeting in Philadelphia, the Confederation Congress had specified that the purpose of the convention was to amend the Articles of Confederation. However, this instruction was ignored almost from the outset as the delegates shifted their focus to drafting a wholly new document.

The Federalists captured control of the convention agenda (the issues to be considered). The Virginia Plan (sometimes called the Randolph Plan, but written in large measure by James Madison) was accepted as the basis for debate, and it called for a much stronger national government. Even the New Jersey Plan (the Paterson Plan), which suggested minimum alterations in the Articles of Confederation, provided for a national government stronger than the one that existed at that time. A stronger central government was seen as essential to solving the three serious deficiencies of government under the Articles of Confederation I mentioned earlier. Table 2.1 lists the key features of these plans; also included are the provisions of the other major proposal considered by the delegates—the Hamilton Plan—along with the comparable provisions of the Constitution.

SEPARATION OF POWERS   Most of the specific proposals concerning the structure of the new government considered by the convention came directly from state constitutions. For example, 9 of the 11 states adopted constitutions that separated the legislative, executive, and judicial departments. In some cases, the Framers felt the states' provisions inadequate and thus they modified separation of powers because, as Madison pointed out in *The Federalist* No. 47, "in no instance has a competent provision been made for maintaining in practice the separation delineated on paper." In other cases, specific articles were lifted directly from state constitutions with only minor adaptations. For example, the executive article was drawn largely from the Constitution of New York.

REPRESENTATION   Perhaps the most difficult issue to resolve was that of representation. The small states feared that the larger states would exert an overriding influence in the new government. This fear led to a compromise involving a **bicameral legislature**, in which there are two chambers, an institutional arrangement now used in 28 other countries and all state govern-

Table 2.1

COMPARISON OF PROPOSALS FOR THE CONSTITUTION

	Virginia	New Jersey	Hamilton	Constitution
Representation Lower House	Based on population and popular election (fixed term)	By implication,* Chosen by state (fixed term) with states equal	Popular election (fixed term)	Based on population and popular election (fixed term)
Upper House	Chosen by the Lower House from nominees of state legislature (fixed term)		Electors, chosen by people (to serve during good behavior)	Two per state, chosen by each state (fixed term)
Executive, selected by	Congress (fixed term)	Congress (fixed term)	Electors, chosen by people (to serve during good behavior)	Electors, each state to decide how chosen (fixed term)
Commerce, controlled by	By implication, national government	National government	National government	National government
Slaves, counted as	Not counted	Three-fifths person for taxation	Not counted	Three-fifths person for taxation and representation

*Implication: Not stated in document, but implied or suggested by a fair reading of it.

Source: Documents Illustrative of the Formation of the Union of the American States (Washington, DC: U.S. Government Printing Office, 1927), pp. 116–19, 204–7, 224–25.

The delegates to the Constitutional Convention in Philadelphia considered three major proposals concerning the structure of the new national government. The most important differences among these plans had to do with the structure of the legislature (Congress) and the basis for representation, the way in which the executive (the president) was to be chosen, and the counting of slaves for purposes of representation.

ments except Nebraska. Representation in the lower house (House of Representatives) was apportioned according to state population, with each slave to be counted as three-fifths of a person. The upper house (the Senate) was based on equal representation, with each state having two representatives.

ROLE OF THE EXECUTIVE   The role of the executive in the new government was also difficult to resolve. Should this office be entrusted to one individual? What powers should it have? How should the executive be chosen? And how long should the president serve? These were major questions. The delegates arrived at the answer to two of these questions rather quickly: the executive branch would be entrusted to one individual—a president—who would have considerable discretion. The question of how the president should be chosen, however, remained a stumbling block throughout most of the convention. More than a dozen proposals were considered, the most serious of which were that the executive should be appointed by the House of Representatives or that the executive should be elected directly by the people. In fact, on more than one occasion the convention voted for the former, but the advocates of the latter were able to whittle this support away by convincing delegates like Madison that it violated the concept of separation of powers. Those in favor of direct election, however, also knew they could not get the votes for their proposal, and so they instead supported the proposal for an electoral college to be composed of representatives from each state who would choose the president. This plan was one of the last items accepted by the convention. The method of determining who the electors would be, however, was left to the states. The length of term issue was tied to whether the president could succeed himself; when the shorter term—four years—was agreed to, the delegates also accepted presidential succession. On one point, however, they were in agreement: Whatever system was adopted, George Washington would be the first president.

SLAVERY   There were other important questions to be resolved. For example, South Carolina insisted that states be allowed to import slaves. As a result, a provision in Article I, Section 9, prohibited enactment of any law restricting free importation of slaves until 1808. (Slavery and where it would be allowed became the defining political issue of the nineteenth century; many would say we are still dealing with its consequences.) In exchange, the southern states agreed to allow the national government to pass navigation acts (prohibitions on foreign ships loading at American ports), a provision favored by the New England states, and to allow it to be accomplished by a majority vote rather than the two-thirds vote favored by the South.

The convention also took up the question of voting qualifications and eligibility. The delegates decided that these matters should be left to the states, with one specification: that those who could vote for members of the lower house in the state legislature must also be allowed to vote for representatives in the Congress.

Having agreed to the formation of a stronger national government, the delegates could compromise on matters of detail. As a consequence, most provisions of the Constitution are ambiguous because they were intended to be; they were so worded to avoid conflict or because the document was pieced together from divergent perspectives. Furthermore, emphasis was on the survival of the American colonies in the immediate future, not on the establishment of a timeless document.

The questions and decisions we have been discussing are those that evoked the greatest controversy at the convention, because the delegates were attempting to draw up a constitution that would define and delineate basic concepts about government and its relationship to individual citizens and to the states—concepts with which most of the delegates who stayed throughout the proceedings generally agreed. Benjamin Franklin's final plea on behalf of the Constitution seems to express the delegates' attitude:

By Burr Shafer, © 1960.

"It is unthinkable that the citizens of Rhode Island should ever surrender their sovereignty to some central authority way off in Philadelphia."

> I doubt too that any other convention we can obtain may be able to make a better constitution. For when you assemble a number of men to have the advantage of their joint wisdom, you inevitably assemble with those men all their prejudices, their passions, their errors of opinion, their local interests, and their selfish views. From such an assemblage can a perfect production be expected? . . . Thus, I consent sir, to this constitution because I expect no better and because I am not sure that it is not the best. The opinions I have of its errors I sacrifice to the public good. (Madison 1966 [1787], 653–54)

Ratification

Having approved the new Constitution, the delegates disbanded, and the document they had framed was presented to the Confederation Congress. The Congress, where the Federalists were well represented, then presented the document for ratification to state conventions called specifically for that purpose, thereby bypassing the state legislatures. This was a radical move indeed, but one which Federalists insisted upon, since in large measure their reason for a stronger national government was an attempt to undercut the growing power of the state legislatures. Article VII of the new Constitution provided that ratification would require approval of only 9 of the 13 states. As a result, ratification was possible even if the large states (Pennsylvania, New York, Massachusetts, and Virginia) voted against passage. Nevertheless, a new government without these states would probably not survive.

The campaign for ratification extended from September 1787 through May 29, 1790, when Rhode Island became the last state to ratify. The intervening period saw a vigorous political struggle between proponents of the new Constitution (the Federalists) and opponents (the Anti-Federalists). Writ-

Figure 2.2

Source: Library of Congress.

While Franklin's first famous 1754 "United We Stand, Divided We Fall" woodcut was done to dramatize his Albany Plan of Union, he did several other versions after the Revolution as a potent reminder that insistence on states' rights might well ruin prospects for ratification of the Constitution.

ing under the pseudonym Publius, three of the more prominent Federalists—Alexander Hamilton, James Madison, and John Jay—wrote and published a series of 85 articles on behalf of the Constitution. Known collectively as *The Federalist* papers, these articles, which appeared in the newspapers of the day, presented the major arguments in favor of adoption. *The Federalist* papers probably did not sway large segments of the population, but the arguments they presented were used by pro-Constitution forces in debates in several of the major state conventions. Today, they remain one of the major sources of the thinking that went into the Constitution and have become an established part of our political legacy.

Like the Federalists, the Anti-Federalists also sought to take their case to the public via the printed word. Long overlooked by scholars and the public alike, their views have recently been given renewed attention (see, for example, Beeman, Botein, and Carter 1987). Also like the Federalists, the Anti-Federalists wrote under pen names, using pseudonyms such as Brutus, Cato, John DeWitt, Sentinal, and "The Federalist Farmer." Brutus, for example, the pen name of Robert Yates, a disgruntled delegate from New York, railed against unlimited power to tax, failure to put a limit on the number of terms a member of Congress could serve, and failure to prevent the government from going into debt (Ketcham 1986). He could as easily have been writing in support of the Republican Party's Contract with America in 1994 as denouncing the document in 1788.

Figure 2.3

THE CONSTITUTION: A CHRONOLOGY OF EVENTS

1776
  July: Declaration of Independence signed
  Drafting of Articles of Confederation begins
1777
  November: Articles of Confederation submitted to the states for ratification
1781
  March: Articles of Confederation become effective when Maryland ratifies
1786
  August/December: Shays's Rebellion
1787
  May: Constitutional Convention opens
  September 17: Constitution submitted to Congress
  December 7: Delaware is first state to ratify the Constitution
  December 12: Pennsylvania ratifies
  December 18: New Jersey ratifies
1788
  January 2: Georgia ratifies
  January 9: Connecticut ratifies
  February 6: Massachusetts ratifies
  March 24: Rhode Island votes not to call a ratifying convention
  April 28: Maryland ratifies
  May 23: South Carolina ratifies
  June 21: The Constitution is adopted when New Hampshire becomes the ninth state to ratify
  June 25: Virginia ratifies
  July 21: North Carolina rejects the Constitution
  July 26: New York ratifies
1789
  June–September: Bill of Rights passed by Congress
  November 21: North Carolina ratifies
1790
  May 29: Rhode Island is the last state to ratify the Constitution
1791
  December 15: Bill of Rights ratified

While the Constitution was drafted during the summer of 1787 and ratified within two years, the historical origins of the new document extend back at least to July 1776 with the signing of the Declaration of Independence.

In many of the small states, victory was gained easily; in the large states, victory came only after considerable debate and maneuvering. Historian Richard D. Brown provides an account of the crucial moves to gain support in Massachusetts. In part, he notes, it was ratified because several opponents had left the convention, in part because the Federalists had won some support by superior debate.

> But it was their compromise maneuver, in which the previously noncommittal convention president, John Hancock, came out in favor of the Constitution with amendments, that was decisive. Perhaps 20 delegates [changed their votes on this alone]. (1987, 125)

Table 2.2

ORDER OF RATIFICATION AND VOTES UPON RATIFICATION

State	Ratification Date	Vote	
		Yes	No
1. Delaware	December 7, 1787	Unanimous	
2. Pennsylvania	December 12, 1787	46	23
3. New Jersey	December 18, 1787	Unanimous	
4. Georgia	January 2, 1788	Unanimous	
5. Connecticut	January 9, 1788	128	40
6. Massachusetts	February 6, 1788	187	168
7. Maryland	April 28, 1788	63	11
8. South Carolina	May 23, 1788	149	73
9. New Hampshire	June 21, 1788	57	46
10. Virginia	June 25, 1788	88	78
11. New York	July 26, 1788	30	27
12. North Carolina	November 21, 1789	195	77
13. Rhode Island	May 29, 1790	34	32

The ratification process occurred from late 1787 through May 1790. The first state to ratify was Delaware. Although adoption of the new Constitution was assured when New Hampshire became the ninth state to ratify on June 21, 1788, two of the most important states, Virginia and New York, did not endorse the new Constitution until later, while both North Carolina and Rhode Island delayed ratification until after the new government had actually convened in April 1789.

Ratification in Virginia was particularly crucial to success; after all, it was basically Virginia's plan. New York's ratifying convention was delayed by Alexander Hamilton, who hoped that Virginia would ratify and that news of her approval would overcome a clear Anti-Federalist bias in the New York convention. Key votes in these states centered on the question of conditional ratification (ratification subject to the incorporation of certain modifications) versus unconditional. In New York, delegates such as Gilbert Livingston and Zephaniah Platt, who were opposed to the Constitution originally, saw that New York could not stand alone. Even though they were dissatisfied with the document, they switched to the side of those who supported its adoption. The votes were 88–80 in Virginia and 31–29 in New York in favor of unconditional ratification. The vote for final passage, as shown in Table 2.2, was by a wider margin in both of these states. Often, the most controversial issue in legislative bodies is a key question—a vote to amend a particular section of a bill—that is decided prior to the vote on final passage.

When New Hampshire became the ninth state to give the Constitution its stamp of approval, the Confederation Congress set into motion the machinery that would effectuate the new government as of March 4, 1789. North Carolina did not formally join the Union until the end of that year, and Rhode Island waited until more than a year later—induced in part by the threat of a tariff against its goods if it did not join.

The Bill of Rights

Massachusetts and Virginia had agreed to ratification only after a side agreement—not part of the basic agreement, but something to which participants are pledged—had been reached that the first order of business under the new Constitution would be to draft and adopt a bill of rights. Protection of individual liberties was not so much the question (several protections had been included in Article I, Sections 9 and 10, of the Constitution). But whether specific kinds of liberties were implied or needed to be enumerated was an issue. James Madison felt there was no need to list every type; Thomas Jefferson, writing from his diplomatic post in Paris, disagreed.

The amendments that would protect these liberties were introduced in the House by James Madison. Considerable discussion and debate centered around the propriety of amending the Constitution so soon after its ratification, and around the question of whether the proposed changes should be incorporated into the original document or be added separately at the end. Madison had circulated a proposed list of 42 rights, 26 of which were incorporated into what became the first 10 amendments. Actually, 12 amendments were submitted to the states for approval (Lutz 1991, 12). Amendments 3 through 12 were the first 10 to be approved and became the **Bill of Rights**.[1] The first 8 of these amendments form the basis of individual rights: 4 are substantive (for example, freedom of speech) and 4 are procedural (such as the right to trial by jury). Amendments 9 and 10 provide for general protection—the first for those rights not enumerated in the Constitution and the second for states' rights. I will discuss these in more detail in chapter 4.

Acceptance of the Bill of Rights on December 15, 1791, ended this period of constitution making. Since then, we have had to deal with the interpretation of the provisions of this document: The extent of national power, the relationship of the three major branches to each other, and the scope of individual liberties.

Constitution by Procedure

Our Constitution has survived for so long primarily because the document we adopted in 1789 is procedural. It sets out the rules for *how* things are to be done—the time and place of elections, who may hold office, for how long, which institution makes which decisions, and so on.

---

1. Not all amendments proposed by Congress have been ratified. Of the first 12 offered in 1789, the two amendments that were not ratified (1) provided for increases in population by setting minimum numbers of representatives and (2) prohibited pay increases for Congress from taking effect until after the next scheduled election. In 1992, this latter amendment was ratified, making it the Twenty-seventh Amendment. In the early 1800s, an amendment rescinding the citizenship of any American who accepted a title of nobility or other honor from a foreign power failed to be ratified. Just prior to the Civil War, Congress adopted an amendment prohibiting limits on state authority that failed ratification. More recently, two amendments proposed by Congress—the Equal Rights Amendment (ERA) and one granting statehood to the District of Columbia—were not ratified.

Figure 2.4

POGHKEEPSIE
July 2d, 1788.

JUST ARRIVED
BY EXPRESS,

The Ratification of the New Conftitution by the
Convention of the State of Virginia, on Wed-
nefday the 25th June, by a majority of 10 ; 88
agreeing, and 78 diffenting to its adoption.

Source: Rare Book Division, New York Public Library.

When news reached New York that Virginia had ratified, the Federalists automatically had more than the requisite nine states for ratification. With the Anti-Federalists outflanked, New York shortly followed suit.

In contrast, most of our state constitutions and the constitutions of other nations are substantive. A substantive document specifies *what* is to be done. For example, many state constitutions contain provisions specifying tax rates, spelling out rights and privileges of citizens in detail, and requiring the government to have a balanced budget. The California experience is illustrative of substantive constitution making; whenever changes are needed to bring policy in line with social changes, the document has had to be changed. Thus, Californians find themselves faced with as many as a dozen constitutional amendments each election year (Price and Bell 1996, 103).

The procedurally oriented federal Constitution has required very little alteration even in the face of changing social and political conditions. If we consider the first 10 amendments—the Bill of Rights—as effectively part of the original document, we have amended our Constitution only 17 times since 1791. Some of these amendments have had a profound impact on our governmental system: the Thirteenth, Fourteenth, and Fifteenth—Civil War Amendments—come quickly to mind. Others, such as the Eighteenth and Twenty-first, instituting and then repealing Prohibition, have been minor.[2]

Most major changes in American society have occurred under essentially the same political framework as that established in 1789. Precedents set by

(Continued on p. 45)

2. Amendments to the Constitution can be initiated in either of two ways: by a two-thirds vote in both houses of Congress or on the petition of two-thirds of the states. Ratification can also be accomplished in either of two manners: approval of three-fourths of the states or by conventions called for this purpose in three-fourths of the states. No amendment has been initiated by the states; only one, the Twenty-first, has been ratified by convention. See Figure 2.5 on p. 46.

Table 2.3

AMENDMENTS TO THE U.S. CONSTITUTION

Amendment	Provisions	Date Ratified
1	Freedom of speech, press, assembly, and religion; right to petition	1791
2	Right to keep and bear arms as part of a "well-regulated Militia"	1791
3	Prohibits quartering of soldiers during peacetime (or during wartime, except as prescribed by law)	1791
4	Prohibits "unreasonable searches and seizures"	1791
5	Protects against double jeopardy or self-incrimination; forbids trial for major crimes without indictment by grand jury; provides for "due process of law," and "just compensation" for crimes against private property	1791
6	Right to trial by jury in criminal cases; right to speedy trial, to be informed of charges, and to secure witnesses	1791
7	Right to trial by jury in civil cases	1791
8	Prohibits excessive bail, fines, and "cruel or unusual punishments"	1791
9	Rights listed in the Constitution do not deny other rights "retained by the people"	1791
10	Powers not delegated to U.S. government are reserved to the states or the people	1791
11	Federal judicial power does not extend to suits brought against a state by citizens of another state	1795
12	Separate ballots to elect president and vice president	1804
13	Abolishes slavery	1865
14	Defines citizenship; protects the "privileges and immunities" of citizens; forbids states to deny "equal protection of the laws" or to deprive anyone of life, liberty, or property without "due process of law"	1868
15	Right to vote shall not be denied because of race, color, or previous condition of servitude	1870
16	Permits a federal income tax	1913
17	Provides for direct election of senators	1913
18	Institutes Prohibition	1919
19	Right to vote shall not be denied because of sex	1920
20	Changes terms of president, vice president, and Congress to eliminate "lame duck" sessions	1933
21	Repeals Eighteenth Amendment	1933
22	Limits presidents to two terms	1951
23	Gives District of Columbia residents the right to vote in presidential elections	1961
24	Outlaws the poll tax in federal elections	1964
25	Provides for filling the office of vice president in case of a vacancy; indicates procedure in circumstances in which the president is unable to carry out his or her duties	1967
26	Provides citizens 18 years or older the right to vote	1971
27	Congressional pay raises cannot take effect until after an election	1992

Since the Constitution was first ratified, successive amendments have clarified its original intent without negating its original principles.

Congress, the president, the courts, and changing political forces, rather than amendments, have been our means of adaptation. Many of the most important rules and procedures that govern us have been established by practice, not the Constitution. As we shall see in later chapters, the constitutional grants of authority are ambiguous, allowing the Constitution to mean many things to many people. For example, some believe the Constitution prohibits governmental regulation of gun ownership; others disagree. Some believe the Constitution requires the executive to have congressional approval to commit American troops to combat; others do not believe it does, and so on. If there is a deep commitment on the part of the American people to the concept of a written Constitution as the basic, fundamental law, it has been tempered by our pragmatism in making it work.

Principles of the Constitution

The governing principles underlying the Constitution have been the subject of considerable debate, as has their meaning. In part, this is a result of the ambiguity of the document and, in part, of the difficulties inherent in putting ideas into practice. As we shall see, the statement of a principle simply is not the same as its application.

The basic principles of the Constitution discussed in this section—constitutionalism, limited government, federalism, separation of powers, and individual liberties—illustrate the underlying ideas of government as well as the ambiguity that pervades the entire document.

Limited Government and Constitutionalism

Perhaps the most basic precept of American politics is the idea that government should be limited and that these limits should be delineated, that is, contained in a basic document. The principle of **constitutionalism** is rooted deep in American politics and culture. All of our states have constitutions, and many of our cities and counties have self-governing charters. Similarly, virtually every club and organization in our society is governed by a constitution. Indeed, a club is generally recognized as official only after its constitution has been drawn up and published. In our society, and in many others, a constitution confers legitimacy.

What are the reasons that might explain our belief in constitutionalism? One is that demands for a written constitution often follow an abrupt change in government. K. C. Wheare develops this argument in explaining the lack of a written constitution in the United Kingdom. He notes that, with one short exception, the United Kingdom had "an unbroken line of development" in its history (1966, 10). A look at other nations that have adopted written constitutions since the American experience confirms Wheare's contention that, after an abrupt change, basic rules will be recorded in a document.

Figure 2.5

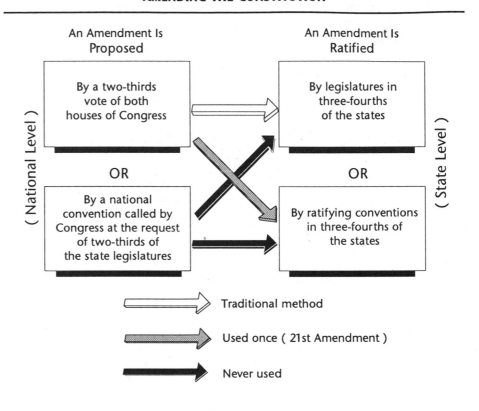

AMENDING THE CONSTITUTION

An Amendment Is Proposed | (National Level)

By a two-thirds vote of both houses of Congress

OR

By a national convention called by Congress at the request of two-thirds of the state legislatures

An Amendment Is Ratified | (State Level)

By legislatures in three-fourths of the states

OR

By ratifying conventions in three-fourths of the states

⟹ Traditional method

⟹ Used once (21st Amendment)

⟹ Never used

The Constitution provides four possible ways of amendment, but only the way shown in the top row has been used extensively.

The American belief in contracts is another possible explanation of our penchant for committing the powers and responsibilities of government to paper. Arthur E. Sutherland points out:

> Here is a logical application of an ancient theory, that the basis of governmental power is a contract between governor and governed. The immense prestige that Magna Carta has acquired over the centuries furnishes one illustration. The existence of this contractual concept in the minds of American colonists is evident from the Mayflower Compact, and from the early prestige of our colonial charters. (1965, 6)

A contract is written evidence between two or more parties of a binding agreement. The Constitution, therefore, is a contract that delineates the powers and responsibilities of the government, as well as the rights and duties of individual citizens.

Our belief in the authority of the law rather than of men is probably another reason for our emphasis on constitutionalism. For example, our courts are empowered to review the official actions of legislators and executives to determine whether their actions conform with our basic law. Finally, the longevity of our present system has served to strengthen our commitment to constitutionalism as a basic precept. We have come to depend on the long-term validity of our Constitution

Federalism

A system of government with two different levels of authority, a central national unit and lower-level regional units, each of which has direct authority over the people and possesses at least one political power independent of the others, is called **federalism**. There are many nations with federal systems of government today. In addition to the United States, these include Canada, India, Malaysia, Nigeria, and Switzerland.

Why adopt a federal system? William H. Riker (1964) gives us two reasons: first, a federal system, as a method of producing a larger, more viable political system, protects against encroachment by foreign powers and, second, is less costly to achieve than military conquest. Most political systems that wish to expand do so by forcefully taking land from their neighbors, which can be costly not only in immediate terms but also as a result of continued costs of maintaining control in the future. The convention's decision to adopt a federal form of government rested on the practical consideration that a union of 13 distinct and independent states would require some degree of centralization to meet the pressures exerted by foreign powers and to establish uniform laws regulating commerce. But the delegates could also foresee considerable opposition to concentrating too much power at the national level. As a result, the Constitution delegated some powers to each level of government.

CENTRALIZATION OF AUTHORITY   In defending the choice of a federal system against opponents who feared the states would lose their autonomy, the authors of *The Federalist* papers argued that, historically, power in federalist governments tended to become concentrated in the constituent units rather than in the central unit. The history of the United States, however, has shown a marked tendency in the other direction, toward national supremacy. But several federal systems in modern times have had central authority challenged: Canada with its separatist movement in Quebec is one illustration close to home; another is the breakup of the former Soviet Union and Yugoslavia. And national supremacy in the United States has been challenged in recent years by demands that many government functions be returned to the states.

REASONS FOR NATIONAL SUPREMACY   Features contained in the U.S. Constitution, as well as political events, have fostered national rather than state supremacy. For example, the Supremacy Clause contained in Article VI reads, "This Constitution, and the Laws of the United States which shall be made in Pursuance thereof; and all Treaties made, or which shall be made, under the Authority of the United States, shall be the supreme Law of the Land." The Constitution also grants certain specific powers to Congress that have contributed to the dominance of the central unit over its constituent parts. Article I, Section 8, enumerates the grants of power to Congress; particularly important is the authority to "regulate Commerce" and to "make all Laws which shall be necessary and proper for carrying into Execution the foregoing Powers." The general trend of court interpretations has been to grant Congress exclusive control over regulating commerce if it wishes, and to interpret the **Necessary and Proper Clause** liberally to include almost any action in which Congress wishes to engage.

Interpretations of the Tenth and Fourteenth Amendments by the Supreme Court have also enhanced the role of the national government. The Court has ruled that the Tenth, through which states have those powers neither delegated to the national government nor prohibited to the states, expresses a simple truism: states have those powers that states have. It does not specify nor even imply what those powers might be, nor does it in any way diminish what is given to or implied as powers of the national government (*United States v. Darby Lumber Co.,* 1941). The Fourteenth Amendment is significant because its Equal Protection and Due Process clauses have been used to apply the protection of the first eight amendments to the states as well as to the national government. Thus, states must now adhere to protections for free speech and freedom of religion found in the First Amendment, provisions of the Fourth against unreasonable searches of one's home or possessions, and other protections of the bill of rights. I will describe these protections more fully in chapter 4, Civil Rights and Civil Liberties. (I should note that most states have a bill of rights with many or most of these provisions in their constitutions, but I will be referring in this book to the "national" Bill of Rights.) The Fourteenth also has been used to provide national intervention into questions of civil rights and apportionment—the determination of how states draw the boundaries of their election districts.

The national government has become far more significant than individual states have, as political problems have become nationalized in the American system. This is partially the result of the physical growth of the American system, producing a larger and more powerful nation that at the same time has diluted the authority and power of the individual states. Furthermore, in the modern era—since the Civil War—most of our economic activities have become nationwide. The national government has had to respond to the people's demands to regulate, control, or promote the economic sphere to the relative exclusion of the states. The Court has interpreted the grant of national power to regulate "interstate commerce" to be exclusive. Once Congress has entered an area of commercial regulation, the states are precluded from it—unless Congress allows the states to exercise some regulatory power (*Gibbons v. Ogden,* 1824). In addition, the United States has become a major world power, and the conducting of foreign affairs is vested exclusively with the national government.

The modern relationship between the national government and the states in which the national, state, and local authorities have had to cooperate with one another in carrying out specific programs and policies will be explored in detail in the next chapter.

Separation of Powers

The Framers of our political institutions were concerned with putting too much power in the hands of any one government decision maker. James Madison expressed this concern in *The Federalist* No. 47:

> The accumulation of all powers, legislative, executive, and judiciary, in the same hands, whether for one, a few, or many, and whether hereditary, self-appointed, or elective, may justly be pronounced the very definition of tyranny.

Louis Fisher, senior specialist in separation of powers for the Congressional Research Service, contends that the Framers saw the need to add a stronger and separate executive branch and court system, in addition to a legislature, to make government work. Thus, it was not just concern for the oppression of the king, or his agents, the colonial governors, that concerned the Framers; they also saw the abuses of state legislatures—such as the printing of paper money with no security behind it—as just as great a threat to successful government.

> Americans discovered that state legislative bodies could be as oppressive and capricious toward individual rights as executive bodies. Also, many delegates to the Continental Congress watched with growing apprehension as the Congress found itself incapable of discharging its duties and responsibilities. (Fisher 1993, 9)

There was another problem that bothered Madison. He wrote Thomas Jefferson in 1788 that "it is a melancholy reflection that liberty should be equally exposed to danger whether the government have too much or too little power" (Padover 1969, 255). It was precisely to avoid these two extremes that our Constitution attempted to balance the powers necessary to successful governance and placed limits on those powers to prevent excess. This would be accomplished by creating a system where "ambition [should] be made to counteract ambition" (Madison, *The Federalist* No. 51). This was needed even in a political system where the people could elect their representatives. Again, Madison states the proposition: "A dependence on the people is, no doubt, the primary control on the government; but experience has taught mankind the necessity of auxiliary precautions" (*The Federalist* No. 51).

The solution to the problems posed above was to create a system of separate institutions: legislative, executive, and judicial branches of government. The first was to have primary responsibility for formulating the laws; the second for administering the laws; and the latter for adjudicating (judging) disputes arising from the law or its administration. The Constitution is assumed to have created a system of separation of powers. Richard E. Neustadt states emphatically, "It did nothing of the sort." What it did create was "a government of separated institutions *sharing* powers" (1990, 29). The distinction is so crucial to an understanding of the relationship among our branches of government that we will explore the concept in some depth before proceeding.

On the one hand, Neustadt is stating an obvious facet of national government: checks and balances. That is, the Constitution has granted one institution the authority to intrude into the affairs of another. Congress passes laws, but the president can veto them, and the Supreme Court can interpret them. The president can appoint members of his administration as well as federal judges, but Congress (the Senate) must advise and consent to the appointment, and so on. In the 1820s, John Adams wrote to a friend that there were eight checks built into the American system:

1. States v. national government
2. House v. Senate
3. Executive v. legislature
4. Courts v. executive and legislature
5. Senate v. executive on treaties and appointments
6. People through elections v. legislature
7. State legislatures through appointments v. Senate
8. Electors v. people in choosing a president.

The last two are not really accurate anymore. States no longer choose senators; they are chosen in popular elections, and presidential electors are chosen by political parties (see chapter 11, pp. 268–269). Checks and balances are still present in these areas; they have just been altered. The first six, however, are still functioning components of our system, one of the Framers' most original contributions to the theory of democratic government. Fisher cites the "rigid and dogmatic" separations found in the French constitutions of 1791 and 1848 as examples of creating systems that cannot work; they each ended in dictatorship (1993, 8). Checks and balances, thus, are integral to a functioning of separate institutions.

On the other hand, Neustadt is saying much more. In effect, one's whole conception of government is different if one accepts Neustadt's definition. It assumes that "power" is more adequate than "powers" in describing national government. The power of government is to make public policy, and each of our three branches is inextricably involved in that process of making binding decisions, ones that affect each of us, and to which each of us must adhere. Our institutions are in constant competition with each other over who will have what share in defining these rules.

There are several immediate conclusions one can draw from this. First, no one, or no single branch of government, is to be allowed to make public policy without some input from the other political institutions. Second, just how much control over any given decision resides with a particular branch of government depends upon the time in history that we are examining. At one time in our history, Woodrow Wil-

Figure 2.6

SEPARATION OF POWERS AND CHECKS AND BALANCES

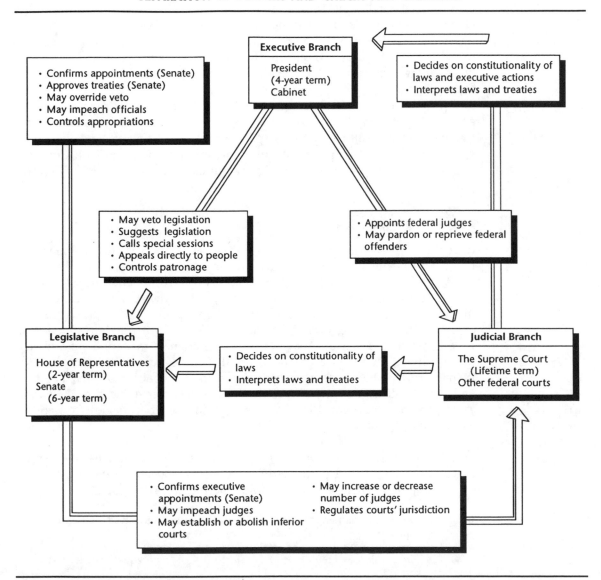

The government created by the Constitution is characterized by branches with distinct spheres of authority and the ability to check or balance each other. Although the phrase "separation of powers" is often used to describe the resulting arrangement, it is perhaps better described as a government of "separated institutions sharing powers."

son, our 28th president, could write a doctoral dissertation entitled *Congressional Government* (1885); at another, Arthur M. Schlesinger, Jr., a noted historian, could write of *The Imperial Presidency* (1974); and in 1975,

Joseph Califano, a ranking official in the Johnson administration, could write of *A Presidential Nation.*

That the relationship among our three major institutions will also change as one moves from policy area to policy area is the third insight gleaned from Neustadt's interpretation. The relationship of Congress, the president, and the courts to one another and to policy varies as we move from determining foreign policy, to deciding upon support for farmers, to assessing the current meaning of the First Amendment to the Constitution. The president may have primacy in foreign affairs, but Congress is not without influence; Congress may have the power of the purse, but the president is no bystander in determining how to spend the nation's money. And the Court may be the major interpreter of our rights and liberties, but both Congress and the president play crucial roles, as the discussion in chapter 4 will clearly indicate.

Individual Liberties

One of the great principles underlying the Constitution is that of individual liberty, the right to act without government interference. Securing liberty for the American people was one of the declared objectives of the American Revolution. It was also one of the most popular, and it remains so today. Indeed, many would contend that the pursuit of liberty is one of the distinguishing characteristics of Western civilization. But liberty, until put into practice, is little more than a slogan. And it is when we attempt to define what liberty means, and to put it into practice, that difficulties are most likely to arise. In part, this is due to another basic value in our concept of civil liberties: Equality. I will explore these in more detail in chapter 4; for now, let's look at how the notion of equality has difficulty moving from its ideal conception to real public policy.

EQUALITY   One of the cornerstones of civil liberties is the idea of equality. It has, however, been a particularly troublesome concept to define in terms of public policy. There are at least four interpretations of equality:

> *Political,* which usually means the right of all adult citizens to vote and participate in the political process.
> *Legal,* which refers to equality before the law.
> *Economic,* which can refer to equal opportunity or to an equal distribution of property.
> *Moral,* which refers to treating a person as an end and not as a means.
> (McClosky 1964, 368)

Some of us believe in each of these, others in only one; even those who support all, when confronted with a choice or conflict involving some other public value—liberty, or freedom from outside interference, for example—might not be willing to grant equality first.

Equality, then, is a concept with more than one practical meaning. Of these, for example, universal suffrage—allowing all people to vote—is probably the most well-established now. But we have needed a civil war, several constitutional amendments, and numerous congressional actions, such as the Voting Rights Acts, to extend the suffrage to women, blacks, and 18-year-olds. The ideal of equality before the law also enjoys wide support, but here again, there are numerous studies to show that our practice is less than ideal. Edward J. Bronson (1989), in his studies of prospective jurors, has found, for example, that many do not afford equal presumptions of innocence to all defendants in criminal cases, especially those who are poor and/or black.

From early attempts at eliminating religious and hereditary distinctions during our colonial days, to current attempts at providing truly equal educational opportunities for all and implementing the concept of one person, one vote, Americans have grappled with the meaning of equality. Garry Wills, in a Pulitzer-Prize-winning book, sees Abraham Lincoln as key to the re-emergence of the centrality of this goal. To Lincoln, the Declaration's "We hold these truths to be self-evident, that all men are created equal" was the prime gift of the era of the founding, and the Constitution an imperfect attempt to implement it. Wills quotes Lincoln:

> They [the fathers] did not mean to assert the obvious untruth, that all men were then actually enjoying that equality, nor yet that they were about to confer it, immediately, upon them. In fact, they had no power to confer such a boon. They meant simply to declare the *right,* so that the *enforcement* might follow as fast as circumstances should permit. (1992, 87)

Lincoln's position was echoed in more recent times by Martin Luther King Jr. In his famous speech on the steps of the Lincoln Memorial in 1963, King said, "I have a dream that my four little children will one day live in a nation where they will not be judged by the color of their skin but by the content of their character."

Wills goes on to show how many at the time saw that Lincoln's conception created conflict with other values—our commitment to equality is often at odds with our commitment to liberty; and liberty is seldom compatible with our commitment to community, another basic value. As a result, we are often faced with the need to choose among ideals. Consider, for example, the ongoing debate over **affirmative action** programs (governmental programs designed to ensure that hiring, admissions, promotion, and other related procedures actively encourage the consideration of minority and other groups traditionally discriminated against by such procedures). Here the conflict is between the ideals of equal access to economic benefits and individual liberty, in this case, the protection against unwarranted government intrusion into the activities of the private sector. For those who argue that liberty is the more important value, affirmative action programs, even if desirable on other grounds, represent a potential threat to individual liberty. For those who favor such programs, equality of economic opportunity is the more important value.

These are not easy choices. They form the basis of the great political debates and major court decisions of our time. As with all choices, they are not neutral in their impact; some will be advantaged with one choice, others with a different choice.

Summary

We can return here to the questions with which we opened this chapter. Why has the Constitution survived? How have we been able to accommodate 200 years of great social and political change while retaining essentially the same constitutional framework? Four factors have been essential to the survival of the Constitution:

1. It created a national government with sufficient authority to deal with problems, one far more effective than the government created by the Articles of Confederation.
2. Many of its doctrines are stated ambiguously and thus, permit interpretation, while much of the content emphasizes procedure rather than substance.
3. The document is difficult to change; in effect, a substantial majority must be in agreement before we can change our fundamental document.
4. It is based on some basic principles of governing that have proven to be successful and, indeed, have been copied by other governments. Moreover, these principles were familiar to Americans of that time from European tradition.

The Constitution has allowed great flexibility. Under this document, our national government has evolved from one that did little and spent even less to one that enters almost every phase of our lives, spends about $1.5 trillion a year (which represents almost a fifth of our gross domestic product), and employs almost three million civilian and more than a million military personnel. Our government began as one with little consequence in world affairs and emerged as the most significant in the world. Our concern throughout the remainder of the text shall be with the adaptations in our political institutions that have been necessary to meet these changing circumstances.

Analytical Exercises

1. A useful device for focusing discussion is to draw some tradeoff curves, indicating how much of one thing a person is willing to sacrifice to obtain another. The graph on the next page indicates the tradeoff between external costs and bargaining or decision-making costs. External costs are ones over which you have no control; decision-making costs are just that: the time and resources needed to reach a decision.

For this exercise, let's forget about costs that might arise between or on account of other countries and concentrate on our internal arrangements. Bargaining costs become higher as the number of people involved increases. That

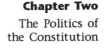

Hypothetical Trade-Off Between External and Decision-Making Costs

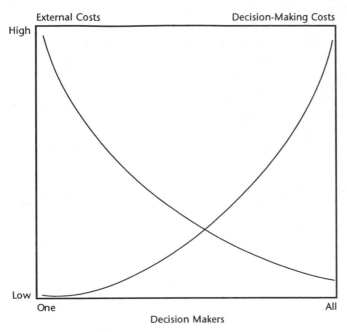

is, an absolute dictator has no bargaining costs—unless he argues with himself. External costs are highest in a society with the absolute dictator; as the number of citizens involved in decision making increases, external costs decrease. When everyone must agree to a society's decisions, we have eliminated external costs, but we have greatly increased the costs of making a decision. Using these concepts, where do you think the optimal tradeoff for a decision rule is for a society when it is: a) selecting representatives for office; b) approving a yearly budget; c) modifying the eligibility requirements for a student loan; d) changing the Constitution; or e) deciding to fight a war. How does our Constitution deal with each of these?

2. Establishing rules binding on every citizen in a society can raise interesting and ambiguous moral issues. Consider the case of the Grudge Informers, as developed by the legal scholar and teacher, Lon Fuller. Your country, which has a long history and established constitution, has come on hard economic times, the result of which is the election to positions of power of the Purple Shirts, a ruthless party of bullies and petty tyrants. The new rulers do not suspend the old constitution or laws, but they do repress dissent by using roving bands of party members as enforcers. They also pass laws designed to produce acceptance of their rule, among them laws making it a crime to listen to a foreign broadcast, read anything but the official newspaper, hoard dried eggs, or to fail to report the loss of an identification card within 5 days. Many of your friends are arrested, tried, and convicted of these crimes, in some cases receiving the death penalty. Some of your neighbors see these new restrictions as a way to get even with those they don't like. In one case, for example, the lover of a married woman reports her husband for failure to replace his ID card—the husband is executed; in another case, a woman who had been in-

sulted reports the person who offended her for hoarding eggs, a crime for which the offender receives 10 years in prison.

Finally, the Purple Shirts are overthrown in a revolt and you are now appointed to the judicial council that must decide how to deal with the recent events. Handling the Purple Shirts themselves is not a problem. They were all killed or fled the country. The most vexing situation is what to do with the Grudge Informers. How do you address their actions without becoming much like the hated Purple Shirts? How do you make actions that took place before certain laws were passed (also known as **ex post facto laws**) illegal? And how do you distinguish between the real Grudge Informer and the mere busybody who simply reported any or all suspicious actions to the authorities (Fuller, 1964)?

Chapter Outline

3

The Federal System

Truly federalism is an unstable relation. . . . A great change in the whole system of institutions has come about, unperceived, by a long series of small changes. The enumerated powers have been supplemented by the implied powers, the compact theory and state pretensions to sovereignty collapsed in the Civil War, and now the only real limits on the functions of the national government are the demands of the people and its own sense of self-restraint.

—William H. Riker, *Democracy in the United States,* 1964

The fifty American states, located between the powerful federal government and the burgeoning local governments in a metropolitanized nation, are the keystones of the American governmental arch. This was the case when the Constitution was adopted in 1789, and it remains so despite the great changes that have taken place in the intervening years.

—Daniel J. Elazar, *The American Mosaic,* 1994

The system of government created by the Constitution has proven remarkably successful in a number of respects. I mentioned two key elements in the last chapter: separation of powers and federalism.

> In the compound republic of America, the power surrendered by the people is first divided between two distinct governments, and then the portion allotted to each subdivided among distinct and separate departments. Hence a double security arises to the rights of the people. The different governments will control each other, at the same time that each will be controlled by itself. (James Madison, *The Federalist* No. 51)

57

That a system of government designed in 1787 should have survived for over two centuries with its basic structural features intact is remarkable. One of the key factors is the federal system, a system of government with several distinct levels, each having its own distinctive set of powers. But to what extent has the relationship between these levels remained the same? The quotes by Riker and Elazar give diametrically different interpretations. Keep these in mind as the federal system is explored in this chapter.

Let's begin by noting the obvious. Over the years, the system of government created by the Constitution has grown in complexity and number of units. A system that in 1789 comprised a single new national government, 13 state governments, and a relatively small number of towns, townships, and counties now encompasses approximately 83,200 governmental bodies. We have a national government (or, as it is commonly known, the *federal* government) and 50 state governments. The remaining 83,000-plus bodies of government are local in nature. They include some 3,000 counties, over 19,000 municipalities, nearly 17,000 townships, just under 15,000 school districts, and about 30,000 special districts that provide services as diverse as fire protection and mosquito control (*Municipal Year Book 1994*, xii).

As the number of governmental units has increased, so has the size of the governmental labor force. Today, the federal government employs just under 3 million civilian employees, of whom the vast majority (all but 65 thousand) are employed by the executive branch (*Budget of the United States Government* 1996, Historical Tables 245). The states employ about 5 million. The local government workforce is even larger, comprising about 11 million workers presided over by some 500,000 elected officials.

Such figures, however, tell us little about the relationships among the various levels of government in our federal system. Invariably, these relationships are dynamic, evolving over time in response to changing circumstances and events and not always in a positive manner. The basic rules were established by the Constitution where certain powers were delegated exclusively to the national government. Others were reserved to the states. Still others, known as **concurrent powers**, are shared by the national and state governments. Figure 3.1 on the next page indicates the specific powers that fall into each of these three categories.

Federal-State Relations

Like other aspects of our government, the nature of the relationship between the federal and state governments has evolved over time. The Constitution, however, imposes certain requirements on both levels of government that affect their relationship.

Constitutional Influences

The Constitution requires the national government to provide certain protections to the states. These are:

(Continued on p. 60)

Figure 3.1

CONSTITUTIONAL POWERS AND PROHIBITIONS

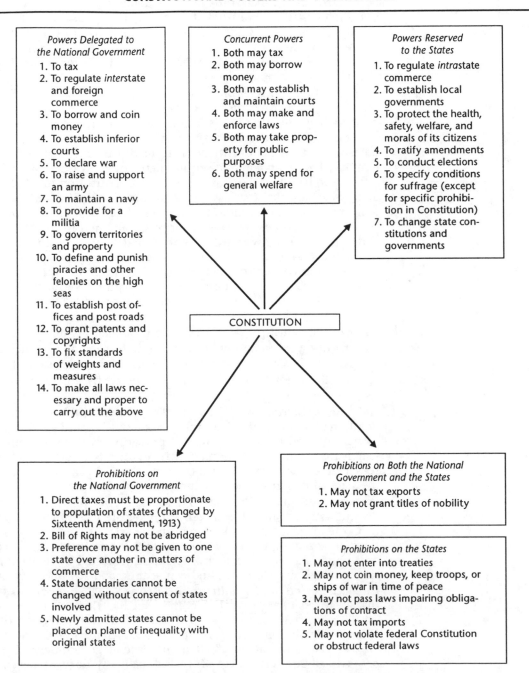

*Powers Delegated to
the National Government*

1. To tax
2. To regulate *inter*state and foreign commerce
3. To borrow and coin money
4. To establish inferior courts
5. To declare war
6. To raise and support an army
7. To maintain a navy
8. To provide for a militia
9. To govern territories and property
10. To define and punish piracies and other felonies on the high seas
11. To establish post offices and post roads
12. To grant patents and copyrights
13. To fix standards of weights and measures
14. To make all laws necessary and proper to carry out the above

Concurrent Powers

1. Both may tax
2. Both may borrow money
3. Both may establish and maintain courts
4. Both may make and enforce laws
5. Both may take property for public purposes
6. Both may spend for general welfare

*Powers Reserved
to the States*

1. To regulate *intra*state commerce
2. To establish local governments
3. To protect the health, safety, welfare, and morals of its citizens
4. To ratify amendments
5. To conduct elections
6. To specify conditions for suffrage (except for specific prohibition in Constitution)
7. To change state constitutions and governments

CONSTITUTION

*Prohibitions on
the National Government*

1. Direct taxes must be proportionate to population of states (changed by Sixteenth Amendment, 1913)
2. Bill of Rights may not be abridged
3. Preference may not be given to one state over another in matters of commerce
4. State boundaries cannot be changed without consent of states involved
5. Newly admitted states cannot be placed on plane of inequality with original states

*Prohibitions on Both the National
Government and the States*

1. May not tax exports
2. May not grant titles of nobility

Prohibitions on the States

1. May not enter into treaties
2. May not coin money, keep troops, or ships of war in time of peace
3. May not pass laws impairing obligations of contract
4. May not tax imports
5. May not violate federal Constitution or obstruct federal laws

The U.S. Constitution provides for a federal system of government by delegating separate powers to the national and the state governments. This chart also shows the concurrent, or shared, powers.

1. *Republican form of government* (art. IV, sec. 4). The republican form of government takes its direction from representatives who are to be elected, as distinct from a direct democracy, where the people rule directly. When confronted with this issue, the Supreme Court stated, "It rests with Congress to decide what government is the established one in a state . . . as well as its republican character" (*Luther v. Bordon*, 1849). If Congress votes to seat a state's representatives, it has, in effect, accepted the state as republican in nature.

2. *Protection from invasion and from domestic insurrection* (art. IV, sec. 4). The opinion in *Luther v. Bordon* also states that Congress is to decide when this situation is imminent. In practice, the president is the one who must act. Presidents in modern times have drawn upon other sections of the Constitution to justify their use of troops. For example, Presidents Eisenhower and Kennedy used troops to achieve integration based on the provisions of the Constitution that the president "take care that the Laws be faithfully executed" (art. II, sec. 3).

3. *New states must be admitted on an equal basis with other states* (art. IV, sec. 3). There was precedent for this contained in the Northwest Ordinance of 1787, where the western lands were to gain statehood on an equal basis with the original ones. But it was a matter of some debate at the convention, and the decision to grant equal status to new states has been important for our nation's development: All citizens within the United States were to have equal standing.

In addition, the Constitution places certain obligations upon the states that must be met in their dealings with other states. In general, all states must respect the legal actions of other states and afford their citizens equal treatment. Three specific obligations that must be observed by all states are:

1. *Full faith and credit* (art. IV, sec. 1). This provision takes a basic idea of international law—that laws valid in one state should be recognized in another—and makes it explicit. It primarily involves ensuring that judgments in one jurisdiction apply in another. For example, all states recognize the validity of marriage and drivers' licenses regardless of the state of origin of these documents.

2. *Privileges and immunities* (art. IV, sec. 2). This provision prevents discrimination against the citizens of one state when they are acting in another state. It is a carryover from the Articles, and most scholars think it was designed to produce a united country. In traveling to or through another state, a citizen can be protected by its laws, have the right of **habeas corpus**, and can acquire and sell property there.

3. *Extraditions (interstate rendition)* (art. IV, sec. 2). This provision states that a citizen charged with a crime who has fled to another state "shall . . . be delivered up . . . to the State having Jurisdiction of the Crime." The Supreme Court in *Kentucky v. Dennison* (1861) held that "it was just a moral duty"; that the Federal government "has no power to impose on a state officer, as such, any duty whatever, and compel him to perform it." This objection was overruled in 1987 when, in *Puerto Rico v. Branstad* (1987), the Court declared that the Constitution required state observance of the extraditions rule.

Historical Development

In 1986 a number of state governors objected to the decision of Ronald Reagan to send their states' National Guard units to Honduras for training exercises. They saw it as a political ploy to provide military support to the Contras, the group opposing the Sandinista government in Nicaragua. The Contras were mostly based in Honduras and received most of their military support from the United States. One governor, Rudy Perpich of Minnesota, took the national government to court, arguing that as head of the state militia he had to agree before his troops could be sent on duty to foreign countries.

In a 1990 case, *Perpich v. Department of Defense,* the Supreme Court unanimously upheld the validity of a 1986 congressional act known as the Montgomery Amendment, which gave the national government the power to "call forth the militia." The Court ruled that "the congressional power to call forth the militia may in appropriate cases supplement its broader power to raise armies and provide for the common defense and general welfare, but it does not limit those powers." Thus, Governor Perpich lost his case.

The Supreme Court's ruling in *Perpich* is consistent with our recent experience. For the past 50 years, the balance of power in federal-state relations has belonged to the federal government. Federalism American-style has been "a nationally dominant system of shared power and shared functions" (Reagan and Sanzone 1981, 157). This has not always been the case. And there is an effort by the new Republican majorities in Congress to return some functions and powers to the states. Most scholars point to three distinct eras in the evolution of American federalism.

1. *The era of* **competitive federalism,** *1789–1836.* Some of our most important Supreme Court decisions are from this era, which includes the first 50 years of the new republic. During this time, in court cases where states attempted to restrict the actions of the national government, the national government generally won. For example, the attempts of Maryland to tax a national bank were forbidden in the case of *McCulloch v. Maryland* (1819). Justice John Marshall in his opinion stated, "The power to tax involves the power to destroy." Since the Constitution envisioned each level of government capable of acting without the other, to let states tax federal activities would in effect give them the power to undercut the independence of the national bank. A similar decision was reached in *Gibbons v. Ogden* (1824), in which Marshall, again speaking for the Court, prohibited the states from regulating commerce that was previously regulated by the national government.

2. *The era of* **dual federalism,** *1857–1936.* This era began with the Dred Scott decision (1857), just prior to the Civil War, although it probably is the view expressed in *The Federalist* papers, and lasted until 1937. The basic view was stated by the Court in *Abelman v. Booth* (1859). Dual federalism may be defined as two levels of government that "are yet separate and distinct sovereignties, acting separately and independently of each other, within their respective spheres."

The *Dennison* extradition case mentioned earlier is illustrative of this. Under this doctrine, national attempts to regulate the activities of states or of private business were struck down as an encroachment on state power. For example, efforts to regulate the hours of employment of women and children were effectively prevented in the case of *Hammer v. Dagenhart* (1918). I should note that not all court decisions during this era went against federal regulation. In *Missouri v. Holland* (1920), for example, the Court upheld the provisions of a treaty between the United States and Canada that restricted the hunting of ducks, an area of regulation traditionally left to the states; the decision rested on the idea that treaties had the same force as the Constitution, placing them above state laws.

3. *The era of cooperative federalism, 1937–present.* The expansion of the role played by government in American life, beginning with the efforts to deal with economic depression in the 1930s and accelerated greatly by the adoption of Great Society programs in the 1960s, has produced an era of federalism in which the different levels of government have had to cooperate to achieve desired goals. Much of the growth in the number of government employees mentioned earlier stems from these added activities that are directed primarily by the federal government, but administered by the states and their local governments. Highways are a good example. The federal government decided in the late 1950s to create an interstate highway system. It did so by providing states with 90 percent of the cost of construction. Currently (1995), the federal government provides about $25 billion a year as grants to states for highway construction and upkeep.

Nevertheless, these cooperative efforts should not obscure the fact that during this same time the federal government has been the clear winner in most disputes with state and local governments. Challenges to federal authority have for the most part been rejected by the Supreme Court. The *Perpich* case is but one in a long succession of victories for the national government. Many of the court decisions upholding dual federalism have been overturned. For example, *Hammer v. Dagenhart* was overturned in 1941 by *United States v. Darby Lumber Co.,* which upheld the Fair Labor Standards Act of 1938, allowing federal restrictions on the use of child labor. In a startling decision, *South Carolina v. Baker* (1988), the Court said that the federal government could tax the income from state bonds, which overturned *Pollock v. Farmers' Loan and Trust* (1895).

Despite winning most of its disputes with state and local governments, the federal government would rather avoid these confrontations when possible. Project Rio Blanco is a good illustration. The federal government detonated three nuclear devices in northeastern Colorado in an effort to tap large underground deposits of natural gas. However, when Colorado citizens voted overwhelmingly in 1974 to prohibit such explosions in their state, the federal government, although not bound by such state actions, did not pursue the program (Winter 1981).

In order to appreciate the dynamic nature of federal-state relations, let's explore some of the advantages enjoyed by the national government. I will briefly trace the developments of the past 50 years.

The Expansion of the Federal Role

In the ongoing competition between the federal and state governments, the national government enjoys several distinct advantages. Some of these are discussed in chapter 2, The Politics of the Constitution. It has, for example, a judicial branch that, when faced with a conflict between state and national interests, will generally side with the national government. It also enjoys certain constitutional advantages, notably the Supremacy Clause and the Constitution's various prohibitions upon state action. Finally, historical factors have also favored the expansion of federal power. As social problems have increased, becoming national in scope, more and more reliance has been placed on the national government to solve them. The economy, as one example, has become a national problem (really an international one). National problems require national solutions.

In addition, the national government, with its broader tax base, has a major financial advantage over the states. Economic difficulties in one section of the country may be offset by better conditions in another. In contrast, most states do not have this diversity; many must rely on the health of a single major industry. Even large states such as Texas (oil) and California (defense industries) have experienced significant economic difficulties when that relied-upon industry slowed economically. The national government relies primarily on income taxes as its principal source of revenue. Taxes based on income respond well to increases in the economy and are less costly to administer than sales taxes, which account for about half of states' revenues, and property taxes that account for about three-fourths of the revenue of local governments.

The scope and significance of the federal government's role in most policy areas remained limited until the mid-1960s. The Northwest Ordinance of 1787 required the new states to set aside land for education—the first real intrusion into state and local affairs. The Interstate Commerce Act in 1889, the Federal Food and Drug Act in 1906, and the Federal Trade Commission Act of 1914 were the first in a series of attempts to establish and ensure compliance with national policy. There were also grants of modest monetary support. These began after the passage of the Sixteenth Amendment to the Constitution establishing a federal income tax in 1913: agricultural extension services (1914), highways (1916), vocational education (1917), and public health (1918). In 1960, the total number of federal aid programs was 44, and, except for highways and welfare, federal aid "did not constitute a sizable proportion of state and local spending" (Advisory Commission on Intergovernmental Relations [ACIR] 1970, 2).

Between 1960 and 1970, however, there was a dramatic increase in federal financial assistance to state and local governments. By January 1, 1967, the number of programs had grown from 44 to 379, including 109 new programs enacted in 1965 alone (Sundquist 1969). The result was an increase in the availability of federal dollars, and a significant expansion of the federal role in a broad range of domestic policy areas, most dramatically in the area of health care.

Types of Federal Intervention

Two types of federal intervention in state and local affairs can be described: fiscal and regulatory. In tracing the development of federalism, I mentioned that the move to federal regulations came first. It was, however, the rise of fiscal federalism in the 1960s that most changed the dynamics of the federal-state relationship.

Fiscal Federalism

Federal financial aid to state and local governments takes one of two basic forms. One involves an outright grant of money in several different types of grant programs. A second, less direct, method of providing such assistance is a **tax expenditure**, a provision in the tax code that benefits a particular class of taxpayers. For example, bonds issued by state and local governments are free of federal taxes, allowing these bonds to compete with private bonds while paying about 3 percent less in interest. As Table 3.1 indicates, these are significant forms of federal aid. By 1995, the total dollar benefit to states and local governments through tax expenditures was over $57 billion.

With respect to direct financial assistance, the national government doubled its financial commitment to state and local governments between 1960 and 1980 (see Table 3.2). During this 20-year period, federal grant-in-aid programs increased from 8 percent of all federal expenditures to 15 percent. The total dollar amount of such programs grew even more rapidly, from $7.0 billion in 1960 to $91.5 billion by 1980. As a result, federal dollars accounted for a steadily increasing share of state and local revenues. By 1980, over one-fourth of all state and local government revenues were being provided by the federal government. In fact, the federal share of state and local revenues grew from 10.4 percent in 1950 to 26 percent in 1980, an increase of over 250 percent.

As Table 3.2 also documents, the federal contribution to state and local governments decreased between 1980–90 as a result of policies initiated by the Reagan administration. Nonetheless, federal grant-in-aid programs still accounted for 20 percent of state and local revenues in 1990. The growth returned in the

Table 3.1

TAX EXPENDITURES AIDING STATE AND LOCAL GOVERNMENTS
(Outlay Equivalents in $ Millions)

Type of Tax Expenditure	1986	1990	1996
Deductions for taxes paid by individuals	33,550	30,455	28,795
Exclusion of interest for state and local debt: loans and bonds	20,290	33,145	28,935

Source: Budget of the United States Government 1996, Analytical Perspectives 51.

Tax expenditures are provisions in the tax code that provide benefits to certain classes of taxpayers. As such, they represent an indirect form of federal aid to state and local governments. Although easily overlooked, such expenditures totaled about $58 billion in 1996.

Table 3.2

FEDERAL GRANTS-IN-AID
1950–1994

Fiscal Year	Total Grants in $ Billion	Grants as a Percentage of State and Local Revenue	Grants as a Percentage of Federal Outlays
1950	2.3	10.4	5.3
1960	7.0	14.6	7.6
1970	24.1	19.2	12.3
1980	91.5	25.8	15.5
1990	135.4	20.0	11.0
1994	210.6	24.0	14.4

Source: Budget of the United States Government 1996, Historical Tables 175.

By any measure, federal grants to state and local governments have increased dramatically since 1950, when they represented just over 10 percent of state and local revenue and only a little more than 5 percent of federal outlays. However, despite continuing increases in the dollar amount of such grants, they declined steadily during the 1980s as a percentage of both state and local revenues and federal outlays. Health costs have led to the recent increases.

second half of the Bush years and continued into Clinton's: the total dollar value of such programs had risen to an estimated $230.6 billion in 1995, 15 percent of total federal outlays, a 4 percent growth from the end of the Reagan era. The most dramatic increase in recent years has been in health care, which has doubled in the past four years alone, to an estimated $101.7 billion in 1995. One of the major controversies between Republicans and Democrats these days is how to reverse this trend—how to limit health and welfare costs.

There are a variety of ways in which the national government assists state and local governments, and there are advantages and disadvantages for each. As a result, the form of assistance can itself become a political issue, even when there is agreement that aid should be given. Congress, the executive branch, and state and local governments often have quite different preferences regarding the form of aid they would like to receive. In general, each can be expected to support the form of aid they find most advantageous to themselves from a monetary or power perspective.

Outright grants from the federal government to state and local agencies currently fall into two basic categories: categorical grants and block grants. In addition, from 1972 through 1987, there was a third type of federal grant aid, general revenue sharing, or GRS. Statistically speaking, categorical grants are the most important of these three forms of federal aid. As can be seen from Table 3.3, categorical grants accounted for 90.1 percent of federal grants in 1972, declined to 79.3 percent in 1980, and then rose to 90.9 percent by 1993. By contrast, block grants never accounted for more than 11.3 percent of federal grants during this same period. General revenue sharing's peak occurred in 1980 when it constituted 9.4 percent of federal grant monies.

GRANTS-IN-AID (CATEGORICAL FUNDING) Grants awarded for specific purposes are called **categorical grants**. Federal aid that is earmarked for a

Table 3.3

PERCENT OF FEDERAL AID TO STATE AND LOCAL GOVERNMENTS BY TYPE
1972–1993

Type of Program	1972	1980	1993
General Purpose (GRS and Other)	1.6%	9.4%	1.7%
Broad-Based (Block Grants)	8.3%	11.3%	7.4%
Other Grants (Categoricals)	90.1%	79.3%	90.9%
Total	100.0%	100.0%	100.0%

Source: Budget of the United States Government 1993, Part One-436.

Despite the rise, and subsequent demise, of general revenue sharing between 1972 and 1993, categorical grants-in-aid held firm as the single largest source of outright grants from the federal government to state and local levels. Today such grants continue to account for almost 90 percent of federal aid dollars.

specific "category" of services, welfare or highway construction, for example, is categorical aid. Funds can be awarded on the basis of some formula—population, for example—or based on a specific project. Because projects are funded on the basis of compliance with objectives set by the federal government, such grants come with more strings attached than those awarded by formula.

The dominance of project grants is a relatively new phenomenon. Prior to 1960, most federal grant programs, in education, for example, were formula in nature, "designed to help state and local governments achieve objectives that primarily were local in nature" (ACIR 1972, 39). Those monitoring the programs were concerned with efficiency and economy rather than with adherence to nationally defined policy.

Categorical grants for specific projects reached their present level of importance during the turbulent decade of the 1960s. Frustrated by their inability to influence the behavior of state and local agencies, national policymakers seized upon categorical aid as a means of ensuring compliance with national policy objectives. Understandably, project grants tend to be more popular with Congress and the executive branch than with state and local officials. The Economic Opportunity Act of 1964, in particular, was enormously unpopular with governors and mayors, who were effectively cut out of the "funding loop." As a result, they could only sit and watch as federal funds went directly to local government agencies or local community groups, many of whom had policy agendas that were, at best, quite different from those of elected state and local figures. The ensuing outcry among the bypassed officials effectively killed the Economic Opportunity Act. It also ensured that future federal programs would not bypass established governmental agencies. Most federal aid today passes through the hands of state agencies.

Nonetheless, categorical aid remains far and away the most common type of federal assistance. By the late 1960s there were at one point 105 separate budget categories and over 500 subcategories of federal categorical aid. While the number and scope of such programs declined during the 1980s, there has since been a gradual increase. In 1993, for example, there were 578 categorical grant programs in operation (Gordon and Milakovich 1995, 108).

GENERAL REVENUE SHARING   Although the program ended in Fiscal Year 1988, as both the Reagan administration and the Congress looked for ways to cut the deficit, **general revenue sharing (GRS)** was an important experiment in federal-state-local finance. Under this program, the federal government awarded monies to state and local governments on an annual basis with virtually no stipulations as to how the money was to be spent. One-third of this money went to the states; the remainder went to local governments. State and local officials liked the program mainly for this reason, and also because they felt that they could better decide how to spend money provided to them than federal officials who were geographically and emotionally distant from their problems; for the same reason, Congress was never a strong supporter.

Nearly $70 billion was distributed to state and local governments via the GRS program over its lifetime. Some of the uses to which this money was put did not play well in Washington. Many state and local governments substituted GRS funds for money that would otherwise have been obtained from their own tax revenues, effectively using federal money to reduce needed increases in state and local taxes.

BLOCK GRANTS   The third type of outright federal grant is a block grant; the first, in 1973, was for Community Development. **Block grants**, which fall somewhere between categorical grants and GRS, are meant to eliminate the fragmentation of categorical aid and provide local areas with some discretion as to how to use the money, while still maintaining broad national policy objectives. Block grants consolidate a number of related categorical programs into a single, larger "block." They come with fewer specific conditions attached than categorical grants, allowing state and local agencies a greater degree of flexibility in determining how the money may be used.

The Comprehensive Employment and Training Act (CETA) of 1976 provides an example of the compromises involved in the block grant approach. It consolidated into a single framework 17 separate categorical programs. However, it remained an administratively complicated program, with 47 separate authorizations administered by 10 agencies (Reagan and Sanzone 1981). Although CETA was intended to provide job training for those lacking adequate skills, CETA funds were used primarily to train workers who already possessed considerable skills. On occasion they were also used to hire people who were already qualified to perform the job for which they were hired. These and other problems led to serious revisions of CETA by Congress and to its ultimate end under the Reagan administration.

One of the outcomes of the CETA experience was a certain dissatisfaction with block grants on the part of Congress. This led to "administrative creep," a term coined by my colleague John Sanzone: the imposition of additional restrictions on how block grant money could be spent. Another result of dissatisfaction was that during the late 1970s neither Congress nor the president made any further attempts to consolidate categorical programs into block grants. At the same time, those block grant programs that remained became more and more similar to categorical grants in terms of the restrictions imposed by Congress.

Block grants again found favor in the 1980s. As part of its initial attempt to reduce the size of the federal government, the Reagan administration succeeded in converting some 77 categorical programs into nine block grants. This effort, along with other related actions, led to nearly a 25 percent reduction in the total number of federal programs in a single year (Saffell 1993, 46). The Reagan administration's real objective was to reduce the total amount of federal outlays and shift funding responsibilities to the state and local level. Thus, while the consolidation effort gave state and local agencies more discretion to determine how to spend federal monies, less money was provided, about 30 percent less in real dollars during the 1980s. The effort by Congress in 1995 to expand block grants follows much the same pattern: Reduce the size of the federal government.

Most governors have applauded this effort, although they know it leads to other major policy problems: Unfunded mandates, to which I will return in a moment, is one; another is "biting the hand that feeds you." Governors have a problem complaining about federal expenditures and then continuing to ask for disaster relief when a flood, hurricane, or earthquake hits, or fighting to prevent a military base closing as part of reductions in defense spending.

Overall, then, the various efforts to reduce the proportion of federal aid provided through categorical grants have had modest success. Taking a second look at Table 3.3 on page 66, data show that categorical grants again constitute 90 percent of all federal aid to state and local governments. Nor is this terribly surprising. Whatever their weaknesses, categorical grants have one great advantage over block grants and experiments such as general revenue sharing. Simply stated, they have been the programs most likely to be approved by Congress and the president. The Republican agenda in 1995 was to put increased emphasis on block grants, for crime prevention and welfare, for example. You may want to investigate how successful this effort has been.

Federal Regulations

The other major form of federal intrusion into state and local affairs is in the form of regulations and mandates. Many of these regulations have a direct impact on the everyday life of the average citizen. Consider, for example, the decision of many state governments to raise the legal drinking age to 21. While partially a result of public pressure from groups such as Mothers Against Drunk Driving, this policy decision was for almost half of the states triggered by a federal directive that insisted that states raise their legal drinking age to 21 or lose a portion of their Highway Trust Fund money.

Recent regulations have also been a major concern to state and local governments because they often impose high cost without federal money to cover their implementation—called **unfunded mandates**. For example, a study by the United States Conference of Mayors found that the total cost to cities of meeting the provisions of the Clean Water Act in 1993 was $3.5 billion

(*CQ Weekly Report,* January 21, 1995, 210). Cities, by the way, also object to the unfunded mandates emanating from their state governments.

There are a variety of forms these regulations take.

1. *Direct orders* Some federal regulations directly order compliance with the provisions of a statute—the Equal Opportunity Act of 1982, for example, which bars job discrimination—or the imposition of criminal or civil sanctions. The constitutionality of these orders is not completely settled, and they are not popular with state and local officials; Congress usually finds a less directly intimidating means to accomplish its will.

2. *Preemption* Some areas of policy the federal government has taken completely unto itself—total preemption. Under the Supremacy and Commerce clauses of the Constitution, the federal government can take total control of an area of regulation. The courts since *Gibbons v. Ogden* (1824) have been quite consistent on this. State regulations are not allowed in a totally preempted area of policy. Examples include the disposal of toxic waste, determining the acceptable weight of trucks on interstate highways, and the regulation of bankruptcy and of airlines.

   At times, the federal government will adopt a partial preemption. Occupational Safety and Health Act provisions are an example. States can regulate any area where there is not a conflicting federal standard; if there is, then the state may not regulate. Environmental protection is another example. Here, the states are allowed to adopt standards that are equal to or greater than those of the federal government.

   I mentioned above the inducement to states for raising the drinking age. A similar federal action led states to lower their speed limits to 55 miles per hour in urban areas. According to Joseph F. Zimmerman (1991), these represent "informal preemptions," awards made to state and local governments based on their agreement to follow certain established procedures. On occasion, the federal effort to influence state and local policy takes the form of incentives. In general, however, these are less effective than sanctions or penalties. For example, when the federal government offered a 1 percent bonus in highway monies in 1965 to states that met or exceeded national highway beautification standards, 20 states responded with the appropriate legislation. When Congress later changed the rules to provide a 10 percent penalty for states not meeting federal standards, all but 3 promptly passed the necessary laws (Reagan and Sanzone 1981, 117).

   States can adopt standards above those dictated by Washington in non-preempted areas. California, Michigan, and New Jersey courts have called for equal per-pupil funding of schools, something the federal courts refused to do. And New York state courts voided police searches for illegal drugs that would have been allowed under the federal standard. Judge Judith S. Kaye stated, "A state court decision that rejects Supreme Court precedent and opts for greater safeguards as a matter of state law does indeed establish high Constitutional standards [but] . . . is a perfectly respectable and legitimate thing to do" (Sach 1992, 1ff).

3. *Cross-cutting regulations* Expanded federal regulations have, on occasion, been the result of a piece of legislation that extends the provisions of one federal grant to other grants received by that governmental entity. The most important of these was the Civil Rights Act of 1964. Title 9 of the Education Amendments in 1972 is another example: schools lose their other federal aid if they discriminate based on gender.

Impact of Federal Aid

The allocation of federal aid is not without its controversies. For one thing, some states have proven more effective than others in the inevitable process of competing for federal dollars. The result is a considerable disparity among states in the amount of federal aid received. As Figure 3.2 illustrates, some states receive more dollars in federal aid than they (and their citizens) pay the federal government in taxes. Others have an actual net loss. In general, rural and southern states (generally poorer than others) fare best, while more urban states (especially those in the North) and the most populous states (regardless of location) fare worst.

The availability of federal dollars has also given rise to controversy over how these dollars should be spent. One such example is the continuing debate over the appropriate use of federal highway funds. Many state officials and citizens of rural areas favor using this money to complete the construction of any remaining unbuilt segments of the interstate highway system and then to help defray the system's ongoing maintenance costs. Urban officials and environmentalists, on the other hand, tend to favor using this money for urban transit. The Transportation Act of 1991 tries to meet all of these concerns by giving state and local governments more flexibility in dealing with completing highways, repairing bridges, developing urban transit, and coordinating efforts with the recently adopted Clean Air Act (McDowell 1992, 6–7). Transportation officials face a formidable task in creating guidelines that will keep those who support each of these diverse activities happy.

The Politics Associated with Federal Aid

As may be evident by now, the politics of federal aid are tied to the types of aid involved. Categorical aid programs aimed at specific functional areas of government, such as health care or education, will receive strong support from specialists in that field at all levels of government. Over time such programs will create their own system of support groups like the health care lobby or the education lobby. From the perspective of such groups, the less interference from general administrators—city managers, for example—the better. After all, presumably, the expert best knows what should be done. The system has strong political support from the academic community as well, since, among other things, many academics are the experts who advise or administer the programs and grants.

Many state and local officials, finding themselves bypassed to a large extent by some grants and programs, have sought alternative forms of federal aid. Indeed, the adoption of GRS was largely a response to the intergovern-

Figure 3.2

FEDERAL AID TO STATES IN DOLLARS

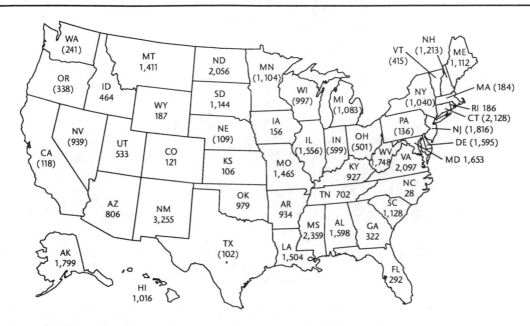

Source: Daniel Patrick Moynihan, *New York State and The Federal Fisc: IXX, Fiscal Year 1994*, July 1995.

Each year Senator Daniel Patrick Moynihan has his staff compute the average amount each resident of a state nets from the federal government. This is computed by taking the total of federal aid allocated to a state, subtracting the total taxes paid from the state, and dividing by the state's population. Thus, in fiscal year 1994, New Yorkers paid in $1,040 more than they got back; those in New Mexico received $3,255 more in federal aid than they paid in taxes.

mental lobby, composed of the National League of Cities, the United States Conference of Mayors, the National Governors' Conference, the National Association of Counties, and the Council of State Governments.

The return of functions and power to the local level has not been without associated problems for state and local officials. Demands once directed at Washington are now directed to them. Often there is not enough money to respond successfully. And officials often find themselves in competition with other states and localities for diminished resources. Let's look at what trends have emerged in the past 15 years.

The New Federalism: Reagan and Beyond

The Reagan administration (1981–1989) sought to return as many functions to state government as possible, but its members were less interested in turning power over to cities. At the same time, aid provided by the national government, in inflation-adjusted terms, was reduced by about 30 percent

©1995 by Luckovich-Atlanta Constitution

over a 10-year period. State efforts to respond to this challenge have been complicated by organized public efforts to lower or put a ceiling on state and local taxes. When successful, these efforts have reduced state revenues considerably. Perhaps the best known of these was Proposition 13 in California. Enacted in 1978, it reduced property taxes by half and placed limits on new taxes. State and local governments in California have not been the same since. The tax burden on California taxpayers was reduced by 22 percent in one year (Dye 1990, 94). This drastically cut available funds to local governments, which were only partly reimbursed by the state. With the recession of 1991–95, California has been forced to cut services severely to balance its budget.

States have been left to their own devices in dealing with these new constraints. But the trend has also placed them in a more significant position to influence certain policies. Elazar's quote at the beginning of this chapter characterizes this perspective. (The facts presented so far largely support the position of Riker: national dominance.) Nevertheless, many policy innovations are first tried by states: term limits, campaign finance reform, contracting for services, motor-voter registration, are all examples of this. Public funding of elections is now provided in 24 states; half of the states limit campaign contributions by PACs (Alexander and Schwartz 1993). In an effort to reduce health costs, states have provided several models that were considered for national adoption during the health care debate in 1994. Hawaii is the most notable example, having adopted employer-mandated health care in 1974, which has resulted in 98 percent of the population being covered, with premiums about one-third lower than the average in the nation.

Faced with continued reductions in federal aid and an inability to raise their own tax revenues, some state and local governments have responded by seeking alternative revenue sources. One of the responses has been to pursue economic development by using tax benefits, gifts of land, or promises of support to entice businesses to locate in their jurisdiction. Frequently, however, this means attracting business away from some other state. For example, when H. J. Heinz, of 57 Varieties fame—now a British firm—was looking to relocate its rice cake production facility, two cities in California and one in Texas were in the running. Heinz selected Gridley, California, because Gridley, which owned its own utilities, could promise low utility rates. While the other two locations offered tax advantages and free land, they were unable to match the Gridley offer. In some cases, winners become losers: The cost of the inducements exceeds the benefits in new economic activity.

While Elazar, in the opening quotation to this chapter, saw states as sources of innovation—laboratories of democracy—some now argue that states are as outmoded as is the federal government. They contend that the new dynamism is to be found in our metropolitan areas. Neal R. Peirce, a respected political writer, calls them *Citistates.* The argument is that today's major metropolitan areas are the communications centers of the new world economy. Peirce tells this story: "When a flood in April, 1992, closed down Chicago's Board of Trade, trading in the London Futures exchange surged as Chicago tried desperately to get back on line and avert a permanent loss of market share" (1993, 3). Telecommunications has become global and instant. With access to an international airport, goods can be moved between any two continents in a single day. My colleague, John G. Sanzone (1994), summarizing various studies on this topic, finds that communities are interested in "knowledge sector" jobs and investments to compete in the new world economy and are ready to engage in cutthroat competition to get them.

Increasingly, the economic development activities of state and local governments extend beyond the domestic arena. Today, only three states do not have economic development offices located in foreign countries; California has five such offices. In a survey of cities, over 80 percent of those with populations in excess of 500,000 had pursued foreign investment (*Municipal Year Book 1992,* 4). This trend raises the interesting question of whether such activities violate constitutional prohibitions on state involvement in foreign policy. States now routinely make arrangements to export their products abroad and contact foreign governments concerning the location of automobile or other manufacturing facilities. Clearly, these are times of change in our federal system.

Federalism in the 1990s

Scholars of intergovernmental relations aren't sure quite what to make of the current condition of federalism. They aren't even sure what to call it. "Cooperative federalism," "picket-fence federalism," "centralized federalism," "competitive federalism," "dysfunctional federalism," "one-way federalism"—all have been suggested as better descriptions than the **"new federalism"** label first provided by the Reagan administration. By whatever name, there is no question there have been significant changes in the past few years that will impact on federalism in the 1990s. John Shannon (1989) suggests three of utmost importance: *Garcia v. San Antonio Metropolitan Transit Authority* (1985), the 1986 tax reform act, and the end of general revenue sharing in 1987.

GARCIA V. SAN ANTONIO METROPOLITAN TRANSIT AUTHORITY   As noted by Shannon, the *Garcia* decision reversed an earlier ruling of the U.S. Supreme Court that allowed state and local governments to set conditions of employment for their own employees. In *Garcia,* a majority of the Court ruled, in effect, that federal regulations could supersede those established by state and local agencies. One of the arguments used by the majority was that because local governments had representatives in Washington, they needed no additional protection from federal authority. That, indeed, was the intent of the Framers. Why, after all, should states need or have special protection from a legislative body that was composed of their representatives?

The *Garcia* decision represents a return to the trend evident since 1937 of national supremacy in areas where Congress has set standards. The *Perpich* decision mentioned at the outset of this chapter is also consistent with this view. It is a view that the Constitution "presumed the existence, not the sovereignty, of the states. The interests of the 'States *qua* [as] States,' for better or worse, however adequately or inadequately, are represented in the national political process" (O'Brien 1989, 417). Recent exceptions to a national approach are *New York v. United States* (1992) and *United States v. Lopez* (1995). The *Lopez* case, in which the Court struck down a congressional action outlawing guns near schools, has some observers claiming that the Court no longer holds a strictly national view.

THE 1986 TAX REFORM ACT   We have already discussed the experiment in general revenue sharing. Some quick inferences can be made about the impact of the 1986 Tax Reform Act. The act reduced the total tax expenditures resulting from the deduction of individuals' state and local tax payments. Indeed, this forced many states to respond by decreasing their own income tax rates. Many, as in California, which had top-end rates in excess of 10 percent, brought them under the 10 percent figure. (In response to the recession, however, California temporarily increased its tax rate to 11 percent on incomes over $250,000 in 1993.) One result can be noted in Table 3.1 on page 64: state and local governments have increased their use of various debt mechanisms such as loans and bonds. Much of this increased debt load has been taken on as a result of the economic development efforts mentioned in the last section.

Other scholars have suggested additional areas of significance for federal-state relations in the 1990s. John G. Sanzone (1989) proposes economic development as the most significant issue facing state and local governments. Among other things he notes is the new mix of private and public activities. This can take two forms. One is discussed at great length in *Reinventing Government* by David Osborne and Ted Gaebler (1992). In it, the authors note the growing competitiveness of the local public sector in the face of difficult economic times. As an example, the city of Phoenix decided to contract with private companies in 1978 for garbage service; it was much cheaper than that provided by the public agency. Rather than just rot away, however, the city's garbage service streamlined its operation and began underbidding the private companies. By 1988 it had won back all of the routes it had lost.

The premise of reinventing government has been picked up by the Clinton administration. Vice President Al Gore headed a commission that has proposed a number of governmental reforms to increase efficiency and productivity. The impact on federalism could be profound. Osborne, who served as a consultant to this commission, describes the goal as "replacing large, centralized, command-and-control bureaucracies with a very different model: decentralized, entrepreneurial organizations that are driven by competition and accountable to customers for the results they deliver" (Posner and Rothstein 1994, 134).

The other area mentioned by Sanzone is hybrid federalism, a model that might fit the goal stated above. Here private companies and local governments join forces to plan projects, secure federal planning grants, and then continue the enterprise on a joint basis. Many local governments already had owned or operated their own utilities—power and water, for example—and provided services such as garbage collection. But here Sanzone is talking about economic activity that until recently was strictly private. An example of this is the joint efforts of local developers and Yolo County in California to create several new towns near the Sacramento airport.

Another problem concerning federalism is that of increased regulations. Some estimates now suggest that as much as 40 percent of local expenditures are needed just to meet federal mandates (*Municipal Year Book 1992*, 51). Joseph Zimmerman calls this the "silent revolution": The control of policy rests with the national government, while compliance remains a state or local problem. The problem, according to Zimmerman, is one of accountability and responsiveness. Local governments are asked to respond to needs, but can hardly be held accountable when they have no control of the policy.

Multistate Regionalism

Our discussion of federalism would not be complete without some mention of regional relationships, particularly multistate arrangements for solving regional problems. Some of these require little attention from the national government other than the constitutional requirement of congressional ratification. Vermont and New Hampshire, for example, can each house prisoners in the other's state. Other cooperative arrangements are more ambitious and thus of greater significance. Among these are regional programs designed to spur economic development, control air pollution, or provide for entire river basin development. The creation of the Port Authority of New York and New Jersey in 1921 provides an illustration of this form of cooperation. Figure 3.3 shows the extent of this governmental empire. Bridges, tunnels, airports, office buildings, in addition to port facilities, now make up the Port Authority. The power of such intergovernmental agencies can even rival that of the states in which they reside. (For a report on this, see the award-winning biography of

Figure 3.3

THE PORT AUTHORITY'S SPRAWLING EMPIRE

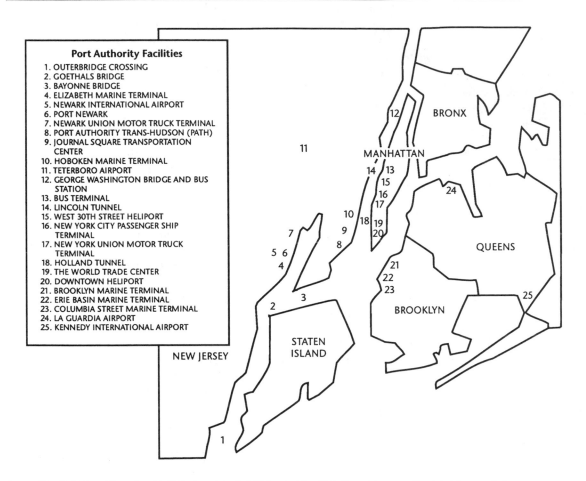

Port Authority Facilities
1. OUTERBRIDGE CROSSING
2. GOETHALS BRIDGE
3. BAYONNE BRIDGE
4. ELIZABETH MARINE TERMINAL
5. NEWARK INTERNATIONAL AIRPORT
6. PORT NEWARK
7. NEWARK UNION MOTOR TRUCK TERMINAL
8. PORT AUTHORITY TRANS-HUDSON (PATH)
9. JOURNAL SQUARE TRANSPORTATION CENTER
10. HOBOKEN MARINE TERMINAL
11. TETERBORO AIRPORT
12. GEORGE WASHINGTON BRIDGE AND BUS STATION
13. BUS TERMINAL
14. LINCOLN TUNNEL
15. WEST 30TH STREET HELIPORT
16. NEW YORK CITY PASSENGER SHIP TERMINAL
17. NEW YORK UNION MOTOR TRUCK TERMINAL
18. HOLLAND TUNNEL
19. THE WORLD TRADE CENTER
20. DOWNTOWN HELIPORT
21. BROOKLYN MARINE TERMINAL
22. ERIE BASIN MARINE TERMINAL
23. COLUMBIA STREET MARINE TERMINAL
24. LA GUARDIA AIRPORT
25. KENNEDY INTERNATIONAL AIRPORT

Source: *New York Times* November 14, 1976. Copyright © 1976 by the New York Times Company. Reprinted by permission.

The Port Authority of New York and New Jersey, created in 1921, is one of the more impressive examples of a multistate compact. Over two dozen major facilities, including bridges, tunnels, and airports, are now owned and operated by this massive agency.

Robert Moses [Caro 1974], who was largely responsible for the expansion of the Port Authority.)

The major rush to join such agreements came during and after World War II: more than 100 compacts were enacted between 1941 and 1975. There are now over 170 of these compacts between states. In an interesting new twist, the national government is now a party to some 30 "federal-interstates," compacts in which the national government has joined with states to address some problem (Saffell 1993, 48). The most significant of these is the Appalachian Regional Commission created in 1965. Spanning a region from Mississippi to New York, this agreement seeks to coordinate a range of federal programs in the areas of sewage treatment, vocational education, water resources, timber aid, conservation, health facilities, and highways. President Clinton proposed spending $187 million in 1995 for this project, down from $247 million in 1994, most of it for highways and economic development.

There does seem to be good reason for attacking some problems, such as air and water pollution, on a regional basis. This is the purpose of the Interstate Sanitation Commission created by New York, New Jersey, and Connecticut. On the one hand, pollution problems usually extend beyond state boundaries. On the other hand, the situation in that region may be unique, and a national solution may be inappropriate. Yet focusing upon and responding to regional differences may pit one region against the other in the quest for scarce federal dollars. In addition, with the current environment of intense competition within and between regions, the likelihood of increased cooperation between states seems much less than it did a decade ago.

Summary

The national government plays an important role in state and local government. The major source of interaction between states and the national government was originally regulatory; it is still significant. But nowadays significant interactions are financial. About a quarter of state and local revenues come from the federal government. Moreover, federal mandates have placed significant financial burdens on state and local governments.

Despite efforts to find alternatives, categorical grant-in-aid programs continue to be the largest source of federal aid, with block grants running a distant second. Almost half of categorical money is directed at three programs: Medicaid, highways, and Aid to Families with Dependent Children (AFDC). General Revenue Sharing, a notable experiment, proved politically unpopular and is no longer available. In a period of continuing change in intergovernmental relationships, regional associations, in which several states combine to attack a common problem, are of increasing importance.

With a reduced commitment from the national government, tax revolts in many states, and an economy going through serious transformations, state and local governments have had to seek alternative sources of income. While there are some important success stories, there has also been cutthroat competition among our states and communites. Increasingly, this competition extends beyond the United States and into the international arena.

Analytical Exercises

1. There is a division of labor that has evolved in the United States among the various levels of government in their provision of goods and services. The

table below shows estimated percentages spent by each on a number of major activities.

	Federal	State	Local
Defense	100	0	0
Health Care/Hospitals	60	18	22
Welfare	36	50	14
Highways	30	40	30
Public Safety	15	13	72
Education	13	20	67

Can you give an explanation as to why these current divisions exist? Do you find any of these that you would like to change? Justify your choices.

2. Assume that you live in a small city that has an annual budget of $20 million and has just received word that it will get a federal grant of $1.2 million. There are no restrictions on how the money can be spent. Immediately, various groups of citizens, city agencies, and the city manager come forward with proposals, listed below, of how to spend the money. As a city council member, you must allocate the funds, realizing the following conditions: all of the suggestions are legal and proper ways to spend the funds; this is the first year of the new program, and there is no guarantee of its continuance next year (the Republicans and Democrats in Congress are divided about it, and while the president supports it, there is a large budget deficit that she is committed to reducing); only those projects with an * can be spent in portions less than that listed in this first year; and all those marked with @ imply costs that will continue after this year. Which options would you support? Why?

- Four new police positions at $35,000 each $140,000*@
- Correct sewer line problem (during storms there is a backup affecting ¼ of the city) 400,000 (if * then @)
- Ladder truck for fire department 220,000
- Matching funds for grant to improve runway at airport (federal government will pay 90 percent) 155,000
- Additional street repair 180,000*
- General pay increase of 5 percent (all employees) 415,000*@
- Equity pay increase (would bring secretaries' pay up to level of custodians) 65,000*@
- Lease office space (Planning Department) 36,000
- Legal services for poor 65,000
- Consultant to write applications for federal grants 40,000
- Emergency housing for homeless 80,000*
- Restore original house of town's founder 80,000*
- New building code enforcement program; two inspectors at $35,000 each 70,000*@
- Fix boiler in City Hall (there's no heat!) 45,000

Chapter Outline

4

Civil Rights and Civil Liberties

If there is a fixed star in our constitutional constellation, it is that no official, high or petty, can prescribe what shall be orthodox in politics, nationalism, religion, or other matter of opinion or force citizens to confess by work or act their faith therein.

—Justice Robert H. Jackson, *West Virginia v. Barnette*, 1943

I would rather be exposed to the inconveniences attending too much liberty than those attending too small a degree of it.

—Thomas Jefferson, 1801

The remarkable events in eastern Europe in 1989 and 1990 and the former Soviet Union in 1991 had many people stating that freedom was breaking out all over—freedom from oppression, freedom from restraint, freedom from a totalitarian state. But not long after, outbreaks of violence, torture, and repression occurred in many of these newly independent enclaves: Bosnia and Chechnya come quickly to mind. And in many other parts of the world, governments do not provide civil liberties to their people. One then might ask whether every human being has a right to expect protection from his or her government and, if so, how it may be guaranteed.

The Framers of the Constitution had to grapple with the same problems. Chapter 2, The Politics of the Constitution, illustrated the debate over the need to include a list of rights in the Constitution and showed how ratification depended on their inclusion. But even at that time there was debate over which rights to include. In this chapter I will develop the bases for an understanding of the concepts of rights and liberties. Their current status in the United States will then be explored. Finally, we'll look at how much popular support there is for various provisions in the Constitution for protecting these rights.

Rights and Liberties: Definitions

The Constitution of the United States guarantees that every citizen has a basic right to freedoms such as personal security, ownership of property, and speech. **Civil liberties** guarantee that government will not illegally interfere with these rights. To simplify a complex concept: civil liberties involve issues of due process of law. These liberties are guaranteed in the Fifth Amendment, and for the first half of our nation's history, this was our basic protection. **Civil rights,** on the other hand, obligate the government to actively ensure that its citizens are not prevented from exercising their rights in the face of unlawful actions of others, whether individuals or government agencies. These rights are based primarily on equal protection of the laws, a concept not added to our Constitution until the Fourteenth Amendment. Voting is one example of a civil right. In practice, the distinctions between liberties and rights may not be so clear-cut; I will treat them as a single subject in the discussion that follows.

There is a fine balance between how much a government should interfere in the lives of its citizens and how much it should not. As a matter of fact, one of the basic principles of the Constitution is limited government. Almost all of us believe that some things reside outside its control. Governments that consider no actions to be outside their concern and control are called **totalitarian** systems. As one way of illustrating this concept, let us consider acceptable government involvement in individual actions, the left-hand side of the area in Figure 4.1. The area across from it represents actions of citizens with which government cannot interfere. There are some areas, however, that continue to be a matter of political disagreement. The shaded area represents these unsettled areas.

Until 1938, this model would have explained constitutional protections. In that year, however, a major change occurred. Chief Justice Stone, in his famous "footnote 4" of *United States v. Carolene Products*, asserted a fundamentally different notion, one that suggested that some constitutional protections were more important than others—they had a preferred position—and that minorities may require special consideration in order to guarantee their rights. The Court, in effect, ended an era in which rights consisted mainly of allowing business to do what it wished and ushered in an era in which individual protections were paramount. This meant that almost all actions of citizens could come before the Court, and citizens could seek relief not just from government but from the actions of other individuals. The Court in recent years has been moving back from this position, giving less attention to individual claims and more to the protection of property. Just how far this trend will go, we do not know; for now, let's try to get some perspective on what has happened and just what protections we have.

Figure 4.1

THE CONCEPT OF LIMITED GOVERNMENT

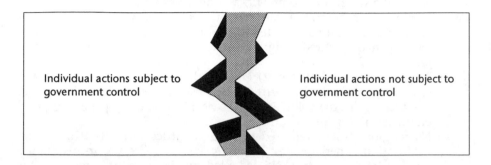

Individual actions subject to government control

Individual actions not subject to government control

The principle of limited government is basic to the U.S. Constitution. The figure above illustrates that there is a clear division between individual actions that are not subject to government control and those that are. In addition, there is an area of behavior, represented by the shaded section, in which it still is unclear whether the government or the individual should have control.

Constitutional Protections

Even in 1787, Americans were a diverse lot. They had come to the United States from different backgrounds and for different reasons. Indeed, in many cases, the rationale for coming to America was to escape from being an oppressed minority. But even here, tolerance was mostly reserved for white Europeans. And despite the fact that particular communities, and even some states, were intolerant of differences, there was a general understanding that different values were supported elsewhere.

Included in the original Constitution as framed in Philadelphia were the following major protections:

- The writ of **habeas corpus** means that an imprisoned person must be brought before a judge, who will determine whether the government is holding the prisoner legally and whether it can continue to do so. This right may be suspended only in time of war (art. I, sec. 9). Literally, it means to produce the body.
- No **ex post facto law** may be passed (art. I, secs. 9 and 10). An ex post facto law is a law that makes criminal an act which was not unlawful when done, or that inflicts a greater punishment than the law provided when the act was committed. One of our fundamental concepts is that the law must be known; the rules cannot be changed after the fact. Thus, in *Calder v. Bull* (1798), the Court rejected a law that changed the rules of evidence to permit conviction with less or different evidence than existed when the crime was committed.
- No **bill of attainder** may be passed (art. I, secs. 9 and 10). A bill of attainder is a legislative action that may "apply either to named indi-

viduals or to easily ascertainable members of a group in such a way as to inflict punishment on them without a judicial trial" (*United States v. Lovett,* 1946). When the legislature acts as a judicial agent, except where allowed in impeachment, as Congress did in the above case by naming in an appropriations bill three officials who were not to receive a pay raise, it has violated this prohibition against attainder. There have been only three congressional actions struck down under this provision.

- **Trial by jury** (art. III, sec. 2) ensures the right to a jury trial in the state where the crime occurred. Long established in English practice and accepted in the colonies was the notion that one's peers can properly determine guilt.
- No **religious test** is required to hold an office (art. VI). This widely held notion is perhaps best stated by Thomas Jefferson in his Statute for Religious Freedom (1786) adopted by the state of Virginia: "Our civil rights have no dependence on our religious opinions."

The Bill of Rights

Most Federalists felt that additional amendments to the Constitution guaranteeing basic individual liberties were unnecessary, since the national government had been delegated only specific powers in the first place. But others, led by Thomas Jefferson, argued that they were absolutely necessary. In order to gain ratification of the Constitution, the Federalists agreed to add these amendments. The House adopted 17, the Senate 12, and 10 were finally ratified by the states in 1791. These 10 have always been known as the Bill of Rights. The major provisions include:

• Freedom of religion	First Amendment
• Freedom of speech	First Amendment
• Freedom of press	First Amendment
• Freedom of assembly	First Amendment
• Protection from unreasonable search and seizure	Fourth Amendment
• No double jeopardy	Fifth Amendment
• Due process of law	Fifth Amendment
• Trial by jury	Sixth Amendment
• Confront one's accusers	Sixth Amendment
• Speedy and fair trial	Sixth Amendment
• No cruel and unusual punishment	Eighth Amendment

Selective Incorporation

There was no question that the Bill of Rights applied to the national government. Did it also apply to the states? In *Barron v. Baltimore* (1833), the Court held that these amendments applied only to the national government.

The city of Baltimore had dumped its excess sand and gravel into the water near Barron's wharf in 1832 and, in so doing, destroyed it for commercial

© 1996 by Sidney Harris

use. Barron took the city to court on the grounds that it violated the "takings" provision of the Fifth Amendment and deprived him of his property without compensation. Chief Justice Marshall disagreed and argued that the amendments applied only to the national government, not the states. Thus, if the national government had destroyed his property, Barron would have won his case. The state of Maryland was not bound by the same constitutional provision, Marshall said, and Barron lost his case. The decision essentially confirmed that each person was a dual citizen, both of the national government and separately of an individual state.

The Fourteenth Amendment, adopted in 1868, clearly states that its equal protection and due process clauses are directed at the states. In 1897, the Supreme Court used these provisions to extend the Bill of Rights to the states. The Court, however, has not taken an all-or-nothing approach as to which provisions are applicable to state and local governments. Determination is made on a case-by-case, clause-by-clause basis. This is called **selective incorporation.** For example, since 1925, state and local governments have not been able to limit speech—at least not to a greater degree than the federal government; since 1931, the press has also been protected from unreasonable state or local interference. In 1913, the Court established what is called the **exclusionary rule** in federal cases: Information obtained illegally cannot be admitted as evidence in court. Agencies such as the FBI and the Treasury Department have been bound by these rules since then. But state and local governments were not until 1961. In that year, in the case of *Mapp v. Ohio*, the Court held that state and local governments were subject to these provisions as well. Figure

Figure 4.2

INCORPORATION OF THE BILL OF RIGHTS

Year	Right	Case
First Amendment		
1925	Freedom of speech	*Gitlow v. New York*
1931	Freedom of press	*Near v. Minnesota*
1937	Freedom of assembly and freedom to petition government	*DeJonge v. Oregon*
1937	Freedom of religion	*Hamilton v. Regents*
1947	Separation of church and state	*Everson v. Board of Education*
Fourth Amendment		
1961	Limitations on search and seizure	*Mapp v. Ohio*
Fifth Amendment		
1897	Right to just compensation	*CB&Q Railroad v. Chicago*
1964	Protection against self-incrimination	*Malloy v. Hogan*
1964	Protection against forced confessions	*Escobedo v. Illinois*
1969	Protection from double jeopardy	*Benton v. Maryland*
Sixth Amendment		
1948	Right to public trial and notice of charges	*In re Oliver*
1961	Right to an impartial jury	*Irvin v. Dowd*
1963	Right to counsel at trial	*Gideon v. Wainwright*
1965	Right to confront witnesses	*Pointer v. Texas*
1966	Right to counsel and to remain silent at arrest	*Miranda v. Arizona*
1967	Right to a speedy trial	*Klopfer v. North Carolina*
1967	Right to compulsory process	*Washington v. Texas*
1968	Right to jury trial	*Duncan v. Louisiana*
Eighth Amendment		
1962	Protection from cruel and unusual punishment	*Robinson v. California*
Ninth Amendment		
1965	Right to privacy	*Griswold v. Connecticut*

The Supreme Court applies provisions of the first 10 amendments—the Bill of Rights—to state and local government on a case-by-case, phrase-by-phrase basis. The figure above gives the year and case in which a provision of the Bill of Rights was applied to the states.

4.2 lists the cases and the sections of the Bill of Rights that have been incorporated.

Notice that the first cases involve the protections of the First Amendment. Justice Benjamin Cardoza noted in *Palko* (1937) a distinction between fundamental and non-fundamental rights; only fundamental rights were incorporated because "the matrix, the indispensable condition, of nearly every other form of freedom" depended on them. Then a gap occurs before a number of significant cases in the 1960s incorporate provisions of the Fourth to Ninth Amendments. When reference is made to the liberalism of the Warren Court—the era from 1953 to 1968 when Earl Warren was chief justice—it is usually

to these cases. However, Henry Abraham (1993), a leading authority on the Court, assigns to Justice Hugo Black the main credit for getting the rest of the Bill of Rights incorporated.

There are only a few provisions of the Bill of Rights that do not apply to the states now. These include the provisions of the Second—the right to keep and bear arms; the Third—quartering of troops; the Fifth—the provision for a grand jury indictment; the Seventh—jury trial in civil cases; and the Eighth—bail and excessive fines. The rest of the provisions have now been extended to all levels of government. The Fourteenth Amendment also has been used to allow national intervention into questions of civil rights and apportionment.

Rights and Liberties in Practice

Two problems arise from trying to implement these provisions. The first is one of definition. Just what do we mean by "a speedy trial," and what is "cruel and unusual punishment"? The second problem occurs when two rights are in conflict; which one takes precedence? The issue of abortion, for example, involves both problems. There is first a matter of definition: Is the fetus a person under the Constitution? And second, there is a matter of priority: Do the rights of the mother take precedence over the right of the state to protect the unborn? Some states, for example, consider the murder of a pregnant woman to be a double homicide. Yet the courts have allowed abortion partly on the basis of the fetus's not yet having full individual rights. In its highly controversial decision, *Roe v. Wade* (1973), the Court used the following to define legal abortions:

1. First trimester (12 weeks). Mother and her physician have complete control over choice of abortion, and the state cannot interfere.
2. Second trimester. Mother can abort, but states can impose regulations to ensure that she does so only under a doctor's advice regarding her health.
3. Third trimester. Mother can only abort to preserve her life or health, and state can impose regulations restricting or barring abortion.

Since 1973, the Court has been faced with numerous cases in which it has had an opportunity to overturn *Roe*. For 23 years, opponents have sought a reversal of this decision, and presidents have appointed justices who have expressed opposition to *Roe*; while the Court has allowed states greater leeway in what they can regulate, it has failed to directly overturn *Roe*. The most recent major challenge came in *Planned Parenthood of Southeastern Pennsylvania et al. v. Casey*, in which a majority held that courts "must protect all of the most fundamental personal liberties, whether or not these are specifically mentioned in . . . the Constitution" (Dworkin 1992, 29).

If you find yourself arguing with others over these provisions, you will have plenty of company. Few issues have divided citizens as clearly as this one. And this brings us to another point: The basic issues of civil liberties are not simple. The definitions are difficult, and each of the conflicting arguments has some merit. The Fourth Amendment provides another illustration. At what point does its protection from illegal search give way to a societal demand that a "presumed culprit should not be allowed to go free simply because," in Justice Cardozo's memorable words, "the constable blundered" (Abraham, 1993, 16)? In recent terms of the Supreme Court, some of the difficult questions that were addressed included:

- Can Congress "encourage" states to adopt a minimum drinking age of 21 years by withholding federal highway funds if they do not? (Yes. *South Dakota v. Dole*, 1987)
- Does the fact that blacks are much more likely than whites to receive the death penalty in Georgia invalidate its use? (No. *McClesky v. Kemp*, 1987)
- Can a public employee be fired for commenting, "If they go for him again, I hope they get him," when informed of the shooting of President Reagan in 1981? (No. *Rankin v. McPherson*, 1987)
- Did a Louisiana law requiring the teaching of "creation-science" along with evolution violate the separation of church and state? (Yes. *Edwards v. Aguillard*, 1987)
- Does a person have a free-speech right to burn the American flag as a protest gesture? (Yes. *Texas v. Johnson*, 1989)
- Can the death penalty be used against a defendant with severe mental retardation? (Yes. *Penry v. Lynaugh*, 1989) Or against a 16-year-old? (Yes. *Sanford v. Kentucky*, 1989)
- Can individuals refuse life-support medical treatment—a so-called right to die? (Yes. *Cruzan v. Missouri Department of Health*, 1990)
- Can federal judges order local governments to increase taxes to remedy constitutional violations such as school segregation? (Yes. *Missouri v. Jenkins*, 1990)

- Can a state provide for testimony in child molestation cases where the accused cannot be present when the child testifies? (Yes. *Maryland v. Craig,* 1990)
- Can a state keep criminals from profiting from books and stories about their misdeeds? (No. *Simon & Schuster v. New York State Crime Victims Board,* 1991)
- Does the forced administration of antipsychotic medication during a trial violate a defendant's rights? (Yes. *Riggins v. Nevada,* 1992)
- Can the United States bring to trial someone kidnapped from his or her country, even if the government of that country protests? (Yes. *United States v. Alvarez-Machain,* 1992)
- Does a prayer at a high-school graduation ceremony violate the separation of church and state? (Yes. *Lee v. Weisman,* 1992)
- Can a state impose an enhanced sentence on someone convicted of a hate crime? (Yes. *Wisconsin v. Mitchell,* 1993)
- Can a city ordinance outlaw animal sacrifices of religious groups? (No. *Church of the Lukumi Babalu Aye v. City of Hialeah,* 1993)
- Can a city require a property owner to dedicate land for a bike and pedestrian path in exchange for a building permit if what is taken is not in "rough proportionality" to the overall value of the development? (No. *Dolan v. City of Tigard, Ore.,* 1994)
- Does a restraining order that establishes a buffer to keep abortion protestors away from clinics violate the protestors' right of free speech? (No. *Madsen v. Women's Health Center,* 1994)
- Can states impose term limits on their members of Congress? (No. *U.S. Term Limits, Inc., v. Thornton,* 1995

These kinds of tough questions are hardly unusual; year after year the Court is faced with the most pressing of our concerns about individual liberty. In 1995–96 the Court will face difficult questions involving the death penalty (when must a petition for *habeas* be filed to be timely?), gay rights (can a state prevent its local governments from protecting gay rights?), and Native American casinos (can Congress force states to negotiate gambling limits with Indian tribes?).

The Fundamental Civil Liberties

Our basic civil liberties are outlined in the Bill of Rights. Here we will examine the protections of the First Amendment—speech, press, and religious freedom, criminal due process as it relates to the death penalty, and equal protection as illustrated by the civil rights movement.

First Amendment Protections

The First Amendment outlines the basic elements of freedom of speech, press, and religion. What the First Amendment has not been able to do, however, is to clearly interpret some of the complications and questions that arise in the practice of these freedoms. Some of these will be discussed in the following section.

FREEDOM OF SPEECH   "Congress shall make no law . . . abridging the freedom of speech." This seems straightforward enough, but there has always been controversy over what constitutes "speech," and there has also been the recognition that freedom of speech is generally not an absolute; there are times when it cannot be protected. Political speech has been protected to a greater extent than commercial advertising, which, in turn, has greater protection than obscenity. But even with political speech, problems arise. What do we do about political speeches that call for the overthrow of the government? As early as 1798, Congress enacted the Sedition Act (of the **Alien and Sedition Acts**), a law prohibiting speech (writing and publishing are included) "with a willful intent to defame the government or excite against it the hatred of the people." A number of prominent Jeffersonian Democrats editors—and writers—were tried under its provision. The Federalists had passed this and a number of other acts in an attempt to undermine Jefferson and his supporters. The Federalist who proposed and passed the laws lost the next election, in part, no doubt, because of the uproar concerning the Alien and Sedition Acts.

There is also the problem of speech versus some other basic right. While speech protection is generally afforded a "preferred position," it still is not unlimited. Justice Holmes said that the Constitution "would not protect a man in falsely shouting 'fire' in a theater and causing a panic" (*Schenck v. United States,* 1919). One's speech is generally protected from prior restraint; that is, it cannot be stopped or censored before it is made. One must, though, still be responsible for one's actions; if what you say slanders someone else, you can be held accountable. One's speech is also protected unless it presents a clear and present danger to others or to society. In *Brandenburg v. Ohio* (1969), the Court limited restrictions on free speech to instances "where such advocacy is directed to inciting or producing imminent lawless action and is likely to incite or produce such action." Any restrictions the government might make must be stated with clarity and apply equally to all.

There are areas of speech that are not protected. Libel is one such area; inciting others to commit an illegal action is another. A recent free-speech issue of interest to most students is the attempt by colleges and universities to deal with racism and sexism on campus. Can individuals or groups be disciplined or expelled for uttering racist or sexist slurs? A number of schools from coast to coast have imposed sanctions on students' speech, from the University of California at Berkeley—the home of the Free Speech Movement in 1964—to the University of Connecticut. The basis for such limitations is the Court's determination that so-called "fighting words" do not enjoy constitutional protection. But a number of recent lower court rulings have struck down such restrictions. The University of Michigan's code that prohibited hate speech about "race, ethnicity, religion, sex, sexual orientation, creed, national origin, ancestry, age, marital status, handicap, and Vietnam-era-veteran status" was ruled in Federal District Court to have gone too far (*Michigan v. Miller,* 1990). Stanford's limitations were also ruled unconstitutional in Federal District Court in 1995; Stanford chose not to appeal. The problem is that what constitutes fighting words is not always clear, and even where some words are clearly offensive and would lead those to whom they are directed to respond violently in some circumstances, when they are uttered in other settings they may simply be deemed vulgar or in poor taste.

More controversial, however, is the issue of obscenity, which is legally defined as visual or written material portraying sexual activities that appeal to prurient interests in a manner that is offensive to public taste and morals. The legal dilemma derives from the conflict of two basic rights: the right of freedom of speech versus the right of a community to restrict what it considers offensive material from being sold and read. After considerable vacillation over what was obscene and what could be done about it, the Court, in *Miller v. California* (1973), set the following standard: to be obscene, a work, taken in its entirety, must to "the average person applying contemporary community standards" appeal to "prurient interest" and depict "in a patently offensive way, sexual conduct specifically defined by applicable state law." It must, as well, lack "serious literary, artistic, political, or scientific value." Obviously these guidelines are confusing, leading many to concur with former Justice Potter Stewart, who contended that he couldn't define obscenity, but he knew it when he saw it.

Even with this standard, or lack of it, if you will, there are many controversies that extend beyond court actions. Recent attention to artistic expression is an example. In 1989, a photo retrospective of the work of Robert Mapplethorpe, in part funded by a National Endowment for the Arts (NEA) grant, became the center of a major political controversy. Mapplethorpe photographs in some cases gave graphic and explicit detail to homosexual acts. Led by Senator Jesse Helms (R-NC), conservatives tried to restrict grants made by the NEA; some tried to do away with the NEA altogether. The arts community saw this as an attempt to limit artistic expression, a form of free speech. James Barrie, the director of the Contemporary Arts Center in Cincinnati, was eventually acquitted of all charges of displaying obscenity in the museum. But the appropriations battle for funding for the NEA continues to be waged in Congress. Senator Wyche Fowler, a Georgia Democrat and member of the Appropriations Committee, said: "The battle will never be over as long as we have critics of any government funding of the arts, and as long as we have artists using public funds producing works repugnant to a sizable portion of American families" (*New York Times* October 18, 1990, C19). With Republicans in control of Congress in 1995, the issue of NEA funding was again in the forefront. The 1995 vote to continue NEA funding for two more years, for example, was 235 to 198 in the House of Representatives. Whether detailed limits are placed on the NEA or other federal programs, there is no question that, henceforth, agencies are going to be cautious about what they fund and whom they support. The point is that while the courts play a major role in defining constitutional protections, other government agencies must also make a determination of what is accepted and acceptable. There is currently wide discretion on the part of the government as to what is given preferred treatment and what does not receive support.

Drawing by Shanahan; © 1993 The New Yorker Magazine, Inc.

"Of course, until they appoint a new NEA chairman I'm in limbo."

FREEDOM OF THE PRESS   The Framers were especially supportive of a free press. Madison, perhaps carrying the argument beyond that of most, claimed "that to the press alone, chequered as it is with abuses, the world is indebted for all the triumphs which have been gained by reason and humanity over error and oppression" (Platt 1992, 285). Thomas Jefferson claimed that if given the choice between "a government without newspapers, or newspapers without a government," he would "prefer the latter." There still can be restrictions, however, on what the press can cover. When a defendant's right to a fair trial is threatened by too much publicity, a judicial hearing can be closed to the press. In the highly publicized case in California of accused mass murderer Charles Ng, for example, the court closed the preliminary hearing to the press when videotapes depicting torture were to be shown.

The press is held accountable for what it prints—it can be sued for libel, although this is especially difficult if the person offended is a "public figure." The Court held in *Sullivan v. New York Times* (1964) that with public figures, not only must the statements be false, but they must have been knowingly printed with malice. Were this not the case, wrote Justice Brennan, "would-be critics of official conduct may be deterred from voicing their criticism, even though it is believed to be true and even though it is in fact true, because of doubt whether it can be proved in court or fear of the expense of having to do so."

Most would agree that the real test of freedom of the press is what government can keep from being printed. In 1971 the *Washington Post* and the *New York Times* came into possession of a work known as the Pentagon Papers. It was a lengthy document that included considerable information about how the United States had made certain decisions concerning its involvement in Vietnam. The Nixon administration went to court to prohibit its publication in order, officials said, to avoid endangering national security. The administration further asserted that only the president was able to determine what constituted such a danger and had complete authority therefore to seek an injunction to suppress publication. The Supreme Court—and this included four justices appointed by Nixon—unanimously held that the government could not exercise prior censorship of the press. Nevertheless, the Reagan administration successfully prevented media representatives from covering the first 24 hours of the invasion of Grenada in 1985, again contending national security reasons; and the press was subject to official direction during the Gulf War.

A somewhat different conclusion from that in the Pentagon Papers was reached in a similar case in 1987 in the United Kingdom. There, a former member of the intelligence community wrote a book called *Spycatcher*, which the government felt violated the State Secrets Act, an act forbidding government officials from publicly discussing any of their actions that the government considered confidential. The Law Lords, England's highest court, sided with the government, not only prohibiting the publication of the book in Britain, but prohibiting any newspaper from commenting on it. The difference between this case and the Pentagon Papers case points to a fundamental difference in our interpretation of liberties. In the United States there is the idea that a liberty is freedom from government action. In Britain the notion is that a liberty is something the law has given the people; the power to make the law is therefore the power to define liberties. Since Parliament is supreme—that is, no other body can overrule it—Parliament defines what liberties are. However, the United Kingdom is also a signatory to the European Convention of Human Rights, whose Court of Human Rights ruled in favor of the newspapers in 1991, arguing that *Spycatcher* was already widely available. However, the court upheld the ability of governments to prevent publication of national security secrets.

FREEDOM OF RELIGION   There are two provisions in the First Amendment affecting religion. The first provides for the free exercise of religion; the other prohibits the government from establishing a religion. There are controversies arising from the **free exercise clause** which, while allowing the freedom to practice any religion, nevertheless prohibits religious activity that is a crime or is contrary to public morals. For example, various religious groups have refused to salute the flag on religious grounds or refused to fight in war. The Court in the flag salute issue first said that states have a right to force compliance, then changed its mind a few years later. In *West Virginia v. Barnette* (1943), the Court allowed religious belief as a basis for not saluting the flag. But the Court has not allowed various religious practices such as refusing medical treatment or vaccination, or encouraging substance abuse, to stand in the way of state laws controlling these practices. In the latter category would be the Court's refusal to protect Native Americans who use peyote for sacramental purposes from prosecution by states for violating narcotics laws (*Employment Division v. Smith,* 1990). Nevertheless, the Court did strike down an ordinance aimed at preventing animal sacrifice by a religious group (*Church of the Lukumi Babalu Aye v. City of Hialeah,* 1993).

The major controversies, however, stem from the **establishment clause,** which prohibits the interaction of church and state. The most problematic area is that of government assistance to church schools. The government cannot establish a religion, nor can it interfere with religious practice. But can it provide textbooks to children attending church schools? The basic test the Court now uses to decide whether or not a law supports a religious purpose was developed in a number of cases in the late 1960s and early 1970s, but draws mainly from *Lemon v. Kurtzman* (1971). The following three provisions determine how a decision is to be made:

- Does the law have a secular purpose?
- Does it enhance or inhibit religion?
- Does it produce excessive government entanglement with religion?

Many critics of *Lemon* hoped that it would be set aside in a 1994 case; however, the Court upheld *Lemon* by ruling that a school district in New York set up specifically to provide special education for a Satmar Hasidic community was unconstitutional in *Board of Education of Kiryas Joel Village School District v. Grumet.*

Prayer is another area of the establishment clause. The Court has consistently struck down religious observances in public schools since *Engel v. Vitale* (1962). But the controversy continues, with various groups attempting constitutional amendments to allow prayer in school, or enacting provisions for one minute of each school day to be set aside "for quiet and private contemplation or introspection." The Court in a 5–4 decision in 1992—*Lee v. Weisman*—ruled that prayers at school graduation ceremonies violated the First Amendment. The Court has, however, provided religious groups access to public schools for meetings if the school allows other nonacademic groups access (*Westside Board of Education v. Mergens,* 1990).

Criminal Due Process

Few areas of civil liberties are more controversial than the protections afforded those accused of criminal activity. Most people would prefer that criminals not be afforded protections because of the element of fear—those who are a danger to society should not be walking our streets—and because of the element of retribution—a criminal should pay for her or his actions. Providing the guarantees of the Constitution to someone accused of a gruesome murder is not easy in the face of widespread hostility toward what is perceived as the Court's being "soft on criminals." The death penalty provides an interesting illustration. In *Furman v. Georgia* (1972), the Court struck down the death penalty in the states. A sharply divided Court gave a variety of reasons, but essentially the rationale was that, as practiced, the penalty was applied in an arbitrary fashion. There was too much discretion in deciding who would be subject to death. For example, more blacks were executed than whites, even though blacks constituted only about 12 percent of the population.

States responded by reenacting death penalty laws—35 of them by 1976— that in many cases took away any discretion as to when the death penalty was applied. The Court struck these down as too narrow (*Gregg v. Georgia,* 1976). In so doing, the Court suggested guidelines that states might follow in meeting the constitutional test. Any state law had to provide for a clear-cut definition of those crimes that were to be capital cases by indicating the circumstances that made them especially heinous. For example, a murder committed during the commission of another felony is considered a special circumstance. There is another aspect that the Court looks for as well. A law must also provide for mitigating factors that would suggest a more lenient sentence. A young person who has never been in trouble but who commits a murder during a car theft might be looked at differently from one who has a long record of car theft, assault, and armed robbery.

Death penalty decisions in individual cases continue in each term of the Court; in 1994 the Court ruled on a number of issues, including jury instructions about life imprisonment without parole and a jury's consideration of the circumstances of the crime, the defendant's criminal history, and defendant's age in deciding on a death penalty (*Sandoval v. California*). As stated above, the constitutional impasse has been removed, and now we are seeing cases that do not challenge the death penalty directly. Rather, these cases concern conditions under which the death penalty is to be applied. For example, in 1989 the Court ruled that a severely retarded individual could still be sentenced to death, as could a 16-year-old. Decisions in 1990 restricted multiple appeals by those convicted and sentenced to death. The Court also prohibited third parties from appealing when the person convicted did not wish appeals to go forward (*Whitmore v. Arkansas,* 1990). More recent controversies have focused on such issues as whether lethal gas is an appropriate method of execution; it was ruled inappropriate in District Court and is working its way to our highest court. With New York's approval of a death penalty, there are now 38 states with capital punishment. The number of executions since 1976 is provided in Figure 4.3.

Civil Rights

We classify things all the time and make discriminating judgments concerning these classifications: For example, your instructor will judge that some of you deserve an A in this course; others will get lower grades. Governments make distinctions also. Not all of these classifications are unconstitutional. For example, people with different incomes pay different levels of tax. But some classifications are not reasonable. In fact, they place an unfair burden on those so classified. Thus, in order to be more just, the Court now uses a concept of a **suspect classification** in which the government must present

Figure 4.3

CAPITAL PUNISHMENT IN THE UNITED STATES

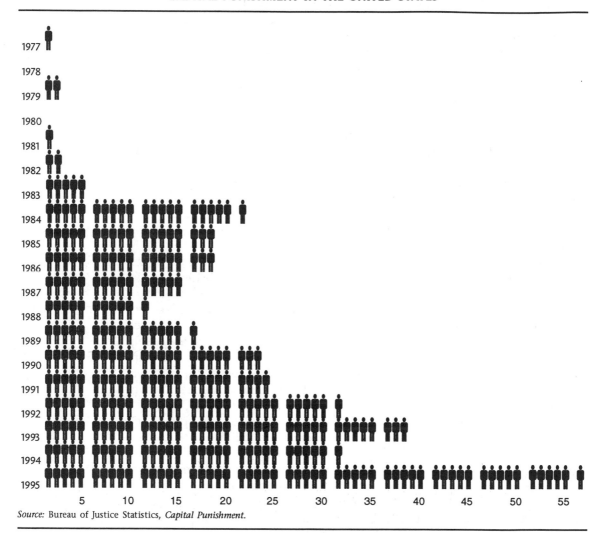

Source: Bureau of Justice Statistics, *Capital Punishment*.

Since the U.S. Supreme Court reinstated the death penalty in 1976, the number of executions has continued to rise. The methods of execution in most states are lethal injection and electrocution, with lethal gas, hanging, and the firing squad also being used in some states.

an especially compelling reason to continue its discrimination. In 1954, for example, the Court made the concept of race a suspect classification. One result of this decision, in the case of *Brown v. Board of Education of Topeka, Kansas* (1954), was that discrimination on the basis of race was ruled unconstitutional in determining the school one attended. The extent of segregation at the time is shown in Figure 4.4; almost half the states were officially segregated!

Figure 4.4

SEGREGATION LAWS IN THE UNITED STATES IN 1954

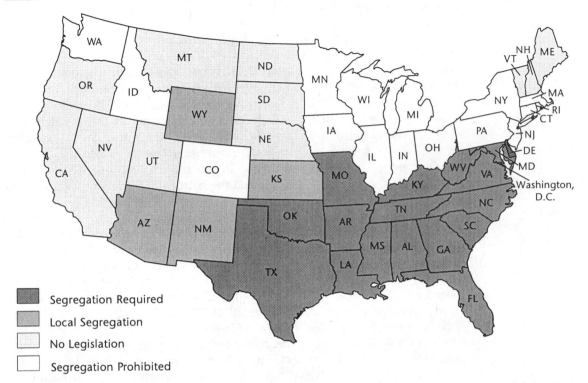

Segregation Required

Local Segregation

No Legislation

Segregation Prohibited

Source: Thomas R. Dye, *Politics in States & Communities,* 6th ed., © 1988, p. 383. Reprinted by permission of Prentice Hall, Inc., Englewood Cliffs, NJ.

Segregation by law denied civil rights to blacks in many states as late as 1954.

VOTING   Perhaps the most basic form of citizen participation is the right to vote. The concept has always been an important American value, but there has not always been agreement on who has a right to vote. In the American colonies, the estimate is that only about eight percent of the adult population could vote. Women, minorities, those without property or who didn't pay taxes, and those who were from the "wrong" religion were excluded. In addition, the Constitution gave little direction as to who should vote, leaving it to the states. There was one exception: Article I, Section 2, required a state to give voting rights in national elections to those who could participate in the election of state legislative representatives—the "most numerous branch" provision.

It took a civil war and considerable political upheaval to change our approach to who may vote. Four constitutional amendments—the Fifteenth Amendment, 1870, removing the qualification of race; the Nineteenth, 1920, gender; the Twenty-fourth, 1964, payment of a poll tax; and the Twenty-sixth, 1971, which extended voting to 18-year-olds—as well as significant legislation such as the 1965 Voting Rights Act and its amendments were necessary for the openness we experience today.

AFFIRMATIVE ACTION   Removing legal obstacles to the full extension of civil rights is one thing; establishing these rights in practice is another. The inability to secure full rights for African Americans led to the concept that the government must do something positive to redress the imbalance produced by segregation. That is, not only should roadblocks be removed, but inducements should also be added. **Affirmative action,** as this is called, has added a new dimension to the controversy over civil rights. Special training or entrance programs implemented for those formerly disadvantaged have brought about a backlash from those in the majority who see these actions as threatening. Although the courts and the national government have adopted some provisions for affirmative action, they have rejected others.

Supreme Court decisions are a good example. In the case of *Regents of the University of California v. Bakke* (1978), a plan that set aside 16 spaces for disadvantaged and minority applicants to the University of California, Davis, Medical School was ruled unconstitutional. A specific quota was regarded as an inappropriate means of enhancing minority enrollment. Based on this precedent, the Justice Department filed suit against the law school at the University of California, Berkeley, in the fall of 1992 for having provided minority applicants unfair advantage. Yet, in *Fullilove v. Klutznick* (1980), a congressional provision that 10 percent of the public works funds be set aside for minority businesses was upheld. The decision in *Metro Broadcasting v. FCC*, 1990, upheld a congressional affirmative action plan to help minorities gain ownership of broadcasting franchises. But *Metro* was overturned in a case challenging preferences for minorities in government contracts—*Adarand Constructors, Inc., v. Pena*, 1995—which suggests that the Court has still not set a clear direction for affirmative action.

Government agencies are still providing affirmative help; in 1994, the Federal Communications Commission issued guidelines for bidding for new broadcasting rights that give minority firms up to a 25 percent credit in their bid and a 15 percent lower down payment than larger, nonminority firms. But in Congress, new Republican majorities in 1995 made affirmative action programs a major political battleground. And in California, a constitutional initiative that undoes affirmative action legislation is scheduled for the ballot in 1996.

The major provisions of civil rights legislation and what each attempted to accomplish are listed in Figure 4.5 on the following page.

Changes in Civil Liberties

Our conception of what is appropriate action on the part of government and what is not has grown during our 200-year history. In some cases, we have modified the Constitution to reflect these changing views. The most dramatic

Figure 4.5

CIVIL RIGHTS: THE MAJOR ENACTMENTS

- Civil Rights Act
  1957
  Established Civil Rights Commission.
- Civil Rights Act
  1960
  Established use of federal registrars in South.
- Civil Rights Act
  1964
  Established Equal Employment Opportunity Commission, barring discrimination in employment and public facilities; parents could now sue to integrate schools.
- Voting Rights Act
  1965
  Extended federal registrars; dropped literacy requirements; adopted preclearance.
- Age Discrimination
  in Employment Act
  1967
  Prohibited job discrimination against 40–65-year-olds. Amended in 1986 to prohibit mandatory retirements.
- Fair Housing Act
  1968
  Barred discrimination in renting or selling houses; prohibited interference with civil rights workers.
- Voting Rights Act
  (Amendments)
  1970
  Extended provisions to North.
  (Amendments)
  1975
  Extended provisions to language of minorities.
  (Amendments)
  1982
  Extended provisions 25 years.
- Rehabilitation Act
  1973
  Added handicapped persons to affirmative action programs.
- Civil Rights
  Restoration Act
  1988
  Restored anti-sex discrimination to 1972 Education Act Amendments.
- Civil Rights Act
  1991
  Protection of workers from discrimination.

These are the major laws enacted by the federal government to protect citizens' civil rights.

change relates to slavery, a practice specifically protected in the original Constitution. We have also amended the Constitution to reflect changing ideas of the right to vote, as mentioned earlier.

Changes have also been accomplished through court decisions. I have already mentioned capital punishment as an area where the courts have grappled with a changing society and its use of the death penalty. Another controversial change brought about by Court interpretation is the warning that suspects must be given prior to interrogation by authorities. An example of the provisions in a "Miranda" warning is given in Figure 4.6. The Court, in the *Planned Parenthood v. Casey* decision mentioned earlier, stated, "Our Constitution is a covenant running from the first generation of Americans to us and then to future generations. . . . We accept our responsibility not to retreat from interpreting the full meaning of the covenant in light of all our precedents."

Perhaps the most dramatic changes in our view of fundamental rights have taken place in the area of women's rights. Women were second-class

(Continued on p. 99)

Figure 4.6

NOTICE OF RIGHTS

NOTICE OF RIGHTS
JD-CR-5 REV. 1-84
PR. BK. 637, 654, 656
GEN. STAT. 54-1b, 54-2a, 54-63c, 54-64b

STATE OF CONNECTICUT
JUDICIAL DEPARTMENT
SUPERIOR COURT

INSTRUCTIONS

TO CLERK OF COURT
1. *Prepare in duplicate.*
2. *Give Original to Defendant.*
3. *Retain copy for file.*

TO OTHER AGENCIES
1. *Prepare in triplicate.*
2. *Give Original to Defendant*
3. *Send a copy to Clerk of Court*
4. *Retain a copy for your files.*

NAME OF DEFENDANT

JUDICIAL DISTRICT OR G.A.

LOCATION OF COURT *(No., Street, Town)*

OFFENSES CHARGED *(Also specify statute number)*

NOTICE OF RIGHTS

1. You are not obligated to say anything, in regard to this offense you are charged with but may remain silent.

2. Anything you may say or any statements you make may be used against you.

3. You are entitled to the services of an attorney.

4. If you are unable to pay for the services of an attorney you will be referred to a Public Defender Office where you may request the appointment of an attorney to represent you.

5. You may consult with an attorney before being questioned, you may have an attorney present during questioning and you can not be questioned without your consent.

6. *(Not applicable if you were arrested on a Superior Court Warrant which specified that bail should be denied or which ordered that you be brought before a clerk or assistant clerk of the Superior Court.)* You have a right to be promptly interviewed concerning the terms and conditions of your release pending further proceedings, and upon request, counsel may be present during this interview.

ADVERTENCIA DE DERECHOS

1. Usted no está obligado a decir nada en cuanto a esta ofensa por la cual se le acusa, pero puede permanecer en silencio.

2. Cualquier cosa que usted diga o alguna declaración que usted haga puede ser usada contra usted.

3. Usted tiene derecho a los servicios de un Abogado.

4. Si usted no puede pagar por los servicios de un Abogado, usted sera referido a la Oficina del Defensor Publico donde puede usted solicitar el asignamiento de un Abogado para representarlo.

5. Usted puede consultar con un Abogado antes de ser interrogado. Puede tener un Abogado presente durante el interrogatorio y no puede ser interrogado sin su consentimiento.

6. *(Esto no aplica si a usted lo arrestaron con una orden de arresto de la Corte Superior que especificaba que se le negara fianza u ordenaba que a usted se le presentara ante el secretario o el ayudante a secretario de la Corte Superior.)* Usted tiene el derecho de ser entrevistado prontamente acerca de los términos y condiciones de su libertad, pendiente a procedimientos adicionales y sobre solicitud el Abogado Consultor puede estar presente durante esta entrevista.

I, the undersigned, have advised the Defendant of his/her rights as stated above:

SIGNED *(Authorized person)*

TITLE

DATE AND TIME ADVISED
/ / ____M.

For Court Use Only
FILE DATE

I have been advised of my rights as stated above and have received a copy of this notice.

He sido instruido acerca de los derechos que aparecen en esta notficacion, de la cual he recibido copia.

SIGNED *(Defendant)*
X

DOCKET NO.

NOTICE OF RIGHTS

The Supreme Court decision *Miranda v. Arizona* (1966) required that defendants be informed of their rights.

citizens until the Nineteenth Amendment to the Constitution in 1920, when women were given the right to vote. But there were still laws that placed women in an inferior position to men. For example, women could be excluded from certain jobs just because of their gender. In some state laws, women were defined as property belonging to their husbands or fathers. Even when laws making invidious comparisons were removed, there still were lingering social norms or patterns of employment that disadvantaged women. Women performing the same job and with the same qualifications did not receive the same salary or opportunity for advancement as men—the "glass ceiling." The issue became one of affirmative action: Must the government help in the assertion of a right or in correcting past abuses? Part of the answer depends on whether one agrees that past wrongs should be made right; if one does, then generally one would support a positive program to correct those past inequities. If one takes the view that the only guarantee should be equal opportunity now, then one would probably not support affirmative action.

Privacy is another area where new viewpoints are in conflict with old. The issue of privacy relates to personal behavior, such as sexual preferences and practices about which government might wish to take action, and personal information that government might wish to acquire. The Bureau of the Census gathers personal statistics from the entire population; the Internal Revenue Service has extensive files about our incomes; the Immigration and Naturalization Service about our travels; the Selective Service about our registration for possible military service; the military about our service record, and so on. Governments at the local level obtain similar kinds of facts. Schools, for example, have extensive information about a person's performance, abilities in tests, family background, and behavior. Modern technology makes this information more readily accessible and more easily transmitted from one agency to another than it was in the past.

Who should have access to this information? And under what conditions? Justice Louis Brandeis, in a dissent in a case in 1928 (*Olmstead v. United States*), called privacy "the right to be left alone—the most comprehensive of rights and the right most valued by civilized men." But he was in the minority then; it was not until 1965 that the Supreme Court accepted the constitutional liberty of privacy. Congressional enactment of the Privacy Act of 1974 was the first recognition of this emerging area by Congress. Your instructor cannot post your grade for all to see, for example, if others can identify who you are.

States have in the past assumed the right to regulate the sexual activities of their citizens. One's sexual preferences and practices have therefore become important areas of controversy for the Court. Beginning with *Griswold v. Connecticut* (1965), the Court ruled that states could not restrict the sale of contraceptives, basing their decision on several constitutional provisions, including the right to privacy. The Court decided that the concept of "privacy" was contained in the Ninth Amendment, which states that we possess rights that may not be enumerated in the first eight amendments. The decision in *Roe v. Wade* was also based on this amendment. But the Court in 1986 upheld a Georgia law that made sodomy a crime, rejecting a claim to privacy regarding what is done between consenting adults behind closed doors (*Bowers v. Hard-*

wick). This decision, as well as more recent ones limiting the scope of *Roe,* indicate that some on the Court are uneasy with the privacy argument.

Support for Civil Liberties

Aside from the difficulty of defining rights and liberties, and the equally difficult task of deciding which has priority when two or more freedoms are in conflict, we also, paradoxically, face the challenging problem of lack of popular support for our basic liberties. In the abstract, most of us support the high ideals of the Bill of Rights; in practice—that is, when we must act to guarantee or protect a basic right—we are not always as supportive.

In a recent nationwide public opinion poll sponsored by the Thomas Jefferson Center for the Protection of Free Expression, over 90 percent of the respondents indicated that the government had no business telling them what to say, while 59 percent favored government censorship—for example, the banning of popular music that condones drug abuse or broadcasts of sexually explicit lyrics. "We found alarming evidence of a double standard, a sense that the First Amendment protects what the speaker wants to say, but not so clearly the views of others," stated the Center's Director, Robert O'Neil (*Sacramento Bee* September 15, 1990, A5). These findings are consistent with evidence gathered over the past 60 years. In the 1950s, a major study found that 58 percent of the population agreed that we should identify all communists even if innocent people might be hurt, while 54 percent would not let a socialist teach at a college or university (Stouffer 1955). In a replication of Stouffer's work, the findings were that "intolerance has by no means disappeared; it has simply shifted targets." Instead of socialists and communists, hostility is now directed more at fringe groups of both the right and left (Sullivan, Pierson, and Marcus 1979, 87). In a major review of over 120 academic studies of public attitudes toward Jews, Tom W. Smith, director of the National Opinion Research Center at the University of Chicago, found that "four in 10 Americans believe that Jews are more loyal to Israel than to the United States," an attitude unchanged in the past 40 years, and "that about one in five believes that Jews 'have too much' power and influence in some spheres of America life." (Morin 1994, 37). It is also true that the level of intolerance is related to education. In a 1992 study of anti-Semitism, results showed that about one in ten respondents with a college education was rated as highly anti-Semitic, while for those with less than a college education the rate rose to one in four (*Los Angeles Times* November 17, 1992, A28).

In a study of over 600 potential jurors in Colorado, Edward J. Bronson (1971) presented respondents with these statements:

- If the police have arrested an individual and the district attorney has brought him or her to trial, there is good reason to believe that the man or woman on trial is guilty.
- If the person on trial does not testify at his or her trial, there is good reason to believe that he or she is concealing guilt.

Bronson found 25 percent and 26 percent, respectively, in agreement, even though our basic premise of justice is a person's presumed innocence. When this study was repeated in California several years later, 31 percent and 48 percent, respectively, concurred (Bronson 1979). Bronson and I have gathered data from over 25 surveys in California in the past four years in which, on average, 42 percent of the respondents felt that, regardless of what the law says, defendants in a criminal trial should be required to testify in their own defense (Bronson and Ross 1991). The Fifth Amendment prohibits self-incrimination; the Sixth Amendment guarantees a fair and impartial jury. But these liberties become harder to realize when such sizable segments of the population do not, in practice, agree with them.

Summary

Many would contend that we fought the Revolutionary War to secure protection of individual liberty. Various provisions were included in the Constitution, but more specific protection was called for. The Bill of Rights added 10 amendments to the Constitution dealing with rights and liberties. Additional amendments have also expanded the basic rights of Americans.

Giving abstract support to such basic provisions as free speech does not mean that everyone would support the free speech of someone they believe is wrong or whose views they fear. Support for the abstract provision also does not guarantee that we can agree on just what each provision means in practice. Moreover, basic rights and liberties often are in conflict—to protect one may mean denying another. Thus, much of constitutional law is now concerned with defining and determining the relative importance of the basic guarantees of rights and liberties in the Constitution. The issues involved represent some of the most significant political controversies we face.

Analytical Exercises

1. Few would dispute the grave social injustices that women and minorities have suffered in American society in the past. The current social problem is what to do about such injustices. Generally these have been dealt with under what we call affirmative action. If public opinion polls are to be believed, most Americans favor affirmative action as an abstract principle. Nevertheless, affirmative action has come under increasing criticism when it involves quotas or other specific plans to provide women and minorities with special treatment. Assume you are a member of a city council that is approached by a group of women employees who work as secretaries. They present data to show that while they must have at least a high school diploma and pass a difficult proficiency test to qualify for their positions, jobs occupied mainly by men, such as janitor or truck driver, require only an eighth-grade education and the passing of a less-demanding exam; yet these positions pay significantly higher wages. The women want compensatory pay and a new, higher base pay that reflects qualifications and responsibility.

Arguments in favor of the women's plan include:
- The goals of the program are appropriate; the means would accomplish these goals.
- Programs like this are necessary to correct past abuses. No one denies that the differences in salary are because occupations historically held mostly by men are paid more highly than those dominated by women. It is especially appropriate for government to be setting the example for appropriate treatment of employees.
- The fundamental principle of pay based on the qualifications necessary for and the responsibility associated with an occupation is an important one.
- The costs would not be that great—less than 1 percent of the city budget.

Arguments against such a plan include:
- Discrimination in any form, even to correct a past injustice, is wrong. The answer is to ensure that women and minorities have equal access to current and future janitorial and teamster positions.
- Pay is based on prevailing market conditions; to adjust this to achieve some social goal is inappropriate. The city has no difficulty attracting good employees with the current salary schedule.
- Adopting this program would artificially raise the costs to private enterprise in the area, since they would have to pay similar wages to attract and keep secretaries.
- Current employees in other occupations should not have to bear the cost of correcting past actions in which they had no part.

Would you vote to initiate the program?

2. On May 17, 1995, three police officers from a large city arrived at the home of John Doe, a student at the local university, to execute a warrant to search the house for suspected narcotics. The judge had granted a search warrant after police had reported a tip from a reliable informant that Doe was making sales of controlled substances from the house.

Approaching the house, officers noticed someone looking at them from the front window. They quickly approached the front door, knocked loudly, identified themselves as police, and demanded admission. They heard noises from inside; they repeated their demand for admission. A young man, later identified as one of four students living at the house, opened the door and was presented with the warrant. The police entered quickly and moved through the house. They came upon a closed bedroom door, and without knocking or identifying themselves, broke down the door. Inside were Doe and his girlfriend; on the bed were a gun and a box containing what was later determined to be marijuana and methamphetamines. Doe was charged with possession of a deadly weapon, which, when found in conjunction with another felony adds 10 years to the sentence, and with possession for sale of marijuana and methamphetamines. At a hearing, his attorney moved to suppress the evidence.

The Fourth Amendment states that the right of people to be secure "against unreasonable searches and seizures, shall not be violated, and no warrants shall issue, but upon probable cause, supported by oath or affirmation and particularly describing the place to be searched, and the persons or things to be seized." The prosecutor contended that the police had a valid warrant, had given proper knock-and-notice compliance, and were not required to do so again for each room within the house. In addition, she asserted that since the officers had been seen, evidence could be destroyed and there was a potential for violence if they did not proceed swiftly through the house. She cited the gun found in the bedroom to support this argument.

The defense claimed that the police did not use good faith in gaining the warrant in the first place—no evidence was presented that the informant was either real or reliable; that even if the warrant was valid, police must still knock and identify themselves before entering a closed room; and finally, that since the gun was not identified in the warrant and was not actually in Doe's possession at the time, its presence should be suppressed regardless of the ruling on the previous points. As the judge hearing these arguments, how would you rule on each?

Chapter Outline

Congress: Structure and Legislation

Like a vast picture thronged with figures of equal prominence and crowded with elaborate and obtrusive details, Congress is hard to see satisfactorily and appreciatively at a single view and from a single standpoint. Its complicated forms and diversified structure confuse the vision, and conceal the system which underlies its composition. It is too complex to be understood without an effort, without a careful and systematic process of analysis.

—Woodrow Wilson, *Congressional Government*, 1885

It could probably be shown by facts and figures that there is no distinctly native American criminal class except Congress.

—Samuel L. Clemens (Mark Twain), 1894

At the Constitutional Convention in 1787, a **bicameral legislature** (one with two houses) was created. The small states feared that if the House of Representatives were allowed to select members of the Senate, as proposed in the Virginia Plan, power would accrue to large, populous states. A compromise was reached: a House of Representatives composed of members who were to be elected every two years in each state, with the number to be based on the population of the state, and a Senate made up of two members from each state who were to be elected to six-year terms. This compromise proposed by Connecticut was a key element necessary to the adoption of the Constitution.

Table 5.1

DIFFERENCES BETWEEN THE HOUSE AND THE SENATE

House	Senate
Represent districts of about 600,000 people	Represent states—2 senators for each state
Larger—435 members	Smaller—100 members
Serve 2-year terms	Serve 6-year terms
Individual members have less power	Individual members have more power
Less debate and restrictive access to the floor	More debate and more open access to the floor
Amendments must be germane to the subject matter of original bill	Amendments do not need to be germane
All tax and appropriations bills begin in House	Ratify treaties and confirm presidential appointments
Members have fewer committee and subcommittee assignments	Members have more committee and subcommittee assignments
Office staff of about 20 with emphasis on casework	Office staff from 20 to 100 depending on size of state—more emphasis on legislation
Less prestige and visibility—representatives run for Senate	More prestige and visibility—senators run for presidency
Presiding officer is an elected Speaker of the House who is the leader of the majority party	Presiding officer is vice president—real power rests with majority leader—elected by majority party

Differences in Perspective

The differences between the House and the Senate are summarized in Table 5.1 and will be discussed at various points in the next two chapters. To begin with, I would like to emphasize how these structural characteristics lead members of the two houses to have different perspectives on the roles they play in government. Even when both are controlled by the same party, there may be little cooperation or agreement on what should be done.

A major distinction between the two houses of Congress is the length of terms of representatives and senators. The two-year term forces House members to campaign almost immediately if they plan to run again. It exposes them to pressures that are not felt by senators, who have three to four years in which to become familiar with their jobs and their committee assignments and to form their areas of expertise. There may be time for senators to correct their mistakes before campaigning for reelection.

Size is another major difference between the House and the Senate. The intimacy of the Senate with only 100 members (two from each of the 50 states) can be contrasted to the House with 435 representatives. Representation in the House is apportioned among the various states according to the **census**, which is taken every 10 years (see chapter 10, Political Parties, Fig. 10.6, p. 253). The Senate engages in debate more frequently and conducts its business in a more informal atmosphere than does the House. Size is also largely responsible for the organization of each body. The House with so many members must find ways to keep control so that a majority can govern. It does this by giving its elected leadership more power. In the Senate, with fewer members, leaders must defer to individual members. The "underlying governing principles of chamber rules—majoritarianism in the House and individualism in the Senate" gives leaders in the House more control of actions; in the Senate consent must be crafted with individual senators in mind (Smith 1992, 128).

Although Alaska, Delaware, Montana, North and South Dakota, Vermont, and Wyoming each have only one representative, states such as New York and California as of 1995 have 31 and 52 representatives, respectively, and only two senators each. Differences in the **constituency** of representatives and senators from these more-populous states have produced striking variations in their perspectives. Representatives might come from a suburb, a predominantly rural area, or a central city. In most cases, they represent the views of their particular districts. Senators must find ways to represent the conglomerate interests of the entire state. Every senator, for instance, represents some farmers but not all representatives do. There are, in brief, more constituency demands on senators compared to House members (Oleszek 1996, 198). Major large states, such as Ohio, Texas, New York, and California, have almost as many conflicting interests and as heterogeneous a population as the nation has. Effective senators, more than representatives, must see how issues are connected. "Thus, we expect senators to be less willing to defer to committees and more insistent on their individual right to contribute to policy outcomes" (Smith 1992, 171).

Until 1913, senators were appointed by their state legislatures; with adoption of the **Seventeenth Amendment** to the Constitution, senators are popularly elected. The change had a profound effect on the prestige of the two bodies. Mark Twain, whose unkind comment introduces the chapter, was particularly miffed at how a Senate seat could be bought from corrupt state legislatures. "I think I can say, and say with pride, that we have some legislatures that bring higher prices than any in the world" (Hodge and Freeman 1992, 13). In the first half-century under the Constitution, the House was the more prestigious: James Madison, the father of the Constitution, ran for and was elected to the first House, and the party caucus of House members nominated our early presidents. Since 1913, popular election, combined with smaller size, longer terms, and larger constituencies, as well as the power to confirm presidential appointments and ratify treaties, has made the Senate the more prestigious of the two houses, and at the same time more vulnerable to challenge in elections. Senate races attract better-known challengers, who are better financed than House challengers, and better able to succeed. Paradoxically, members now face the criticism raised by Twain and others a century ago that their seats are bought. In our time, candidates depend on contributions for the large sums of money needed to compete for a seat in Congress, especially a Senate seat. I will return to this issue in chapter 10.

Constitutional Powers

The Constitution explicitly grants Congress a number of powers. Most of these are enumerated in Article I, Section 8, of the Constitution (see p. 357) and were designed to correct shortcomings in the Articles of Confederation. Congress is empowered to establish and maintain armed forces, to declare war, to raise taxes, and to spend money. In addition, Congress controls interstate commerce under the Commerce Clause, which it has used to strengthen federal power in relation to state governments. Finally, Congress is given constitutional authority to pass those laws "necessary and proper" to carry out its explicit grants of authority. Federal courts have interpreted this as a broad grant of authority, giving Congress great latitude in the content of legislation with which it can deal.

This constitutional framework places Congress squarely in competition with the executive branch. According to Neustadt's thesis of "sharing powers" (see chapter 2, p. 50), the agencies, offices, and programs of the executive branch must first be created by Congress. The armed forces, for example, commanded by the president, are created and financed by Congress. Indeed, through the **appropriations** process (see pp. 125–127), Congress becomes concerned with all actions of the executive, since presidents and bureaucrats must enlist Congress to gain financial support for their programs. The Senate has some special constitutional rights that involve it in executive decision making. In the area of foreign affairs, the Senate must ratify treaties proposed by the president. Moreover, the Senate must advise the president and consent to most nominations made by him or her, confirming all federal judges, ambassadors, cabinet members, and other officials. Congress also has the power to impeach executive and judicial officials and to remove them from office upon conviction. Although I suggest in chapter 9 (p. 220) that this grant is seldom used, its threat has had an impact on the actions of justices and presidents. President Nixon, for example, resigned when confronted with sure impeachment and conviction in 1974. The process is slow, however, and is used only as a last resort.

Internally, Congress is authorized to establish its own organization and rules. Article I, Section 5, states that "Each House shall be the Judge of the Elections, Returns and Qualifications of its own Members, . . . punish its Members for disorderly Behaviour, and, with the Concurrence of two thirds, expel a Member." Having a grant of authority and exercising it are two different things, as the 1974 Senate election in New Hampshire indicated. The vote was so close—Louis C. Wyman (R) 110,926; John A. Durkin (D) 110,924—that the decision rested on how to count about 100 disputed ballots. The Senate gave up the effort after 42 roll-call votes failed to resolve the issue, and called for a new election, which Durkin won handily. In the House, however, a disputed election in Indiana in 1984 resulted in a House committee's counting disputed votes and deciding on a winner who had only two votes more than his opponent. Republicans were so incensed at that decision that they walked out of the chamber and refused to return for several days.

On occasion, both houses have refused to seat a member. The most recent instance was the exclusion of Adam Clayton Powell (D-NY) from the House during the 90th Congress for misuse of public funds. Powell took his case to court: in *Powell v. McCormick* (1969), the Court ruled the House action unconstitutional. Expelling an already seated member is another matter. Representative Michael Myers of Pennsylvania was expelled in 1980 after his felony conviction in the Abscam scandal—the only member of Congress to be unseated in the twentieth century. The Senate was prepared to expel Harrison Williams (D-NJ) after his conviction on corruption charges, but he resigned in 1983 before a vote was taken. In 1988, the House was prepared to expel Mario Biaggi (D-NY), convicted of taking bribes in the Wedtech scandal, had he not resigned. Most recently, Senator Bob Packwood (R-OR) finally gave up his seat in September 1995 when the Senate ethics committee voted to expel him for making unwanted sexual advances toward female staff members.

Discipline less than expulsion can include reprimands up to censure. Each house now has an ethics committee, responsible for investigating suspected wrongdoing. In the Senate, recently, Dave Durenberg (R-MN) was "denounced" for staying in his own condominium on trips to Minnesota and billing the Senate for lodging. In most cases, a member chastised in this manner simply does not seek reelection. Of the five senators who were reprimanded for their dealings with Charles Keating of the failed Lincoln Savings and Loan, only Senator DeConcini (D-AZ) sought reelection, and he won.

Legislation

The Constitution formally grants "all legislative power" (art. I, sec. 1) to Congress. The complicated process by which Congress considers and passes legislation is shown in Figure 5.1. The remainder of this chapter will describe the various steps in this process. You might wish to mark this figure and refer to it often as we move through the chapter.

Conducting Legislative Business

Congress can act on bills, resolutions, and executive documents. Of these, bills are considered most frequently. They may be either public or private; if they are passed and approved, they become acts of Congress.

BILLS   Public bills concern class actions, whereas private bills relate to actions on behalf of and relating to a named individual, primarily immigration cases or claims against the government. At one time, private bills numbered several hundred a year; now fewer than 20 every two years are passed. This is mainly the result of changes in immigration law and increased responsibility of administrative agencies. During the past decade, approximately 10,000 public bills have been introduced in each term, of which Congress passes about 500 (Ornstein, Mann, and Malbin 1996, 165). A term of Congress lasts two years, divided into two sessions. In January 1995, the 104th Congress—the first was in 1789—began its first session. I should note, however, that while the total of bills passed has remained about the same, the length of the bills passed has increased dramatically, from about 2,000 total pages in the 1960s to over 7,500 total pages in 1993–94 (165).

(Continued on p. 110)

Figure 5.1

HOW A BILL BECOMES LAW

This shows the most typical way in which proposed legislation is enacted into law. There are more complicated, as well as simpler, routes, and most bills never become law. The process is illustrated with two hypothetical bills, House bill No. 1 (HR. 1) and Senate bill No. 2 (S. 2). Bills must be passed by both houses in identical form before they can be sent to the president. The path of HR. 1 is traced by a solid line, that of S. 2 by a broken line. In practice most bills begin as similar proposals in both houses.

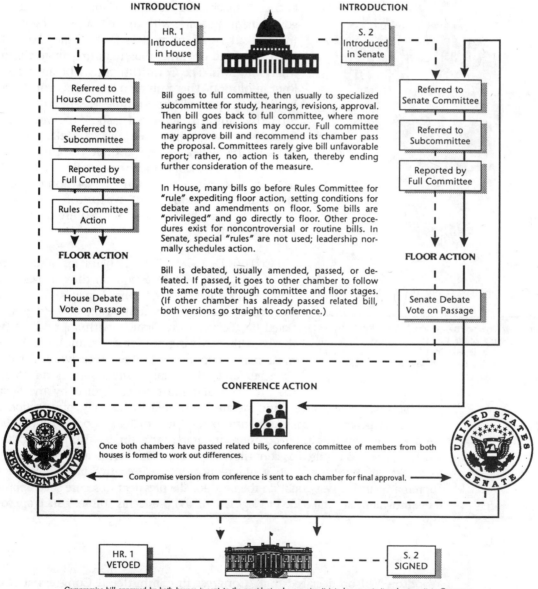

INTRODUCTION

HR. 1
Introduced
in House

INTRODUCTION

S. 2
Introduced
in Senate

Referred to
House Committee

Referred to
Subcommittee

Reported by
Full Committee

Rules Committee
Action

FLOOR ACTION

House Debate
Vote on Passage

Bill goes to full committee, then usually to specialized subcommittee for study, hearings, revisions, approval. Then bill goes back to full committee, where more hearings and revisions may occur. Full committee may approve bill and recommend its chamber pass the proposal. Committees rarely give bill unfavorable report; rather, no action is taken, thereby ending further consideration of the measure.

In House, many bills go before Rules Committee for "rule" expediting floor action, setting conditions for debate and amendments on floor. Some bills are "privileged" and go directly to floor. Other procedures exist for noncontroversial or routine bills. In Senate, special "rules" are not used; leadership normally schedules action.

Bill is debated, usually amended, passed, or defeated. If passed, it goes to other chamber to follow the same route through committee and floor stages. (If other chamber has already passed related bill, both versions go straight to conference.)

Referred to
Senate Committee

Referred to
Subcommittee

Reported by
Full Committee

FLOOR ACTION

Senate Debate
Vote on Passage

CONFERENCE ACTION

Once both chambers have passed related bills, conference committee of members from both houses is formed to work out differences.

Compromise version from conference is sent to each chamber for final approval.

HR. 1
VETOED

S. 2
SIGNED

Compromise bill approved by both houses is sent to the president, who can sign it into law or veto it and return it to Congress. Congress may override a veto by a two-thirds majority vote in both houses; the bill then becomes law without the president's signature.

Source: 1994 Congressional Quarterly Almanac, C-4.

Drawing by Stan Hunt; © 1977 The New Yorker Magazine, Inc.

"There are days, Hank, when I don't know who's President, what state I'm from, or even if I'm a Democrat or a Republican, but, by God, I still know how to bottle up a piece of legislation in committee."

RESOLUTIONS   Congress also considers various types of resolutions. The most important are **joint resolutions**, which must be passed by both houses of Congress. Important joint resolutions are used to extend or suspend existing legislation, and if they are approved by the president they then become public laws. During recent years when the president and Congress have not been able to agree on spending decisions or budget cutbacks, for example, Congress has extended government spending with the use of joint resolutions. Indeed, only once from 1985 to 1995 has the budget been approved on time, thus requiring these continuing resolutions. The Constitution may be amended by joint resolution. This requires a two-thirds vote in both houses; if approved, the measure is sent to the states for ratification. In Figure 5.4 I show the vote on the Balanced-Budget Amendment, which fell two votes short in the Senate in 1995. **Simple resolutions** must pass only the house in which they are introduced. They deal with matters of concern to that house, such as changing rules. **Concurrent resolutions** are expressions of opinion by Congress and require only the approval of both houses.

EXECUTIVE DOCUMENTS   Congress is also authorized or required to take action on three types of executive documents. First, the Senate's advice and consent is necessary for ratification of treaties negotiated by the executive branch, with approval of two-thirds of those voting needed for ratification. Second, most major appointees to the executive and judicial branches and all military officers are nominated by the president and must be confirmed by the Senate. Appointments to executive positions are considered individually, after action has been recommended by the appropriate committee; military appointments usually are considered en masse, on occasion, thousands at a time. A simple majority of senators present is required to confirm nominations. Third are plans by the executive to implement legislation that would reorganize the executive branch. While the Supreme Court has cast doubt on the need for the president to secure such approval, these provisions are still added to legislation, and presidents still seek such approval.

Committees

Woodrow Wilson declared that "Congress in committee is Congress at work" ([1885] 1956). Early in its development, Congress went to a system of **standing committees**, those that carry on from year to year, for the consideration of legislation. The House started the process at the turn of the nineteenth century; the Ways and Means Committee became a standing committee in 1802, Public Lands in 1805, and the Post Office in 1808. In 1816, the Senate established the major components of a standing committee system for, among other things, finance, foreign relations, and armed services. Recently, committees have been added to deal with ethics, science, technology, and the budget.

The Power of Committees

Once a bill is introduced, it is sent to a committee for consideration. Herein lies the primary power of the committee system. It is within the committee that the basic decisions are made about whether and in what form a piece of legislation is going to move forward. A growing volume of legislation and a need for expertise in evaluating that legislation have made Congress reliant on specialized standing committees. While this is more true of the House than of the Senate, the reliance on committees holds for all but a few major issues: those stemming from presidential or partisan politics and ideological or even interpersonal conflicts.

SUBCOMMITTEES   Specialization has led to a breakdown of the tasks facing committees into small categories considered by **subcommittees**. A subcommittee is composed of fewer members than the full committee and considers only some of the issues facing the full committee. A typical House member will have two committee and four subcommittee assignments; a Senate member usually has three committee and eight subcommittee assignments. A senator, then, has little time to develop expertise in a topic, while a half-dozen members in the House may have such expertise. This more recent result in the Senate is stated by Barbara Sinclair in *The Transformation of the U.S. Senate,* an award-winning study. "The typical senator no longer specializes; he becomes involved in a broad range of issues, including ones that do not fall into the jurisdiction of his committees" (1989, 2).

The unwritten rule that governed congressional action in the past, and which still is important, is **reciprocity**, in which one is given control over his or her area of specialization and defers to others in their area of specialization. Only on issues that are highly publicized and crucial to a member's constituents or to national politics, in areas of dispute between the two parties, or on questions concerning the president's program is the unwritten rule of reciprocity likely to be broken.

IMPLEMENTING THE LAW   Committees also have a duty to see that the laws Congress makes are properly implemented. Some feel that this primary function of Congress is even more important than the legislative function. Congressional committees not only investigate highly publicized transgressions of the executive branch, as they first did in 1792 in looking at the government's dealings with Native American Indian tribes, and as they have done more recently with respect to Watergate, Iran-Contra, the savings and loan failures, and Whitewater, but committees also hold formal investigations or hearings to determine whether the bureaucratic decisions that implement current legislation are in line with congressional intent and purpose. It is true that Congress cannot always compel administrative officials to talk, but as Richard Allan Baln states, "It can make them wish they had" (1989, A10). Congress still controls the purse; it can reward or punish; it can change the jurisdiction or organization of agencies; it can decide not to reauthorize programs. Most agency administrators find it to their advantage to follow closely the wishes of their respective oversight committees, those responsible for an agency's legislation. Presidents have sometimes felt that this function represents an unnecessary intrusion of the Congress into program administration. Congressional reforms in 1970 and 1974, however, added specific legal power for committees to conduct investigations. And the courts have generally supported this congressional power. There are many scholars who think this is the most important thing that Congress does. They point to John Stuart Mill, the British philosopher, who stated back in 1861:

> Instead of the function of governing, for which it is radically unfit, the proper office of a representative assembly is to watch and control the government: to throw the light of publicity on its acts: to compel a full exposition and justification of all of them which any one considers questionable, and, if the men who compose the government abuse their trust, to expel them from office. This is surely ample power, and security enough for the liberty of the nation. (Mill [1861] 1958, 8)

Critics of Congress suggest that "**oversight**" all too often means overlooking rather than watching over administrative actions. For example, "Senator John Glenn (D-OH) noted that members of Congress 'may have been derelict in our duty . . . in not being on top of those things more' " when commenting on an estimated half-billion-dollar-per-plane cost overrun in the B-2 bomber program (Ripley and Franklin 1991, 163).

In addition to formal investigations, Congress can control budget decisions at the authorizing and appropriating stages, or it can audit specific program expenditures to determine what improvements might be made in future legislation. Informally or in hearings, a member of Congress can make "suggestions" to agency heads that some course of action be pursued. Such nonstatutory control of administration can also be accomplished through the committee report. Appropriations subcommittee reports are an example. Found therein are such directives as "the Committee . . . directs the Department to change its practice and procedure," "funds . . . should be earmarked for establishing a market news service on fruits and vegetables," and "it is directed that such funds not be used directly or indirectly to impose regulations relative to wages" (Kirst 1969, 33–35). "[T]he verbs 'expects,' 'urges,' 'recommends,' 'desires,' and 'feels' display in roughly descending order how obligatory a committee comment or viewpoint is intended to be" (Oleszek 1996, 308). Appropriations bills each year contain numerous directives; typical would be 1989, when 19 were added. Each directive has a specific meaning of which bureaucrats are well aware and to which they respond appropriately. But such a system is fragile, depending on the good faith of agency officials.

Table 5.2

COMMITTEES AND SUBCOMMITTEES OF THE 104th CONGRESS

House Committees	Number of Subcommittees
Agriculture	5
Appropriations	13
Banking and Financial Services	5
Budget	0
Commerce	5
Economic and Educational Opportunities	5
Government Reform and Oversight	7
House Oversight	0
International Relations	7
Judiciary	5
National Security	5
Resources	5
Rules	0
Science	1
Small Business	4
Standards of Official Conduct	0
Transportation and Infrastructure	6
Veterans Affairs	0
Ways and Means	5
Senate Committees	
Agriculture, Nutrition, and Forestry	4
Appropriations	13
Armed Services	6
Banking, Housing, and Urban Affairs	0
Budget	0
Commerce, Science, and Transportation	6
Energy and Natural Resources	4
Environment and Public Works	4
Finance	6
Foreign Relations	7
Governmental Affairs	3
Indian Affairs	0
Judiciary	6
Labor and Human Resources	4
Rules and Administration	0
Small Business	0
Veterans Affairs	0

Source: Congressional Staff Directory (Washington, DC: U.S. Government Printing Office, 1995).

"Violations of that trust may result in budget cutbacks, restrictive language in statutes, and itemized appropriations" (Fisher 1993, 99).

STANDING COMMITTEES   In the 104th Congress, there were 19 standing committees in the House of Representatives and 17 in the Senate. These are listed in Table 5.2 along with the numbers of subcommittees attached to each (a total of 141). The degree to which committees have subdivided their activities became an issue in 1994–95 when Republicans gained control of Congress. In the House, the new majority made major changes, reducing the number of committees and subcommittees. The Senate did not make any significant changes in their committees. The penchant of Congress to divide tasks minutely will become apparent shortly.

SPECIAL AND SELECT COMMITTEES   In addition to standing committees, **special and select committees** are sometimes established to investigate particular problems and are dissolved after issuing their reports. A select committee is chosen for its specialized knowledge or ability to deal with some particularly troublesome problem (for example, the Select Committee on Intelligence). Recent cuts in the congressional budget have all but eliminated their use.

JOINT COMMITTEES   Primarily administrative, **joint committees** consist of an equal number of senators and representatives and are created by concurrent resolutions. They are designed to attack an important national problem, such as taxation or economics, or to supervise congressional housekeeping, such as the Joint Committee on Printing. The chair is held alternately by a senator and a representative. Joint committees function as communication links between the two houses and limit control over certain policy areas to a few members.

CONFERENCE COMMITTEES   Like joint committees, **conference committees** consist of both senators and representatives and are constituted on an ad hoc basis to resolve differences in measures passed by both the House and the Senate. While conference committees usually involve just a few key members from each house, the House sent 250 conferees in 1981 to the conference on the budget and over 100 to a conference on the 1990 Clean Air Bill.

COMMITTEE OF THE WHOLE   Finally, the House organizes the **Committee of the Whole**, in which all revenue and appropriations measures, as well as other types of legislation, are considered. The Speaker excuses himself from this committee, but his exclusion is primarily a parliamentary device to facilitate expeditious handling of debate and drafting of amendments to important legislation. Only 100 members are needed for a quorum in the Committee of the Whole as compared to 218 in the full House. Until 1971, votes were not recorded, but the Legislative Reorganization Act of 1970 provided for recorded votes, which need only be requested by 25 members. Actions taken in the Committee of the Whole are then presented to the House for final passage.

The Legislative Process

A **bill** is merely the formal draft of a law presented to Congress for enactment; a bill that has been passed by Congress and approved by the president is a **law**. Bills can be introduced in either house of Congress, but the Constitution gives the House of Representatives the exclusive power of initiating revenue measures (taxes). By custom, appropriations bills (spending) also originate in the House. Identical bills can be introduced simultaneously in both houses as **companion bills**. When a bill has been introduced and "read" (merely printed by title in the *Congressional Record*), it is sent to the appropriate committee. Determination of the committee to which it will be assigned is rigorously defined in the rules of both the House and the Senate. Legislation has become so complex that bills are sent increasingly to more than one committee, a practice called **multiple referral**. Should some question arise, determination of the appropriate committee is made by the Speaker of the House or by the presiding officer of the Senate.

Often, competing bills concerning a policy area are introduced: the administration's proposal, the other party's countermeasure, a bill submitted on behalf of some interested organization, and bills from members whose districts or states are directly affected by that legislation. Because the committee will report favorably on only one bill for consideration by the full house, I will simplify the description of what will happen to a bill by assuming that the committee is considering only one proposal. The committee will send the bill to a subcommittee concerned with the substantive area covered by the bill, although, again, there may be overlapping jurisdictions. The subcommittee can: (1) do nothing; (2) hold hearings; (3) approve the proposal unchanged; (4) approve the proposal with amendments; (5) write and approve a new bill, called a clean bill; or (6) report negatively on the bill (seldom done).

Drawing by Handelsman; © 1995 The New Yorker Magazine, Inc.

"You've been around here longer than I have. What *are* 'congressional ethics'?"

Subcommittee Action

Most legislation dies a quiet death through subcommittee inaction (**pigeonholing**). Over 9,800 measures were processed in 1993–94, of which only 473 became law. Failure to consider legislation is sometimes a polite method of allowing a member to introduce a bill that will satisfy campaign promises for constituents (even though there is no real intention of pursuing it seriously) without impairing the effectiveness of the committee system. Failure to consider legislation can also represent attempts to block key legislation that would otherwise be approved by a majority of members. Civil rights legislation was delayed by such tactics in the late 1950s.

Major bills before the subcommittee are usually given extensive coverage in public hearings to gain a perspective on public and expert opinion. Representatives of the political executive, the appropriate bureaucratic agencies, and political interest groups are generally invited to attend the hearings. Such exposure not only provides a basis for congressional action but, as part of the legislative history of an act, can provide information for later court tests of the legislation's intent. The subcommittee is required to give seven days' notice of impending hearings to allow all interested parties time to prepare.

Following the hearings, the subcommittee deliberates the bill, discussing it line by line. At this point, amendments can be made. Some feel that this phase, known as **markup sessions**, is the most significant step in the process. Once always closed to the public, markup sessions now can be closed only by a majority vote. Nevertheless, there has been a greater tendency to keep these meetings closed than was true 20 years ago. Major legislation, such as the Tax Reform Act of 1986 and the Budget Reconciliation Bill in 1990, was deliberated behind closed doors. Republicans, in winning control of Congress in 1994, pledged to have a more open process, but conflicts over legislative priorities forced them to use closed sessions. After considering the legislation, the subcommittee can report favorably or unfavorably on the bill. Unfavorable reporting occurs only rarely; it is easier just to pigeonhole a bill not supported by a majority of the committee.

The full committee can take any of the actions concerning the bill mentioned above. Committees generally accept their subcommittee's recommendations. As a result, the authority to write legislation has for the most part been delegated to the subcommittees of Congress. The full committee also deliberates, votes, and issues a report. The bill is then placed on a calendar to await consideration.

Calendars

Proposals that have been studied by committees and are ready for a decision of either the House or the Senate are placed on the appropriate **calendar**. The Senate has two calendars—the *Executive Calendar,* for nominations and treaties, and the *Calendar of General Orders,* on which all other legislation is placed. The majority leader, in consultation with his or her party's policy committee and the minority leadership, can move to consider items from the General Orders Calendar in whatever order he or she wishes.

The House of Representatives is far more structured in scheduling legislation for consideration on the floor. In the House, bills are placed on one of five major calendars.

1. *The Calendar of the Whole House on the State of the Union.* This calendar, usually called the Union Calendar, is for all revenue and appropriations bills.
2. *House Calendar.* The House Calendar is for all public bills not pertaining to revenue or appropriations.
3. *Private Calendar.* All private bills (relating primarily to immigration, suits against the government, and so on) are placed on this calendar. Such bills are considered on the first and third Tuesdays of each month and are usually approved by unanimous consent.
4. *Consent Calendar.* Bills that are not controversial can be placed on the Consent Calendar. If no objection is made when a bill is called,

it passes. If a bill is objected to twice on the Consent Calendar, it will be referred to the Union or the House Calendar. The Consent Calendar is called on the first and third Mondays of each month.

5. *Discharge Calendar.* Any member may present a motion to discharge a bill from committee consideration, including the Rules Committee, to force House action, if the bill has been referred to the committee at least 30 days before the motion is filed. The petition is posted, and if a majority of the 435 members sign it, the bill is placed on the Discharge Calendar. On the second and fourth Mondays of each month, a representative may call for consideration of any bills that have obtained the necessary 218 signatures, and the House will vote on the motion. Some five or six petitions are filed each session, but seldom do they obtain the necessary number of signatures, and seldom do the bills discharged become law—three since 1911. Until 1993, the list of those who had signed was kept secret, but a rules change, which itself was brought to a vote through the discharge process, opened it to public scrutiny. This led to an interesting political confrontation over budget reductions in 1994. A proposed law with 230 cosponsors was being held up by the House leadership; a discharge petition was filed, but only 178 of the original 230 signed on. Talk show hosts railed against the obstruction, but it was a series of *Wall Street Journal* editorials listing those sponsors who had not signed, referring to them as "hypocrites," that led to a quick increase to 203 signatures. Quickly, the House leadership made a number of concessions; indeed, concessions are more the norm than outright adoption of the disputed bill.

Bills in the House also can be considered under a *suspension* of the rules, permissible on the first and third Mondays of each month or the last six days of a legislative session. In order to approve motions for suspension of the rules, two-thirds of the members present must vote for suspension. With important or controversial items, this procedure is seldom used. In part this is because gaining two-thirds support on a controversial measure is unlikely; in part, also, this is because suspensions leave a measure open for floor amendment.

Preparing for Floor Consideration

Most floor activities are conducted under **unanimous consent agreements**; that is, no objection is raised to waiving the rules, inserting an article from a local newspaper into the *Congressional Record,* or allowing members to revise and extend their remarks. Indeed, most daily procedures, such as reading the previous day's *Journal,* completing quorum calls, and the like, are dispensed with by unanimous consent. A legislator's time is limited; to debate or even to record a vote on a high proportion of proposals would be impossible. Legislators must decide which of the multitude of issues deserve to be considered seriously on the floor. With private bills, legislators usually defer to the judgment of their colleagues—each party selects three monitors (or objectors) who are present when private bills are considered. The rules become important only when they are needed to resolve conflicts on issues of importance.

THE HOUSE RULES COMMITTEE   Up to this point, the procedure for considering a bill would hold for either the House or the Senate. It differs from this point on, with the House giving the **Rules Committee** major control over access to the floor; in the Senate this power rests with the majority leader (see p. 129). The House Rules Committee has roughly the same options that other committees have with respect to legislation. It can ignore or reject proposals, return them to the substantive committee seeking modifications, or adopt a rule favorable to the legislation. The rule assigned can be **open**, which would allow amendments to be made; **closed**, which precludes all amendments; or **restrictive**, which allows only certain amendments, or only those made by some designated member, such as an originating committee member. The House leadership basically controls the Rules Committee and, on important legislation, will carefully craft which amendments, and by whom, they are willing to consider. Even committees with privileged access to the floor, such as the Committee on Ways and Means, seldom get legislation to the floor without a rule. The purpose here is simply that:

> the Rules Committee is the only body which is empowered to fix terms of debate. Traditionally, and for the purpose of avoiding excessive **logrolling** on the floor of the House, the Ways and Means Committee has asked for, and received, a closed rule from the Rules Committee which bars all amendments other than committee amendments on the House floor. (Froman 1967, 51)

Increasingly long and complex legislation has produced rules to match. Beginning in 1978, with the energy bill of that year, the Rules Committee began to use restrictive rules, which placed special conditions on the consideration of a bill (Bach and Smith 1988). For example, I have included as Figure 5.2 the rule in 1990 for consideration of aid to Nicaragua and Panama. This rule allowed one and a half hours of general debate, and waived any points of order against putting substantive comments in an appropriations bill. It then specified the amendments that could be offered. (Note: the five-minute rule is the standard amount of time allowed for debate on an amendment in the Committee of the Whole.) Finally, it indicated that after consideration by the Committee, the bill would be voted on by the House and then substituted in its entirety into a Senate bill. This meant that when the bill was returned, the Senate would technically be considering amendments to its own bill, which allows it to move directly to the floor of the Senate (see Figure 5.2).

Even under the open rule, there are precedents and procedures that allow the committee leadership largely to control what happens to their legislation. "These rules nearly always allow the proponents of legislation to respond to an opponent's amendment, mitigating the potential damage of the latter" (Weingast 1989, 795). Committees that have a fairly sound working relationship with the Rules Committee and are granted the rules they request have much better control over their area of specialization. Committees with more controversial legislation are more likely to need protective rules.

Figure 5.2

RULE FOR CONSIDERATION OF AID TO NICARAGUA AND PANAMA

PROVIDING FOR CONSIDERATION OF H.R. 4636, SUPPLE-MENTAL ASSISTANCE FOR EMERGING DEMOCRACIES ACT OF 1990

Mr. MOAKLEY. Mr. Speaker, by direction of the Committee on Rules, I call up House Resolution 395 and ask for its immediate consideration.

The Clerk read the resolution, as follows:

H. RES. 395

Providing for the consideration of the bill (H.R. 4636) to authorize supplemental economic assistance for fiscal year 1990 to support democracy in Panama and Nicaragua, and for other purposes.

Resolved, That at any time after the adoption of this resolution the Speaker may, pursuant to clause 1(b) of rule XXIII, declare the House resolved into the Committee of the Whole House on the State of the Union for the consideration of the bill (H.R. 4636) to authorize supplemental economic assistance for fiscal year 1990 to support democracy in Panama and Nicaragua, and for other purposes, and the first reading of the bill shall be dispensed with. All points of order against consideration of the bill are hereby waived. After general debate, which shall be confined to the bill and which shall not exceed one and one-half hours, with one hour to be equally divided and controlled by the chairman and ranking minority member of the Committee on Foreign Affairs, and with thirty minutes to be equally divided and controlled by the chairman and ranking minority member of the Committee on Rules,

the bill shall be considered as having been read for amendment under the five-minute rule and all points of order against the bill are hereby waived. No amendment to the bill shall be in order except the amendments printed in the report of the Committee on Rules accompanying this resolution. Said amendments shall be considered in the order and manner specified in the report, may only be offered by the Member specified or his designee, shall be considered as having been read and shall be debatable for the time specified in the report, equally divided and controlled by the proponent and a Member opposed thereto. All points of order against the amendments printed in the report are hereby waived. Said amendments shall not be subject to amendment except as specified in the report. The amendments numbered one shall be considered en bloc and shall not be subject to a demand for a division of the question in the House or in the Committee of the Whole. If both amendments numbered four and five are adopted, only the latter amendment which is adopted shall be considered as having been finally adopted and reported back to the House. At the conclusion of the consideration of the bill for amendment, the Committee shall rise and report the bill to the House with such amendments as may have been adopted, and the previous question shall be considered as ordered on the bill and amendments thereto to final passage without intervening motion except one motion to recommit with or without instructions. After passage of H.R. 4636, it shall be in order to take S. 2364 from the Speaker's table and to consider said bill in the House. It shall then be in order to move to strike out all after the enacting clause of S. 2364 and insert in lieu thereof the provisions contained in H.R. 4636 as passed by the House, and all points of order against said motion are hereby waived.

Source: Congressional Record May 22, 1990, H2654–55.

This is a transcript from the *Congressional Record* indicating the specific rules the House must follow in its consideration of a bill to appropriate aid to Nicaragua and Panama.

The Rules Committee is now closely tied to the House Republican leadership, rather than being an independent source of power. It was once seen as a bottleneck for important legislation favored by a majority.

SENATE FLOOR PROCEDURES   In the Senate, where the setting is more relaxed and informal, the rules are not as stringent as they are in the House, but they are equally important. Some of these rules specify the powers and responsibilities of committees and govern debate, along with the circumstances under which debate may be stopped. In general, debate in the Senate is unrestricted; it need not be **germane** to the issue at hand, as it must be in the House. Opponents of a bill can **filibuster**, a process by which a minority might talk about a bill long enough to prevent a vote or to secure desired changes in it. Relevance is not necessary to the filibuster: one senator once read the Washington telephone directory aloud; another recited his recipe for "potlikker." Debate, or nondebate, in the Senate can be cut off only by invoking a rule of **cloture**, a procedure that has met with some success in recent times. Two steps are necessary to invoke cloture: first, a petition signed by 16 senators must be filed; second, after a two-day lapse, an absolute three-fifths must elect to stop the debate (if the issue is a change in the Senate rules, then an absolute two-thirds is necessary). Such major issues as civil rights and defense spending have prompted filibusters in the past, and at times still do. But the filibuster is no longer regarded as a southern conservative device to prevent civil rights legislation; it has now become almost a standard tactic by members of either party and any political persuasion to force the majority to accede to their demands—and it has worked. Table 5.3 lists the number of successful attempts at cloture. In the 103rd Congress alone, there were 42 attempts to invoke cloture, 14 of which were successful (Ornstein, Mann, and Malbin 1996, 169).

"Senate rules protect individuals' and the minority's right to participate far more than do House rules. The rights to filibuster and to offer nongermane amendments on the Senate floor give senators leverage with committees and party leaders that representatives do not have" (Smith 1992, 172). The Senate leadership thus does not have the manipulative powers of House leadership. Indeed, a determined minority can effectively bring Senate business to a standstill. Senate Republicans in the 1990s, for example, were able to effectively thwart efforts by the majority to pass a variety of reform measures, frustrating Democrats; a record total of 91 cloture votes was taken. They were so effective that when Republicans became the majority party in 1995 and attempted to push through their proposals, Democrats found the filibuster more to their liking, stopping, for example, the Balanced-Budget Amendment.

The determination by the majority leader in consultation with the minority leader over when and under what circumstances legislation is to be considered must encompass the concerns of other senators. The Senate functions under unanimous consent for most of its actions. Figure 5.3 provides an example of the use of unanimous consent by the majority leader of the Senate, Bob Dole (R-KS). In the first maneuver, he is trying to expedite consideration of a joint resolution, but objection is made; in the second, he is setting the agenda for the next legislative day.

Just as important in the legislative process, but harder to define explicitly, are the informal codes governing behavior. "Congress is not a temporary convocation. It is an ongoing social system, which must preserve itself intact and which deals with problems on a long-run, rather than a one-shot, basis" (Dexter 1972, 427). The powers of political parties to select committee members on the basis of seniority (or any other criteria, for that matter) are not to be found in the Rules of Procedure in either house. The importance of these norms may be less today than it was 40 years ago. One review of recent scholarship on the subject found that recently elected members of the Senate were less attached to the institution than those of a previous generation (Harris 1993).

Table 5.3

SENATE CLOTURE VOTES, 1919–1994

	1919–1930	1931–1940	1941–1950	1951–1960	1961–1970	1971–1980	1981–1990	1991–1994
Number of Cloture Votes	10	3	8	2	26	112	137	91
Number Successful	4	0	1	0	4	43	53	37

Source: Adapted from *Vital Statistics on Congress, 1995–96*, p. 169.

Cloture is a procedure used in the Congress to prevent a filibuster or an extended debate from interfering with the enactment of legislation. Cloture needs the petition of 16 senators and, after a two-day lapse, an absolute three-fifths vote. Thus, the success rate of Senate cloture votes is considerably less than initial attempts.

Attempts to reform either the formal or the unwritten rules have met with only occasional success. The Legislative Reorganization Act of 1970 was adopted only after more than five years of study and debate. The results were to make more activities open to the public, including most markup and conference sessions. In the House Appropriations Committee, for example, half of the subcommittees held open markups in 1994; those that didn't were mostly concerned with national security issues. Most floor votes are now recorded. "This made floor votes visible to the public, gave legislators incentives to overturn committee recommendations, and led to a dramatic increase in the frequency of floor amendments and the importance of floor action in congressional policy-making" (Quirk 1992, 312). This trend continued with major changes in the rules of the House in 1995, designed to open legislative proceedings. However, other reforms, such as campaign finance, are debated regularly and just as regularly rejected.

Consideration of Legislation

We have now covered several steps in the process. A bill has been considered by the appropriate committees, a report explaining the legislation and giving recommendations for its consideration has been prepared and issued, the bill has been assigned to a calendar, and, in the House, it has cleared the Rules Committee. It is now ready for consideration on the floor. Here is where debate will occur and votes will be taken to decide whether the bill should be adopted.

DEBATE   Debate in the House of Representatives is usually limited to one hour, with the time being divided equally between opposing sides. In both houses, debate allows a member to make his or her position public, in part for the benefit of constituents. But more importantly, debate allows the dimensions of the proposed legislation to be recorded. When administrators and courts are called upon to implement or to interpret a law, they use the record of a debate as one indication of what was intended. Members now have more impact on legislation during floor debate than they did 20 years ago. There

Figure 5.3

THE USE OF UNANIMOUS CONSENT

Mr. DOLE. Mr. President, I understand that Senate Joint Resolution 28, introduced earlier today by Senator JEFFORDS, is at the desk.

The PRESIDING OFFICER. The Senator is correct.

Mr. DOLE. I ask for its first reading.

The PRESIDING OFFICER. The clerk will read the resolution for the first time.

The assistant legislative clerk read as follows:

A joint resolution (S.J. res. 28) to grant consent of Congress to the Northeast Interstate Area Compact.

Mr. DOLE. And I now ask for its second reading.

Mr. FORD. Mr. President, I object.

The PRESIDING OFFICER. Objection is heard.

The second reading will occur on the next legislative day.

ORDERS FOR FRIDAY, MARCH 3, 1995

Mr. DOLE. Mr. President, I ask unanimous consent that when the Senate completes its business today, it stand in recess until the hour of 10 a.m. March 3, 1995; that following the prayer, the Journal of proceedings be deemed approved to date, and the time for the two leaders be reserved for their use later in the day; that there then be a period for the transaction of morning business not to extend beyond the hour of 1 p.m., with Senators permitted to speak therein not to exceed 5 minutes each, with the following exceptions: Senator CRAIG, 1 hour; Senator DASCHLE, 30 minutes; Senator LIEBERMAN, 20 minutes; Senator GRAHAM of Florida, 15 minutes; Senator GRAMS, of Minnesota, 5 minutes.

The PRESIDING OFFICER. Without objection, it is so ordered.

Source: Congressional Record March 2, 1995.

This is a transcript from the *Congressional Record* indicating how the majority leader of the Senate would proceed according to the rule of unanimous consent.

are more amendments offered, and more approved. For example, Rep. Henry Hyde (R-IN) was instrumental over a number of years in shaping legislation affecting the funding of abortion, using amendments from the floor even though he was not a member of the committee considering these funds.

In addition, in the Senate the individual member has several key rights that give added power during floor consideration. Senators can place a **hold** on unanimous consent agreements, preventing their implementation. If the leadership decides to move on legislation anyway, then the individual member has further power through the debate process.

A filibuster can be an effective strategy, especially if there is a sizable minority filibustering, or if one occurs in the closing days of a legislative session. In the summer of 1994, for example, Republicans were able to prevent consideration of a crime bill—a major issue—until Democrats dropped a controversial death penalty provision; in the late fall of 1993, Senator Mitch McConnell (R-KY) was able to prevent the Senate from considering five nominations to diplomatic posts—clearly a minor matter—until leaders promised his concerns on a related issue would be considered. "Thus, as the House was moving with special rules to recover some of the autonomy its committees had lost to the floor, the Senate was moving in the direction of further entrenching individualism at the expense of committee autonomy" (Smith and Deering 1990, 191).

VOTING   Seldom is a major piece of legislation considered without at least one recorded vote: the yeas and nays must be recorded in a **roll call vote**. In the Senate, the request of one-fifth of the members present will produce a recorded vote. Figure 5.4 is an example of a roll call vote in the Senate on the Balanced-Budget Amendment of 1995. If a roll call is not requested, there is a voice vote. In the House, 100 members can request a recorded vote. A recorded vote is now required on any appropriation or bill raising taxes. And if the Speaker cannot distinguish the winner in a voice vote, a division of the House can be called. Those in favor are asked to stand first, then those who are opposed. In the House, **teller votes**, in which members would file past "tellers" and indicate their votes, were used in the Committee of the Whole prior to 1970; now most teller votes are recorded and published along with other recorded votes in the *Congressional Record*. Electronic voting was among the most dramatic changes of the Reorganization Act of 1970. The *Congressional Quarterly Weekly Report* also publishes all recorded votes by each house of Congress, and it is available to the public. Your library probably has this publication.

A legislator who will be absent during recorded voting can arrange with another member, who would vote in opposition, to refrain from voting so as to exercise a **pair**. Pairs are announced by the floor leaders before voting begins. In this way, the representative is able to state a position on a bill publicly in his or her absence from the House.

AMENDMENTS   In the Senate, legislation is open to **amendment** on any subject a member might wish. Thus, attached to a bill raising the national debt in 1995 were amendments to restrict death penalty appeals and to balance the budget, provisions that led President Clinton to veto the bill. These are known as **nongermane** amendments or **riders**. The House, however, does not allow nongermane amendments to be attached to a bill. Instead, the use of amendments on the floor of the House is limited by the rule that accompanies the bill. Committees and the House leadership may wish that their efforts not be tampered with on the floor. There had been an increased use of the closed rule by the Democratic leadership in the early 1990s; almost half of those bills adopted in recent years were closed, compared with about 20 percent 10 or 15 years ago. Yet, during an extended political controversy over budget cuts in 1994, Republicans won concessions from the leadership, so that only 2 of the 13 appropriations bills would come to the floor with closed rules. Republicans had promised that as the majority they would use open rules. But to keep Democrats from undermining their Contract with America, they, too, were forced to use closed rules.

Following its passage in one chamber, a bill follows a similar course through the other house: it is introduced; sent to the appropriate committee; assigned to a subcommittee; and, after hearings and reports, scheduled for consideration. With so much to do, there is frequently an unwritten agreement

Table 5.4

SENATE VOTE ON BALANCED-BUDGET AMENDMENT

ALABAMA		**INDIANA**		**NEBRASKA**		**SOUTH CAROLINA**	
Shelby	Y	*Coats*	Y	Exon	Y	Thurmond	Y
Heflin	Y	*Lugar*	Y	Kerrey	N	Hollings	N
ALASKA		**IOWA**		**NEVADA**		**SOUTH DAKOTA**	
Murkowski	Y	*Grassley*	Y	Bryan	Y	*Pressler*	Y
Stevens	Y	Harkin	Y	Reid	N	Daschle	N
ARIZONA		**KANSAS**		**NEW HAMPSHIRE**		**TENNESSEE**	
Kyl	Y	*Dole*	N	*Gregg*	Y	*Frist*	Y
McCain	Y	*Kassebaum*	Y	*Smith*	Y	*Thompson*	Y
ARKANSAS		**KENTUCKY**		**NEW JERSEY**		**TEXAS**	
Bumpers	N	*McConnell*	Y	Bradley	N	*Gramm*	Y
Pryor	N	Ford	N	Lautenberg	N	*Hutchison*	Y
CALIFORNIA		**LOUISIANA**		**NEW MEXICO**		**UTAH**	
Boxer	N	Breaux	Y	*Domenici*	Y	*Bennett*	Y
Feinstein	N	Johnston	N	Bingamon	N	*Hatch*	Y
COLORADO		**MAINE**		**NEW YORK**		**VERMONT**	
Brown	Y	*Cohen*	Y	*D'Amato*	Y	*Jeffords*	Y
Campbell	Y	*Snowe*	Y	Moynihan	N	Leahy	N
CONNECTICUT		**MARYLAND**		**NORTH CAROLINA**		**VIRGINIA**	
Dodd	N	Mikulski	N	*Faircloth*	Y	*Warner*	Y
Lieberman	N	Sarbanes	N	*Helms*	Y	*Robb*	Y
DELAWARE		**MASSACHUSETTS**		**NORTH DAKOTA**		**WASHINGTON**	
Roth	Y	Kennedy	N	Conrad	N	*Gorton*	Y
Biden	Y	Kerry	N	Dorgan	N	Murray	N
FLORIDA		**MICHIGAN**		**OHIO**		**WEST VIRGINIA**	
Mack	Y	*Abraham*	Y	*DeWine*	Y	Byrd	N
Graham	Y	Levin	N	Glenn	N	Rockefeller	N
GEORGIA		**MINNESOTA**		**OKLAHOMA**		**WISCONSIN**	
Coverdell	Y	*Grams*	Y	*Inhofe*	Y	Feingold	N
Nunn	Y	Wellstone	N	*Nickles*	Y	Kohl	Y
HAWAII		**MISSISSIPPI**		**OREGON**		**WYOMING**	
Akaka	N	*Cochran*	Y	*Hatfield*	N	*Simpson*	Y
Inouye	N	*Lott*	Y	*Packwood*	Y	*Thomas*	Y
IDAHO		**MISSOURI**		**PENNSYLVANIA**			
Craig	Y	*Ashcroft*	Y	*Santorum*	Y		
Kempthorne	Y	*Bond*	Y	*Specter*	Y		
ILLINOIS		**MONTANA**		**RHODE ISLAND**			
Moseley-		*Burns*	Y	*Chafee*	Y		
Braun	Y	Baucus	Y	Pell	N		
Simon	Y						

KEY
Y Voted for (yea).
N Voted against (nay).
Democrats
Republicans

Source: Congressional Quarterly, March 4, 1995.

This proposed constitutional amendment, a joint resolution, would have required a balanced budget by the year 2002 or two years after ratification by three-fourths of the states. A two-thirds majority vote of those present and voting, 67 in this case, was required. The vote was 65 for and 35 against.

between the two houses as to which will study particular legislation more fully. For example, a 1985 pipeline safety bill that had been studied by three House committees was sent directly to the floor of the Senate without any committee consideration at all.

CONFERENCES   Major differences in bills passed by the House and the Senate are resolved in a conference committee composed primarily of the ranking committee or subcommittee members from each chamber. A study of the 99th Congress found that 9,267 bills and resolutions had been introduced, with only 664 signed into law. Of these, 72 percent passed when one chamber adopted without amendment the version sent to it by the other; 20 percent passed after one chamber agreed to amendments offered by the other; and 8 percent went to conference (Congressional Research Service, 1987). The House and the Senate may instruct their conferees on how to deal with the issues to be negotiated or, more frequently, allow the conferees to use their own judgment.

Members of the conference committee can even undo some of the changes made on the floor. This procedure is known as an **ex post veto**. With more complicated legislation and with multiple referral of bills, conferences can also become quite complicated. Some conferees deal with special sections of legislation either exclusively or in conjunction with the general conferees. For example, the conference on the savings and loan bailout bill in 1989 was composed of "eight senators from two committees (five from Banking, three from Finance) and ninety-four House members from five committees, including all fifty-one members of the House Banking Committee" (Smith and Deering 1990, 196). Finance members were there only for the tax provisions. A successful conference sends a report back to each house. Upon acceptance of the Conference Report, the bill is sent to the president for signature (see Figure 5.1 on page 109). Although compromise is the rule, some issues produce intractable positions in both houses. When agreement cannot be reached, proponents must start the process over again, and look for ways to break the deadlock.

APPROPRIATIONS   Once a program has been authorized by Congress and approved by the president, funds must be appropriated to implement it.

Substantive legislation can authorize a program for any length of time, although five years is typical. The administration has the authority to carry out its provisions. But the Constitution is quite clear that "No Money shall be drawn from the Treasury, but in consequence of Appropriations made by law" (art. 1, sec. 9, clause 7). The president submits a budget in January that is sent to the Appropriations committees and parceled out to 13 subcommittees to be considered for the next fiscal year. About one-half of appropriations are made for one year only. That means that even though a program may be authorized, there is no guarantee that it will be funded fully, or at all. The other half come automatically under existing law: a permanent appropriation, which accounts for most of the spending mentioned in the next paragraph.

Although they are among the most powerful committees in Congress, Appropriations face some serious constraints. A major limitation is the extent to which the budget is uncontrollable. Before you say, "Of course it's uncontrollable," let me define what is meant by this technical term. There are some funds that are going to have to be spent in any given year, and neither the president, Congress, nor the Appropriations committees have much control

Permission granted by Fred H. Thomas

"I had an awful nightmare last night! I dreamt that every taxpayer in the country ran out of money!"

over them. The major sources and the approximate amounts of uncontrollable outlays in 1995 were:

1. Interest on the national debt ($234 billion).
2. Contract authority—decisions made in previous years to build a new aircraft carrier or a sewage treatment plant that are now due ($187 billion).
3. Social Security and other retirement ($358 billion).
4. Medical care ($259 billion).

Added together, these expenditures are about two-thirds of the total budget. This is why cutting the budget in the short term is so difficult: Congress can only deal with the remaining third. Instead of finding a way to cut, say, $50 billion from a $1.5 trillion budget, in fact, it is really only able to cut from $500 billion—a probably unrealistic 10 percent to cut in one year.

The difficulties with substantial budget reductions were brought to a head in 1990 and again in 1995 when the federal government floundered for several months while Congress and the president battled over cuts and plans to balance the budget in the future. In 1990, the crisis came as a result of lower-than-expected revenues and significantly higher costs to bail out the savings and loan industry, which led to a projected $300 billion deficit. President Bush and most Republicans in Congress did not want to raise taxes;

Democrats in Congress did not want to cut domestic programs too drastically. The compromise solution called for some new taxes, cuts in most federal programs, and over the five-year period, some reductions in the uncontrollable outlays, such as medical care. The proposed goal was a balanced budget in 1995. President Bush paid dearly for his willingness to compromise. And conservative Republicans became more insistent on balancing the budget. In 1995, with Congress under Republican control and a Democrat in the White House, the battle came not only over the size of cuts but over a new plan to balance the budget by early next century. It will be a very difficult task to achieve, even in a decade.

The other factor limiting Appropriations committees is the emergence of the Budget committees as competing sources of power. The combination of budget reform and the extensive budget deficits of recent years has limited the ability of Appropriations committees to spend money freely. Yet the Appropriations committees have some room to maneuver. As Steven S. Smith and Christopher J. Deering state, "translating budget resolutions into guidelines for appropriations is not a straightforward process" (1990, 26).

Because appropriations relate to almost all committee activities, the Appropriations committees have organized themselves around subcommittees that substantially parallel substantive committee organization. Rarely are the decisions of subcommittees overturned by the full committee. "We tend to be," states George Mahon (D-TX), former chair of the House Appropriations Committee, "more an aggregation of autonomous subcommittees than a cohesive Appropriations Committee" (Fenno 1966, 135). Since the appropriations process begins in the House, the House committee has become more significant in the appropriations process than has the Senate committee, which is looked on more as a "court of appeals" for appropriations passed in the House.

Parties and Leadership

The political party has some functions that are of real importance for the members of Congress, but a member can and does survive in legislative politics without much support from his or her party. What does the party do? Randall B. Ripley (1967), summarizing the findings of a number of studies on Congress, points to the importance of party as the basis for friendships among members and as the single most important factor in voting. Formally, the primary significance of parties is in the organization of the House and the Senate. Before a session, each party holds a caucus and elects from among its members the leaders of Congress. Invariably, caucus decisions are ratified by the full House and Senate. The selection of leaders, unlike the choice of committee chairpersons, does not rest entirely on length of service. In this century, however, an important transition has occurred in the length of service of leadership in the House. Before 1900, most members had served *less* than 10 years before they were selected as Speaker: in addition to the first Speaker, one—Henry Clay in 1811—had no previous experience at all. Since 1900 all have served at least 16 years and most considerably more. Newt Gingrich (R-GA) served 16 years prior to becoming Speaker of the House.

Each party has special committees to carry out its business. The party caucus, or conference as it is called in the House, includes all the members from the same party. Its official functions are to elect leaders and to ratify committee assignments, which are made by committees on committees in the House and the Senate (see chapter 6, p. 150). Each party has a policy committee, which was designed originally to develop and promulgate the party's position on legislation, but usually plays a minor role in this function. Finally, there are party campaign committees that have served as a means of campaign support relatively independent of the president and national party. With some of the campaign finance reforms, to be mentioned in chapter 10, Political Parties, they have become important sources of funds for candidates.

The power of elected leaders stems from their ability to influence colleagues and to use certain institutional advantages effectively rather than from formal grants of authority. This is evident from an examination of the two most influential leaders—the **Speaker of the House** and the **majority leader** of the Senate.

Speaker of the House

At one time the Speaker of the House was the single most important official in Congress; the Speaker had complete control over the assignment of members to committees, over the assignment of legislation for consideration to particular committees, and over the order of consideration on the floor. But the position's institutional authority was diluted following a revolt in 1911. Although the Speaker still assigns bills to committees, House rules rigidly specify to which committee legislation may be assigned, and the Speaker may exercise personal discretion only when there is doubt as to the proper committee. Assignments of members to standing committees are now made by the party, not by the Speaker, although reforms in 1975 have placed the Speaker back in an important role in committee selections. The Speaker is authorized to appoint conference committee members, but well-established tradition usually determines which members are to be selected. The power of presiding over a legislative body and controlling its debate is limited in an arena where debate is little more than a token step in the legislative process. The Speaker can cast a vote, but usually does so only to break a tie or an expected tie, as Tom Foley did on May 23, 1992, on a balanced-budget constitutional amendment. When not presiding, the Speaker appoints a replacement—for example, when the House meets as the Committee of the Whole. In some instances this has an impact on how a bill is considered, but it is not the crux of legislative leadership.

Taken individually, then, the powers of the Speaker are not of great consequence. Nevertheless, "because the procedural controls of the Speaker extend fairly broadly across the stages through which legislative proposals must pass before they emerge as law, the scope of this person's procedural influence is probably more important than its weight at any one point" (Fenno 1965, 59). Furthermore, an effective Speaker such as Newt Gingrich, who has the support of his party, can have a significant impact. Gingrich, for example, was able to keep his party members organized and moving on their agenda when Republicans took power in 1995.

Senate Majority Leader

The most influential position in the Senate is the majority leader, not the presiding officer. The Constitution gives the role of presiding officer to the vice president. Except when his or her vote may be needed to break a tie, as Al Gore's was on June 25, 1993, to break a tie on the president's budget proposal—this was the first since 1987—vice presidents usually spend their time at the White House or on the road on behalf of the president. The duties of presiding then fall on the president pro tempore of the Senate, who by custom is the most senior member of the majority party. Even this person does not spend much time in the chair and, since the position has no real political power, delegates the responsibility to the most junior members of the Senate.

The majority leader has considerable influence over the workings of the Senate. He or she controls the scheduling of bills for consideration on the floor. The individual power of each member, however, requires a coordinated effort by both parties to get things done. Thus an efficient leader has traditionally made scheduling a bipartisan effort (Oleszek 1996, 200–203). The classic description, by Ralph Huitt, is still the norm: the majority leader's authority derives in part from the fact that "he is the center of the senatorial party's communications network and has access to the president if they are of the same party. The leader knows more than other senators and can share what he knows as he chooses" (1965, 80). Note the similarity of powers of the Speaker of the House and the majority leader. Access to information, control over communications and agendas, and intimate knowledge of their institutions are the chief means by which congressional leaders acquire effective leadership. Skillful use of these parliamentary resources gives the leader added influence, as does her or his ability to bargain, reach compromises, and, on occasion, manipulate activities and events.

Presidency and Legislation

We have seen that, constitutionally, some of the activities of Congress are directly related to executive activities such as nominations and treaties. As you will see in chapter 7, Presidency, much of the major legislation considered by Congress has been formulated in the executive branch. Often the president, in his legislative messages, outlines bills he would like to see introduced in Congress. Each such bill is then introduced by a member, usually the chair, of the standing committee to which it is referred. Consideration of the president's program is handled in the same manner as is other proposed legislation; it is studied in detail, and a report is written by a committee for consideration by the full membership. Issues of national concern, however, become the domain of the House or the Senate as a whole. A great many of the president's proposals are of this nature, and Congress then becomes a forum for debating

Table 5.5

HIGHLIGHTS OF THE 103rd CONGRESS (1993–1995)

Accomplishments

Abortion Clinic Access	Criminalizes the use of force or the threat of force to intimidate women entering abortion clinics.
Brady Bill	Requires a five-day waiting period and background check before the purchase of a handgun.
California Desert	Protects nearly eight million acres of wilderness and creates three national parks.
Crime Bill (PL 103-322)	Allocates $30 billion to toughen penalties, increase prevention programs, build more prisons, hire more police officers, and ban assault weapons.
Deficit Reduction	Cuts about $180 billion in spending and increases taxes by about $250 billion in an effort to balance the budget.
Earned Income Tax Credit	Expands program to provide tax credits to low-income families.
Family and Medical Leave	Requires employers to provide unpaid leave to workers for child raising and family health care.
GATT	Implements the Uruguay round of trade agreements and creates a World Trade Association among member states.
Motor-Voter Registration	Links voter registration with securing a driver's license or registering for some other government service.
NAFTA	Creates a free trade zone between Canada, the United States, and Mexico.
National Service	Provides educational assistance for individuals who perform community service.
Student Loans	Creates direct loans from government to students, removing banks and other agencies traditionally providing these funds.

Setbacks

Campaign Finance	Would have set limits on congressional campaign expenditures.
Economic Stimulus Package	President Clinton's proposal to spend $16 billion on public works, summer jobs, and other social programs to stimulate the economy.
Health Care	President Clinton's health care package guaranteeing universal coverage and reducing costs.
Lobbying Restrictions	Proposed limits on gifts and more stringent disclosure rules.

Source: CQ Weekly Reports November 5, 1994, 3146–47.

the president's program. When this is the case, the formal rules associated with legislation are not as crucial as is the fact that Congress—or even one member of Congress—has decided to use that body as a forum in which to question a program that has been proposed by the president.

The minority party, for example, has always used Congress as a launching pad for its attacks on the administration. In recent years, presidential candidates from the Senate have increasingly done this. However, presidential hopefuls are not always the loudest critics of presidential programs; indeed, potential candidates have a proclivity for straddling the fence on controversial issues. Usually the strongest opposition comes from other members, even those from the president's own party. During the Johnson administration, many of the most outspoken critics of the Vietnam War were Democrats, and

Senator Jesse Helms, conservative Republican senator from North Carolina, was a persistent critic of Presidents Reagan and Bush, especially in the area of foreign policy. Presidents often seek congressional support to ensure joint sharing of responsibility. To gain this support, however, may take considerable time, energy, and political resources on the part of the administration. Congress may reject the proposal or alter it so that it becomes unacceptable to the president. Thus, the temptation is always present for the president to move ahead without involving Congress. At times this has led to disaster, as it did when the Reagan administration provided aid to Nicaraguan Contras in the mid-1980s. Congress had specifically forbidden aid, but the administration secretly sought other sources of funding, which when made public led to an embarrassed administration and a major congressional inquiry. In late 1990, President Bush faced just this dilemma with respect to his policy regarding the Iraqi invasion of Kuwait. Bush had, in fact, dispatched 430,000 U.S. troops to the Persian Gulf without congressional approval. Shortly after the Congress convened in January, however, both Houses (the Senate by a narrow margin) passed resolutions authorizing the president to use military force against Iraq after January 15, 1991. And late in 1995, President Clinton decided to secure congressional support for his use of troops in Bosnia.

The Legislative Veto

Congress has attempted to maintain control of the rules and decisions that affect legislative enactments in the face of presidential opposition. Starting with presidential reorganization plans under President Hoover, Congress adopted a strategy of requiring the presidential plan or proposal to be submitted to Congress for approval before it could be implemented. This **legislative veto** allowed Congress to reject any proposal by majority vote. By 1983 there were as many as 300 veto provisions in force. Presidents frequently used their own veto powers to reject legislation containing a legislative veto (the creation of a National Science Foundation was held up for five years in this way).

The issue came to the Supreme Court in the case of *INS v. Chadha* (1983). In this case the legislative veto provision allowed one house to reject decisions of the Commissioner of Immigration and Naturalization on deportation appeals. Many scholars saw constitutional problems with a one-house veto; Congress is bicameral, and action usually requires both houses. The Court went further, however, ruling that not only one-house vetoes, but all legislative vetoes were unconstitutional because the Constitution calls for legislation to be presented to the president for his or her signature before it becomes law; legislative vetoes did not allow for this.

The problem with this decision was that these provisions had grown up largely with the agreement of those involved—except that of the president.

Members of Congress liked legislative vetos, because Congress could pass general law and then look at the provisions of the implementation process before allowing them to go into effect. Bureaucrats liked them because they kept members of Congress happy and gave them flexibility to administer their programs. For example, Congress required the Agency for International Development to obtain the approval of the Appropriations Committees when it wished to move funds from one appropriated account to another. This amounted to a legislative veto (actually, a committee veto); after *Chadha,* the Office of Management and Budget (OMB) objected. Congress agreed and struck the provision allowing the transfer of funds. OMB backed down when they saw an administrative nightmare ahead, and the committee veto was included in new legislation. (Fisher 1993, 83). In other cases, administrative agencies informed congressional committees that they would continue past practices with informal "side agreements." As summed up by Louis Fisher,

> With or without the legislative veto, Congress will remain a partner in "shared administration." It is inconceivable that any court or any President can prevent it. Call it supervision, intervention, interference, or just plain meddling, Congress will find a way. And government is not the worse off for it. For the most part, statutes can define only the broad contours of public policy. The specific application of funds will remain a joint enterprise between executive agencies and congressional committees. Contrary to the Court's doctrine, future legislative control will not be exercised solely through public laws. We should not be too surprised or disconcerted if after the Court has closed the door to the legislative veto, we hear of a number of windows being raised and perhaps new doors constructed, making the executive-legislative structure as accommodating as before for shared power. (1993, 152)

Summary

Differences in size, constituency, and length of term have led to differences in perspective between the House and the Senate. The Constitution also specifies different functions for each: treaties and appointments are the exclusive domain of the Senate, while tax measures and, by custom, appropriations, originate in the House.

By forming specialized standing committees, Congress has found a way to master the complexities of legislation in the modern world. Also, it has provided a means for keeping watch over the administration of our programs and policies. Specialization has fostered an expertise among members that at times rivals the bureaucracy. Later, I will consider the difficulties encountered by the political executive in controlling the bureaucracy; there is much to be said, then, for the control Congress can exercise over the bureaucracy. Congress is particularly well suited for this task, because it is closely associated with the actual operations of the bureaucracy; Congress not only can investigate bureaucratic activity rigorously, but it also has the legislative power to finance bureaucratic activity. Unfortunately, it does not always keep as close a watch as we might want.

The conduct of business is under the direction of the party leaders in each house—Speaker of the House, Senate Majority Leader—whose powers and effectiveness stem more from control of informal communications networks than from formal rule-making ability. In the House, where the rules of procedure and calendars of business are well defined, effective control of these can give a Speaker considerable power, as shown by the current Speaker, Newt Gingrich. Debate is more significant in the Senate, where the scheduling of legislation and the opportunity for individual input is more a matter of making arrangements with the leadership. Individual members have more power in the Senate: Consent must be gained from members before moving on most items.

The president's influence on the agenda of Congress is great. Some have suggested that the executive is our chief source of legislation; others prefer to place more emphasis on a range of institutions, including Congress, for the origin of policy proposals. Certainly, at the beginning of the 104th Congress, the executive was on the defensive; it was Congress, and especially the House, which set the agenda. Regardless, the president is a significant component of the legislative process.

Analytical Exercises

Every public officeholder must decide on questions of compromise and conscience, and those decisions are usually the toughest of all. As a member of Congress, what would you do in the following situations?

Situation One. As an individual, you oppose legalized gambling. You believe that it can lead to organized crime and promote the kind of strike-it-rich fever that leads desperate heads of households to squander family resources in order to take just one more chance. However, you have the results of a public opinion poll reporting that most voters in your district favor a national lottery as a way to raise money. One of your colleagues has introduced a bill to create such a national lottery. Given the serious budget deficit, the alternative to a lottery will be either to pass a general tax increase or find some programs to cut. Most of the calls to your office, as well as the mail from constituents, are in favor of this bill. What would you do?

- Vote your conscience. No one expects you to agree with the majority of *Senate*
  your constituents all the time, and when faced with questions like this,
  you have to do what you think is right.
- Vote for the bill, since most of your constituents want it. *House*

Situation Two. Local elections will soon be held in your hometown, and Jane Dillon, a woman you've known and respected for many years, is running for mayor. Dillon asks for your public endorsement. But she is *not* a member of your political party. Your party has nominated a former White House aide who had to resign his post over allegations of wrongdoing. You believe he acted illegally and lied to Congress about it. Yet, party leaders now want you to give him your endorsement. What would you do?

- Stay out of it. It's best for national officials not to get involved in partisan
  local elections. Besides, this is a no-win situation.
- Give Dillon your endorsement. A member should be free to support
  other candidates for office and try to get the best-qualified people into
  local government. Besides, it's a free country and, as an individual, why
  should you be afraid to express your opinion?

- Stick with your party. You don't need angry members of your party; you have enough from the other side. After all, even though you don't care for the candidate, he did get the nomination from local party members.

Situation Three. You have been a critic of covert (secret) government actions in the past, and in part because of that, you have just been appointed to the committee that oversees any covert actions of the administration. In part, also, you were appointed because your party is now in control of the White House and you have been a close supporter of the current administration. In a briefing by the CIA, you are informed of several billion dollars in aid being sent to a rebel group fighting the established and popularly elected government of a small African country. This aid is hidden in various other appropriations, and other members of Congress and the American public do not know of its existence. In fact, rumors in the press that such assistance is occurring have been vigorously denied by the administration.

When you ask why we are supporting the rebellion, you are informed that the president objects to that government's confiscation of all foreign-owned property in the country; individuals and corporations have had many millions of dollars taken from them. In addition, the government of that country has refused to repay numerous loans made to the previous government by the United States and has used government police to harass Americans living there. What would you do?

- Endorse the administration's actions. We cannot let other countries violate basic rights of Americans.
- Support the administration, but reluctantly; after all, the president has more information about the situation than you do, and you do not want to embarrass your president.
- Object to these actions and seek support for your position from other members of the oversight committee as well as from friends of yours in the administration.
- Go public by either leaking the information to the press or making a speech in Congress opposing the actions of your government. Interfering in the domestic affairs of a democratically elected government is unconscionable.

Chapter Outline

6

Congress: Individual Power and Actions

I have come to the conclusion that one useless man is called a disgrace, that two are called a law firm, and that three or more become a Congress.

—Stone and Edwards, *1776, A Musical Play.*
John Adams opens the show with this comment.

A congressman was once asked about his attitude toward whiskey. "If you mean the demon drink that poisons the mind, pollutes the body, desecrates family life, and inflames sinners, then I'm against it. But if you mean the elixir of Christmas cheer, the shield against winter chill, the taxable potion that puts needed funds into public coffers to comfort little crippled children, then I'm for it. This is my position, and I will not compromise."

—Lender and Martin, *Drinking in America: A History*, 1987

In the previous chapter I emphasized the structural components of Congress with special attention to the passage of legislation. In this chapter I will consider the representational side of Congress: To what extent is Congress representative of and responsive to the American people? One of the most significant changes in Congress over the past 20 years has been the increase in power of the individual members of Congress. The leadership is still important, and Newt Gingrich's start as Speaker reminds many of the control and power of those in the 1950s—Sam Rayburn in the House or Lyndon Johnson in the Senate. These elected leaders, along with the chairs of the standing

135

committees, used to dominate congressional action. Reforms, however, have placed more power in the hands of subcommittees and individual members. Most members of the majority party in the Senate (87 percent in 1995) chair at least one subcommittee. In addition, individual members now see themselves as being able to act independently of other politically powerful people, especially in the Senate. They now have more resources at their disposal to help formulate legislation and to allow them to represent their constituents more effectively, which in turn makes reelection easier. Indeed, it is this relationship between members of Congress and their constituents that has primarily reshaped the congressional system. A paradox of this relationship is that constituents regularly reelect their representative while also supporting limits on how long a member can serve: 23 states have now adopted some form of term limits. Moreover, opinion polls consistently show respect for Congress at an all-time low: only 34 percent of respondents in a *Washington Post*-ABC News poll approved of the way Congress is doing its job (Morin and Broder 1994, A1).

Characteristics of Members

Let's first look at who gets elected to Congress. The elections of 1992 and 1994 were especially significant in influencing the characteristics of members. To understand the significance of these elections, some background is necessary. The most important measure of electoral success in the past has been the advantage that incumbency provides. The figures have been dramatic. In 1990, only one senator seeking reelection—Rudy Boschwitz (R-MN)—lost; of the 407 members of the House seeking reelection, 391 were returned to office—96 percent. This was the fourth straight election in which more than 95 percent of House members seeking to return had been reelected.

With an increasing public distrust of government, along with some specific complaints about their representatives, voters in 1992 were in a restive mood. Moreover, congressional districts had been redrawn after the 1990 census, placing many members in less desirable districts. A large number of members chose not even to seek reelection—52 representatives and 7 senators—a modern record! Of those who did choose to run, 19 members of the House and one senator were not even renominated by their party, while an additional 28 were unsuccessful in the general election. Challengers have the best chance against members who are old, who have been brushed by scandal, or who come from one of the truly competitive districts. The off-election of 1994 continued this trend. Once again, a large number retired without seeking reelection—9 in the Senate and 47 in the House—while 2 House members were defeated in primaries. Republicans were successful in ousting 35 Democrats in the House and 2 in the Senate. Even with this, 90 percent of incumbents seeking reelection in the House and 92 percent in the Senate were reelected.

Differences between House and Senate members and possible explanations of who is now capable of winning election in American politics can be determined by considering the religion, occupation, age, gender, and race of members of the 104th Congress as they took office in January 1995. (These

Table 6.1

RELIGIOUS AFFILIATIONS OF MEMBERS OF CONGRESS, 1965 AND 1995

| | House | | Senate | | General Population |
Religion	1995	1965	1995	1965	1995
Catholic	125	94	20	14	24.0%
Jewish	25	15	9	2	1.7%
Protestant					
Baptist	57	42	10	12	14.4%
Episcopal	34	54	14	15	1.0%
Methodist	50	69	11	22	5.4%
Presbyterian	47	56	8	11	1.5%
Other (including other Protestant)	97	105	28	24	9.0%

Sources: Congressional Quarterly Special Report November 12, 1995, p. 11; Information Please and World Almanacs 1995; Congressional Almanac 1965.

The religious affiliation of members of the 104th Congress is compared to that of the 89th Congress (1965). Some facts are immediately striking: Presbyterians, Episcopalians, Methodists, and Jews are all present in Congress in much higher proportions than in the general population.

numbers change slightly during a Congress, as a few members will die, others will take positions in the executive branch, and a few may even be forced to resign. Vacancies in the House are filled by special elections, in the Senate by gubernatorial appointment.)

Religion

Table 6.1 presents religious preferences of the members of the 104th Congress, compared with the 89th Congress 30 years ago. The most dramatic change over this period of time is the increase in Roman Catholic and Jewish representation and the corresponding decrease in Protestant representation. More interesting, though, is a comparison with religious membership among the general population. If our concern is representativeness, several factors are striking. Members of Congress are more likely to come from long-established, high-status Protestant groups. Notice that Episcopalians account for less than 1 percent of the general population but about 8 percent of the House and 14 percent of the Senate. Methodists, Presbyterians, and Jews are also present in much higher proportions in Congress than in the general population. The most striking comparison, however, concerns whether or not members have a religious affiliation. Almost all members of Congress claim one; nearly 30 percent of the general population do not. This may be an unfair comparison, since members of Congress might find belonging to a church politically expedient. One study did find religiousness of members at or above that of the population, but this particular study suggests that knowing their denominations "does not tell us very much about [a member's] religious beliefs" (Benson and Williams 1982, 82). Benson and Williams subjected a number of

Table 6.2

OCCUPATIONS OF MEMBERS OF CONGRESS, 1965 AND 1995

Occupation*	House		Senate	
	1995	1965	1995	1965
Law	171	247	54	67
Business and Banking	162	161	24	25
Public Service/Politics	102	**	12	**
Agriculture	20	44	9	18
Education	75	68	10	16
Journalism	15	43	8	10
Real Estate	28	**	3	**
Other	19	18	1	4

*Members can list more than one occupation, so that numbers exceed size of chamber.

**New category; some, but we don't know how many, would have listed this in 1965.

Source: Congressional Almanac 1965; Congressional Quarterly Special Report November 12, 1995, p. 11.

The number of lawyers elected to Congress has fallen in the past 30 years, while those in business and banking have remained about the same. Together, these two occupational categories still dominate the list.

common assumptions about members and religion to investigation and found that many stereotypes were wrong: Congress is not a hotbed of secular humanism; members do find religion meaningful in their lives. Do members vote on some issues based on their religious preference? In Benson and Williams's study, 50 percent said that they do.

Occupation

The occupations of members of Congress are presented in Table 6.2. There is a clear similarity between the two houses and a disproportionate number of lawyers and other professionals compared to the population as a whole. But the percentage of lawyers has been falling over the past 30 years. In 1965, lawyers constituted 67 percent of the Senate and 57 percent of the House; in 1995, this has fallen to 54 percent of the Senate and 39 percent of the House. Occupation presents a much more difficult characteristic to assign meaning to than religion: For one thing, members can have multiple occupations. How do we categorize someone who is a lawyer, served as a government official, and now owns a farm in Minnesota? Do we count only his or her most recent occupation, or all, or some?

Let's take a real case to make the point. Fred Thompson (R-TN) is listed as an actor and lawyer. He is, perhaps, best known for portraying the White House Chief of Staff in Clint Eastwood's movie *In the Line of Fire*. He campaigned as the outsider against the Democratic nominee, Representative Jim Cooper. But Thompson got his start in politics as the chief minority counsel on the Senate Watergate Committee, and for years had been a lobbyist in

Washington. How do we categorize Thompson? And once we do, does occupation influence voting behavior as religion does? Some would say it does. Occupation becomes a matter of concern when members of specific committees and subcommittees are responsible for legislation affecting their profession or business. An example is banking. We now are aware of how both Congress and the executive branch looked the other way concerning activities of banks during the 1980s; it is going to cost us hundreds of billions of dollars to pay for these mistakes.

There is one rather dramatic change occurring in congressional career patterns: the emergence of the professional politician. Increasing numbers of former congressional aides and those who set out on a political career as their vocation (Thompson would fit this designation as well) are being elected to Congress. After law, business, and banking, this has become the largest category, with 114 members listing public service and politics as their occupation in 1995. The category was not even given in *Congressional Quarterly Weekly Report* until recently. New House Republicans in 1995, however, were less likely than candidates in recent years to have had previous political experience.

Age

The average ages of members in the House and the Senate differ somewhat: House members average 51 years in 1995 and senators 53. The average ages in the House and Senate had been going up in the past few years and were at their highest in 20 years as members kept getting reelected. However, during the early 1980s the average age in the House dipped below 50. Membership was in flux during this period; members were retiring, and in some elections a higher percentage of incumbents than usual were defeated. The same thing happened in 1992: a large number, 65, did not seek reelection; in 1982, it was 53. Of those who did not run in 1992, some were seeking other offices, governor and senator for the most part; while others lost in the primary; but a surprising number simply decided to leave office. For some, to be sure, there were greater rewards in private life, based in part on the contacts and experience of having served in Congress. Some left to become lobbyists or Washington lawyers. Others wanted to be out of the fishbowl that is now Capitol Hill; not to be in the evening news; to have some time for themselves and their families; to have time to reflect, to enjoy life—to avoid the "red-eye" flights between Washington and home.

There is a possibility that the changes in number of members seeking reelection go in cycles. For example, few members left in 1984, 1986, and 1988; 27 House members left voluntarily in 1990. But in 1992 we had another upheaval: 52 retired voluntarily, while another 43 were defeated in their reelection attempts; in 1994, the numbers were 56 retiring, 38 defeated. Over half the Republicans in the House in 1995 had been there two years or less.

Whether age makes any difference in terms of the kind of policy effected depends on how different the new members are from the ones they are replacing. The election of 1980 brought in generally more conservative members. Fred Harris (1993), a former senator and current author, calls these direction-changing elections. He also considered the 1958 election to be one. In both cases, members elected in those years were not only younger, but different in political perspective from their predecessors. More recent results have been less dramatic in terms of political orientation. The results of 1986 produced a membership with a more liberal tendency, while in 1988 those elected maintained the status quo; 1990 again showed modest liberal gains. Results in 1992 produced what many think was a more moderate orientation, while 1994 not only gave Republicans control of Congress for the first time in 40 years, but was viewed by some as representing just such a direction-setting election. Certainly the first year produced major changes in direction for national government.

Gender and Race

Women and minorities make up a small percentage of the membership of Congress. An increasing number of women were elected to Congress during the 1950s, reaching a high of 18 members in 1959–60. Women's membership fell to a low of 11 in 1969–70 but increased steadily in the 1970s to 20 by the end of the decade. The 1992 elections brought more women and African Americans: there were 48 women in the House, 6 in the Senate; African Americans numbered 39 in the House and one in the Senate (see Table 6.3). The elections of 1994 saw the numbers of women increase to 49 and 8, respectively. While women make up about 53 percent of the adult population and African Americans about 12 percent, they are represented in Congress by 11 percent and 9 percent respectively.

In addition to women and African Americans, the representation of other groups in society has been increasing. Latinos in the 104th Congress numbered 18 members in the House (5 from Texas and 4 from California), one of whom is nonvoting,* and none in the Senate; Asian and Pacific Islanders had 6 in the House, 2 nonvoting, and 2 in the Senate. There is one Native American in the Senate. These figures have been improving over the past decade, in part because the Voting Rights Act has helped to ensure registration of minorities and requires federal approval of any changes in voting districts and procedures. There is a base of minority representation because some districts have a concentration of minority voters. But because minority candidates do not fare well in districts that are mostly white, increases in minority representation will occur mostly in districts that have increased the proportion of their minority population to a point—some say about 65 percent—where such candidates are electable. The Voting Rights Act, which I discuss in more detail in chapter 11, has provided increased minority representation by adding minority voters and by making it more difficult for a white majority to alter districts to a minority's disadvantage. Indeed, most controversies now come from the claim by whites that they have been disadvantaged by districts drawn to increase minority representation. Recent court cases in North Carolina and Louisiana have, in fact, overturned such districts. Exactly what the Court will support in the way of minority-majority districts is now unclear.

*Nonvoting members can propose legislation and vote in committees.

Table 6.3

GENDER AND RACE IN CONGRESS 1939–1995

Year	Women				Blacks			
	House		Senate		House		Senate	
	Dem	Rep	Dem	Rep	Dem	Rep	Dem	Rep
1995	31	17	5	3	37	2	1	0
1993	36	12	5	1	38	1	1	0
1991	19	9	1	1	24	1	0	0
1989	14	11	1	1	24	0	0	0
1979	11	5	1	1	16	0	0	0
1969	6	4	0	1	9	0	0	1
1959	9	8	0	1	3	0	0	0
1949	5	4	0	1	2	0	0	0
1939	4	4	1	0	1	0	0	0

Source: Congressional Quarterly Weekly Reports for appropriate years.

Women and blacks have gained representatives in the House much more rapidly than in the Senate, but still constitute a small portion of the total membership. Considering that there are 100 members in the Senate and 435 in the House, in 1995 blacks constituted 9 percent of the House and women 11 percent. Women constituted 8 percent of the Senate, while blacks were represented by just one.

Women are rather evenly distributed in the country but, like minorities, have a problem of competing against incumbents, most of whom are male, and most of whom win. Of course, if the woman is an incumbent, she will be just as likely as a male incumbent to win—the problem is to become the incumbent in the first place. This suggests that the real problem women must overcome is one of making their way into positions from which to launch a political career. And this has traditionally been the high-status professions from which most successful male politicians are drawn. Women have better prospects of doing this than minorities—about half the students in law and medical schools are now women—and are potential challengers in every district in the country. The 1992 elections saw not only more women and minorities elected, but serious challenges to incumbents across the country. The elections of 1994, however, saw few gains.

Members of Congress still tend to be male, white, have middle- to upper-class incomes, and enjoy high-status positions in society. The women and minorities who are elected tend to reflect these status and income characteristics as well. They are well educated and tend to be conservative in the sense that they are the successful products of the type of society that they support.

Congressional Benefits

Both senators and representatives receive basically the same types of financial support, although the amounts differ considerably. We will consider salary and fringe benefits, offices, staff, franking, travel, and institutional support.

Salary and Fringe Benefits

The basic perquisites of congressional life are extensive. Besides a salary of $133,600 as of 1995, members receive office space in Washington and in their district or state; office allowances for staff, travel, rent, stationery, and so on; free mailing privileges; the use of gymnasiums, television and radio studios, subsidized restaurants, and free parking facilities. A representative has $568,560 for staff—up to 22—while senators' allotments vary from $2,037,500 to $2,312,400, depending on the size of the state. Office expenses for a representative average $193,000 a year, while a Senate office varies from $90,000 to $250,000. In total, the congressional budget for 1996 is $3 billion.

Faced with public concern over the salaries of public officials, members have been reluctant to accept the amounts specified by the employment cost index, which by law has determined congressional as well federal civil service pay scales. Indeed, they have removed themselves from automatic increases on several occasions. This has also placed a cap on what senior executive and congressional staffers can receive because, as is not true in many state systems, they cannot earn more than members of Congress. In an attempt to deal with the sensitivity of this subject, members of Congress built some controls into their pay raise voted in 1989. In 1991 the House, and in 1992 the Senate, eliminated honoraria as a source of income. But these moves were not enough to prevent the necessary states from ratifying the Twenty-seventh Amendment to the Constitution, which requires an election to be held before pay increases can go into effect.

Offices

Members divide their staff between an office in Washington and those in the district or state (up to three for a congressperson, five for a senator). How many and what functions each performs is an individual preference. The norm, however, is to have the Washington office, with about 60 percent of the staff, handle the more important cases and perform most of the functions of representation. District offices, then, become conduits for information and problems to flow to Washington.

CASEWORK   The office of a member is mostly geared to providing constituent services: casework, tracking of legislation, and projects in the state or district. **Casework**, a typical constituent service, refers to requests from individuals who have problems with their government. Most often these are Social Security recipients or veterans concerned with their benefits. A congressional office will devote at least one and usually several staff members just to dealing with these individual cases. Problems can go beyond these two major sources: a squatter being evicted from National Forest land, a family trying to get a relative admitted to the United States in excess of immigration quotas, a family with an emergency or death requesting that a son or daughter on active military duty be sent home immediately, a savings and loan executive distressed with the pace of a regulatory agency investigation; these are just some of the problems facing the typical House and Senate office. In some countries, and in some cities in the United States, there is an **ombudsman**, a special governmental official who hears citizen complaints against the government. But in Washington, members of Congress handle these problems themselves. Casework, perhaps the least significant of activities when one views government's broader actions and significance, is at the heart of what makes a member successful today. Government is seen by most citizens as distant, even alien; the congressional office provides a place where not only the rich executive, but also the poor widow and the disabled veteran can seek a clear answer or secure a fair hearing. Most members see to it that their mail is answered quickly, because responsiveness keeps constituents happy. Members received a total of over 58 million letters and 32 million larger mailings in 1991 alone, not including bulk postcards from interest groups (Ornstein, Mann, and Malbin 1994, 164). In addition, most agencies, such as Social Security, Veterans Affairs, and the armed services, have regular offices set up just to deal with inquiries from congressional offices.

Congressional offices are bombarded with interesting requests from constituents in addition to the types of cases previously mentioned. One of my university interns working in a congressional office, for example, was asked by a constituent, a college student doing a paper on the topic, to provide information on the member's role in introducing and securing passage of the pay raise bill in 1989. As another example, when I served as a faculty intern on the Hill, I dealt with a complaint from a local air force base where many families had signed up for a vacation to Hawaii through the base's Non-Appropriated Funds Committee, which had contracted with a local travel agent to make the appropriate arrangements. All the money had been paid, the travel agent had gone bankrupt, and a number of angry constituents were demanding congressional office support to gain refunds. In one of my more inspired moments, I asked my assistant to check the address of the individual who had written. While the air base was in our district, the letter writer lived a block over the line in another congressional district! Congressional protocol is clear: you don't tamper with the problems of another member's constituent. We packed up the file, marched it across the hall to the appropriate member's office, and said goodbye to what was a messy, no-win situation.

PROJECTS   Projects are of importance also. In any state or district there is federal construction—a new post office, a sewage treatment plant, an extension of the runway at the airport—as well as grants, loans, emergency aid, at least a hundred things going on simultaneously. Some move expeditiously; others require an occasional inquiry; still others require additional appropriations or some other legislative action to complete. Projects that benefit one, or just a few, districts or states are often called **pork-barrel** projects. While such projects may not fit neatly into national policy, they are important to many in the district or state. The member of Congress must stay on top of each project and inform his or her constituents of the results; the member who does not will quickly hear from them with a phone call, letter, or even a personal visit. Since the people back home must be informed when a project is funded, agencies allow all of their announcements of funding to be made first by the congressional office. One could also argue, quite rightly, that the folks back home could easily wait an extra day and hear the good news from the appropriate agency, to save time and staff in a member's office.

LEGISLATIVE INFORMATION   Finally, constituents are interested in various bills and seek information. Each member assigns staff to answer inquiries, keep up with where major pieces of legislation are in the legislative process, and inform him or her of the sentiments of the people back home.

The result of all these narrowly focused activities has been a fundamental change in the functioning of national government. Morris Fiorina's observation is apt.

> [T]he growth of an activist federal government has stimulated a change in the mix of congressional activities. Specifically, a lesser proportion of congressional effort is now going into programmatic activities and a greater proportion into pork-barrel and casework activities. As a result, today's congressmen make relatively fewer enemies and relatively more friends among people of their district. (1989, 44)

Staff

The number of congressional and committee staff members has grown dramatically, from about 4,000 in 1960 to over 17,000 in 1994. One of the pledges of the new Republican majority was to reduce staff by one-third; a rule adopted in the House early in 1995 mandated such a reduction. Staff can be assigned to a member's Washington office, district or state office, or a committee. A typical office would have an administrative assistant concerned with organizing and running the office and directing the activities of other staff. Then there would be staffers concerned with casework, project development and oversight, and legislative affairs. In a House office this latter position would mainly be for tracking legislation for constituents and keeping the member informed about what is happening with current legislation. In a Senate office, more staff would pay attention to policy issues than in a House office; most people write their representative, not their senator, when they have a problem with their government. And since senators have an interest in a variety of policy issues, staff is needed to provide information on them. Senator Bob Graham (D-FL) is probably typical, employing legislative assistants responsible for issues in education, health, immigration, and the environment. Under each are several legislative analysts doing research.

COMMITTEE STAFF   Those on the committee staff possess a high level of formal education, since their concerns tend to be policy-oriented. One study conducted in 1988 found that 42 percent had law degrees and 22 percent had Ph.D.s (*Roll Call* July 25, 1989, 1ff).

Much of the increase in committee staff was related to the growing use of subcommittees and to the desire of Congress to have its own source of expertise to offset that of the executive branch. Committee staff have increased

Table 6.4

INCREASES IN THE SIZE OF CONGRESSIONAL STAFF AND SPENDING

	1961	1993
Office Staff	3,556	11,538
Committee Staff	910	3,141
Leadership Staff	—	2,596
Numbers of Pieces of Franked Mail	85,100,000	458,000,000 (1992)
Congressional Budget	$140,000,000	$2,302,924,000

The growth in congressional staff and its budget can be attributed primarily to the growth of committees that are needed to deal with more complex issues and legislation than in the past.

750 percent, from 400 in 1947 to almost 3,200 in 1994. It should be added that these numbers do not include those in support positions in the **Congressional Research Service,** nor the **General Accounting Office,** nor the **Congressional Budget Office** (see p. 147), which are major sources of expertise in dealing with executive requests. Republicans have pledged to cut these numbers significantly.

CONGRESSIONAL OFFICE STAFF   It is in the personal or office staff that we see the most dramatic of the increases (see Table 6.4). Because very little in the way of legislation emanates from the office itself, especially in House offices, we would have to conclude that the main purpose of these increases is to allow the member to campaign for reelection! The reelection rates cited earlier provide a clear test of the success of this strategy. Glenn R. Parker and Roger H. Davidson give an indication of "why Americans love their congressman so much more than their Congress" (1979, 53). They contend that members are considered favorably mostly for the services they perform for constituents and receive negative ratings, as Congress as an institution does, when examined for the policies they enact or fail to enact.

But as with most things, there is another side. Staff expand the number of issues a member can handle, provide oversight of executive agencies, and can act as effective "surrogates for their 'bosses' " (Malbin 1980, 239). For challengers seeking to unseat incumbents, this staff support may seem patently unfair, but for constituents, a responsive congressional staff may be the most effective governmental service they receive.

Capitol Hill is an exciting place, with thousands of bright, interested, and interesting people working in a pressure-packed environment. It would be a mistake to imply that this intensity exists only on the Hill, and not at the White House. But there are downsides as well. Burnout and disillusionment occur regularly as staffers work too long and too hard and, at times, see little or no success in what they are doing. There is a high rate of turnover in positions. There are also none of the job security measures that many enjoy in other public or even private employment. One serves at the pleasure of the member, the committee chair, or the president's chief of staff; there is no set pay scale. The reason, at least for members of Congress, is both simple and quite important: they had exempted themselves from most of the labor laws imposed on other federal employees because they did not wish to be under the control of executive agencies. Those on the outside complained that Congress had set itself above the law—that members should be subject to the same conditions they impose on others. This became a campaign issue in 1994, and one of the first actions of the new Congress in 1995 was to bring itself under the same rules as others.

Franking and Travel

A useful addition to the member's arsenal of perks is the frank. The privilege of free mail use, **franking**, was given to members to enable them to keep in touch with their constituents on official business. It is used for more than that: It is now a major factor in campaigning. Mass mailings and targeted mailings are significant new additions to campaign techniques. Both are completely paid for by the public. Mail increased in volume to about 950 million pieces in the 1984 election year. Budget deficits and complaints from challengers have led to recent attempts to reduce expenditures for the frank and to limit the number of bulk mailings a member can make. Volume is now about half of what it was at its peak.

Another perquisite is government-paid travel to the home state or district. This has increased tremendously over the past several decades. Air travel is a prime factor; members from the East Coast could always go home on weekends, but those from greater distances could do so only during major breaks in legislative activity. Now even West Coast members can catch a plane home for a quick three days with constituents. Congress organizes its workload in such a way that members know when votes will be scheduled—these are almost always between Tuesday and Thursday. In addition, members get extended periods of time in their district or state during the year. Known as "district work days," these can amount to as much as two weeks in the spring and early summer to a month in August.

Institutional Support

Support services for Congress have grown with the increased volume and complexity of legislation. The major sources of expertise are the Congressional Research Service of the Library of Congress, the General Accounting Office, the Congressional Budget Office, and the **Office of Technology Assessment**.

CONGRESSIONAL RESEARCH SERVICE (CRS)   Created in 1914, the Congressional Research Service has about 850 personnel providing research services for individual members and committees, ranging from a mundane request from a constituent who wants information about elementary education in Great Britain to studies or background papers on such significant policy issues as impeachment, impoundment, separation of powers, and presidential war powers. CRS has one of the most respected staffs in national government;

many of the names found frequently in these pages—Johnny H. Killian, Walter J. Oleszek, and Louis Fisher, for example—are senior analysts for the CRS.

GENERAL ACCOUNTING OFFICE (GAO)   The General Accounting Office (GAO) was created in 1921 to audit and report to Congress on the functions of the executive branch. Its role has been expanded by Congress as the federal government and its programs have grown. It now possesses additional functions of evaluating program effectiveness, efficiency, and economy. The **Comptroller General** indicates:

> GAO auditing includes not only examining accounting records and financial transactions and reports but also checking for compliance with applicable laws and regulations; examining the efficiency and economy of operations; and reviewing results of operations to evaluate whether the desired results, including legislatively prescribed objectives, have been effectively achieved. (Hearings on GAO Effectiveness 1975, 110)

Joseph Pois (1979), in his study of the GAO, notes that in 1966 only 8 percent of the workload of the GAO represented special requests from members and committees; in 1977, 34 percent of the workload was in the form of special requests. During this same time, the professional staff increased from about 2,400 to 3,800. It is now just over 5,000, with about one-third concerned with congressional requests. Administrators are made clearly aware that their actions are the subject of congressional scrutiny and no doubt react accordingly. For example, in early 1990 members of Congress were distressed with $2.2 billion in proposed budgetary deferrals that had been sent to Congress from the Bush administration. A request was made of the GAO to see whether these proposals conformed to the law relating to deferred items. "The agency, an arm of Congress, concluded that $1.3 billion of the proposed deferrals did not meet the legal requirements" (*CQ Weekly Report* February 24, 1990, 605).

To keep the GAO as independent as possible, the Comptroller General is appointed for a 15-year term by the president, with the advice and consent of the Senate. His or her term is fixed and long, and he or she retires at full pay, as does a federal judge.

CONGRESSIONAL BUDGET OFFICE (CBO)   The Congressional Budget Office (CBO) is relatively new, and relatively small—with about 225 employees—created by the Budget Reform Act of 1974. Designed to assist the budget committees, it has taken on a role of much greater proportions, projecting costs and inflationary impact of proposed legislation, for example. It has become a major source of economic forecasting to counter that of the executive branch's Office of Management and Budget. And because its figures have proven to be somewhat more reliable than those of the OMB, it is looked to for more information than just that needed by the committees on the budget. Indeed, recent administrations have been forced to use the CBO's estimates for budget requests when the original figures are disputed.

OFFICE OF TECHNOLOGY ASSESSMENT   The Office of Technology Assessment was created in 1972 to provide Congress with the technological expertise to deal with such issues as energy, the environment, nuclear reactor safety, and the impact of technology on public policy. The office, with the smallest staff of the agencies mentioned—about 150—had about a dozen areas of technical assessment with which to assist Congress. It did not survive the budget cuts of 1995 and no longer exists.

Gaining Support at Home

Members can communicate with the folks back home without leaving Washington. Congress provides studios where they can be videotaped or recorded with messages for their constituents. Some local papers, looking for fillers, have weekly reports filed by a member, which are, of course, written by a staffer. However, it is members' actual presence at home that directly affects their constituents and hence their reelection.

Political scientists, inspired by the work of Richard Fenno, have recently begun to look systematically at how members of Congress present themselves to their constituents. Fenno's classic study, entitled *Home Style*, describes how members deal with their constituents. As Fenno notes, "It is the style, not the issue content, that counts in the reelection constituency" (1981, 153).

Fenno postulates that representation becomes basically presentation of self. This concept refers to the image presented by the member to constituents. It involves a style, and it requires a presence. Washington is no longer remote, and people expect to see their representatives. True, they can see them on television on the House or Senate floor and on the news, but they like to think that the member cares enough to spend time at home. Thus the trip home for members cannot be spent quietly with family and friends, but must include considerable publicity, with visits to new projects, appearances before various groups, and interviews with the media. Members must generally give the appearance, at least, of actively looking out for the needs of their state or district.

Thus, in recent years members of Congress have increased the number of trips home. Several factors have contributed to members' tendency to spend more time in their districts than in Washington. Fenno has found that the styles representatives use in relating to their constituents usually do not change much after their election. Those that do so change for very interesting reasons—when there has been redistricting, personal goals have changed, or when the incumbent has faced a close primary or general election—all factors that increase the likelihood of not being reelected.

One of the major ways to maintain visibility and control in the district is to maintain offices that provide immediate constituent support service (although many cases must be forwarded to Washington for resolution). Frequent trips to the state or district are now required by members to handle office administration chores as well as to visit with constituents. The reaction of members to being home is often interesting. Representative Philip R. Sharp (D-IN), for example, stated, "Every time I come back here [to Indiana] I am

CONGRESS
IN
ACTION

Permission granted by Fred H. Thomas

struck again—and humbled—by how different the two worlds are" (Maraniss 1983, 15).

Senators command more media attention than representatives, especially in the major media markets, and tend, therefore, to place a higher premium on press conferences. Representatives, who spend more time in the field, are sometimes distressed by this grandstanding, feeling that they do all the work and the senators get the attention. I remember one incident when I worked in a representative's office and received a call from one of the state's Senate offices asking what we knew about problems on the Trinity River. We knew a great deal and had an extensive file, which I indicated I would be glad to share. But when I asked what the senator's interest in it was, I was told that he was going to hold a news conference in San Francisco the next day; he had heard that there were some problems with the river and wanted to make a statement. I decided against giving him much information and, as one member told me, no representative from his state would give him much help either; they felt that he had not done his share of the work, nor helped them with problems in their districts. He lost the next election.

But he probably lost for a much more profound reason than my somewhat cynical portrayal suggests. Again, I return to Fenno (1994) for an explanation. Fenno sees a fit between a senator's character and his electability. Presentation of self is not just media gloss. First, the "prepolitical" career is important in shaping the political career. Second, a candidate's character is the most important element in gaining support in the electorate. Finally, a member's survival depends on maintaining a congruence between that character and the policy role the member plays. To return to my example above, voters were able to evaluate the absence of a congruent character/policy/representational role and voted someone else into the job.

Committees: Membership and Selection

In the last chapter the importance of standing committees in the legislative process was developed. For members, assignment to a key committee(s) is paramount; to exercise effective power they must use their committee assignments to advantage.

Selection

Congressional representatives are assigned to committees by their respective parties. Within each party, this responsibility is delegated to a **committee on committees**, each of which has different characteristics:

- *House Republicans.* Each state with a Republican representative has a member on the committee, but he or she casts a number of votes equal to Republican representatives from that state.
- *House Democrats.* Their Steering and Policy Committee is elected by the caucus and headed by the minority leader.
- *Senate Republicans.* Their committee includes a panel of about 14 members appointed by the conference chair.
- *Senate Democrats.* Their Steering Committee (about 25 members) is appointed by the floor leader.

These committees are often criticized as being unrepresentative of the entire party caucus. A young, recently elected representative or one from a vigorous two-party district is not likely to be a member of these committees. Selection is strongly influenced by the party leadership, since the nominees must be elected by the party caucus. House Republicans from small states, for example, have complained of being overpowered by larger states.

Assignments to standing committees made by the committees on committees are based on several factors: seniority, geography, interest and expertise of the member, and philosophy or ideology.

SENIORITY   The assignment to choice committees, those considered the most powerful and influential, was once based completely on length of uninterrupted service, or **seniority**, in the Senate. When Lyndon Johnson became majority leader in 1953, he initiated what is now known as Johnson's Rule: each new Democratic senator received at least one major committee assignment. In 1965 the Republicans adopted a similar rule. Both now support a 2A-1B rule, giving members two major and one minor committee assignment; some exceptions can be granted to this rule. In the House, assignment to a major committee like Appropriations will usually be a member's only assignment. House members on less prestigious committees may have two.

Congressional seniority is still a major factor in determining committee assignments. The person who has been in Congress for more terms, or even more days, than another, will be given a preferred committee. Members accrue two types of seniority: one with their party based on length of service in that house of Congress; and one with each committee to which they are assigned based on length of service on the committee. Thus, a member who has served on a committee for a number of years seldom requests changes in assignments (unless the current assignment is not to the member's liking or an opening occurs on a more desirable committee), because his or her seniority would be forfeited, along with the accompanying privileges of, say, a subcommittee chair. In the Senate, where a member has more assignments, trading one less desirable for a more prestigious one is accomplished more frequently and with less loss of prestige than in the House. Senator Orrin G. Hatch (R-UT), for example, was in 1995 the sixth ranking Republican on the Finance Committee, the second ranking Republican on the Judiciary Committee, and the next to least senior Republican on Indian Affairs. He became chair of Judiciary, however, because the ranking member preferred to be chair of Armed Services.

GEOGRAPHY   Committees on committees do make some attempt to balance assignment of members geographically and to assign members to committees that are particularly important to the interests of their states or districts. Consider, for example, agriculture. The Senate subcommittee on Agricultural Production and Price Competition in 1995 consisted of members from Mississippi, Virginia, North Carolina, Georgia, Kansas, Arkansas, South Dakota, Montana, and Nebraska (see Table 6.5). Functional representation has been standard practice for some time, and agriculture is not the only example.

EXPERTISE   Consideration of an individual's expertise or major interest is also important in making assignments. A banker, for example, might want to serve on the Banking and Commerce Committee. With the autonomy of standing committees over the legislation in their field, many have concluded that special interests have been given too much attention. Nevertheless, this is not always the case.

IDEOLOGY· Another consideration in making committee assignments is the philosophy or ideology of the member. "Committees that are carefully balanced between liberal and conservative interests can be tilted one way or the other by the [committee assignment process]" (Davidson and Oleszek 1996, 209). These authors go on to cite Rep. Henry Waxman (D-CA): "There are enormous policy implications in the committee selection process."

Committee Chairs

Traditionally the chairs of standing committees are awarded to the committee member of the majority party with the longest record of uninterrupted service on that committee.

Table 6.5

SENATE COMMITTEE ON AGRICULTURE—SUBCOMMITTEE ON PRODUCTION AND PRICE COMPETITION, 1995

Republicans	Democrats
Cochran (MS)	Pryor (AR)
Warner (VA)	Daschle (SD)
Helms (NC)	Baucus (MT)
Coverdell (GA)	Kerrey (NE)
Dole (KS)	

Each party's committee on committes tries to balance appointees geographically and to assign members who have an ideological, professional, or constituent interest in the committee's area of responsibility.

This seniority system evokes criticism and controversy year after year. Its proponents point out that the system provides experienced, knowledgeable leadership with a minimum of political infighting within the party caucus. Opponents of the seniority system contend that the leadership it provides is not reflective of contemporary society or responsible to majority opinion—that a bias toward areas of one-party control is evident.

In my opinion, the major drawback of seniority is that it precludes accountability. Failure to adopt some measure of democratic control over committee leaders speaks badly for an institution that takes pride in its democratic nature. There has been some effort to deal with the problem by striking a balance. On several occasions, Democrats in the House have by-passed seniority. The most recent occurrence was in 1994, when effective control of the Appropriations Committee was taken from 82-year-old William Natcher (D-MO), who had been put in charge over the more senior Jamie Whitten (D-MS) just the year before. Whitten had served in Congress since 1942 and was in poor health. Natcher developed health problems as well; the Democrats by-passed the third ranking member in favor of the fifth, David R. Obey (D-WI). Republicans in the House picked three chairs in 1995 who were not the most senior members. Republicans in the Senate have stayed with seniority. Senator Jesse Helms (R-NC) became chair of Foreign Relations in 1995, although Richard Lugar (R-IN) and Helms had been appointed to the committee on the same date. Helms was given seniority for longer service in the Senate.

The impact of seniority on the substance of legislation stemming from Congress can be seen in the power of standing-committee chairs. I have noted that much power has passed, in part, to subcommittees, and to individual members in the Senate. Yet the chair of a committee still has considerable power. She or he still controls most of the staff, can dominate the agenda and the timing for consideration of legislation, and represents the committee on the floor and in the conference chamber. There have been reforms since 1970 to make committees more democratic, including those that provide for majority votes to decide issues and that give the minority one-third of the staff positions. With the proliferation of subcommittees, much of the power is diffused, but the chair of the committee still has considerable influence.

Committee Staff

At one time, committee chairs had complete control over appointing the staffs of their committees. This has been somewhat modified, so that now minority members appoint certain staff members. Staff members are generally loyal to the committee chair, and despite the recent reforms, ideological and political minorities continue to be slighted. Committees dealing with particularly complex legislation and those that are burdened with a heavy workload (such as Appropriations) have large staffs that are used extensively. While the staff of a committee with high turnover in membership, such as Post Office and Civil Service, has considerable responsibility and power, the staff of a committee with little turnover, like the House Rules Committee, is unimportant (Manley 1968). Staff aides can not only assist in writing legislation, but are also called upon to accompany the member to the floor when their legislation is being considered, to assist in debate, and to handle negotiations that might be necessary.

Congress in Perspective

How one views Congress depends on one's point of view. On the one hand, members have gained considerably in power and influence as they have secured resources to assist them in their work. Large staffs, both in the office and in the committees, provide needed support services and technical assistance. Thus, members are able to confront legislative tasks more effectively. Yet much of the resources go to support services for the constituency. There is much to be said for providing citizens with needed support, and most members do it well. They are then rewarded with reelection. But most analysts agree that because of the time spent with local issues, members have little time or inclination to deal with the great national issues.

On the other hand, a few political scientists provide an entirely different perspective on Congress. Nelson Polsby contends, for example, that the Senate "is increasingly a great forum, an echo chamber, where great issues, and some not so great, are debated; that, indeed, many issues are kept alive here, waiting for the right political mix to move them from the floor to public policies" (1977, 99).

What then is to be said for Congress as an institution if, for the most part, it diffuses its power to committees, subcommittees, and even to individual members and allows them to work their will almost unchecked? Four important activities can be discerned: *legitimation, obstruction, amendment,* and *issue crystallization.*

LEGITIMATION   Although the executive branch might initiate legislation or accomplish most of the task of determining its content, Congress must approve that legislation. Justice William J. Brennan states the issue clearly in addressing a troublesome case on telecommunications before the Supreme Court: "As we so often admonish, only Congress can rewrite this statute" (*Louisiana Public Service Commission v. FCC,* 1986). As I will note in chapter 7, the president frequently asks for congressional approval of actions that need none. Most legislative actions are not acceptable to the American people, or do not appear to be legitimate, unless they have been approved by Congress.

OBSTRUCTION   Of course, Congress can refuse to act. "But the President, with his advantageous position and vast resources, does not *legislate.* . . . [Indeed] in the age-old way, *a majority must be created for every issue*" (Lowi 1965, xiv). This is true even when the majority in Congress is of the same party as the president, as President Clinton found in 1994 as he tried to craft majorities to pass his crime and health care legislation. "Congress can defend its autonomy only by refusing to legislate," states Samuel P. Huntington (1965, 6). Invariably, a refusal to act and approve a president's program brings heated criticism, at least from the president, but often from the public as well. Yet this may be the only way to preserve the independence of the legislature.

AMENDMENT   In addition, proposals that do come from the administration can be altered. Indeed, as noted in chapter 5, Congress: Structure and Legislation, committees can alter proposals more to their liking, and not all committee actions are rubber-stamped. Debate is important primarily in the consideration of amendments, and most of the more important proposals facing Congress are amended on the floor to some extent.

ISSUE CRYSTALLIZATION   Finally, Congress serves to define and debate national issues. The president has been preeminent with respect to setting the agenda of government, but Congress also plays a role, as Republicans showed after becoming the majority in 1995. At times, indeed, Congress has raised opposition to national policy to a legitimate and debatable plane, as it did when it took the national concern over the Vietnam War from the campuses and streets into the halls of its own debating chambers toward the end of the Johnson administration. During the mid-1980s, Congress was the center for debate and opposition to the president's policies in Central America. Efforts by some members to get Congress in the fall of 1990 to play a major role in policy making with respect to Iraq and Kuwait were not successful, but early in 1991 President Bush asked and Congress did authorize him to use force against Iraq, in effect providing him with an advance declaration of war. A balanced budget, welfare reform, and changes in Medicare and Medicaid became central issues in 1995 because of Congress's actions, not the president's.

Summary

Recent elections have sent more women and minorities to Congress. Nevertheless, members are still overwhelmingly white, middle-aged males. And members are overwhelmingly well educated and from high-status occupations and religions.

There are many support services available to help the member in the two prime functions of Congress: legislation and representation. Staff in Washington, in the member's office, and with committees, help in the drafting and passage of legislation. In addition, Congress has created organizations independent of the executive to provide it with information needed for either legislating or investigating the performance of the executive.

The representational role of members of Congress is centered in their district or state. A member's office(s) responds to individual cases, projects, and the tracking of legislation. Casework, in particular, is more often the concern of members of the House. Members are generally quick to respond to constituents' requests for assistance—it pays off at election time.

In assessing how effectively members perform these major functions, there is general agreement that members are better representatives than they are legislators.

Analytical Exercises

You will find as a member of Congress that conflicting demands on your time force constant evaluation of your priorities and responsibilities. What decisions would you make in the following situations?

Situation One. Congress is in recess, and the House Transportation and Infrastructure Committee has just scheduled emergency oversight hearings in San Francisco to learn more about possible misuse of flood and earthquake disaster relief funds in California. If you attend the hearings, you will have to spend three days away from your district, where you have been tentatively scheduled to meet individually with 10 constituents, speak to a group of insurance brokers about how new laws will affect them, have breakfast with the city council of the largest city in your district, and present an award to a local school whose programs have received national recognition. What would you do?

- Skip the hearings. You have little enough time to spend in the district anyway, and the people who elected you have a right to meet with you as often as possible. You can always send a staff member to the hearings.
- Given the importance and high profile of the subject, you should participate in these legislative hearings. A staff member could give you a briefing, but you would obviously be missed. And you can always reschedule the district activities.

Situation Two. During your campaign for office you criticized your opponent—who was the incumbent—for not being present to vote all of the time.

You now find that attending the annual Fiesta Parade in your hometown will mean missing a day of voting in Washington. You check the bills scheduled to be voted on that day, and you are assured by your party's leadership that your vote will not be critical on any of these measures. What would you do?

- Go to the Fiesta Parade. Although voting is a primary responsibility of a legislator, it is appropriate to participate in district cultural and civic activities on special occasions.
- Skip the parade. A legislator should always be in Washington when Congress is in session. Ceremonial responsibilities just aren't worth missing votes.

Situation Three. Representative Martin is celebrating her 60th birthday, and you have been invited to a small dinner party in her honor. As chair of the House Ways and Means Committee, she is one of the most powerful members in the Congress. To date you have not had an opportunity to get to know her very well, and the party provides a rare opportunity for you to establish a personal relationship with her that could be of political benefit in the future. However, the Department of Education has scheduled a working session on the same evening to prepare amendments to the bilingual education program, a program which affects a large number of your constituents. What would you do?

- Accept the party invitation, realizing that good personal relationships are essential to being an effective legislator. You can send a staff member to the Department of Education. You'll have a chance for input when the proposals are brought to Congress.
- Decline the invitation and attend the work session. You can have more effective input at the inception, which a staff member could not do; once submitted to Congress, a proposal becomes more difficult to change.

Situation Four. You were elected by a narrow 51 percent majority in the last election, and your opponent is continuing to raise money for the next challenge to your seat. You have been busy trying to do your job as a member, but now the campaign is gearing up. Your campaign manager indicates that you need $100,000 immediately to begin a TV ad campaign to counter an aggressive ad campaign by your opponent. A local business executive, who you know is under investigation for bribery and illegal campaign contributions to another campaign, offers to organize a benefit dinner that he assures you will raise the necessary money.

- Accept the offer. You can find a way to minimize the contributor's role if he should become a political embarrassment.
- Refuse the contribution. Even if you lose, it just isn't worth accepting money from those who don't play by the rules.

7

Presidency

We give the President more work than a man can do, more responsibility than a man should take, more pressure than a man can bear. We abuse him often and rarely praise him. We wear him out, use him up, eat him up. And with all this, Americans have a love for the President that goes beyond loyalty or party [or] nationality; he is ours, and we exercise the right to destroy him.

—John Steinbeck, *America and Americans*, 1966

A prince, wrote Machiavelli, must imitate the fox and the lion, for the lion cannot protect himself from traps, and the fox cannot defend himself from wolves. One must therefore be a fox to recognize traps, and a lion to frighten wolves. Those that wish to be only lions do not understand this.

—James MacGregor Burns, *Roosevelt: The Lion and the Fox*, 1956

Few Americans fully understand the significance of the institution we call the presidency. Paradoxically, this is probably because the president, as a personality, is so well known. The media constantly feature the president at work and at play, and because of this exposure we tend to think of the person as all there is to the executive function.

The method of electing the president contributes to this emphasis on the individual. Presidential elections since Franklin D. Roosevelt have become personal campaigns organized around the candidate rather than the political party. (This development, as well as the procedures we use to elect presidents, will be discussed in more detail in chapter 10, Political Parties.) Theodore Lowi, a leading observer of American government, refers to this development as the rise of "the Personal President," whereby the American people "concentrate their hopes and fears directly and personally upon him" (1985, 96). "The lines of responsibility run direct to the White House, where the president is personally responsible and accountable for the performance of the govern-ment" (99). This development places great demands on the president for man-agement and leadership and requires quality assistance from the agencies of government if he or she is to succeed. It also makes the president central to legislation and the output of Congress. Finally, the president is required to maintain our standing and status in the world. Each of these areas—organizing and managing government, legislative leadership, and foreign affairs—will be explored in detail.

The Political Executive

Effective governing in today's complex world requires the president to "hit the ground running" after election. "Only the *authority* of the presidency is transferred on January 20; the *power* of the presidency—in terms of effective control of the policy agenda—must be consciously developed" (Pfiffner 1988, 4). Central to the taking of power is the appointment of those who will act on the president's behalf. This key staff, the advisers and administrators who serve at the pleasure of the president, those who can be removed from, as well as appointed to office by the president, I will call the **political executive**.

One person cannot consider, study, or decide more than a few of the fundamental issues that must concern a president. Certain tasks may be dele-gated to close advisers, who in fact perform many of the activities we associate with the president. Most of these advisers are appointed to serve in official positions close to the president, in the White House. Some occupy ranking positions elsewhere in the executive branch—a cabinet secretary, for example. However, the president may rely on the advice and services of anyone: officials in other branches of government (members of Congress and Supreme Court justices) and individuals outside of government who have specialized knowl-edge. Illustrative, but we hope not typical of the use of outside experts, was the report that Nancy Reagan consulted an astrologer before allowing her husband to make various moves. In the 1992 campaign, the extent to which a spouse might influence policy making became a contentious issue. Indeed, Republicans tried to make Hillary Clinton an issue when Bill Clinton ask his wife to play a major role in health care policy. The point is that an organi-zation chart is not always going to show who has the ear of the president. I remember asking Ed Meese, who had been appointed attorney general after serving as a political adviser in the Reagan White House, if he then felt cut off from the president. His reply was, "No, I spend half of each day here [at the White House] anyway."

The Institutionalized Presidency

President Franklin D. Roosevelt knew he faced serious problems in managing the sprawling governmental establishment that had mushroomed during his first term in answer to the challenge of the Depression. He appointed Louis Brownlow to head the Commission on Administrative Management. In 1937,

Figure 7.1

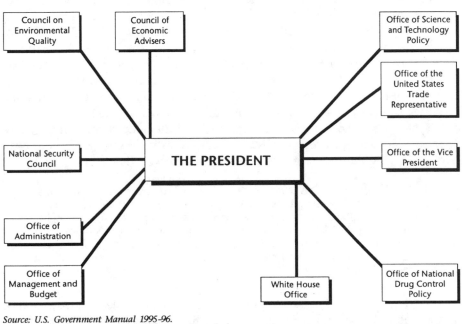

EXECUTIVE OFFICE OF THE PRESIDENT

Council on Environmental Quality	Council of Economic Advisers		Office of Science and Technology Policy
			Office of the United States Trade Representative
National Security Council	**THE PRESIDENT**		Office of the Vice President
Office of Administration			
Office of Management and Budget		White House Office	Office of National Drug Control Policy

Source: U.S. Government Manual 1995–96.

The Executive Office of the President (EOP) is composed, in 1995, of 10 offices with approximately 5,000 employees who provide the president with help and advice in carrying out his major responsibilities. The EOP was created by President Franklin D. Roosevelt in 1939.

the Brownlow Commission opened its report with the simple declaration that "the President needs help." It went on to recommend more presidential control of the administration. Congress reluctantly agreed, after withholding approval for two years. Executive Order 8248, issued by Roosevelt in 1939, created the **Executive Office of the President (EOP),** consisting of the presidential staff agencies that advise the president and help carry out his or her responsibilities; in 1995, the EOP accounted for 10 offices, as shown in Figure 7.1, and about 5,000 employees. The political executive has continued to expand, primarily as a result of the growth of the American system, the increased complexity of issues, and the position the United States occupies in world affairs.

The major offices of the EOP are extremely vital to policy formulation, organization and management of budgets and legislation, and communication among agencies of the government.

1. *The White House Office.* This loosely organized institution is composed of about 50 advisers, assistants, counselors, deputy assistants, special assistants, and others—and their staffs. These most trusted confidants of presidents have in recent years included: in foreign affairs, such names as Henry Kissinger in the Nixon administration and former air force general Brent Scowcroft in the

Bush administration; in domestic policy, Roger Porter in the Bush administration; in politics, Ed Rollins in the Reagan administration. The advantage of such an organization is that a president can use it as he or she sees fit. The size of the White House Office, the functions assigned to it, and its significance in American government vary from one president to another.

2. *The Office of Management and Budget.* Created in 1970, the **Office of Management and Budget** superseded the Bureau of the Budget. Its principal duty is to assist the president in preparation of the budget and in formulation of fiscal policy for the federal government. It is also charged with supervising and controlling the administration of the budget by coordinating departmental activities, improving efficiency in government, and implementing the president's program. The name change in 1970 reflected the relative importance of these management functions. Few offices are as necessary. Richard E. Neustadt, a leading authority on the presidency, observed that:

> The making of the budget is still the prime general-purpose decision-and-action-forcing process yet institutionalized in the executive. The budget process, as it stands, is so firmly a fact of government life, so thoroughly assimilated in legislative and administrative practice and expectation, that its continuation goes unquestioned; its institutional embodiment, "The Budget," commanding everywhere a healthy measure of respect, if not always regard. (1954, 669)

Under President Reagan, the OMB became responsible for the clearance of all proposals from the executive branch to Congress. It is supposed to be the gatekeeper, responsible not only for controlling the flow of money but also for regulating its use. For example, agencies and departments must submit their proposed legislation to OMB. It then determines if the proposal is "in accordance with the president's program." If so, the proposed legislation is sent to Congress to be introduced by a member friendly to the administration's policies (only members of Congress can introduce legislation). Originally the OMB required agencies and departments to secure its approval of all rules and regulations issued by the agencies. This practice, however, was overturned by the Supreme Court in a 7–2 decision, in *Dole v. Steelworkers* (1990). In this case the steelworkers, joined by Public Citizen, a Ralph Nader affiliate, had objected to the fact that OMB had blocked work safety rules to which the steelworkers and Labor Department had agreed. The Court held that Congress, in its legislation giving the Labor Department regulatory authority, had not specified that a third party (OMB) could intrude in the issuing and reporting of rules and regulations.

3. *The National Security Council.* This group was created in 1947 to consider policies and to make recommendations to the president on questions of national security. It has varied from a significant policy-making and deliberative body under President Eisenhower to a seldom-convened and insignificant office early in the Kennedy administration. After the 1962 Cuban missile crisis, the need for high-level policy-and-planning agencies such as the National Security Council became apparent. The president's special assistant for national security affairs in the White House Office became the prime mover in foreign policy, at times

exceeding the secretary of state in power and prestige. This was certainly the case with Henry Kissinger during the Nixon administration. President Reagan's National Security advisers Robert McFarlane and Admiral John Poindexter got both themselves and their president into considerable difficulty by taking on operational control of various foreign policy initiatives, rather than maintaining their advisory roles as first envisioned.

The Iran-Contra affair in 1986 best illustrates this situation. It was alleged that the Reagan administration, without congressional approval, had sold arms to the government of Iran, who, it was hoped, would then work for the release of American hostages in Lebanon. In addition, the armaments were sold at higher than normal prices and the profits were used to fund the Contras in Nicaragua. This led in 1986–87 to a constitutional crisis of major proportions. The issue of who was making American foreign policy, what role Congress was to play, and what accountability the president must bear for actions taken in his name produced a dramatic hearing before a Select Committee of Congress. Actually, these hearings were more drama than substance. The most damaging finding came from an earlier investigation headed by former senator John Tower. The Tower Commission found that the National Security Council had, indeed, illegally sold arms in negotiation for the release of hostages and had funded the Contras beyond the limits set by Congress. It further exonerated President Reagan, indicating he was unaware of this foreign policy process. It found, as well, that certain White House staff members sought to cover up the incident. The immediate result was the resignation of Donald T. Regan, the president's chief of staff. There were also criminal convictions of various key figures, such as Robert McFarlane and Lieutenant Colonel Oliver North. Some of these were overturned on appeal.

The Central Intelligence Agency, originally an arm of the National Security Council, still provides the council with information concerning national security affairs, but now also coordinates the intelligence activities of the government. Although presumably the CIA is organized at a level lower than that of the council, few agencies in American government match its notoriety, and few are so hidden from the view of the American public and from most decision makers in the American system (Woodward 1987). Few in the administration and only a small committee in Congress are privy to the expenditures of the CIA, and even these folks are probably unaware of most of its activities. Even with the recent investigations concerning links between the CIA and drug dealers and the arrest of a high-ranking CIA official for selling secrets to Russia, the scope of CIA actions still seems obscured. Indeed, one director of the CIA, William Colby, was fired by President Gerald R. Ford for being too candid with Congress about CIA activities.

Managing the Political Executive

In attempting to implement administrative programs, the president must rely heavily on the EOP. This is true partly because the departments of the executive branch have statutory mandates to carry out. Indeed, at times these may run counter to what the president would like to see happen, as when in 1939 the secretary of the interior, Harold Ickes, "refused to approve the sale of helium to Germany despite the insistence of the State Department and the urging of President Roosevelt. Without the secretary's approval, such sales were forbidden by statute" (Neustadt 1990, 321). Moreover, cabinet members can quickly become captives of their departments, advocates for the programs and perspectives found therein, and thus seen by the White House as disloyal.

Increasingly, then, presidents have relied on staff members close at hand to carry out directives. The role of the president's close advisers may bring them into conflict with other political agents, as the following classification of their activities illustrates:

> At times they are buffers to absorb pressures which the President must avoid or divert. Some serve as catalysts to expedite administrative or political action when it is in danger of being bogged down by resistances of various kinds. They are liaison men and fixers with the press, congressmen, administrators, party leaders, doing the "cementing" job of negotiation and discussion for the President. They are "needlers" [teasers, inciters] who, acting for the President, may expedite action at key points where bureaucratic resistance threatens. (Seligman 1956, 412–13)

But the complexities of modern government have led to a functional differentiation among White House staff as well. As Thomas E. Cronin has suggested, "the day of the 'general purpose aide' with an entirely undefined portfolio seems a thing of the past," having been replaced with specialists in at least five areas: congressional relations, administrative and public relations, national security and foreign policy, budget and economic policy, and domestic policy and legislative programs (1970a, 603). Yet Cronin also points out that too much specialization will leave the presidency "unable to provide what should be the essential presidential contributions: the capacity to integrate, synthesize, and comprehend diverse policies and their costs, their liabilities and their effect" (1980, 154).

Presidents have adopted different management styles to deal with the institutionalization of the political executive. Richard T. Johnson (1974) suggests three:

1. formalistic, with an emphasis on order and established lines of communication
2. competitive, where overlapping jurisdictions create conflict
3. collegial, with an emphasis on the sharing of responsibility

Each style has its associated benefits and costs for effective presidential decision making, as summarized in Figure 7.2, but most authorities suggest that Franklin D. Roosevelt's competitive style provides the president with the most options and the best chance of making the ultimate decision (Neustadt 1990). But Roosevelt was operating in a much smaller setting than that facing the modern president. John F. Kennedy relied on the collegial model; most presidents since Kennedy have relied on the formalistic. Each president approaches the task of management style with different values and perspectives. There does not seem to be complete agreement on which is best in all cases. However, as Johnson (1974) notes, Nixon's formalistic style trapped him in isolation, producing decisions that ultimately led to his disgrace and resignation, and it seems to have been this style that caused Reagan much of his difficulties with the Iran-Contra affair and other problems as well.

WHITE HOUSE CHIEF OF STAFF   Key to making the formalistic style work is the appointment of a top-quality administrator and savvy politician to head the White House Office. In June of 1994, Bill Clinton made a major shuffle in his administration, naming Leon Panetta as his new Chief of Staff, a position first held by Clinton's boyhood friend from Arkansas, Mack McLarty. The Clinton administration had been under serious attack from two sides: The one from Washington insiders who found Clinton's White House lacking focus and direction; the other from the right, concentrated in the talk shows and cable television of religious broadcasters who criticized administration positions. Panetta had the kind of Washington experience deemed necessary for this role, having been a well-respected member of the House, serving as Chair of the Budget Committee. Clinton had originally appointed him as director of OMB. On his advice, the president shifted to a more formalistic style.

   Under a formalistic style, presidents have become increasingly reliant on their White House chief of staff. In recent times, that administrator has become almost as powerful as the president. Richard Neustadt remarks:

> The duties of the chief of staff derive from nothing more than personal delegation. Constitutionally he is and has to be the president's mere dogsbody, to borrow a British term. Practically, however, he cannot help being more than that. For while he holds his boss's confidence he will be, in effect, a presidential deputy, sometimes even a substitute. (Kernell and Popkin 1986, xiv)

   For one thing, the chief of staff controls access to the president—what the president reads, whom he or she sees, which policy proposals are going to make it to his or her desk. For another, the chief of staff makes most of the appointments in the White House. One estimate given in a speech at the White House by John Kerry, the assistant to the first chief of staff in the Bush administration, John Sununu, had the president making about 80 appointments in the White House. The remaining 600 were made by the chief of staff. He went on to describe the three main functions of the White House Office:

1. the care and feeding of the president
2. the development of policy, including domestic, economic, and foreign
3. the marketing and selling of the president and his or her programs

   The first relates to the logistics of presidential time, travel, and well-being; the second, to the very core of what an administration plans to do and

Figure 7.2

THREE MANAGEMENT MODELS

Formalistic Approach

Benefits	*Costs*
Orderly decision process enforces more thorough analysis.	The hierarchy which screens information may also distort it. Tendency of the screening process to wash out or distort political pressures and public sentiments.
Conserves the decisionmaker's time and attention for the big decision.	
Emphasizes the optimal.	Tendency to respond slowly or inappropriately in crisis.

Competitive Approach

Places the decisionmaker in the mainstream of the information network.	Places large demands on decisionmaker's time and attention.
Tends to generate solutions that are politically feasible and bureaucratically doable.	Exposes decisionmaker to partial or biased information. Decision process may overly sacrifice optimality for doability.
Generates creative ideas, partially as a result of the "stimulus" of competition, but also because this unstructured kind of information network is more open to ideas from the outside.	Tendency to aggravate staff competition with the risk that aides may pursue their own interests at the expense of the decisionmaker.
	Wear and tear on aides fosters attrition and high turnover.

Collegial Approach

Seeks to achieve both optimality and doability.	Requires unusual interpersonal skill in dealing with subordinates, mediating differences, and maintaining teamwork among colleagues.
Involves the decisionmaker in the information network but somewhat eases the demands upon him by stressing teamwork over competition.	Risk that "teamwork" will degenerate into a closed system of mutual support.
Places substantial demands on the decisionmaker's time and attention.	

Source: Managing the White House by Richard T. Johnson. Copyright © 1974 by Richard Tanner Johnson. Reprinted by permission of HarperCollins Publishers.

The three basic management styles adopted by U.S. presidents have both positive and negative aspects. No one approach is used exclusively, but serves to identify the style of the president and creates the environment in which he works.

how it plans to do it; the third is concerned with the public reception of the president and his or her policies.

The Vice President

Discussion of the political executive would be incomplete without some mention of the vice president. Senator Robert J. Dole (R-KS) was asked at a speech to a group of students why he wanted to be vice president in 1988. He replied,

Table 7.1

VICE PRESIDENTS WHO SUCCEEDED TO THE PRESIDENCY

Predecessor	Vice Presidential Successors
	Elected after completing term as vice president
George Washington	John Adams (1797)
John Adams	Thomas Jefferson (1801)
Andrew Jackson	Martin Van Buren (1837)
Lyndon B. Johnson	Richard M. Nixon (1969) [after losing an attempt in 1960]
Ronald W. Reagan	George H. W. Bush (1989)
	Assumed presidency upon death of predecessor
William Henry Harrison	John Tyler (1841)
Zachary Taylor	Millard Fillmore (1853)
Abraham Lincoln	Andrew Johnson (1865)
James A. Garfield	Chester A. Arthur (1881)
William McKinley	*Theodore Roosevelt (1901)
Warren G. Harding	*Calvin Coolidge (1923)
Franklin D. Roosevelt	*Harry S. Truman (1945)
John F. Kennedy	*Lyndon B. Johnson (1963)
	Assumed presidency upon resignation of predecessor
Richard M. Nixon	Gerald R. Ford (1974)

*won election to another term

The office of the vice president of the United States becomes significant when we consider the number who have succeeded to the presidency.

"Well, it's inside work and there is no heavy lifting." Thomas Jefferson, while serving as vice president, stated in a letter, "The second office of this government is honorable and easy, the first is but a splendid misery" (Ford 1896, vol. 7, 120). The vice presidency might be "the most insignificant office that ever the invention of man contrived or his imagination conceived" (Young 1965, 5), as John Adams contended, were it not for the fact that 14 vice presidents have become president: 5 were elected after completing their term, 8 assumed the office upon the death of the president, and 1 took office following a presidential resignation. When added to the number of presidents who have almost died—of illness, as Woodrow Wilson and Dwight D. Eisenhower; or of assassination attempts, as Franklin D. Roosevelt, Harry S Truman, Gerald R. Ford, and Ronald W. Reagan—the above figures become even more significant. The old saying that "the vice president is only a heartbeat away from the presidency" is not just a possibility but has been a reality. There is a certain irony in this situation when one considers the reluctance with which these future presidents accepted second place on the ticket. Seldom has selection of the vice president been based on the possibility of that person's becoming president. Usually, a candidate is chosen for his or her ability to balance the party's presidential ticket either geographically or ideologically. For example, John F. Kennedy from the Northeast chose Lyndon B. Johnson from the Southwest to serve as his running mate. Walter Mondale named the first woman, Geraldine Ferraro (D-NY), to be the vice-presidential candidate of a major party in 1984. The 1992 Democratic selection of Al Gore was unusual, since he is from the same region of the country, the same religion, and the same age as Bill Clinton.

The fact that there was no provision in the Constitution to deal with vacancies in the vice presidency, or with presidential disability, led to the adoption of the Twenty-fifth Amendment in 1967. Procedures were established for filling the office of vice president when a vacancy occurred and for the vice president to take on the duties of the president upon the inability of the president "to discharge the powers and duties of his office." This amendment proved vital to the functioning of American government when Spiro T. Agnew resigned as vice president on October 10, 1973, amid charges of bribery, extortion, and income tax evasion. He pleaded no contest in a negotiated settlement with the Justice Department (Cohen and Witcover 1973). President Nixon then nominated Gerald Ford to be vice president; he took office following favorable votes in both houses of Congress. Ford then assumed the presidency upon Nixon's resignation and nominated as vice president Nelson A. Rockefeller, who was also approved by Congress. We were thus faced for the first time in our history with an unelected president and vice president.

The vice president's official duty is to preside over the Senate. Recent presidents, however, have used the vice president to chair policy-making bodies, such as the National Aeronautics and Space Council, and to serve as a member on other councils, such as the National Security Council. Politically, the vice president can play a minor or a major role in the government. On the one hand, FDR seldom relied on his vice president; Truman knew nothing of our nuclear capabilities until after he became president. On the other hand, recent presidents have used their vice presidents for more important things than ceremonial purposes. Dan Quayle, under George Bush, staked out a major policy role in regulatory politics as chair of the President's Competitiveness Council; Al Gore, under Bill Clinton, has been deeply involved in environmental policy and government reform, as head of the National Performance Review Commission. Yet, even with all the advantages of name recognition and media attention, as well as claims to significant political roles, the fact is that George Bush was the first vice president since Martin Van Buren in 1836 who was able to move directly into the White House after his term was up.

The President and the Policy-Making Process

The president of the United States is both a symbolic head of state and a very real head of government. Thus, he or she may participate in ceremonial duties such as greeting heads of state, meeting championship Little League teams, and proclaiming National Chicken Week. At the same time, the president exercises real power at cabinet-level meetings, negotiates with representatives of world powers, and signs or vetoes bills. The position, then, as head of the political executive is a major source of policy making and policy decisions for American government.

*—Symbolic
—executive*

Presidential Powers

The office of the president was a successful creation of those who sought to ensure a more effective national government than had existed under the Articles of Confederation. The proposals at the Constitutional Convention for the nature of the presidency ranged from the creation of a near-monarchy to an executive completely subordinate to the legislative branch. The presidency, as finally created by the Constitution, allowed for the acquisition of significant power. Aside from the very specific age and citizenship qualifications the president must meet (be at least 35 years old, a natural-born citizen, and 14 years a resident of the United States), the president's powers and position in federal government were not delineated, in contrast to the more highly defined functions and methods of the legislative powers found in the Constitution. The president has been allowed greater freedom in which to grow and to meet the changing demands of the American system. Edward S. Corwin, considered one of our most important interpreters of the office, stated that executive power "is the most spontaneously responsive to emergency conditions; conditions, that is, which have not attained enough of stability or recurrency to admit of their being dealt with according to rule" (1957, 3).

Presidential power is derived from four sources: two are formal grants of authority—under specific provisions in the Constitution and in delegations of authority from Congress; the other two are political—precedents set by former presidents and informal power involving the ability to bargain and persuade.

Formal Basis of Power: The Constitution

The constitutional grants of authority seem straightforward enough: "be Commander in Chief," "grant Reprieves and Pardons," and "take care the Laws be faithfully executed" (art. II, secs. 2 and 3). When we read these in conjunction with other constitutional provisions, however, the ambiguity in the president's power becomes apparent: Congress must pass the laws to be "executed" (art. I, sec. 7); the Senate must approve treaties by a two-thirds vote (art. II, sec. 2); and Congress must raise and support the military establishment of the commander in chief (art. I, sec. 8). Furthermore, the executive branch over which the president nominally presides is created and funded by Congress. As a result, the president and Congress have been traditional antagonists throughout much of American history.

Nonetheless, the presidency has been granted five major constitutional powers:

1. Legislative leadership
2. Conduct of our foreign relations

Courtesy of Edgar Soller, California Examiner

3. Control of our armed forces
4. Appointment and removal of officials
5. Execution and enforcement of law

1. *Legislative leadership.* According to the Constitution, the president's involvement in legislative affairs is limited to vetoing legislation, recommending items for congressional consideration, providing a State of the Union address, determining the time of adjournment when the two houses of Congress cannot agree, and calling special sessions of the legislature. Except for the **veto**, these powers are not extensive. The president must submit proposals for major legislation to Congress. It has become customary for the president to suggest general proposals and priorities in the State of the Union address, a message now televised nationwide. This is followed by more detailed and specific legislative proposals. Most major legislation, then, is first proposed by the executive and subsequently submitted to Congress for adoption. Legislative initiatives such as the Taft-Hartley Act of 1947, which originated in Congress and passed despite the president's veto, have been the exception, not the rule. In 1995, however, a cohesive and activist Republican majority in the House dictated the agenda, pursuing the legislation suggested in their Contract with America. After this flurry of activity, the president once again emerged as a major source of the issues considered by Congress. Congress may alter the president's suggestions, and may even be dominant in giving shape to the final legislation, but the president's ability to set the agenda and to first express the terms for debate of legislative activity cannot be overlooked. Congress responds to presidential initiative; even where ideas originate in the legislature,

Figure 7.3

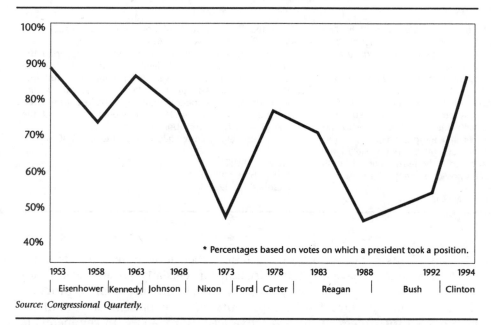

PRESIDENTIAL SUCCESS ON VOTES, 1953–1994*

* Percentages based on votes on which a president took a position.

1953 1958 1963 1968 1973 1978 1983 1988 1992 1994

| Eisenhower |Kennedy| Johnson | Nixon |Ford| Carter | Reagan | Bush | Clinton

Source: Congressional Quarterly.

This graph depicts the percentage of successful congressional votes on which the president has taken a position.

they seldom get very far until and unless they become a part of the president's program (Johannes 1972). The adage, "The president proposes, Congress disposes," still expresses the fundamental relationship.

The president is the only elected *national* official. The president is expected to implement the programs advocated in the campaign, assisted, of course, by an extensive advisory system. One of the difficulties in passing legislation is the fact that members of Congress represent districts or states, not the nation as a whole, and thus have their own local agendas. Moreover, as we saw in chapter 5, their legislative functions are less attuned to program formulation than are those of the executive. These differences can result in a stalemate between these two institutions—what Ross Perot repeatedly referred to during the 1992 campaign as "gridlock." Figure 7.3 shows the percentage of bills enacted for each of nine presidents on which the president had stated a position. Note the difference between Democratic and Republican presidents. Republicans controlled both houses of Congress during Eisenhower's first two years, and again in 1995–96; Reagan had only a Republican Senate. All other Republicans have had to face a Democratic Congress. If we look at data on actual policy proposals from the presidents, they have had much less success; seldom have more than half of these proposals been approved.

Figure 7.4

USE OF THE PRESIDENTIAL VETO

President Bush vetoed the fiscal 1990 appropriations bill (HR 3026) for the District of Columbia because of language that would have permitted the District to use locally raised taxes to fund abortions for poor women.
Following is the White House memorandum of disapproval:

I am returning herewith without my approval HR 3026, the "District of Columbia Appropriations Act, 1990."
I informed the Congress earlier that I would veto this bill if it permitted the use of appropriated funds to pay for abortions other than those in which the life of the mother would be endangered if the fetus were carried to term. The limitation I proposed is identical to the one

Source: Congressional Quarterly November 1989.

included in the District of Columbia Appropriations Act for 1989 (Public Law 100-462).
This year, regrettably, the Congress has expanded the circumstances in which Federal funds could be used to pay for abortions. Moreover, unlike Public Law 100-462, HR 3026 would also permit payment for abortions with local funds, which under current law must be appropriated by the Congress. Thus, HR 3026 would not restrict the use of such funds for abortion in any way.
I am, therefore, compelled to disapprove HR 3026.

GEORGE BUSH
THE WHITE HOUSE
October 27, 1989.

Presidents not only suggest legislation, they actively seek its adoption. Modern presidents have a special assistant for legislative affairs, who heads an office concerned primarily with moving the president's program through Congress. Presidential representatives are present at committee hearings, in the offices of the legislative leadership, and with key members on issues important to the president. Presidents spend much of their time entertaining members of Congress, at White House breakfasts, for example, or calling them on the telephone in order to gain support for legislative proposals.

If the legislation passed is not to the president's liking, a veto can be used. The president can return a bill to Congress with his or her objections. Figure 7.4 shows a veto message from President Bush stating his objections to a bill that failed to prohibit abortions with funds appropriated for the District of Columbia. If a veto should occur, then each house of Congress must pass the bill again, this time with a two-thirds vote, for it to become law. This does not happen often. The president has 10 days in which to sign a bill or return it to Congress; if the president does neither and Congress is still in session, the bill becomes law without a signature. This does not happen often, either. But if Congress has adjourned, then the bill is considered to have been vetoed—called a "pocket veto." Pocket vetoes have been so controversial with members of Congress, especially when they occur during short recesses or between the two sessions of a Congress (each Congress lasts two years and has two regular sessions), that members have taken the president to court on these issues and won. President Bush claimed pocket veto powers at any time when Congress was not in session. Congress objected, but was never able to challenge this practice successfully. President Clinton, like others before him, used the threat of a veto to gain objectives in legislation when faced with congressional proposals he didn't like. Table 7.2 gives the veto records of presidents along with the number of successful overrides. Since

Democrats controlled Congress for most of the past 50 years, the fact that Democratic presidents have had fewer overrides should come as no surprise. But even President Ford, a Republican facing a large Democratic majority, and in a weakened position as an appointed president in the wake of the **Watergate scandal** (1972–74), had only about 20 percent of his vetoes overridden!

2. *Conduct of our foreign relations.* Presidents are also responsible for the conduct of U.S. foreign relations through the maintenance of diplomatic relations with foreign nations, the negotiation of treaties, and the surveillance of situations potentially dangerous to the country. Presidents are privy to more information than any person or group in the country. They have an extensive foreign service bureaucracy and intelligence apparatus to serve and advise them, and they can respond to crises with dispatch. Neither Congress nor any other political institution has these advantages.

Although the Senate must ratify treaties, presidents can avoid this constitutional requirement by negotiating **executive agreements**, which do not need senatorial approval. President Franklin Roosevelt used this technique to provide destroyers to the United Kingdom prior to our involvement in World War II. Richard Nixon negotiated our withdrawal from Vietnam under executive agreement. These enactments are increasingly used by the executive to avoid embarrassing fights with Congress, or simply to keep information secret. They are also used to implement the provisions of treaties and laws, which is the purpose for which they were intended.

The president, rather than Congress or the judiciary, has emerged as the primary political institution in American government, partly because the formal grants of authority have been best suited to meet the changing conditions of modern government, especially in the area of foreign affairs. Coupled with the significance of world politics in our time, this has become the area of public policy most dominated by executive leadership. Well-known political scientist Aaron Wildavsky noted some time ago that "serious setbacks to the President in controlling foreign policy are extraordinary and unusual" (1979, 449).

While presidents still have special advantages in foreign affairs, Vietnam and Watergate have opened the doors to increased congressional initiatives in foreign affairs (Franck and Weisband 1979). Attempts to control the actions of the executive have usually been only partly successful. Even where Congress has specifically forbidden actions in certain foreign affairs, presidents have not always complied. For example, as mentioned earlier, when President Reagan wanted to continue support for the Contras in Nicaragua in the face of congressional restrictions, his chief advisers simply took actions under cover.

3. *Control of our armed forces.* As the commander in chief of the armed forces, the president is empowered to move the troops of the United States in almost any fashion that he wishes. With respect to domestic uses, the Court has established that the president's discretion extends to incidents of insurrection and that the commander in chief may respond as forcefully as he

(Continued on p. 173)

Table 7.2

NUMERICAL SUMMARY OF BILLS VETOED, 1789–1995

President	Congresses Coincident with Terms	Regular Vetoes	Pocket Vetoes	Total Vetoes	Vetoes Overridden
George Washington	1, 2, 3, 4	2		2	
John Adams	5, 6			0	
Thomas Jefferson	7, 8, 9, 10			0	
James Madison	11, 12, 13, 14	5	2	7	
James Monroe	15, 16, 17, 18	1		1	
John Q. Adams	19, 20			0	
Andrew Jackson	21, 22, 23, 24	5	7	12	
Martin Van Buren	25, 26		1	1	
W. H. Harrison	27			0	
John Tyler	27, 28	6	4	10	1
James K. Polk	29, 30	2	1	3	
Zachary Taylor	31			0	
Millard Fillmore	31, 32			0	
Franklin Pierce	33, 34	9		9	5
James Buchanan	35, 36	4	3	7	
Abraham Lincoln	37, 38, 39	2	5	7	
Andrew Johnson	39, 40	21	8	29	15
Ulysses S. Grant	41, 42, 43, 44	45	48	93	4
Rutherford B. Hayes	45, 46	12	1	13	1
James A. Garfield	47			0	
Chester A. Arthur	47, 48	4	8	12	1
Grover Cleveland	49, 50	304	110	414	2
Benjamin Harrison	51, 52	19	25	44	1
Grover Cleveland	53, 54	42	128	170	5
William McKinley	55, 56, 57	6	36	42	
Theodore Roosevelt	57, 58, 59, 60	42	40	82	1
William H. Taft	61, 62	30	9	39	1
Woodrow Wilson	63, 64, 65, 66	33	11	44	6
Warren G. Harding	67	5	1	6	
Calvin Coolidge	68, 69, 70	20	30	50	4
Herbert Hoover	71, 72	21	16	37	3
Franklin D. Roosevelt	73, 74, 75, 76, 77, 78, 79	372	263	635	9
Harry S Truman	79, 80, 81, 82	180	70	250	12
Dwight D. Eisenhower	83, 84, 85, 86	73	108	181	2
John F. Kennedy	87, 88	12	9	21	
Lyndon B. Johnson	88, 89, 90	16	14	30	
Richard M. Nixon	91, 92, 93	26	17	43	7
Gerald R. Ford	93, 94	48	18	66	12
Jimmy Carter	95, 96	15	16	31	2
Ronald W. Reagan	97, 98, 99, 100	39	39	78	9
George H. W. Bush	101, 102	29	17	46	1
William J. Clinton	103, 104*	5	0	5	0
Total		1,455	1,065	2,520	104

*As of September 1, 1995.

Sources: Presidential Vetoes 1789–1976 (Washington, DC: U.S. Government Printing Office, 1978). Recent data from *Statistical Abstract of the United States: 1995* (Washington, DC: U.S. Bureau of the Census, 1995) and *Congressional Quarterly* 1995.

deems necessary. The president "must determine what degree of force the crisis demands" (*The Prize Cases*, 1863).

The use of troops on foreign soil is a different matter. In spite of strong opposition from many members of Congress who believed that the president was specifically and legally precluded from taking military action into Laos and Cambodia in 1970, the president prevailed. But his action did lead Congress to pass the **War Powers Act** in 1973, which sets the conditions under which the president can commit U.S. troops without congressional approval. The two key provisions require consultation with Congress prior to engaging troops in hostilities and in order to maintain a force there for longer than 60 days. This did not prevent Presidents Ford, Carter, and Reagan from using troops without informing Congress, however. And it has been difficult for Congress to require the president to admit that our troops are in a hostile environment. President Bush used American forces to escort food shipments in Somalia in 1992 without invoking the War Powers provisions, even though casualties were possible. Part of the problem, according to Michael J. Glennon, stems from sloppy language in the original act. The law doesn't specify at what point a president should file a report on "hostilities," "introduction of troops," or an increase in size of troops. Since only a report filed on hostilities triggers the 60-day provisions of the War Powers Act, Congress must assert its position if it feels the need for a War Powers Resolution; but since it would have to do so at the very time when support for the president's actions is greatest rather than 60 days later, Congress is at a disadvantage (1984, 571–81).

Presidents do, nevertheless, strive for congressional support, especially in times of war and in foreign activity that does not have formal congressional sanction. Thus, Eisenhower gained congressional approval of the Eisenhower Doctrine in 1957 and subsequently used this as the basis for sending U.S. troops to invade Lebanon in 1958, and President Johnson sought congressional approval for his expanded activities in Vietnam with the **Gulf of Tonkin Resolution** in 1964. President Reagan gained congressional approval under War Powers Act provisions for his use of troops in Lebanon in 1985, President Bush sought congressional approval before embarking on attacks against Iraq in 1991, and President Clinton asked for congressional support for troops in Bosnia in 1995.

4. *Appointment and removal of officials.* The president's ability to control his own administration is somewhat limited, because Congress must create the bureaucracy, define its functions, and fund it. The president can, however, exert influence through control of budget formulation and expenditures and by appointments to the federal judiciary and recommended commissions for officers of the armed forces. Earlier I defined the political executive as those the president could remove from office as well as those he or she could appoint. Congress, when it creates elements of the bureaucracy, specifies the conditions of appointment, the need for Senate confirmation, and whether the position is at the pleasure of the president. As with most elements of our national government, however, things are not always so neat. For example, on the one hand, President Bush wanted more day-to-day control in the bailout of the savings and loan industry. The administrator of the Resolution Trust Corporation, L. William Seidman, a Reagan appointee, could not by law be

removed by Mr. Bush. Yet, enough pressure was exerted from the White House that he resigned (*New York Times* May 2, 1990, A1ff.). On the other hand, a position over which the president does have the power of removal, the director of the Federal Bureau of Investigation, was, during the days of J. Edgar Hoover, almost immune to presidential displeasure. Lyndon Johnson was reportedly asked by an associate why he didn't get rid of Hoover, to which Johnson allegedly replied, "It's probably better to have him inside the tent pissing out, than outside pissing in."

Major appointments require the consent of the Senate. Although senators generally accede to a president's nominees, there are occasions when they are turned down. Only 12 cabinet-level appointments have been turned down, the last in 1989, when John Tower was rejected as secretary of defense. However, there have been many examples of presidents withdrawing a nomination that was doomed. Bill Clinton faced this problem when his first selections for Attorney General were withdrawn after significant opposition arose. And presidents have had many rejections at the subcabinet level. Sometimes this is for reasons of competence, as in the case of Edward A. Curran, who was rejected as chairman of the National Endowment for the Humanities in 1985 because key senators perceived him as lacking the qualifications for the job. At other times it represents a political dispute, as when conservative Republicans in the Senate blocked President Reagan's nomination of Melissa F. Wells to be ambassador to Mozambique in 1986–87 because members of the Senate disagreed with the administration over U.S. policy toward that country or when President Clinton's 1995 nomination of William Foster as Surgeon General was blocked because of opposition to Foster's use of abortion. Presidents have countered at times with the use of **recess appointments** made when Congress is not in session; they are good until the end of the next session without Senate confirmation. For example, during his first term Reagan made 139 recess appointments, compared to 69 by Carter (*CQ Weekly Report* October 12, 1985, 2065).

5. *Execution and enforcement of law.* In line with the president's executive functions, the Constitution indicates that the president is to ensure "that the laws be faithfully executed" (art. II, sec. 3). In fact, this is the only provision specifically directing the president to exercise authority in the protection of the law. This ambiguous phrase has been a source of controversy, since presidents have great leeway in deciding which laws to emphasize. For example, no recent president has liked the idea of busing to achieve racial integration; each has directed his education and justice departments to place a low priority on enforcement and not to penalize districts that do not comply. But President Eisenhower went so far as to use federal troops in Little Rock, Arkansas, in 1957 to enforce school desegregation.

Congress often allows the executive the option of whether or not to exercise the grant of authority and in what manner to implement it. For example, Congress has given the executive discretionary power over tariff rates on imported goods. Frequently the president uses the **Executive Order** (a directive) to exercise these delegated powers. On August 15, 1971, for example, President Nixon issued Executive Order 11615, a wage-price freeze based on a previous year's authorization from Congress. But presidents have also used the order to go beyond the law or even to work in opposition to it. Executive Order 11286, designed to provide opportunities for minorities by establishing quotas in minority hiring, clearly violated provisions of the Civil Rights Act of 1964, which banned discrimination based on race, color, religion, or national origin in employment and in any program receiving federal funds (Fisher 1985).

Political Basis of Power: Precedent

While the Constitution has established the areas of basic presidential power, certain customs have developed over the years that have set precedents for establishing other types of powers. For example, precedents set during the two terms of George Washington are sometimes overlooked, but they have had a tremendous impact on the presidency. Washington's definition of the executive's proper role has survived throughout our history. He initiated the practice of proposing legislation to Congress, established the convention that he was master of his official family (that is, the cabinet), took the initiative and assumed dominance in foreign affairs, limited himself to two terms of office, and used the full power of the federal government in domestic disorders. Other presidents have made important contributions to developing and delineating the power of the presidency, but few have been as significant as these initial conceptions established by Washington. Andrew Jackson extended the veto and removal powers to ensure the development of executive programs. Jackson was also instrumental in severing selection of the president from congressional control; he implemented a system that rested instead on selection by a national convention, thus laying the foundations for a more democratic office. Abraham Lincoln must be credited with establishing the **war powers**—the president's authority to initiate war to ensure the security of the nation. Presidential initiatives in legislation and congressional delegation of many powers to the executive resulted in a strengthened presidency during the terms of Theodore Roosevelt and Woodrow Wilson. Wilson also extended the concept of the war powers beyond those used by Lincoln during the Civil War.

> But it is the second Roosevelt who beyond all twentieth-century presidents put the stamp both of personality and crisis on the presidency. In the solution of the problems of an economic crisis—"a crisis greater than war"—he claimed for the national government in general and the president in particular powers hitherto exercised only on the justification of war. Then when the greatest crisis in the history of our international relations rose he imparted to the president's diplomatic powers new extension, now without consulting Congress, now with Congress's approval; and when at last we entered the Second World War he endowed the precedents of both the Civil War and the First World War with unprecedented scope. (Corwin 1957, 311)

Under Eisenhower, who had experience in military staff organization, the political executive—a president served by a complex advisory organization—became an institutionalized component of American government.

Informal Bases of Power: Persuasion and the Media

Informal powers of the president are less restrictive than are the formal powers granted by the Constitution. As the only nationally elected official, the president speaks for the American people and has access to the major symbols of the American system. President Clinton spoke for all Americans in expressing his outrage at the bombing of a federal building in Oklahoma City in 1995. Appeals to patriotism and to other basic values of the American system are powerful weapons in the hands of a president. Adroit presidents quickly learn to use symbols to secure support for both their programs and their reelection. Of course, use of these symbols can also become abuse. Critics of Presidents Johnson and Nixon contend that these presidents perpetrated such abuses in their attempts to discredit critics of the Vietnam War. In a speech in South Dakota in 1969, for example, President Nixon attacked those demonstrating against the war in Vietnam by stating, "To those intoxicated with the romance of violent revolution, the continuing revolution of democracy may seem unexciting" (Edelman 1971, 71).

PERSUASION   One commentator on the American presidency, Richard E. Neustadt (1990), contends that the president's power of persuasion is the principal power, rather than formal constitutional powers. His point is well taken. A president must use the advantages and resources of the office to induce members of the professional bureaucracy, Congress, decision makers in the private sector, and our allies abroad to accept the president's leadership or legislation before programs can be implemented. The key to Neustadt's theory is the impact of current decisions on future prospects for exercising power. But the assets at a president's disposal to influence directly the bureaucracy and Congress, while substantial, are not unlimited. In formulating a total program (particularly the federal budget), the president can reward those who are supportive and chastise those who actively oppose or merely fail to lend their support. More frequently the president negotiates with important bureaucratic officials and members of Congress to obtain their support for administration programs. Successful presidents are expert bargainers. The president can reach even those with whom there is no direct contact if he or she establishes a reputation for effective power. Figure 7.5 charts my interpretation of Neustadt's conception of presidential leadership.

THE MEDIA   One major resource of the president is the ability to approach the people through the mass media to secure popular support for programs. Presumably, elected officials such as members of Congress will respond to the swell of popular sentiment. One author has suggested that this use of media—going public, as he calls it—represents a fundamental shift in the power relationships between presidents and Congress (Kernell 1993). This places a tremendous burden on modern presidents and at the same time provides an extraordinary opportunity for them to exercise moral leadership. In times of war, presidents have always worked to mobilize the nation's support and to provide moral leadership. Generally this applies also to the entire area of foreign affairs. With respect to domestic legislation and affairs, presidents find themselves prone

Figure 7.5

NEUSTADT'S MODEL OF PRESIDENTIAL LEADERSHIP

Type of Power	Activity	Costs	Risks
1. Persuasion (most effective)	Convince others that it is in their interest to do what the president wants	Time and skill	None
2. Bargaining	Negotiate with others; offer to compromise, support their position on another issue; or promise campaign funds or other support	Political capital	Depletes resources; potential to overpay; can backfire if public knows too much
3. Sanctions	Use strategic advantages to threaten someone to effect compliance	Political capital	Can easily backfire; resentment from those on whom imposed; might not work
4. Commands (least effective)	Order others to follow directive based on constitutional or congressional authority	Puts administration on the line; even if wins battle may lose war	Humiliates others; makes enemies; might not work; shows weakness in not using 1, 2, or 3 successfully

Source: Adapted from Richard E. Neustadt (1990). *Presidential Power and the Modern Presidents.* New York: Free Press.

Richard E. Neustadt feels that the greatest presidential power may reside in his or her ability to persuade others to a particular point of view, a style compared here with three other approaches.

to partisanship and seek to use their influence and control of the news to improve their own positions vis-à-vis competing parties and programs. Certainly one of the major controversies facing modern American government is the chief executive's use of his or her tremendous persuasive and moral powers either for the benefit of all Americans or for only a limited number.

Limits to Presidential Power

The president is powerful, yet is neither infallible nor omnipotent. One reason we mistakenly assume omnipotence is because some things a president can do are of great consequence, such as instituting the use of nuclear weapons

Figure 7.6

THE PRESIDENT'S CABINET— EXECUTIVE DEPARTMENTS

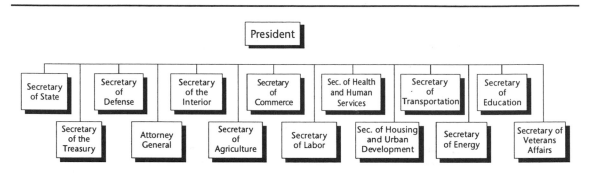

Fourteen cabinet departments serve as advisers to the president and are directly answerable to him. They carry out much of the nation's business, from national defense and foreign policy to matters once left almost entirely to state and local authorities, such as education, housing, and health.

and sending U.S. troops to areas of conflict. But the president doesn't have unlimited power. The internal affairs of most other countries cannot be controlled, nor can the cost of living in our own country be completely within a president's control. "It is misleading to infer from a president's capacity to drop an A-bomb that he is similarly powerful in most other international or domestic policy areas" (Cronin 1970, 43).

We have already discussed the president's limitations in exercising authority, observing that because of a lack of time, the president can seriously consider only a handful of major policy items. With the expansion of the presidency to include a host of presidential advisers, many more issues can be considered, but only major legislation and programs are given serious attention. These same advisers, however, may isolate the president from events and people, thus obstructing access to accurate and complete information on which to base decisions (Reedy 1970). Presidents also can be misled by these advisers. We may never know the complete story, but from the Iran-Contra hearings in 1987 we can assume that President Reagan was not kept informed of the dealings by his close associates. Much worse, the advisers themselves may not have understood the issues, as Daniel Patrick Moynihan suggests in his critique of the Johnson administration's antipoverty programs.

> *The Government did not know what it was doing. . . .* [It] at this time was no more in possession of confidential knowledge as to how to prevent delinquency, cure anomie, or overcome that midmorning sense of powerlessness, than was it the possessor of a dependable formula for motivating Vietnamese villagers to fight Communism. (1969, 170)

Some presidential appointees have disagreed with the programs and policies they were to implement. Furthermore, the appointee simply may fail to

understand what the president is trying to accomplish. Moynihan, in his remarks to the cabinet upon leaving his post as a presidential adviser in 1970,
said, "It comes to this. The presidency requires much of those who serve it,
and first of all it requires comprehension. . . . Time and again, the president
has said things of startling insight, taken positions of great political courage
and intellectual daring, only to be greeted with silence or incomprehension"
(*San Francisco Examiner* December 27, 1970, A22). Often a president com-
pounds these difficulties by failing to communicate effectively with subordi-
nates. This was President Reagan's explanation for how his policy of not
providing goods to terrorist states became a policy of arms-for-hostages in the
Iran arms disaster in 1985–86.

IMPEACHMENT   Presidents are not only constrained by certain institutions,
they are subject to impeachment by Congress. Officially, the House of Representatives votes to impeach and the Senate sits in judgment. Congress has
moved to impeach a president only once: Andrew Johnson was accused and
tried in 1867, but the Senate acquitted him by a margin of one vote.[1] Most
scholars agree that Richard Nixon would have been impeached had he not
resigned the presidency in 1974.

CONGRESS   The three branches of government are on an equal level in our
constitutional arrangement. Consequently, the president has only a certain
amount of influence over Congress and its members, and Congress can meet
the tactics of an executive with maneuvers of its own in a tug-of-war for
policy control. Congress, moreover, created all the offices and agencies in the
executive department, and seldom has it been in the interest of Congress to
make these too responsive to executive leadership. Each year a president must
seek congressional approval of policies and programs; even when the president
and Congress are controlled by the same party, approval often comes grudg-
ingly and, when control is divided, as it has been for 14 of the past 16 years,
support can be lukewarm at best. (Refer again to Figure 7.3 on p. 169.)

Even strong-willed, active presidents find that influencing the bureaucracy
is difficult. Peter Drucker asserts that John F. Kennedy, for example, "had no
impact whatever on the bureaucracy" (1969, 221). Furthermore, independent agencies such as the Federal Reserve Board or the Postal Service are able to conduct
much of their activity without considering the president's goals or wishes.

Presidents' claims of **executive privilege**—assertions by presidents that some
matters are of such national importance that information regarding them can be

1. The House of Representatives hears the case and has the power to impeach by majority vote. The
analogy is to a grand jury returning an indictment. A trial is held before the Senate, which can convict
by a two-thirds vote. The presiding officer is the chief justice of the Supreme Court if the case involves
the president. Only 14 officials have been impeached; of these, 7 were convicted. Most (11) have been
federal judges, most recently Judges Harry Claiborne of Nevada in 1986 and Aylcee Hastings of Florida
in 1989. Conviction leads to removal from office. The Senate can decide whether the person convicted
is barred from office for life. Hastings went on to be elected to the House after his impeachment. An
impeached official is still subject to criminal prosecution. Claiborne, for example, was serving a prison
term for income tax evasion when removed from office. Nixon was pardoned by President Ford in 1974
for any and all criminal acts he might have committed.

withheld from Congress or the courts—have met with mixed success. President Eisenhower was able to withhold information from Senator Joseph McCarthy in 1954 when the senator's Government Operations Committee searched for Communist sympathizers in government; President Nixon was forced to turn over incriminating White House tapes in 1974 to the congressional committees investigating the Watergate break-in (*United States v. Nixon,* 1974).

Advisers close to the president confirm the limitations on presidential power. More than half of Kennedy-Johnson staff members felt that the president's impact on policy was selective at best (Cronin 1970). More significantly, two-thirds of those interviewed felt that to serve as an educator and to set priorities selectively was the proper role of a president.

Finally, presidents are limited by their highly political position. They respond to political pressures. They must be aware of shifts in sentiment in the electorate; they must be wary of the opposition party that will discredit them when possible; and they must maintain control over their own political party—a goal more easily stated than achieved.

Summary

The president is no longer a solitary leader, but the head of a major institution called the political executive—the offices and agencies directly responsible to the president. The president's job is increasingly one of managing.

The success of this task is based in part on making quality appointments to the numerous positions within the executive branch responsible for devising and implementing the president's program.

Presidents do have formal powers conferred by the Constitution or delegated by Congress: war powers, Commander in Chief; powers of appointment, formulating the budget, and overseeing the administration of the law are the most notable. But much of a president's success depends on the use of informal powers, the ability to control the agenda of government, to persuade others to follow the president's lead. A president's power is probably greater in the public eye than it is in fact. Significant constitutional and political forces limit what even the boldest of presidents can accomplish. Most significant of these would be the extent to which Congress is in line with or in opposition to the president's programs.

Analytical Exercises

1. Listed below are the career paths to the presidency of recent presidents.

	Last job before:	Second to last:	Third to last:
Roosevelt	Governor	Navy Ass't Sec	State Senator
Truman	Vice President	Senator	Businessman
Eisenhower	College Pres	General	
Kennedy	Senator	Representative	Journalist

Johnson	Vice President	Senator	Representative	Presidency
Nixon	Lawyer	Vice President	Senator	
Ford	Vice President	Representative	Lawyer	
Carter	Governor	State Senator	Businessman	
Reagan	Governor	Trade Ass'n President	Actor	
Bush	Vice President	Ambassador	National Party Chair	
Clinton	Governor	State Attorney General	Law Professor	

Do you see any pattern? Is there an advantage to any particular occupation or office if one wishes to run for the presidency? Has this changed over the past few decades? Look at the career paths of those running for president in 1996; what advantages or disadvantages did various careers confer on the candidates?

2. Presidents have numerous political appointments to make, subject to Senate confirmation. The choice is seldom easy, because any action has serious political repercussions. Suppose as president you need to appoint a new ambassador to Mexico under the following conditions:

- The leading opponent to your reelection next year has strong ties to the Latino community, especially in Texas and California, two states that together will send one-seventh of the delegates to your party's national convention.
- Latino leaders are irritated at your failure to nominate a Latino to a ranking position in your administration.
- One of your campaign pledges was to open government positions to disadvantaged groups, and you have been attacked for your overall record on affirmative action.
- The State Department strongly supports the notion of appointing career diplomats with language skills and experience in the area as opposed to diplomatic amateurs, especially in a sensitive position such as this.
- One of your campaign pledges was support for experienced career diplomats.
- Relations with Mexico are strained at best. Mexican gas and oil are the major sources of revenue to repay the loans we made during recent economic crises in Mexico, and you are hoping for improved trade relations with Mexico.
- Mexican officials refer to Americans of Mexican descent with the derogatory term of "pochos," and have repeatedly said the appointment of one as ambassador would be patronizing.
- A distinguished panel of advisers has submitted two names to you for your consideration: The first choice is an Anglo, a career diplomat with years of distinguished service in Latin America, including time in Mexico, and a graduate degree in economics; the other is a highly respected Latina academic, a prize-winning poet, who is now president of a major university in Texas.

Whom would you pick?

8

Bureaucracy

Between the idea
And the reality
Between the motion
And the act
Falls the Shadow

—T. S. Eliot, *The Hollow Men,* 1925

The Treasury is so large and far-flung and ingrained in its practices that I find it is almost impossible to get the action and results I want—even with Henry [Morgenthau, Secretary of the Treasury] there. But the Treasury is not to be compared with the State Department. You should go through the experience of trying to get any changes in the thinking, policy, and actions of the career diplomats and then you'd know what a real problem was. But the Treasury and the State Department put together are nothing compared with the Na-a-vy. The admirals are really something to cope with—and I should know [Roosevelt had been Secretary of the Navy]. To change anything in the Na-a-vy is like punching a feather bed. You punch it with your right and you punch it with your left until you are finally exhausted, and then you find the damn bed just as it was before you started punching.

—Franklin D. Roosevelt, in Neustadt,
Presidential Power and the Modern Presidents, 1990

Government programs must be put into effect; that is, someone must implement them. Departments, agencies, and offices have been created to do this. These institutions are organized in a pyramid-shaped fashion, with tasks divided into smaller and smaller components to allow for more efficient implementation and with responsibility flowing up to the higher unit. We call this organization **bureaucracy** and those who work in it and administer these programs **bureaucrats**. At the top of the pyramid is the president and his or her chief political appointees—the political executive. Below these are professional bureaucrats, who have made government service their careers and are not subject to presidential appointment or removal. These distinctions in real life are not quite so neat, but for now they are a good starting point in our discussion of the federal bureaucracy. Figure 8.1 provides an illustration of this organizational arrangement or hierarchy.

Understanding the role of the bureaucracy is important, because much of what governs us now really comes from the bureaucracy and because, to adapt the T. S. Eliot opening quote, implementation is in the "shadow." The bureaucracy is in essence removed from direct political control and is often overlooked because of the nature of its decision-making processes. Bureaucrats seldom make the headlines, and they encourage this inattention by the media in part to increase their control over the areas of expertise that they manage.

Our understanding of government is also clouded because we see our national bureaucracy as being under the president and political executive. "Even Washington reporters, White House aides, and congressmen are not immune to the illusion that administrative agencies comprise a single structure, 'the' executive branch, where presidential word is law, or ought to be" (Neustadt 1990, 33–34). Why this is not always the case, and the impact this has on policy and on the proposals enacted into law, will be the important subject of this chapter.

The Professional Bureaucrat

In chapter 7, discussion centered on the political executive—the personnel in the executive branch appointed by and responsible to the president. They serve at the pleasure of the president, and can be removed or reassigned at will by presidential directive. In this chapter we are talking about the professional bureaucrats—those whose positions are governed by civil service rules (or those in a similar setting in the postal, foreign, or other services). They receive appointment and hold office independent of a particular president.

Civil Service

Federal employees prior to 1883 were appointed and/or replaced by the president. In this system supporters of the winning party and candidate were rewarded with government office. The control of such appointments was called **patronage**; the system was referred to as the **spoils system**. It had two major defects: There was no assurance that those appointed had any skill or aptitude for the job, and there was a constant turnover as party and candidate fortunes changed. **Civil service**, adopted through the Pendleton Act of 1883, was designed to change this by ensuring the selection of qualified applicants and

Figure 8.1

DEPARTMENT OF THE INTERIOR

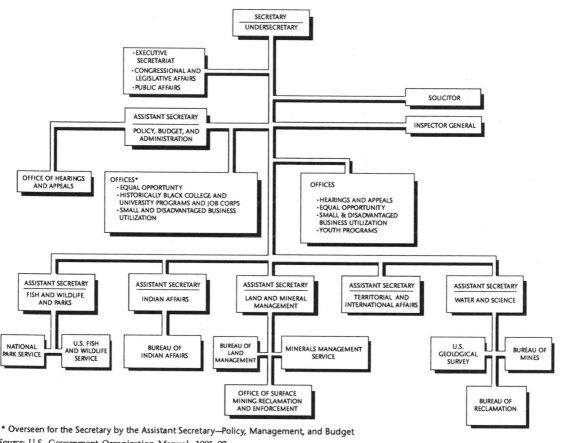

* Overseen for the Secretary by the Assistant Secretary—Policy, Management, and Budget

Source: U.S. Government Organization Manual, 1991–92.

Most government organization charts look similar to this one for the Department of the Interior. The organization is headed by a secretary under whom come the various offices and agencies arranged in a hierarchy, with lower units reporting to and responsible to higher units.

by basing promotion on merit. Both of these reforms were to be based on test results, and the chosen applicant had to be among the top three scorers in an exam. Moreover, a civil servant could not be removed except for cause, making each, in effect, a lifetime employee.

Civil service had a profound effect on political parties. George Washington Plunkett, a leading figure in the New York City Democratic organization, Tammany Hall, at the turn of this century, portrays it vividly:

This civil service law is the biggest fraud of the age. It is the curse of the nation. There can't be no real patriotism while it lasts. How are you goin'

THE CIVIL SERVICE AS IT IS.

Hon. Member of Congress presenting a Few of his Constituents for Office.

Source: Library of Congress.

Prior to the Pendleton Act of 1883, jobs were awarded to political supporters, seen here presenting themselves for consideration.

to interest our young men in their country if you have no offices to give them when they work for their party. . . . This ain't no exaggeration. I have good reason for sayin' that most of the Anarchists in this city today are men who ran up against civil service examinations. (Riordan 1963, 11)

About the only presidential appointments that are similar today to the old system of patronage are those of ambassadors. There have been numerous complaints from career diplomats in the Foreign Service and from congressional committees that all too many Reagan and Bush appointees were people whose major qualification for the job was as fund-raisers for the political party (*CQ Weekly Report* July 15, 1990, 2275).

High-ranking civil service positions, grade GS-15 or above, or those who serve in independent offices for fixed terms established by Congress, have a considerable say in policy making. (GS refers to **General Schedule**, with positions graded to 15. There are other classifications—for instance, Foreign Service, as well as those on an hourly wage—but most of the agency personnel discussed here are placed in a position on the General Schedule.) In 1995, a beginning position (GS-1, Step 1) paid $12,141 per year; those holding policy-making positions within the professional bureaucracy (GS-15) were paid up to $88,326 per year. Above this level is the **Senior Executive Service (SES)**, with pay grades ranging from $97,991 to $122,014. The SES is definitely policy oriented, but also much more political. Those who accept SES positions are subject to transfer or removal by political executives. Moreover, exceptions are permitted under the civil service rules that allow many of these positions in the SES to be filled by political appointees, not by career bureaucrats. Performance reviews and assignments can also be politically directed. The original idea, however, was to create a high-level service based on merit. Indeed, most high-ranking civil servants have spent their careers in government service, working their way up through the ranks and usually remaining with the agency in which they started their careers. Thus, we would expect a high level of expertise but with the potential for a narrowness of perspective.

Advancement and Promotions

Initial selection of bureaucrats at lower-level positions in the federal service apparently is objective and open. Nevertheless, transfers of personnel from major positions in private industry and the military into related positions in civil service are common. Former ranking members of the military, for example, may occupy high positions as civil servants in the Defense Department. A recent GAO report noted that 20 percent of political appointees had been given special help in transferring to civil service positions—"burrowing into career jobs," the authors call it (Causey 1991, D2). In an earlier study it was found that 102 former oil people were staffing the new Federal Energy Office. The report went on to say, "There's barely a U.S. department bureau, office, or division dealing with oil or natural gas that hasn't been infiltrated from the top by oilmen" (*San Francisco Examiner* November 17, 1974, A17).

Primarily, bureaucrats for ranking positions are selected by other civil service career officers. Appointments may be made on an objective basis, but promotions may not. One complaint lodged against HUD field offices in 1992 was that 16 of 76 executive positions were filled with people related by marriage or blood. While the government does not have rules against nepotism, these numbers "may seem familiar to some Washington area federal workers," says Mike Causey, "who complain that when it comes to raises, promotions and better assignments, blood is often thicker (and more effective) than good performance" (*Washington Post* July 14, 1992, D2). Of particular concern is the advancement, or nonadvancement, of women and minorities. Figure 8.2 shows the composition and changes in the General Schedule workforce during the 1980s. While there have been modest advances, the general rule is still that women and minorities occupy the lower-level positions, whereas white males are in the policy-making positions.

Figure 8.2

THE FEDERAL WORKFORCE: CHANGES IN THE 1980s

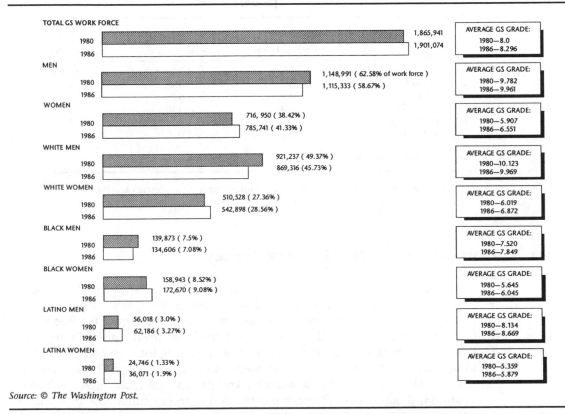

Source: © *The Washington Post.*

This figure of the General Schedule shows the percentage of various categories of the population working in civil service positions. The grade for the General Schedule refers to the work level one has achieved, with GS-18 being the highest.

The point is best made by looking at the smaller numbers of particular agencies. The FBI, for example, did not have a female agent until 1972. In 1992 only five percent of the agents were African Americans. A white agent would receive a promotion in 6 years on average, while a black agent could expect to wait 10 to 14 years (LaFraniere 1992, A1). In 1992, the Bureau settled a discrimination suit brought by black agents to provide more opportunities for minority advancement. The Department of State shows a similar situation. A comparison of State Department jobs is shown in Table 8.1. Notice the large percentage of women and minorities in what are basically the secretarial positions, with only a small percentage in the Career Foreign Service. The same pattern occurs in other departments as well. This does not speak well for a government that has mandated improvement in opportunities for women and minorities.

Table 8.1

EMPLOYMENT CHARACTERISTICS OF STATE DEPARTMENT
January 1991

	Civil Service	Foreign Service	Career Senior Foreign Service
White Males	25.3%	62.5%	88.6%
White Females	28.4	25.2	6.2
Black (M & F)	38.2	5.5	3.6
Latino (M & F)	3.4	3.8	1.2
Asian (M & F)	3.1	2.2	0.1
Other (M & F)	1.6	0.8	0.3

Source: Department of State, January 1991.

The positions at the State Department are ranked from least prestigious—civil service—to most prestigious and best paid—career senior foreign service.

Organization of the Federal Bureaucracy

The federal bureaucracy is made up of an extensive array of departments, bureaus, and agencies employing almost three million full-time, permanent employees. Theoretically, bureaucracies are hierarchical. Figure 8.1 (see p. 184) illustrates the hierarchical bureaucracy of the Department of the Interior. The simplicity of this diagram should not mislead you into oversimplifying the bureaucratic structure. Some departments, such as Health and Human Services, are conglomerates of diverse agencies and offices that make effective coordination difficult at best. Others are composed of agencies that have independent political support, for example, the Federal Bureau of Investigation (FBI) in the Department of Justice. Some departments are so large that effective management is hard to accomplish; the Defense Department, for one, employs almost one million civilian employees, in addition to about one and one-half million in the services themselves. Government employment figures given in Table 8.2 indicate the size of the federal government. Some of the largest employers are independent agencies, such as the Postal Service, which command considerable uncontrollable financial support but are not directly accountable to elected officials.

Creating the Bureaucracy

Congress has responded to requests for bureaucratic agencies in a number of ways: by creating line agencies within the major departments of government, by creating staff agencies primarily to advise and assist the executive, and by creating independent agencies that are not placed in specific departments and are not always under the direct control of the president. Apparently, with respect to independent agencies, Congress would prefer not to grant the president much control over the activities to be administered. For regulated indus-

Table 8.2

PAID CIVILIAN EMPLOYMENT IN THE FEDERAL GOVERNMENT

Branch of Government	Number	Percent of Total
Legislative Branch	35,537	1.2
Judicial Branch	28,035	1.0
Executive Branch	2,804,654	98.0
Total	2,868,226	100.0

Executive Branch Paid Civilian Employment

Department/Agency	Number	Percent of Total
Executive Office of the President	1,544	*
Executive Departments		
Agriculture	118,100	3.9
Commerce	35,700	1.3
Defense[1]	800,600	28.5
Education	5,100	.2
Energy	20,800	.7
Health & Human Services	125,800	4.5
Housing & Urban Development	12,600	.4
Interior	76,200	2.7
Justice	109,200	3.9
Labor	17,900	.6
State	24,800	.9
Transportation	64,400	2.3
Treasury	162,200	5.8
Veterans Affairs	230,100	8.2
Independent Agencies		
Environmental Protection Agency	18,900	.7
NASA	23,200	.8
Office of Personnel Management	5,500	.2
Small Business Administration	4,800	.2
Tennessee Valley Authority	16,400	.6
Postal Service	822,754	29.3
All others	119,600	4.3
Total	2,804,654	100.0

[1]Defense Department figures are for nonmilitary personnel only.

Source: Analytical Perspectives, U.S. Budget, pp. 180–181. Figures are estimates for 1996 and change regularly.

The executive branch contains 98 percent of the total civilian government workforce. Within this branch, the Department of Defense and the Postal Service employ the greatest numbers of people.

tries in particular, Congress shuns executive control. Congress has met popular demands for regulation of powerful industries such as railroads and banking only halfway; some controls were added, but these industries were also instrumental in discouraging introduction and enactment of bills that would further

Table 8.3

INDEPENDENT ESTABLISHMENTS AND GOVERNMENT CORPORATIONS

ACTION
Administrative Conference on the U.S.
African Development Foundation
American Battle Monuments
  Commission
Appalachian Regional Commission
Board for International Broadcasting
Central Intelligence Agency
Commission on Civil Rights
Commission of Fine Arts
Commodity Futures Trading
  Commission
Corporation for National and
  Community Service
Consumer Product Safety Commission
Environmental Protection Agency
Equal Employment Opportunity
  Commission
Export-Import Bank of the U.S.
Farm Credit Administration
Federal Communications Commission
Federal Deposit Insurance Corporation
Federal Election Commission
Federal Emergency Management
  Agency
Federal Home Loan Bank Board

Federal Labor Relations Authority
Federal Maritime Commission
Federal Mediation and Conciliation
  Service
Federal Reserve System, Board of
  Governors of the
Federal Retirement Thrift Investment
  Board
Federal Trade Commission
General Services Administration
Inter-American Foundation
Interstate Commerce Commission
Merit Systems Protection Board
National Aeronautics and Space
  Administration
National Archives and Records
  Administration
National Capital Planning Commission
National Credit Union Administration
Nation Foundation on the Arts and
  the Humanities
National Labor Relations Board
National Mediation Board
National Railroad Passenger
  Corporation (Amtrak)
National Science Foundation
National Transportation Safety Board

Nuclear Regulatory Commission
Occupational Safety and Health Review
  Commission
Office of Government Ethics
Office of Personnel Management
Office of Special Counsel
Panama Canal Commission
Peace Corps
Pennsylvania Avenue Development
  Corporation
Pension Benefit Guaranty Corporation
Postal Rate Commission
Railroad Retirement Board
Resolution Trust Corporation
Securities and Exchange Commission
Selective Service System
Small Business Administration
Social Security Administration
Tennessee Valley Authority
Trade and Development Agency
U.S. Arms Control and Disarmament
  Agency
U.S. Information Agency
U.S. International Development
  Cooperation Agency
U.S. International Trade Commission
U.S. Postal Service

Source: *U.S. Government Organization Manual* 1995–96, 48.

Listed above are the offices and agencies not directly under one of the major departments of government. They include relatively minor commissions and agencies, such as the American Battle Monuments Commission; major regulatory agencies, such as the Securities and Exchange Commission; government businesses, such as the Tennessee Valley Authority; and other independent agencies, such as the Central Intelligence Agency.

regulate them. This type of organization in particular raises the issue of accountability: to whom are regulators responsible?

Independent Offices

The **independent agencies** listed in Table 8.3 and all components of the executive branch are also created by Congress. There are three major types of independent agencies: single-purpose organizations, government corporations, and regulatory commissions. The Selective Service System, NASA, and the United States Information Agency are independent offices each headed by a single administrator appointed by the president. These organizations have been responsive to presidential control and usually implement programs in line with those requested by the political executive. Such government corporations as the Tennessee Valley Authority and the Federal Deposit Insurance Corpo-

Table 8.4

SELECTED GOVERNMENT REGULATORY AGENCIES

Agency	Year Created	Regulates
Agencies that regulate specific industries:		
Interstate Commerce Commission (ICC)*	1887	Railroads, trucking, pipelines, barges, express carriers
Federal Reserve Board (FRB)	1913	Banks
Federal Power Commission (FPC)	1930	Public utilities
Food and Drug Administration (FDA)	1931	Food, drugs, cosmetics
Federal Communications Commission (FCC)	1934	Radio, television, telephone, telegraph
Federal Aviation Administration (FAA)	1967	Airline safety
National Highway Traffic Safety Administration (NHTSA)	1970	Motor vehicles
Nuclear Regulatory Commission (NRC)	1974	Nuclear energy and weapons
Agencies that regulate specific functons:		
Securities and Exchange Commission (SEC)	1934	Sales of securities
National Labor Relations Board (NLRB)	1935	Labor-management relations
Equal Employment Opportunity Commission (EEOC)	1964	Hiring practices
Environmental Protection Agency (EPA)	1970	Pollution of the environment
Occupational Safety and Health Administration (OSHA)	1971	Conditions in workplaces
Consumer Product Safety Commission (CPSC)	1972	Design and labeling of goods

*Congress voted in 1996 to eliminate the ICC.

Regulatory commissions are some of the most powerful agencies of the government.

ration are created to provide quasi-commercial services. These corporations have their own sources of revenue and, although their activities are annually reviewed by Congress and the president, control by these political agents seems minimal. The government is also involved in a number of mixed enterprises, part public and part private, such as the National Railroad Passenger Corporation, to which the president appoints some directors, but over which he or she exercises no real control.

Perhaps the most politically powerful of the independent agencies are the **independent regulatory commissions** such as the Federal Trade Commission, the Federal Aviation Administration, and the Federal Reserve Board.

Presidents appoint, with the advice and consent of the Senate, the members of these commissions' governing boards. Members of the board serve for fixed terms of office (for example, seven years on the Federal Trade Commission), and often a new president has little impact on their composition until he or she has served for several years.

Regulatory commissions are unique in another sense. Congress has granted to regulatory commissions considerably more power than to most components of government. An indication of the range of regulatory activities is shown in Table 8.4 above, which lists some of the more significant agencies along with the function each performs. Some regulatory agencies are housed within established departments, such as the Food and Drug Administration in Health and Human Services, but few are as powerful as the independent commissions. In chapter 3, the growth of federal activity was documented. One consequence is the increase in federal regulation; one study, for example, found that in 1979, 10 major economic and 18 major social regulatory agencies spent over $8 billion, required 77,497 pages of the *Federal Register* to publish their regulations (almost four times the number required in 1970), and were governed by an estimated 90,000 pages in the U.S. Code (Clark 1980). While recent administrations have attempted to cut back on regulations, and the current majorities in Congress have pursued legislation to strip regulatory agencies of much of their authority, these agencies and commissions still play a major role in governing our behavior. Because they have the authority to make policies and decisions, these agencies function as legislatures. And because they act as trial courts to hear complaints against the regulations they have issued, they serve in a quasi-judicial capacity. They are also charged with implementing their decisions, thus functioning in an executive capacity. Therefore, the three major functions of government—to legislate, to adjudicate, and to administrate—are performed by some regulatory agencies over which elected officials exercise only minimal control.

Functions of Bureaucracy

We may complain about bureaucracy, but imagine the difficulty of accomplishing complex tasks without such an organization or with an organization that is collegial, like Congress, rather than hierarchical. Max Weber, one of the first sociologists to study bureaucracy, noted that a modern capitalistic economy demands bureaucratic arrangements (Gerth and Mills 1946). It allows for the possibility of carrying out special functions according to objective criteria, presumably with calculable results and without regard for who is carrying them out. The more complex the society, the greater the need for the objective expert. As important, I might add, is the need for democratic controls to direct and oversee the expert.

Policies, Regulations, and Routines

As a source of policy, the bureaucrat is thrust into the mainstream of American political activity, "for it is in the crucible of administrative politics," states Francis E. Rourke, "that public policy is mainly hammered out" (1987, ix).

Bureaucratic agencies are often granted considerable power in formulating policy because, in many instances, an act of Congress furnishes only general guidelines, leaving an agency of the bureaucracy to fill in the specifics. A good example is Title IX of the Education Amendments of 1972. It took the Office of Education three years and required 14 pages of fine print in the *Federal Register* to summarize the rules and regulations for this one-sentence mandate forbidding sex discrimination in schools that receive federal money. In part, the delay resulted from the controversial nature of the amendment, but it was also the result of breaking new ground in administrative regulations. Normally regulations have been based on an extensive legislative history of what Congress intended, experience with other regulations, and court rulings on administrative law. Courts, however, have usually granted considerable discretion to the administration of congressional delegations of authority. For example, the Supreme Court held that Congress was specific enough in stating that an administrator could fix prices for goods and services during wartime that were "generally fair and equitable" (*Yakus v. United States,* 1944), or that the War Department could determine whether or not a defense contractor was making "excessive profits" (*Lichter v. United States,* 1948).

In addition, many administrative agencies in the bureaucracy are given the responsibility to act as judges in disputes that arise over implementation of a particular policy. Thus, if you as an individual attempt to override a bureaucratic decision, you will be listened to by the agency itself. If you lose there, you can pursue your claim in a court of appeals. Kenneth J. Meier asserts that adjudication is used by most regulatory agencies, and he provides the following illustration:

> The National Highway Traffic Safety Administration uses an adjudicatory process to remove vehicle models with safety defects from the road. When NHTSA suspects that a certain vehicle has a safety defect, it informs the manufacturer and holds a hearing. . . . When recalls involve large numbers of vehicles, manufacturers are understandably hesitant to agree to a recall, and NHTSA must go to court to enforce it. (1987, 81)

The bureaucracy must also implement policies. Even in cases where the law is specific, the administrator of an agency in the bureaucracy has considerable leeway in choosing methods to apply it. And the Supreme Court has supported this discretion. In *Chevron, U.S.A., v. Natural Resources Defense Council* (1984), the Court said that administrators need only adopt a rule or regulation that is reasonable under the law, not necessarily the best or most obvious one implied by the law. Prior to this decision, the standard was how "faithful to the statute's purpose" the proposed regulations might be. Just how far the Court is willing to allow bureaucratic interpretation to go can be seen in *Rust v. Sullivan* (1991). Funds for family planning had been included in the 1970 Public Health Service Act; the regulations called for both pre- and postconception counseling and assistance. In 1988, the Secretary of Health and Human Services announced new rules that allowed only preconception planning and information and forbade the discussion of abortion by those receiving Title X monies. Congressional critics claimed these changes were not supported by the legislation governing these funds, and the medical profession saw it as a violation of a doctor's free speech and professional responsibility. The Supreme Court ruled that the administration's position was a "reasonable" one under the *Chevron* test, and allowed it to stand. However, the Clinton administration rescinded the rules against postconception counseling.

Sometimes additional congressional action, or court action, is required to alter the implementation of programs. In fact, the *Rust v. Sullivan* decision is a classic case where the Court, under its own rules for considering statutory versus constitutional interpretations, should have overturned the rules and regulations and invited Congress to pass legislation that clearly spelled out just what types of activities it wished to fund. The courts could then have decided whether this was constitutional or not. Food stamps provide an illustration of how this process would work. Under the guidelines established by Congress, about 38 million people were qualified to receive food stamps in 1974, according to the Institute for Research on Poverty at the University of Wisconsin, but only about 18 million used the program. In large measure this was due to the Department of Agriculture's hostility toward the program, leading some critics to claim "deliberate maladministration" (Chapman 1975, 25). The program was not given wide announcement, recipients had to be recertified every three months, and local officials had allegedly been warned by department representatives to keep the number of recipients down. Both court cases and specific directions from Congress upon reauthorizing the program were necessary to change these administrative actions.

Economic Policy: A Budget as a Case Study in Bureaucracy

The budget provides an excellent case study of just where the bureaucracy fits with respect to Congress and the president. Budgets represent policies in terms of what will be done, who will do it, and what resources will be committed. Because little can be done without money, the making of the budget is "the number one political and priority" activity of the government (Shuman 1992, xiv). Figure 8.3, page 195, shows the process involved in preparing the budget.

The president's most effective control of the bureaucracy occurs because he or she recommends the budget to Congress. Most agencies rely on the amount requested for them in the executive budget, although as we have seen, some may approach Congress directly for increased funding. As a result, bureaucrats must rely to some extent on the president for a favorable or at least neutral attitude toward their activities. Administrators who allow an agency's projects to deviate too far from the president's policy will probably find the president's displeasure reflected in the curtailment of the agency's budget. But control over the budget is a more effective way for the president to continue the bureaucratic programs than it is for him or her to curtail the programs supported by the professional bureaucracy. The funding for most agencies begins with a base, or the amount received the previous year, to which only modest adjustments, that is incremental adjustments, are made each year. This style of policy making is referred to as **incrementalism**.

Much of the federal budget each year is already committed to uncontrollable outlays, as noted in chapter 5, pp. 125–127. Figure 8.4 on page 196 shows the percentage of mandatory outlays and their growth. In 1995, 64 percent of the budget fell into the category of uncontrollable outlays.

(Continued on p. 196)

Figure 8.3

FORMULATION OF THE PRESIDENT'S BUDGET

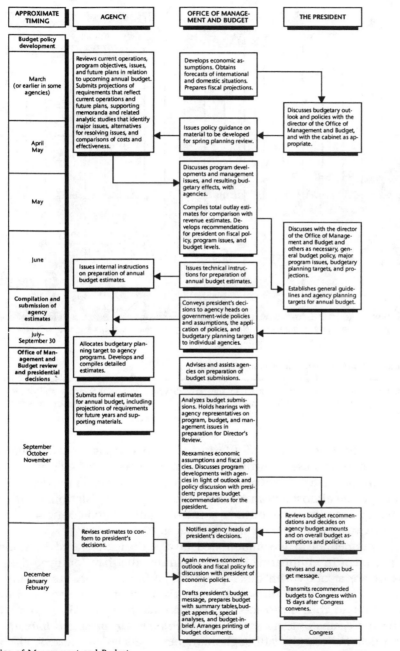

Source: Office of Management and Budget.

The president recommends the amount of money allocated to agencies of the government. Most agencies, therefore, are hesitant to disagree with the chief executive for fear of cutbacks in their proposed budgets.

Figure 8.4

CONTROLLABILITY OF THE FEDERAL BUDGET

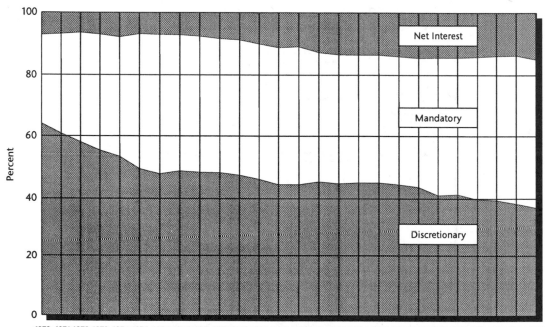

Source: Historical Tables, The Budget of the United States Government 1996, p. 97.

Net interest has doubled as a percentage of the federal budget in the past 25 years, as Social Security and other entitlement programs have increased mandatory expenditures nearly as much. Discretionary spending has dropped dramatically as a result.

There is little possibility of altering these percentages in the near future, because most represent ongoing programs such as Social Security, unemployment compensation, farm price supports, and interest on the debt—programs that continue almost automatically under existing legislation. Another major source of uncontrollable outlays is the obligations and contracts incurred in previous years that are now due and payable.

Incrementalism is compounded by the difficulty faced by Congress or the president in eliminating current programs that have outlived their usefulness or are at odds with other programs. Administrators are usually able to rally enough political support to keep their programs going. An interesting illustration of this is provided by Herbert Kaufman (1976), who studied the births and deaths of agencies, in *Are Government Organizations Immortal?* Kaufman's data indicate that although many new agencies are created—142 between 1961–73—few are ever abolished. Bradley R. Schiller describes a recent example: "The Office of Navajo and Hopi Indian Relocation still employs 97 people, although its mission ended in 1982" (1992, 24). Both the president and Con-

Figure 8.5

MAJOR STEPS IN THE BUDGET PROCESS

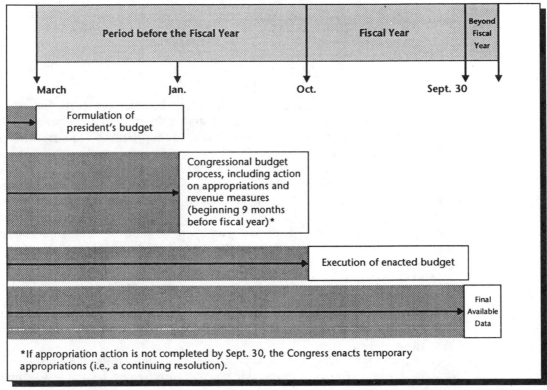

Source: Office of Management and Budget.

It takes almost a year to prepare a budget, and then nine months for Congress to consider its proposals before it takes effect on October 1.

gress have recently addressed this problem, but from different angles. Vice President Gore's National Performance Review Task Force has led an effort at "reinventing government" that has recommended numerous consolidations in programs and the elimination of various agencies. In one recent action they eliminated 16,000 pages of regulations. The Republican majority in Congress has used both its budget authority as well as legislation to go after programs and agencies it feels are no longer needed. You might want to explore whether either or both of these efforts have a real effect on the number of government programs and agencies.

Looking again at the constant interchange between the Office of Management and Budget (OMB) and each agency (or department), we see that bureaucrats are deeply involved in budget formulation. The president makes decisions concerning overall fiscal and program policy, but the appropriate agency and the OMB make most program decisions.

Relations between agencies and the [OMB] are important . . . in particular the relation between each agency and the [OMB's] examiners assigned to it. On the one hand, the agency is reluctant to incur [OMB] disfavor, for the [OMB's] recommendations to the president do carry weight. Congress usually exceeds the president's appropriations recommendations with some reluctance and more commonly cuts them. At the same time, the [OMB] cannot restrain the agencies too much, for "end runs" by agencies to Congress to get funds disapproved by the [OMB] are not unusual. So both parties are constrained and the end result is usually somewhere between what each would prefer. (Ott and Ott 1977, 32)

The OMB is not the only place to which agencies can turn. Indeed, in bypassing the OMB, many bureaucrats, and even cabinet secretaries of the executive departments, can negotiate their appropriations requests directly with the White House Office.

The president submits a budget to Congress in January of each year. From Figure 8.3 on page 195 we can see that it takes almost a year to prepare. Congress will now have 9 months to consider it. Figure 8.5 gives a better picture of the time period to which I refer. For each budget year, which goes into effect on October 1, there has been about 18 months of preparation and refinement. This drawn-out process also favors only incremental adjustments to the budget. A president is beginning the second half of his or her term before really working with his or her own budget, and by then is submitting plans and proposals that will not become reality until his or her successor is in office—or until the incumbent's second term. This gives greater power to those who will be there year after year: professional bureaucrats and members of Congress.

Bureaucrats can not only appeal their case directly to the president or the White House; they can and will also attempt to get favorable treatment from Congress. When the president decides how much to request from Congress, the appropriations are closely scrutinized, particularly by subcommittees of the Appropriations Committee. Now bureau chiefs are able to present their cases, to defend the money given them in the executive budget, or to attempt to gain sufficient legislative support to increase their authorizations. David Stockman, who had been a member of Congress for six years before becoming the director of the OMB in 1981, gives us the following insight:

What I did not know then [when he had been a member of Congress] was how little weight the paper recommendations of a presidential budget carry on Capitol Hill . . . particularly when you've got a whole department of bureaucrats, including the top one, working the other side. (1986, 116)

Several agencies, because of their close liaison with Congress, are often more successful than others in obtaining amounts greater than the executive allocated. Notable in their success before Congress have been the Army Corps of Engineers and the Federal Bureau of Investigation. The success of the Corps is attributed to its ability to provide benefits for almost all congressional districts. Armed with the political support from these districts, such an agency can increase its appropriations. Projects that even the Corps is skeptical about sometimes find their way into the budget. The FBI usually receives the amount it requests, and on occasion has been awarded more than it requested. Members find it hard to vote against law enforcement requests.

Bureaucracy and the President

How to control the bureaucracy is a problem that has plagued presidents since the New Deal. Presidents, as the constitutional agents in charge of the executive branch, have attempted to provide the necessary coordination and control over a sometimes unresponsive and large bureaucracy, but none of the attempts has proved to be satisfactory. The issue is an important one: If bureaucrats are not accountable to democratically elected leadership, to whom are they accountable?

Early in his administration, Richard Nixon, for example, had found little success with his legislative proposals to control bureaucracy. He then adopted a strategy in which all domestic policy proposals and policies were directed and run by White House staff. But, Nixon soon realized, as he stated in his memoirs, that "we had failed to fill all key posts ... with people who were loyal to the president and his programs" (1978, 284).

There is always the problem of loyalty among appointees. One Carter assistant secretary is quoted as saying,

> There is a belief that some assistant secretaries are in business for themselves. Officially, when they testify on the Hill, they say the right things.
> ... But privately, they tell committee staff members, "I don't really think that." (Bonafede 1978, 1853)

Rewarding various constituencies for electoral support by appointments in a new administration may make for good politics; it makes for poor administration, at least where good administration means clear, consistent follow-through on presidential directions. "Making the right appointments at the outset of a new government is one of the keys for a president in getting a managerial grip on the office" (Nathan 1983, 90). Nathan thinks Ronald Reagan did a good job of getting the right people for the job from the first appointments—people committed to the president and his policies. The Reagan solution, as explained by his personnel director Robert Tuttle, was the control of the appointment of political executives by the White House. If there was disagreement between a cabinet secretary and the personnel director, it went to the president. But the strategy of centralizing appointments seemed to produce a political executive responsive to Reagan's wishes. These agents, in turn, attempted to place politically responsive personnel in the professional bureaucracy, sometimes in violation of the spirit if not the letter of the rules. Senator John Glenn (D-OH), then chair of the committee overseeing the professional bureaucracy, presented a report showing that many departments were approaching the 25 percent limit in political appointments to high-level bureaucratic positions (high-level executive service can have political appointees, but there is a limit to the number permitted). A GAO report also indicated that there was a growing use of **Schedule C** (positions that are classified as politically sensitive), particularly in the Justice and Education departments and in the United States Information Agency (*Washington Post* August 6, 1987, A4). In addition, a federal court blocked the administration's use of **Schedule B** (positions that are special, to be filled by temporary appointments) as a means of bypassing the regular examination and appointment process of the civil service (Havemann 1987). The ability of these appointees to effect control over the professional bureaucracy, however, is more difficult to assess.

Another Reagan administration strategy was to take control of regulations. Under Executive Order 12291, issued in 1981 and since overruled by the Supreme Court, the OMB was responsible for clearing all regulations issued by bureaucratic agencies to ensure that they were in line with administration policy. The Reagan administration also used regulations to bypass congressional involvement in policy when Congress had failed to support administrative requests for legislative changes. Regulations that had been in force since 1907 with respect to labeling and packaging of products were changed by new rules after Congress refused to act. In an even more controversial move, the Clinton administration issued new regulations concerning gays in the military, a decision unpopular with both military and congressional leadership.

The use of the budget as a means of gaining bureaucratic compliance with administrative wishes has already been discussed; it is effective, especially in an era of limited government resources, but there are ways for an affected agency to continue to receive support if strong ties with Congress remain. Finally, the executive can attempt to reorganize the bureau or agency in an attempt to bring its actions in line with administration wishes. William Penn Mott Jr., Director of the National Park Service, for example, in 1986 wrote a memorandum to the secretary of the interior that was critical of attempts by the political appointees in the Interior Department to alter Park Service performance, reviews, and reorganization plans.

> I feel compelled to reiterate my concerns about the way your staff has handled this reorganization. People have been offered jobs that are encumbered or do not exist. . . . I find it incomprehensible that the changes of bonuses, ratings, and the assignment of conditional ratings would occur without consultation with me. (Cahn and Cahn 1987, 28–29)

Attempts by the Clinton administration to control the bureaucracy have been mixed. For one thing, the appointment of ranking political executives was slow; many positions were unfilled after more than a year in office. However, Clinton is given high marks for actively delegating authority and responsibility to department and agency decision makers and not trying to micromanage affairs from the White House (Blakesley 1995, 249). In addition, Blakesley concludes that "the accessibility of the Oval Office to top administrative officials, and President Clinton's high regard for systematic program evaluations all suggest [that he will be] relatively effective . . . as he attempts to monitor policy implementation" (269).

But the extent to which any administration can grasp the reins of control is always limited. Professional bureaucrats have the political resources available to protect their domains, and there are interest groups in society intent on keeping programs or regulations as they are, and willing to take the administration to court to ensure this. Also the media are always ready to take up a controversy and give it national attention. Most importantly, Congress is as much a part of bureaucratic control as is the executive. For example, as the 1992 election approached, the Senate brought the confirmation process to a standstill, leaving many bureaucratic and judicial positions unfilled. Democrats wanted to see if they would win control of the White House. The control of Congress by Republicans, starting in 1995, has placed the Clinton administration's appointments in jeopardy. A number of appointments were withdrawn after the 1994 election; others required major political battles. The most widely reported conflict was the nomination of Dr. William Foster to be the Surgeon General, a battle the president lost.

Bureaucracy and Congress

The president is the chief executive. It is Congress's business to make the laws. But we have seen that the president is a much more active source of law than Congress. In another reversal of roles, Congress is a much more effective check on the bureaucracy than is the president. What presidents wish to do—that is, control the actions of the bureaucracy—is exercised daily by Congress.

Formally, of course, Congress does create the bureaucracy, can reorganize it, and, most importantly, must fund it. But as with other formal powers, these are shared with the executive; indeed, as indicated, most initiatives emanate from the executive branch. However, the most effective sources of control stem more from organizational arrangements between Congress and the bureaucracy. Day-to-day contact between Congress and the bureaucracy occurs for two reasons. Individually, the member seeks to serve his or her constituents, the ombudsman feature of congressional offices we looked at in chapter 6. For the most part, though, casework relates to only a few agencies, such as the Defense and Veterans Affairs departments and the Social Security Administration, those agencies that have the broadest impact on individual citizens. Nevertheless, congressional inquiries to any agency can have a profound effect on that agency. One former senator phrased it this way: "The very knowledge by executive officials that some Congressman is sure to look into a matter affecting his constituents acts as a healthy check against bureaucratic indifference or arrogance" (Davidson and Oleszek 1996, 267). Projects in a state or a district represent another reason for contact between Congress and the bureaucracy. A member of Congress may be in constant contact with an agency during a major construction project, or if he or she is seeking and coordinating emergency aid

Table 8.5

THE 13 SUBCOMMITTEES OF THE HOUSE APPROPRIATIONS COMMITTEE

Agriculture, Rural Development, FDA and Related Agencies
Commerce, Justice, State, and Judiciary
District of Columbia
Energy and Water Development
Foreign Operations, Export Financing and Related Programs
Interior
Labor, Health and Human Services, Education
Legislative
Military Construction
National Security
Transportation
Treasury, Postal Service, and General Government
Veterans Affairs, HUD–Independent Agencies

Source: *Congressional Staff Directory* 104th Congress, 1995.

The subcommittees of the House Appropriations Committee handle the budgets for various agencies in the House. Those under the jurisdiction of one subcommittee, such as Commerce, Justice, State, and Judiciary, must deal with the problems and concerns of the others.

during a disaster. No doubt both House and Senate members may pursue contact with agencies on the same projects.

But neither projects nor casework are regular or systematic; both enhance the link between Congress and the bureaucracy but do not provide the key to control, which comes from the committee system. Congress organizes itself basically along the same lines as those in which the bureaucracy is organized. Committees and their subcommittees are responsible for the various government agencies that they oversee. There is a Department of Veterans Affairs, and both the House and Senate have a committee on veterans affairs; there is a Department of Agriculture, and both the House and Senate have a committee on agriculture; and so on. The subcommittees in Congress, then, reflect in large measure the breakdown of functions within a department. The relationships are not totally neat or completely correspondent: some committees oversee more than one department, and the problems facing some departments are dealt with by more than one committee, but as a general rule congressional organization and the bureaucracy are quite similar. To change the organization of the bureaucracy is to disrupt the existing power relationships on Capitol Hill. A major theme from the discussion of Congress was that a member's legislative power stemmed mostly from committees. Members are just not very enthusiastic about doing away with programs or components of the bureaucracy that serve as their bases of power.

An additional congressional control over bureaus and agencies is the appropriations process. The budget is broken into 13 sections, which are dealt with by a subcommittee of the appropriations committees from each house. Table 8.5 lists those of the House Appropriations Committee. The Defense

Department requires two subcommittees to handle its affairs—Defense and Military Construction. Other departments, such as Commerce, Justice, State, and Judiciary, are combined under the jurisdiction of one subcommittee. When multiple departments are represented by the same subcommittee, each is drawn into the problems and battles of the other. For example, when funds for abortion administered by the Department of Health and Human Services were held up in the late 1970s as the House and Senate attempted to resolve their differences, it was as much a problem for the Education Department, which also faced a delay in getting its appropriation because it was part of the same bill. In the fall of 1995, government agencies were technically out of money while Congress and the president haggled over how to solve the budget crises. The budget resolutions were not actually adopted until several months after the start of the new fiscal year. While most observers agree that the most important link between Congress and bureaucracy is that between substantive committee and agency, appropriations subcommittees and the budget committees play an important role. Recent budget crises, in fact, have given the Appropriations and Budget committees a more equal role in defining what is to be done. Congress devotes much time to committee work, as we noted in chapter 5; it is their source of power within Congress. The bureaucracy gives them the information and provides them with the expertise necessary for power. But the bureau and agency are dependent on the members of Congress for support, programmatic and financial, as well as protection from other agencies and programs and the attempts of the president to control their actions. In this reciprocal relationship, members and bureaucrats have largely shared goals and objectives.

The White House, however, views the relationship of Congress and administrative agencies of the bureaucracy somewhat differently. Theodore Sorensen, special assistant to President Kennedy, expressed it this way:

> We knew about the sweetheart contract [cozy working relations] which the FBI had with Capitol Hill; it took us a little longer to learn about those of the Bureau of Reclamation, the Passport Office, the Forest Service, the Park Service, the Army Engineers, and several others. (1975, 43)

Relationships between the administrative agency and members of Congress or committee staff can become too close, resulting in legislators' making administrative decisions or attempting to micromanage agency programs. The result can be complaints from the White House, as well as from students of sound administration. President Bush, and later President Clinton, complained often and loudly about congressional restrictions on bureaucratic discretion, claiming it to be excessive. Illustrative of this problem is the Foreign Aid Authorization for 1996, in which House Republicans not only cut spending and eliminated several agencies, but also required the president to recognize Tibet as an independent country, among many other specific directives. All of this led to a threatened presidential veto.

Substantive committees exercise control primarily through setting conditions in the initial legislation that will direct how a program is to be carried out. When a program comes up for renewal, members can inject additional controls based on their previous experience. Programs that have been in existence for considerable time are thus refined to a mutually acceptable status. In addition, Congress has used the legislative veto, although it has had to make adjustments of its own based on *INS v. Chadha* (1983) (see the discussion in chapter 5 on pp. 131–132). But the contact and influence of members need not be so direct; study tours, hearings, or informal conversations often provide members of Congress with the opportunity to set the direction for how programs are to be administered.

Appropriations subcommittees' control is not as firm as that of the substantive committees. In part, this is because the substantive committee defines the legislative mandate. Appropriations subcommittees nevertheless can and do exert substantive control through the appropriations process by inserting language that directs or emphasizes some activities rather than others. Bureaucrats read with care the reports and language of the budget bills for clues as to how to avoid alienating key members on those committees (Oleszek 1996, 308). However, congressional control of administrative agencies is limited by the extent to which government expenditures are in fact uncontrollable, or fixed by existing law or prior commitments, as discussed previously in this chapter.

Administrators have the means at their disposal to influence congressional actions. They can ensure that key members, those crucial to the coalitions supporting the agency, receive benefit: "Ordinarily, bureaucrats choose to allocate disproportionate shares of benefits to members of those committees that have jurisdiction over their programs" (Arnold 1979, 207).

Congress and the bureaucracy are closely allied; they need each other. And the actions of each are designed to enhance not only their own position but to secure support from the other. Both members of Congress and bureaucrats have a much longer tenure in office than those directing departments and agencies from the political executive. Thus, these reciprocal relations are developed over a long period of time, are relatively stable, and tend to dictate ongoing administration of programs to a greater degree than could any administration that might be in the White House.

Summary

The federal bureaucracy, caught in the political competition between the president and Congress, has, nonetheless, emerged as a major source of power and policy in its own right. Bureaucracies take on a life of their own. Many bureaus and many bureaucratic positions have outlived their usefulness or received a disproportionate share of public expenditures, leading to serious critiques of government waste, as well as significant efforts at reform, such as Vice President Al Gore's National Performance Review. Professional bureaucrats acquire office by appointment, are protected by civil service, and most make government service their life's work. They may not be accountable to the president or to his or her political appointees who oversee their office or agency. Government employees have become a significant and organized portion of the electorate. Public employees at all levels of government number about 16 million—about one-sixth of the workforce. Three million of these work for the federal government.

Implementing our laws is the function of the bureaucracy. Since many laws need considerable interpretation before they can be put into operation, bureaucrats have a major role in what is ultimately done or not done. As bureaucrats are insulated from direct democratic control, this power over policy poses a problem for democratic government.

The president and Congress each have considerable influence on bureaucratic performance, although Congress is able to more closely monitor what is going on. Recent presidents, in an attempt to increase their own control, have attempted to alter appointment patterns, rule making, and reorganizations within the bureaucracy. In some cases they have been successful. And states and local governments have called for the return of many of the governmental functions recently performed by bureaucracies at the federal level. In some cases, these efforts have succeeded. But at whatever level, modern societies cannot function without the organizing advantages of bureaucracy.

Analytical Exercises

1. As the director of an agency in the federal bureaucracy, you are confronted with the following situations. What decision would you make in each case?

A. Your staff has investigated a proposed project in upstate New York and found that it does not meet the minimum criteria for inclusion in your list of projects to be funded in next year's budget. However, the chair of the subcommittee that oversees your agency is the congressman from that upstate district. Do you include the project or not?

B. Your proposed budget is in trouble on Capitol Hill. The president has pointed to your agency as central to the administration's new programmatic emphasis, and the opposing party that is in control of Congress has singled out your budgetary requests for deletion in order to embarrass the president. You can retain your agency's budget authority if you will agree to testify publicly that the new initiatives are unnecessary or unwise. If you don't, you may lose most of your agency's budgetary authority. What do you do?

C. You have just learned from an old friend now serving in the White House that the administration is planning a new program that will supersede the major task assigned to your agency. This new program will be given to another agency in the bureaucracy. The president's plan, however, includes a number of other controversial moves involving reorganizing the bureaucracy and/or reassigning responsibility for programs. From past experience you know that you have a good chance of killing these changes if you leak your information to the media. What do you do?

2. Charges of conflict of interest that accompany the appointment of industry personnel to powerful positions in agencies and regulatory commissions leave the appointing official in a dilemma. Those making the appointment want to ensure competence and expertise in the substantive area of the position, but it is often difficult to find a candidate who has both expertise and no close

ties to the industry involved. We see this especially in areas of banking, energy, and defense, for example. Is it possible to staff highly specialized and technical positions with disinterested appointees who were not trained in the businesses and institutions affected by the agency's programs or policies? From where would they be recruited? And if they are to come from the affected industries, is there a way to ensure that they are now acting in the public interest?

One answer would be to draw from academic institutions, but if you choose this strategy, how would you weigh an appointee's previous role in research grants, contracts, or consulting relationships with the private-sector industries to be regulated? If you suggest the appointment of staff members from the congressional committee having jurisdiction over the policy area, how do you weigh the possibility that the staffer is still more loyal to Congress than to the agency? What effect would a requirement barring employment in an affected industry or a position lobbying Congress or former colleagues in the executive branch for five years after leaving public service have on your ability to secure applicants for the job? You might want to investigate the difficulties the Clinton administration encountered in writing such restrictions.

9

Supreme Court

However the Court may interpret the provisions of the Constitution, it is still the Constitution which is the law and not the decision of the Court.

—Charles Warren, *The Supreme Court in United States History*, 1932

I do not think the United States would come to an end if we lost our power to declare an Act of Congress void. I do think the Union would be imperiled if we could not make that declaration as to the laws of the several States.

—Justice Oliver Wendell Holmes, 1934

The Supreme Court was formerly an institution unique to the United States. As many as 70 other countries have now adopted something similar (Abraham 1993a, 270–71), but nowhere has a court demonstrated the power and independence of the American original. The desire to establish a rule of law as expressed at the Constitutional Convention dictated that someone should be responsible for interpreting the law. Thus, the Court has enjoyed a prominence in the American system unrivaled by judiciaries in other nations. The power of the Court to interpret law has been both its strength and its weakness. In areas in which the law is ambiguous, unsettled, or affected by changing circumstances, the Court is a major source of public policy. But there are two sides to the Court's position. It has removed itself from areas that have been largely settled in points of law but are still major battlegrounds for policymaking in the American system, such as the relative war powers of the Congress and the presidency. The Court limits its own power because excessive use of its authority could render it ineffectual. This somewhat para-

Figure 9.1

FEDERAL JUDICIAL CIRCUITS

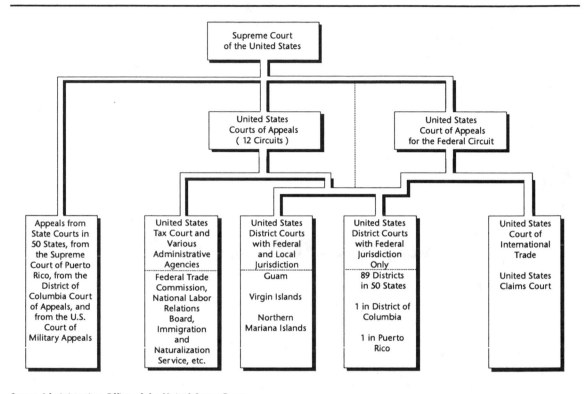

Source: Administration Office of the United States Courts.

The United States is divided into 12 judicial circuits, each of which has a court of appeals. Each court of appeals has from 6 to 28 permanent judgeships, depending on the amount of work in that circuit. The circuit courts hear appeals from decisions reached in lower federal district courts.

doxical situation and the resulting dilemma facing the Court will be my topic in this chapter.

Organization and Jurisdiction

Organization and jurisdiction of the federal judiciary is shown in Figure 9.1. The Supreme Court has jurisdiction of both original cases and appeals from lower court decisions. Original jurisdiction means that the case is begun in the Supreme Court and has not been heard in another court. The Supreme Court has original jurisdiction in all cases that affect "Ambassadors, other public Ministers and Consuls, and those in which a State shall be Party" (Constitution, art. III, sec. 2). These account for only a small number of cases, about one a year. Some involve a question of national importance, as in *South*

Carolina v. Katzenbach (1966), where the Court upheld the major provisions of the Voting Rights Act of 1965. More typical would be the 1992 case *United States v. Alaska*, a dispute between Alaska and the Army Corps of Engineers over who owned land created by the construction of the port facilities at Nome. Except for legal disputes between two or more states, Congress has also given jurisdiction in state cases to other federal courts, allowing the Supreme Court to avoid these if it wishes. And the Eleventh Amendment to the Constitution, adopted in 1798, exempted from Court consideration suits brought against "States by Citizens of another State."

Most cases on the **docket** or calendar are those brought under appellate jurisdiction as a result of decisions of the lower courts. Three methods may be used to bring cases under appellate jurisdiction: certification, appeal, and certiorari. Certification is a seldom-used technique whereby a lower court asks the Supreme Court for guidance in a particular case. One example of this rarely used technique occurred when the Fifth Circuit Court of Appeals asked whether its criminal contempt citation of Mississippi governor Ross R. Barnett required a jury trial. The appeals court was divided 4–4 on the issue; the Supreme Court voted 5–4 that it did not require a jury trial (*United States v. Barnett*, 1964). Normally, if the case raises important questions, the Court itself considers and decides those questions instead of offering its guidance to the lower court. Appeals are another avenue under appellate jurisdiction. Appeals arise when cases involve statutorily defined characteristics (such as a state court upholding a law against a challenge that the law conflicts with the Voting Rights Act). There were at one time a number of cases that, because of their subject matter, had a right of mandatory appeal to the Supreme Court. Congress virtually eliminated them in 1988. Left are appeals from Voting and Civil Rights Act violations and a small number of federal antitrust cases. In 1992, a major decision on appeal involved a challenge by Montana to the method used to apportion seats for the House of Representatives. A three-judge panel of district judges—whose decisions have automatic appeal to the high court—had ruled for Montana; the Supreme Court overturned that decision, leaving Montana with only one representative as a result (*U.S. Department of Commerce et al. v. Montana et al.*).

Almost all cases now heard by the Court under appellate jurisdiction are presented by means of a petition for a **writ of certiorari**. A writ is an order issued in the name of a court, and *certiorari* means to make more certain, in effect, to call up for a review. One reason for granting such a writ might be that a lower court had upheld a state law against a challenge that it conflicted with a federal law. There are certain criteria for granting certiorari (published in the Rules of the Court); basically, the case must involve a substantial federal question. The Court itself decides what is substantial. That is, the Court now has the discretion to decide which cases and how many to hear each year. Four justices must vote to consider a case before certiorari is granted. The Court may refuse a case if it is considered trivial or insubstantial. With the removal of most appeals, the Court now gives extensive consideration to, and issues written opinions in, about 100 cases a year, a 50 percent reduction from a decade ago.

Lower Federal Courts

The establishment of a national court system with its own jurisdiction was a major accomplishment of proponents of stronger national government at the Constitutional Convention in Philadelphia in 1787. As the national government expanded its activities into more and more areas, the federal judiciary was faced with questions that were formerly the exclusive concern of the states, such as criminal justice, voting qualifications, and education.

Competition between the two court systems—state and federal—ensued from their overlapping jurisdiction. In some circumstances litigants can choose the system in which they will initiate proceedings. Under the direction of recent chief justices, the availability of federal courts to hear cases that are justiciable in state courts has been limited. Nevertheless, major questions of public policy tend to deal with federal statutes or the Constitution; thus, the federal judiciary has become the focal point of most important litigation.

At the lower level, the federal court system has expanded in response to the growing volume of litigation. There are now 89 district courts in addition to 1 district court for the District of Columbia and 4 district courts serving territories (Puerto Rico, Guam, the Virgin Islands, and the Mariana Islands). Although these courts serve as the trial courts of the federal judiciary, they were also intended to be, and are, supportive of state and local interests. In fact, district court jurisdictions

> were drawn along state boundary lines. . . . Thus, from the outset, the federal judiciary was state-contained, with the administrative and political structure of the states becoming the organizational structure of the federal courts. . . . [Furthermore,] the federal judge was, therefore, a local resident, approved by senators, adjudicating in his home area, and subject to the continuing influence of his environment. (Richardson and Vines 1970, 21)

Because of these circumstances, considerable tension between local communities and the federal courts has occurred when the courts have been called on to decide cases that conflict with the prevailing communal sentiment. Indeed, at times judges have maintained community values at the expense of federal law. The most notable example would be school desegregation in the late 1950s and early 1960s, where some district judges in the South did not enforce desegregation.

Reviewing the decisions of district and special courts such as the U.S. Tax Court are the 12 U.S. Courts of Appeals (1 for each of the 11 circuits plus 1 for the District of Columbia). Created in 1891 to relieve the Supreme Court of much of the appellate burden, our circuit courts today handle most appeals. Figure 9.2 shows the jurisdiction of each appeals court. In 1925, the Judiciary Act reduced the burden of the Supreme Court and moved appellate activity mainly to the courts of appeals. With much of the Supreme Court's review and control over lower federal courts circumscribed, the circuit courts exercise considerable influence over the administration of justice in the federal court system in addition to their role in interpreting the Constitution.

Figure 9.2

ORGANIZATION AND JURISDICTION OF THE FEDERAL JUDICIARY

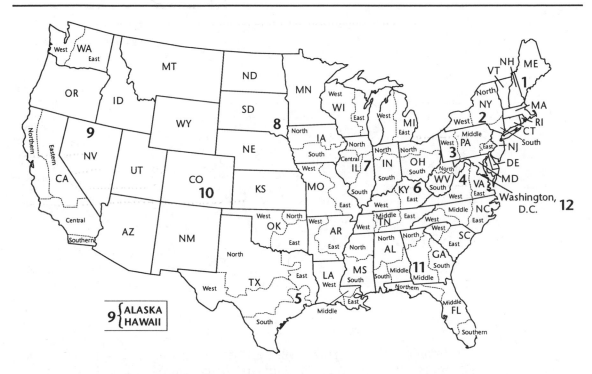

Source: Adapted from *The Federal Courts as a Political System* by Sheldon Goldman and Thomas P. Jahnige. © 1985 by Harper & Row Publishers, Inc. Reprinted by permission.

Cases move from district courts to higher courts of appeal serving regions of the country shown in the figure above.

There is also a U.S. Court of Appeals for the Federal Circuit, which hears appeals from a variety of special courts: the U.S. Court of Claims, for example (see Figure 9.1). These special courts present an interesting adaptation in the court system. Most are legislative courts; that is, they are created by Congress from constitutional grants of authority other than Article III. For example, the U.S. Court of Military Appeals is based on Article I powers of Congress. Another aspect of legislative courts is that judges do not necessarily serve for life: Judges on the U.S. Court of Claims, for example, serve for 15-year terms.

Powers of the Court

As we have seen, the Supreme Court sits alone at the top of an extensive federal court system. While lower courts frequently exercise the same powers as the Supreme Court, their actions are subject to review by the higher court.

Figure 9.3

NUMBER OF WOMEN AND BLACKS APPOINTED TO THE FEDERAL BENCH

	Number of Blacks	Number of Women	Appointing President
	0	1	Coolidge
	0	1	Roosevelt
	1	1	Truman
	1	1	Eisenhower
	4	1	Kennedy
	9	3	Johnson
	6	1	Nixon
	3	1	Ford
	37	40	Carter
	8	31	Reagan
	11	37	Bush
	34	51	Clinton*
Total:	114	169	

*As of October 1, 1995.

Source: Alliance for Justice, *Judicial Selection Project*, October 1995.

The president appoints federal court justices with the consent of the Senate. There are now approximately 850 Article III judges.

Three areas of Court power will be discussed in this section: judicial review, statutory interpretation, and boundary maintenance.

Judicial Review

The most effective power in the hands of the Supreme Court is **judicial review**. Constitutional scholar Henry Abraham calls it the "most awesome and potentially the most effective weapon in the hands of the judiciary" (1991, 55). It was a "bold and in many respects original expansion of central government power which helped to raise the courts, the law, and the legal profession to a governing role unprecedented then and unequaled elsewhere today" (Dolbeare and Metcalf 1987, 131). It is a controversial power and not always understood, but basic to any interpretation would be the following:

> Judicial review is the ultimate power of any court to declare unconstitutional and hence unenforceable: (1) any law; (2) any official action based upon a law; and (3) any other action by a public official that it deems to be in conflict with the Constitution. (Abraham 1991, 55)

Squaring the enactments of legislators or presidents with the Constitution might appear on the surface to be an objective and relatively nonpolitical technique. But if we accept Justice Felix Frankfurter's claim that the words of the Constitution "are so unrestricted by their intrinsic meaning or their history or by tradition or by prior decision, that they leave the individual justice free, if indeed they do not compel him, to gather meaning, not from reading the Constitution, but from reading life" (Prichard and MacLeish 1930, 30), or Justice Charles Evans Hughes's contention that "the Constitution is what the judges say it is" (Pusey 1951, 204), the power of judicial review becomes a considerable grant of authority.

It was not explicitly decided at the Constitutional Convention that the Supreme Court should be the final arbiter of what laws and actions were in conformance or in conflict with the Constitution, although a reading of the debates leaves one thinking that the Framers intended such a power for the Court. Many who helped write the Constitution felt that the Court had been given this power. This was especially true of those who favored strong central government. Alexander Hamilton, for example, in *The Federalist* No. 78, argues that:

> The complete independence of the courts of justice is peculiarly essential in a limited Constitution. By a limited Constitution, I understand one which contains certain specified exceptions to the legislative authority; such, for instance, as that it shall pass no bills of attainder, no ex post facto laws, and the like. Limitations of this kind can be preserved in practice no other way than through the medium of the courts of justice, whose duty it must be to declare all acts contrary to the manifest tenor of the Constitution void. Without this, all the reservations of particular rights or privileges would amount to nothing.

Later in the same paper, Hamilton writes:

> It is far more rational to suppose that the courts were designed to be an intermediate body between the people and the legislature in order, among other things, to keep the latter within the limits assigned to their authority. The interpretation of the laws is the proper and peculiar province of the courts. A Constitution is, in fact, and must be regarded by the judges as a fundamental law. It therefore belongs to them to ascertain its meaning as well as the meaning of any particular act proceeding from the legislative body. If there should happen to be an irreconcilable variance between the two, that which has the superior obligation and validity ought, of course, to be preferred; or in other words, the Constitution ought to be preferred to the statute, the intention of the people to the intention of their agents.

The Judiciary Act of 1789, which created the lower federal court system and established jurisdictions, also gave the Supreme Court judicial review. The act of 1789 specifically gave the Supreme Court the power to affirm or reverse on appeal any decision of the high court of a state holding a state law valid and constitutional or a federal law unconstitutional.

The mention of judicial review in *The Federalist* papers and the Judiciary Act of 1789 created the basis for this prerogative of the Court, but not until John Marshall's momentous decision in *Marbury v. Madison* (1803) was the principle firmly established in precedent. While the threat of using some power may, at times, produce the desired actions, a threat must be credible. Until the Court used it, judicial review was no power at all. Moreover, if the power was a grant of the legislature, it could also be revoked by the legislature.

Marshall had to find the basis for judicial review in the Constitution in order for the Court to have its independence. The case was an interesting one and deserves some discussion.

MARBURY V. MADISON   President John Adams appointed William Marbury to the federal court at the close of his administration in 1801, but Adams's secretary of state, John Marshall, failed to deliver Marbury's commission. Thomas Jefferson, succeeding Adams, instructed *his* secretary of state, James Madison, not to deliver the commission to Marbury. Marbury, on behalf of himself and three others who had been appointed to the position of justice of the peace of the district court in Washington, all of whose appointments had died on Marshall's desk, took his case to the Supreme Court, asking for a writ of mandamus (a writ requiring a public official to perform a specified duty) under Section 13 of the Judiciary Act of 1789, which had given the Court original jurisdiction in such cases.

The Court was dominated by Chief Justice John Marshall (who coincidentally had been instrumental in initiating the dispute through his failure to deliver the commission). Marshall was faced with a perplexing political problem. The Court was the last bastion of the Federalist party in a nation in which the Jeffersonian Democrats had come to political power over the Federalists. Moreover, the Court was uncertain and unsettled in its role in the American system.

Marshall's solution was that Marbury should, by all standards of what was right, receive his commission, but that Section 13 of the Judiciary Act of 1789 exceeded the constitutionally specific instances in which the Court has original jurisdiction. Since Section 13 violated the Constitution, it was null and void. Marbury had a right to his commission, but he did not have the right to bring an original action in the Supreme Court. By ruling on the constitutionality of Section 13, Marshall established the precedent of judicial review. President Jefferson was placed in the interesting position of having the Court rule in his favor, basing its decision, however, on the principle of judicial review, a principle with which he was hardly in agreement, and one that placed the Court, dominated as it was by the opposing party, in a position to seriously challenge Jefferson's programs. Nevertheless, Jefferson had little choice but to accept the Court's precedent-setting decision.

JUDICIAL REVIEW SINCE *MARBURY*   Judicial review has been sparingly used, however, with respect to federal laws, because relatively few matters actually have been placed in the context of violating the Constitution. Not until *Dred Scott v. Sandford* (1857) did the Court again rule an action of Congress to be unconstitutional. I should note, however, that few decisions have had such a profound impact on American politics and history as did *Dred Scott*. In that case the Court ruled that the Missouri Compromise of 1820, which had outlawed slavery in the territories, was unconstitutional, stating that it deprived masters of their property without due process of law. By upsetting a very delicate compromise between the North and the South, the Court in no small way contributed to the outbreak of the Civil War.

In total, through 1995, the Court has struck down 129 acts of Congress in full or in part (Killian and Costello 1996). Between 1890 and 1936, 46 statutes, mostly economic regulations (for example, the child labor laws), were declared unconstitutional. During this time, the Court was primarily concerned with the protection of property and the prohibition of government impositions on its use. In most cases in the past 50 years, acts have been held unconstitutional on the basis that they violated the Due Process Clause of the Fifth Amendment. A major decision in 1995 struck down the Gun-Free School Zones Act of 1990, which forbade "any individual knowingly to possess a firearm at a place that [he] knows . . . is a school zone" (*United States v. Lopez*). Chief Justice Rehnquist, writing for a 5 to 4 majority, said that the act exceeded Congress's commerce clause authority (Art I, Sec 8, clause 8). The decision was important because the Court had been supportive of a wide-ranging use of the commerce power to effect national goals, and the Court, as evidenced by cases cited in the last chapter, has generally deferred to the other branches, especially in areas specifically given them in the Constitution.

The modern Court has proscribed numerous state and local government actions that violate specific mandates of the Constitution; more than 1,100 state acts and local ordinances have been voided through 1995 (Killian and Costello 1996). In recent years, these represented a failure on the part of state and local governments to comply with the specific individual rights listed in the first eight amendments and applied to the states through the Fourteenth Amendment, rights that were described in chapter 4.

Boundary Maintenance

Constitutional interpretation historically occurs on the boundaries between the separate institutions of national government, between the federal and state governments, and between appropriate government action at any level and areas where government is to leave the citizen alone. This concept of boundary maintenance was developed in chapter 4, Civil Rights and Civil Liberties. In recent decades the Court has also become involved in deciding what private individuals can do to one another. In a limited government, many areas of citizen behavior are beyond the purview of government control. Some of these are more obvious than others. Not many dispute the protection that individuals have from torture or from laws that hold them responsible for their actions before those actions were made illegal. Nor would many dispute the right of government to imprison those duly convicted of crimes, or to tax incomes. But there is much dispute over the government's right to regulate private sexual practices between consenting adults or to require a woman to bring a fetus to term. There is also no consensus on requirements that private employers provide family leave or that timber companies protect spotted owls. It is in these gray, unsettled areas of policy that the Court is often called upon to determine boundaries.

In the arena of settling disputes that arise between institutions and levels of government, the Court is seen as an umpire, determining what the Constitution intended. Walter Murphy stated it this way:

A political system which combines separation of power and federalism needs an umpire if it is to function. The justices of the Supreme Court quickly utilized both traditional and legal arguments to place themselves in the role of arbiter between the other two branches, between the states and the nation. (1964, 13)

With respect to states, the Court has argued primarily for national supremacy. Edward S. Corwin, in his introduction to *The Constitution of the United States of America*, says that "the purpose which it serves more and more exclusively is the purpose which it was originally created to serve, the maintenance of the principle of national supremacy" (Killian 1995, 23). The Court has been much more willing to use its authority in defining the boundary of legitimate government action against state and local governments (as I explained in chapter 3, The Federal System, in some detail), leaving national institutions more leeway in arriving at political resolutions. But, when pressed, the Court has stepped in to decide a major boundary dispute at the national level. It did this in *United States v. Nixon* (1974), for example, by requiring the president to provide certain documents for use in federal court cases. Nixon had claimed that executive privilege allowed him to evade doing so. Nevertheless, when the president has been overruled, he has frequently already achieved his purposes. The classic case illustrating this phenomenon was *Ex parte Milligan,* decided in 1866. Milligan was charged with a host of crimes, including conspiracy, giving aid and comfort to the Confederacy, inciting insurrection, and disloyal practices. He was convicted of resisting the draft and stealing arms and ammunition from a federal arsenal. Milligan had been tried under martial law in Indiana in 1864 and was appealing the suspension of habeas corpus and imposition of martial law by President Lincoln. The Court ruled in Milligan's favor, but by then the war had been over for two years, and Lincoln and Milligan were dead.

The modern Court has gone beyond the maintenance or determination of boundaries. It has also engaged in a determination of the relative position of constitutional protections. I developed this notion in chapter 4, Civil Rights and Civil Liberties. That is, some constitutional protections, free speech, for example, are given a preferred position in the Court's interpretation of the Constitution.

Statutory Interpretation

Not all issues facing the Supreme Court involve an interpretation of the Constitution. In some cases the Court is called upon to give clarification to a statute passed by Congress or a rule or regulation issued by the executive branch. In many cases, ambiguity in a law is intentional: it enables the legislative body to duck specific issues and to leave the responsibility for interpreting its terms to the courts or the executive. In other instances, interpretation by the Court is necessary because formulation of a clearly defined, rational mandate of policy is often not possible in a legislative system composed of diverse interests and people. Acts of Congress represent the compromises and ambiguities found in the legislative arena. Abner J. Mikva, a former member of Congress, federal judge, and presidential counsel, says that members do not confront "the most difficult value conflicts in society." This leaves interpretation to the courts. "Such behavior by Congress is both an abdication of its role as a constitutional guardian and an abnegation of its duty of responsible lawmaking" (1983, 610).

The impact of a Supreme Court determination on the administration of government programs can be illustrated with what is an obscure, but to many a rather significant, case, *Goldberg v. Kelly* (1970). John Kelly, a disabled welfare recipient, had his benefits terminated without notice for moving from where he had been placed by his caseworker. Justice Brennan, speaking for the Court, said, "Termination of aid pending resolution of a controversy over eligibility may deprive an *eligible* recipient of the very means by which to live while he waits." The Court's remedy was to require a hearing before aid could be terminated, a practice that now affects some 75,000 people a year (*New York Times* May 11, 1990, B12).

Interpretation of our laws is the responsibility of our courts. As government expands its activities into new and varied fields, there is a great need to clarify the exact scope of governmental action and to determine the relationship of such action to existing programs and laws. The judiciary can delineate and reinterpret legislative action even though the legislative intention is clear, although when courts do so they are subject to the charge of making rather than interpreting law. The Court can, of course, duck the specific issues and refuse to address the actions of Congress or of the administration.

The Success of the Court

The Supreme Court has been successful in maintaining control over its own sphere for a number of reasons. First and foremost, political power in the United States is diffuse. In a politically fragmented society, a concentrated majority is not easily mustered. As a result, the Court usually is insulated from strong political and public pressure, allowing it some freedom to maneuver. Where strong majorities have been recruited, the Court has been careful not to move too rapidly or too far in ruling against them. Robert G. McCloskey observed that "At no time in its history had the Court been able to maintain a position squarely opposed to a strong popular majority" (1994, 132). Remember that one of the major fears of the Framers was the tyranny of the majority; the courts were, in part, to counteract this danger. Yet, courts have not always been vigorous in fulfilling this role. The modern Court is no exception. Two decisions rendered at the height of national hysteria over the communist threat, in *American Communications Ass'n v. Douds* (1950) and *Dennis v. United States* (1951), exemplify the way in which strong public sentiment can sway the Court. In the *Douds* and *Dennis* decisions, a majority of the

Court gave support to government prosecution of communists and ex-communists. During the same period, however, the Court expanded the permissible areas of behavior in what McCloskey terms "non-seditious free speech" (1994, 132). As the clamor over communism subsided, the Court began to dismantle government statutes that limited freedom of expression. For example, the *Douds* decision was overruled in part by *Killian v. United States* (1961), and the *Dennis* decision was reversed in part by *Yates v. United States* (1957).

Generally the Court is able to secure the political support of important divisions of American society on behalf of its decisions. The Court is partly able to muster this support because of its relationships with other political institutions. Louis Fisher, a senior specialist in American government with the Library of Congress, expresses it this way: "Judicial decisions rest undisturbed only to the extent that Congress, the President, and the general public find the decisions convincing, reasonable, and acceptable" (1985, 746). Alexander Bickel called this a "continuing colloquy," in which constitutional principles "evolved conversationally" between the public and decision makers in our political institutions (1962, 244). Fisher contends that this give and take between the Court and other political institutions is what allows an undemocratic Court to function in the American system.

In periods of transition, when political realignments are taking place or when the courts support values not endorsed by other institutions, court decisions are called into question. For example, many decisions of the Warren Court (1953–69) have been noticeably unpopular. The Court's school desegregation decisions in *Brown v. Board of Education* (1954 and 1955) are a case in point. Even before the Court handed down its desegregation guidelines in 1955, many districts (in excess of 600) had begun to integrate their schools. The Court's guidelines, however, were ambiguous. In addition, a Congressional Manifesto issued March 11, 1956, by most of the southern delegation in effect declared political war on the Court's decision. The executive branch had never expressed great enthusiasm for the *Brown* decision. Southern leaders stiffened in their resolve against integration; federal troops were required to enforce the Court's decree in Little Rock, Arkansas, in 1956; and even now, some 40 years after *Brown,* this touchy and bitterly contested political issue has not been resolved.

The manner in which the Court makes its decision can also have an impact. Richard C. Cortner (1970) offers a number of reasons why the Court's position was more acceptable in reapportionment and redistricting cases but still contested in desegregation. His most persuasive arguments are that in reapportionment cases: (1) the Court made a definitive statement of "do it now"; (2) lower courts accepted the rulings and enforced them; and (3) technically, compliance was easy. Desegregation cases have not met any of these three criteria.

The Court's prestige is attributable partly to its vigilance in perpetuating its authority. That is, it has removed itself from areas and controversies that do not lend themselves to a judicial solution. Louis Fisher notes that the Court has succeeded by leaving some issues of constitutional interpretation to the other branches of government. An example of this concept of "coordinate construction" is the president's ability to remove department heads, something about which the Constitution is unclear, and which was resolved by the first Congress (Fisher 1990, 62).

The Court has also relied on precedent to add an aura of constitutional history to its pronouncements. (The Court has only overruled itself some 200 times in our 200-year history [Killian and Costello 1996].) Moreover, Americans have elevated the Supreme Court to the same level as the Constitution. Because the Court is guardian of the Constitution, we equate the two institutions, although we should heed the words of Charles Warren that opened this chapter: It is the Constitution that is the law, not the decision of the Court. The caliber of those who have been justices has also contributed to the prestige of the Court. Justices have developed concepts of American democracy through their judicial opinions, books, and other forms of communication. In addition, the number of outstanding and gifted legal scholars who have sat on the Court has imbued the decisions and actions of the Court with an aura of respectability and legal soundness.

Limitations on Judicial Power

The Court is neither free to rule on all controversies in American society nor capable of correcting all injustices. Not only do institutional obstacles prevent the Court from considering certain major questions, but even when it has the authority, the Court exercises considerable self-restraint. Judicial restraint can be based on philosophical as well as on practical considerations. The concept of *stare decisis* (let the decision stand), or the upholding of past precedents of the Court, is a strong influence on justices. There is also the restraint that a fair reading of the Constitution or of a statute requires a particular ruling. "Despite their deep personal opposition to the death penalty, for example, Harry Blackmun, Lewis Powell, and Potter Stewart all voted to uphold capital punishment laws," states Lawrence Baum in his study of the Supreme Court, because "in their view, the Eighth Amendment could not be interpreted otherwise" (1992, 135). Justice Kennedy, in a decision striking down a Texas law prohibiting the burning of the flag, stated "that sometimes we must make decisions we do not like" (*Texas v. Johnson*, 1989). Furthermore, many justices believe certain types of questions should not be considered by the Court. Perhaps the most well-known illustration is Justice Felix Frankfurter's opposition to considering reapportionment cases. Frankfurter had written the opinion prevailing for 16 years on staying out of "political thickets," that is, leaving these decisions to the political branches—the legislature and executive—in the case *Colegrove v. Green* (1946). The Court, however, overturned this position with *Baker v. Carr* (1962), with Frankfurter dissenting. He continued to object to Court consideration of these cases until his death.

Political Restraints

The political restraints on judicial power are considerable. The president appoints federal court justices by and with the consent of the Senate; Congress

Jeff Stahler; reprinted by permission of Newspaper Enterprise Association, Inc.

determines the number and jurisdiction of courts. Although the public debate over the appointment of a justice is frequently clothed in terms of qualification, as with the controversial nominations of Robert Bork by President Reagan in 1987 and Clarence Thomas by President Bush in 1991, a study of disputes concerning confirmations indicates that invariably they are political (Biden 1987). The rejection of Bork by a vote of 42–58 and the withdrawal of the nomination of Douglas Ginsburg in 1987 were only the 27th and 28th nominations to be rejected or withdrawn.

The size of the Court has been another political issue. Although the number of justices varied from six to ten before the mid-nineteenth century, since 1869, nine justices have become traditional: the chief justice and eight associates. Attempts to change it have met with formidable opposition. Most fluctuations were the result of maneuvering for purely political purposes. The most recent attempt to alter the size of the Court was made by President Franklin D. Roosevelt, in an unsuccessful "court packing" scheme in 1937. Congress, however, does have the power to change the size of the Court if it wishes.

Justices of the Supreme Court and of the other federal courts are not elected and are the only members of the national government who hold their jobs for life. There are no constitutional requirements for the justices as there are for the other two federal branches. Nevertheless, they are subject to political pressure and can be impeached. Impeachment is by majority vote in the House of Representatives, with a two-thirds vote in the Senate necessary for conviction. Impeachment has been used against federal officials 16 times. Only once has a Supreme Court justice been impeached—Samuel Chase in 1804 for behavior unbecoming a justice—and he was acquitted. Of 13 federal judges impeached, 5 were acquitted, 7 were convicted, and 1 resigned before a vote could be taken. In addition, Congress has created Judicial Councils in each appellate circuit to investigate charges against judges—though they still can't be removed short of impeachment (Carp and Stidham 1991, 126). The behavior of other judges has been questioned or investigated by the House. An awareness by judges and justices of these investigations cannot help but inhibit their independence. Most judges are sensitive and responsive to social problems and public opinion, and mindful that they represent an undemocratic institution in a democratic system.

Court decisions can be negated by political institutions and processes short of the impeachment of justices. In the past 30 years, the House of Representatives (but not by the necessary two-thirds majority) voted to amend the Constitution to allow prayer in schools, to prohibit busing, and to prohibit flag burning, practices that in the Court's **opinion** violated the Constitution. Congress has proposed amendments to the Constitution that were ratified and designed to overturn Court decisions. The Eleventh Amendment, ratified in 1795, was in response to the Court's accepting jurisdiction in a suit against one state by a citizen of another state in 1793 (*Chisholm v. Georgia*). The decision by the Court in 1895 invalidating an income tax (*Pollock v. Farmers' Loan and Trust Co.*) led to numerous attempts to pass a constitutional amendment, successfully culminating in ratification of the Sixteenth Amendment in 1913. This amendment authorized Congress to implement and collect taxes "from whatever source derived." The 1970 amendments to the Voting Rights Act of 1965 lowered the voting-age qualification in all elections to 18. The Court's ruling in *Oregon v. Mitchell* (1970) invalidated the portion applying to all but federal elections. Congress proposed, and sufficient states quickly ratified, the Twenty-sixth Amendment in 1971 that reestablished 18 as the age qualification in all elections.

More frequently, Congress has attempted to alter the law as a means of changing court rulings. For example, the Older Workers Benefit Protection Act of 1990 was designed to overturn a court decision, *Public Employees Retirement Fund v. Betts* (1989), by prohibiting discrimination in employee benefits based on age. But the Court can, on occasion, strike back, as it did in 1995, overturning a congressional action designed to overturn a Court decision (*Plant v. Spendthrift Farms, Inc.*). Congress can also alter the jurisdiction of the courts, the number of members, or seek appointment of new justices or judges more closely in line with congressional thinking. Presidents involve themselves in such appointments, of course. Presidents can also direct their administrations to enforce a Court decision vigorously; or they can direct that a Court decision not be enforced vigorously. Recent presidents have taken both positions with respect to court-ordered busing of school children.

There is one further political check. The Court has been considered a unitary institution when, in fact, it is composed of nine distinct individuals. To secure a majority in the Court is no easy matter. Hence, most decisions are made as they are in other types of policy-formulating institutions in which an effective coalition is necessary to win. This process is time-consuming, it involves considerable compromise, and it limits the Court's ability to move too far from established precedent. Outside observers point to the importance of the social contact among justices in producing like-minded opinions—Justices Scalia and Rehnquist play poker regularly, for example—but law clerks of the justices claim these contacts have no influence on their decisions (author's personal interview with law clerks). Even justices of the same political leanings do not necessarily share the same views about certain issues. One indication of internal conflict is scathing comments directed at other justices or their opinions. These are usually found in dissenting opinions. But Justice Blackmun in a concurring opinion states, "The Chief Justice's criticism of *Roe* follows from his stunted conception of individual liberty" (*Planned Parenthood v. Casey*, 1992).

The Court appears more fragmented than in the past. David M. O'Brien, in his major study, *Storm Center* (1993), points out that more justices wrote separate opinions during the Burger years (1969–86) than in all previous courts combined.

One indication of the level of dispute among the justices is the number of 5–4, or one-vote-margin decisions. These have comprised about 20 percent of the decisions in recent years—the highest was in 1989, when 37 of 131 were decided by a one-vote margin, compared with about 10 percent in previous years (Epstein et al. 1994, 163). These close votes are usually on the most important issues considered: prayer in schools, abortion, affirmative action, and the use of the death penalty.

Let's consider for a moment, "Who are the justices?" Without doing an exhaustive evaluation of the social backgrounds, training, or political perspectives of our nation's highest jurists, we could easily summarize their sociological characteristics as basically conservative—conservative in the sense that justices come from families of relatively high social status, are educated at our more conservative law schools, and have administered and served the law, which itself is a stabilizing and conservative force. Table 9.1 lists the current members of the Court with their education and career patterns. Yet, justices of the Court must often look at questions of considerable moment, at times reaching decisions that lead us in new political directions.

> As for the modern Court's espousal of civil rights as a substitute for the economic rights it once so cherished, this too was less a matter of deliberate choice than of predictable response to the wave of history.... The Court has always tended to focus on the great open questions that plagued America as a whole.... To be sure, there are some such "great issues" which are probably not meet [i.e., proper] for judicial treatment. The slavery question in the 1850s seems in retrospect one of these; the question of foreign policy in modern circumstances is, for rather different reasons, another. But within the limits of what it regards as its capacities, the Court can be expected to preoccupy itself with the issues that most preoccupy America. (McCloskey 1994, 210)

Legal Restraints

The Court is bound by a number of self-imposed rules and procedures that limit its power. These rules are spelled out in *Ashwander v. TVA* (1936): there must be injury involved; persons who question the constitutionality of a law from which they have benefited have no standing to sue; there must be real adversaries; the Court will give no advisory opinions; it will rule only on the

Table 9.1

JUSTICES OF THE SUPREME COURT

Justice	Colleges	Appointed	Previous Position
William H. Rehnquist (1924)	Stanford, Harvard Stanford Law (#1 in Class)	1972 1986 (Chief)	Ass't Attorney General
John P. Stevens (1920)	Chicago, Northwestern Law	1975	U.S. Court of Appeals
Sandra Day O'Connor (1930)	Stanford, Stanford Law	1981	Arizona Court of Appeals
Antonin Scalia (1936)	Georgetown, Harvard Law	1986	U.S. Court of Appeals
Anthony Kennedy (1936)	Stanford, Harvard Law	1988	U.S. Court of Appeals
David H. Souter (1939)	Harvard, Oxford (Rhodes Scholar), Harvard Law	1990	U.S. Court of Appeals
Clarence Thomas (1948)	Holy Cross, Yale Law	1991	U.S. Court of Appeals
Ruth Bader Ginsburg (1933)	Cornell (Phi Beta Kappa) Harvard Law, Columbia Law	1993	U.S. Court of Appeals
Stephen G. Breyer (1938)	Stanford, Oxford (Marshall Scholar), Harvard Law	1994	U.S. Court of Appeals

Justices appointed to the Supreme Court come from high-status educational backgrounds and from occupations of relatively high social standing. They must decide issues of great moral and legal complexity.

case involved; it will rule on a case in the narrowest sense possible; it will decide which issues are justiciable and which are not. The Court has left some questions for resolution by other components of the political system, calling them **political questions**. For example, it has remained aloof from questions of foreign policy, it has refused to consider what represents a republican form of government in the states, and it has left untouched questions relating to the ratification of constitutional amendments. The technique of referring to some cases as political questions outside the purview of judicial scrutiny can also be used to avoid controversial issues. I mentioned earlier the reapportionment thicket and the *Baker v. Carr* decision.

The Court is also limited in the manner in which it must consider most cases. The Court controls the recording of facts only when it has original jurisdiction. Usually it is called on to review the activities of a lower court in order to determine whether that court erred in making a particular decision—for example, to determine whether or not a confession should have been admitted as evidence or whether a lower court should have allowed a defendant to be represented by counsel. The Supreme Court, then, returns a case it has tried to the court of origin with instructions to either correct its procedure or retry the case. Incorrect interpretation by lower courts can be rectified only by bringing decisions of the lower court back to the Supreme Court or the Court of Appeals for clarification or correction.

The conclusion from this rather lengthy listing of limitations is that the Court does not have the final say. Our system is one of competing powers. Louis Fisher, a leading student of separation of powers, provides the following additional categories where the Court is not the only or the final arbiter of what may be done:

1. The fact that the Supreme Court upholds a measure does not mean that there is an obligation on the legislature or executive to adopt the measure in the future. In 1990, for example, the Court held that states could require parental notification for a minor to obtain an abortion; states did not have to adopt such a measure. This ruling, however, did make parental notification a major issue in some states, such as Kansas, South Carolina, Vermont, and Wisconsin.

2. A Court decision that some practice is not unconstitutional does not prohibit the legislature or executive from restricting it. "Rights unprotected by the courts may be secured by Congress and the President." The Civil Rights Restoration Act of 1988, discussed in chapter 4, is an example where Congress extended protection not afforded by the Court.

3. A Court conclusion that an action has no constitutional protection at the federal level does not prohibit a state court from finding such protection in the state's constitution. For example, the Supreme Court ruled that education was not a fundamental right under the U.S. Constitution; the California Supreme Court ruled that it was one under the state constitution. In chapter 4, I mentioned a New York decision that extended greater free-speech protection to the state's citizens than the Supreme Court has been willing to extend nationally.

4. Many constitutional issues are resolved through rules of evidence, statutes, customs, and accommodations—a common law method of settling disputes; practices in which the Supreme Court may play little role (1988, 278–79).

The Supreme Court in Action

The actual processes by which cases are selected and heard can have an impact on their determination. In this section I discuss the selection, hearing, and decision processes leading to the disposition of cases brought before the Supreme Court.

Case Selection

As a result of the 1925 Judiciary Act, specifically granting the Court authority to consider those cases that represent a substantial federal question, the Supreme Court spends a good deal of time determining which questions it will hear. It has complete control over its docket. This is an instance of a political institution, the Court, increasing its power by limiting the scope of its activities. On most occasions, the Court will exercise its discretion even when its jurisdiction is unquestionable—appeals, for example. The writ of certiorari is the major vehicle for discretionary action. What cases does the Court hear? There are guidelines to help the justices decide this question. Rule 19 of the Supreme Court's Revised Rules gives the Court the following bases for consideration in granting review on petition for a writ of certiorari.

(a) Where a state court has decided a federal question of substance not theretofore determined by this court, or has decided it in a way probably not in accord with applicable decisions of this court. (b) Where a court of appeals has rendered a decision in conflict with the decision of another court of appeals on the same matter; or has decided an important state or territorial question in a way in conflict with applicable state or territorial law; or has decided an important question of federal law which has not been, but should be, settled by this court; or has decided a federal question in a way in conflict with applicable decisions of this court; or has so far departed from the accepted and usual course of judicial proceedings, or so far sanctioned such a departure by a lower court, as to call for an exercise of this court's power of supervision. (90 S.Ct. 2273, 2288)

These guidelines seem clear, but other considerations—such as the subject matter of the case—influence the Court's selection of cases. The decision not to hear a case lets stand the decision of the lower court. The Court may refuse to exercise its jurisdiction because the majority is in basic agreement with the original or the appeals decision, because they do not think the issue ripe for Court consideration, or because they think the issue trivial. The Court's main function is to consider special and important cases, not simply to correct technical errors.

To Decide or Not to Decide

There are no constitutional or political provisions for forcing the Court to decide a particular issue. Even when it would be difficult for the Court to deny a hearing, it can duck the controversial issues of a case by ruling on a technicality and ignoring the other issues. *Maxwell v. Bishop* (1970) is an example. The case involved the imposition of the death penalty in the rape of a white woman by a black man. There were a number of issues that could have been addressed: Was the death penalty cruel and unusual in a nonhomicide case; was the death penalty as administered biased against black defendants? The court chose to narrow its consideration to two important questions:

1. The jury had determined the two issues of guilt or innocence and of a life or death sentence in a single proceeding, thereby precluding Bishop from presenting evidence pertinent to the question of penalty without subjecting himself to self-incrimination in the guilt phase.
2. The jury had been given no standards or directions of any kind to guide it in deciding whether to impose a sentence of life imprisonment or death.

To rule on these issues necessarily would involve consideration of the death penalty itself—a controversial issue; the Court evaded such a ruling by stating that "in the action we take today, we express no opinion whatever with respect to the two questions originally specified in our grant of certiorari." *Maxwell* was decided instead on the technical ground that jurors who objected to the death penalty on moral or religious bases had been excluded from the jury. "In short," Walter Murphy has succinctly stated, "one can bring a case before the Court, but no litigant, not even a governmental official, can force the Court to take the case, or once the Court has taken the case, to decide the substantive issues" (1964, 19).

Proceedings

The Supreme Court term opens on the first Monday in October and ends in June. The Court hears cases for several weeks and then recesses for several weeks to write opinions. Monday is decision day, and after a recess many opinions are published. The Court convenes in secret session each Friday, and only the justices may attend. In **conference**, the Court decides which cases it will hear and reaches decisions in the cases it has heard. Consideration of which cases it will hear begins with an initial screening of cases. Every year most cases are rejected; many of those selected only require or receive a judicial order or unsigned opinion. For example, in the 1993 term there were 6,336 cases filed with the Court (*Harvard Law Review* 1994, 376), and about 120 were selected for careful review. Confidants of some justices have said that they pay particular attention to this stage of the process, while others have contended that screening is primarily performed by law clerks (Massachusetts School of Law Symposium 1995). Once the Court has decided to consider a case, which requires a vote of four of the justices, it moves into the hearing stage. Written arguments from both sides—**briefs**—are called for. Often, other interested parties are allowed to submit briefs stating their position on the case at hand: called *amicus curiae* or friend of the court. In 1987 over 80 percent of the major cases had amici (Baum, 1992, p. 86). Contending parties present their cases in **oral argument** before the Court, in a setting that differs from that of trial courts. In oral argument, justices frequently engage in close and bitter exchange, interrupting an attorney's presentation at will in attempting to determine the salient points in his or her argument. Oral argument is considered so important that a justice who misses one will not take part in the decision in that case.

When the case is being considered in conference, the chief justice presents the case to be decided. Here the role of the chief justice is of crucial importance. He or she begins the discussion and states what he or she feels are the major issues raised by the case and how they should be handled. Following the chief justice's presentation, each justice in descending order of seniority gives his or her opinion verbally concerning the case. After all aspects of a case have been discussed, the voting begins in reverse order of seniority, with the newest associate voting first, the chief justice last. The chief justice assigns the writing of the opinion to one of the associates or to him- or herself if he or she voted with the majority. If not, the senior associate of the majority view assigns the opinion. This is followed by a period when opinions are drafted and passed around for comment. Considerable behind-the-scenes maneuvering can occur during this period. At times, clear-cut majorities can dissolve during this process. The *Maxwell* decision, discussed on the previous page, is an example in which a majority against the death penalty became a sharply divided Court that could decide the case on only very narrow grounds. They left the issue of the death penalty unresolved. The Pennsylvania abortion case in 1992, *Casey,* provides another illustration. According to published reports, Chief Justice Rehnquist had already written a draft of a plurality opinion overturning *Roe v. Wade,* when Justice Kennedy changed his position and sided with O'Connor and Souter to create a new plurality that maintained *Roe* (Reuben 1992, F1).

There is no restriction on the number of opinions, either dissenting or concurring. The written opinion is extremely important, because it tells why the judges decided as they did and because it delineates the scope of the decision. The average number of dissenting or concurring opinions fluctuates, depending on the ideological compatibility of the justices. During the early tenure of Chief Justice John Marshall (1800–35), most decisions were unanimous. Recently there have been more divided opinions, and justices have had a proclivity for expressing their individual viewpoints; cases involving the Pentagon Papers (the 1971 joint cases *United States v. Washington Post Co.* and *New York Times Co. v. United States*, for example) elicited written opinions from each of the justices deciding the case. Interpreting these opinions in such close cases can be difficult at best.

In the key abortion decision in 1990 (*Hodgson v. Minnesota,* involving parental notification), here is the court reporter's account of the decision:

> Stevens announced the judgment of the court and delivered the opinion of the court with respect to Parts I, II, IV, and VII, in which Brennan, Marshall, Blackmun and O'Connor joined; an opinion with respect to Part III, in which Brennan joined; an opinion with respect to Parts V and VI, in which O'Connor joined; and a dissenting opinion with respect to Part VIII. O'Conner filed an opinion concurring in part and concurring in the judgment; Marshall filed an opinion concurring in part, concurring in the judgment in part, and dissenting in part, in which Brennan and Blackmun joined. Scalia filed an opinion concurring in the judgment in part and dissenting in part. Kennedy filed an opinion concurring in the judgment in part and dissenting, in part, in which Rehnquist, White and Scalia joined.

Trying to seek guidance from such results is difficult.

Summary

The first thing to remember is that the courts are largely removed from many areas of policy. The Supreme Court cannot deal with every controversy or resolve all disputes. In some cases, such as foreign policy, this is by choice; in other cases, in areas such as budget policy, this is because the decisions more appropriately fall to other branches of government. As former chief justice Earl Warren stated, "In our democracy it is still the Legislature and the elected

Executive who have the primary responsibility for fashioning policy consistent with the Constitution" (1962).

Nevertheless, our courts do have a profound impact on some policy areas. Most significant, of course, would be civil liberties. Since the 1930s, the Court has taken this area as one of special concern and has a preponderance of determination of what we mean by "freedom of speech" or of "religion." In particular, the Court has been aggressive in dealing with state and local governments, limiting their actions with some frequency.

And as we are governed more and more by the rules and regulations of the bureaucracy, the courts have become a major participant in determining what those rules look like.

The unique power of the Court is its ability to rule that actions taken by the legislature or executive are unconstitutional. Yet, as Louis Fisher points out, constitutional interpretation really involves a dialogue among our major institutions. The Court is also called upon to define laws and to settle disputes over the boundaries between political institutions. The Court has succeeded in these areas in part because it has limited itself in the number and types of cases it will consider. In addition to this self-imposed selectivity, the Court is limited by legal as well as political restraints. Even in areas where it has limited power, the Court can serve to preserve just claims against excesses and to maintain the accepted boundaries of permissible behavior.

Analytical Exercises

1. The choice of a justice for the Supreme Court is made by the president but must be approved by the Senate. Let us assume that you are a senator from the president's party who will be seeking reelection this year. You barely won six years ago, and you know that your opponent this time is a strong candidate. In the summer of the election year, the president sends a nomination for the Supreme Court to the Senate for confirmation. The nominee is rated as "well qualified," the highest rating used by the American Bar Association. He has written a number of books on constitutional law and has been a law professor at a distinguished law school. This nominee is currently serving as a judge on the federal court of appeals and has written some major decisions.

However, a number of groups have come before the Senate in opposition, claiming the nominee is openly hostile toward women and minorities. For example, the nominee has held membership in several clubs and groups that do not admit Jews or minorities. (Since being appointed to the federal bench the nominee has dropped these memberships.) The nominee, in one of the books mentioned above, claimed that there was no constitutional basis for affirmative action and indicated disapproval of the Court's decision in *Brown v. Board of Education* (1954). He has also been an outspoken opponent of abortion, a position on which there has been considerable comment, both for and against, by those appearing during the confirmation hearings.

You personally have sponsored legislation to improve school desegregation and are on record as favoring a woman's right to abort a fetus under most circumstances. The vote for confirmation is going to be close, and the president has invited you to the White House to discuss the nomination. What is your position going to be? What factors would you consider in arriving at that position?

2. The courts frequently confront complicated questions of law and serious ethical and moral questions as well. Moreover, the jurist is aware that his or her decisions are not made in a political vacuum. Professor Lon Fuller has provided an interesting hypothetical case that incorporates all of these elements.

While deep in the recesses of a limestone cave, five amateur explorers, spelunkers, were trapped when a landslide occurred near the entrance. When the men failed to return home, a search party was sent out and discovered the cave-in. Volunteers with special equipment attempted to extricate the trapped men. The work was hampered by further cave-ins, one of which killed 10 of the workers in the rescue party. Several days later, those on the outside discovered that the explorers had a two-way radio with them, and within a short time contact was established. An assessment was quickly made of the time necessary to complete the rescue and the amount of supplies available inside the cave. It was clear to all that the men could not survive that long. One of the explorers, Whetmore, asked, "If one of the five were sacrificed, could the others last until rescued?" The answer from the attending physicians was yes, but when asked to permit the sacrifice, no one on the outside would give consent. Whetmore himself started to have second thoughts, but the other four were prepared to proceed with the plan. Lots were drawn, and since Whetmore would not participate, one was drawn for him. He lost! The rescue was completed on the schedule that had been indicated, and the four remaining spelunkers were brought out, only to be arrested and put on trial for the murder of Whetmore. The facts stated above are agreed to by all parties to the case (Fuller 1948). How would you rule, and what reasoning would you give if you were the judge?

10

Political Parties

There is not much difference in basic temperament between a good tight end and a successful politician. They both go down in the pit and do whatever has to be done—then come up smiling, and occasionally licking blood off their teeth.

—Hunter S. Thompson, *Fear and Loathing on the Campaign Trail '72*, 1985

Republicans are the party that says that government doesn't work, then they get elected and prove it. Democrats are out there saying the government can make you richer and taller and smarter and take the chickweed out of your lawn and add 20 pins to your bowling average. And somewhere in there, they've got to be lying.

—P. J. O'Rourke, *A Parliament of Whores*, 1992

Political parties were not anticipated by the Framers at the time the Constitution was being drawn up. Indeed, the Constitution made no specific provision for political parties, yet the type of government it established requires some formal organization to obtain the majorities necessary to nominate and elect a president and to pass legislation. To assume that these coalitions would simply disband after each election or vote is naive. Thus, even at this early stage of our political history, there were two basic sides—Federalists, who supported the adoption of the Constitution, and Anti-Federalists, who opposed the adoption; only the Federalists operated in a coherent, coordinated fashion. As I pointed out in chapter 2, The Politics of the Constitution, this was one of the reasons for their success, especially in some key states where they were probably in the minority. It was not until the actual implementation of programs by the new government in the early 1790s that two sides formed on most policy issues and these opposing groups organized to elect their members to government positions.

The first American party system was composed of Federalists, led by George Washington, John Adams, and, in particular, Alexander Hamilton; the Democrat-Republicans' were Thomas Jefferson, James Madison, and James Monroe. Their differences were for the most part over Hamilton's plans as Secretary of the Treasury to pay the national debt and create a national bank. In essence, Federalists supported economic development that favored commerce and bankers—city interests; Democrats supported farmers, people on the frontier, and debtors hostile to banks—country interests. A strong central government was favored by the former, a weaker one by the latter. By the election of 1796, these two sides were running candidates for president and Congress and making other decisions based on a group approach to government policy.

Organizations that select candidates, conduct election campaigns, staff the appointed offices of government, and seek to implement a broad-ranging policy agenda will be our working definition of **political parties**. Although since the eighteenth and nineteenth centuries the line between parties and political interest groups has blurred, this definition is still viable. Today we have two major parties—Republicans and Democrats—who year in and year out field candidates for political office and, if successful, fill positions of government with their supporters and push for the enactment of their own political platforms.

Political Party Systems

Many party allegiances have shifted, and several name changes have occurred since the 1790s. Scholars suggest that we are now in our fifth or sixth party system. By **party system**, political scientists mean a fairly stable set of issues by which people distinguish between parties and decide for which to vote. There are several major variables that divide the electorate, and these divisions persist from election to election. When major alterations in these basic alignments occur, a new party system emerges.

Figure 10.1, based on a detailed study of the maps and data from each congressional election in our history, divides party history into 17 distinct periods. Different party systems are not hard to discern, however. By the War of 1812, the Federalist party had largely disappeared; the first party system between the Federalists and the Democrat-Republicans no longer existed. There was then a transition period when the major political issues were fought out among the Democrats. With the emergence of Jacksonian Democrats beginning in 1829, a rival party, the Whigs, also emerged; this era lasted until just before the Civil War. The third party system occurred with the rise of the Republicans to challenge the Democrats in the late 1850s. Once the Civil War and Reconstruction had run their course, this new party system competed on a national basis and held until 1896. The election of 1896 inaugurated an era of extreme sectionalism. The two parties stayed the same in name, but fundamental changes had occurred. The election of 1932 produced another such change in the basic configuration of support for the two parties; most analysts call this the start of the fifth party system in our history.

Figure 10.1

PERIODS IN AMERICAN PARTY HISTORY

1789–95	Pre-party
1795–1801	Rise of Federalists and Democrat-Republicans; sectional split
1801–12	Triumph of Democrat-Republicans
1812–15	War of 1812
1817–23	Era of Good Feeling
1823–29	Fractionalization of Democrat-Republicans; sectional split between eastern and western wings of party
1829–37	Triumph of Jackson
1837–55	Whig-Democrat Era; national competition and close elections
1855–57	Demise of Whigs and rise of Northern Anti-Slavery party
1857–61	Formation of Republicans; sectional split
1861–65	Civil War
1865–75	Reconstruction; almost all Republican
1875–95	Gilded Era; national competitive elections, but strong sectional bias
1895–1931	Era of Extreme Sectionalism; South solidly Democratic; North, Republican
1931–47	The New Deal; Democratic dominance, but still strong sectional splits
1947–65	Post-War Era; fairly even competition between parties but still sectional
1965-Present	National competitive two-party system; breakdown of the solid South

Source: Adapted from a Library of Congress exhibit (summer 1990) based on the work of historical cartographer Kenneth C. Martis.

Political parties in the United States have evolved in several stages to the basic two-party system that is currently in use. The figure above divides our political history into 17 different periods, each of which had an effect on determining the focus and structure of the party of that time.

Types of election:

To understand better the emergence of different party systems, I will use a formulation by V. O. Key. Key argued that there are three types of elections: maintaining, deviating, and realigning. Maintaining elections occur when the majority party remains in power and the underlying basis of support for the political parties also stays the same. The elections of 1976 and 1992 are examples; the majority party, the Democrats, won. Deviating elections occur when the minority party wins office, but the underlying social support for the political parties is unaffected. The election of Republican Dwight D. Eisenhower as president in 1952 would be an example: People did not change their underlying attachment to the Republican or Democratic parties, they simply chose a president who was a Republican. A realigning election occurs when the minority party wins and the fundamental social cleavages of the previous era change. The election of Democrat Franklin D. Roosevelt in 1932 would fit this definition. The Democratic Party emerged as the new majority party, a position it has maintained for 60 years. Because some elections are more important than others in this formulation, Key uses the term critical elections for those where fundamental changes occur in the electorate (1958, 198–210).

The basic components of the reordering in 1932 came from changes in immigration beginning early in this century, and from the Great Depression, which had begun in 1929, and for which Republicans, who had been in power during that decade, were generally blamed. But the election could have been simply a deviating one had not Franklin D. Roosevelt consciously gone about building a new political coalition. The foundations of Democratic support stemming from the New Deal were as follows:

- White Southerners. These voters had supported the Democrats since the Civil War; the New Deal solidified their support. They also became crucial to Republican success in the 1980s, when they were known as "Reagan Democrats."
- Blacks. One of the reasons the white South had been Democratic was the role that Republicans had played in Reconstruction, imposing northern military government on the defeated South following the Civil War. Many blacks supported the Republican Party, the party of Lincoln, the party that attempted to give them political power under Reconstruction. But Roosevelt made it a policy to help minorities, calling for integration of our armed forces during World War II, for example; and it was the Democratic Party that started advocacy of civil rights following that war. The Great Society programs of Democrat Lyndon B. Johnson, aimed at aiding minorities, the poor, and the disadvantaged, and Democrats' support of civil rights in the 1960s solidified the support of black voters for the Democratic Party. (It also produced the defections of the white Southerners mentioned above.) No other social group has been as Democratic; as many as 90 percent of black voters usually choose a Democratic candidate.
- Farmers. This group was particularly hard hit by the Depression, and Franklin Roosevelt's New Deal farm legislation wedded farmers to the Democratic coalition.
- Urban working groups (labor). Since the late nineteenth century labor had been trying to organize, only to meet management resistance supported by government policy. Urban workers who had been Republican swung to the Democratic Party with the strong labor legislation of the New Deal.
- Immigrant (ethnic) groups. Here was another major change from the previous party system: Ethnic groups were Republican after the realignments of 1896, but heavily Democratic after 1932. This was primarily because two shifts occurred in immigration patterns: The bulk of immigrants started coming from Southern Europe, and they were likely to stay in the larger metropolitan areas. Democratic strength in these areas, along with New Deal programs aimed at urban problems, led to Democratic support.
- Roman Catholics and Jews. These groups became Democratic with the New Deal and, for the most part, continue to vote Democratic. In addition, Democratic control of big cities, where most immigrants settled, led to a relationship that has lasted almost a century.
- Intellectuals. The excitement of the New Deal and the adoption of a conscious policy of using government to solve major social problems attracted intellectuals, who have remained strongly Democratic.

Let me return to the data in Figure 10.1. There has been a vacillation in loyalty between parties, based either on sectional interests or national in-

Table 10.1

PARTY CONTROL IN CONGRESS

Congress	Years	President	Senate	House
89th	1965–67	Johnson (D)	D	D
90th	1967–69	Johnson (D)	D	D
91st	1969–71	Nixon (R)	D	D
92nd	1971–73	Nixon (R)	D	D
93rd	1973–75	Nixon/Ford (R)	D	D
94th	1975–77	Ford (R)	D	D
95th	1977–79	Carter (D)	D	D
96th	1979–81	Carter (D)	D	D
97th	1981–83	Reagan (R)	R	D
98th	1983–85	Reagan (R)	R	D
99th	1985–87	Reagan (R)	R	D
100th	1987–89	Reagan (R)	D	D
101st	1989–91	Bush (R)	D	D
102nd	1991–93	Bush (R)	D	D
103rd	1993–95	Clinton (D)	D	D
104th	1995–97	Clinton (D)	R	R

Source: Clerk of the House of Representatives and Secretary of the Senate.

Consistent party loyalty is difficult to determine when we observe from this table that Republicans have held the presidency for 20 of the past 28 years, from 1969 to 1997. Democrats, on the other hand, controlled the House until 1995 and the Senate for 20 years during the same time period.

terests as manifested in a nationally competitive two-party system. The current situation—the last entry in the table—suggests that we now have a competitive two-party system. These data refer to congressional elections. Most often, presidential elections follow the same trends. This was not true from 1968 to 1988, however. At the presidential level, there has been a clear sectional preference for the Republican candidate. Southern states and those west of the Mississippi supported the Republican candidate during this era. The 1992 election saw Clinton win 8 of 13 western and 6 of 13 southern states. This makes recent elections difficult to categorize in terms of party loyalty. As of the end of 1995, Republicans have held the presidency for 20 of the past 28 years. Table 10.1 gives these data. Democrats have controlled the House of Representatives for all but the most recent two years, and the Senate for 20 of the 28. Democrats have also controlled a majority of state legislatures and governorships. One might view many of the presidential elections in Table 10.1, then, as the deviating type.

But if you think about the underlying support for political parties, you may detect something else going on. Everett Carll Ladd Jr. calls this a period of **dealignment**. A look at Table 10.2 may give you an indication of what he is referring to. Support for Democrats has dropped in recent years, but voters have not necessarily swung their allegiance to the Republican Party. Rather, a great many have begun to remain independent of both. The old New Deal coalition has been seriously eroded by these changes: Many working-class

Table 10.2

PERCENTAGE OF SUPPORT BY POLITICAL AFFILIATION, 1952–94

	1952	1960	1968	1976	1984	1994
Democrats	47%	46%	45%	40%	40%	33%
Republicans	27	30	24	23	29	34
Independents	22	23	30	36	29	31
Apolitical	4	4	1	1	2	2

Source: Data from the American National Election Studies, Center for Political Studies, University of Michigan.

This table suggests that support for the two major parties is declining and that people are referring to themselves as independents.

people have either supported Republicans or are no longer strongly Democratic; ethnic groups also show weaker support; and white Southerners are no longer solidly Democratic voters. In the preface to an extended treatment of this phenomenon, Ladd provides a summary assessment.

> A somewhat paradoxical result of this is that the Democrats have lost their ascendancy of the New Deal years—surely in the presidency and perhaps in all visible and personality-oriented contests—without, in nominal terms, being supplanted as the majority party. And the source of the paradox arises in the transformation of the character of party allegiance. It is a fact of contemporary American electioneering that party loyalties have become increasingly divorced from actual voting behavior. The electorate continues to move away from stable, predictive attachments to the parties, and thus it responds to each succeeding election as though the contest were a world unto itself. (1982, viii)

The supporters of Ross Perot in the 1992 election provide one visible manifestation of this phenomenon. As summarized by Stanley B. Greenberg, pollster for President Clinton, "these [are] detached voters who both hate government and demand government action, who resent both political elites and economic elites." These contradictory tendencies provide a challenge to both political parties, because these voters' "world view is not easily accommodated by the dominant parties—one associated with political elites and government activism and the other with economic elites and government indifference" (1995, 259). Greenberg worries that a failure to incorporate these disaffected voters will "yield a harvest of angry alienation." The disaffection is not just among Perot voters. E. J. Dionne Jr. claims that the "great American middle felt cheated" by a liberal agenda that "demeaned its values," and a conservative agenda that "shortchanged its interests" (1991, 345).

Challenging this view is Raymond Wolfinger, a noted authority on voting and elections from the University of California, Berkeley, who with his students has analyzed the independent voters and found that most of them lean

Table 10.3

PORTRAIT OF THE ELECTORATE

% of '92 total		1976 Carter	1976 Ford	1980 Reagan	1980 Carter	1980 Ander-son	1984 Reagan	1984 Mon-dale	1988 Bush	1988 Duka-kis	1992 Clinton	1992 Bush	1992 Perot
	Total vote	50	48	51	41	7	59	40	53	45	43	38	19
46	Men	50	48	55	36	7	62	37	57	41	41	38	21
54	Women	50	48	47	45	7	56	44	50	49	46	37	17
87	Whites	47	52	56	36	7	64	35	59	40	39	41	20
8	Blacks	83	16	11	85	3	9	90	12	86	82	11	7
3	Latinos	76	24	33	59	6	37	62	30	69	62	25	14
1	Asians	–	–	–	–	–	–	–	–	–	29	55	16
22	18–29 years old	51	47	43	44	11	59	40	52	47	44	34	22
38	30–44 years old	49	49	55	36	8	57	42	54	45	42	38	20
24	45–59 years old	47	52	55	39	5	60	40	57	42	41	40	19
16	60 and older	47	52	54	41	4	60	40	50	49	50	38	12
49	White Protestant	41	58	63	31	6	72	27	66	33	33	46	21
27	Catholic	54	44	50	42	7	54	45	52	47	44	36	20
4	Jewish	64	34	39	45	15	31	67	35	64	78	12	10
17	White born-again Christian	–	–	63	33	3	78	22	81	18	23	61	15
14	Family income under $15,000	58	40	42	51	6	45	55	37	62	59	23	18
24	$15,000–$29,999	55	43	44	47	7	57	42	49	50	45	35	20
30	$30,000–$49,999	48	50	53	39	7	59	40	56	44	41	38	21
20	$50,000–$74,999	36	63	59	32	8	66	33	56	42	40	42	18
13	$75,000 and over	–	–	63	26	10	69	30	62	37	36	48	16
24	From the East	51	47	47	42	9	53	47	50	49	47	35	18
27	From the Midwest	48	50	51	41	7	58	41	52	47	42	37	21
30	From the South	54	45	52	44	3	64	36	58	41	42	43	16
20	From the West	46	51	53	34	10	61	38	52	46	44	34	22
2	Liberal Repub.	17	82	78	17	5	88	11	73	27	17	54	29
15	Moderate Repub.	11	88	83	10	7	93	7	87	12	15	63	21
18	Conservative Repub.	6	93	91	5	3	95	4	95	4	5	82	14
5	Liberal Inde.	64	29	26	51	17	40	58	26	71	54	16	30
14	Moderate Inde.	45	53	53	30	14	57	42	51	47	42	28	30
7	Conservative Inde.	26	72	75	18	6	85	13	77	20	18	54	28
13	Liberal Demo.	86	12	14	73	10	11	88	6	93	85	4	11
20	Moderate Demo.	77	22	27	67	5	22	78	18	81	76	10	14
6	Conservative Demo.	64	35	39	56	4	46	54	34	65	60	24	16
68	Employed	47	51	54	37	7	60	39	56	43	42	38	20
5	Full-time student	–	–	–	–	–	52	47	44	54	50	35	15
6	Unemployed	65	34	39	51	8	32	67	37	62	56	24	20
8	Homemaker	–	–	–	–	–	62	38	58	41	36	45	19
13	Retired	–	–	–	–	–	60	40	50	49	51	36	13

Source: New York Times, November 5, 1992. 1992 data were collected by Voter Research and Surveys based on questionnaires completed by 15,490 voters leaving 300 polling places around the nation on election day. 1976 data were based on a survey conducted by CBS News with questionnaires from 15,300 voters. Data for other years were based on surveys of voters conducted by the *New York Times* and CBS News: 15,201 in 1980; 9,174 in 1984; and 11,645 in 1988. Copyright © 1992 by The New York Times Company. Reprinted by permission.

toward the Democrats or Republicans. Wolfinger claims that only about 11 percent of the electorate is truly independent, about the same as his data suggest was true 40 years ago (1992, A44).

Figure 10.2

HOW TO TELL REPUBLICANS AND DEMOCRATS APART

Republicans usually wear hats	Democrats usually don't
Democrats buy banned books	Republicans form censorship committees and read them
Democrats eat the fish they catch	Republicans hang them on the wall
Republicans study the financial pages of the newspaper	Democrats put them on the bottom of the bird cage
On Saturday Republicans head for the golf course, the yacht club, or the hunting lodge	Democrats get a haircut, wash the car, or go bowling
Republicans have guest rooms	Democrats have spare rooms filled with old baby furniture
Republicans hire exterminators	Democrats step on the bugs
Republicans sleep in twin beds—some even in separate rooms	That is why there are more Democrats

Source: Republican Congressional Campaign Committee Newsletter.

This classic comparison of Republicans and Democrats is based on historical stereotypes, but politicians, nevertheless, enjoy citing these differences as if they were real.

Dealignment and **realignment** are not the only possibilities to emerge from these recent trends. Another concept of Key's is a **secular realignment**, in which the changes to a new majority party take place over a longer period of time. Thus we would not have a critical election, but, over a decade or so, a new majority party would emerge (Key 1955). Still another possibility is advanced by Gerald Pomper (1980), that of a **converting election**. Pomper is referring to the situation where fundamental shifts do occur in party support, but where movement to one party is offset by movement to the other. The result is a new set of partisan alignments—a new party system—but the same party remains the majority. Given the fluctuations in voter behavior over the past 15 years or so, we need to monitor the trends in party support in coming elections before we can determine which of the concepts mentioned best describes the current state of our political parties.

Democrats received 54 percent of the vote in 1990, for example. But in 1994, the edge was 53 percent Republican to 47 percent Democratic. This corresponds with recent presidential elections—a good measure of the underlying support for political parties—where samples of voters, shown in Table 10.3, show the support of various groups for our two parties. We can also see from this table some of the obvious tensions that exist within each party as it tries to please its constituency: Republicans, the more affluent and the religious right; Democrats, Southerners, Catholics, liberals, women, and minorities.

Despite the somewhat facetious differences between the Democrats and Republicans listed in Figure 10.2, there are real differences. Figure 10.3, summarizing the party platforms of 1992, gives an indication not only of how the parties differ, but also of how they try to position themselves to attract voters. You can also see some of the obvious tensions such positions create among their own supporters. For example, strong advocates

(Continued on p. 239)

Figure 10.3

KEY DIFFERENCES IN REPUBLICAN AND DEMOCRATIC 1992 PARTY PLATFORMS

REPUBLICANS	DEMOCRATS

Abortion

"The unborn child has a fundamental individual right to life which cannot be infringed. We therefore reaffirm our support for a human life amendment to the Constitution. ... We oppose using public revenues for abortion and will not fund organizations that advocate it."

"Democrats stand behind the right of every woman to choose, consistent with *Roe v. Wade*, regardless of ability to pay, and support national law to protect that right."

Investment

"Our economy is people, not statistics. ... We launched an era of growth and prosperity such as the world had never seen—20 million new jobs in the longest peacetime economic expansion in the history of our nation."

"The only way to lay the foundation for renewed American prosperity is to support both public and private investment. We must strive to close both the budget deficit and the investment gap."

Defense conversion

"Rather than admit their mistakes of the past, the same liberal Democrats who sought to disarm America against the Soviet threat now compound their errors with a new campaign—half audacity, half mendacity—to leave the nation unprotected in a still dangerous world. Republicans call for a controlled defense drawdown, not a free fall."

"Our economy needs both the people and the funds released from defense at the cold war's end. We will help the stalwarts of that struggle—the men and women who served in our armed forces and who work in our defense industries—make the most of a new era."

Welfare

"Welfare is the enemy of opportunity and stable family life. Today's welfare system is anti-work and anti-marriage. It taxes families to subsidize illegitimacy. It rewards unethical behavior and penalizes initiative."

"Welfare should be a second chance, not a way of life. We want to break the cycle of welfare by adhering to two simple principles: No one who is able to work can stay on welfare forever, and no one who works should live in poverty."

Affordable health care

"Republicans believe government control of health care is irresponsible and ineffective. We believe health-care choices should remain in the hands of the people. ..."

"All Americans should have universal access to quality, affordable health care—not as a privilege, but as a right."

Civil and equal rights

"Asserting equal rights for all, we support the Bush administration's vigorous enforcement of statutes to prevent illegal discrimination on account of sex, race, creed or national origin. Promoting opportunity, we reject efforts to replace equal rights with quotas and other preferential treatment."

"We don't have an American to waste. Democrats will continue to lead the fight to ensure that no Americans suffer discrimination or deprivation of rights on the basis of race, gender, language, national origin, religion, age, disability, sexual orientation, or other characteristics irrelevant to ability."

Strengthening the family

"Our national renewal starts with the family."

"Governments don't raise children, people do."

Real differences do exist between Republicans and Democrats, as seen in some of the major issues of the two party platforms in 1992.

Table 10.4

PERCENTAGE OF TWO-PARTY VOTE AND PERCENTAGE OF SEATS IN THE HOUSE FOR REPUBLICANS AND DEMOCRATS, 1970–1994

Party	1970 Vote	1970 Seats	1980 Vote	1980 Seats	1990 Vote	1990 Seats	1994 Vote	1994 Seats
Democrats	54%	59%	51%	56%	54%	61%	47%	46%
Republicans	46	41	49	44	46	39	53	54

Source: Computed from *Statistical Abstract of the United States* 1994, 232; *Congressional Quarterly Weekly Report* November 11, 1994.

Districting results in an interesting phenomenon where the percentage of votes for a particular party does not necessarily translate into the same percentage of seats in the House for that party.

for women's rights and Roman Catholics have been traditionally Democratic; women's rights advocates gained adoption of their position on abortion as a fundamental right of free choice on the party's platform. What does a devout Catholic, who is also a Democrat, but morally opposed to abortion, do?

The Two-Party System

The American system has been characterized by two major political parties. The most important structural basis for this is our system of electing only one representative from each electoral district, called **single-member districts (SMDs)**, combined with our use of a **plurality rule** for winning; that is, the candidate with the most votes, regardless of the percentage, wins. Maurice Duverger proposes that plurality rules are supportive of the two-party system; countries like Canada and the United States use this rule and have two-party systems. Political systems using other types of voting techniques tend to have multiparty systems. Germany and Italy, for example, which have used proportional representation, have multiple parties. While more reflective of the diversity of the electorate, multiparty systems sometimes have trouble creating coalitions that can effectively govern; Italy, for example, has had a governing coalition fall apart about once every 18 months over the past 50 years. Duverger argues that the single-member district is one of the major factors in preserving a two-party system because in a situation where only one wins, the only safe collection of voters is a majority (1963, 217). Douglas W. Rae (1967) provides a comparative study of 107 elections in 20 Western democratic systems that supports Duverger's propositions. His findings show a strong association between the type of electoral system used and the type of resulting party system. Most two-party systems have plurality rules—23, compared to just 4 with some other voting rule—and most multiparty systems—73 compared to just 7—have proportional voting rules and multimember districts.

In the United States, members of the House of Representatives, about half of the state legislators, and over a third of the city councils are selected from single-member districts. While single-member districts have one elected

representative from each electoral district, **multimember districts (MMDs)** have more than one representative per district or have all officials elected at large (members elected from the entire city or state). Approximately 45 percent of the state legislators and over 60 percent of city council members come from multimember districts (*Municipal Yearbook* 1991, x).

In addition, the majority party in a two-party system tends to be over-represented in the legislature—that is, the percentage of its legislators exceeds the percentage of its voters in the population. Although Rae suggests that this is a result in all electoral systems, it is more obvious in single-member districts. To illustrate this phenomenon, Table 10.4 shows the results of several congressional elections from 1970 to 1994. In 1980, for example, we can see that Democrats carried 56 percent of the districts, while Republicans were successful in 44 percent. By contrast, the popular vote (the total vote for Republicans and Democrats) gives an advantage of only 2 percent (51 to 49) for the Democrats. But in 1994, when Republicans gained 53 percent of the popular vote, they won only 54 percent of the seats. A number of explanations are offered for this phenomenon. One is that the majority party is able to draw voting-district boundary lines to their advantage—called **gerrymandering** (see p. 254 later in this chapter)—in many states. However, some states use appointed nonpartisan commissions rather than their legislatures to set boundary lines. In addition, the courts have been called upon to make many of the reapportionments in recent years. The district boundaries resulting from either of these methods are assumed to be fair to both parties. In the United Kingdom, where a nonpartisan commission is also used, there is the same evidence of overrepresentation.

Another explanation of this phenomenon of overrepresentation is that there are more pockets of one-party support for the majority. There were 45 Democrats elected to Congress in 1986 who ran unopposed by a major party challenger. There were only 9 Republicans in the same situation. However, in 1994, only 17 Democrats compared to 31 Republicans were without a major party challenge, and Democrats lost control of Congress.

In all likelihood, a combination of factors produces these results; as noted, Rae found that even in proportional-representation systems the majority party was overrepresented; single-member districts no doubt play a part, as do the political advantages that accrue to the majority party.

The inability of minor or third parties to succeed under this type of electoral system is even more strikingly apparent. Clinton Rossiter cites one example:

> In New York City in 1935 the City Council had sixty-three Democrats, two Republicans. In 1936, the voters of New York, having reduced the number of members, decided that it would be more sporting to try a system of proportional representation. Results of a characteristic election (1945): Democrats fourteen; Republicans three; American Labor Party two; Communists two; Liberals two. These two Communists were two too many for most persons in New York and in 1947 the City beat a retreat to the single-member district. The result of the next election (1949): Democrats twenty-four; Republicans one—which proves that the single-member district might be hard on the second party but is death on third parties. (1960, 9)

The practical consequences of such a system should be evident. Conventional wisdom has it that candidates who stray from the mainstream of American politics have difficulty in securing the nomination of their party because it must appeal to the most voters in a particular district to win. Those who attempt to go it alone in a third party are, for the most part, unsuccessful in the American system.

Third or Minor Parties

While we have had two major parties for most of our history, we have also had a number of third or minor parties participating in elections. Third parties traditionally lack the support or following of enough people to win major elections in the United States. Minor parties fall into two major categories: followers of a dynamic leader and proponents of a single issue.

An example of the first type would be the Bull Moose party of 1912, headed by Theodore Roosevelt. Roosevelt had been president from 1901 to 1909 as a Republican. When he decided to run again in 1912, he was unable to secure the Republican nomination; he joined the Progressives (Bull Moose) and came in second, behind Woodrow Wilson (Democrat) and ahead of William Howard Taft (Republican), with 27 percent of the vote. No minor party has done as well before or since. More recent examples of one-man appeals would be the efforts of George Wallace in 1968 and Ross Perot in 1992. Perot was an especially interesting case: He had not even officially announced his candidacy, yet at one point in the late spring of 1992 he actually led both

Source: Library of Congress.

The Socialist Party candidates Eugene V. Debs and Ben Hanford are shown above in a campaign poster for the 1904 election.

President Bush and Governor Clinton in the opinion polls. Supporters qualified Perot for the ballot in 50 states; he received 19 percent of the vote.

One-issue parties have been a regular feature of American elections, such as the Theocratic, Gold Standard, and Prohibitionist parties. They get some free publicity for their causes, but have no serious chance of winning a national election. There are also some small parties that function as political entities but without the support necessary to win elections in American politics. The Socialists are probably the most persistent of these, although we also have Libertarians, Liberals, and Conservatives. Below the presidential level, such parties have had only limited, and usually regionally isolated, success. In 1990, Bernard Sanders, a Socialist, was elected to the House from Vermont. He caucuses with and receives committee assignments from the Democrats. In the Senate, James Buckley (R-NY) (1968–74), was first nominated by the Conservative party and listed himself as such. He was also the nominee of the Republicans and was given his committee assignments by the Republican Party in Congress. Ralph Nader has recently urged third parties to adopt the strategy of nominating a candidate who will also be the nominee of one of the major parties; he thinks it will give third parties added weight in American politics, by helping to ensure that party members need not waste their votes on a sure loser.

Third parties serve as a safety valve for those dissatisfied with the two major parties, and they can be the source of new and untried ideas. They also bring, according to one major study, new groups into the political system (Rosenstone, Behr, and Lazarus 1984). The election of 1992 provides an illustration of how important this aspect of minor parties can be. Much of the

Table 10.5

VOTES CAST FOR MINOR PARTIES AND INDEPENDENTS SINCE 1892*

Year	Candidate	Party	Percentage of Vote
1892	John B. Weaver	Populist	8.5
	John Bidwell	Prohibition	2.3
1900	John G. Wooley	Prohibition	1.5
1904	Eugene V. Debs	Socialist	3.0
	Silas C. Swallow	Prohibition	1.9
1908	Eugene V. Debs	Socialist	2.8
	Eugene F. Chafin	Prohibition	1.7
1912	Theodore Roosevelt	Progressive	27.4
	Eugene V. Debs	Socialist	6.0
	Eugene F. Chafin	Prohibition	1.4
1916	Allen Benson	Socialist	3.2
	J. Frank Hanley	Prohibition	1.2
1920	Eugene V. Debs	Socialist	3.4
	Parley P. Christensen	Farmer-Labor	1.0
1924	Robert M. La Follette	Progressive	16.6
1932	Norman Thomas	Socialist	2.2
1936	William Lemke	Unionist	2.0
1948	J. Strom Thurmond	States' Rights	2.4
	Henry A. Wallace	Progressive	2.4
1968	George C. Wallace	American Independent	13.5
1972	John Schmitz	American Independent	1.4
1980	John B. Anderson	Independent	6.6
	Ed Clark	Libertarian	1.1
1992	H. Ross Perot	United We Stand	19.0

*Only candidates with more than 1 percent are included.

Source: Congressional Quarterly Guide to U.S. Elections.

Third-party candidates for national office seldom have a sufficient number of votes to affect the outcome of the race. The only exception was Theodore Roosevelt in 1912.

increased turnout at this election has been attributed to Ross Perot. Perot was able to tap a widespread disaffection with politics-as-usual among potential voters. Perot received 30 percent of the vote in Maine, and even came in second behind Bush in Utah with 27 percent. Table 10.5 shows third-party candidates in the past century.

Political Parties: Organization

One of the major difficulties in discussing parties is that they can represent three distinct entities: officeholders, formal party organizations, and those citizens who are party members or identify with the party (Key 1958). For the remainder of this chapter, we will deal with parties as organizations. National parties are really confederations of state and local organizations, held together rather loosely by National Committees (Epstein 1987). Traditionally,

Influential political cartoonist Thomas Nast depicted the Republican Party as an elephant in *Harper's Weekly* in 1874. He was also responsible for awarding the Democratic Party with the donkey.

the task of the party organization was to provide candidates to run for office. This role, however, is increasingly being preempted by candidates with their own organizations who vie for the party's endorsement in popular primaries. These candidate-centered organizations have become the principal sources of power and patronage in national politics and in many lesser political arenas as well. Walter Dean Burnham, a leading analyst of elections, offers this assessment:

> [T]he electoral market today is largely organized by the media and by individual candidates, together with their apparatus of professional "hired guns" in the polling and political-advertising trades. In a media age, the relevance of party as a channel for voting decisions has disappeared among the very large fraction of those adult citizens who still bother to vote at all under these conditions. (*Wall Street Journal* November 26, 1986, 20)

The growth of these candidate-centered organizations is a result of the following:

1. Direct primaries, which have removed candidate selection from traditional party control.
2. Television, which can provide positive exposure for any candidate skilled in its use.
3. Restrictions on campaign financing that have limited the regular party's spending and resulted in the growth of numerous ad hoc committees responsible to the candidate for raising money.

Figure 10.4

ORGANIZATION OF POLITICAL PARTIES

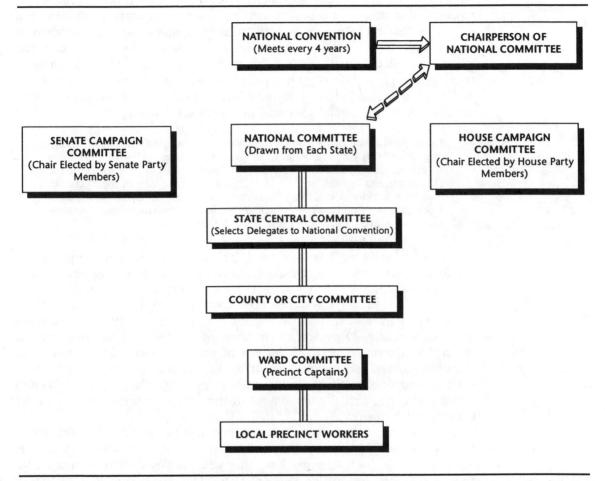

This chart shows party organization from the precinct to the national level. While the role of the party may be changing, it still provides an organization that can develop campaign funds and support for a candidate.

4. The unwillingness of many candidates to be labeled as a party man or woman because of the stigma of corruption many have come to associate with these labels.

5. The inability of regular party organizations to sanction members or even to define who is a member of the party.

6. Various reforms producing nonpartisan local politics that have taken away the parties' access to local government positions.

These characteristics have led some to proclaim that national party organizations are declining in popularity and importance. Figure 10.4 shows a typical party organization. While these changes have produced party structures different from previous eras, Joseph A. Schlesinger, who was the first to report the important changes in the nature of the modern party, argues persuasively that they have produced parties of greater importance than several years ago. His argument proposes that today people are more independent in their voting and, with each candidate unable to count on a guarantee of votes, organization becomes all the more important; parties provide that organization. Schlesinger further suggests that parties are important sources of money and fund-raising and are able to provide technical support and other organizational skills that candidates could not acquire elsewhere.

> In the second half of the twentieth century a "new" party has been emerging, one that is more national in scope, more active, and with clear signs of greater linkage among its [constituent parts]. This is true for both the Democrats and Republicans. . . . [A]n increasing instability in the electorate and thus a more competitive party system has accompanied [campaign] rules changes. As a result . . . officeseekers have increasingly found organization in all of its facets more necessary. (1985, 1160)

If members have a greater need for party organizational support, we would also expect to find a greater likelihood of their voting along party lines, the definition of party voting. *Congressional Quarterly* has tracked party voting in Congress for some time now. Over the past several decades, there has been an increase in party votes; for example, in the 1970s, party votes occurred less than 40 percent of the time; in the 1980s, it had risen to just under 50 percent; in 1993, 65 percent of the votes were along party lines (Ornstein, Mann, and Malbin 1996, 199). Republicans in the past few years have been especially cohesive in their voting. In early 1995, for example, House Republicans were virtually unanimous in their votes on various parts of their Contract with America.

In the conclusion to one recent study reporting on these changing roles, L. Sandy Maisel states that parties "persist and adapt to changing conditions because, like all such organizations, they are composed of individuals who have a stake in their survival" (1990, 308). One adaptation is a campaign committee for each party in the House and Senate, as well as political action committees headed by well-known senators—Kennedy (D-MA) and Helms (R-NC), for example—or House Speaker Newt Gingrich's GOPAC, in addition to the traditional national party organization, each raising money and providing campaign support for candidates.

While it is not mentioned by Schlesinger, there is another factor supporting his position. Incumbents still have an advantage, but there is more competition, both local and national, between the parties. In 1992, for example, while the Democrats won the presidency, there was a change of over 48 seats in Congress: 25 went from Republican to Democratic; 23 went from Democratic to Republican. In 1994, however, Republicans won 22 open seats that had been Democratic, while losing only 4; they also defeated 34 incumbent Democrats. Most attibute these gains to successful fund-raising by the party, as well as fielding strong candidates.

Figure 10.5

TWO TYPES OF BALLOTS

OFFICIAL BALLOT

A

PRESIDENT AND VICE PRESIDENT

	Vote for One Party	
ROSS PEROT for President / **JAMES STOCKDALE** for Vice President	Independent	+
HOWARD PHILLIPS for President / **ALBION KNIGHT** for Vice President	American Independent	+
RON DANIELS for President / **ASIBA TUPAHACHE** for Vice President	Peace & Freedom	+
BILL CLINTON for President / **AL GORE** for Vice President	Democratic	+
GEORGE BUSH for President / **DAN QUAYLE** for Vice President	Republican	+
ANDRE MARROU for President / **NANCY LORD** for Vice President	Libertarian	+
for President / for Vice President		+

UNITED STATES SENATOR

Full Term	Vote for One
JEROME 'JERRY' MC CREADY, American Ind. Businessman	+
BRUCE HERSCHENSOHN, Republican Television Commentator/Educator	+
GENEVIEVE TORRES, Peace & Freedom Cancer Researcher	+
BARBARA BOXER, Democratic Congresswoman	+
JUNE R. GENIS, Libertarian Computer Programmer	+
	+

UNITED STATES SENATOR

Short Term	Vote for One
RICHARD B. BODDIE, Libertarian Adjunct Professor/Mediator	+
PAUL MEEUWENBERG, American Independent Marketing Consultant	+
GERALD HORNE, Peace & Freedom Teacher	+
DIANNE FEINSTEIN, Democratic	+
JOHN SEYMOUR, Republican Appointed United States Senator	+
	+

UNITED STATES REPRESENTATIVE

2nd District	Vote for One
WALLY HERGER, Republican Congressman/Rancher	+
HARRY H. PENDERY, Libertarian Medical Doctor	+
ELLIOT ROY FREEDMAN, Democratic Criminal Defense Attorney	+
	+

B

Vote on the Questions

	1		2	
	YES	NO	YES	NO
	1. Shall the constitution of the state be amended to authorize the enactment of legislation to make procedures for absentee admission as an elector available for all applicants?		2. Shall the constitution of the state be amended to impose a limit on state expenditures?	

OFFICES ➡	1 Presidential Electors for	2 United States Senator	3 Representative in Congress
A CONNECTICUT PARTY	1A	2A Christopher J. Dodd	3A Rosa L. DeLauro
REPUBLICAN	1B Bush and Quayle	2B Brook Johnson	3B Tom Scott
DEMOCRATIC	1C Clinton and Gore	2C Christopher J. Dodd	3C Rosa L. DeLauro
CONCERNED CITIZENS	1D	2D Richard D. Gregory	3D
AMERICANS FOR PEROT	1E Perot and Stockdale	2E	3E
LIBERTARIAN	1F Marrou and Lord	2F Howard A. Grayson, Jr.	3F
NEW ALLIANCE	1G Fulani and Munoz	2G	3G

Two major types of ballot are shown in Figure 10.5. The office bloc ballot (A) lists candidates according to the office they are seeking and the party column ballot (B) lists candidates according to their party affiliation, thus making it relatively easy to vote a straight party ticket. Neither method is entirely equitable in the manner in which it places candidates on the ballot. People still tend to vote for those whose names are at the top of the list or in a prominent position on the ballot.

Parties and Election Machinery

A source of power still available to party organizations is control of elections. The actual mechanics of elections in the United States are primarily in the hands of the major political parties. This serves as a source of patronage and places the party in a quasi-governmental position for the handling of elections.

Major parties are usually placed in an advantageous position in terms of the mechanical aspects of actual voting. Studies have indicated that ballot position and the type of ballot used are important variables in success in American elections. The **party column ballot** (B in Figure 10.5) places the candidates in a direct line with the party label, facilitating straight party voting. On some ballots, in fact, one check in the appropriate box will register a straight party vote for each office. Another commonly used is the **office bloc ballot** (A in Figure 10.5) that lists candidates according to elective offices. Because people tend to vote for the first name on long ballots, or for the first contests, and sometimes leave the remaining contests blank, ballot position is a major influence on chances for success. Some states have required that names be listed on the ballot alphabetically, and in many local or nonpartisan elections, candidates with names starting with letters beyond J or K have little opportunity for success. The switch to machine voting has not really altered these basic facts of political life. Candidates listed in the upper left-hand corner receive the greatest attention, and as the listing moves toward the lower right-hand corner, the attention of the voter decreases. Some states allow voters to add names not on the ballot. Write-in candidates can seldom succeed, although Rep. Joe Skeen (R-NM) was first elected to Congress in 1980 as a write-in candidate.

Most states make it difficult for third parties to gain a position on the ballot. A required number of voters must register with the party, or the party's candidate must receive a required number of votes in the previous election. In California, for example, new parties such as the American Independent or the Peace and Freedom Party had to secure either a registration of 1 percent of the voters in the state or a petition signed by 10 percent of the electorate in order to be listed. Other states make qualification even more difficult. Pennsylvania originally required signatures of only 0.5 percent of the voters to qualify. This was increased to 2 percent after the Peace and Freedom Party qualified in 1968. In the District of Columbia, a party must reapply for each election unless it has elected a president at some time since 1950 (Jacobson 1987). The Supreme Court has not objected to these restrictions. In a case in Washington, for example, a party had to secure at least 1 percent of the vote in a primary to be listed on the ballot in the general election. The Socialist Workers Party challenged the law. Justice Byron White, writing for the Court, said, "States can properly reserve the general election ballot for 'major struggles' by conditioning access to the ballot on having a modicum of voter support" (*Munro v. Socialist Workers Party*, 1986).

Attempts of groups that wish to run as third parties are costly, time-consuming, and unbelievably frustrating. Eugene McCarthy was able to qualify in only 29 states in 1976; John Anderson and Ed Clark in 1980 became the first since 1916 to secure a spot on the ballot in all states. Ross Perot supporters put him on the ballot in 50 states. But these high-profile examples are the exceptions that prove the rule: It is exceedingly difficult to gain official recognition unless one is a Republican or a Democrat.

Indicative of the independence of the two major political parties in writing their own rules is another case that came before the Court in 1986. Here, the Republican Party wished to allow independents to vote in its primary election, even though a state law precluded it because, presumably, unattached voters would then be attracted to its cause. The Court held that states may not limit a party's decision to allow independents to vote in its primary even though the state has a closed primary law, basing its decision on the First Amendment protection of free association (*Tashjian v. Republican Party of Connecticut*, 1986). In California the Democratic Party got a federal court to overturn a state constitutional provision prohibiting endorsements by parties in nonpartisan elections.

Methods of Selecting Party Candidates

Candidates for elective office are chosen in a variety of ways. In some cases the power of selection is in the hands of party leaders, while other methods of selection make party organizations almost irrelevant.

SELF-ANNOUNCEMENTS   In local nonpartisan elections (where one's party affiliation cannot be listed on the ballot), personally announcing one's candidacy is the basic way of getting on the ballot. In those states where the parties hold primaries, conventions, or other systems of nomination, a candidate announces the desire to be considered by his or her party for the nomination. Parties have little control over who does seek office, especially in primary states where anyone can announce and run for office. Gary C. Jacobson provides a colorful assessment:

> Few congressional candidates find opposition from the local party leaders to be a significant handicap, neither is their support very helpful. The nomination is not something to be awarded by the party but rather a prize to be fought over (when it seems worth having) by freebooting political privateers. (1987, 19–20)

CAUCUSES   The first method used extensively by political parties in the selection of candidates for national office was the party **caucus** (also known as the smoke-filled-room method, where party leaders maneuvered to nominate a candidate of their choice). This was the political parties' principal method of choosing presidential candidates prior to 1830, when the caucus was composed of the party's representatives in Congress. Today the caucus remains an important method of selection in various local campaigns, but the meeting is open to all party members. Some states use the local caucus to select delegates to district and state conventions where candidates are nominated to run in the general election. Delegates for the **national party conventions** are also chosen in the caucuses. Because the Iowan presidential caucuses occur first in the nation, they attract considerable attention. Those candidates who wish to be the presidential nominee of their party must spend an inordinate amount of time there in order to gain the votes and the prestige of winning early in the race. Twelve states use the caucus for both parties; another five have either a Republican or Democratic caucus, depending on the choice of the party in that state.

PRIMARIES   All states now use the primary to select at least some candidates for public office. A **primary** is basically an election held before a general election for the purpose of nominating a party's candidate for office. In order to make the parties more democratic, and to reduce the control of party organizations, reformers have advocated a **direct primary**, where the voters, rather than the caucus, choose the candidates. The method with the most widespread use, however, is the **closed primary**, where only registered members of the party can vote. This method excludes a sizable segment of the electorate who are registered independents. Some states get around this problem by allowing an independent to vote in a party primary. These **open primaries**, used in 10 states, allow voters, regardless of their registration, to select the party primary in which they wish to participate. **Blanket primaries** are used in 2 of these states. Here voters get only one ballot listing all of the candidates by party affiliation for each office. The voter can vote in only one party primary per office, but can switch from one party to the other as he or she moves down the ballot. Finally, Louisiana uses a nonpartisan primary, open to all voters; if no one receives a simple majority, a second election is held several weeks later between the top two vote-getters, regardless of party.

Presidential primaries are not without their supporters and detractors. Supporters of the presidential primary system say it may be most representative of the voting public; it provides an opportunity for a larger number of people to participate in the nominating procedure than does the caucus process.

It might be said, in addition, that the primary system allows a greater diversity of candidates to run for office. Candidates with limited funds or from smaller states may test their viability with the voters by running in a limited number of primaries. Once successful there, they acquire media exposure, thus gaining popularity and additional campaign funds.

Because the media are so crucial in bringing the qualities of the candidates before the public, and because there are so many primaries, proponents of this system argue that it is one good method of judging the character of the candidate. He or she must be able to organize campaigns, communicate well, be knowledgeable about current state politics, and be personable and charming as well—the same qualities, they argue, that are necessary in running the government.

Detractors of the primary system, on the other hand, argue that, while more voters may participate in primaries than in caucuses, the quality of their participation may be minimal. For example, they may pay more attention to personalities than to issues, and their knowledge of the issues may be colored by media interpretation and focus rather than by solid research and information.

Critics also suggest that the primaries are poorly scheduled and that the whole process throughout the country may take too long, as it is drawn out over a five-month period from February to June, with candidates becoming exhausted and making costly errors and the electorate becoming bored and disinterested. Early primaries get greater notice and have more impact on who is chosen—one reason for a number of states to move their selection process to an earlier time. I will return to this in the next chapter.

The first move to primaries was an attempt to secure the Republican nomination for Theodore Roosevelt in 1912 over the opposition of party leadership supporting William H. Taft. But dissatisfaction with this method of selection occurs when the candidate who appears to be most popular fails to secure the nomination. For example, those who supported the 1968 movement for Eugene McCarthy criticized the system for its lack of responsiveness to popular support, although there is little evidence to suggest that McCarthy was the choice of a majority of rank-and-file Democrats. However, the rules for Democrats were changed in 1972 to ensure an open selection process for delegates. In effect, control of the nomination was taken completely from established party leadership and handed to those who would actively work in the primary process. Since that time, there has been a gradual return to more input from party leaders. All members of the Democratic National Committee were delegates in 1992, as were a larger number of Democrats who held elective office. In addition, some states have dropped the use of primaries as the means of selecting delegates, in another move that strengthens traditional party leadership. Still, the selection of delegates is mainly in the hands of party activists, who, critics claim, may not represent the average Republican or Democrat. Analyst William Schneider portrays it this way:

> The problem is that most people do not bother to participate in primaries and caucuses. The ones who do tend to be motivated by ideology and special interest. We have ended up with a process that is elitist in a different way. Issue activists and interest groups have replaced bosses and machines. (1987, 1)

CONVENTIONS   This method of selecting candidates was initiated in 1831 by the Anti-Mason party and was quickly adopted by the major national parties for the selection of presidential candidates. It involves the delegates from the various state political parties meeting once every four years to nominate candidates for president and vice president, to draft and vote on a party platform, and to make their candidates and policies attractive to the voting public. This technique is often used also for choosing candidates for lesser offices in states, districts, cities, and other units. The convention has certain merit over the caucus. Caucuses are informal, ad hoc groups, while conventions consist of duly elected representatives from the constituent units of party organizations. However, the presidential primary system has had the effect in recent years of placing the convention in a position where it merely ratifies the candidate who has already received the highest number of delegates in the primary. The convention's processes are available, however, in case the primary proves indecisive.

In an attempt to have the best of both worlds—some party control through a convention and democratic participation—some states only allow voters to choose from candidates selected at a pre-primary convention. Some form of designating assemblies (pre-primary conventions) has been adopted by Colorado, Idaho, Massachusetts, New Mexico, Rhode Island, and Utah and represents an interesting innovation in the nominating process. In Utah, for example, the two leading candidates from the convention are placed on the primary ballot—unless one receives more than 70 percent of the convention vote, in which case the primary is canceled.

Electoral Districting

One way in which parties have attempted to control their relative position in a state is through control of the drawing of electoral districts. Few political activities are as divisive or disruptive. The Constitution, Article I, Section 2, states that representatives shall be chosen "by the People of the several States," and "shall have the Qualifications requisite for Electors of the most numerous Branch of the State Legislature." What this basically means is that each member of the legislature should represent the same number of people. Dividing each state into districts with the population evenly distributed among all districts is supposed to accomplish the goal of one person, one vote. The biggest problem, of course, is that most people don't stay in the same place for very long. By the turn of the century, for example, the influx of immigrants to the cities had already begun to unbalance the proportion of people in urban districts to those in rural districts. In 1921, Congress chose to ignore the constitutional requirement to reapportion seats in the House because of the political consequences of this imbalance. By 1960, the largest legislative district in every state was at least twice as populous as the smallest district. For example, in Tennessee at that time, the smallest district had a population of 3,400 and the largest had 79,000. Those rural residents, including a county judge named Charles W. Baker, petitioned the state to reapportion or redistribute the districts. The Supreme Court ruled, in *Baker v. Carr* (1962), that **reapportionment** should take place and in *Gray v. Sanders* (1963) formulated the rule of one person, one vote. In the case of *Wesberry v. Sanders* (1964), the same mandate was extended to congressional House districts. House districts must be mathematically precise; the Court has invalidated variations as small as 1 percent. But in districts for state officials, a deviation as high as 15 percent has been accepted, in part because noncongressional elections are judged under a different section of the Constitution—the Fifth Amendment as incorporated by the Fourteenth.

After every 10-year census, federal law states that the number of representatives for each state must be reapportioned depending on population. The problem of drawing new lines every 10 years was complicated by the fact that the House froze its membership at 435 in 1909. It provided a mechanism for

Figure 10.6

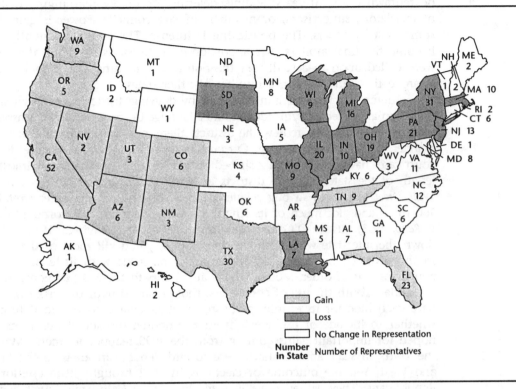

GAIN OR LOSS IN HOUSE OF REPRESENTATIVES, BASED ON 1990 CENSUS

The gain or loss of representatives in the House is based on the census, which is taken every 10 years. The shift in population growth during the 1980s from the upper Midwest and Northeast to the Southwest and West is shown by the shaded areas of the map.

reapportionment in 1929, after failing to do so following the 1920 census. This law, as amended, still governs the process. If a state gets additional seats—that is, if the number of representatives increases—it more easily solves the problem of representation by carving out new districts; if the state has to work with the same number of districts or, as is the case now in the Northeast and Midwest, a smaller number, reapportionment becomes rather bloody. In the 1992 election, after the 1990 reapportionment, nine districts had two incumbents fighting to remain in office.

Under all conditions, reapportionment can lead to attempts by one party or the other to benefit itself by the manner in which the lines are drawn. Figure 10.6 presents the assignment of seats in the House based on the 1990 census and indicating a gain or loss in each state compared to 1980. The combined eastern and midwestern delegations have lost 19 representatives in the past 10 years, while the far West and South have gained those seats. Over a longer time frame, California has grown from 30 districts in 1950 to 52 as a result of the 1990 figures. New York has dropped from 43 districts in 1950 to 31 in 1990. And this trend still continues.

Reapportionment has significance not only for national politics but for state and local politics as well. For all but the most static states, lines must be redrawn every 10 years, adding, deleting, or simply rearranging districts of legislators, supervisors, or members of city councils. Power is gained by some, lost by others. The politicking is intense. The courts frequently have become the final arbiters of reapportionment decisions. In 1990, the courts were called upon to actually set the boundaries in nine states; they had to approve the maps draw in a number of other states.

Attempts to take partisan advantage by drawing districts of unusual shape or design are called gerrymandering, after Elbridge Gerry, governor of Massachusetts. In 1812, after he redrew the districts there, one looked much like a salamander, hence gerrymandering. Current attempts are almost as bizarre. Recent court cases have challenged a Z-shaped district in Louisiana that runs almost the length of the state, and two districts in North Carolina: one described by the *Wall Street Journal* as "a bug splattered on a windshield," the other stretching 160 miles and "for much of its length, no wider than the I-85 corridor" (*Shaw v. Reno*, 1993). Justice O'Connor quotes one legislator as saying, "If you drove down the interstate with both car doors open, you'd kill most of the people in the district." But subtle adjustments can be made with little or nothing appearing out of order. Modern usage also refers to these adjustments as gerrymanders. With the use of computers, those charged with the task can compare each bloc for its ethnic, partisan, or other characteristics to determine whether to include or exclude it from a proposed district. Republicans had hoped for important gains coming from the 1990 reapportionment. Most of the shifts in seats among states were toward Republican areas in the South and West. Yet, the outcome of elections in 1992 brought little comfort to Republicans: They gained only 10 seats. In fact, in California, which gained 7 new seats and where a Republican-dominated state court drew the lines, the results left the state with 30 Democratic and 22 Republican representatives. It had been 26 to 19 before reapportionment; in 1994 the two parties were split 26-26. One of the most successful recent examples of reapportionment was in Illinois, where the Democrats produced a plan approved by the court that had a maximum divergence of 171 people. Even though Democratic areas lost more of their population than Republican areas, the plan gave the Democrats a two-seat advantage. The plan "eliminated two Republican districts even though population decline in Illinois came from the Democratic bastion of Chicago" (Bullock 1982, 435). One reason was the Supreme Court's unwillingness to dilute minority representation. Recently, the Court has changed its position, questioning race as a basis for representation. With either all or part of 35 states under the jurisdiction of the Voting Rights Act, the Justice Department must agree to district changes, and these may not dilute minority representation. The results of reapportionment can have far-reaching effects on a state's politics for the ensuing decade.

But does reapportionment need to be so intense and partisan? Not always. What happens in many states is an agreement among all interested parties to maintain the status quo, to enhance the reelection chances of all incumbents.

Summary

Political parties are organized attempts to select candidates and win elections. They have been a constant feature of our political system since the early 1790s. Our two major parties, the Republicans and the Democrats, have competed with each other for power since 1860. Even though we still have Republicans and Democrats as our two major parties, they do not attract the same voters or stand for the same issues as they did in earlier days. And they have alternated as the choice of a majority of the electorate over these years. We are now at the end of what most political scientists call our fifth political party system. The emergence of a new alignment must be qualified, since it is just emerging, but most would agree we are entering an era of Republican dominance, with a conservative, anti–big-government ideology.

Parties no longer occupy the position of importance they once did. Modern elections are more candidate-centered, and the media have some influence on who wins and who loses. Voters are not as attached to parties as they once were, and direct primaries have taken the choice of party candidates out of the parties' control. Parties do, however, still maintain control of the legal mechanics associated with elections. This gives them advantages, especially with respect to challenges from minor parties or independents.

Analytical Exercises

1. In chapter 1, I introduced a game that showed how each member of society benefited from joining a social contract. The rules of the game were defined as follows: There are five players who are assigned to one of two groups in each round. One group is composed of three players (G3), the other of two (G2); players are assigned to groups in a regular sequence, that is, a player would be in G3 for 3 rounds, then in G2 for 2 rounds for each set of 5 rounds. There are 10 rounds, and in each the players get to nominate a group to win the round. The banker, who manages the money, gets to choose a winning group from among those nominated. The players in the winning group each get $10; those in the other group each have to pay $10.

In the earlier example, players lost money ($20) if they did not act in concert with each other; if they did act in concert they could each come out a $20 winner. Now let's add the concept of a political party to the game. Assume that three members belong to a political party and agree to always nominate the group that has two party members in it. Now what happens to the distribution of rewards and costs to each member of the society? Do you think this result is socially desirable?

2. Assume that you have sole responsibility for redistricting the four congressional districts in your state. You must comply with the Supreme Court test that each district have equal numbers and contiguous boundaries. Contiguous means that there is no physical space between parts of the district. In the example below, you can meet the test by joining any county that is next to, above, or below another county. You cannot join counties only on a diagonal. To simplify the problem, the state's 2.4 million people are equally distributed among 20 counties, each with 120,000 people, of whom 60,000 are registered

voters; thus each district composed of five counties will have a population equal to the others. The number of registered Democrats and Republicans varies from county to county, and statewide Democrats outnumber Republicans 629,000 to 571,000. What is the most favorable number of districts composed of five counties each that could be drawn for the Democrats? For Republicans? Which combination would be best for the Republicans? The Democrats?

	A		B		C		D
D	32,000	D	45,000	D	30,000	D	39,000
R	28,000	R	15,000	R	30,000	R	21,000
	E		F		G		H
D	36,000	D	39,000	D	13,000	D	29,000
R	24,000	R	21,000	R	47,000	R	31,000
	I		J		K		L
D	24,000	D	44,000	D	15,000	D	34,000
R	36,000	R	16,000	R	45,000	R	26,000
	M		N		O		P
D	30,000	D	33,000	D	45,000	D	18,000
R	30,000	R	27,000	R	15,000	R	42,000
	Q		R		S		T
D	42,000	D	15,000	D	45,000	D	21,000
R	18,000	R	45,000	R	15,000	R	39,000

Chapter Outline

11

Electoral and Voting Systems

Bad officials are elected by good citizens who do not vote.
        —George Jean Nathan, *The American Credo,* 1921

I called on a certain rural constituent and was shocked to hear him say he was thinking of voting for my opponent. I reminded him of the many things I had done for him as prosecuting attorney, as county judge, as congressman, and senator. I recalled how I had helped get an access road built to his farm, how I had visited him in a military hospital in France when he was wounded in World War I, how I had assisted him in securing his veteran's benefits, how I had arranged his loan from the Farm Credit Administration, how I had got him a disaster loan when the flood destroyed his home, etc., etc.

"How can you think of voting for my opponent?" I exhorted at the end of this long recital. "Surely you remember all these things I have done for you?" "Yeah," he said, "I remember. But what in hell have you done for me lately?"

        —Alben W. Barkley, *That Reminds Me,* 1954

Despite the fact that we pride ourselves on being a participatory democracy, most Americans find elections commonplace and even boring. Even the most interesting—presidential elections—bring out only about half the eligible voters, and most of those do not take an interest until the last weeks of the campaign. The presidential election of 1992 generated more interest than most, yet only 55 percent of eligible voters participated. The off-year elections of

257

1994 brought 39 percent to the polls. Yet, these recent elections brought out more voters than had gone to the polls in the last decade. We elect over 500,000 officials in the United States. We don't always recognize or understand that a wide variety of **decision rules** govern the outcome of the process of voting and greatly affect the choices we make.

Decision Rules

We have become so accustomed to our electoral apparatus that few of us think about the consequences of the decision rules used in our elections. Majority rule is the basic rule for decision making in legislative bodies and on various ballot propositions facing the voters in popular elections. There are several different types of majority. With a **simple majority**, the winner must receive 50 percent plus 1 of the total votes cast. We use simple-majority rules in the few popular elections that require a majority. The Democratic Party primary in southern states and nonpartisan elections in California use simple-majority rule, for example. In legislatures, such as Congress or a city council, most decisions are based on this rule. An **absolute majority** requires 50 percent plus 1 of those eligible to vote. This can be a prohibitive requirement in popular elections. For example, if there are 100 potential voters, 51 votes are required to win regardless of the number who vote. If less than half of those eligible vote, no one could win. In the 1988 presidential election, only 50 percent participated; George Bush would have to have been the unanimous choice of the voters to win under this rule. We do, however, use it in some legislative voting. For example, most legislatures require an absolute majority to conduct business—called a quorum.

Although electoral decisions are easier to obtain under simple-majority rules rather than absolute rules, most elections for public office are not decided under the simple-majority criterion either. This may surprise those who assume majority rule is basic to democratic government. Instead, *plurality* is usually the rule for decision making. Under a plurality rule, the candidate simply must receive more votes than does any other candidate in the race, regardless of the percentage received.

An alternative to majority or plurality rule is **proportional representation**, used in many western European countries. This system gives representation to groups in proportion to their electoral strength—if a party got 12 percent of the vote, it would get 12 percent of the seats. It has never been favored by the majority, and most of the 19 cities in the United States that once used it have turned to other methods. To award a party with these exact divisions, there must be multiple representatives elected from each electoral district. We call these multimember districts, as opposed to single-member districts, where only one candidate is elected from each district. I have noted the link between proportional representation and multiparty systems. No doubt our reluctance to embrace proportional representation is partly a result of our having only two major parties. Indeed, Congress requires that all of its representatives come from single-member districts. When all representatives are elected from the entire jurisdiction—a city or a school district, for example—we refer to this as an at-large election.

Some decision rules require extra majorities; a two-thirds rule is the most frequently used form of this in the American system. In the U.S. Senate, a two-thirds majority is needed to approve treaties and to convict civil officials in impeachment trials. In state and local affairs, two-thirds of the voters must approve various ballot propositions such as bond issues and tax overrides. The Supreme Court held in *Gordon v. Lance* (1971) that these extra majorities—usually two-thirds—do not violate the equal protection provisions of the Constitution. You might compare this line of reasoning with the one person–one vote standard discussed in the last chapter on page 252.

Historical Development of Voting Rules

Majority rule is accepted as a basic decision rule in the American system, but we find its use is limited. Surprisingly, voting at the Constitutional Convention was by majority rule, since the Articles of Confederation required a two-thirds majority to initiate congressional action and unanimous approval to pass amendments. As our country developed, the most significant applications of majority rule have been in the formal adoption of legislation by Congress and other legislative bodies, and in selection of the president by the electoral college.

One of the real fears of the Framers, however, was giving the majority too much power. A close look at our political system finds other rules in operation a great deal of the time. Election to the House has always been determined by plurality. Because there are usually only two serious candidates running for each seat, the practical result is that the winner secures a simple majority, but in 1994 there were 21 members who won with less than a majority. Originally election of senators was by state legislatures, but since the passage of the Seventeenth Amendment in 1913 they, too, have been chosen by plurality. Four senators in 1994 were elected with less than a majority. Although presidents need a majority in the electoral college, they are frequently chosen by only a plurality of the popular vote: There have been 16 presidential elections, including 1992, in which the winner did not get a simple majority.

There are many other features of the American system that are not based on majority rule. Legislation in Congress must be passed by two separate legislative bodies, and, even then, it can be vetoed by a single individual—the president. In addition, extra majorities are required to enact certain measures, such as the approval of treaties by the Senate. Much of our public policy is determined not by a majority of the people, but by a bureaucracy insulated from majoritarian pressures, by committees and subcommittees of Congress whose actions need not reflect the preferences of a majority of their colleagues, and by judges who are appointed for life and are not directly subject to democratic control.

Sixteen states require extra majorities (two-thirds or three-fifths) for the passage of various revenue bonds; in some states, extra majorities are required of state legislatures to enact appropriations and tax measures. Amendments

Table 11.1

IMPACT OF VOTING RULES

Candidate:	Allyson	Brooks	Cassandra	David	Evie
<u>Voter</u>					
Prescott	1	5	4	2	3
Smythe	2	3	5	1	4
Travis	3	4	2	5	1
Quinones	5	1	4	2	3
Carter	4	1	3	5	2
Sum of Ranks	15	14	17	15	13

This table shows how different voting rules will result in the election of a different candidate. The numbers in the table represent the rank given each candidate by the voter. Under a plurality rule, Brooks would win. Under a majority rule, a runoff election would be needed, since no one has a majority of votes. Under a Borda Count rule, Evie would win.

to the Constitution, moreover, must pass through a laborious process requiring substantial agreement among the American people.

Impact of Decision Rules

An indication of how various rules influence the outcome of voting decisions can be seen from an analysis of Table 11.1. The table portrays a voting environment with five voters, listed on the left of the table, and five candidates, listed across the top. The numbers in the boxes represent the ranking of the candidates by the voters. Prescott, for example, ranks Allyson first, David second, Evie third, and so on. If we assume that voters will choose a more preferred candidate over a less preferred, the following results obtain. Under a plurality rule, Brooks has two first-place votes; Allyson, David, and Evie each have one: Brooks would win. If we switch to a majority rule, then no one has enough first-place votes and we are going to need to go to a second election between two candidates. Brooks is in the runoff, but there were three candidates with one vote each in the first election. We need a method to decide which of them will run against Brooks. In France, for example, where this second stage—*à deux tour*—of voting is used, the various parties would get together and make the decision among themselves as to who has the best chance of winning. We could do that by taking the candidate that is the most preferred of the three. In this case, Allyson has three of five voters preferring her to David, and David is preferred to Evie, but Evie is preferred to Allyson. We have a problem! It's an interesting one in political theory, and it has real importance in the functioning of a democratic system. I will get to it later. For now, the three candidates are able to see that only Allyson can beat Brooks in a head-to-head competition. In the runoff election, Allyson is preferred to Brooks by three of the five voters—a majority. Another way to decide the election would be to compare ranks and pick the candidate with the lowest combined score. That is, we would add up the rank scores, the lowest being the winner. (In academic terms, this is called a Borda Count.) Under this rule, Evie wins with a low score of 13. There are many more possible rules—and for those interested I have provided some of these adaptations in the Analytical Exercises—but the point should be clear: different rules can produce different results, even though the underlying preferences of the voters do not change.

Expansion of the Franchise

There are few stronger ideas being expressed in the world today than that the people of a country should be able to decide their own future. This was certainly a major issue as we formed our government 200 years ago. Arthur Sutherland writes that our system encourages "rule by the unconverted many, regardless of their wisdom or momentary unwisdom, their impatience or vulgarity. The first constitutional principle of our people is their right to make and ultimately (one hopes) to correct their own mistakes" (1965, 5).

Nearly all those over the age of 18 have voting rights, but this has not always been the case. In fact, popular participation has developed rather slowly in the American system. Restrictions on the **franchise** (right to vote) have been effective and persistent throughout our history, and only through long and sometimes difficult negotiations have restrictions been lifted and the franchise extended. In the colonies, prior to the Revolution, as little as two percent of the population was able to vote (McKinley 1905), namely, white males who owned property and paid taxes. Table 11.2, next page, provides graphic illustration of how some of these restrictions prevailed. Pennsylvania required a tax payment until 1933.

RACE   In an attempt to restrict blacks from voting, many states instituted literacy tests, character tests, and poll taxes as prerequisites for registration. These restrictions were instituted in southern states in the late 1800s, after Reconstruction. Literacy tests were administered so poorly in some states that even some black college graduates were prevented from voting. Good character tests required prospective registrants to have two people already registered vouch for them. Of course, most white voters would not vouch for blacks. The tax required of those who were going to the polls to vote was designed to keep not only blacks from voting but also poor whites.

The Voting Rights Act of 1965 extended the franchise to many of those in minority groups who were once excluded from voting. It suspended literacy and character tests in the six southern states and parts of four others where less than half of those eligible had registered or voted in the 1964 election. Later amendments to the Voting Rights Act extended the ban on such tests. The Twenty-fourth Amendment to the Constitution, passed in 1964, prohibits the use of poll taxes by the states.

Few laws have had the dramatic impact of the Voting Rights Act. Registration figures for minorities in southern states were exceedingly low before adoption of the act and are now close to those of other states. In Mississippi, only 6.7 percent of blacks were registered prior to the law; by 1976 their

Table 11.2

REMOVAL OF PROPERTY-OWNING AND TAXPAYING QUALIFICATIONS

	Property	Tax Payment
South Carolina	1759	1810
Pennsylvania	1776	1933
New Hampshire	1784	1792
Georgia	1789	1798
Delaware	1792	1897
Maryland	1810	None required
Connecticut	1818	1845
New York	1821	1826
Massachusetts	1821	1891
Rhode Island	1842	None required
New Jersey	1844	None required
Virginia	1850	None required
North Carolina	1856	1868
Ohio (admitted 1803)		1851
Louisiana (admitted 1812)		1845
Mississippi (admitted 1817)		1832

Source: E. M. Sait, *American Parties and Elections,* © 1952, renewed 1980. Reprinted by permission of Prentice Hall, Inc., Englewood Cliffs, New Jersey.

The voting rights we have come to take for granted did not always exist in this country for everyone. This table shows when the requirements for owning property and paying a tax in order to vote were removed in various states.

number had increased to 67.4 percent! It is now legal for the federal government to investigate wherever registration falls below 50 percent of the eligible population or where the non–English-speaking population exceeds 10 percent, so as to improve access to registration. Thirty-five states are now or have been under the jurisdiction of Voting Rights Act provisions. This act will be with us for some time to come, as Congress extended it for 25 years in 1982. Approval did not come easily, however. The Reagan administration objected to, but ultimately accepted, the Justice Department review provisions of the act. I mentioned these provisions and their impact on reapportionment in the last chapter. Preclearance requires any jurisdiction covered by the act to gain the approval of the Justice Department before it changes any district boundaries or the rules under which elections are held—from single-member to at-large, for example. This is done primarily to protect the voting power of minorities by proving that the changes do not dilute their representative numbers. Traditionally, at-large elections have been used for this purpose.

RESIDENCY Residency requirements also have been reexamined. In our mobile society, these requirements disfranchise many potential voters. The Supreme Court invalidated Tennessee's one-year residency requirement (*Dunn v. Blumstein*, 1972), but allowed a 30-day requirement for residence in the local district to stand. Apparently, all states must now conform more closely to the 30-day standard, although a 50-day requirement in Idaho has been upheld

(*Marston v. Lewis*, 1973), and Colorado recently adopted a 60-day requirement. Individuals can easily miss the deadline if they are unaware of upcoming elections. Title II of the Voting Rights Act Amendments of 1970 established a national 30-day residency requirement for voting in presidential elections.

AGE   Traditionally most states required that voters reach the age of 21 to be eligible to vote. In the late 1960s, however, when so many 18-year-olds were fighting and dying in the Vietnam War, public opinion changed—if 18-year-olds can fight and die in a war for their country, then they should be able to vote. Initial legislation resulted in confusion, since the Supreme Court ruled that Congress could apply voting-age legislation only to the federal level. Thus, you could be one age and vote for president, but might have to be another age to vote for state officers. Then in 1971, Congress proposed and the required number of states quickly ratified the Twenty-sixth Amendment, lowering the voting age to 18 in all elections.

CITIZENSHIP   In the nineteenth century, 22 states and territories allowed aliens to vote. Gradually, all states required that voters be citizens. The 1928 election was the first in which only U.S. citizens could vote. This fact would not at first glance seem to have an effect on the outcome of an election, until we realize that more than 12 million residents could not vote in 1992 because they were not American citizens.

REGISTRATION   Advocates of democracy would agree that we have made progress in democratizing the American system but argue that there are serious shortcomings yet to be overcome. In most states a potential voter must register a specified number of days before an election, usually 30 days. If you fail to comply—out of ignorance of the requirement or physical inability to do so—you will not be eligible to vote. Moreover, official reluctance to encourage registration, which is evident in many college and southern communities, lessens participation. Many states do not allow college students to register at their campuses and instead require them to use their parents' address. Another difficulty for the voter is **absentee voting**. Those who are going to be away from their voting districts on election day must file for absentee ballots. Applications are usually due at least a week in advance, and in many states the ballot must be *notarized*, or your signature witnessed, and returned by election day. These restrictions hinder voters and lower the proportion of those who vote.

Various efforts have been made to increase participation. Michigan adopted a "Motor-Voter" plan, where applicants for drivers' licenses are also given the opportunity to register to vote. This plan was adopted on a national basis in 1993, but several states, including California, have refused to implement it. The federal government is now pursuing action against these states in the courts. Maine, Minnesota, and Wisconsin use same-day registration: prospective voters simply go to the polls on election day. Still other states, such as California, have gone to postcard registration, where one does not have to physically go to the county clerk's office but can simply submit a postcard registration form and be eligible to vote. In Europe, many countries make registration to vote automatic upon the individual's turning 18 years of age. Each of these alternatives has improved the number of those eligible to vote in elections.

Reasons for nonvoting are many and varied, but there do seem to be several major generalizations that can be made. In chapter 1, I presented data indicating a list of reasons for nonvoting. Let me put these into a more systematic analysis. The basic assumption about those who don't participate is that they see little at stake in the political arena. "If you don't benefit," states M. J. Avery in a study of voter demobilization, "you drop out" (1988, 125). The Field Research Institute, which conducts the California Poll, has developed the following systematic categories of nonvoters:

> *Political Passives.* About 40 percent of nonvoters are completely out of the political mainstream. They tend to be low-income, poorly educated minorities, and young adults.
> *Politically Alienated.* About 20 percent of nonvoters feel they are unable to control or affect government. Many who vote also feel this way; the California poll finds them likely nonvoters in the future.
> *Contented Apathetics.* These people see little reason to vote because they are largely content; their lives will stay much the same whoever wins. They cut across the entire social spectrum.
> *System Disenfranchisees.* This group, about 10 percent of nonvoters, are those who have moved or in some other way are prevented from voting because of the institutional constraints we put on voting. (Field Institute Report, June 5, 1990, 2–4)

Social class, as measured by income, education, or occupation, seems to be the most important variable in voting. A recent study suggests that the discrepancies in voter turnout based on class have remained remarkably stable over the past 30 years (Leighley and Nagler 1992, 725).

If we explore the influence of social class more closely, we find that education shows the highest relationship to voting (Wolfinger and Rosenstone 1980, 9). "Education, for example, is important for some political activities because it enhances political interest and civic skills, while income is important for other activities because of the monetary resources it provides" (Brady, Verba, and Schlozman 1995, 271). Brady, Verba, and Schlozman go on to explore the importance of "*resources: time* to take part in political activity, *money* to make contributions, and *civic skills* (i.e., the communications and organizational skills that facilitate effective participation)" (271). They show that these are differentially distributed among groups in the United States and, thus, give an underlying explanation for why social class is so important to participation. They also show that the acquisition of social skills is least related to social class, which helps explain the higher than expected participation among some lower-class religious groups (285).

While recent efforts by civil rights groups, aided by the Voting Rights Act, have increased minority registration, there are still disparities in the percentage who vote. Figure 11.1, on page 266, compares percentages of whites, blacks, and Latinos who reported voting. The gap between white and black

Drawing by Stevenson; © 1993 The New Yorker Magazine, Inc.

"I'll tell you one thing. Nobody had to pay *me* not to vote."

voters was below 10 percent in 1992; the gap between white and Latino voters was nearly 35 percent.

Rules in Action: Presidential Selection

Let me return to the selection of a president to illustrate decision rules in action. There are two distinct phases of such elections: the one constitutional, involving winning electoral votes; the other political, with delegates to a national convention needed for winning nomination. Let's begin with this political phase.

Presidential Nominating Procedures

The campaign season begins in February of a presidential election year with a caucus in Iowa, followed by a primary in New Hampshire the next week. But modern campaigns begin long before this. In 1995, there were seven active Republicans seeking the nomination, making extended visits to these early primary states:

Iowa (caucus)	February 12
New Hampshire	February 20
New York	March 7

Figure 11.1

**REPORTED VOTERS AS A PERCENTAGE OF THE VOTING-AGE POPULATION,
BY RACE AND LATINO ORIGIN: 1972–1992**

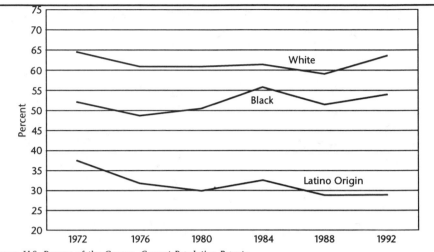

Source: U.S. Bureau of the Census, *Current Population Reports.*

The Voting Rights Act has increased minority registration. But while the gap has narrowed between whites and blacks, it still remains great between whites and Latinos.

Super Tuesday	March 12
Ohio, Michigan, Illinois	March 19
California	March 26

The laws and procedures governing presidential primaries vary from state to state. Some states hold a presidential preference poll that may or may not be binding on the states' convention delegates. Other states select delegates to the national conventions by election. In some cases, the slates of delegates are pledged to a particular candidate; in others, they are listed as favorable to an aspirant; while in still others they are unpledged. At present, 38 states and the District of Columbia hold some form of presidential preference primary (Federal Election Commission *Record*). Recently, there has been a movement to establish a national primary for presidential candidates, a movement designed to eliminate the confusion caused by differing state laws. It would also lessen the chances that leading state party officials might influence the selection of delegates from their state.

DELEGATE SELECTION RULES   Different selection or decision rules can produce different election results. Political parties have been torn between the decision to make the selection process more democratic and their desire to maintain some control. One illustration of this is the differences produced by primaries and caucuses. "Caucuses do tend to measure intensity of support

Table 11.3

COMPARISON OF PRIMARY AND CAUCUS WINNERS IN 1992

Candidate	Primaries Won	Caucuses Won
Clinton	31*	5
Tsongas	4	5
Brown	2	3
Harkin	0	3
Kerrey	1	0

*Three of these were "beauty contests" with no delegates. Clinton also won the primary in the District of Columbia. One beauty contest was won by Ross Perot.

in a way primaries do not," said Michigan Democratic chairman Rick Wiener (*Congressional Quarterly Weekly Report* June 4, 1988, 1523). Some indication of the impact of caucuses is shown by comparing three states in the 1988 election where Democratic voters had an opportunity to engage in both a caucus and a primary: Texas, Vermont, and Idaho. Michael Dukakis won the primary in each state, and ultimately the nomination, but the Reverend Jesse L. Jackson won the caucus in Texas and Vermont (*CQ Weekly Report* June 4, 1988, 1527). Voter turnout can be as much as eight times higher in a primary as compared to a caucus.

Jackson was highly critical of the delegate selection process used by his party in primary states. Some states use a single-member-district system to award delegates, which again shows the impact of rules. For example, in Pennsylvania, New Jersey, and Illinois, Jackson won 28 percent, 33 percent, and 31 percent of the popular vote, respectively; he received, however, only 8 percent, 8 percent, and 21 percent of the delegates in those states. It is nevertheless true that Jackson came closer in 1988 to claiming delegates in proportion to his electoral support—28 percent of the vote, 26 percent of the delegates—than in 1984. It is also true that Dukakis won the most caucuses; even if all states used caucuses, the results would have yielded the same winner, but with a difference in the closeness of the contest.

An interesting reversal in the nominating process has occurred. Whereas in the early part of this century the caucus was dominated by the party organization, and challengers such as Theodore Roosevelt in 1912 had to go to the primary as a means of beating the organization, now caucuses have become the refuge of the outsider against the party's organization. This was the case for Jackson and Republican Pat Robertson in 1988, and it was also true for several Democrats in 1992. If we look at Table 11.3, we see that Tsongas, Brown, and Harkin all did well in caucus states but were overwhelmed in the primaries by Bill Clinton.

States attempt to increase their roles in selection by adjusting the timing and types of selection processes used. And both of these factors can make a difference. In an attempt to gain influence over the nomination, southern states adopted a strategy in 1988 of holding their selection on a common date, which became known as Super Tuesday. California, the largest state, had until 1996 one of the last state primaries, in June, long after the choice of a candidate was usually made. In an attempt to have a greater impact, California moved to March 26. But this led to similar attempts by other states to move to earlier dates. Several attempts involved extended melodramas, such as Louisiana Republicans' effort to move ahead of Iowa, and Delaware's choosing a date just after New Hampshire's. If these attempts, which were still in progress in December 1995, are successful, California will once again make its selection near the end of the process.

The Republican primary in New Hampshire was won by George Bush in 1992. But Pat Buchanan got 37 percent of the vote. This was perceived as a victory by most observers. This perception of how a candidate does relative to his or her expected performance is something candidates try to alter or influence. If candidates portray themselves as underdogs going in, and do well, then they can gain momentum for the next state on the primary circuit. Candidate representatives, called **spin doctors**, are constantly telling the media how they should be interpreting the results. The importance of the media in politics is discussed in detail beginning on page 305.

In addition to the importance of victory, or the appearance of victory, the early primaries serve as a winnowing process. Candidates who do not do well lose not only momentum but campaign contributors and supporters. Since the selection process extends across the country during a five-month period, success in the long run depends not only on enough success in early contests to remain politically viable, but on an organization that can campaign in each state. Good organization, sufficient money to maintain it, and a cadre of committed supporters are what lead to the nomination.

NATIONAL PARTY CONVENTIONS   With all of the mystery gone from who will be each party's nominee, the national conventions have become a starting point for the general election campaign. Indeed, we have not had a convention decision go beyond the first ballot since 1952. Leading political scientists Nelson Polsby and Aaron Wildavsky suggest that conventions now are for consolidating forces for the general election (1991, 174); they have, in effect, become the first shots in the campaign. The nominees' acceptance speeches are crucial in allowing the candidate his or her first effort at succeeding with the public. Most experts agree that the Bush speech in 1988, written by Peggy Noonan, made the most lasting impression; thus, Bush was able to gain considerable momentum coming out of the convention and never relinquished his lead in that election. The 1992 election was very different. What most remember from Houston was the dominance of the conservative wing of the Republican Party in the platform and in the speeches. Bush came out of Houston trailing in the polls and was never able to regain the lead. Thus national conventions are important not for who is nominated, but for setting the tone and direction of the campaign.

Electing the President

The formal, constitutional rules for the actual election of the president and vice president are focused in the **Electoral College**, which is composed of presidential electors, chosen by elections held in each state. The number of presidential electors in each state is equal to the number of representatives and senators from each state—except in the District of Columbia, which has 3 votes (in accordance with the Twenty-third Amendment)—for a total of 538 electors. The electors meet following the general election and cast their ballots for president. They then cast a separate ballot for vice president. All states except Maine and Nebraska operate under a unit rule, which means the candidate who gets the most popular votes (plurality) receives all the electoral votes (unanimity) from that state. Because each candidate has a separate slate of electors, voters vote, in effect, for the slate pledged to the candidate when they go to the polls. But not all states require the electors to vote for their party's candidate. This has produced an occasional "unfaithful elector," as happened in 1968, 1976, and 1980. Unpledged electors—that is, electors not pledged to any candidate—have also been chosen in some states as they were in Mississippi in 1960, where they received more votes than those pledged to Republican or Democratic candidates.

If no candidate receives an absolute majority of the electoral vote (270), then the election is decided by the House of Representatives, using a rule that gives each state one vote. In this case, an absolute majority (26) is needed to be elected.

As a historical note, I would add that the House of Representatives has chosen the president on two occasions. In 1800, Thomas Jefferson was the presidential candidate and Aaron Burr the vice presidential candidate of the Democrat-Republicans. They each had the same number of electoral votes. In the original Constitution each elector had two votes, but there was no way to distinguish the intent of a first and second choice for president. Burr and some Federalists (the losing party) decided to try to prevent Jefferson's election in the House; it took 36 ballots before Jefferson finally won. The members of Congress quickly realized the problem, and a constitutional amendment was proposed and ratified—the Twelfth—to separate the vote of the electors, one for president, the other for vice president. The other case of selection in the House occurred in 1824 when the supporters of Henry Clay joined with those of John Quincy Adams to secure Adams's victory. The popular vote winner and the candidate with the most electoral votes was Andrew Jackson, who ran again four years later and won an overwhelming victory.

With the Twelfth Amendment, some method was needed to handle the case where no candidate received an absolute majority of the College's vote for vice president. The Senate was given this responsibility, with each senator having one vote and an absolute majority necessary to win. Once, in 1836, the Senate had to perform this duty when Martin Van Buren's running mate, Richard Johnson of Kentucky, failed to get the necessary majority. Van Buren's Democrats controlled Congress and selected Johnson.

After each election, attempts have usually been made to change the Constitution as it relates to selecting the president, so far with no success. In part, there is a hesitancy to change the Constitution. But to a larger degree, there is a consideration of the political impact of the Electoral College system on various groups and states. Some argue that the present system is biased against small states, while others suggest that small states would become irrelevant

Table 11.4

FIVE ALTERNATIVES FOR PRESIDENTIAL SELECTION, 1960 ELECTION RESULTS

	Electoral Votes	Popular Votes	Proportional Representation	District Plan	National Bonus Plan
Kennedy	303	34,227,000	262.671	245	405
Nixon	219	34,108,000	263.631	278	219

Some would argue that any system of selecting a candidate for president is inequitable. The search continues, however, for the best method. This table shows what effect each system would have had on the final results of the presidential election of 1960.

under suggested alternatives. African American groups have argued that their effectiveness would be diluted under reforms. They see more effective political strength in being pivotal voters in several key states than in being 10–12 percent of the overall electorate in a nationwide popular vote for president. Study of the 1976 election would tend to confirm this view. Jimmy Carter won 90 percent of the black vote, which provided his victory margin in 13 states, states that had a total of 216 electoral votes (*CQ Weekly Report* April 22, 1978, 972).

A look at some of the major proposals and their impact on the 1960 election should give some indication of the difficulty in selecting a completely equitable method. The most frequently suggested alternative is direct election, in which the candidate with the highest number of popular votes wins. If you look at Table 11.4, you will see that, in a direct election, Kennedy would have won the election by 119,000 votes (although there is some debate over the accuracy of this figure). Another proposal is to assign electoral votes based on the proportion of the vote received in each state. This would be a precise mathematical calculation in which the proportion of electoral votes received would be exactly the same as the proportion of the popular vote received; the individual electors would be eliminated. Using this plan, Nixon would have been the victor in 1960! Another frequently mentioned alternative is the District Plan now used by Maine and Nebraska. Each congressional district would have one electoral vote assigned to the candidate receiving a plurality of the popular vote in that district. In addition, two votes would be awarded to the candidate receiving the most votes statewide. Under this proposal, Nixon again would have been the victor (*Congressional Digest* March 1979). Under a plan proposed by a task force of the Twentieth Century Fund, in which the popular vote winner nationwide is awarded a bonus of 102 electoral votes, Kennedy would have won with 405 votes (Cronin 1980). By adding this bonus, we would, in effect, always be selecting the popular vote winner as president.

Clearly, electoral decision rules have an impact on the type of political system that is created and on the political organization within that system. It is essential to understand these rules if we are to understand other types of institutional arrangements, such as our political parties, and if we are to appreciate the critical role of elections in the American system.

Candidate Selection

Elections are a means of access to a political career. Control over that access, then, is crucial to a potential candidate. In other countries, candidates may spend many years in parliament or on government committees learning how the system of government works and building a "good résumé." In this country, candidates may declare themselves eligible for office without benefit of prior government service. There are, however, social, legal, and political restraints to seeking nomination for elected office in this country.

Social Restraints

There are no social restraints to candidacy imposed by the Constitution. However, to be successful at the polls, a candidate must appeal to a broad spectrum of voters. Until recently, this has effectively excluded women, nonwhites, non-Christians, and those who have been divorced. Ronald Reagan, divorced and remarried, won the presidency in 1980 and 1984. The Roman Catholic faith was a social barrier to office until Al Smith was nominated in 1928 and John F. Kennedy was elected in 1960. Geraldine Ferraro was the first woman nominated for vice president in 1984, and the Reverend Jesse L. Jackson was the first nonwhite to make a serious bid for the Democratic nomination for president in 1984 and again in 1988. We can probably expect that in the future these arbitrary social barriers will continue to disappear.

Legal Restraints

Candidates for public office must meet certain objective criteria. For example, the Constitution specifies that the president must "have attained to the Age of thirty five Years" (art. II, sec. 1), that "No Person shall be a Representative who shall not have attained to the age of twenty five Years" (art. I, sec. 2), and that "No Person shall be a Senator who shall not have attained the Age of thirty Years" (art. I, sec. 3). For most offices, states require that a person have lived within the confines of his or her district for a specified length of time. But rules vary: for example, a five-year residency requirement for County Boards of Supervisors was unreasonable to California's court, but a seven-year requirement for the New Hampshire Senate was upheld by the Supreme Court (*Sununu v. Stark*, 1975). And meeting these objective criteria does not ensure a candidate's spot on the ballot. The legal procedure for placing a candidate's name on the ballot is cumbersome if that person is not the endorsed candidate of a major party (see chapter 10, Political Parties, p. 242).

Political Restraints

Potential candidates are faced with a number of political restraints as well as with the social and legal limitations we have noted. These generally fall into the categories of time, party affiliation, and finances.

TIME   The large amount of time involved in seeking elective office is another restraint on aspirants to elective office. Those of us who hold 8-to-5 jobs are effectively hindered because we have little spare time and usually are not able to leave our jobs for several months in order to become serious candidates. This leaves the way open for candidates who have more free time to spend in political campaigning. Lawyers seem to be particularly drawn to political office. Although they certainly have a special interest in the formulation of public policy because of their legal training, their workload is basically self-arranged, so they have a distinct advantage over others who cannot arrange their own working hours. Some business executives and self-employed professionals enjoy similar advantages.

PARTY AFFILIATION   Competition for elective office varies with the office being sought. At the national level, analysts of Congress consider most seats for the House of Representatives to be solidly controlled by one or the other of our major parties, with incumbents generally retaining their seats. Many states tend to be largely controlled by one party. One study covering the period 1974-80 classifies 22 states as basically split between the two parties, with the remaining 28 giving a distinct advantage to one party or the other (Bibby et al. 1983). Seeking a political career in such a state, therefore, dictates that the candidate belong to the majority party, because members of the minority party are unlikely to gain elective office. When we consider political offices at the local level, we find that one party is usually more dominant. Thus, if someone disagrees with party policy or chooses to run as an independent, unaffiliated candidate, his or her chances of winning the election are minimal. Still, it is not impossible for an independent candidate to succeed. In the 1990 gubernatorial races, for example, two independents won election: Walter J. Hickel of Alaska and Lowell P. Weicker Jr. of Connecticut, although each was a well-known public figure who had held office as a Republican.

FINANCES   Campaigns for any major elective office in the United States are extremely expensive, and candidates must be either independently wealthy or capable of securing considerable financial backing. Costs per vote—dividing the amount spent by the number voting—have quadrupled in congressional elections since 1954. Veteran campaigners in California suggest that at least $250,000 is now (1996) needed to run for the state legislature. Even more staggering are the costs of running for Congress. In 1990, the average expenditure by the winner of an open-seat contest for the House of Representatives was $600,000 (Federal Election Commission *Record* March 1992). In addition, incumbents are able to raise many times as much as challengers, making it extremely difficult to defeat an incumbent. Part of the increase in campaign costs is the result of inflation and the need to reach an expanding electorate. However, if we take these two factors into account, it would still appear that the cost of each vote cast has almost doubled in the past decade. Thus, without adequate financing, a candidate's chances of success are nil.

   Money is a frequently misunderstood aspect of political campaigns. That is, while enough money is important to run a successful campaign, it is just

Drawing by Jeff MacNelly, ©1995. Reprinted by permission: Tribune Media Services

as important to use whatever money one does have wisely. Candidates must be able to reach the electorate, to have an effect on them. This can be done if someone is already well known in a community; it can be done door-to-door, walking precincts in the old style of campaigning; or it can be done expensively through slick media advertising, targeted mailings, and the use of other campaign materials. If one candidate spends large amounts of money, the important variables are how well it is spent and how expenditures compare with those of one's opponent. In Ross Perot's multimillion-dollar campaign for the presidency in 1992, he spent an estimated $60 million of his own money in his unsuccessful bid for the White House. And in California, Michael Huffington spent $26 million of his own money in an unsuccessful attempt in 1994 to unseat Senator Dianne Feinstein. Huffington's comparative advantage in money overcame low name recognition, an ill-defined program, and a failure to make appearances around the state, to bring him within about 150,000 votes of Feinstein.

To assess campaigns one must take all of the relevant factors—money, candidate appeal, party support, campaign organization, volunteers, issues—and look at the comparative advantages of one candidate over the other. It may well be that a candidate with lots of money is faced with a more appealing opponent who has lots of volunteers. Financial backers are fully aware of the modern demands of selling a candidate. To be successful in modern politics, a candidate must be marketable. That is, there is a cluster of characteristics—physical appearance, voice, mannerisms—that makes for an attractive candidate in the era of media politics. Most analysts agree that, on the basis of media attractiveness, Abraham Lincoln would have great difficulty succeeding in modern politics.

Election Reform

To most advocates of democratic government, elections should be the pure expression of voter preference. We have seen that results can vary depending upon the rules used. In addition, results can also be made to vary by fraudulent methods such as ballot-box stuffing, intimidating voters, and having support-ers vote more than once. The old adage of the political machine was "vote early and vote often." Through various reforms we have been able to correct the more flagrant abuses. In the late 1800s, the secret ballot (sometimes called the Australian Ballot) was introduced, with the result that voters could no longer be easily intimidated to vote for a particular candidate. The use of machine voting has made it difficult to alter votes. But an innovation in elections to improve turnout—mailed ballots—has raised the issue of increased fraud. Several states now allow such elections; Oregon used one in 1995 to elect a replacement for Senator Robert Packwood, who had resigned. Partici-pation was about 10 percent greater than in prior special elections, the state saved $500,000, and fraud was apparently minimal. In addition, most states now require voters to register; those who don't participate are removed from the voter rolls.

Reform of Political Parties

The second area that has drawn the attention of reformers is that of preventing distortions in voter preference. One of these areas of concern was the political machine, the party organization that dictated candidates and controlled votes. A number of reforms were introduced in the late 1800s and early 1900s to deal with this problem. One of the most successful reforms was the introduc-tion of the direct primary as a means of selecting party candidates. No longer could the party bosses just pick whomever they wished. In some states, the party cannot even pick sides in a primary contest. Recall the discussion of this topic in the last chapter.

Some states adopted nonpartisan local elections to reduce the influence of the party organization. And many of these same states introduced direct democracy in the form of the initiative, recall, and referendum (discussed on p. 278), so that citizens could bypass party-controlled legislatures.

If anything, these reforms were too successful. Not only did they reduce the influence of political bosses, they undermined all political party organi-zations. The move in recent years has been to return some power and control to the political party, which has also become significant as a source of funding elections.

Financing Campaigns

Perhaps more important to the operation of the political system have been campaign finance reforms. As we have seen, campaigns are expensive. In an attempt to deal with the role of large contributors, limits have been placed on the amount of money one person can give and on what a party can give (see Figure 11.2). We have also adopted public funding as a means of con-trolling expenditures.

One major innovation attempting to gain control of the expenditure of money has been public financing. Campaign reforms adopted in 1973 after Watergate put limits on contributions and party expenditures; they also pro-

Figure 11.2

MAJOR FEDERAL CAMPAIGN-FINANCE RULES

General

• All federal election contributions and expenditures are reported to a six-person Federal Election Commission with power to investigate and prosecute violators.
• All contributions over $100 must be reported, with name, address, and occupation of contributor.
• No *cash* contributions over $100 and no foreign contributions.
• Candidate or campaign may spend any amount (unless a presidential candidate accepts federal funding).

Individual Contributions

• Limit of $1,000 to any candidate in any election per year.
• Limit of $20,000 per year to a national party committee or $5,000 to a political action committee.
• No limit on individual expenditures for "independent advertising."

Political Action Committees (PACs)

• A corporation, union, or other association may each establish one PAC.
• A PAC must register 6 months in advance, have at least 50 contributors, and give to at least 5 candidates.
• PAC contributions to a candidate may not exceed $5,000 per election, or to a national party, $15,000 per year.

Presidential Primaries

• Federal matching funds, dollar for dollar, are available for all money raised by candidates for individual donors giving $250 or less.
• To be eligible, a candidate must raise $5,000 in each of 20 states in contributions of $250 or less.

Presidential Election

• Federal government will pay all campaign costs (up to a certain ceiling) of major-party candidates and part of the cost of minor-party candidates (those winning between 5 and 25 percent of the vote).

Source: Federal Election Commission

vided for public funds to run presidential campaigns. The general election in 1992 had each major candidate receiving just over $55 million; the national parties received about $10 million to spend in that campaign. In addition, each major party received about $11 million to run its national convention. Finally, all candidates who met a threshold received federal matching funds during the nomination process. Winning candidates Bush and Clinton received over $10 million; loser Jerry Brown got about $4 million. Even minor party candidates obtained funding: Lenora Fulani of the New Alliance Party received about $1.5 million. The threshold these candidates must reach is a total of $5,000 from contributions of $250 or less in at least 20 states. The trade-off for candidates is that they must stay within the spending limit imposed by the FEC, which in 1992 was about $30 million total for the primaries and caucuses.

But there are ways around such limitations. One is called "soft money." That is, money collected for state and local party organizations that will be used for voter registration drives and get-out-the-vote activities does not come under the limitations imposed on individuals or parties. In 1992, these expenditures were estimated at $68 million (Wayne 1996, 47). National presidential candidates can charge off state-level staff workers to these accounts and not

Table 11.5

GROWTH OF POLITICAL ACTION COMMITTEES, 1974–1994

Year	Total Number of PACs	Corporate	Labor	Non-connected	Trade/Membership/Health	Other	Contributions to Congressional Candidates (in millions of $)
1974	608	89	201	–	318	–	$ 12.5
1976	1146	433	224	–	489	–	22.6
1978	1653	784	217	165	451	36	35.2
1980	2551	1204	297	378	574	98	55.2
1982	3371	1467	380	746	628	150	83.1
1984	4009	1682	394	1053	698	182	104.9
1986	4157	1744	384	1077	745	207	132.2
1988	4196	1806	355	1066	766	203	167.8
1990	4511	1908	365	1282	758	207	159.3
1992	4094	1738	338	1083	742	193	180.3
1994	3954	1660	333	980	792	189	178.8

Source: Federal Election Commission *Record.*

Political action committees were formed by the labor unions during and after World War II. There are two categories of PACs: (1) the segregated-fund type that solicits money from its parent organization and not the general public, and (2) the nonconnected type that raises money from the general public to independently support candidates. This table shows the various types of PACs that have developed since 1974.

have to use their public funds to pay for them. Individual contributors can give as much as they want to these types of activities.

Another way of dealing with the limits on personal and party spending is to form a **political action committee (PAC)**, an organization that raises funds and then distributes them to political candidates. For example, in 1994, PACs contributed over $150 million to House candidates. Unions developed these organizations after World War II to encourage and acknowledge their power, but as Table 11.5 illustrates, unions are now a distinct minority and have lost a good deal of their influence. Shown are the five categories of political action committees as designated by the Federal Elections Commission. Ironically, unions were instrumental in securing the changes allowing corporate donations (Sabato 1985).

Major corporations, trade associations, and ideological groups are now the major users of the PAC form of organization. Numbers do not tell the whole story. Looking at the donations of PACs in recent campaigns points more eloquently to their pervasiveness and importance as a source of funds. Figure 11.3 provides the figures for a recent congressional election. As candidates look for new money beyond their traditional source of contributions, the significance of PACs takes on an even greater role. Indeed the reform providing for public funding of presidential campaigns "had the effect of concentrating PAC money on congressional campaigns" (Sabato 1985, 9). Since individual contributions to a candidate have been limited in size, the PAC has become a dominant force in congressional elections. PACs gave the average

Figure 11.3

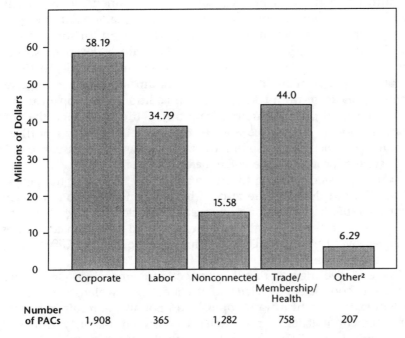

CONTRIBUTIONS TO CANDIDATES BY PACs[1]
(January 1989–December 1990)

[1]Ranked according to total amount contributed to candidates between January 1, 1989, and December 31, 1990.
[2]"Other" category consists of PACs formed by corporations without capital stock and PACs formed by cooperatives.

Source: Federal Election Commission, June 1991.

incumbent receipts of $230,000 out of $501,142 in 1994. Challengers raised $159,327, of which only $21,697 had come from PACs. In 1994, Republicans benefited from strong candidates and increases in both PAC support and individual support.

The public has become more concerned with PACs' influence, but when the subject is investigated, PACs are frequently hidden behind innocuous titles, such as the Citizens Non-Partisan Good Government Committee, a PAC of the Coca-Cola Company. Even with limits of $1,000 on individual contributions, candidates now find them more desirable, in part to avoid the stigma of a close relationship with PACs.

Most reforms have had the result of weakening the traditional party system. Whether we really wanted to weaken parties, as we have, or simply to eliminate the effects of boss rule, is another question. The result is a party system largely unable to pick its candidates, a system where individuals are self-selected for candidacy, and a system in which the candidates provide their financing and staffing largely from outside the formal party apparatus.

Elections and Policy

Just under half of the states have adopted direct democracy: the use of elections to make laws or remove officials from office. In an **initiative**, the citizen is permitted to write laws or even constitutional amendments and, if supported by the petition of enough other citizens (usually about five percent), can have that proposal voted upon at the next election. In some states, such as California, Oregon, and South Dakota, there are a dozen or so of these measures each election. Citizens can also petition to have a legislative enactment put to a vote of the people—a **referendum**—in which a negative vote prevents the measure from taking effect. In addition, the people can petition to have an elected official removed from office. If enough sign the petition, a **recall election** is held to see whether the official is to stay in office. State and local governments can also propose tax increases or the issuance of bonds that must be approved by the voters before they take effect.

Daniel Webster, referring to Congress, stated, "Here, Sir, the people govern." Most of our decisions are reached by representatives we have chosen in elections: a republican form of government. How closely linked, then, are the choices of citizens expressed through elections and the ultimate policies that are adopted by government? This is an important question, for it goes to the heart of the system.

The evidence suggests that the connection is imperfect. On the negative side, there is considerable evidence that issues upon which there has been a consistent expression of majority opinion do not always result in corresponding government policies. For example, a consistent majority expressed the opinion during the 1980s that we should not interfere in the internal affairs of Central American countries. Yet, American policy just as consistently condoned such intervention. In some cases, the political leadership of the country is just out of step with the views of most citizens. Ronald Reagan was one of the most popular presidents in recent history, yet most Americans disagreed with his policy positions most of the time. This was the case in the Central American example above. It was also true of issues such as abortion, environmental protection, and so on.

On the positive side, there is much evidence that, however imperfectly, a good many of the majority opinions in the country do get translated into government policy. Most would agree, for example, that the programs of the Great Society, adopted in 1965–66, could not have happened without the election of a large number of liberals in 1964. But the groundwork for this liberal shift can also be traced to 1958, when there was also a liberal swing. From 1959 until 1965, there was a growing clamor for more attention to urban problems and more liberal social policies championed by this group. With additional liberals elected in 1964, Congress enacted a sweeping array of liberal legislation. The election of 1980 provides another instance where the electorate gave a fairly consistent indication of the type of policies they wished enacted. Not only did Ronald Reagan win the presidency, but a number of well-known liberal members of Congress were defeated. During 1981–83, there was a working conservative majority in

Congress: Reagan was able to secure passage of the major tax and budget components of his agenda. The election of 1994 resulted in major policy initiatives coming from the new Republican majority. Some were clearly favored by the voting majority that elected them; others, as they became known, did not have majority support.

Most elections do not give a clear message for a very simple reason: There is no clear, consistent policy position held by the electorate. To state the same problem somewhat differently, much of the indecision toward various policies in Washington is a reflection of a diversity of positions among the American electorate. There are those who would place environmental protection ahead of other policy choices, for example; there are others who would choose economic growth ahead of the environment. There is no real way to enact legislation that would please every constituency.

Summary

Rules governing elections have a major impact on who is elected as well as on the structure and number of political parties. For congressional and most legislative elections, we use the single-member district under plurality rules. This system favors a two-party system. In addition, legal and political restraints structure the opportunity for individuals seeking a political career.

We use a variety of rules to elect our president. Beginning with popular primaries and caucuses in the spring, candidates are winnowed out, usually early in the process. The winner is usually apparent long before the national party conventions, but conventions do serve as an important campaign event. Party nominees then compete for electoral votes; selection as president requires an absolute majority, or 270, to win. Attempts to reform elections and parties have largely failed to work, although they have had an impact on how elections are conducted and how money is raised. Election outcomes can have an impact on public policy, but it usually takes several elections for a transition to occur, and the connection between election outcomes and policy is modest, at best.

Analytical Exercises

1. The difficulties of implementing majoritarian principles in practice are compounded by logical difficulties. For example, let us assume that a committee composed of three members, Rachel, Kim, and John, is faced by three alternatives to a problem: A, B, and C. The choice is to be made by majority rule; that is, two votes are needed to win. For a majority to express itself, that option must be able to defeat all other options in one-on-one comparisons. That is, the committee will first consider whether it prefers A to B, then B to C, and finally A to C. Further, let us assume that the committee members have the following preference orderings of the three alternatives:

Member	1st Choice	2nd Choice	3rd Choice
Rachel	A	B	C
Kim	B	C	A
John	C	A	B

Notice that we are in the same situation as found on page 260 when we were trying to choose a second candidate to face Brooks in a runoff election. Which alternative is preferred by a majority of the committee? In real political situations, we seldom have a vote concerning each possible pairing; rather, one pair is voted upon first and then the winner is placed against the next alternative. Assume that Rachel is chair of the committee and can control the order of one-on-one comparisons. Is there a way for her to schedule the vote so that her first choice, A, wins? Is there a way for Kim and John to prevent A from winning? Is there a generalization you can reach about which option in a sequence of votes has the best chance of success? About the importance of controlling the agenda?

2. One problem with our election system—and with most methods of voting—is that there is no way to express the intensity of one's feelings toward each candidate. I may rank Allyson first and Brooks second, but there is no way I would want Brooks to win, nor would I ever vote for him. You may have the same rank order, but to you there is so little difference between them that it doesn't really matter who wins; you would be happy with either.

This exercise uses voting rules that try to account for intensity. I have added some additional information for this exercise. Below each rank is a score that indicates the distance between each choice. I have assigned a "1" to each first choice and a ".5" to each fifth-place vote. The amount given the second-, third-, and fourth-place candidates is determined by the distance between them in each voter's mind. For example, for Prescott the difference between Allyson and David is not great, but after that there is a wide gap; for Smythe, after first place there is a wide gap—the middle three candidates are all closely rated, but at the bottom of the scale.

One interesting voting rule, proposed by political scientist Stephen Brams, is called approval voting. In this system, you can cast a vote for all of those candidates of whom you approve. Let's say that all voters are willing to cast a vote for any candidate rated .75 or higher. Who would be the winner? (By the way, some organizations—the American Statistical Association, for example—are

Candidate Voter	Allyson	Brooks	Cassandra	David	Evie
Prescott	1 1.0	5 .50	4 .55	2 .95	3 .60
Smythe	2 .61	3 .60	5 .50	1 1.0	4 .59
Travis	3 .70	4 .55	2 .80	5 .50	1 1.0
Quinones	5 .50	1 1.0	4 .65	2 .90	3 .71

adopting this system as the fairest technique in elections where there are multiple candidates.)

Another voting rule, proposed by the nineteenth-century philosopher Jeremy Bentham, would have us add the preference scores (not the ranks, but the scores that range from .5 to 1). Who wins in this case?

A variation on this rule, proposed by Nash in the 1950s, is to multiply each of a candidate's preference scores to create a new score. Who wins now?

Condorcet, an eighteenth-century mathematician and philosopher, proposed that elections be decided in pair-wise comparisons. Any candidate who could beat all the other candidates in these two-person races would be the winner. A variation of this would be to declare as winner the candidate who wins the most of these pair-wise comparisons. Who would that be?

12

Interest Groups

The only people that come to my office are dedicated, veteran patriots. . . . The other departments get lobbyists.

—Edward J. Derwinski, Secretary of Veterans Affairs, July 28, 1989

I seen my opportunities and I took 'em. My party's in power in the city, and . . . I'm tipped off; say, that they're going to lay out a new park at a certain place. . . . I go to that place and I buy up all the land I can in the neighborhood. Then the board of this or that makes its plan public, and there is a rush to get my land, which nobody cared particular for before.

Ain't it perfectly honest to charge a good price and make a profit on my investment and foresight? Of course, it is. Well, that's honest graft.

—George W. Plunkett, in W. L. Riordon, *Plunkett of Tammany Hall*, 1963

Working with others to further our mutual interests has been a feature of the American system since its beginning. Alexis de Tocqueville, in his travels to this country in the 1830s, noted, "In no country of the world has the principle of association been more successfully used, or applied to a greater multitude of objects, than in America" (1956, 95). Nor was this unforeseen by the Framers. James Madison, in his famous paper *The Federalist* No. 10 (1787), states:

> A landed interest, a manufacturing interest, a mercantile interest, a moneyed interest, with many lesser interests, grow up of necessity in civilized nations, and divide them into different classes, actuated by different sentiments and views. The regulation of these various and interfering interests

forms the principal task of modern legislation and involves the spirit of party and faction in the necessary and ordinary operations of government.

Madison believed that the most significant interests were related to property, and he pitted those with it against those without it. Please keep this assumption in mind as we explore this topic to see whether Madison's contention holds true today.

Political Interest Groups and Political Parties

Political interest groups are organizations that seek to influence public policy. They may be classified into two major categories: institutional and individual membership.

Institutional interest groups may represent corporations, governments, foundations, and universities. Sometimes they act in concert with other institutions under umbrella organizations. Some examples of these are the American Cotton Manufacturers Institute, the United States Chamber of Commerce, the American Council on Education, and the American Public Transit Association. These groups basically are attempting to influence government actions in a way that would be beneficial to their own organizations.

Individual membership interest groups are formed and joined on the basis of an individual's sense of obligation or loyalty to a cause represented by the group. Thus people might join and help to finance such groups as the National Association for the Advancement of Colored People (NAACP), the National Organization for Women (NOW), the Sierra Club, or the Christian Coalition. The essential difference between membership groups and institutional groups is in the source of power and direction of the leadership. Both try to influence those who make decisions in government. Leaders of individual membership groups are in some ways constrained by what their members want or are willing to do. They derive legitimacy from the group as a whole, and their actions are thus directed by the needs of the individual members of the group. Institutions, on the other hand, have lives of their own, independent of any membership. Their leaders make decisions based on the needs of the institution, not necessarily of those who make up the institution. For example, in responding to institutional concerns, Congress allowed savings and loan banks to make investments previously prohibited, investments that proved to be so risky that we are now faced with huge costs to keep the industry alive. The failure of the savings and loan industry is costing American taxpayers about $200 billion. While part of the cost, and of the reason for bailing out the industry, is to protect individual depositors—those who made deposits in thrifts that failed are guaranteed their initial investments—the major reason is to protect the entire banking system. Although the concerns of the bank employees were considered in this action, as were the interests of the workers when Chrysler Corporation was bailed out several years ago, the request from the bankers and the government's response were largely independent of the people concerned.

The primary objective of our two major political parties is to win elections. To do this requires a pragmatic nature, an ability to find consensus or common ground among conflicting or competing interests in order to secure the votes to win elections. This pragmatism makes it difficult for our party system to represent the interests of relatively small numbers of people. Interest groups are more concerned with specific policies, often giving support to both parties in hopes of gaining favorable decisions. "You buy war bonds on both sides," stated Peter Barton, president of the nation's largest cable TV company (Auletta 1995, 53). Nevertheless, in an effort to influence an administration as well as help to form it, political interest groups often give support to a particular political party; they may in fact be an important constituent in the party itself.

Some interest groups have always been concerned with the selection of candidates from within their membership, in order to influence or even gain control of the party apparatus for group advantage. Unions have always had political interests; religious groups have had them as well. A politician from Detroit, for example, does not arrive in Congress without union support, and it would be difficult for someone who was not a Mormon to win elected office in Utah. Conservative Christian groups have made significant inroads in taking control of and naming the candidates of the Republican party in a number of states. A study conducted by *Campaigns and Elections* found that the Christian Right is the dominant force in the Republican Party in 18 states and has substantial control in 13 others (Persinos 1994, 22). Thus, from within the ranks of a union or a religious group comes a candidate for office who supports that particular group; he or she will then be in a position to work for legislation that will be advantageous to that group and to block what would be disadvantageous to the group.

Interest Groups and Elections

Most political interest groups are ill-suited to manipulate elections in the United States. Either they are so dispersed or their memberships are so small that they are unable to wield much influence over elections. Such groups, however, can and do provide many services that make parties more effective and provide much of their needed personpower. This applies particularly to organizations that have large memberships. The American Federation of Labor and Congress of Industrial Organizations (AFL-CIO) consistently has been a strong supporter of the Democratic Party, and it provides much of the personpower to organize, distribute campaign literature, raise money, and assure the party of the presence of Democratic voters at the polls. Nevertheless, a union, or any other group for that matter, must present issues that clearly and directly affect the basic interests of the group in order to deliver the votes in elections.

Interest Groups and Money

With the changes in campaign finance laws, as well as other reforms that have weakened traditional party structures, mentioned in chapter 10, candi-

Table 12.1

LARGEST PAC CONTRIBUTORS TO CONGRESSIONAL CANDIDATES 1985–1994

Industry	Contribution
Banking and Finance	$56,096,840
Energy: Oil, Gas, Coal, and Utilities	50,494,379
Agribusiness and Food Processors	48,901,280
Transportation Unions	45,928,239
Insurance	42,120,605
Real Estate	40,692,087
Communications and Media	37,994,112
Government Employee Unions	37,443,503
Doctors', Dentists', and Nurses' Associations	36,831,744
Transportation Companies	30,148,453

Source: Common Cause, 1995.

PACs were formed to provide a legal method of contributing money to political campaigns. Over the past 10 years, such major groups as the American Bankers Association, American Medical Association, National Education Association, and Realtors PACs have been regular contributors to congressional candidates.

dates have been drawn to group support in the past two decades. The amount of money that a group or an individual can contribute to a political campaign is limited by law (see the discussion in chapter 11, Electoral and Voting Systems, pp. 274–277). We saw that in spite of this limitation, major political interest groups spend hundreds of thousands of dollars to secure the election of candidates they support. Table 12.1, for example, gives the top 10 PAC contributors to congressional candidates in the last decade. Year after year the PACs of realtors, physicians, and public employee unions lead the list of contributors. One of the most influential Washington lobbyists, Tommy Boggs, son of former representatives Hale and Lindy Boggs, gives one explanation for continued contributions by groups.

> "Contributions are more a defensive than an offensive tool," Boggs said. "In my case, if I don't give money to a member, his or her attitude is, 'Why did you contribute to Senator X and not to me?' You must contribute enough so that some member won't complain that you're not participating. Then, even if you don't give enough to be recognized as one of the inner circle, you won't be treated like an outcast, either." (Birnbaum 1992, 163)

Continued negative publicity about interest groups and PACs has led to a fall-off in their contributions and an increase in individual support—often orchestrated by affected interests. Charles R. Babcock found that "the average PAC donation in 1992 was about $1,600 according to FEC; the median was $1,000; the mode was $500. There are members 'who can raise $200,000 at one event from wealthy individuals writing $1,000 checks,' states Rep. Corrine Brown" (1994, 15).

Groups have also found other ways to give financial support to decision makers, such as making "soft-money" contributions, also noted in chapter ll. Financial support given by groups to decision makers as gifts, travel and honoraria—payments for a public official's appearance or speech, usually at a group's convention or corporate retreat—have become especially controversial. In an attempt to deal with the problem, Congress, in exchange for a general pay increase in 1991 and 1992, required honoraria to be given to charity. In addition, gifts and other financial support to government officials are limited and must be disclosed. Attempts to forbid free travel and resort living failed in 1994, but were adopted in 1995, along with major changes requiring that lobbyists register and submit reports. These new rules are expected to increase the number of registered lobbyists by 3 to 10 times beyond the 6,000 who are now obliged to register under existing laws (Clymer 1995).

The Growth of Interest Groups

Individuals who have particular needs or demands have found it to their advantage to join other like-minded individuals to secure advantage. And, as noted by Tocqueville, political interest group activity has been widespread in the United States from its inception. But in recent years we have witnessed a great increase in the number of political interest and **clientele groups**, or those that benefit from government programs. V. O. Key was one of the first to recognize that:

> Increased specialization [in society] almost inevitably means increased governmental intervention to control the relations among groups. In turn, governmental intervention, or its threat, stimulates the formation of organized groups by those who begin to sense a shared interest. . . . Almost every proposed law represents the effort of one group to do something to another. . . . Organization begets counter-organization. (1958, 143)

While we have had the organized promotion of interest for some time, there are indications that events of the past decade or so have made the representation of interest fundamentally different from what it was 35 years ago. Specialists in the field indicate that the following changes have occurred:

1. A great proliferation of interest groups since the early 1960s.
2. A centralization of group headquarters in Washington, D.C., rather than New York City or elsewhere.
3. Major technological developments in information processing that promote more sophisticated, timely, and specialized grass-roots lobbying.
4. The rise of single-issue groups.
5. Changes in campaign finance laws (1971, 1974) and the ensuing growth of political action committees (PACs).
6. The increased formal penetration of political and economic interests into the bureaucracy (advisory committees), the presidency (White

House group representatives), and the Congress (caucuses of members).

7. The continuing decline of political parties' abilities to perform key electoral and policy-related activities.

8. The increased number, activity, and visibility of so-called public interest groups, such as Common Cause [a group concerned with governmental reform and instrumental in the campaign finance reforms] and Ralph Nader–inspired public interest research organizations (Loomis and Cigler 1983, 1–2). **Public interest groups** seek to support causes from which they receive no direct economic gain. The benefits are to be enjoyed by the public at large.

This listing suggests two things of particular importance here: there are many more groups than ever before, and they are concentrated in Washington. The citation by Key above indicates that increased government activity leads to more groups; we can trace this growth in part to a change in our philosophy of government with the Depression of the 1930s and the programs President Roosevelt instituted to combat it. But it was the great leap of national government intrusion into our lives with the adoption of Great Society programs of the mid-1960s that has led to present group activity. Not only were there significant amounts of money to be spent on education, health care, and economic infrastructure, for example, but there were significant increases in the rules and regulations governing our lives.

The Bias of the Interest Group System

Groups are unevenly distributed throughout society. E. E. Schattschneider, in his classic study of groups, notes that "if everybody got into the act the unique advantage of this form of organization [political interest groups] would be destroyed, for it is possible that if all interests could be mobilized the result would be a stalemate" (1960, 35). Indeed, as Schattschneider contends, political interest groups are biased in favor of higher-income groups; even citizens' groups that rely on financial contributions from individuals reflect this bias. For example, of the more than 6,000 lobbies registered with Congress in 1994, over two-thirds were related to corporate and business interests (*CQ Almanac* 1994). Not only do business interests represent the most numerous type of lobby, they are also considered the most effective.

The multitude of blue-collar workers, consumers, white-collar workers, and farmers are organized only in special circumstances, but business interests are organized as a general rule. *In other words, the groups most likely to express interest in our nation's government represent those that already have secured most of the benefits of American society.* A sizable segment of the population—Schattschneider suggests about 40 percent—simply is not included in the material rewards of society. Madison's insight about property and moneyed interests, quoted at the beginning of the chapter, holds true today, perhaps to a greater degree than in 1787.

Drawing by Joseph Farris; © 1993 The New Yorker Magazine, Inc.

"A <u>very</u> special interest to see you, Senator."

Even for those individuals who are well-off, organized political effort requires time, energy, and resources, and the payoff may not be enough to justify these investments. Institutions, then, which have already organized for whatever other purpose, can undertake political action more easily.

Access to Decision Makers

How do political interest groups secure the benefits dispensed by the government? Figure 12.1, next page, provides a graphic portrayal of the process. Access, or the ability to reach and talk to decision makers, is crucial. "Power of any kind cannot be reached by a political interest group, or its leaders, without access to one or more key points of decision in the government," states David Truman in a classic study of the role of groups (1951, 264).

The importance of campaign contributions as a means of access is candidly portrayed by former senator Alan Cranston (D-CA), who was the source of considerable controversy after revelations of his intervention on behalf of Charles Keating and Lincoln Savings and Loan, a failed S&L. Keating had contributed a total of $1.4 million to the campaign funds of Cranston and

Figure 12.1

HOW INTEREST GROUPS WORK

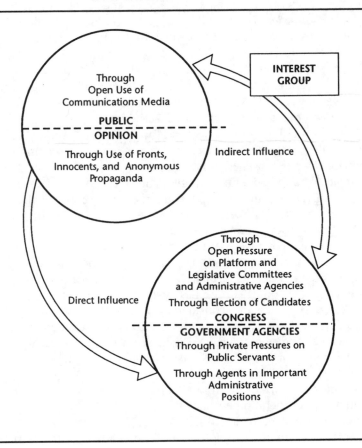

four other senators in exchange, it was charged, for seeking the delay of administrative action that would have effectively shut down the Lincoln Savings and Loan. "Realistically," Cranston said, "somebody who knows you does get access, whereas someone you've never heard of, or who hasn't helped you in the campaign, may not get direct access to you" (Liebert 1989, A29). Just as candid was Justin Dart, founder and chair of Dart Industries: "Talking with politicians is a fine thing, but with a little money they hear you better" (*Wall Street Journal* August 15, 1978, 1).

For several reasons, political interest groups' accessibility to key decision makers is greater in the United States than in other countries. First, there are over 500,000 elected officials in the United States, each representing a potential alliance of political interests. Second, a system of separate institutions at the national level proliferates the number of decision makers and, consequently, points of access. Finally, our federal system provides further entry points for the expression of interest. Many interests need only secure support on a local, state, or regional basis, at least to begin with. "Because their outlets exist almost everywhere, fast-food companies become embroiled in political battles on many fronts [governments at the state and local levels] other than Washington" (*Washington Lobby* 1982, 123). The federal system provides a decision-making framework for this type of lobbying to be accomplished. There are over 80,000 local governing bodies, including school districts and special districts, as well as cities, counties, and states. Contrast this federal system with the centralized parliamentary system in the United Kingdom, where effective power resides in the executive departments in the nation's capital, and most groups concentrate their activities there.

The trend toward greater concentration of interest group activity in Washington is also accounted for, "because the cost of rent seeking—lobbying government for special subsidies, privileges, and protections—is less in Washington, in relation to the benefits available from national legislation, than the combined cost of rent seeking at eighty-three thousand subnational centers. . . . Lobbying in Washington is efficient" (Dye 1990, 53). In the first chapter, I introduced the story of the Tragedy of the Commons, one aspect of which was a situation where costs were dispersed over the whole group and benefits concentrated in a few. Here we see the same situation. National decisions disperse costs; special interests gain individual benefit for a minimal investment in lobbying. This point can be best seen by looking at a specific policy area like tobacco subsidies and considering what the case would be if that special advantage did not exist. Economist Randall G. Holcombe speculates that the tobacco subsidies granted by Washington to North Carolina farmers would not be voted for by the residents of that state if they had to pay the full costs of these subsidies (1986, 174).

As with most important questions of policy, there is another side to the nationalization of conflict. Some policies can be handled only at the national level—they are too expensive for smaller units of government, or there are serious external costs imposed by other governmental units that can be overcome only by concerted national effort. There can also be subunit policies to which a national majority takes great moral exception—abridging civil rights for African Americans would be the most dramatic example—and that can be dealt with effectively only at the national level.

Political decisions are seldom neutral in their effect: some people are going to benefit, while others are going to pay the cost. Changing a decision from a national to a subnational responsibility has consequences for the relative advantage and disadvantage of various groups. The same is true of the decision to make a given policy area a matter of public decision. Where decisions in private arenas are favorable to a group, a continuous effort is maintained to persuade the government not to interfere. Groups that have been disadvantaged by privately reached decisions are, of course, among the most eloquent proponents of expanding the arena of public policy. The effort by farm workers to be covered by the same laws that protect industrial workers is a recent example.

Although numerous avenues of access have led to a proliferation of group activity, not all groups have an equal chance to influence government decisions. Because resources vary, a group must maneuver in such a manner that the resources available to it exert the greatest possible influence. For example, a small group with specialized knowledge, such as a professional association, is most effective in lobbying the bureaucracy, while a group with a sizable voting membership is more effective in directly influencing elected officials. Groups with a small, homogeneous membership and limited interests might want to keep to themselves access to decision makers. One way to do this is to get a separate bureaucratic agency or congressional subcommittee to deal entirely with the concerns of the special interest. In such a situation, "communications will be relatively easy. . . . The agency, in reaching its decision, will have access to a limited amount of information from a single point of view," and, furthermore, "the regulated interests, in presenting arguments, will not have to compete with opposing interests" (Zeigler and Peak 1972, 163).

One solution to counteract this interest group effect is to provide public goods and services at the lowest level of government possible. This concentrates the cost of lobbying on the smallest group of taxpayers that will gain from the concentrated benefits (Holcombe 1986, 174). Certainly, one of the consequences of Republican efforts, once they gained control of Congress in 1995, to return numerous government functions to state and local governments would be to alter the basic power and strategies of political interest groups.

State and local governments, as a general rule, are more responsive than the federal government to the preferences of taxpayers, who are usually more cost conscious than benefit conscious. "This greater responsiveness is not only a product of competition [competing demands for support and competing units of government at the state and local level] but also a result of institutional arrangements in these governments that link taxing and spending decisions" (Dye 1990, 96).

Influencing Decisions: The Lobbyists

The image of a cigar-smoking, rotund, greasy character waiting in the halls of Congress to ply his trade may come to mind when we think of a lobbyist, but it hardly fits reality now, if it ever did. Literally thousands of firms, associations, groups, government agencies, and foreign governments have representatives who attempt to influence legislation. These representatives are called **lobbyists**. Lobbying is the choice:

a. When there is a reasonable likelihood that Congress will take action that will affect policy in the preferred direction.
b. When the organization has enough available resources so that it can afford to invest time, energy, money, and good will in lobbying.
c. When lobbying or its results do *not* run a great risk of becoming counterproductive. (Dexter 1969, 56)

The lobbyists' three major weapons are inside supporters, information, and money. Insiders are members or staffers sympathetic to the interests at hand. For many, their interest was their business before they came to Congress, or it is a major factor in their district or state. In administrative agencies, many ranking bureaucrats are drawn from the industry being dealt with and to which they usually expect to return after government service. Using this base of support, an interest group is able to build a coalition of support for its position.

Information is at the heart of legislative power. Bruce C. Wolpe, in his study of congressional lobbying, notes that "Lobbying is the political management of information" (1990, 9). Wolpe gives five commandments for successful lobbying in Table 12.2. Lobbyists are valuable sources of expertise. And most of them play on this aspect of their role, ensuring that members of Congress are provided with studies and other data supporting their group's position. But there is more: Much of the legislation passed by Congress is first written by lobbying groups. For example, the revisions to the Clean Water Act in 1995 included significant modifications long sought by industry groups. "This is because the bill's sponsors and a committee of lobbyists worked side by side on the bill, inserting one provision after another to satisfy industry groups like the Chemical Manufacturers Association"(Cushman 1995, A-1). In addition, much of the testimony given at hearings and much of the orchestrated activity on behalf of a piece of legislation emanates from lobbying groups. Illustrative of this latter point was a demonstration of the difference in quality between Mexican and American tomatoes by lobbyists for Mexican interests. They dropped a sample of each on the floor before a congressional panel: The Mexican tomato splattered; the American one bounced knee high. "The point was not lost on committee members" (Wittenberg and Wittenberg 1989, 112).

A lobbyist can be an official of an organization with an office in Washington or a ranking official from the home office. But as specialization increases, the lobbyist is more often a Washington lobbyist, a lawyer with one of the major firms or a former government official in a public relations firm, who represents a variety of organizations. An organization can secure the services of extremely influential people this way. For example, sugar interests in 1965 secured the services of these advocates:

> Oscar Chapman, attorney, former Secretary of the Interior under President Truman, chairman in 1964 of a national fund-raising group called "Johnson for President"; Donald Dawson, attorney, "a former Truman aide" . . . ; Robert L. Farrington, "former general counsel at the Agriculture Department during the Eisenhower Administration"; Robert Shields, . . . former Assistant Secretary of Agriculture; [and] Irvin A. Hoff, formerly a "top assistant to Senator Warren Magnuson (D-WA) . . . [who] in 1964 ran the presidential campaign in the western states." (Hall 1969, 6)

Why they might want such high-powered representation is explained in Philip M. Stern's account of the cost of the sugar quota to American consumers: $3 billion a year. In 1990, the average price of sugar in the world market "was seventeen cents per pound; in the United States the price was twenty-three cents per pound" (1992, 170).

The importance of having former government officials as lobbyists is evident from a glance at Hall's list. The transition from an important position

Table 12.2

THE FIVE COMMANDMENTS OF SUCCESSFUL LOBBYING

1. Tell the truth.
2. Never promise more than you can deliver.
3. Know how to listen so that you accurately understand what you are hearing.
4. Staff is there to be worked with and not circumvented.
5. Spring no surprises.

Source: Bruce C. Wolpe, *Lobbying Congress: How the System Works* (Washington, DC: CQ Press, 1990, pp. 9–15).

in an executive bureau or from Congress to a lobbying position on behalf of major corporations or groups is fairly easy. Alan Rosenthal, a leading student of lobbying, claims that "Lobbying is an appealing trade because political practitioners want to stay in politics and legislators and legislative staff want to continue playing roles in the process" (1993, 31). Rosenthal cites data from Robert Salisbury, a leading authority on the subject, that half of the lobbyists in Washington have had previous government employment (29). He indicates that the money that can be made is appealing as well. Despite attempts to prevent a "revolving door" between Congress and lobbying by requiring a year's cooling-off period before former members or staffers can lobby their former colleagues, there still seems to be a steady interchange. Four out of ten departing members in 1992 joined firms or started consulting businesses in the capital. "Even during the cooling-off period, ex-members aren't barred from devising legislative strategy for their clients," and "Nothing in the law ever prevented the ex-members from lobbying the executive branch" (Calmes 1995, A16). Previous government service may not always be an asset, though. For example, Dean Acheson, after his term as secretary of state from 1949–53, felt he had become too "controversial" to be an effective drawing card for his law firm (Goulden, 1970, p. 57).

Influencing Decisions: The Insiders

The elected official poses another problem for understanding the representation of interest. After all, elected officials can and do represent others—their constituents, a major economic interest in their district, and some other special interests. But they can also act on their own. William C. Mitchell writes:

> Office-holders are the major articulators on policy matters, raising and shaping issues themselves, even if in conjunction with key external groups. It is they, after all, who have the most direct "access," namely, the means and perquisites of their own office. (1962, 284)

Interest groups are often seen by analysts as being outside the system and working their will on it; officials respond to group pressures; laws are the outcome of the groups' struggles. But the key to an understanding of interest groups is the concept of representation: Interests are represented at times by lobbyists or advocates of groups, at times by officials of institutions, and at times by government representatives themselves.

Interest groups have also been active in creating organizations within Congress, such as the Black or Women's Caucus. These caucuses can be simply conduits for information among members or they can serve as the bases for efforts to affect legislation. The Steel Caucus, for example, was instrumental in having the Clean Air Act of 1981 amended to allow exemptions to steel mills in meeting clean air standards. Congressional Republicans discontinued providing space and support to these organizations in 1995, the impact of which is yet to be determined.

Many groups have legal advantages conferred on them just as parties do and are given governmental functions to perform. Licensing boards in most states, such as those administering the bar and medical exams, are really interest groups themselves, controlling entry into the groups.

REGULATION OF LOBBYISTS   Those concerned with the propriety of government decisions have suggested that more regulation of lobbyists is necessary, but the action to accomplish this end has had little consequence. By a 1946 law, the Federal Regulation of Lobbying Act, any person engaged in lobbying must (1) register with the House Clerk or the Senate Secretary, and (2) file quarterly reports concerning his or her receipts and expenditures for lobbying. The Justice Department in 1988 indicated that it had processed only five cases for violation of this particular act, and only one—concerning the natural gas lobby—had ended in conviction (*Lobbying* 1990). Regulation is difficult, even questionable, because it essentially infringes on the constitutional rights of free speech and petitioning the government.

The very nature of lobbying poses difficulty in controlling it through statutes. Public myth would have it that most lobbies and lobbyists use bribery to secure votes. There are other more effective, and legal, methods, however. Any lobbyist counts on the good will of members who are basically in agreement with the position taken by the group the lobbyist represents. This can be because of shared interests stemming from former employment of the member or from basic needs of the district or state. It can also come from support by the interest group. For example, the Campaign Research Center found that from 1986 to 1990, "PACs affiliated with commercial banks gave $2.7 million to the 51 members of the Banking Committee, or $53,737 per member" (*CQ Weekly Report* August 24, 1992, 2315). This study also showed similar contributions to members of the Senate Banking Committee as well as contributions from insurance PACs to members of the Energy and Commerce Committee. Building on such a nucleus of sympathetic members, lobbyists for bankers might secure support for their programs. With PACs getting negative publicity, however, there is now an increased use of private donations from individuals within an affected area. Health care reform provides an illustration. During the recent debates over changes in our health care system, contributions from health and insurance PACs increased 23 percent over the previous reporting period (*CQ Weekly Report* May 21, 1994, 1332). However, contributions from health care professionals increased by 52 percent. Often these individual contributions are "bundled" by the lobby group, or individuals from the affected policy area make a point of showing up at a politician's fund-raiser—informal bundling (1333). In the area of individual contributions, lawyers and lobbyists are the biggest contributors, usually on behalf of business or corporate interests. Indeed, in 1992 individual contributions on behalf of business exceeded PAC contributions; individual union members, by contrast, make virtually no contributions (Markinson and Goldstein 1994, 22).

Contacts between lobbyists and members of Congress tend to be informal, perhaps by telephone, meetings in the halls of Congress, or being at the same social event. Having a personal relationship with key decision makers is invaluable, as is having entrée to those places where decision makers will be.

Some groups make no direct contact at all; instead they direct public relations campaigns to a member's constituents. With modern telecommunications, groups can generate considerable mail from the district or state directed at the member. There are times when, in fact, the connection between a group's desires and those of a member's constituents is legitimate.

Frequently lobbyists try to convince a member that it is in his or her district's best interest to support a particular bill. If successful, of course, they have won an ally at minimal cost.

In addition, formal appearances at committee hearings are important, because at these hearings the factual foundation of legislation is recorded. Lobbyists are often effective in the legislative arena primarily because of their ability to provide the expertise that a busy and harried member has not acquired. With an inside knowledge of Congress and the government, a good lobbyist is able to present a point of view successfully.

Even with these skills, however, one still needs the fortuitous event to make things happen. One lobbyist sums it up as follows:

> When you lobby for something, what you have to do is put together your coalition, you have to gear up, you have to get your political forces in line, and then you all sit there and wait for the fortuitous event. For example, people who were trying to do something about regulation of railroads tried to ride the environment for a while, but that wave didn't wash them in to shore. So they grabbed their surfboards and they tried to ride something else, but that didn't do the job. The Penn Central collapse was the big wave that brought them in. As I see it, people who are trying to advocate change are like surfers waiting for the big wave. You get out there, you have to be ready to go, you have to be ready to paddle. If you're not ready to paddle when the big wave comes along, you're not going to ride it in. (Kingdon 1984, 173)

Despite the pressure lobbyists are able to bring on members of Congress, they cannot easily influence legislation. Undeniably, members with homogeneous districts or states that have overriding economic or social interests ignore lobbies at the peril of losing their jobs at the next election. Members from such districts do not need to be pressured into supporting their districts: in all likelihood, they have been in tune with their constituents from the start. Nevertheless, a member usually represents a diverse economic and cultural constituency, which allows him or her, on the one hand, to be harassed by the many factions in his or her district, and, on the other hand, of necessity, to be selective. In this way, the member remains essentially free to select those issues he or she wishes to represent.

For example, "when insurance companies stood to take a large tax increase they called out their heavy hitters but to no avail. After visits to leading legislators, 'Those meetings produced some sympathy, but most of them shrugged their shoulders and wished you well,' [lobbyist Wayne] Thevenot said. 'They were pretty honest about it: There wasn't much they could do' " (Birnbaum 1992, 291). Another account claims that a leading member of the House Ways and Means Committee had so many requests to meet with lobbyists that he was able to see only about five percent of them (Rosenheim 1986, 1). Louis Dexter, in a classic study, refers to lobbying as "emergency fire-fighting," most effective in short-term crises, especially if the issue involved is vital to the interests of the group (1972, 345).

The view of lobbyists as limited actors may be accurate and yet still miss the point. The lobbyist remains able to provide some information, some help, some push, that will result in the desired legislation, often at great cost to the general public, and often at odds with generally accepted social policy.

Interest Groups, Bureaucracy, and Courts

"There are a number of instances in which [interest groups find that] aid by legislative action is harder to get than aid in some other way" (Dexter 1969, 75). Because many bureaucratic agencies have legislative and judicial functions in addition to their administrative duties, political interest groups are usually prepared to represent their interests to the agencies that directly affect them. Independent regulatory commissions receive special attention from economic interests because of the significant economic advantage gained by favorable rulings and the relative assurance that the commission's decisions and activities will seldom be challenged in court or by Congress or the president. United Air Lines, for example, in competition with several other major carriers in 1990, secured a lucrative air route to Tokyo from the Civil Aeronautics Board.

Political interest groups are able to maneuver and operate behind the public scene within the offices and agencies of the federal bureaucracy. Thus it is fairer to criticize interest-group activities among the bureaucracy than anywhere else. Part of the criticism stems from the reasonably free interchange of personnel between industry and bureaucratic agencies in the executive branch. "Subcabinet appointments tend to mirror the diverse clientele groups, dependencies such as defense contractors, construction companies, educational institutions, and professional organizations that constitute an agency's constituency" (Seidman 1970, 104). Or, to take another example, the prestigious Washington law firm of Covington and Burling has what amounts to a permanent slot reserved for one of its lawyers in the Solicitor General's office. "There are twelve lawyers in the office, and for the past two decades one has always come from Covington and Burling—generally for a two-year term with a partnership when he returns to private practice" (Goulden 1970, 56). The importance of such a position becomes apparent when you realize that the major function of the Solicitor General's office is to determine which federal cases are to be appealed to higher courts.

Another area of growing concern is the use of a private contractor to study some problem or to perform some govenment function. With Republicans calling for "privatization" and Democrats supporting "reinventing government," there is an increased use of the private sector. This opens the way for fierce competition over who is to perform what. If decisions are based strictly on the merits—the best service at the lowest price—there is no problem; if the decisions are used to favor one's friends or those who have contributed the most, we may all pay dearly.

Iron Triangles and Issue Networks

One of the more important relationships in the political system involves three basic groups. Interest groups in society, offices and agencies in the bureaucracy, and committees and subcommittees in Congress are linked together by a common interest. There is great advantage to each in these relationships. Groups get government policies adopted that are favorable to them; bureaucrats get programs to administer; and members of Congress get power—power to control the distribution of benefits to the other two. The name most commonly given to such relationships is **iron triangles**, or what some refer to as "cozy little networks" or "issue networks" (Adams 1982). Figure 12.2 is a graphic depiction of this alliance. The lines of the triangle link each of the other two components, and the relationship is reciprocal; it flows in each direction. While the figure depicts a relatively simple reciprocal relationship, iron triangles are actually quite complicated. There are close to 200 committees and subcommittees in Congress, each with jurisdiction over an even larger number of bureaucratic agencies and programs. There are literally thousands of groups attempting to influence government decisions in Washington.

But not all government decisions fit into this neatly closed system. There are some policy areas where considerable controversy exists and where there is the need for outside advice or consultation. In agriculture, water, and public works policies, Hugh Heclo claims that "the iron triangle concept is not so much wrong as it is disastrously incomplete" (1990, 88). Heclo's explanation posits a more open system in which expertise is the key. "Washington's reliance on indirect administration has encouraged the development of specialized subcultures composed of highly knowledgeable policy-watchers" (99). What these subcultures have in common is a "detailed understanding of specialized issues that comes from sustained attention to a given policy debate" (99). Heclo calls these **issue networks**. They are characterized by a large number of participants moving in and out of the process constantly and finding satisfaction from an intellectual or emotional commitment to the issue more than from a direct economic benefit (102). While defense procurement may be the very definition of iron triangles, welfare policies resemble more closely

Figure 12.2

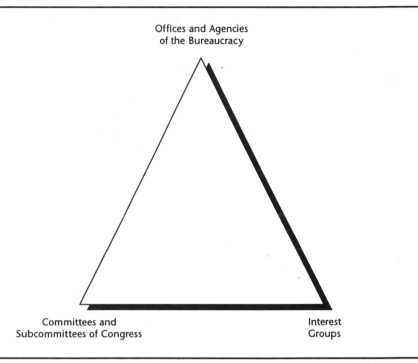

THE IRON TRIANGLE

Offices and Agencies
of the Bureaucracy

Committees and
Subcommittees of Congress

Interest
Groups

The iron triangle is a term meant to show the connections among congressional committees, bureaucratic agencies, and interest groups in the formulation of government policy.

the issue network. Many policy areas probably fall somewhere in between, more structured than Heclo states, but less tight-knit than the term iron tri-angles implies. But they are all fought out in the lower recesses of government.

The advantage in having government agencies deal with narrow interests is that the groups have their own agencies when they need support, and the agencies have group support for programs that they wish to perpetuate. Congressional subsystems, as well, have areas of policy responsibility that they wish to preserve. These groups, then, have interrelationships, shared interests and goals, constant interaction, and the willingness to cut off interference from the outside.

There is a tendency to be protective of such relationships, to keep them from public view, and to prevent others from siphoning off resources that sustain the programs involved. Networks and triangles are made all the more impene-trable by the almost-daily interaction that is an inevitable facet of these relation-ships. Indeed, many of the people involved spend many years working together. Each understands the needs of the others, can communicate easily and effectively because of the shared interests, and will come to the defense of the others. Yet no institution or group of institutions has complete power in the American system.

OVERCOMING SUBSYSTEM DECISIONS   It is possible to break into these networks under several conditions. One such condition is when the combined impact of social and/or budgetary decisions exceeds the resources available to meet them. Someone, then, must decide which of the many lower-level decisions are to be favored and which are not. This raises such decisions to a level above the iron triangle where the president, Congress—in its collective capacity—and the political party system decide. With significant deficits in recent years, there have been numerous attempts to reduce the costs of decisions reached at lower levels of decision making. In efforts to reduce the deficit, Republicans in 1995 first attempted to control the deficit through a constitutional amendment; when this failed, they used the budget process to limit subsystem control of appropriations.

Another occasion when decisions are taken out of the hands of the smaller groups is when the issue is one in which our political parties anticipate partisan advantage. There are not many of these; they usually revolve around the presidential race and are frequently issues raised by candidates rather than by the parties themselves. The budget again represents such an issue. Republicans essentially took the issue from President Clinton, who had made it a priority in his first two years in office, and made it theirs. In forcing a confrontation with Republicans over their plans to cut deeply into welfare, health care, and education spending, Clinton regained some of the advantage in 1995, as the two parties positioned themselves for the 1996 campaign.

Still another occasion is when the cost of the subsystem decision is so great that a higher level of decision making must intervene. Locks and Dam 26, at Afton, Illinois, on the Mississippi River provides a good illustration. In 1972, the Army Corps of Engineers wanted to replace the facility with one that was not only larger but that would accommodate vessels with greater draft. Since a single lock of such proportions would be of no use, what acceptance of the Army Corps of Engineers' plan really meant was a change in the entire Mississippi River system; instead of a $400-million decision, it was a multibillion-dollar decision. But until this became clear, the issue had been handled within the iron triangle of the Army Corps of Engineers, barge owners, and the Public Works committees. Ultimately, the issue was resolved, but the actions of the entire Congress and numerous pressure groups on both sides of the issue, as well as the intervention of Presidents Carter and Reagan, were required (Reid 1980). As with most compromises, no one was completely happy: A new locks and dam system was constructed—although it was not fully operational until 1994—but a greater draft was rejected, and barge fuel was taxed for the first time in our nation's history.

Courts and Interest Groups

Litigation has become a means of altering public policy when other forms of group activity have proved unsuccessful. Most notable in this respect has been the litigation brought by the National Association for the Advancement of Colored People (NAACP). In *NAACP v. Button* (1963), the Court recognized the right of a group to relief through the courts. Justice William J. Brennan Jr., speaking for the Court, said:

> Litigation . . . is a means for achieving the lawful objectives of equality of treatment . . . for the Negro community in this country. It is thus a form of political expression. . . . Litigation may well be the sole practicable avenue open to a minority for redress of grievances.

While civil rights groups pioneered the use of litigation, it can be and recently has been used by any group that has been defeated in other arenas.

Groups interested in spending money in support of their ideological position won a significant victory in the case of *FEC v. NCPAC* (1987). An unusual coalition of the National Conservative PAC and the American Civil Liberties Union took the Federal Election Commission, which was supported by the Democratic Party and Common Cause (a public interest group concerned with fairness in elections), to court over the campaign contribution limits of the 1974 Campaign Finance Law. The Court held that such restrictions on independent political groups violated free-speech protections of the First Amendment.

Groups can influence court decisions in several ways. They can work for the appointment of sympathetic justices. Failing this, they can see that nominees who are unsympathetic or biased are not appointed. Civil rights and women's groups vigorously opposed the selection of Robert Bork to the Supreme Court in 1987. They formed an umbrella group, the Alliance for Justice, to oppose the nomination and lobbied the Senate, which was considering confirmation. Not to be outdone, the White House secured the services of Tom C. Korologos, a Washington lobbyist who had helped the administration with other nominations before the Senate, to lobby on behalf of Bork (Wolpe 1990, 114). The Bork nomination was turned down by a narrow margin. Another close vote occurred in 1991 with the controversial confirmation of Clarence Thomas. Groups have "vetoes" over appointment to other positions as well. Earlier we noted the role of groups in the selection of political executives, judges, and the professional bureaucracy.

Interest Groups in a Democratic System

Interest groups are often referred to in a derogatory fashion, and some groups do engage in deceptive and unethical practices. Tobacco company executives testified before Congress in 1994, for example, that tobacco was not addictive and that no evidence had proven that their products caused death or serious disease. Yet documents were presented at these same hearings showing that company executives had possessed evidence of these contentions from their own research 31 years earlier (Hilts 1995).

Moreover, membership in most groups is dominated by the middle or upper classes in American society, so that the expressions of a group's interests and its maneuvers to gain advantages leave a significant segment of the popu-

Table 12.3

THE ENVIRONMENTALISTS

National Audubon Society (founded 1905)
Members: 516,220
Budget: $32,852,672
Staff: 337
Offices: 16

Defenders of Wildlife (founded 1947)
Members: 80,000
Budget: $4.5 million
Staff: 30
Offices: 4

Environmental Action (founded 1970)
Members: 20,000
Budget: $1.2 million
Staff: 24
Offices: Washington only

Environmental Defense Fund (founded 1967)
Members: 125,000
Budget: $12.9 million
Staff: 100
Offices: 6

Friends of the Earth (founded 1969)
Members: 50,000
Budget: $2.5 million
Staff: 35
Offices: 2

Greenpeace (founded 1971)
Members: 1.4 million
Budget: $33.9 million
Staff: 1,200
Offices: 30

Izaak Walton League of America (founded 1922)
Members: 50,000
Bugest: $1.8 million
Staff: 26
Offices: Washington and St. Paul, Minn.

League of Conservation Voters (founded 1970)
Members: 15,000
Budget: $500,000
Staff: 40
Offices: 3

National Clean Air Coalition (founded 1974)
(Coalition group, made up of 35 other groups)

National Parks and Conservation Association
(founded 1919)
Members: 100,000
Budget: $3.8 million
Staff: 30
Offices: 4

National Wildlife Federation (founded 1936)
Members: 5.6 million members and supporters
Budget: $85 million
Staff: 700
Offices: 12

Natural Resources Defense Council (founded 1970)
Members: 125,000
Budget: $13 million
Staff: 125 (40 lawyers)
Offices: 5

Sierra Club (founded 1892)
Members: 553,246
Budget: $28 million
Staff: 185
Offices: 16, plus 57 chapters divided into 355 groups

The Wilderness Society (founded 1935)
Members: 330,000
Budget: $20 million
Staff: 130
Offices: 15

Source: Robert Clayton, *CQ Weekly Report* January 20, 1990.

Interest groups are formed to promote legislation favorable to the group's philosophy. Concern for the preservation of the environment has resulted in the formation of many groups, which often lobby together for desired legislation.

lation at a disadvantage. The impact of large amounts of money flowing into politics from groups is also a concern in a democratic system.

Yet some contend that interest groups are essential to the proper functioning of a democratic system. Harmon Zeigler said that "democracy is therefore a system in which, through compromise, the competing demands of interest may be satisfied while the decision-making mechanisms of government continue to operate" (Zeigler and Peak 1972). An even more dramatic claim in support of interest groups is given by John R. Commons, who states categorically that economic pressure groups are "more truly representative than the Congress elected by territorial divisions" (1950, 33). Since most government actions do not reach the spotlight but remain obscured in committees, bureaucratic agencies, or regulatory commissions where the public has little voice, the degree to which democratic representation occurs is hard to tell.

One defense of groups in a democratic society is the ability of opposing interests to organize and enter political competition. The formation of one group for the purpose of gaining some type of benefit invariably produces countergroups opposed to such action. Groups work on both sides of most major public issues. In the battle over revising the Clean Air Act, for example, a battle that extended from 1988 until 1990, those supporting tougher standards included environmental groups (see Table 12.3); health groups, such as the American Lung Association; administrative organizations, such as the State and Territorial Air Pollution Program Administrators; and various state and local governments—California and New York, for example, were advocates of stronger auto-emission standards. Those aligned on the other side included the auto industry and their unions; utilities, especially those in the Midwest that would have to do the most to clean up their emissions; and the chemical industry. These industries worked individually as well as through their trade associations, such as the Motor Vehicle Manufacturers Association. They also joined together in an umbrella organization, the Clean Air Working Group, to coordinate their efforts. In addition, various states supported these efforts—auto states, like Michigan; mining states, like West Virginia; and oil states, such as Louisiana.

Mobilization is thus best done by those who stand to gain or lose large amounts, whereas it is more difficult to mobilize a group when the costs or benefits are distributed in small amounts over a large number (Minar 1974). A good illustration of this would be milk subsidies, as reported by Philip Stern. In 1985, Congress had a choice between two plans on milk subsidies; they chose the one that benefited 200,000 dairy farmers and over a five-year period would have cost the taxpayers $2.77 billion and consumers $11.5 billion (1992, 171). The dairy interests had spent about $3.3 million in campaign contributions. Opposing public interest groups such as those mentioned above are often the only source bringing attention to these high-cost subsidies.

Not only are there groups on each side of most conflicts, but individuals are seldom members of only one group. As a result, David B. Truman, in first bringing this to our attention, stated, "No individual is wholly absorbed in any group to which he belongs. Only a fraction of his attitudes is expressed through any one such affiliation, though in many instances a major fraction" (1951, 157). When the interests of various memberships conflict, we may be subject to **cross-pressures**. For example, a member of the Republican Party who is also pro-choice faces a dilemma when a Democratic presidential candidate strongly supports choice, while the Republican candidate opposes it.

Some individuals experiencing conflicting pressures respond by staying with their party, others switch parties, and a few refrain from participation.

Summary

What Tocqueville noted in the 1830s is even more true today: We belong to a large and diverse number of groups. Political interest groups attempt to have an impact on some public decisions. They are formed mainly by those with the most to gain or lose by government action, which accounts for the preponderance of business, professional, and trade associations among those groups active in politics. This preponderance was predicted by Madison, who noted the importance of property in *The Federalist* No. 10. Groups have become increasingly active in elections through the use of political action committees (PACs). The main thrust of groups, however, is still in dealing with legislative and bureaucratic decision making by lobbying government on behalf of their group's interest. Attempting to influence government action or elections has always been a source of controversy, especially by those who emphasize the undemocratic aspects of making decisions in this manner. Attempts to limit such influence, however, run counter to constitutional protections of speech, assembly, and petitioning government.

Analytical Exercises

1. Assume you are a ranking official in a government agency, and the president of a trade association that your agency monitors suggests that you would be an excellent speaker at the association's annual convention in Bermuda. The president thinks you would be the best person to bring the membership up to date on the proposed new regulations that will affect the association. The association would fly you and your husband down in their private jet and put you up at the resort hotel where the meeting is taking place. They would pay all other incidental expenses. Would you accept the offer to speak? Would you accept the expenses-paid trip? Given the close association between what you do as a government official and decisions that affect the association, do you think it would be appropriate to have a law that prevents your accepting gratuities from groups, prohibits you from seeking employment in that industry for two years after you leave government service, and prevents you from lobbying your old associates at the government agency on behalf of the interest group for five years after you leave your post?

2. Assume that you head an interest group faced with the following situations. What strategy(ies) would you propose as the most effective?
   a. Your group wishes to secure a change in the tax code giving the group benefits similar to those that foreign companies receive from their governments.

b. New regulations that your group views as detrimental to their interests have just been announced. They will go into effect in 30 days.

c. The administration has introduced a bill in Congress that your group enthusiastically supports and that would provide members of your group with important benefits.

d. Several members of Congress have consistently opposed efforts by your group to secure a new piece of legislation. Their opposition has prevented consideration of your bill.

13

Political Culture, Media, and Public Opinion

You tell me whar a man gits his corn-pone, an' I'll tell you what his 'pinions is.
      —Mark Twain, "Corn-Pone Opinions," *Europe and Elsewhere,* 1900

The media have replaced the party as the principal link between the candidates and the voters.

      —Dye, Zeigler, and Lichter, 1992

Connie Chung entices the mother of Speaker of the House Newt Gingrich to confide what Mr. Gingrich has said about Hillary Clinton. Lesley Stahl discusses the United Nations' policy of sanctions in the Middle East with the secretary of state. H. Ross Perot announces his availability as a candidate for the presidency in 1992 on the *Larry King Live* show. Perhaps more dramatic, and an image known to us all, was the scene in Baghdad during the evening of January 16, 1991, when Bernard Shaw, John Holliman, and Peter Arnett described for us the bombing taking place around them as the air war in Iraq began, hanging a microphone out the window to capture the sounds of battle and crawling from one side of their hotel room to the other to report what was happening.

These examples show the importance of media in our political life, as well as some of the changes in their use. Newscasters for the national networks are constructing a political reality for those of us who watch them. The decisions they and their editors make about what is "news" and what is not are based, in turn, on their construction of the world, of what they think is important. Our view of the political environment is therefore, in part, influenced by how others interpret the world for us. We see that some behavior is acceptable and is rewarded; other behavior is punished. In part, our views of politics are based on what kind of information is presented to us, and in part on how each of us as individuals processes that information. We filter events through our own particular lenses; we give attention to some things and not to others. This important insight was first noted by Walter Lippmann over 70 years ago:

> For the most part we do not first see, and then define, we define first, and then see. In the great blooming, buzzing confusion of the outer world, we pick out what our culture has already defined for us, and we tend to perceive that which we have picked out in the form stereotyped for us by our culture. (1922, 31)

Let me begin this chapter with an assessment of our political culture—how we acquire it and how it is perpetuated. I will then turn to the role of media in transmitting information as well as in helping to define our political culture.

Political Culture

Culture is the shared beliefs, traditions, myths, and forms of personal interaction of a group of people. It is passed on from generation to generation. **Political culture** relates those patterns of thought and behavior to government and politics—the making and implementing of binding rules for a society.

There are some common themes present in American political culture with which almost all are in agreement: liberty, equality, democracy, civic duty. They stem from the American Revolution and are enunciated in the great documents of that period: the Declaration of Independence and the Constitution. These themes have been stressed by observers of the United States for over two centuries—from Thomas Paine during the late eighteenth century, to the French writer Alexis de Tocqueville in the 1830s, to recent accounts of American society by David Brion Davis and Seymour Martin Lipset. Lipset, for example, notes the differences between a society emphasizing liberty, independence, and the pursuit of happiness, as expressed in the Declaration of Independence, and one that emphasizes "peace, order, and good government," the basic concerns of the founders of the Canadian Confederation (1990). Lipset sees these differences as influencing different societal actions: The emphasis in the former is on transcendental goals that might encourage the use of violence to achieve them, as we have seen in recent years with right-wing militias; in the latter it is on an empirical order of rules designed to encourage the peaceful attainment of goals.

EQUALITY   In chapter 2, I developed four types of equality: political, legal, economic, and moral. Political and legal equality is now an accepted part of our heritage; the others are still problematic. With respect to economics, the

**Chapter
Thirteen**

Political
Culture, Media,
and Public
Opinion

early American concern for equality was not so much in redistribution of income or property (Davis 1990), but in equal opportunity.

Even today, equality is "the fundamental theme and characteristic of American civilization" (Wood 1990, 33). Most Americans realize that people cannot be equal in every respect. As a matter of fact, individualism and uniqueness are highly respected American traits. Economic equality, then, as a basic theme in American political culture, has come to mean the right of every citizen to equal opportunity. But even here there are still major differences in just what that means: Affirmative action and comparable worth are subjects of bitter controversy.

LIBERTY   Freedom from the control of others and the independence to do whatever one pleases, as long as it doesn't hurt others, is considered a basic human right and one that Americans have staunchly defended.

DEMOCRACY   Most Americans feel that our form of government is the most appropriate—that others should emulate ours rather than another model of government. For some, this way of governing was the result of a rational choice after having considered and rejected other options, and it represents the best choice a people could make.

CIVIC DUTY   Many feel that where each individual has the right and privilege of participating in the government, he or she also has the duty to participate in community affairs. That is, each individual should find a way to make a complicated system work most efficiently for most of its citizens.

This concept of civic duty is not a new one or one limited to American experience. Pericles, speaking in Athens over 2,500 years ago, stated:

> We do not say that a man who takes no interest in politics is a man who minds his own business; we say he has no business here at all.

But while there are these shared beliefs in our fundamental values about governing, there are differences as to which of these values is most important and about how each is to be put into practice. Various political cultures exist in the United States that emphasize different aspects and values of our political heritage. There are even groups that simply do not accept some, or all, of them. How many of these people there really are, we don't know, since not all of them are willing to expose their opposition. And that opposition can take many forms, from the gentle Amish in Pennsylvania and Ohio, to revolutionary groups—communists were one of the most obvious groups in past history—or in recent times neo-Nazis like the Skinheads, black separatist groups such as the Nation of Islam, or, most recently, the militias arming in anticipation of a takeover of the United States by the United Nations.

The most common way of describing our political differences is by the terms "liberal" and "conservative." When these designations emerged in Great Britain in the late eighteenth and early nineteenth centuries, the conservative was one supporting the status quo, in favor of a class system, of a hierarchy run by the upper class and the monarchy—the ultimate in class standing. Liberals were for change, for the individual, especially against governmental action, against class and hierarchy, and supporting representative government. In the new United States, there was no class system as such (titles of nobility were forbidden in the Constitution, for example), those advocating change were now in power, and thus the designations of liberal and conservative became somewhat muddled.

Liberals are now usually for government protection of the individual from corporate power. They favor the provision of environmental, health, and old-age security by the government. They are suspicious of large business. Equality is the major issue to liberals. Conservatives are generally concerned with limiting the role of government. They believe that individuals and businesses should be left on their own to make it or not. Liberty is the real issue to conservatives. A real problem exists in using these terms and in accepting such facile definitions: There is great ambiguity involved. In popular usage, a conservative could be a member of a group attempting to remake American society in its own image—Pat Robertson's Christian Coalition, for example; a member of a group that exercises strong control in the American economy such as the Business Roundtable; or a member of the Libertarian Party that wishes no government interference in individual actions. A liberal might be a union official bitterly opposed to affirmative action, or a feminist deeply committed to it; it might be a populist farmer from Iowa opposed to social welfare, or a democratic socialist in California condemning our lack of full national health insurance. It is also hard to distinguish between them sometimes, because both may support the same issue or program. We wonder what is going on. But, upon inspection, we find that their support is for totally different reasons.

Since these terms dominate our political discourse, it is important to have a grasp of what they mean. The distribution between liberals and conservatives has varied only slightly over the past few decades. Figure 13.1 shows the relationship. The first point is that there are more people who consider themselves conservative, by almost a two-to-one ratio. The second is that movement in one direction or the other is really not that great.

These data may help us in looking at popular elections; we know that slight shifts one way or the other can lead to the election of Republicans or Democrats. But I'm not sure that the terms "liberals" and "conservatives" do much for our understanding of political culture. Let me go into this a little more deeply, to conceptions about the underlying foundations of a society.

Philosophers have noted a continuum between a society based on hierarchy and one based on individualism. Most societies in the Middle Ages were decidedly hierarchical. The Enlightenment, the predominant thinking at the time of the American Revolution and the framing of the Constitution, was one of individualism.

The analysis of cultures proposed by Aaron Wildavsky and various students and coauthors over the past decade argues that this continuum from hierarchy to individualism is important, but not enough; it does not explain other cultural phenomena. They argue for another dimension, one relating to

Figure 13.1

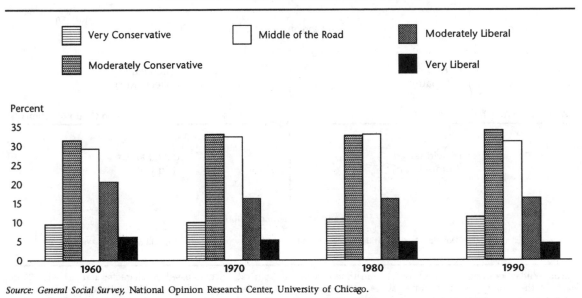

POLITICAL IDEOLOGY IN AMERICAN POLITICS

Source: General Social Survey, National Opinion Research Center, University of Chicago.

When asked about their political views, many Americans identify themselves as conservative, as these survey results show.

imposed norms in a society. Wildavsky suggests that we analyze cultures along two dimensions: identity and behavior, where

> the dimensions of cultural theory are based on answers to two questions: "Who am I?" and "How should I behave?" The question of identity [Who am I?] may be answered by saying that individuals belong to a strong group, a collective, that makes decisions binding on all members or that their ties to each other are weak in that their choices bind only themselves. The question of action [How should I behave?] is answered by responding that the individual is subject to many or few prescriptions, a free spirit or one that is tightly constrained. (1987, 6)

The answers to these questions result in the two-dimensional matrix shown in Figure 13.2, where five cultural types are outlined: fatalism, hierarchy, egalitarianism, individualism, and autonomy. The last type would be exemplified, according to Wildavsky, by a hermit who lives apart from society.

In a culture where there are strong, imposed norms but weak or no group attachments, individuals have no basis for changing their condition and hence develop a feeling of apathy toward the polity. These *fatalists* are controlled from without. In our own society, a nonunionized worker without other social attachments would be a good example. Where individuals belong to strongly defined groups with an imposed order, they are in a *hierarchical* society, one in which the relationships among all groups are well defined,

Figure 13.2

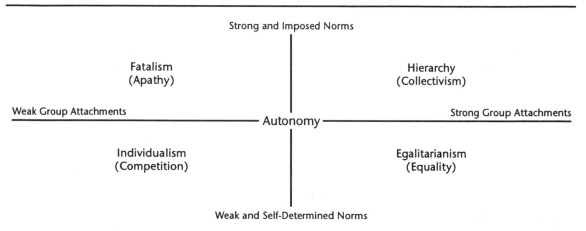

WILDAVSKY'S POLITICAL CULTURE TYPES

Source: Adapted from Mary Douglas, *Natural Symbols,* 1982, and Michael Thompson, Richard Ellis, and Aaron Wildavsky, *Cultural Theory,* 1990.

Aaron Wildavsky et al. have proposed one method of defining political cultures based on character and behavior. Thus, each of the four types diagrammed above is determined by a combination of how weakly or strongly one identifies with a group and whether one behaves within strong or weak group norms.

and where movement between groups is limited. Thompson, Ellis, and Wildavsky suggest the caste system of Hindu society (1990, 7); I would add those of Bali or Taraja in Indonesia as good examples. In *egalitarianism,* which has no strong norms, strong group membership has difficulty finding leadership; all who belong are equal. These groups can withdraw from society, as in some communes, or can attempt to transform society into the vision shared by the group. We could look to the abolitionists of Civil War time, or to groups such as the Religious Right in modern politics. Finally, there is the *individualist* culture. It is characterized by weak prescriptions and weak group attachments, a situation where bargaining and market decision making are necessary in a competitive environment. Here the individual is responsible for his or her own success or failure.

Thompson, Ellis, and Wildavsky contend that their formulation is theoretically useful in defining political cultures and is a realistic portrayal of the societies we know. Not only are various combinations of these found in all societies, but Wildavsky et al. also argue that democracy depends on a good mix of all but fatalism. Indeed, too much fatalism can be devastating to democracy; it needs the social criticism of the egalitarians, the competitiveness of the individualists, and the social organizing characteristics of a hierarchical society.

We now see why there is some confusion with the terms liberal and conservative. In fact, those at both extremes of the group variable are now called conservative, the one supporting a hierarchical society, the other calling for the absence of all hierarchy (libertarians). But you can tell the difference quickly by asking one or two questions: What do you think of government restrictions on abortion? What do you think about government regulation of marijuana use? The individualist will reject both attempts at government control. Party labels are only partly descriptive; they are also in part historical accident. And the party with which we identify is in part a pragmatic decision; it is really where we see advantage to ourselves; it does not usually have much to do with principle. Thus our practical political position may at times conflict with our general cultural beliefs. My colleague William Stewart (1988) refers to this as "paradigm conflict." In fact, he claims that no one is able to keep all of his or her various beliefs [understandings of reality] and practical considerations from overlapping, and thus all of us have some conflict to deal with.

Socialization

That we acquire the proper orientation to the political system is a matter of some concern for those wishing society to be maintained. All societies wish to perpetuate themselves. How do they achieve this? Since members of a culture already agree with its basic assumptions, they pass them on to their children. The family, therefore, is the first, and many think the foremost, agent of socialization. It should not be surprising that most of us share the same political perspective as our parents. One major study compared the political views of families in 1973 to what they were in 1965. "Time has, if anything, worked to bring them closer together" (Jennings and Niemi 1975, 1333). Where there were changes, the attitudes of both parents and children moved in the same direction.

School is also an important factor in our socialization. Schools reflect the dominant social values of a society in their organization, in their patterning of accepted behavior, in the myths and stories presented, and in the manner in which children are taught. The importance of the school as a socializing agent is best seen in the attempts of those with differing cultures or beliefs to secure their own school systems. It is expensive; it requires considerable effort; but those with a fundamentally different viewpoint think it is worth it—and not because these schools have a better way to teach algebra.

Our peers are important to our socialization as well. Few of us can resist the dictates of our in-group, as it defines who is in, who is out, what should be worn, or what should not. A classic study of peer impact found that it has great influence on our perspective of life (Newcomb et al. 1987).

The groups we belong to can be influential also. Churches and synagogues are a major source of our values; when these same values are consistently espoused in the home and school, they become a powerful force. Catholics and Lutherans have known this for some time. In our current politics, fundamentalist groups are the main ones intent on maintaining close ties to denominational schools and family units. We may also belong to such clubs or groups as Boy or Girl Scouts, Rainbow Girls, DeMolay, even a Little

League or Pop Warner football team, that help define our values, especially as we first reach out beyond our family and close friends. As we grow older, the more likely scenario is that we join groups that reinforce our values. They are usually composed of those with similar economic and social positions.

Of crucial importance in socialization also are the media. Today's young people read less than previous generations, but they watch and listen more. An estimated 80 percent of the people in the United States use radio and/or television every day.

In terms of both socialization and political activity, television is more significant than radio. Says media expert Doris Graber, "Television's greatest political impact, compared with that of other media, is its ability to reach millions of people simultaneously with the same image" (1993, 149). It reaches children from the time they are babies. "In the winter," Graber informs us, "youngsters between two and eleven years of age spend an average of thirty-one hours a week in front of the television set—more time than in school" (150). Of importance to our discussion of political socialization is that about 80 percent of what children watch is intended for adults. The child sees military combat, space launchings, funerals—all things that differ substantially from the child's own personal experience. I will return to the importance of this in a moment. Television has become the principal source of information as children grow older, replacing the parents in this role and becoming what Graber calls "the new parents" (121).

The conclusion, then, is that the mass media play an important role in our political socialization. The impacts, however, are different for different media. Newspapers are generally more analytical than other media, and those who have wide exposure to print media are typically better informed and more politically active than those who have little access to them. Television, however, reaches more people. In addition to the very young, television also reaches those who are functionally illiterate—some 23 million adults—and those with language barriers—recent immigrants, for example. Coverage of issues is rather superficial, but for millions who formerly would know nothing of the world around them, it still is a dramatic change. One of the most incongruous sights encountered in poverty-ridden rural Indonesia are the satellite dishes on so many rooftops.

Not only are there differences in the impact of different media, but different types of news are better presented and absorbed by different media. In a study reported recently, Crigler, Just, and Neuman found that "people do not have equal levels of interest in all topics . . . nor do all people have similar interest patterns" (1990, 15). Because of its visual nature, television is best utilized for low-interest stories, while the analytical nature of print media is more useful in covering stories of high interest. "Print and television can each optimize learning, but only for certain issues" (16).

In analyzing the impact of the media on our understanding of the political system, we need to recognize that we don't pay attention to all the news presented to us. In a study of how individuals process the news, Doris Graber's data suggest that we assimilate only one out of three stories (1988, 249) and even then, we select only bits and pieces to file away in memory.

The selection is not random, however. Each of us has a strategy for understanding the world around us and for processing the information we receive.
It is called **schematic thinking**—a patterned way of thinking, of viewing the
world, based on our cultural perspective. These patterns are developed relatively early in life and do not change much over our lives.

> It allows individuals to extract only those limited amounts of information
> from news stories that they consider important for incorporation into their
> schemata. The schema process also facilitates integration of new informa-
> tion into existing knowledge. (Graber 1988, 250)

In part, then, we hear and see what we want to hear and see. For example,
in a study of the 1984 election, media observers found that far more media
comments were negative to President Reagan than they were to the challenger,
Walter Mondale (Clancy and Robinson 1985). Yet in the public's perception
of how the media treated the two candidates, the results were reversed: Reagan
was seen as having gotten the most favorable coverage.

Media and Politics

Not so long ago, a text on American government would have mentioned media
only in passing. Few things have changed so dramatically in the political
arena as the use of media and their impact on the political process. Several
important areas need to be explored: first, the role the media play in the
constitutional scheme of things; second, the ability of the media, or those
who use the media, to make news; third, the concentration of media in the
hands of only a few major sources and the biases this introduces into the first
two areas; and finally, media's impact on campaigns and elections.

But first, a few definitions are in order. **Media** here refer to the print
and electronic means of disseminating information. These include television,
radio, newspapers, magazines, books, and now computers. Some of these are
clearly more important in politics and public affairs than others.

The Constitutional Setting

Newspapers were the main source of information among the small reading
elite of the American colonies. And it was the desire to protect the newspapers'
role in portraying government action that led to the First Amendment protection of a free press (see the discussion of Freedom of the Press in chapter 4,
Civil Rights and Civil Liberties, pp. 90–91). Jefferson expressed the view of
most of the Founders in a letter to Edward Carrington:

> I am persuaded myself that the good sense of the people will always be
> found to be the best army. They may be led astray for a moment, but will
> soon correct themselves . . . [if given] full information of their affairs thro'
> the channel of the public papers, and . . . those papers should penetrate
> the whole mass of the people. The basis of our governments being the

**Chapter
Thirteen**

Political
Culture, Media,
and Public
Opinion

opinion of the people, the very first object should be to keep that right; and were it left for me to decide whether we should have a government without newspapers, or newspapers without a government, I should not hesitate a moment to prefer the latter. (1787, 414–15)

CURRENT PRACTICES   Newspapers and magazines need no license to publish. The Constitution is clear in the First Amendment in giving "freedom" to the press, and the Supreme Court has generally ruled in its favor. One problem the press faces is the attempt by government to prevent information from being printed, especially when it is critical of government performance. The U.S. courts have not supported this notion of "prior restraint" (see chapter 4, pp. 90–91). In the important case that applied these provisions to states, *Near v. Minnesota* (1931), Chief Justice Charles Evans Hughes wrote:

> The administration of government has become more complex, the opportunities for malfeasance and corruption have multiplied, crime has grown to most serious proportions, and the danger of its protection by unfaithful officials and of the impairment of the fundamental security of life and property . . . by official neglect, emphasizes the primary need of a vigilant and courageous press, especially in great cities.

Hughes went on to explain that some may take advantage of this fundamental guarantee, but that does not justify doing away with the protection. Near's paper, for example, not only charged public officials with connections to organized crime, it was also blatantly anti-Semitic and racist. The answer to offensive content, Hughes asserted, is that the press is still responsible after publication for what it has printed.

> The fact that the liberty of the press may be abused by miscreant purveyors of scandal does not make any the less necessary the immunity of the press from previous restraint in dealing with official misconduct. Subsequent punishment for such abuses as may exist is the appropriate remedy, consistent with constitutional privilege.

The idea of punishment after the fact of publication was carried to its extreme in the case of *Patterson v. Colorado* (1907), in which the publication of something that was acknowledged to be true was the basis for punishing Mr. Patterson with contempt of court and a fine. Writing for the Court, Justice Oliver Wendell Holmes stated, "The preliminary freedom [to publish without prior restraint] extends as well to the false as to the true; the subsequent punishment may extend as well to the true as to the false."

The Court no longer holds this view, however. The press is now given great latitude in areas of potential libel, especially if the person involved is a public figure. The basic rule comes from the case of *Sullivan v. N.Y. Times* (1964). Justice Brennan stated that the "right of free public discussion of the stewardship of public officials . . . [is] a fundamental principle of the American form of government." Only criticism that was knowingly false *and* maliciously published could be the subject of criminal or civil actions. This view is quite similar to that of Madison, who argued that the government cannot be li-

**Chapter
Thirteen**

Political
Culture, Media,
and Public
Opinion

beled—citizens can say what they want about their government and their governors.

The press is not subject to some of the restraints placed on electronic media. For example, in the case of *Miami Herald v. Tornillo* (1974), the Court rejected the claim that the press must provide space for a public figure to respond to an editorial critical of him. For the electronic media, the right of reply does exist, as the Court asserted in *Red Lion Broadcasting v. FCC* (1969): A Pennsylvania station had broadcast a scathing critique of a book critical of Senator Barry Goldwater, and the author wanted to respond.

Government officials often do not like books or pamphlets that are critical of their activities and have not always supported their publication. While there are no restrictions on who can publish a book, there have been some restrictions on what can be published. Government servants in the intelligence community are required to sign declarations that they will not publish material about their jobs. For example, the work of Philip Agee, a former CIA official, was prohibited from publication by the Court based on a challenge from the CIA. A similar situation exists in the United Kingdom, where the Government Secrets Act prohibits the publication of material deemed sensitive by the government. In 1987 Prime Minister Margaret Thatcher's government went to court to prevent the sale of *Spycatcher*, an account by Peter Wright of his years in the British Secret Service (even though the book was published and available to readers in the United States and in other countries). Some have argued, however, that Thatcher's real concern was to prevent Wright from describing how the Secret Service under a Conservative administration attempted to discredit the leader of the Labour Party.

ELECTRONIC MEDIA   The electronic media, a modern phenomenon, have always been viewed somewhat differently from print media by our government. The basic concept is that the air is publicly owned, and its use should therefore serve the public's needs. There is also only so much freqency band width available. Hence, a government agency representing the public, the Federal Communications Commission (FCC), assigns licenses for radio or television stations; we have always had some restrictions on what stations could do. I mentioned the right of reply a few paragraphs ago, an extension of what is called the **fairness doctrine**. Licensees have also been bound by the equal-time provision: If a station sells time to one candidate, party, or group, it must provide an equal opportunity to opponents. News broadcasts are exempt from this requirement, however, so a station could, if it wished, provide unequal coverage of candidates or positions. Until 1984, stations were required to provide a certain number of hours of public service broadcasting, and advertising was limited to 16 minutes for every hour; the move to deregulation removed these restrictions. Since 1949, stations had been required to provide outlets for alternative expressions on controversial issues, free if the group could not afford it, again based on the fairness doctrine. When Congress passed a bill in 1987 that would have made the fairness doctrine permanent, President Reagan vetoed it on the grounds that regulation of broadcasters violated the First Amendment. The FCC dropped the requirement in 1987, although there have been attempts in Congress to reinstate it. Thus, a license is still necessary to broadcast, but the various restrictions have been loosened.

One of the major changes in the electronic media is the emergence of cable companies providing both television and radio transmissions. Cable companies were originally regulated by local government, but were deregulated in the 1980s. The rapid increase in subscription rates led to legislation by Congress to give communities some control over rates and service. Indeed, Congress overturned a veto of cable regulation by President Bush in 1992, the only veto override in Bush's presidency. Cable has had a dramatic impact on the major networks, providing competition in the form of 24-hour news and information channels, such as CNN and C-Span. CNN can even be seen in China today. Some of the dramatic events I mentioned at the beginning of this chapter were broadcast by CNN, which most people in the country thought gave better coverage of the Gulf War than any of the three major networks. Indeed, the impact of instant, worldwide television coverage of international crises is even called "the CNN factor" (Gowing 1994, 19). And the FCC has just opened the way for telephone companies to begin providing programs over phone lines to compete with cable companies. With a satellite dish, and an unobstucted view of the sky, any individual can now receive literally hundreds of TV channels; even with the major networks, the subscriber can choose ABC from Miami or Denver or Seattle, for example. Another major change has been the emergence of public radio and television as respected sources of news. For example, most Americans rate the *MacNeil-Lehrer News Hour* on public television as the most believable source of news (Robinson 1986, 45). In case you are unfamiliar with MacNeil-Lehrer, the fact that it seldom mentioned the O. J. Simpson trial might give you some idea of the difference between it and the standard network news show. The Corporation for Public Broadcasting was one of the major casualties in budget reductions enacted in 1995, with funds reduced by almost half.

With a modem, a telephone line, and a computer, individuals can now access information from around the world. Exchanges among "pen pals" almost anywhere can be nearly instantaneous. Whether hooked to the Internet, or the World Wide Web, from your campus, or as a subscriber to various services that provide access, you can, and most of you probably have, joined free-flowing discussion groups, browsed through information on various countries, accessed the Library of Congress, read a column by a favorite writer in a distant newspaper, or even shopped for holiday gifts. Since this medium is growing exponentially, it is hard to project just where it will lead us, but there is no question that it will be influential.

Media Concentration

There are about 1,000 television stations in the United States; in addition, about 60 million people are connected to 6,000 cable television systems. Radio stations number about 10,500, and there are 1,800 daily newspapers. Magazines of every type and political persuasion abound. Many of the stations and papers are locally owned, and all provide local news, often in excess of national coverage.

Yet these facts obscure a fundamental change that has emerged in recent years: concentration of information in the hands of a basic few, and limited alternatives for sources of information. First, let's look at what has happened in the way of competitiveness and the emergence of national media; then we can begin to assess whether this is or is not a problem. Although most major cities used to have competing daily papers, they, like medium- and small-sized communities, usually now have only one.

The major sources of news in the United States are few. There are three major national networks with which most local stations are affiliated. These networks, in turn, are usually multimedia conglomerates. General Electric owns NBC, Disney owns ABC, and Westinghouse hopes to gain approval to purchase CBS. The major networks own individual stations as well. The FCC does limit the number of stations that can be owned in each media market— new rules allow 12 television, 12 FM, and 12 AM stations to be held by the same company. But the major networks own their stations in the largest of our media markets—areas served by the same papers or television channels— accounting for about 40 percent of the total. There is no national press as such, but some papers, such as the *Washington Post* and the *New York Times,* have considerable influence because they are read by most decision makers, and through their news services provide news and commentary to most other papers. The *Washington Post* owns *Newsweek,* five television stations, and a dozen cable companies. Times Mirror Company, which publishes the *Los Angeles Times, Newsday,* the *Hartford Courant,* and the *Baltimore Sun,* also owns TV and cable companies. Time Warner, one of the nation's largest conglomerates, is involved in almost all phases of publishing and film and record production, in addition to owning numerous cable companies. In fact, most small newspapers also belong to large conglomerates. The 10 largest chains own about 50 percent of the 1,800 daily newspapers in the country. Only about 400 newspapers are independent. And almost all papers get their non-local news from a few sources, such as the *Washington Post* or *New York Times* news services; or the one remaining wire service, the Associated Press, which supports a corps of reporters around the world and provides news stories for subscribing members.

I should note that the level of concentration of ownership in this country is nowhere near what is found in Europe. In Italy, one person, Silvio Berlusconi, controls all three private television channels and the country's largest advertising agency. Berlusconi is also the head of Forza Italia, a leading political party; indeed, Berlusconi was prime minister for seven months in 1994 before his ruling coalition fell apart over the issue of media control. Rupert Murdoch controls 37 percent of the daily newspaper market in the United Kingdom, as well as Fox Broadcasting in the United States. And in Germany, Leo Kirch and Bertelsmann A.G. control the three major commercial TV networks (Viciano 1995, A8ff).

IMPACT ON THE NEWS Does this concentration and lack of competition pose a problem? Many think so. One problem is that each of these sources is concerned first with profit. I remember once giving a reporter an important local news story, only to be told it would not appear in the next day's paper because of a "news hold." That meant advertising material had already been laid out in the local newspaper, and the space remaining for news was already full.

A second problem is that much of what we read or see as "news" is created. Out of the many events that occur in a given day, some are selected as "newsworthy." This is a bigger problem for television and radio than it is for newspapers. If a station or network has committed resources to a particular story, then, in all likelihood, it will be presented regardless of its significance. There are only so many cameras, lights, and microphones; there are only so many times the reporter can be shot with a lead-in—the picture of her or him in front of the White House or Capitol. I vividly remember being in the Dirksen Senate Office Building when former attorney general John Mitchell was to testify before a Senate committee during the Watergate investigation in 1973. A major commitment was made by the networks and local stations, with as many as 15 microphones set up for impromptu interviews in the second-floor hallway. There were at least 100 reporters and technicians present starting at about 9:30 A.M. Mitchell arrived about 10:00 A.M. and entered the building by a back door to avoid questioners; he was behind closed doors the entire day; when he appeared at about 5:30 P.M., he said "No comment!" and left. What does a station do now? Rather than focus on another story of significance, it stretches what little it has of this event to fill the allotted time. Much the same was true for the **Iran-Contra affair** hearings during the summer of 1987. Hundreds of newspeople were present daily; as many as 12 television cameras were set in an alcove of the Rayburn House Office Building for interviews during and after the hearings. But there was little information available. Mostly, media people just waited for something to happen.

Biased News

Bias may result from the format in which news is presented, giving us cues as to what is important and what is not so important. Newspeople use

> a series of prominence cues (for example, story placement, headline size, story length, pictorial treatment, and frequent repetitions) to attract attention to news that political leaders and media gatekeepers deem significant. (Graber 1988, 250)

Those who pick the stories we read, where they are placed, and how they are presented are called **gatekeepers**. Who chooses what news is reported is important, in part, because what we see as important is based on what the media present. "Our point of departure is the agenda-setting hypothesis: those problems that receive prominent attention on the national news become the problems the viewing public regards as the nation's most important" (Iyengar and Kinder 1991, 2). But the importance goes beyond this agenda setting. Coverage of some issues but not others influences our judgment of candidates and public officials. Iyengar and Kinder call it "priming" (63). There is evidence "that individuals' explanations of political issues are significantly influenced by the manner in which television news presentations 'frame' these issues" (Iyengar 1987, 815). Iyengar and Kinder also explore how the framing of these issues influences public opinion and how we assign responsibility for political issues based on how the media present them.

Ownership of the media is generally conservative. However, when it comes to reporters, television producers, and television news personalities, most are liberal in their orientation. Doris A. Graber, in her study of media and politics, states that among journalists,

> Economic and social liberalism prevails, as does a preference for an internationalist foreign policy, caution about military intervention, and some suspicion about the ethics of established large institutions, particularly government. (1993, 62)

Perhaps the most thorough study of the differences between opinions of readers and those of news staffs was conducted by the *Los Angeles Times* in 1985. The data are presented in Table 13.1. Note that on many issues, news staffs and readers are about the same: in support of labor, and of efforts at income-gap reduction between rich and poor. But there are areas of significant difference also. News staffs are much less likely to support prayer in public schools and more likely to support civil rights issues.

What difference does it make? Certainly the endorsement of a major newspaper—and here we are speaking usually of an ownership decision—has an impact, especially in election contests about which the public has little information. Editorial support for Clinton may not have had a great effect on his election, because voters had independent sources of information, but in the less well-publicized races of representatives, state legislators, and city and county officials, the endorsement of the local paper can be crucial.

The research data are confirmed by my own experience. When I first ran for trustee of the local school district, I was endorsed by both local papers and came in first among five candidates, with several thousand votes more than my closest rival. When I ran for reelection, the local daily saw fit not to support me. I had become a "cat in the tuna factory," although I still had the support of the weekly paper. I won, but came in third (of three to be elected) and only a few hundred votes above my closest rival. The third time I ran, I again had the support of both papers and won with 6,000 votes to spare. While I would like to think my outstanding qualifications and fine, professional campaign accounted for the first and third election results, with the second being a fluke, I know better. Not very many people get elected to local, nonpartisan office in the face of opposition by the local daily newspaper.

Do liberal reporters give a bias to the news? Probably not much. There are a number of factors that argue against it. One is ownership; reporters are not going to do an obviously biased job when their bosses do not share their political perspective. Another factor is professionalism: reporters, producers, and news anchors are visible, public figures themselves, who share standards that they violate only at the risk of losing professional standing. In many cases

(Continued on p. 321)

Table 13.1

DO JOURNALISTS HAVE A LIBERAL BIAS?

Opinions of newspaper readers compared with the staff of the paper they read.

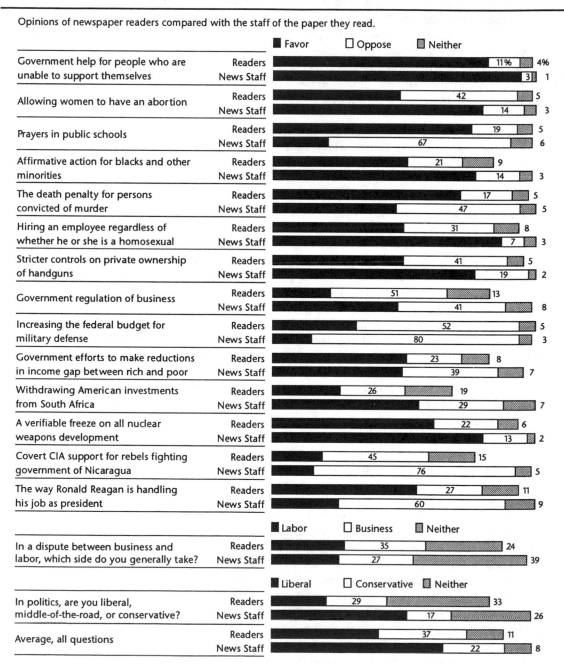

■ Favor   ☐ Oppose   ▨ Neither

		Favor	Oppose	Neither
Government help for people who are unable to support themselves	Readers		11%	4%
	News Staff		3	1
Allowing women to have an abortion	Readers		42	5
	News Staff		14	3
Prayers in public schools	Readers		19	5
	News Staff		67	6
Affirmative action for blacks and other minorities	Readers		21	9
	News Staff		14	3
The death penalty for persons convicted of murder	Readers		17	5
	News Staff		47	5
Hiring an employee regardless of whether he or she is a homosexual	Readers		31	8
	News Staff		7	3
Stricter controls on private ownership of handguns	Readers		41	5
	News Staff		19	2
Government regulation of business	Readers		51	13
	News Staff		41	8
Increasing the federal budget for military defense	Readers		52	5
	News Staff		80	3
Government efforts to make reductions in income gap between rich and poor	Readers		23	8
	News Staff		39	7
Withdrawing American investments from South Africa	Readers		26	19
	News Staff		29	7
A verifiable freeze on all nuclear weapons development	Readers		22	6
	News Staff		13	2
Covert CIA support for rebels fighting government of Nicaragua	Readers		45	15
	News Staff		76	5
The way Ronald Reagan is handling his job as president	Readers		27	11
	News Staff		60	9

■ Labor   ☐ Business   ▨ Neither

		Labor	Business	Neither
In a dispute between business and labor, which side do you generally take?	Readers		35	24
	News Staff		27	39

■ Liberal   ☐ Conservative   ▨ Neither

		Liberal	Conservative	Neither
In politics, are you liberal, middle-of-the-road, or conservative?	Readers		29	33
	News Staff		17	26
Average, all questions	Readers		37	11
	News Staff		22	8

Source: Los Angeles Times, August 11, 1985, p. 12. Copyright 1988, Los Angeles Times. Reprinted by permission.

Three thousand editors and reporters and three thousand members of the general public were interviewed. Reporters and editors were substantially more liberal on a variety of social and political issues than their readers.

**Chapter
Thirteen**
Political
Culture, Media,
and Public
Opinion

it would be difficult to report stories in a slanted manner; others are there reporting on the same event. Another reason is that even if they did, the public would not necessarily notice it. I mentioned earlier in the chapter how individuals filter news through their particular set of lenses. Yet the assumption that news coverage is biased has turned many people away from it. The established national media are seen as part of the problem—as "them," part of a government elite. Surprisingly, many people indicate that they listen to talk radio's Rush Limbaugh in order to get the news. Whatever merits Limbaugh's broadcasts may have, news is not one of them.

One reason for the charge of reporter bias is the emergence in the last 30 years of interpretive reporting, which has replaced descriptive reporting as the dominant type of political coverage. Because interpretive news stresses the "why" rather than the "what" of events, writers have more control over the content of stories than they did in descriptive reporting (Patterson 1993).

More important than any bias on the part of owners or reporters is the general notion that people will only take notice if the news is bad. An old adage is that for most people, no news is good news, and that for those in the media, good news is no news. Hence there is a predilection to report acts of violence, sex scandals, or the embarrassments of celebrities. We observe this in the *National Enquirer* and *People* as we stand in line at the supermarket. But a close inspection of our major newspapers and of the evening news on television also shows a fascination with catastrophe, with human foibles, and with exposés of government action or of public figures. The O. J. Simpson case dominated much of the media for over a year! More people could identify Lance Ito (64 percent) as the judge in the O. J. trial in one recent poll than could name the Speaker of the House, Newt Gingrich (50 percent) (Kurtz 1995, 6). A major study from Harvard University calls reporters the "stockbrokers" of Washington policy debates, more interested in keeping things interesting than in keeping us informed (Linsky 1986).

GOVERNMENT AND NEWS   Our understanding of political events is also skewed by the daily briefings by press secretaries at the White House or the Defense Department, news conferences held by public officials, press releases, reports issued by government agencies and Congress, and, of course, the "leak." Although in many cases government officials are interested only in getting out the facts, they may also be preparing for the next election or attempting to enhance a policy or image position of the administration. Reporters are caught in a trap. They need and, indeed, cultivate, sources for their stories, but they also know that at times they are being used by the administration as it tries to discredit an opponent or shift public attention away from a mistake. The Gulf War provides a remarkable illustration. I mentioned at the outset the indelible pictures from Baghdad as the war began. The American military, however, had been planning ways to keep the press from interfering—as they felt reporters had in Vietnam—for some time. Indeed, during the invasion of Grenada in 1983, the press was not allowed to accompany any of the military activity. What happened in the Gulf War was a classic case of managed news. Reporters were kept away from most actions, only pool re-

Reprinted by permission: Tribune Media Services

"On second thought, I want maximum media coverage on that information. Cancel the press conference and leak it."

porters were allowed to travel, and then only under strictly guided conditions. The military released footage of the effectiveness of its "smart bombs." Nothing was allowed to interfere with a well-coordinated public relations campaign directed by the Pentagon.

One of the most successful individuals at combining political advertising with the use of the free media (news programs, talk shows, and the like) was Roger Ailes, widely credited with masterminding the Bush media campaign in 1988. He had also been instrumental in the campaigns of Richard Nixon and Ronald Reagan. In 1988 Ailes created the "revolving door" ads, which gave us the images of convicted murderers being released to commit additional violent crimes. One analyst called it "The single most dominant ad in the campaign" (Levine 1995, 232). Ailes stated recently on National Public Radio, "Sure, we target the media, because the free media . . . are total suckers for pictures and events and drama and will put anything on the screen that gives them a better picture than the next guy, and they'll do it under the guise of news. So you can create paid political advertising for the suckers in the news division" (*Morning Edition* October 29, 1992).

Leaks are an especially interesting phenomenon. One type of leak, called a trial balloon, happens when a public official, usually from the administration, tells a selected journalist of some plan and then waits to see how the journalist's readers react. If there is a positive reaction, the plan can proceed; if negative, the administration can bury the plan. President Clinton used this technique to "float" the names of people being considered for high-level positions. In a number of cases, however, this led to "unnecessary embarrassment for both the candidates and the president when second thoughts were publicly aired and the names of candidates were withdrawn"(Blakesley 1995, 248). There is also the strategic leak from opponents of a proposal. There is nothing like public knowledge of a previously secret government action to get it stopped. This is an especially effective technique of bureaucrats who are opposed to administration plans. Surprisingly, Congress is only a minor source of leaks in government; information and secrets emanate from Congress, to be sure, but as one study found, about two-thirds come from the executive branch. Former *New York Times* columnist James Reston said that the administration "leaks the baloney it thinks people will swallow, and threatens to sue anybody who publishes information it wants to suppress" (May 21, 1986).

TERRORISM   The very real power of the media, and hence the urgent need to be covered by them, is perhaps best realized when the media report terrorist actions. Terrorism has become a ubiquitous occurrence in the modern political arena. There is considerable debate as to just what constitutes terrorism. A number of critics of both the media and the actions of American government suggest that we have limited our definition of terrorists to only those whose actions we oppose. We view the former Soviet Union's supplying arms to Libya, for use in killing political opponents, as an act of terrorism; we view our supplying arms to El Salvador, also for use in killing political opponents, as supporting democracy. The argument goes on to blame the mainline media for accepting these definitions and failing to see both actions as properly fitting the concept of terrorism (Herman and Chomsky 1988).

For an objective and comprehensive definition of terrorism, most agree that it must have the following components:

- The use or the threat of the use of violence.
- A type of surreptitious warfare separate and distinct from conventional warfare.
- Actions aimed at inducing a state of fear in the victim. (Grosscup 1991, 13)

There is an interesting relationship between the media and political actions we define as terrorism. Terrorism would not have much effect if it did not provoke widespread abhorrence. Those wishing to gain attention for their activities or the plight of their group or nation can do so instantly by staging acts of violence that are then reported by modern telecommunications throughout the world. Indeed, most experts agree that modern terrorists deliberately engage in staged media events—more theater than reality. News organizations recognize this, but are trapped in a no-win situation: To report it may result in continuing terrorism, but not to report it would be a disservice to the public that depends on the media for information.

Media and Elections

Among the media, television is central to modern politics because, as Thomas Dye, Harmon Zeigler, and Joseph Lichter contend, "television is our most sig-

Figure 13.3

EXPENDITURES FOR CAMPAIGN SERVICES

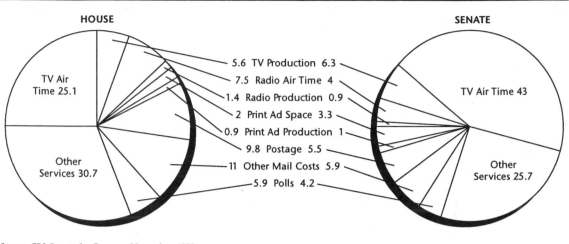

HOUSE   SENATE

TV Air Time 25.1

Other Services 30.7

5.6 TV Production 6.3
7.5 Radio Air Time 4
1.4 Radio Production 0.9
2 Print Ad Space 3.3
0.9 Print Ad Production 1
9.8 Postage 5.5
11 Other Mail Costs 5.9
5.9 Polls 4.2

TV Air Time 43

Other Services 25.7

Source: *CRS Report for Congress*, November 1990.

This figure shows what percentage of the campaign dollar in the 1988 general election was spent for specific services. "Other services" refers to overhead and related expenses. Television advertising consumes a large part of the budget, particularly for candidates for the Senate.

nificant form of *mass* communication—that is, communication that reaches nearly everyone: the poor, the illiterate, the aged, the sick, children" (1992, 4). There are two major factors affecting the use of television: expense and campaign direction. A 30-second spot in Los Angeles can cost up to $20,000. In much smaller markets, a 30-second spot may only cost $300 to $500. Even here, costs mount quickly. Figure 13.3 shows a recent distribution of campaign costs. The cost to produce a quality commercial may be anywhere from about $10,000 up to $100,000.

Still, television is the most cost-effective way to reach the public. A congressional district today includes about 600,000 people. Consequently, knocking on doors is no longer an effective way to reach voters. (Candidates and their supporters still do this, of course, but it is in part for show, in part for reaching specific sectors of a community. And it relies on a large cadre of workers who are willing to give up their evenings and weekends to canvass for the candidate or party. Only a few candidates are lucky enough to have so many volunteers.) Since there is a television set in 98 percent of the households in America, candidates can, with the use of sophisticated demographic profiles, tailor-make their appeals to the voters. That is, not only is the appeal tailor-made, but the specific program, station, and/or time of day is targeted.

The second factor is what the use of television has done to the structure and organization of the campaign. Central to a campaign organization now is the expert in public relations, the media consultant, the public opinion

Chris Curtis, DCI Publishing, Inc./Connection Newspapers

pollster (to be discussed in the next section), and the fund-raiser. Ed Rollins, who directed President Reagan's successful reelection campaign in 1984 and for a while was an adviser to the Dole campaign in 1995, claimed in a discussion with the author that he could take data from a public opinion poll conducted one evening and, based on what was found, have a television commercial running the next night that answered some question raised by those responding or dealt with some problem in the campaign spotted the night before. This type of campaign activity requires the coordination and contributions of all the experts involved: pollsters, analysts, marketing specialists, TV producers and directors, media consultants, and campaign directors.

William Schneider, a political analyst for CNN and the American Enterprise Institute, suggests that the American system has been transformed by changes in the rules and by changes in technology.

The emphasis on media, and the power of media in elections, has also led a number of serious students to suggest that they have replaced the party as a major participant in American politics. Dye, Zeigler, and Lichter assert that "the media have replaced the party as the principal link between the candidates and the voters" (1992, 125). Candidates can bypass parties, even at the local level, and appeal directly to the voter. Only candidates who can appeal on television are seriously considered. Making the same point is Gary R. Orren, of Harvard University, who sees the United States as having a "media democracy" (Linsky 1986, 1).

One of the themes of this book has been political participation. What impact does television have on participation? There is considerable evidence to suggest that it is one of the causes of our falling rate of participation. One explanation is that television is such a passive medium, a cool medium as some describe it, that it elicits a passive response. People watch; they don't participate (Robinson 1972, 23). Another critique of the role played by television is given by Neil Postman:

> Television as the command center of American Culture erases literacy, reduces the level of public discourse, atomizes all sense of a cohesive society responsible for its history or future, rewards emotion over thought, substitutes spectacle for analysis, symbols for ideas; it celebrates the market as a proxy for democracy and ultimately and inexorably turns citizens into mere consumers. TV Culture is the New World Order. (1992, 19)

There is also considerable evidence that television has changed the way institutions perform. Congress acts differently when under the glare of TV cameras; television opens access to a larger public for those not in leadership positions. Most commentators do not think the effect is for the better. Norman Ornstein contends:

> As media coverage expanded, the number of members of Congress who were brought to public attention mushroomed, and more and more of the publicized members came from the rank and file.... No longer did a member have to abide by insider rules to receive inside rewards or avoid inside setbacks. One could "go public" and be rewarded by national attention; national attention in turn could provide ego gratification, social success in Washington, the opportunity to run for high office, or, by highlighting an issue, policy success. (1983, 202)

In his book on the relationship of news to lawmaking, Timothy E. Cook states that "making news, in short, has become a crucial component of making laws" (1989, 168). But he does not see this as necessarily bad. It has changed the way laws are made, and it has changed the power relations within Congress, but it has not necessarily led to poorer lawmaking.

Public Opinion

Most of us have opinions about politics. In the past, unless you were an activist in politics—one who spoke at meetings, wrote letters to public officials or newspapers, or otherwise expressed yourself—your opinions were important to politicians only at election time. They needed your vote and looked for ways to get it, such as paying attention to what you thought. With the introduction of widespread **public opinion polling**, politicians now think that it is possible to know what the public's attitudes are toward many issues, such as sending troops to the Persian Gulf, eliminating affirmative action programs, and negotiating with Russia on reducing nuclear weapons.

Public opinion represents the thinking of groups of people concerning issues that affect them. There are many groups that have opinions on many different policies in a society as large and complex as ours. Some analysts thus use the term "publics" when talking about opinions. On some issues, of course, there is a consensus of opinion. Why are some perceptions widely shared? In part, as I have suggested, our political culture dictates our response to issues. This is one reason why successful politicians try to define issues in ways that trigger a cultural response. George Bush was quite successful in the 1988 election in associating his opponent with certain symbols, such as "liberal." Indeed, politicians constantly search for ways to convey their positions so as to create a cultural response. Jarol B. Manheim calls it "strategic communication." Politicians aren't the only ones, though. For example, Manheim analyzes the use of the terms "freedom of choice" and "right to life" by opposing sides in the abortion controversy (1991, 15–16). These terms are carefully chosen to try to tap deep-seated cultural biases. Perhaps the most famous example of getting people to view an issue symbolically, regardless of its real content, involved a proposal by President Harry Truman for national health insurance. In the aftermath of World War II, all Western democracies adopted some version of national health insurance. In the United States, the American Medical Association hired the public relations firm of Whitaker and Baxter to campaign against such a proposal. Whitaker and Baxter pinned the label "socialized medicine" to the plan. In fact, they were so successful in creating a negative opinion that no serious politician would touch the issue of health insurance until the 1960s (Greenberg 1971).

Opinion is also influenced by the media. Media frame issues for us, give us a look at national figures, report on their actions, set the agenda: what the issues are, what is important. Most would agree that our use of troops in Somalia was in response to media images of starvation in that country. Not only do the major media set the agenda, it is a remarkably similar agenda across electronic and print sources. Notice sometime when you are browsing at a newsstand how similar the emphases are in *Time* and *Newsweek*, and how often that week the same subjects have been the focus of television news.

Public Opinion Polls

Finding out what we think about public issues has become a regular feature of American politics. Reports of Gallup, Harris, CBS, the *Washington Post*, the *New York Times*, or *USA Today* polls are regularly given in newspapers and on the evening news. The linkage of these opinions to government decisions is unclear, although there are cases in which decisions seem to follow public opinion. There are also cases in which decisions do not. Pollsters can state results about opinion with some confidence because of the techniques they use in selecting samples and by making those samples of large enough size to be useful.

Most polling is done by telephone, because it is more cost effective for the polling organization than personal interviews. Thus polling can be done from any place in the country, rather than having interviewers located in each community. (The Survey Research Center at the University of Michigan, for one, still uses face-to-face interviews for some of its studies, which requires a network of trained interviewers around the country.) It is estimated that there is a telephone in 94 percent of the households in the United States. Remember the factors associated with voting—income, education, employment status—from the discussion of participation. The fact that telephone subscription is also related to these factors means that for voting studies, at least, pollsters can reach almost all households with registered voters. Larger organizations now use a CATI (Computer Assisted Telephone Interviewing) system in which they can have people's answers to a questionnaire loaded directly into a computer, from which analyses can be instantaneous.

Pollsters must pay particular attention to the wording of questions so that bias is not introduced, and so that the questions do not lead respondents to arrive at particular answers. The care given to constructing questions used by academic and professional pollsters can be contrasted with the type of questionnaire you, or your parents, might receive from your elected representative or from various interest groups. A recent questionnaire I received asked, for example, "Do you support the Clinton Administration's proposal to change federal immigration law and allow foreigners infected with the AIDS virus to enter the United States?" A more neutral wording might have been, "Do you support the Clinton Administration's proposal to eliminate the requirement that all individuals asking to emigrate to the U.S. be tested for AIDS/HIV?" Question wording has an impact, and not only with the use of loaded words. When asked "Do you favor or oppose the proposal for a constitutional amendment to require a balanced Federal Budget by the year 2003 and every year after that?" 70 percent were in favor. But when the question read "Do you favor or oppose the proposal for a constitutional amendment to require a balanced budget that cuts government spending on Medicare by 20% over the next 7 years?" only 31 percent were in favor (*New York Times* June 5, 1995, A1).

Polling samples are selected using various techniques designed to make them representative of a large population. For example, most phone polls use a technique known as "random-digit dialing." First the pollsters determine how many phones share each prefix (the first three numbers) used in the area being surveyed. Then an attempt is made to eliminate businesses and institutions that have been assigned blocks of numbers, so as to avoid repeated calls to the same location. Then the computer can be programmed to assign the remaining digits randomly. The advantage of this technique is that unlisted numbers are included—in some urban areas over 50 percent of residential phone numbers are unlisted—as are recently assigned numbers that would not be in the telephone directory.

Most major polling organizations use **random samples** of about 1,000–1,500 people for nationwide surveys. Many state polls attempt to talk to about 700 people. Local surveys are usually happy with a sample of around 400 people. The basic theorem of sampling is that the larger the sample, the more likely that the results obtained are reflective of those of the larger population. Pollsters speak in terms of probabilities: "I am 95 percent sure that the true population numbers are within 3 percent plus or minus of my sample results." To be that sure, a pollster needs a sample of about 1,100 people. To reduce the rate of error to 2 percent would require a sample of about 2,500. The sample size of 400, mentioned above, would have a sampling error of about plus or minus 5 percent. There is a trade-off between the cost of a survey and the associated error. Major pollsters, nevertheless, have been quite accurate in recent presidential elections. In the 1992 election, five of the six major polls had Clinton at 44 percent. The sixth predicted 43 percent, the actual amount for Clinton.

How is polling information used? In campaigns, especially presidential ones in which polling is done daily, major decisions are based on perceived strengths or weaknesses of the candidate and his or her opponent, or the emergence of different issues as salient to voters. In many cases, the decision to run at all is based on early polling data indicating support, name recognition, and what the key issues might be. Douglas Wilder withdrew from the 1992 race based on negative polling data. Academics use the polls as a means of tracking a campaign or support for a particular issue as they attempt to explain what happened in an election and why it happened.

While public opinion polls can be useful in campaigns and in gauging the public's opinions toward various issues, some would argue that we should not place too much emphasis on them as a source of public policy. In an informal discussion in 1991 on the role of polling in White House decision making, David F. Demarest Jr., then communications director in the Bush White House, stated that opinions are not a good indication of policy preferences. The reason is that policy is complex and involves considerable bargaining and compromise, things that are not the subject of polling, nor things in which most people are interested. This fact can be viewed in several ways by political analysts. A classic study found only a modest connection between a representative's position on issues and that of constituents (Miller and Stokes 1963).

Some even question whether policy makers need to be in touch with constituent interests. Public opinion polls during the Reagan years, for example, consistently found that Reagan was popular with the public, and that people thought he was doing a good job, but that the same public did not agree with most of his major policy positions—on abortion, for example, or aid to the Contras in Nicaragua. The same kind of ambivalence has been shown in attitudes toward other issues. Policy makers, these analysts would argue, should do what they think best, not what is expressed in the most recent public opinion poll.

On the other hand, some would say that average citizens do not have time to interpret the specifics of policy or the processes of its adoption, but that they do have clear notions of what the outcomes of those policies should be—a viable economy, a cleaner environment, safer streets, a more peaceful world, and so on. Failure of decision makers to achieve these goals leads to punishment at the polls. A look at the electoral consequences for President Carter in 1980, when his economic and world political accomplishments were seen as negative, is an indication of how public opinion can result in defeat. In 1992 strong negative feelings among the public gave President Bush difficulty in Republican primaries, opened the way for a serious third-party candidate, and resulted in his defeat in November. Congressional elections in nonpresidential years more often than not result in the party in power in the

White House suffering from lack of support if things are not going well. But few off-year elections are as dramatic as in 1994, where voters were fed up with Washington and its failure to deliver on preferred policies.

To carry the argument farther, not only is there popular opinion reflected in who is elected and who is turned out of office, but the policies we adopt are imperfect, though often accurate, reflections of public opinion. A symposium in 1994, sponsored by the American Political Science Association, found all authors agreeing that opinion influences policy choices; some more than others, to be sure, but at times, quite closely (Jacobs et al. 1994). Policy makers, according to these analysts, know about and respond to what is expressed by the public.

Given the technology presently available, it is now possible to conduct an instant "vote" or popular referendum on government actions. That is, either with telephones or television, citizens are able to record their preferences for particular policies, which can be tallied instantaneously and serve as the basis of government decisions. During the 1992 presidential campaign, Ross Perot suggested that he would hold "electronic town meetings" to resolve policy issues. Whether or not this would be a desirable addition to our political system is another and quite controversial question.

Summary

There are common values held by most of us concerning the basic distribution of resources and power in our society. These are instilled in us by our families, schools, friends, groups, and the media. We tend to view those who do not adhere to our values with varying degrees of tolerance. These cultural norms are also the basis of our political involvement, leading us to participate or not participate in government, and to support various types of government decisions that affect our way of life. Since there are several cultures, there is always some conflict over which decisions we want government to make.

Much of our information concerning politics now comes from the media, especially television. Television also plays a major role in modern elections, requiring candidates to compete through this medium. It has raised the cost of political involvement considerably. It has also altered our way of viewing the world, and it has changed how governmental institutions function.

Public opinion has also become more of a factor in the governing of America. This is the case because the technologies to collect it have become less costly and are sufficiently widespread. These new technologies have also made it possible for us to know about the results quickly. Politicians know this, and there is some suggestion that they behave accordingly. But the connection between the opinions expressed by various publics through polls and policy making is not so close. In part, this is a result of a republican form of government, in which representatives are somewhat removed from the people. In part, also, it is a result of the imperfect manner in which information is presented in polls, and in the lack of the qualification and subtlety that are required to actually produce public policies.

Analytical Exercises

1. This exercise would be better done by the class as a whole, although each student can analyze it individually. You and another student with whom you are paired are required to reach a decision, but you cannot communicate with each other; instead, a problem is posed and you must write a solution, after which you can compare answers to see if you came to the same decision.

Situation 1. You and your partner are to meet on campus tomorrow, but each of you has forgotten where and at what time you were to get together. Where would you go and when would you go there?

Situation 2. You and your partner have received a $100 tax assessment for a piece of property you jointly own. Each of you must decide how much of the bill to pay. If the total you both pay is $100, there is no problem; if it is less, the tax collector will penalize you an additional $100; if you pay more, the tax collector will keep it as a voluntary contribution. How much do you pay?

Situation 3. The situation is the same as #2 above. In this example, however, assume that you are a member of a society that places a high premium on generosity. In fact, in your culture a reputation for generosity is more important than wealth or knowledge in giving a man or woman status in the community. Given this situation, how much of the tax bill do you pay?

After each situation, compare your answers and then discuss how you reached the solutions that you did. How much of each solution do you think is based on cultural factors?*

2. For the following questions, indicate whether you strongly agree, agree somewhat, disagree somewhat, or strongly disagree.
- Regardless of what the law says, the defendant in a criminal trial should be required to prove his or her innocence.
- One shouldn't believe the testimony of a police officer more than that of other witnesses at criminal trials.
- Local public schools should be free to have prayers at their graduation ceremonies if the local school board approves.
- The state has a moral obligation to prevent the abortion of a fetus except in cases where the mother's life is in danger.
- The death penalty is an appropriate punishment for particularly heinous crimes.
- The individual needs governmental regulations to protect him or her from false advertising, contaminated food, and infectious diseases.

How do you think you developed these opinions? What factors were the most important? Have your attitudes changed any in the past year or so?

*Source: Seth Thompson, "Exercises in Tacit Coordination," in Charles Walcott, ed. (1980). *Simple Simulations II*. Washington DC: American Political Science Association, pp. 154–57.

14

Public Policy Making

The really basic thing in government is policy. Bad administration, to be sure, can destroy good policy, but good administration can never save bad policy.

—Adlai E. Stevenson, speech before the Los Angeles Town Club, 1952

All wise princes should consider not only present but also future discords and diligently guard against them; for being foreseen they can easily be remedied, but if one waits till they are at hand, the medicine is no longer in time, as the malady has become incurable; it happens with this as with those hectic fevers, as doctors say, which at their beginning are easy to cure but difficult to recognize, but in the course of time when they have not at first been recognized and treated, become easy to recognize and difficult to cure. Thus it happens in matters of State; for knowing afar off (which it is given to a prudent man to do) the evils that are brewing, they are easily cured.

—Machiavelli, *The Prince and the Discourses*, [1532] 1950

So far, I have given two different meanings to a concept of democracy. Beginning in the first chapter, I have emphasized participation, especially in voting. Simply put, this view says that if sufficient citizens are enfranchised and exercise that franchise, then the system is democratic. A different view, explicitly stated in chapter 12, states that so long as the system is open to a multitude of groups, a pluralistic system results that is the closest approximation we can have to democracy. Neither of these depends much on the outcomes of the political struggle, so long as the structure is open and participation or competition occurs. In the participative model, we assume that left in the hands of their citizens, governments will provide beneficial policies; in the pluralistic model, the outcomes are seen as similar to a scorecard, recording which groups have been the most successful.

There is another view of democratic systems that does concentrate on the outcomes of our political decisions. Do those decisions make people better off? Economists have an entire field of study devoted to just this question: if at least one person is made better off while no one else is made worse off, we have a Pareto Optimal situation, an ideal for which we should strive. For political scientists, emphasizing the results places us in the study of public policy. To be sure, there is emphasis on how those results are obtained, but the real concern is what happens when governments attempt to achieve some goal: Does it work? And is it the most efficient manner to provide the good or service? Having weighed the results against these standards, we can look at what changes we might make in the process to effect better results.

Lawrence M. Mead, whose work helped to crystallize some of the notions above, summarizes policy analysis: "The moral is that if policy is to be improved, the policy-making institutions must also be changed" (1995, 1).

The Policy-Making Process

There is a process—a series of steps followed—in arriving at a policy in our society that includes recognizing and defining a problem, securing a place on the government's agenda to consider it, identifying the institutions and actors in national government that must deal with the problem, finding ways to effect whatever policy choices are made, and, finally, fine-tuning the policy in response to its impact on society. In simplest terms, a problem exists and government attempts to solve it. This idea was first presented in political terms by David Easton, one of the most influential political thinkers of our time, back in 1953. The diagram below portrays this.

Social problem ———▶ Government action ———▶ Impact on society

We know that in real life, things are not so simple and straightforward. Certainly Easton did, although critics were wont to condemn him for oversimplification. For example, first we must recognize a situation as a problem. We may be unaware of its existence, we may see it but not see anything wrong with it, or we may see it as a condition of modern life, not as a problem in and of itself. Only when a situation is seen as a problem can it be placed on the social agenda. But seeing something differently usually requires a dramatic event or series of events that forces our attention to the issue. The social agenda, then, refers to those issues that concern a community and about which there is a feeling that something can be done. In other words, the emergence of a social problem should look more like that in the diagram below.

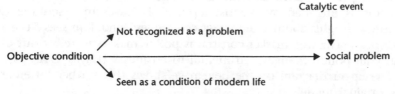

But just seeing that a problem exists does not guarantee that that issue will come to the attention of government. In the face of the inherent resistance of the political system to admit new issues for consideration and the glut of old issues already on the political agenda, there must be a real push on the part of the initiators or entrepreneurs to bring the problem before government. Cobb and Elder describe the process as follows:

> For example, a mine disaster itself does not create an issue. Many times in the past such an event has occurred with no ameliorative action. A link must be made between a grievance and an initiator who converts the problem into an issue for a private or a public reason. (1983, 85)

There are several reasons for this. One is the fact that there may be some in the community with sufficient power to prevent an issue from being considered—they can contain consideration. In the literature on policy making this is referred to as a nondecision.

There may be institutions that we have created to pick and choose from among various problems those that will be considered by government. We refer to these as **gatekeepers.** Seeking to overcome these obstacles and have a particular issue dealt with by government is the task of the **political entrepreneurs.** I shall use the term entrepreneur and use the definition provided by Norman Frohlich and Joe A. Oppenheimer. "A political entrepreneur is an individual who invests his own time or other resources to coordinate and combine other factors of production to supply collective goods" (1978, 68–69). (The term entrepreneur is taken from business and refers to those who invest their time and energy to bring together sufficient resources to address a problem.) Their task is to get their chosen issue past the gatekeepers and on to the agenda of government. One of the factors, then, that must be present is the initiator or entrepreneur. Eyestone describes the process:

> Along the line from issue generation to governmental response and issue resolution, there must be a number of critical people who facilitate movement in the issue translation process. Though their actions would not be sufficient to bring off the whole enterprise by themselves, these "issue entrepreneurs" are necessary parts of the process. (1978, 88–89)

All forms of political organization are biased in favor of the exploitation of some kinds of conflicts and the suppression of others, because "*organization is the mobilization of bias.* Some issues are organized into politics while others are organized out" (Schattschneider 1960, 71). All political systems, then, are conservative, in that their agendas favor society's best-organized groups. One illustration is provided by theorist Michael T. Hayes in describing Charles Lindblom's insights about free-market economies. Lindblom sees "The Market as Prison. . . . The free market constrains policy makers to reject out of hand virtually all policy changes detrimental to business" (Hayes 1992, 63).

The upper diagram on the next page shows this further differentiation of the original model.

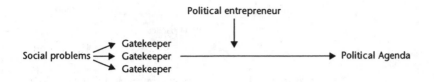

The list of those items being considered for public resolution is called the **political agenda.** Items on the agenda can be considered in two different arenas of decision making. I have called the one in which most decisions are made, and which is largely obscured from public view, the **minimal decision-making arena.** To it are assigned routine decisions and monitoring and making minor adjustments to existing policies. Seldom are new policies the result of this level of decision. Nevertheless, on occasion new policy emerges, as it did in the case I recounted in chapter 12 of a major modification of the locks and dam on the Mississippi River. And of greater importance, the constant adjustment to policy over a period of time can produce fundamentally different policies. A prime example would be the extension of tax breaks and tax expenditures to numerous groups and interests.

The other, what I have called the **maximal decision-making arena**, can consider only a few issues at a time and is highly visible. It is the stuff of most political controversies we see on the evening news or in the papers. It is where most new policies emerge and where fundamental changes in policy making occur. These concepts are illustrated in the diagram below.

The policies produced in the minimal and the maximal decision-making

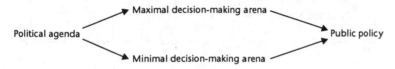

arenas must be put into effect. **Implementation**—taking general rules and putting them into a format for specific application—is a significant part of the political process. Frequently, policy is general in nature; the specifics must be added for it to be useful. These specifics are sometimes as important as the original policy decisions—they give shape and direction to a policy. There are rules and regulations that need to be formulated. They are often formulated in the minimal arena, with congressional committees and interest groups involved. There may even be the need for new government organizations—bureaus, offices, agencies—to carry out a policy. This aspect of policy is portrayed in the upper figure on the next page.

Finally, these actions by government have an impact on society and affect the objective situation, which in turn leads to modified demands placed on government. In fact, this **feedback loop** as it is called, can affect any or all of the steps in the process. For example, as a policy is implemented, the specific rules and regulations are worked out in minimal decision arenas, where those involved further refine the policy and how it will be perceived

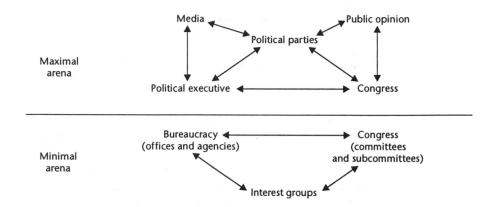

in society. The more accurate, complete model of policy making is presented in the diagram below.

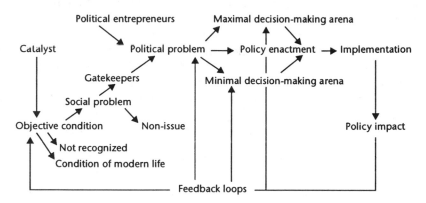

My colleague Robert J. Waste argues that policy should be seen as a life cycle, "which spans the distance from the shift of a potential issue from a community 'condition' to a community 'problem' and through enactment and implementation to evaluation and feedback or termination" (1989, 7). He calls this an ecological approach. In other words, while the stages of policy making look rather dry and inanimate on the pages in this chapter, policy is made by real people, confronting real problems. John Gaus gives the classic definition of the "ecology of government":

> An ecological approach ... builds ... quite literally from the ground up; from the elements of a place—soils, climate, location, for example—to the people who live there—their numbers and ages and knowledge, and the ways of physical and social technology by which, from the place and in relationship with one another, they get their living. It is within this setting that [policy] ... should be studied. (1947, 8–9)

To get a notion of just how large some of the problems we will be considering are, we can look at the scope of federal domestic policy as seen

Table 14.1

OUTLAYS BY AGENCY
(in billions of dollars)

Agency	1994 Actual	1995	1996	1997	1998
		Estimate			
Legislative Branch	2.6	2.8	3.0	3.0	3.0
The Judiciary	2.7	3.1	3.3	3.4	3.4
Executive Office of the President	0.2	0.2	0.2	0.2	0.2
Funds Appropriated to the President	10.5	10.9	10.8	10.8	10.7
Agriculture	60.8	62.3	62.3	62.7	61.3
Commerce	2.9	3.6	4.1	4.4	4.6
Defense—Military	268.6	260.3	250.0	246.1	244.2
Defense—Civil	30.4	31.2	31.9	32.6	33.6
Education	24.7	32.9	30.7	29.3	28.5
Energy	17.8	16.1	15.8	15.5	14.5
Health and Human Services	278.9	301.4	331.4	357.5	384.6
Housing and Urban Development	25.8	26.9	26.3	29.6	30.1
Interior	6.9	7.3	7.3	7.2	7.1
Justice	10.0	11.8	13.5	15.5	16.7
Labor	37.0	31.9	35.9	37.5	37.8
State	5.7	6.3	5.5	5.5	5.4
Transportation	37.2	38.0	37.3	36.8	36.5
Treasury	307.6	351.8	386.1	406.1	425.5
Veterans Affairs	37.4	38.2	38.0	39.5	39.7
Environmental Protection Agency	5.9	6.3	6.6	7.0	7.2
General Services Administration	0.3	1.1	0.6	0.6	0.7
National Aeronautics and Space Administration	13.7	14.2	14.1	14.0	13.7
Office of Personnel Management	38.6	40.3	42.8	44.8	47.5
Small Business Administration	0.8	0.7	0.4	0.5	0.1
Social Security Administration	345.8	363.4	381.7	404.6	426.5
Other Independent Agencies	11.5	8.6	14.3	18.2	17.5
Total	**1,460.9**	**1,538.9**	**1,612.1**	**1,684.7**	**1,745.2**

Source: U.S. Government Budget for Fiscal Year 1996, p. 10a.

in the budget for fiscal year 1996. Table 14.1 lists the proposed expenditures in the major categories of the budget. Looking down the column headed 1996, you can see proposed expenditures of about $62 billion for agriculture, $282 billion for defense, $31 billion for education, $331 billion for health and human services, and $382 billion for Social Security. These figures are estimates; they will be adjusted by Congress and these particular agencies before adoption, as actual expenditures are made. Efforts to reduce expenditures in these areas are difficult because of mandates. Required spending for agriculture is $45 billion, for example. The efforts at serious reductions—in 1990, when Congress and the executive agreed to major cuts of about $40 billion for fiscal year 1991 and an estimated $500 billion over the next five years; and again in 1994, when President Clinton and congressional Democrats produced cuts of another $450 billion over a five-year period—have still left us with massive deficits in the $150 billion-a-year range. In 1995, congressional Republicans

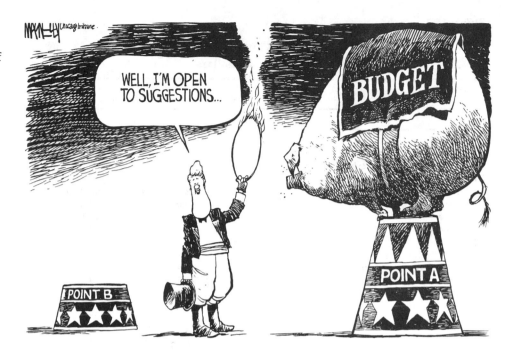

By Jeff MacNelly for the *Chicago Tribune*. Reprinted by permission: Tribune Media Services

forced Clinton to accept a seven-year plan to eliminate the deficit, against the president's nine-year plan. At this writing, the details are not yet settled, but even the more substantial cuts proposed by the Republicans are primarily scheduled to occur in the last two years of the plan, after the elections of 2000.

Government and Economic Policy

The relationship of government to the economy is an area of such importance, one so constantly on the agenda, and one about which we make so many adjustments each year, that I will use it for the remainder of the chapter to illustrate the terms of policy making.

Guy Peters identifies four major goals of government economic policy: "economic growth, full employment, stable prices, and a positive balance of payments from international trade" (1993, 174). In addition, some would add the distribution of wealth as a goal. Economic growth means that we are able to increase productivity with what we currently have, or that we can increase our productive capacity in some way. We may become more productive because our workforce is better trained, or a new method of production is introduced, or a change is made from a less to a more productive use of some resource. Increasing capacity means building new plants or expanding old ones.

The concept of full employment has been official government policy since 1946, when Congress adopted the Full Employment Act. But just what does this mean? At any given time, some people are between jobs either by choice or by circumstances; others want to work but are unable to work because they do not possess the appropriate skills or training. This is called structural unemployment. Most agree that between three and five percent unemployment is about as good as we can get. Governments engage in education and job training programs precisely to deal with this problem. The government can provide signficant inducements to encourage participation in new careers. Many of your parents went to school with National Defense Education Act grants, designed to encourage people to take up careers in science and math; others may have benefited from service in the military that provided educational opportunties both during and after active service.

The goal of stable prices refers to the value of our money. If the costs of goods and services increase, then the value of our money has decreased. The result is what is called inflation. We need more money just to buy the same things. If the costs of goods go down, then our purchasing power has gone up. We have deflation; our money is worth more.

The international economy is where we purchase goods and services from other countries, and we sell our goods and services to them. If we purchase more than we sell, as has been the case for some time now in the United States, then we have a negative balance of payments. Money is flowing out of the country. The goal is to have more sales than purchases, so that a positive balance obtains. This is easier said than done, especially when other countries are able to produce desired products at lower prices than we can. One way countries deal with this is to impose a tariff—a tax, an added cost—that increases the prices consumers must pay for the imported goods to make domestic products more attractive. The problem is that if one country does this, the inducement is for others to retaliate and do the same. I will return to this problem later in the chapter. Recently, our government policy has been to encourage open markets worldwide; only when faced with serious imbalances, as we currently have with Japan, where evidence exists that the Japanese have prevented the free importation of American goods, has the United States threatened to impose trade sanctions.

The distribution of wealth in the United States has raised significant political disputes in recent years. That's because evidence suggests that the gap between the rich and the poor has grown over the past 15 years. Using 1993 data, the most recent available, we find that "the highest-earning 20 percent of households" gained about $10,000 on average during this time frame, while "the 20 percent of households at the bottom of the income ladder" received an average of $1,200 less (Pearlstein 1995, 6). The plans of Republicans in Congress to lower taxes, about 50 percent of which would go to those earning $100,000 a year or more, would only add to the gap. They argue that while this will increase the disparity in the short run, the increased economic growth created by the tax reductions will improve the imbalance in the long run. Democrats are not so optimistic.

How do governments manage their economies to achieve the goals I listed above? To simplify our discussion, I will divide the discussion into monetary, fiscal, and regulatory policy. Monetary policy relates to the money supply— how much of it there is, how easy it is to get, what you have to pay for it. One thing governments have done when faced with the need for money is to print more of it. In chapter 2, I pointed to the great fear of leaders like Madison that the states would print their own money. Without anything else happening in the economy, of course, printing more money simply debases the value of the currency. Those who are in debt are happy, because they can repay with cheaper money; those who have loaned money are not happy, because what they will get back is not worth as much as what they loaned.

In the United States, we turned most of our monetary policy over to the Federal Reserve System, created in 1913. The Board of Governors of the Federal Reserve System (known as the Fed) is composed of seven members, appointed by the president with the consent of the Senate, who serve for 14-year terms. There are 12 regional Reserve Banks, whose presidents must be approved by the Board of Governors of the Fed. Technically, the regional Reserve Banks are owned by the member banks in that region, but with various changes in the law, real power rests with the Board of Governors of the Fed, and especially with the Chairman of the Board, a position currently held by Alan Greenspan.

The Fed, one of the most powerful of the independent regulatory agencies I introduced in chapter 8, is able to determine the supply of money and its cost by adjusting three variables. One is the amount of money a bank must have in its reserves. For example, if banks are required to have a 12 percent reserve, then they can loan out only 88 percent of what you and I deposit with them. By adjusting the reserve requirements, the Fed can make more or less money available for use. Another variable affects the amount banks must pay to borrow on a short-term basis from a Federal Reserve Bank. For example, in 1994 the Fed raised its discount rate seven times to keep inflation in check. The interest rates that banks charged for car, home, or business loans increased accordingly. The economy slowed, although some contend it slowed too much; rather than a soft landing in which no serious recession would ensue, some felt that by early 1996 we would, indeed, be in a modest recession. Since we are always guessing how these policy decisions will affect us, you might look at the situation today as you study this chapter.

The seven members of the Fed along with five regional bank presidents (the president of the New York Reserve Bank and four others who rotate) compose the Federal Open Market Committee (FOMC), which determines the amount of government securities to purchase. When the FOMC decides to buy securities, it increases the money supply; when they decide to sell, it decreases the supply. Here's why. When the Fed buys a U.S. government security, the selling bank gains increased reserves. When the Fed sells its securities, the buying bank has less money on reserve. Thus, greater or smaller reserves are available for loans.

By a careful combination of reserve requirements, discount rates, and the activities of the FOMC, the Fed is able to control the money supply.

Fiscal policy is primarily the province of the principal political institutions of national government: the president and Congress. Fiscal policy relates to how much we spend, on what, and how we pay for it. One side of the equation of fiscal policy is the budget. I developed the timelines and the interactions involved in formulating a budget in chapter 8. Remember that budgets are priorities, those policy areas we have decided to fund. The budget can encourage some activities by providing them funds; it can discourage others by failing to provide funds. Given the mandatory nature of so much of what is in the budget, however, there is little room for maneuvering. And there is no guarantee that behavior will change in the way anticipated by budget decisions.

In chapter 3, I discussed the extensive nature of federal grant-in-aid programs. Subsidies and grants represent a major vehicle for accomplishing economic goals. While the cost of subsidies has been brought down, and those receiving them must demonstrate more need, there is still the question of whether or not we should subsidize. Agriculture provides a nice illustration. Basic commodities are guaranteed government support; these are defined as corn, cotton, wheat, rice, peanuts, and tobacco. Nonbasic commodities receiving support are honey, milk, barley, oats, sorghum, sugar, and oilseeds, to which legislation in 1954 added wool and mohair. Larry Myers is a lobbyist for the honey, wool, and mohair producers, who have received more than $2 billion in the last decade. "It's a hard job [for me], because the original rationales behind the subsidies—beeswax to waterproof World War II military hardware, and wool and mohair for uniforms—rotted away decades ago" (Greve 1992, A14). The wool and mohair subsidies were just eliminated in 1994. And it seems ironic that we consider tobacco a basic commodity, granting subsidies for its production, but we also fund a smoking-cessation program—to the tune of $111 million in 1993.

Most of our arable land and farm subsidies go to corn and wheat production. And despite the popularity of pasta and corn tortillas, most of our grain—70 percent—goes to feed livestock. One study suggests that we have destroyed most of our grassland to grow these crops, even though we could feed beef cattle just as well with grass (Manning 1995). Republican efforts in 1995 to phase out farm subsidies were opposed by farm-state Republicans and a few Democrats, despite studies showing that sizable payments go to some of the nation's wealthiest farmers (Engelberg 1995).

Cotton and rice make especially interesting stories, since we provide support for them not only in direct subsidies, but in less obvious ways as well. You may not have realized that the major agricultural product in dry, sun-baked Arizona is cotton. It grows in the desert because of federal water projects costing hundreds of millions of dollars. In California, agriculture is the largest user of water—85 percent, in fact. The water used to irrigate cotton would provide enough to maintain both Los Angeles and San Francisco's needs (Reisner 1986). About 37 percent of all farmland irrigated by Bureau of Reclamation water produces surplus crops! In 1992, we paid California rice farmers $100.5 million in crop-subsidy payments—almost a third of which went to 900 rice farmers under the "prevented from planting" or "50/92" program. The 50/92

Table 14.2

1994 TAX RATE SCHEDULES

Schedule X—Use if your filing status is **Single**

If the amount on Form 1040, line 37, is: Over—	But not over—	Enter on Form 1040, line 38	of the amount over—
$0	$22,750	15%	$0
22,750	55,100	$3,412.50 + 28%	22,750
55,100	115,000	12,470.50 + 31%	55,100
115,000	250,000	31,039.50 + 36%	115,000
250,000		79,639.50 + 39.6%	250,000

Schedule Y-1—Use if your filing status is **Married filing jointly** or **Qualifying widow(er)**

If the amount on Form 1040, line 37, is: Over—	But not over—	Enter on Form 1040, line 38	of the amount over—
$0	$38,000	15%	$0
38,000	91,850	$5,700.00 + 28%	38,000
91,850	140,000	20,778.00 + 31%	91,850
140,000	250,000	35,704.50 + 36%	140,000
250,000		75,304.50 + 39.6%	250,000

Schedule Y-2—Use if your filing status is **Married filing separately**

If the amount on Form 1040, line 37, is: Over—	But not over—	Enter on Form 1040, line 38	of the amount over—
$0	$19,000	15%	$0
19,000	45,925	$2,850.00 + 28%	19,000
45,925	70,000	10,389.00 + 31%	45,925
70,000	125,000	17,852.25 + 36%	70,000
125,000		37,652.25 + 39.6%	125,000

Schedule Z—Use if your filing status is **Head of household**

If the amount on Form 1040, line 37, is: Over—	But not over—	Enter on Form 1040, line 38	of the amount over—
$0	$30,500	15%	$0
30,500	78,700	$4,575.00 + 28%	30,500
78,700	127,500	18,071.00 + 31%	78,700
127,500	250,000	33,199.00 + 36%	127,500
250,000		77,299.00 + 39.6%	250,000

program, created by 1985 legislation, allows a farmer to plant up to 50 percent of his acreage and still receive a 92 percent deficiency payment for the entire acreage. About 1,600 cotton farmers received $13.9 million under these same programs (Cony 1992, A22).

We have here, as with the tobacco and smoking example above, policy making that works at cross-purposes. We spend billions of dollars building dams that provide cheap water to develop arid land, and then we pay the

Table 14.3

MAJOR TAX EXPENDITURES IN THE INCOME TAX, RANKED BY TOTAL 1996 REVENUE LOSS (in millions of dollars)

Provision	1996
Exclusion of employer contributions for medical insurance premiums and medical care	66,620
Net exclusion of employer pension plan contributions and earnings	59,010
Deductibility of mortgage interest on owner-occupied homes	54,165
Step-up basis of capital gains at death	29,480
Deductibility of nonbusiness state and local taxes other than on owner-occupied homes	28,795
Deductibility of charitable contributions (all types)	24,145
Accelerated depreciation of machinery and equipment (normal tax method)	20,850
Deferral of capital gains on home sales	17,850
Exclusion of OASI benefits for retired workers	17,395
Deductibility of state and local property tax on owner-occupied homes	15,680
Exclusion of interest on public purpose state and local debt	12,690
Exclusion of interest on life insurance savings	11,160
Exclusion of interest on state and local debt for various nonpublic purposes	7,405
Net exclusion of Individual Retirement Account contributions and earnings	6,375
Capital gains (other than agriculture, timber, iron ore, and coal) (normal tax method)	6,205
Earned income credit	5,740
Exclusion of capital gains on home sales for persons age 55 and over	4,920
Exclusion of workmen's compensation benefits	4,860
Net exclusion of Keogh plan contributions and earnings	4,825
Accelerated depreciation of buildings other than rental housing (normal tax method)	4,385
Exception from passive loss rules for $25,000 of rental loss	4,170
Graduated corporation income tax rate (normal tax method)	4,120
Deductibility of medical expenses	3,965
Exclusion of social security benefits for dependents and survivors	3,730
Premiums on group term life insurance	3,020

Source: Budget of the United States, 1996.

landowners not to produce crops on it. Farmers are given cheap water, which encourages them to use it on crops that are not economically viable. These same crops are in some cases overproduced, and we ask farmers to set aside some acreage and not farm it. In other cases the crop raised does not reach its market-target price, and the government makes up some of the difference. The result is a contradictory set of policies that encourage waste, unproductive use of resources, and squandering of public money. These policies allow production of what we don't need, and we must then pay people not to produce these same crops. No one said policy making was easy.

There is also taxing policy. Tax codes are not neutral; some people are advantaged, others disadvantaged. Earlier in this chapter I mentioned the proposal of congresssional Republicans in 1995 to provide a large tax break for upper-income groups and the impact this would have on income distribution. Table 14.2 shows the tax rates currently used—how much you pay for various amounts of income, depending on your marital status. But what you pay also depends on how you earn your money. The table is for earned income; if your money comes from tax-free municipal bonds, you pay nothing. If you make your money investing and then selling things for a profit, you pay a capital gains tax that is now 28 percent, but that would be lowered significantly if the Republican tax plan were adopted. If your business is a corporation, you operate under one set of rules; if you conduct your business as a sole proprietorship or a partnership, you are governed by another.

There are also rules that allow you to deduct certain types of expenses and not pay taxes on that money. For you, it's a deduction—a credit or exemption; for the government, it's lost revenue—called a tax expenditure. In chapter 3, I indicated the importance of these tax expenditures to state and local governments. Table 14.3 on the previous page gives the largest tax expenditures and the amount of tax revenue lost thereby. Notice the favorable treatment given home ownership (and the most affected industries of real estate and savings banks, which depend on home sales and loans), or life insurance companies. We would have no deficit if these were all eliminated!

Finally, we try to achieve our economic goals by regulations that encourage some activities and discourage others. The Fed is responsible not only for monetary policy but also for regulating the behavior of banks. The sale of stocks is monitored by the Securities and Exchange Commission. Nevertheless, there are many who see the regulatory activity of government as working against the achievement of economic goals such as growth and full employment. The quality of our water and air is monitored by the Environmental Protection Agency, the medicine we take by the Food and Drug Administration, nuclear energy by the Atomic Energy Commission. These and other agencies have sometimes come under fire for promulgating rules and regulations that affect economic activity in a negative fashion. Let's look at one of the more important illustrations of how regulations impact on our economy: the failure of savings and loan banks in the 1980s.

The Savings and Loan Scandal: A Case Study in Policy Making

Sam Epstein, an 80-year-old from the San Fernando Valley of Los Angeles, received a check for $24,050 on November 23, 1992. It represented 37 percent of the money he and his wife, Lillian, had invested in high-interest bonds with Lincoln Savings and Loan in Irvine, California. Lincoln had been seized by government officials in April 1989. It was insolvent. The Epsteins had been lured from insured savings to risky junk bonds, in part, because Lincoln had assured them that the bonds were insured. They and others won a lawsuit against Lincoln and, after three and a half years, recovered only about one-third of their investment. Those with insured savings were repaid by taxpayers—you and me—to the tune of about $2 billion. This was the largest bank failure in what we have come to call the Savings and Loan Scandal. John Kenneth Galbraith, a noted economist, said

Figure 14.1

S&L CLEANUP: A REPORT CARD

Nonrecoverable losses to U.S. government, to date	$158 billion*
Additional funds needed to complete cleanup	$50 billion**
Number of seized institutions sold or liquidated	653
Number of insolvent institutions under government control	73
Value of S&L assets sold as of Sept. 30, 1992	$287 billion
Value of unsold assets	$106 billion

*Includes deals before the Resolution Trust Corp. was established.
**According to Timothy Ryan, director of the Office of Thrift Supervision.

Source: © 1992 *The Washington Post*, November 23–29, 1992, p. 20, reprinted with permission.

that "the scandal will stand as one of the most appalling such events in our civil history, and undoubtedly as the most expensive, . . . [a] looting . . . of government-supplied money" (1990, 15). The total cost to taxpayers now appears to be about $200 billion.

Caught up in the scandal were several prominent individuals. The Keating Five were a group of senators investigated for attempting, on behalf of Lincoln Savings, to prevent investigations into the bank's insolvency. They had done so in exchange for campaign contributions. When Vernon Savings and Loan went under in Texas, the former Speaker of the House, Jim Wright, was forced to resign his post in 1989, in part because of his activities on behalf of failed Texas thrift institutions. These failures in Texas indicated that the problem was widespread, and it required tremendous amounts of money to resolve it. Texas alone accounted for about $30 billion in bail-out funds. More recently, President and Mrs. Clinton have been under investigation for their financial dealings with the head of a failed thrift institution in Arkansas. But the scandal has not been limited to Democrats. Senator Phil Gramm (R-TX) was under investigation for allowing a builder who owned three troubled thrifts to charge Gramm only half the cost of building his new vacation home in Maryland (*New York Times* Dec. 7, 1992). Former president Bush's son, Neal, was among those investigated for another large bank failure, that of the Silverado Bank in Colorado. The younger Bush helped secure a loan of several hundred million dollars for a close friend, who used the money for highly speculative ventures. This was one contributing factor leading to the bankruptcy of Silverado (Kwitny 1992, 31).

Just how did we end up in such a mess? One factor, no doubt, was greed, leading to outright theft. Independent auditing failed to note the problems. Ernst and Young, one of the nation's biggest accounting firms, agreed to pay the federal government $400 million on December 7, 1992, to settle claims that its auditors had failed to warn of financial problems in some of the country's most troubled thrifts. Ernst and Young had been accountants for Lincoln, Silverado, and 10 other failed thrifts (Cushman 1992, A1).

But our concern here is government policy. Why did it fail? To answer this we need to look at the regulation of banks prior to and after 1980.

The first savings and loan in the United States was founded in 1831. The idea is really quite simple and laudable: small, local banks would collect savings from area citizens and make loans to build, particularly housing. The local community and the bank would be closely connected. To encourage such enterprises, the federal government gave savings banks permission to grant a quarter-percent bonus on savings interest above what a full-scale bank could give. The amount that could be paid was capped by the government, starting in 1933. In addition, banks could not locate in more than one state. (This piece of legislation, the McFarren Act, was aimed at the rapidly growing Bank of America, which other banks feared would overwhelm them.) Most Americans, of my age particularly, remember opening an account from our piggy banks at the local thrift office.

Deregulation

Eliminating regulations governing various economic activities did not start with banks, nor did it begin in the Reagan administration. In the late 1970s, during the Carter administration, we saw the first efforts at deregulation with trucking and airlines. The banks' interest-rate cap was removed, and the government agreed to insure savings up to $100,000. But deregulation was a cornerstone of the Reagan approach to government. The theory was that individuals free of government interference would invest their money wisely, and we would all benefit. Congress went along, and in 1982 savings and loans were freed of many more restrictions.

Steven Pizzo, Mary Fricker, and Paul Muolo, in their study of the scandal, cite the following changes:

- S&Ls could invest up to 40 percent of their assets in nonresidential real estate loans. Commercial lending is far more risky than home loans, but the potential returns are greater.
- The rule requiring that an S&L have 400 stockholders, none of whom owns more than 25 percent of the stock, was abolished. This allowed one major stockholder (Charles Keating, for example, of Lincoln Savings and Loan) to do as he pleased without fear of veto by other stockholders.
- Entrepreneurs could buy a thrift with noncash assets. This helped land developers who had "extra land" that they had not been able to develop. "Four years after deregulation, noncash assets on S&L books included good will, customer loyalty, market share and other 'warm fuzzies,' which accounted for 40 percent of their net worth. 'Voodoo accounting,' say traditional accountants."
- S&Ls could make real estate loans anywhere. "Heretofore, they financed home-building in their own market area."

- S&Ls did not have to get traditional down payments from borrowers. They could provide 100 percent financing, so the borrower did not have to invest a dime of his own money. (1989, 12–13)

So, write Pizzo, Fricker, and Muolo, "Instead of majoring in financing family homes with 30-year mortgages, the enterprising new owner used S&L resources to finance exotic projects: hotels, shopping malls, mushroom and windmill farms, tanning salons, Arabian horses, restaurants, hot-tub spas. Many of these new ventures, especially in Texas, were in out-of-the-way places, on poor land with insufficient populations or tourist attractions to support them. They are now flopping in the breeze in various stages of incompleteness" (15). The irony is that the ordinary person could never have obtained a small-house loan with the backing S&Ls were willing to use for collateral in large-scale projects such as ski area condominiums or high-rise office buildings.

There were other contributing factors in the collapse of S&Ls. Loans made to your parents returned six percent or seven percent interest to the banks, while these same banks gave five percent interest to depositors—a nice profit margin. But then deregulation created serious competitors for their deposits: Brokerage houses created money-market funds that paid significantly higher interest than savings banks did. Small depositors could now invest in treasury notes that had once been the province of large financial institutions. The effect was "catastrophic," according to Michael M. Thomas (1991, 31). S&Ls went from a positive net loan balance to a negative net worth in one year, 1980. As interest rates increased to squeeze out inflation, S&Ls were left to their own devices: How could they continue to carry low-interest loans on houses and still attract depositors with high interest rates? One solution was to buy junk bonds that paid especially high rates of interest. The S&Ls did this in part to secure large ($100,000) deposits that were distributed by Wall Street brokerage firms; the trade-off was that the banks had to invest in the firms' bonds. When the economy began to slow, many of the bonds proved to be literally "junk," as did many of the speculative real estate ventures. We now had an S&L crisis (public officials had helped create the problem by delaying the closing of failed thrifts), and a scandal.

Government Regulators

As I pointed out earlier, the U.S. government engages in numerous regulatory activities. Our food is inspected; airplanes are cleared for landing and takeoff; campaign contributions are noted; and banks' books are audited. The Reagan administration's approach was to do away with regulations, or, where they remained, to reduce the number of government employees monitoring regulations. As a result, those in the banking industry recognized that there was only a slight chance of being caught if they engaged in shady activities. Bank regulators from the Federal Home Loan Bank Board were aware of some of the problems that were being created by the proliferation of banks and the flimsy funding behind them. But they could deal only with a few, and then they had to confront an array of lobbyists, lawyers, and politicians acting on behalf of the banks.

Table 14.4

ECONOMIES OF THE G-7 AND THE WORLD

Country	Gross Domestic Product—1992
United States	$ 5.9 trillion
Japan	$ 3.7 trillion
Germany	$ 1.8 trillion
France	$ 1.3 trillion
Italy	$ 1.2 trillion
United Kingdom	$ 0.9 trillion
Canada	$ 0.5 trillion
G-7 Total	$15.4 trillion
Russia	$ 0.4 trillion
World Total	$23.0 trillion

Source: World Development Report, 1994. New York: Oxford University Press, 1994, pp. 166–67.

Congress

Members of Congress are expected to bring the concerns of their constituents to the attention of appropriate government officials. This is the representational function mentioned back in chapter 6. We would probably not reelect a representative who didn't go to bat for Mrs. Smith, who was ruled ineligible for Social Security, or for Mr. Jones, who did not get his disability payments from the Veterans Administration. And it shouldn't surprise us that Mr. Keating would go to his representatives when he was under investigation by bank examiners.

Yet, even with the reduced government role in regulating such activities, agencies of the federal government began to issue warnings about the activities of savings and loan bankers. The first such warning came from Texas, where Empire Savings and Loan failed in 1984. Within a year, examiners had determined that an additional 191 banks were in danger of insolvency. Lobbyists for the banking interests went to their friends in Congress to seek relief from regulators. In the most egregious case, the so-called Keating Five senators went to bat for a savings and loan that was on the verge of failing. The evidence suggests that their efforts were in part a response to generous campaign contributions from the head of Lincoln Savings and Loan, Charles Keating. The prime benefactor of this was Senator Alan Cranston of California, who was in a tough reelection compaign in 1986 and needed the support. But he was hardly alone: Every district in the country has S&Ls, and it is clear that there was no groundswell of support for tighter control of their activities.

International Economic Issues

We have moved from an era where strategic concerns dominated our foreign policy to one where economic issues are at the forefront. Indicative of this is the emergence of the **Group of Seven (G-7)** countries—the major economic democracies of Canada, France, Germany, Italy, Japan, the United Kingdom, and the United States (and some would contend that within a year or so, Russia)—as the major decision makers concerning the world economy. Economic summits among the leaders of these countries have been held for the past 20 years. The size and resources of these countries compared with the rest of the world is shown in Table 14.4. The figures are for 1992 and show the United States with the largest economy, creating $5.9 trillion of goods and services. Note should be made that if the European powers fully implement the Treaty of Maastricht and combine their economic resources in a European Community, their combined economy would be worth about $7.5 trillion with a population of about 350 million. The recent rise in nationalism has slowed the movement toward unification. Most observers expect a continuing slower move toward integration.

North/South Divisions

The makeup of the G-7 typifies another major concern: the division between the countries of the Northern and Southern hemispheres. Sometimes these are referred to as the "haves" versus the "have-nots." Most of the wealth resides in the northern countries of Western Europe, the United States and Canada, and Japan. The greatest poverty exists in countries to the south. Most of these southern countries are former colonies. The colonial powers were concerned mainly with the extraction of raw materials or with controlling trade, not with making the colonies' economies viable to stand on their own. (It is also true that the northern-tier states have many geographic advantages over their southern rivals in terms of a variety of resources and climate.) Internal strife and poor government have left most of these countries even more destitute than under colonialism. Stephen Ambrose sees our shift in attention to North/South problems coming mainly because of the changing nature of world economics.

> The emergence of black Africa, and the discovery of abundant raw material in both Africa and South America, helped turn American eyes from the northern to the southern half of the globe. This shift emphasized the fundamentally changed nature of the American economy, from self-sufficiency to increasing dependency on others for basic supplies. America at the end of the 1980s was richer and more powerful—and more vulnerable—than at any time in her history. (1993, xv–xvi)

Conflicts arising from conditions of hunger, poverty, and economic dependency in poor nations were frequently seen by us as attempts by communist countries to exploit these conditions in order to gain political power. But the instability of developing nations can also be seen as a political problem independent of communism. And with the end of major aid from communist systems, as well as replacement of the Communist Party in these countries as the major power, there is no longer either an ideological or an economic basis for blaming communism. Most Western nations provide aid of some form in attempts to shore up the economies of **Third World** countries (so called because they were distinct from the Western and Eastern blocs). In addition to aid, Western banks have made billions of dollars of loans to Third World countries. Dramatic increases in private lending occurred in the early 1970s; for example, 70 percent of lending in Latin America came from banks, compared with 8 percent in 1968. Many of these countries are on the brink of bankruptcy. It is of interest to note that at congressional hearings in the summer of 1987 the question was asked, "Are banks in effect making foreign policy for the United States?" The answer from the chairman of the Federal Reserve System was "no," but he acknowledged the strain these loans have made on the banking system, and the tremendous pressure on the government not to have countries default on their loans. This issue arose again in 1994, as Mexico verged on bankruptcy and required major economic aid. Many felt aid was given to protect American banks as much as it was to protect our neighbor to the south.

In many cases the northern countries need the raw materials found in southern countries. Some Third World countries have been able to join together to force higher prices for their produce—the most successful being **OPEC**, the Organization of Petroleum Exporting Countries. But other Third World countries with economies based on coffee or sugar have been less successful and are to a large extent at the mercy of the prices Western nations are willing to pay and the quantities they are willing to buy.

Third World countries have also become major sources of Western corporations' manufacturing operations. These countries provide cheap labor and land, frequently free of significant tax assessments. Most major corporations have plants or production facilities in several different countries, and usually in different regions of the world. This creates several serious problems for the American economy. The first is the loss of jobs in the United States. The loss of a manufacturing base is considered by some to be a significant deterioration of the front-ranking economic position of the United States. The second problem raised is the possibility of the United States' needing to use force to keep the flow of goods open. There is certainly some suggestion that this was at the heart of the quick and overwhelming response to Iraq's move into Kuwait: dependence on oil and a fear concerning its control and supply.

International Economic Organizations

A major part of U.S. foreign policy is economic, and there are a number of international organizations that we use to accomplish foreign policy goals. A major conference at Bretton Woods, New Hampshire, toward the end of World War II, set the stage for international economic assistance following the war. Stemming from agreements there, the **International Monetary Fund (IMF)** and the **International Bank for Reconstruction and Development** (the **World Bank**), were established in 1946. Today these institutions have about 150 members each. The IMF attempts to stabilize exchange rates and provides liquidity to countries with payment problems. The World Bank makes loans to devel-

oping countries, about $17 billion to 50 countries in 1993. Two related or-
ganizations make loans to private sector companies in these countries (International Finance Corporation) and no-interest loans to the very poorest
countries (International Development Association) (Rourke 1995, 546–47).
These loans often come with demands to change the host country's policies;
they also often lead to better trade for the United States. India is an example.
"IMF and World Bank loans backed by demands for policy changes" have
turned around a country on the brink of bankruptcy, to a point where it is
now seen as a major market for U.S. exports, which "jumped by 45 percent
from 1992 to 1993" (Denitzer 1995, 45).

These institutions are not without their critics, with the issues revolving
around North/South divisions. One criticism: the voting power in each is
based on the contribution a member state makes to the funds. Thus the United
States has 20 percent of the vote in both the World Bank and the IMF; with
the remaining G-7 countries added, there is majority control. Third World
countries object. One of the major reasons they object is that there are usually
strings attached to loans, requiring these countries to adopt economic strategies approved by the IMF or the World Bank, which, in effect, means the
United States and other G-7 countries.

But this does not mean that the G-7 is always in agreement, or that it
always gets its way with less-developed nations. The **General Agreement on
Tariffs and Trade (GATT)** was established in 1947 and in 1994 consisted of
106 members. A number of other states are observers, several of which are
applying for regular membership. The desire to join stems from several of
GATT's provisions. Members must extend "most favored nation" rights to
other members; that is, they cannot set higher trade restrictions on one member compared to another. Second, there is a mechanism for settling disputes
that allows smaller countries a chance of securing a favorable decision against
one of the major powers. For example, Venezuela was able to get an unfavorable import restriction on oil imposed by the U.S. reversed in a GATT settlement.

GATT is primarily concerned with establishing freer trade among nations
and removing unfair competition. The most recent round of talks, designed
to solve remaining issues of trade barriers, was held in Uruguay and ended
with no agreement on the pressing issues of agricultural subsidies. The United
States objected to Japan's refusal to allow rice imports and to European countries' agricultural subsidies. Trade issues are one of the major sources of tension
in current international relations. Some of these were ultimately resolved, and
the current GATT agreed in 1994 to create a World Trade Organization to
replace the GATT structure.

Summary

I have developed a number of new concepts in this chapter. Basically, I have traced the trajectory of an issue as it moves from the social to the political agenda and then back, affecting society.

The model of policy making has emphasized the importance of some triggering event to get issues on the political agenda. There are numerous forces that work toward keeping issues from reaching agenda status.

Once adopted, policy must be defined by administrators in order to be implemented. Rules and regulations must be adopted.

The impact that policies we adopt have on society serves to alter the social condition. In the rare case where a policy is instantly successful, the need for further government attention may dissipate. More frequently, policy must be dealt with again and again as we adjust and adapt in an attempt to solve the changing social situation that led to the need for policy in the first place. The relationship of government to the economy is one such area, one constantly on the agenda, and one about which we make adjustments each year.

Monetary and fiscal policy are the major tools of government to try to achieve the goals of economic growth, stable prices, full employment, and a favorable balance of payments. We can no longer be concerned just with our own economy. Complicating the world situation is the economic condition of a sizable portion of the world's population. Unstable economic and political conditions threaten peace in vast areas of Eastern Europe, Africa, South and Central America, South and Southeast Asia, and the Middle East. Attention to these problems is taking an increasingly large share of our resources; it is also taxing our ability to lead in a world where many nations view the United States as an economic imperialist, if not a colonial power.

Analytical Exercises

1. Public policies have a differential impact on individuals, varying with each policy. Some people are made better off, others worse off, while still others are unaffected. Let us assume that the most desired policy would be one where some (or at least one person) are made better off, while no one is made worse off. (Economists call this a Pareto Optimal solution.) Consider the options listed below. For this exercise, let us also assume that the benefits and disadvantages are proportionate: that is, the total benefits are exactly matched by the total costs imposed. Which policy would you choose and why? (Adapted from Mitchell 1971a.)

Policy	Made better off	Made worse off	Unaffected
P1	$1/3$	$1/3$	$1/3$
P2	$1/10$	$8/10$	$1/10$
P3	$1/2$	$1/4$	$1/4$
P4	$2/3$	$1/3$	0

2. Let's assume that there is increased demand, which has led to a large increase in production of the following private goods: automobiles; hallucinatory drugs; small, private aircraft; private pleasure boats; hand guns; bubble gum. (Recall from chapter 1 the differences between public and private goods.)

Which public goods are most likely to experience an increased demand in response to the increase in each of the private goods? Why? How should we pay for these public goods? Should we impose any regulations concerning by whom and under what conditions the private goods can be used?

STUDY GUIDE

Each chapter of this guide begins with a list of key terms—the words and phrases that are boldfaced in the text—along with their definitions. These glossary terms are also indicated with boldfaced page numbers in the General Index so that you can review how they were used in context.

The chapter contents are then summarized in numbered paragraphs, followed by study questions that could guide you in taking notes as you review the chapter.

Finally, each chapter includes a set of quizzes—true-false, multiple-choice, and matching questions—to test your knowledge of the material. Answers are provided on the last page.

1 STUDY GUIDE

Politics, Participation, and Public Policy

Key Terms

authoritative describing a societal decision that people feel compelled to obey.

collective (public) goods goods or services provided by government for all citizens.

democratic describing a political system in which most adult citizens are eligible to participate in governmental decisions by voting.

direct democracy a system in which all eligible citizens participate in making policy decisions. See also **representative democracy**.

free rider one who receives the benefits of a societal group's decisions without paying for them.

government an institution established by society to make policies and enforce laws.

indivisible goods goods and services that cannot be divided up and sold individually in the marketplace.

institution a formally established way of making and carrying out decisions.

legitimacy term describing government when citizens believe that those making the laws have the right to do so.

misery index the inflation rate plus unemployment at the end of a presidential term.

off-year elections elections that take place in the two-year interval between presidential elections.

participation actions through which citizens influence or attempt to influence governmental outcomes.

political science the study of how societies make public decisions through their government.

private goods benefits or assets produced and held by individuals, as distinguished from **public goods**.

public (collective) goods goods or services provided by government for all citizens.

representative democracy (republic) a form of government in which a few individuals are designated to make political decisions on behalf of the entire society.

sanctions punishments, or threats of punishment, that are designed to prevent people from doing something.

Chapter Highlights

1. The 1992 presidential election highlights many important themes in American politics. The manner in which Americans select their leaders is a long and drawn-out process that thoroughly scrutinizes the past record and personal character of individual candidates. Through party primaries, live television interviews, and frequent public appearances, Bill Clinton proved that his personal charisma, coherent message, and campaign organization were superior to those of his Democratic challengers and his Republican opponent, incumbent president George Bush. The unpredictable nature of politics was represented by the on-again off-again presence of Ross Perot and his independent movement. The prominence of the national economy and

impact of the budget deficit as the defining issues in the campaign are examples of factors that influence the outcome of policy debates and elections in America. Finally, despite a slight upturn in voter interest, the relatively low voter turnout illustrates the continued problem of apathy and dissatisfaction that many Americans feel toward mainstream politics.

2. The 1994 off-year election swung control of both houses of Congress to the Republican Party and was the first election since 1946 to unseat more than 50 representatives of the party that had been in control. Republican Speaker of the House Newt Gingrich initiated a congressional movement that was tantamount to a referendum on Washington politics and the Clinton presidency.

3. When choices are being made that affect citizens' fundamental well-being, we assume that most of those citizens will want to take part in making those decisions. Yet political participation varies a great deal around the world. In some countries, decision making is restricted exclusively to members of a royal family; in others, a select group of military officers or the leaders of a ruling party have complete control. Societies that allow the general public to take part in making decisions that affect everyone are called democratic systems. The manner in which public participation is channeled into government can also vary. In a direct democracy, all citizens are expected to participate personally. Because this is impractical, all such societies today are representative democracies, in which governing responsibility is given to a small number of people who are elected by the citizens to represent them.

4. The preconditions for a truly representative democracy include frequent elections, multiple candidates who represent alternative ideas, and allowance for all citizens to vote and influence the decisions that will be made by their representatives. Despite the fact that voting is a relatively simple act, only a limited number of eligible Americans take the time to participate in this activity, especially in off-year elections. Other forms of public participation in politics are even more uncommon among the general population. Citizens most likely to participate can be distinguished by regional differences, age, income, and education. In general, participation is more likely to occur as individuals perceive themselves to have a larger stake in their community.

5. Political participation ultimately rests on the shoulders of single individuals who are working to bring about some desired change to their community. Aside from professional politicians, there are many cases of single individuals who have greatly changed the course of history through their voluntary participation in politics. Daniel Shays helped to organize a farmers' protest against unjust debts that developed into an armed rebellion. Fears of impending civil war brought about calls for a stronger national government and the Constitutional Convention of 1787. Rosa Parks, a seamstress at a Montgomery, Alabama, department store, refused one day to relinquish her seat on the bus to a white passenger. Local and federal political pressure,

along with the power of Martin Luther King Jr.'s powerful rhetoric, made Parks a symbol of resistance against Montgomery's segregation laws. A long and ultimately successful boycott of the city's buses brought the first civil rights victory to Montgomery in 1956. Finally, Ralph Nader used his legal and oratorical skills to publicize the prevalence of unsafe consumer products. After winning a nationally prominent lawsuit against Chevrolet, he established dozens of public interest groups and inspired a generation of lawyers and activists to work hard for safer consumer products and more democratic governance. It is important to recognize that in each case, these individuals overcame significant obstacles that included opposition by well-entrenched, powerful groups and dissension within their own organizations.

6. There is a long tradition in America of suspicion and deep skepticism about government that goes back to the earliest years of our history as a nation. So how do we explain the ongoing prevalence of this institution in our society? Two morality stories help us to understand the answer. In the Tragedy of the Commons, fellow villagers attempted to create a system of voluntary compliance for limiting grazing on their large meadow. The purpose of this system was to preserve the right of all to continue to use this collective good while preventing overgrazing. In the Story of the Lighthouse, residents of a fishing village pooled their money to build a lighthouse that would prevent their boats from wrecking in foggy conditions. In each case, however, problems arose that well-meaning community members could not solve successfully without a higher authority to act as intermediary and rule maker. In the shepherding village, some community residents sought to continue increasing the size of their flocks out of self-interest. In the fishing village, new community members who had not contributed to the collective good in the first place refused to pay their share, becoming, in effect, free riders. Government arises out of the need to provide a central authority to make and enforce decisions on behalf of all members of society.

7. Political science is the study of how societies determine the way in which they will govern themselves. It focuses our attention on those who have the authority to allocate values for the rest of society. This encompasses both the formal, authoritative institutions of government and those private individuals and groups that seek to shape the debate over policy decisions.

Study Questions

1. What specific hurdles did Bill Clinton face in running for president in 1992?
2. Explain why President George Bush was unable to win reelection.
3. What kind of influence did Ross Perot have on the 1992 presidential campaign?
4. Explain how Bill Clinton was able to win so decisively in 1992.
5. Distinguish between a direct and an indirect democracy.

6. What are the essential attributes of a democracy?
7. What trend has been taking place in voter turnout in America over the past 30 years?
8. Who is most likely to vote in America?
9. Why do many Americans refuse to vote?
10. What kind of rule changes could increase voter turnout?
11. Identify Milbrath's three categories of American political participants.
12. How did Daniel Shays's participation shape the future of American politics?
13. What changes were brought about by Rosa Parks's refusal to give her seat on the bus to a white passenger?
14. What issues have been of concern to Ralph Nader?
15. What general attitude do Americans have about government?
16. Explain why the shepherding village's solution to overgrazing worked to benefit those engaged in immoral actions.
17. Why did the agreement reached by the fishing village simply lead to further arguing and dissension?
18. Give some examples of indivisible goods other than those provided in the text.
19. What is the difference between public and private goods?
20. What is the goal of studying political science?

Quizzes

True-False Questions

____   1. Bill Clinton was never able to articulate a clear message to the voters during the 1992 campaign.
____   2. The state of the national economy was an important factor in the 1992 presidential race.
____   3. Democratic societies are defined simply as those that have elections.
____   4. The vast majority of Americans participate actively in politics.
____   5. More Americans would vote if voting were made more convenient.
____   6. Daniel Shays took part in writing the Constitution.
____   7. Americans have a long tradition of not trusting their own government.
____   8. Free riders are people who receive benefits without paying for them.
____   9. Indivisible goods are those that cannot be seen.
____ 10. Sanctions can be threats of punishment designed to prevent people from doing something.

Multiple-Choice Questions

____   1. Bill Clinton's 1992 presidential candidacy had all of the following advantages except:
  a. good organization and fund-raising.
  b. an untroubled marriage and impressive military record.

    c. a well-orchestrated party convention.

    d. effective use of live interviews on TV talk shows.

____ 2. The main reason that George Bush lost his race for reelection in 1992 was:

    a. that he got the U.S. involved in the war against Iraq.

    b. the challenge from the right wing of his party.

    c. charges of marital infidelity and draft evasion.

    d. that he had no plan for reviving the economy.

____ 3. In Milbrath's hierarchy of political involvement, what activity appears at the top?

    a. making a monetary contribution to a party

    b. voting on a regular basis

    c. holding public and party office

    d. exposing oneself to political stimuli

____ 4. What kind of American is most likely to vote?

    a. an 18-year-old person from the South

    b. a middle-aged person with a college degree

    c. an unemployed worker from the West

    d. a 75-year-old without a college degree

____ 5. All of the following changes would improve voter turnout except:

    a. reducing the number of candidates on the ballot.

    b. holding registration just before an election.

    c. permitting voting by mail.

    d. placing fewer issues on the ballot.

____ 6. Ralph Nader has been influential in American politics because:

    a. he has won several elections to prominent offices.

    b. he has raised a lot of campaign donations.

    c. he helped to organize several public interest groups.

    d. he has been willing to work with private enterprise.

____ 7. The shepherding village faced a tragic situation because:

    a. some herders were constantly criticizing others.

    b. some herders were just beginning their flocks.

    c. some herders' flocks were larger than others.

    d. some herders continued to increase their flocks.

____ 8. The fishing village had a problem with free riders because:

    a. nobody was wrecking their boats any longer.

    b. newcomers were not paying for the lighthouse.

    c. there were more newcomers than residents.

    d. the harbor tax would only apply to newcomers.

____ 9. Valuable goods and services that cannot be sold individually are called:

    a. private goods and services.

    b. selective goods and services.

    c. government goods and services.

    d. indivisible goods and services.

____ 10. Politics can be defined as all of the following except:
   a. the fulfillment of the emotional needs of a society.
   b. the authoritative allocation of values.
   c. who gets what, when, and how.
   d. how society's decisions are made and by whom.

Matching Questions

1.

____ H. Ross Perot   a. ran on the single theme of change
____ David Duke   b. focused attention on the deficit
____ Bill Clinton   c. had no plan for reviving the economy
____ George Bush   d. was a right-wing Republican challenger
____ Patrick Buchanan   e. was a Ku Klux Klan leader from Louisiana

2.

____ authoritative   a. decision making is in the hands of a country's citizens
____ government   b. ordinary members of a political system influence or attempt to influence outcomes
____ participation
____ institution   c. makes and enforces policies obeyed by everyone
____ democratic system   d. describes a decision people feel compelled to obey
     e. is a formal way of making and carrying out decisions

3.

____ direct democracy   a. term indicating citizens' belief that those making the laws have a right to do so
____ sanctions
____ republic   b. system in which a few individuals are designated to make political decisions for everyone else
____ misery index
____ legitimacy   c. system in which all citizens are eligible to participate in making policy decisions
     d. inflation rate plus unemployment at the end of a presidential term
     e. punishments or threats of punishment designed to prevent people from doing something

4.

____ Daniel Shays   a. became symbolic leader of a bus boycott
____ David Easton   b. believes that most citizens are political spectators
____ Rosa Parks   c. believes that politics is the authoritative allocation of values
____ Ralph Nader   d. felt that courts were unjustly taking farmers' land
____ Lester Milbrath   e. felt that consumers are threatened by unsafe products on the market

5.

____ free rider

____ indivisible goods

____ political science

____ private goods

____ public goods

a. recipient of the benefits of a group decision without paying for them

b. benefits or assets produced and held by individuals

c. benefits or assets provided by the government for the benefit of society

d. benefits or assets that cannot be divided up and sold individually

e. the study of how societies make public decisions through government

Answers

True-False

1. F, 2. T, 3. F, 4. F, 5. T, 6. F, 7. T, 8. T, 9. F, 10. T

Multiple-Choice

1. b, 2. d, 3. c, 4. b, 5. a, 6. c, 7. d, 8. b, 9. d, 10. a

Matching

1. b, e, a, c, d   2. d, c, b, e, a   3. c, e, b, d, a   4. d, c, a, e, b   5. a, d, e, b, c

2 STUDY GUIDE

The Politics of the Constitution

Key Terms

absolute majority requirement of the approval of 50 percent plus one of those eligible to vote to pass a measure.

affirmative action government programs to ensure that historically disadvantaged individuals are considered for hiring, admissions, promotions, and other decisions.

Annapolis Convention a gathering called to address trade issues among the states in 1786 that failed to draw enough attendees to succeed.

Anti-Federalists those who feared a stronger central government, believing that power should be retained by the states. They opposed ratification of the new constitution.

Articles of Confederation the nation's first constitution, adopted in 1781 and in effect until the ratification of the U.S. Constitution in 1789.

bicameral legislature a legislature with two separate chambers or houses, each of which must pass identical bills in order for a measure to become law.

Bill of Rights the first 10 amendments to the Constitution, which enumerate specific protections that individuals have from government actions.

constitutionalism the belief that the basic rules by which we are governed should be in written form.

ex post facto laws any laws that make a formerly legal action criminal or increase the penalty for a crime after it has been committed.

federalism a political system in which at least two levels of government have independent political power and can exercise authority directly over citizens.

Federalists those who supported the creation of a stronger central government and were in favor of ratifying the new constitution. This name was later adopted by the political party that emerged in the 1790s, led by John Adams and Alexander Hamilton.

Founding Fathers (Framers) the delegates who participated in the Constitutional Convention of 1787 and authored the U.S. Constitution.

Necessary and Proper Clause Article I, Section 8 of the Constitution, which gives Congress the authority to enact all legislation necessary to carry out its purposes. Sometimes called the Elastic Clause because of its discretionary nature.

quorum the number of persons who must be present before a group can officially conduct business or enact legislation.

suffrage the right to vote.

Chapter Highlights

1. The Articles of Confederation were the first constitution adopted by the newly independent citizens of the United States. The document was a loose arrangement designed to give the state governments most power over decision making and to leave the national government weak and ineffective. Despite some notable achievements, it proved inadequate in the face of severe problems facing the new nation. Among the most significant of these problems were the continuing threat of European aggression, domestic un-

rest triggered by disgruntled farmers, an unmanageable national debt, and commercial disputes among the states.

2. The Constitutional Convention of 1787 was called to propose changes to the existing constitutional arrangement, but the delegates in attendance decided to write up an entirely new document. The Framers, among whom wealthy elites were overly represented, shared a commitment to creating a stronger central government, and they were highly apprehensive about granting real power to the masses. Nonetheless, the convention was frequently divided over key issues, with lines being drawn on a sectional basis, over rival economic interests, or between populous and less-populous states. Only an overriding spirit of compromise saved the convention from disbanding. Chief among the new principles enshrined in the document was the establishment of three separate branches of government, a bicameral legislature, and a chief executive to be chosen by means of an electoral college. Other important issues dealt with the future status of slaves, restrictions on foreign imports, and voting qualifications.

3. The decision to adopt the new constitution was neither quick nor easy. State conventions met throughout 1787–1788 to consider the merits of the document. Those in favor, called Federalists, argued that it created a more solid foundation for the country through a more powerful, but limited, central government. Americans who were opposed, called Anti-Federalists, railed against what they perceived as excessive and unlimited powers given to the central government. In the smaller states, ratification came easily, but many of the larger states approved the document only after considerable debate and political maneuvering. In the end, ratification was assured only after an agreement was reached that a bill of rights would be adopted by the first Congress and submitted to the states.

4. One of the truly remarkable features of our Constitution is the fact that it has stood the test of time with relatively few changes. It has survived for so long primarily because its content is procedural rather than substantive. It is also framed in brief and ambiguous language. Most major changes in American society have therefore been accommodated within this framework, with precedents for governmental change set by Congress, the president, the courts, and changing political forces rather than through amendments. In addition, the amendment process is slow and cumbersome.

5. Our Constitution can be understood in the context of a deep-rooted commitment to limited government and a belief in written, binding contracts between leaders and the people. This principle of constitutionalism is derived from Americans' conviction that contracts of all kinds confer legitimacy, our belief in the authority of law over that of men, and the longevity of our present system of government.

6. Another important feature of the Constitution is federalism. The establishment of a political system in which authority is shared between different levels of government reflects the Framers' desire to preserve the

ongoing existence and legitimacy of state governments while creating a central government powerful enough to resist foreign pressures and establish uniform laws regulating commerce. Although the balance was initially viewed as even, the central government has steadily increased its power and standing over the past two centuries. This has come about because the Constitution grants the national government supremacy over state laws, permits Congress the leeway to pass virtually any legislation it considers necessary, gives the federal government control over interstate commerce, and authorizes substantial federal intervention in state affairs in questions of civil rights because of the Fourteenth Amendment.

7. The Constitution also mandates a separation of powers among the three branches of the national government. The Framers clearly intended this mechanism to counterbalance competing ambitions among rival political figures in the central government. Although this works to prevent possible abuses of power, it also serves the purpose of involving each of the three branches intimately in the process of making policy. Just how much say each branch has over policy is a function of historical factors and of the distinction between foreign and domestic policy issues.

8. Finally, the Constitution contains important guarantees of individual liberty to prevent potentially abusive governmental interference. While the concept of liberty remains popular among Americans, struggles continue over exactly how the concept should be defined in the context of political, legal, economic, and moral considerations. Even more troublesome has been the implementation of the concept of equality, which is often at odds with the commitment to absolute personal freedom that liberty implies. Current debates over affirmative action illustrate how this conflict can create problems.

Study Questions

1. What kinds of hurdles confronted the First Congress when it met in New York in March 1789?
2. Explain how the Articles of Confederation governed the nation.
3. Identify some of the severe problems facing the United States in the mid-1780s.
4. Why did the Articles of Confederation prove to be inadequate for the needs of the new nation?
5. Who attended the Constitutional Convention, and why were the proceedings kept secret?
6. What evidence is there that the Framers were deeply suspicious of granting power to the people?
7. What key issue divided the Federalists and Anti-Federalists?
8. Identify how the Virginia, New Jersey, and Hamilton plans differed from each other.
9. Why was the issue of legislative representation so divisive?
10. How did the delegates settle the issue of slavery?

11. What was the purpose of *The Federalist* papers?
12. Why did the Anti-Federalists oppose ratification of the new constitution?
13. Explain why a bill of rights became the first order of business for the First Congress.
14. Why has our Constitution survived for so long with so few changes?
15. What is the principle of constitutionalism, and why is it so deeply rooted in American politics?
16. Why did the Framers adopt a federal system?
17. What accounts for the gradual trend toward national supremacy?
18. What was the purpose of establishing a separation of powers?
19. Why does a separation of powers lead to shared responsibility over the making of public policy?
20. What was intended by the Framers when they included individual liberty in the Constitution?
21. Citing the case of affirmative action, explain why individual liberties have always been difficult to define?

Quizzes

True-False Questions

____ 1. There was no national executive or judiciary under the Articles of Confederation.
____ 2. Delegates to the Constitutional Convention refused to allow the general public and news media to attend.
____ 3. Federalists opposed adoption of the new Constitution.
____ 4. The new Constitution abolished slavery forever.
____ 5. The Constitution has survived for so long because it is primarily procedural in nature.
____ 6. Federalism is a system of government in which all power is in the hands of the central government.
____ 7. The Fourteenth Amendment has vastly expanded the authority of the central government.
____ 8. Separation of powers refers to the division of power between the states and the central government.
____ 9. Each of the three branches of government is involved in making public policy.
____ 10. Affirmative action presents no conflict with the ideal of individual liberty.

Multiple-Choice Questions

____ 1. The Articles of Confederation did not work well for the country because they:
    a. led to high taxes for the people.

b. did not provide enough unity among the states.

c. mandated life terms of office for the judiciary.

d. gave too much power to the executive branch.

____ 2. All of the following problems faced the country in the mid-1780s except:

a. the inability to raise sufficient revenues.

b. disputes between the states.

c. the threat of foreign invasion.

d. extremely high federal taxes on the people.

____ 3. The Framers attending the Constitutional Convention can be considered "radicals" for their time because:

a. they all wanted to see the country governed by democracy.

b. they all advocated giving more power to the central government.

c. they all wanted to abolish slavery as inhuman.

d. they all were in favor of redistributing wealth from the rich to the poor.

____ 4. The major issue that divided the Federalists and Anti-Federalists was:

a. the abolition of slavery.

b. the power of the central government.

c. the right of people to vote.

d. the separation of powers.

____ 5. Several states refused to ratify the new Constitution unless:

a. a clause abolishing slavery was added.

b. they could select the first president.

c. a bill of rights was added.

d. authority over voting was given to the states.

____ 6. The Constitution has stood the test of time, with very few amendments being adopted, because:

a. Americans have faced few serious political crises over the years.

b. the Constitution is largely substantive in nature.

c. elected politicians have found ways of getting around its provisions.

d. the Constitution focuses primarily on procedural matters.

____ 7. A federal system of government was incorporated into the Constitution because:

a. of the need to protect against encroachment by foreign powers.

b. of the need to protect and promote civil liberties.

c. of the desire to trust in the authority of law rather than men.

d. of the longstanding belief in the legitimacy of written contracts.

____ 8. National supremacy has expanded because of all of the following parts of the Constitution except the:

a. Supremacy Clause.

b. Fourteenth Amendment.

c. Necessary and Proper Clause.

____ d. Ratification Clause.

____ 9. When James Madison wrote that "ambition should be made to counteract ambition," he was referring to:

    a. civil liberties.

    b. constitutionalism.

    c. separation of powers.

    d. federalism.

____ 10. The issue of equality is complicated because it has been defined in
all of the following ways except:

    a. economic.

    b. historical.

    c. moral.

    d. legal.

Matching Questions

1.

____ quorum

____ suffrage

____ constitutionalism

____ absolute majority

____ elastic clause

a. 50 percent plus one of those eligible to vote

b. belief that basic rules by which we are governed should
be written down

c. number of persons who must be present before a group
can officially conduct business

d. right to vote in elections

e. authority to enact all legislation that is necessary and
proper

2.

____ Articles of Confederation

____ Framers

____ Anti-Federalists

____ Annapolis Convention

____ Federalists

a. delegates who participated in the Constitutional
Convention

b. those in favor of ratifying the new Constitution

c. gathering to address trade issues among the states

d. the first constitution of the U.S.

e. those who opposed ratification of the new Constitution

3.

____ Delaware

____ Virginia

____ Rhode Island

____ New Jersey

____ South Carolina

a. other states threatened a tariff against its goods if it did
not ratify the Constitution

b. insisted that states be allowed to continue to import
slaves

c. was the first state to ratify the Constitution

d. offered a plan that created a single-chamber Congress

e. demanded that a bill of rights be added to the
Constitution

4.

____ bicameral
____ ex post facto law
____ bill of rights
____ affirmative action
____ federalism

a. legislature with two separate chambers
b. measures to ensure that historically disadvantaged individuals are considered
c. concept of two levels of government with independent political power
d. legislation making an act criminal even though it was legal at the time it was committed
e. protections individuals have from government actions

5.

____ constitutionalism
____ federalism
____ separation of powers
____ individual liberties
____ suffrage

a. privilege left up to the states to determine
b. right to act without government interference
c. concept of balance among rival branches for successful governing
d. government with two different levels of authority
e. a belief in contracts

Answers

True-False

1. T, 2. T, 3. F, 4. F, 5. T, 6. F, 7. T, 8. F, 9. T, 10. F

Multiple-Choice

1. b, 2. d, 3. a, 4. b, 5. c, 6. d, 7. a, 8. d, 9. c, 10. b

Matching

1. c, d, b, e, a   2. d, a, e, c, b   3. c, e, a, d, b   4. a, d, e, b, c   5. e, d, c, b, a

3 STUDY GUIDE

The Federal System

Key Terms

block grants federal aid consolidated into broad categories and awarded to state and local governments to be used for specific purposes.

categorical grants federal aid to state and local governments that is targeted to achieve some specific goal.

competitive federalism a system of government in which the states and national government openly compete for authority over issues of joint concern.

concurrent powers constitutional powers that both national and state governments may exercise, such as levying taxes.

cooperative federalism a system of government in which the states and national government cooperate to achieve desired goals.

cross-cutting regulations rules that extend the provisions of one federal grant to other grants received by the same governmental entity.

direct orders federal regulations that demand total compliance by the states.

dual federalism a system of government in which the national and state governments act separately and independently of each other.

general revenue sharing federal aid to state and local governments that carries no specifications

as to how funds should be spent. This program was ended in 1987.

habeas corpus (writ of) a court order requiring a warden or police officer to bring a prisoner before a judge and explain the reason for his or her detention.

multistate regionalism an arrangement among several states located in the same region to work together to solve joint problems like pollution or harbor management.

new federalism an effort by the Reagan administration to return many federal functions back to the state and local governments.

preemption the federal government's action to take total control over an area of regulation away from the states.

tax expenditure provision in the tax code that provides for a reduction in the amount of tax owed by an individual or corporation.

unfunded mandates legal requirements from a higher government to a lower one, usually from the federal to the state level, that require certain actions but do nt provide the money needed to perform them.

Chapter Highlights

1. The Constitution provides the framework upon which our federal system of government is built. It provides considerable detail concerning the relationships among the multiple levels of government. For example, certain powers are delegated to the federal government, others are reserved for the states, and still others can be practiced by both. In addition, the federal government is required to provide certain guarantees to the states that include a republican form of government, protection from invasion and domestic insurrection, and admission to the union on an equal basis. Each state is further obligated to respect the legal actions of other states and to afford their citizens equal treatment.

2. The relationship between the federal government and the states has shifted dramatically over the course of American history. In the earliest era, federal authority was frequently challenged by the states in the courts, which ultimately led to the Civil War. In the era of dual federalism, the two levels of government were viewed as being separate and distinct, each with their own sovereign areas of responsibility. From the time of the Great Depression on, the states and the federal government have come into a far more cooperative relationship, sharing in the funding and administration of every type of public policy. Relations have not been uniformly harmonious, despite the fact that most challenges to federal supremacy have been rejected by the Supreme Court.

3. The most notable trend in the past 50 years has been the steady expansion of the federal government into affairs formerly handled solely by the state and local governments. This expansion has been made possible by a number of factors, including a judicial branch that consistently sides with the federal government, the Supremacy Clause and related provisions of the Constitution, the major financial advantages enjoyed by the federal government, and the emergence of serious social and economic problems that have defied the capability of the states to solve. As a result, federal intervention has increased substantially, first in areas like economic regulation, agricultural extension, vocational education, and highways, and later to welfare, urban development, and environmental regulation.

4. The gradual expansion of federal intervention in public affairs has taken two different forms. Fiscal federalism refers to outright grants of federal funds to the states, along with tax expenditures. The manner in which funds are distributed can vary from specific, tightly controlled grants to those that have few strings attached and allow the states considerable discretion in the way they spend the money. Over the years, Congress has preferred to keep a tight rein on its funding, while the state and local governments have argued for more self-determination. Regulatory federalism refers to federal monitoring and supervision of private-sector activities. The extent to which the federal government takes responsibility for regulation can also vary, from total control and preemption of state authority to more cooperative, flexible arrangements. This, too, has been the source of considerable federal-state tension, as the states complain of the high costs of compliance to federal rules without sufficient federal money to cover implementation. In both fiscal and regulatory federal intervention, the states have been largely ineffective in warding off federal supremacy because of their dependence on the federal government for continued financial aid.

5. In response to many complaints about insensitive and overbearing federal intervention, attempts were made by the Reagan administration in the 1980s to move federalism in a new direction. New legislation returned functions to the states, consolidated grant programs, and cut back on the share of federal funds. This in turn led to short-term hardships for the states by the

end of the decade. They have responded to the crisis with a variety of policy innovations that include economic development initiatives and seeking out alternative revenue sources. Much of this new dynamism is found in large metropolitan governments.

6. Federalism in the 1990s is undergoing major changes as a result of a number of important policy developments. The Supreme Court's decision in *Garcia v. San Antonio Metropolitan Transit Authority* firmly established the notion that federal regulations could supersede those in force at the state and local levels. *Garcia* was followed by the 1986 Tax Reform Act and the termination of general revenue sharing in 1987. Both of these changes have forced states to become increasingly reliant on their own sources of revenue while competing harder for ever-scarcer federal aid funds. Finally, a growing number of states have found it convenient and fiscally responsible to enter into multistate agreements as a way to deal with problems that are beyond the scope of their limited resources.

Study Questions

1. What powers does the Constitution give exclusively to the federal government?
2. Which important powers are reserved to the states?
3. What protections is the federal government obligated to guarantee for the states?
4. Describe the obligations each state must honor in dealing with the other states.
5. What kinds of relationships existed between the national government and the states during the eras of competitive and dual federalism?
6. How did the relationship between the national government and states change during the era of cooperative federalism?
7. What factors enabled the national government to expand its authority over the years?
8. Explain the difference between federal grants and tax expenditures.
9. How are categorical grants administered?
10. Why have state and local governments been frustrated by the proliferation of federal categorical grant programs?
11. What is general revenue sharing, and why was it ultimately ended by Congress?
12. How do block grants differ from the other types of grant programs?
13. Why do state and local governments frequently complain about federal regulatory intervention?
14. Describe the four different forms that federal regulations may take.
15. What accounts for the disparity among the states in receiving federal aid?
16. Why do some groups favor categorical grants over all others?
17. What kinds of changes were made by the Reagan administration under the new federalism?

18. How have the states responded to changes in federalism over the past decade?
19. Explain the impact of the *Garcia* case and the 1986 Tax Reform Act for the future of federalism.
20. What kinds of changes in federalism have been proposed by the Clinton administration?
21. Give some examples of the trend toward multistate regionalism.

Quizzes

True-False Questions

_____ 1. The federal government has exclusive authority to grant patents and copyrights.

_____ 2. Each state must respect the legal actions of all other states.

_____ 3. The era of dual federalism ended with the Vietnam War.

_____ 4. The federal government has been the clear winner in most disputes with state and local governments.

_____ 5. The expansion of federal fiscal aid to the states ended by 1960.

_____ 6. Categorical grants are preferred by state and local governments.

_____ 7. The federal government forced the states to raise their legal drinking age to 21.

_____ 8. The Reagan administration sought to reduce the total amount of federal aid to the states.

_____ 9. The *Garcia v. San Antonio* decision ended the requirement that states comply with federal requirements.

_____ 10. Multistate regionalism is a way for states to cooperate on problems that cross their borders.

Multiple-Choice Questions

_____ 1. The federal government is delegated all of the following responsibilities by the Constitution except the power:
    a. to fix standards of weights and measures.
    b. to regulate interstate trade.
    c. to conduct elections.
    d. to raise and support an army.

_____ 2. According to the Constitution, the states may not:
    a. pass laws interfering with intrastate commerce.
    b. pass laws impairing obligations of contract.
    c. pass amendments to the U.S. Constitution.
    d. pass laws specifying conditions of suffrage.

_____ 3. The Full Faith and Credit Clause of the Constitution specifies that:
    a. states may not pass laws violating freedom of religion.
    b. states may extend credit to financial institutions.

c. states must extradite citizens charged with a crime to another state.

d. states must recognize the laws of other states.

___ 4. During the era of dual federalism:

a. federal regulations were permitted to supersede those established by the states.

b. federal efforts to establish a national bank were turned back by taxes imposed by the states.

c. federal financial aid to the states expanded dramatically.

d. federal attempts to regulate private business were struck down.

___ 5. The first attempts by the federal government to establish and ensure compliance by the states occurred in the area of:

a. commercial regulation policy.

b. foreign trade policy.

c. affirmative action policy.

d. vocational education policy.

___ 6. The most popular form of financial grants to the states in Congress is:

a. general revenue sharing.

b. categorical formula grants.

c. categorical project grants.

d. block grants.

___ 7. Block grants were created by Congress for all of the following reasons except:

a. to consolidate related categorical programs into a single grant.

b. to tighten the amount of federal supervision in the way funds were spent.

c. to reduce fragmentation while still maintaining broad national goals.

d. to permit the states greater flexibility in how funds would be spent.

___ 8. The intent of President Ronald Reagan's new federalism initiative was to:

a. impose additional restrictions on the way in which federal funds were spent by the states.

b. shift more responsibility to the states in funding and administering programs.

c. expand the amount of federal funding in return for more responsible state supervision.

d. increase the level of general revenue sharing while reducing the number of block grants.

___ 9. Federalism in the 1990s has been influenced by all of the following recent events except:

a. the reduction in federal tax expenditures for state and local tax payments.

b. the continued reliance on categorical grants.

c. the termination of general revenue sharing.

d. the ongoing increases in federal grant funds to state and local governments.

____ 10. The Supreme Court ruled that federal regulations supersede those of state and local governments in:

a. *McCulloch v. Maryland.*

b. *Perpich v. Department of Defense.*

c. *Hammer v. Dagenhart.*

d. *Garcia v. San Antonio.*

Matching Questions

1.

____ dual federalism
____ cooperative federalism
____ new federalism
____ competitive federalism

a. states and national government work together to achieve desired goals

b. states and national government openly vie for authority over issues of joint concern

c. federal government returns many functions to the state governments

d. national and state governments act separately and independently of each other

2.

____ prohibited power
____ federal power
____ state power
____ concurrent power

a. borrow money
b. establish post offices
c. tax exports
d. conduct elections

3.

____ *McCulloch v. Maryland*
____ *Garcia v. San Antonio*
____ *Gibbons v. Ogden*
____ *Perpich v. Department of Defense*

a. states may not regulate commerce in areas previously regulated by the federal government

b. states cannot levy a tax on federal banks

c. state regulations do not supersede those imposed by the federal government

d. state governors cannot restrict the movements of their National Guards out of state

4.

____ concurrent powers
____ cross-cutting regulations
____ direct orders
____ federal preemption

a. federal rules that demand total compliance by the states

b. situations in which the national government takes total control over an area of regulation

c. powers that both national and state governments may exercise

d. rules that extend the provisions of one federal grant to others

5.

____ general revenue sharing
____ formula grants
____ block grants
____ project grants

a. federal aid distributed on the basis of population
b. federal aid with no specifications as to how funds should be spent
c. federal aid targeted to achieve some specific goal
d. federal aid consolidated into broad categories

Answers

True-False

1. T, 2. T, 3. F, 4. T, 5. F, 6. F, 7. T, 8. T, 9. F, 10. T

Multiple-Choice

1. c, 2. b, 3. d, 4. d, 5. a, 6. c, 7. b, 8. b, 9. a, 10. d

Matching

1. d, a, c, b 2. c, b, d, a 3. b, c, d, a 4. c, d, a, b 5. b, a, d, c

4 STUDY GUIDE

Civil Rights and Civil Liberties

Key Terms

affirmative action government programs to ensure that minorities and women are considered for jobs, admissions, and other opportunities.

Alien and Sedition Acts laws enacted by Federalists in 1798 to prevent criticism of their foreign policy and to make it more difficult for immigrants to gain citizenship.

bill of attainder a law alleging that specific individuals or groups have committed crimes and allowing them no opportunity to defend themselves in court.

civil liberties basic individual freedoms of speech, press, religion, assembly and petition, as well as the right to jury trials and protection from unjust arrest and prosecution.

civil rights rights of citizens to vote, to receive equal treatment before the law, and to share in public facilities.

establishment clause prohibits governmental support of any organized religion.

ex post facto law any law that makes a formerly legal action criminal or increases the penalty for a crime after it has been committed.

exclusionary rule prevents evidence that is illegally obtained by the authorities from being used in court.

free exercise clause permits individual freedom to practice religion as long as the activities are not of a criminal nature.

habeas corpus (writ of) a court order requiring a warden or police officer to bring a prisoner before a judge and explain the reason for the offender's detention.

religious test a requirement imposed by many of the colonies that one must belong to an officially recognized religion in order to vote or hold public office.

selective incorporation gradual extension on a phrase-by-phrase basis of the Bill of Rights to the states by the Supreme Court.

suspect classification Supreme Court concept that arbitrary categories based on race, gender, religion, or ethnicity may not be used in laws to discriminate against such groups.

totalitarian system of government in which all actions of citizens are subject to government control.

trial by jury the right of an accused person to have a selected group of other citizens determine his or her guilt or innocence.

Chapter Highlights

1. The Framers saw to it that the Constitution guaranteed basic civil liberties to all citizens. In the body of the original document and through the addition of the Bill of Rights, Americans are protected from government interference with their fundamental freedoms. Other important guarantees for citizens, called civil rights, were incorporated into the Constitution at a later date through the Fourteenth Amendment. These obligate the government to ensure that citizens are not treated unjustly by others.

2. The Bill of Rights clearly restricts the actions of the national government, but do these restrictions apply to state governments as well? For many years, the Supreme Court held that the first 10 amendments applied only to the federal government. With the addition of the Fourteenth Amendment and many related Supreme Court decisions over the ensuing 50 years, the guarantees of the Bill of Rights were selectively incorporated by the courts to include the actions of state officials as well. This process is not complete, however, and continues today.

3. There has always been a fine balance between how much our government should interfere in the lives of its citizens and how much it should allow them to enjoy their personal freedoms. Both civil liberties and civil rights remain controversial because of this tension. In addition, questions frequently arise about interpretation when two rights appear to be in conflict.

4. The Bill of Rights comprehensively describes our civil liberties. The First Amendment outlines the basic elements of freedom of speech, press, and religion. Each of these liberties has been hotly debated, since none can be viewed in absolute terms. An examination of the Supreme Court's record indicates that some limitations have always been placed on these freedoms when someone's individual expression could harm another person or could pose a serious threat to civil order or national security. The protections afforded in the Fourth, Fifth, Sixth, and Eighth Amendments to those accused of criminal offenses have also been controversial, since few members of society feel much sympathy for people who may be lawbreakers.

5. The Fourteenth Amendment calls upon the national government to protect individuals from unjust and discriminatory treatment. The concept of civil rights has been further refined through the addition of several other constitutional amendments, as well as federal legislation. While the right to vote is now firmly in place, such rights-related federal policies as affirmative action and set-aside contracts for minorities remain highly controversial.

6. Our conception of what is appropriate action on the part of government to protect civil rights and civil liberties has undergone constant change for more than 200 years. One source of change has been formal amendments to the Constitution, and alterations have also been accomplished through Supreme Court decisions. Women's rights have expanded dramatically, but the issue of privacy remains extremely controversial and subject to continued debate.

7. A major problem in the ongoing debate over civil rights and civil liberties is the uncertainty and shifting attitudes of the general public toward these issues. Polling and surveys indicate that significant numbers of the public express intolerance toward those with controversial viewpoints and toward the rights of the accused, despite clear-cut protections outlined in the Constitution. Essential liberties are hard to ensure when sizable segments of the population do not agree with them.

Study Questions

1. Explain the fundamental difference between civil liberties and civil rights.
2. How does our notion of limited government conflict with the beliefs of totalitarian societies?
3. What basic freedoms are guaranteed in Articles I, III, and VI of the Constitution?
4. What additional freedoms are guaranteed in the Bill of Rights?
5. How did the Fourteenth Amendment contradict the earlier court opinion in *Barron v. Baltimore?*
6. What portions of the Bill of Rights still do not apply to state and local governments?
7. Describe the basic position of the Supreme Court with regard to government regulation of abortion.
8. Why has interpreting the meaning of civil liberties been so controversial?
9. Identify the types of speech that are not protected by the First Amendment.
10. Is the government ever permitted to censor the press?
11. Distinguish between the two First Amendment guarantees regarding religious freedom. In what ways has each of these concepts been controversial?
12. Why are civil liberty guarantees regarding criminal due process so controversial?
13. What is the current position of the Supreme Court on the death penalty?
14. How has our notion of who has the right to vote changed in the course of 200 years?
15. Explain why affirmative action remains controversial.
16. How do changes in our understanding of civil liberties come about?
17. How have new concepts of rights had an impact on issues related to women and privacy?

Quizzes

True-False Questions

____ 1. Civil rights are basic freedoms relating to speech, press, religion, and due process.
____ 2. Governments that consider no actions to be outside of their control are called totalitarian.
____ 3. A bill of attainder guarantees any person the right to a jury trial.
____ 4. The exclusionary rule permits police to exclude certain types of evidence from a case.
____ 5. Some portions of the Bill of Rights do not apply to the states.

_____ 6. Speech that poses a clear and present danger to society is not protected by the Constitution.

_____ 7. The courts upheld the right of the Nixon administration to prevent national secrets from being published.

_____ 8. Affirmative action involves efforts by government to redress the racial imbalances created by segregation.

_____ 9. *Roe v. Wade* resulted in the banning of abortion.

_____ 10. Significant numbers of Americans disagree with civil liberty guarantees in the Constitution.

Multiple-Choice Questions

_____ 1. The Constitution explicitly forbids all of the following government actions except:
   a. bills of attainder.
   b. writs of habeas corpus.
   c. ex post facto laws.
   d. religious tests.

_____ 2. The Fifth Amendment gives citizens the right to:
   a. trial by jury in civil cases.
   b. confrontation with their accusers.
   c. freedom from cruel or unusual punishment.
   d. due process of law.

_____ 3. The Supreme Court has selectively incorporated the Bill of Rights based on:
   a. the First Amendment.
   b. the civil rights movement led by Martin Luther King.
   c. the Fourteenth Amendment.
   d. a number of civil rights laws passed by Congress.

_____ 4. The Supreme Court has ruled that the First Amendment does protect citizens whose speech:
   a. deliberately offends other people.
   b. incites others to commit illegal actions.
   c. presents a clear danger to society.
   d. contains fighting words of a racist or sexist nature.

_____ 5. In *Miller v. California,* the Supreme Court ruled that obscenity
   a. could not be banned because it defied any precise definition.
   b. could not be banned unless Congress voted not to continue NEA funding.
   c. could be banned if it lacked serious literary, artistic, political, or scientific value.
   d. could be banned if it seriously offended enough people to result in a formal petition.

_____ 6. The courts have allowed all of the following limitations to be imposed on the press except:

a. closing off a judicial hearing to the press.

b. filing a lawsuit against a newspaper for libel.

c. limiting the press to official military supervision on a battle-field.

d. prohibiting publication of a story to avoid endangering national security.

_____ 7. In exercising their religious freedom, the Supreme Court has permitted individuals to:

a. refuse medical treatment or vaccinations.

b. refrain from saluting the flag on religious grounds.

c. use peyote and other drugs for sacramental purposes.

d. take part in human sacrifices.

_____ 8. With regard to the death penalty, the Supreme Court has recently ruled that:

a. it is no longer constitutional.

b. it may not be applied to severely retarded persons.

c. it may not be applied to 16-year-olds.

d. multiple appeals may be restricted.

_____ 9. A major source of controversy in women's rights is the "glass ceiling," which means that:

a. women do not receive the same advancement opportunities as men, despite equal qualifications.

b. women are defined as property in the courts, belonging to their husbands or fathers.

c. women are denied the right to choose whether or not to seek an abortion.

d. women are given jobs as a result of affirmative action quotas rather than personal qualifications.

_____ 10. The constitutional right to privacy is recognized in all of the following sources except:

a. *Griswold v. Connecticut.*

b. the Ninth Amendment.

c. *Barron v. Baltimore.*

d. *Roe v. Wade.*

Matching Questions

1.

_____ bill of attainder

_____ ex post facto law

_____ religious test

_____ writ of habeas corpus

a. voters and candidates for office were required to meet it

b. prisoners have right to see a judge about their incarceration

c. singles out individuals or groups as alleged criminals

d. pronounces an individual guilty after the fact

2.

____ civil rights

____ free exercise clause

____ civil liberties

____ establishment clause

a. prohibits governmental support of any organized religion

b. guarantees rights of citizens to vote, to receive equal treatment before the law, and to share in public facilities

c. guarantees freedom to practice religion

d. guarantees freedoms of speech, press, religion, and prohibits unjust arrest and prosecution

3.

____ First Amendment

____ Fourth Amendment

____ Sixth Amendment

____ Fourteenth Amendment

a. protects freedom of religion, speech, press, and assembly

b. protects right to a speedy and fair trial

c. guarantees equal protection of the laws

d. protects freedom from unreasonable search and seizure

4.

____ exclusionary rule

____ suspect classification

____ selective incorporation

____ jury trial

a. determines a person's guilt or innocence through a selected group of citizens

b. describes categories of people vulnerable to discrimination

c. states that illegally obtained evidence may not be used in court

d. extends the Bill of Rights to the states

5.

____ *Brown v. Board of Education*

____ *Miranda v. Arizona*

____ *Griswold v. Connecticut*

____ *Barron v. Baltimore*

a. suspects must be warned of their rights when arrested

b. segregation of public facilities is not enforceable

c. the protections of the Bill of Rights do not apply to the states

d. states cannot restrict the sale of contraceptives

Answers

True-False

1. F, 2. T, 3. F, 4. F, 5. T, 6. T, 7. F, 8. T, 9. F, 10. T

Multiple-Choice

1. b, 2. d, 3. c, 4. b, 5. a, 6. c, 7. b, 8. d, 9. a, 10. c

Matching

1. c, d, a, b 2. b, c, d, a 3. a, d, b, c 4. c, b, d, a 5. b, a, d, c

5 STUDY GUIDE

Congress: Structure and Legislation

Key Terms

amendment a change to a bill, usually in the form of an addition or correction.

appropriations the provision of funds for specific programs authorized by a bill.

bicameral legislature a legislature with two houses, each of which must pass identical bills in order for a measure to become law; in addition to Congress, all states except Nebraska have bicameral legislatures.

bill a proposed law introduced in either house of Congress.

calendar a time schedule that indicates when a bill will be considered on the floor of the legislature.

census a count of all persons in the United States taken every 10 years, the constitutional purpose of which is to determine the number of representatives for each state.

closed rule a procedure in the House that does not permit any amendments to the bill under consideration.

cloture a process to cut off debate on the floor of the Senate; requires the affirmative vote of 60 senators (a three-fifths majority).

Committee of the Whole a committee formed in the House of Representatives to consider legislation under more relaxed rules than the formal requirements of its regular session, such as having a quorum of one-half the membership.

companion bills bills with identical provisions introduced in both houses of Congress.

concurrent resolutions expressions of opinion by Congress that do not have the force of law. They require approval by both houses of Congress but not by the president.

conference committees ad hoc committees composed of senators and representatives chosen to reconcile differences between similar bills passed by both houses so that a single version may then be resubmitted for adoption.

constituency the voters of a district represented by an elected official, or the district itself.

ex post veto conference committee method of undoing changes to congressional bills or resolutions.

filibuster tactic in the Senate that allows unlimited debate on proposed legislation to prevent or delay its further consideration; can only be stopped by invoking cloture.

germane debate that is pertinent to or has bearing on the subject.

hold action permitted in the Senate to block unanimous consent agreements.

joint committees committees composed of equal numbers of representatives and senators that consider matters of mutual concern to both houses.

joint resolutions actions to extend or suspend existing laws or to amend the Constitution; must be passed by both houses of Congress.

Journal a daily record of the official actions of each house of Congress.

law a bill that has been passed by both houses of Congress and signed by the president, or, if vetoed, repassed by a two-thirds majority in both houses.

legislative veto procedure in which Congress rejects by majority vote a presidential or executive agency act or regulation. The Supreme Court ruled such vetoes unconstitutional in 1983 in *INS v. Chadha.*

logrolling the trading of votes among members of Congress.

majority leader the leader of the majority party in the House or Senate who has previously been elected by party caucus. In the Senate, this person is very influential in setting the Senate agenda.

markup sessions stages in the legislative process when committees consider bills line by line and decide where amendments are in order.

multiple referral instance in which a bill is sent to more than one committee for consideration because its content transcends committee boundaries.

nongermane riders amendments to a bill that are not relevant to the bill's content; prohibited by House rules but occur frequently in the Senate.

open rule an order that allows amendments to be made to a bill under consideration on the floor of the House.

oversight the power of congressional committees to review and investigate the actions of the executive branch to ensure that laws are being faithfully executed.

pair an agreement by two members of Congress on opposite sides of an issue to have their positions announced if one or both will be absent.

pigeonholing a tactic used by committee members to avoid dealing with a bill; involves putting the bill aside for an indefinite time, intending never to take it up again.

reciprocity the practice of deferring to others in their areas of expertise in the expectation of receiving the same deference in one's own area of expertise.

restrictive rule an order that restricts the number and type of amendments that can be attached during the consideration of a bill on the floor of the House.

riders See **nongermane riders**

roll call vote a method of tallying up votes in which the position of each legislator is publicly recorded when he or she answers either yes or no by voice vote or electronic means.

Rules Committee a powerful committee in the House that controls access to the floor. It has authority to determine when and under what conditions bills will be taken from the calendar for consideration.

Seventeenth Amendment adopted in 1913 to change the manner of selecting senators from appointment by the state legislatures to direct election by voters.

simple resolutions majority votes passed by one chamber of Congress, ordinarily dealing with that chamber's rules or prerogatives.

Speaker of the House the presiding officer of the House of Representatives, selected by members of the majority party.

special and select committees those named on an ad hoc basis to consider a particular problem or when special expertise is needed on the part of members; usually disband after concluding their reports.

standing committees permanently established committees that are responsible for all legislation within a certain policy or subject area.

subcommittees small groups of legislators who all come from larger (full) committees. They conduct initial hearings and investigations on more narrowly defined subjects and report their findings back to their full committees.

teller votes an old method of voting in the House, where members passed by tellers (counters) who recorded each member's position on an issue. Most teller votes are now recorded electronically and published in the *Congressional Record*.

unanimous consent agreements time-saving legislative procedures applied to noncontroversial measures, in which party leaders reach agreement to adopt a bill without a vote.

Chapter Highlights

1. The Framers designed a two-chamber Congress to satisfy the demands of both small- and large-population states. The differences they incorporated into each chamber in terms of office, styles of deliberation, and constituencies have led to distinctive characteristics for the Senate and House of Representatives. Congress has many important constitutional powers, including complete control over taxing and spending, the regulation of interstate commerce, and maintaining the armed forces. The Senate has additional powers related to executive decision making.

2. Much of the work of legislators revolves around proposals for action that come in the form of bills, resolutions, and executive documents. They handle these responsibilities by breaking up into a multitude of standing com-

mittees and more specialized subcommittees. Here they devote themselves to detailed investigations into the activities of the executive branch. Such oversight can result in substantial changes in policy, since congressional committees ultimately have authority over authorization and continued funding for government programs.

3. The legislative process formally begins when a bill is submitted by a member of Congress and ends with the president's decision to accept or reject it. In the interim, many competing bills and alternative ideas are considered and debated. Much important initial work takes place in committees. The relatively few bills that survive this stage are then sent on to the floor to be considered by all members of each chamber. Detailed rules are worked out in advance by powerful members to determine what kinds of changes will be allowed and when a bill will appear for debate and floor votes. Any differences between House and Senate versions of a measure then must be worked out by conference committees before additional votes and submission to the president.

4. The fate of legislative bills can be greatly influenced by the dynamics of party politics and the roles played by influential leaders in each chamber. Parties are the basis of personal loyalties and voting patterns and they control committee membership and the appointments of chairpeople. While nowhere near as powerful as they once were, leaders such as the Speaker of the House and the Senate majority leader may exercise considerable influence through their access to information, control over communication, intimate knowledge of procedural rules, and ties to the president.

5. The president has always occupied a prominent place in the legislative process, despite the formal separation of the executive branch from the legislature. Indeed, most major initiatives originate in the executive branch, and Congress always gives the president's opinions top priority in crafting any major changes to policy. Yet there is always tension between the two branches, and the temptation for presidents to act without the consent of Congress is always strong. It is for this reason that Congress has made frequent use of the legislative veto in recent years.

Study Questions

1. Why did the Constitutional Convention create a bicameral legislature?
2. Describe how the perspectives of the House and Senate differ.
3. What was the long-term impact of the Seventeenth Amendment on the Senate?
4. List the formal constitutional powers granted to Congress. What additional powers does the Senate have?
5. What is the difference between a bill and a resolution?
6. Why are congressional committees so powerful?
7. What specific functions do committees serve in Congress?

8. What options do subcommittees have when they receive a bill for consideration?
9. What kinds of issues are dealt with in the legislative calendar?
10. Describe the powers of the House Rules Committee.
11. In what ways are Senate floor procedures far less stringent than those of the House?
12. How does floor debate differ in the House and Senate?
13. Explain why amendments and voting procedures could be important to the passage of a bill.
14. What is the purpose of conference committees?
15. Explain why appropriations committees are constrained in their ability to alter budgetary outlays.
16. What significance do the political parties have in Congress?
17. In what ways can the House Speaker and Senate majority leader use their positions to exert influence on legislation?
18. What role does the president play in the legislative process?
19. How does the legislative veto work?

Quizzes

True-False Questions

____ 1. The Senate conducts its business in a more rigid and formal atmosphere than the House.
____ 2. Membership in the Senate is more prestigious than that in the House.
____ 3. Each chamber of Congress determines its own organization and internal rules.
____ 4. Most bills submitted to Congress are passed and become law.
____ 5. Committees have much influence over which bills reach the floor for a vote.
____ 6. The Rules Committee is the single most powerful committee in the Senate.
____ 7. Filibusters are permitted only in the House.
____ 8. Most of the annual federal budget is uncontrollable.
____ 9. The Speaker of the House determines all committee assignments for individual members.
____ 10. The Supreme Court ruled that legislative vetoes were unconstitutional.

Multiple-Choice Questions

____ 1. Which of the following characteristics does not apply to the Senate?
   a. members have very diverse constituencies
   b. members are more relaxed and cordial with one another
   c. members frequently engage in formal debate with each other
   d. members must begin campaigning almost immediately after winning their seats

_____ 2. The House of Representatives has all of the following powers except:

a. the power to review and confirm all presidential appointees.

b. the power to pass all laws it deems necessary and proper to carry out its grant of authority.

c. the power to create agencies, offices, and programs.

d. the power to establish and maintain the armed forces.

_____ 3. A committee that has been temporarily created to investigate a particular problem is called a:

a. joint committee.

b. committee of the whole.

c. special or select committee.

d. conference committee.

_____ 4. When both chambers vote to extend or suspend existing legislation without the president's signature, they have passed a:

a. public bill.

b. joint resolution.

c. unanimous consent agreement.

d. legislative veto.

_____ 5. In practice, most legislation considered by Congress is not adopted because of:

a. frequent presidential vetoes.

b. subcommittee pigeonholing.

c. poor coordination between the House and Senate.

d. opposition by the House Speaker or Senate majority leader.

_____ 6. The powerful House Rules Committee has control over all of the following except:

a. returning bills to committee for rewriting.

b. scheduling the time permitted for floor debate.

c. determining the committee assignments of House members.

d. choosing to adopt open or closed rules for bills.

_____ 7. Conference committees are called when:

a. the two chambers of Congress cannot agree on the same wording for a bill.

b. two or more members of Congress want to exchange views.

c. an important bill fails to pass with the necessary majority in either chamber.

d. the president needs to ask Congress for additional funds.

_____ 8. Political parties are important in Congress because:

a. rules require members always to vote with the party's official position.

b. all members of Congress are required to have a party caucus affiliation.

c. members of Congress will not win reelection if they vote against their party leaders.

d. parties form the basis for many friendships and personal loyalties.

____ 9. The Senate majority leader is influential for all of the following reasons except that he or she:

a. is at the center of party communications.

b. possesses an intimate knowledge of parliamentary rules and procedures.

c. presides over the Senate in the absence of the vice president.

d. negotiates unanimous consent agreements with the minority party.

____ 10. Congress has attempted to limit the influence of the executive branch by:

a. requiring the president to submit an annual budget.

b. prohibiting the president from sponsoring a bill.

c. enacting legislative vetoes.

d. assigning executive branch functions to the House Speaker.

Matching Questions

1.

____ Committee of the Whole
____ standing committee
____ select committee
____ Rules Committee

a. exists in the House and controls when and under what conditions bills will be considered on the floor

b. is named on an ad hoc basis to consider a particular problem or where special expertise is needed

c. is permanently established to be responsible for all legislation within a subject area

d. is formed in the House to consider legislation under more relaxed rules than the formal requirements of a regular session

2.

____ closed rule
____ open rule
____ ex post veto
____ restrictive rule

a. permits amendments to a bill

b. limits the number and type of amendments to a bill

c. permits no amendments to a bill

d. removes portions of a bill or resolution already passed by one or both chambers

3.

____ Speaker
____ House of Representatives
____ Senate
____ vice president

a. has a powerful Rules Committee

b. is presiding officer of the Senate

c. permits filibustering

d. is presiding officer of the House

4.

____ filibuster
____ hold
____ rider
____ germane

a. amendment to a bill that has no relation to its content or purpose
b. unlimited debate on a proposed bill to prevent or delay further consideration
c. debate that is pertinent to or has bearing on the subject
d. tactic that permits members to block unanimous consent agreements

5.

____ unanimous consent
____ rule of cloture
____ concurrent resolution
____ joint resolution

a. vote by both chambers of Congress to extend or suspend existing laws or amend the Constitution
b. statement of opinion that does not have the force of law
c. agreement among party leaders to adopt a bill without a formal vote
d. vote to end debate on the floor of the Senate

Answers

True-False

1. F, 2. T, 3. T, 4. F, 5. T, 6. F, 7. F, 8. T, 9. F, 10. T

Multiple-Choice

1. d, 2. a, 3. c, 4. b, 5. b, 6. c, 7. a, 8. d, 9. c, 10. c

Matching

1. d, c, b, a   2. c, a, d, b   3. d, a, c, b   4. b, d, a, c   5. c, d, b, a

6 STUDY GUIDE

Congress: Individual Power and Actions

Key Terms

casework legislators' efforts to solve individual constituents' problems with such government benefits as Social Security.

committee on committees committee organized by the party caucuses in both the House and the Senate that is charged with determining assignments to standing committees.

Comptroller General head of the General Accounting Office, a congressional agency that audits executive branch performance.

Congressional Budget Office created by the Budget Reform Act of 1974; assists Congress by providing economic analysis and projections.

Congressional Research Service located in the Library of Congress; provides research and policy analysis to assist members of Congress.

franking free postage provided for members of Congress for communicating with constituents.

General Accounting Office (GAO) independent agency set up to assist Congress in auditing expenditures by government agencies.

Office of Technology Assessment agency that assisted Congress in the study of technological policy issues; now disbanded.

ombudsman government officer responsible for investigating complaints by citizens about government; usually operates independently of executive control.

pork-barrel describing government projects that disproportionately favor certain districts, states, or private groups; usually added to spending bills by lawmakers in order to curry favor with supporters.

seniority length of service of a lawmaker in Congress or as a committee member or chair.

Chapter Highlights

1. An increasing degree of public distrust in government and general dissatisfaction with Congress has led to falling support for incumbents. Despite recent changes in its composition, Congress remains largely unrepresentative of the American public with regard to the religious affiliations, occupational status, race, and gender of its members.

2. The perquisites enjoyed by members of Congress are extensive. Members receive large salaries, generous allowances for office space and staff, free mailing privileges, travel subsidies, use of television studios, and many other benefits. The need to maintain offices both in Washington and the home state bolsters these large budgets. In addition, most staff and other resources are devoted to constituent service. Members of Congress have found that this ombudsman role is critical in securing reelection.

3. Staff needs have also expanded as Congress has sought to increase its expertise to offset the power of the executive branch. Each of the many com-

mittees has its own extensive budget and staff. In addition, Congress has created special research agencies to assist its members, such as the Congressional Research Service, General Accounting Office, and Congressional Budget Office.

4. Committee assignments are vital to individual members of Congress. The two parties in both the House and Senate have devised different means for determining who sits on which committee. A number of factors are taken into consideration when assignments are made, including seniority, geography, ideology, and the interests and expertise of members. But the most important factor remains seniority in Congress and on a particular committee.

5. Traditionally, committee chair positions were awarded to the member of the majority party with the longest record of uninterrupted service on that committee. Criticism of the seniority system has led to alterations in the selection process among Democrats, although Republicans retain the seniority principle. A more significant change has been the removal of many powers formerly concentrated in the hands of committee chairs.

6. Congress has been criticized for spending too much time with local issues and constituent requests, while neglecting important national issues. Nonetheless, it continues to serve important functions in its role of legitimating, obstructing, or amending executive decisions. Congress also helps to provide definition of national issues, crystallizing public opinion for or against executive policies.

Study Questions

1. What are some reasons for recent declines in the number of incumbents returning to Congress?
2. Which religious groups are overrepresented in Congress?
3. Which occupational groups are most numerous in Congress?
4. Explain why women and minorities are underrepresented in Congress.
5. What kinds of fringe benefits does each member of Congress receive?
6. What is casework, and why is it so important to members of Congress?
7. Why do individual members of Congress eagerly seek funds for pork-barrel projects?
8. What important functions do legislative staffs fulfill?
9. How do members of Congress use franking and travel privileges to their advantage?
10. What kinds of specialized research agencies does Congress have?
11. Explain how members of Congress use their home styles to win re-election.
12. How are committee assignments apportioned in the House and Senate by each party?

13. What factors are influential when committee assignments are considered?
14. How are committee chairs selected, and why has the system been criticized?
15. What kinds of independent powers do committee chairs have?
16. Describe four important ways that Congress influences executive decision making.

Quizzes

True-False Questions

_____ 1. The level of support for incumbents has fallen in recent years.
_____ 2. Women and minorities are well represented in Congress.
_____ 3. Members of Congress devote much staff time to casework.
_____ 4. Most people dislike Congress but like their own representative.
_____ 5. The free mailing privilege is supposed to be used only for correspondence with fellow members of Congress.
_____ 6. The General Accounting Office assists members of Congress with constituent casework.
_____ 7. In recent years, members of Congress have increased the frequency of trips to their home districts and states.
_____ 8. Seniority is no longer a factor in the assignment of committee seats to members of Congress.
_____ 9. Most staff work in Congress is devoted to great national issues.
_____ 10. Congress may refuse to act on the president's proposals.

Multiple-Choice Questions

_____ 1. The level of support for congressional incumbents has been falling because of:
    a. increasing numbers of women and minorities elected.
    b. steadily rising campaign costs.
    c. declining interest in the major political parties.
    d. increasing public distrust of government.

_____ 2. The majority of members of Congress are characterized by all of the following except:
    a. an age of 60 or over.
    b. a high-status occupation.
    c. a strong religious affiliation.
    d. being a white male.

_____ 3. Women are underrepresented in Congress because:
    a. voters overwhelmingly prefer male candidates.
    b. few women are interested in running for office.
    c. women are not often found in professions that lead to election.

d. women often have more difficulty raising enough campaign funds.

_____ 4. Members of Congress spend a lot of time with casework because:

a. they want to appear helpful and responsive to constituents' needs.

b. they wish to embarrass the executive agencies directed by the president.

c. they have few other significant responsibilities.

d. they have access to free mailing and travel subsidies.

_____ 5. Which of the following items would *not* be considered a pork-barrel project?

a. a new post office for a small town

b. additional benefits for recipients of food stamps

c. a job training program for unemployed pearl divers

d. an extension of a city highway

_____ 6. A member of Congress from a rural Kansas district would be likely to seek out an assignment on the House:

a. Merchant Marine and Fisheries Committee.

b. Science, Space, and Technology Committee.

c. Agriculture Committee.

d. Judiciary Committee.

_____ 7. Which of the following would *not* be a criterion used to determine a committee assignment?

a. length of service in Congress

b. past professional experience

c. home state of residence

d. temperament and personality

_____ 8. Determining committee chair assignments on the basis of seniority is beneficial because:

a. it provides leadership that is reflective of contemporary society.

b. it minimizes political infighting within the party caucus.

c. it limits the bias of one-party control over Congress.

d. it lessens the influence of political parties in Congress.

_____ 9. Committee chairs are still quite powerful because of:

a. their ability to control committee staff.

b. their absolute power over subcommittees.

c. their power to appoint new members to their committees.

d. their right to a seat in the powerful committee on committees.

_____ 10. Congress as an institution has all of the following impacts on executive decisions except:

a. obstruction.

b. amendment.

c. commutation.

d. legitimation.

Matching Questions

1.

____ congressional office staff
____ senior members of Congress
____ congressional committee staff
____ junior members of Congress

a. are highly educated and deal mostly with policy matters
b. spend a lot of time on casework and public relations
c. frequently seek a better committee assignment
d. often chair committee meetings

2.

____ franking
____ pork-barrel
____ casework
____ ombudsman

a. looking after the needs of the voters
b. projects favoring certain states, districts, or private groups
c. free postage provided for members of Congress
d. investigates citizen complaints about government

3.

____ Congressional Research Service
____ General Accounting Office
____ Office of Technology Assessment
____ Congressional Budget Office

a. assists Congress in analyzing the impact of the budget and taxes on the national economy
b. was created to analyze energy, environmental, and scientific research
c. assists Congress in auditing expenditures by government agencies
d. provides research and policy analysis to assist members of Congress

4.

____ House Republicans
____ House Democrats
____ Senate Republicans
____ Senate Democrats

a. determine committee assignments through a committee that includes a 14-member panel appointed by the party caucus chair
b. determine committee assignments through a special committee, which has seats for any state with a party member in the chamber
c. determine committee assignments through a steering committee appointed by the floor leader
d. determine committee assignments through a special committee elected by party caucus and headed by the Speaker

Answers

True-False

1. T, 2. F, 3. T, 4. T, 5. F, 6. F, 7. T, 8. F, 9. F, 10. T

Multiple-Choice

1. d, 2. a, 3. c, 4. a, 5. b, 6. c, 7. d, 8. b, 9. a, 10. c

Matching

1. b, d, a, c   2. c, b, a, d   3. d, c, b, a   4. b, d, a, c

7 STUDY GUIDE

Presidency

Key Terms

executive agreements international agreements reached by the president with other countries that do not require the approval of the Senate.

Executive Office of the President (EOP) cluster of staff agencies created in 1939 to help the president in the formulation, evaluation, coordination, and monitoring of government policy.

Executive Order a presidential directive implementing provisions of a statute or treaty.

executive privilege assertion by the president that some matters are of such national importance that information regarding them can be withheld from Congress, the courts, and the public.

Gulf of Tonkin Resolution a resolution passed by Congress in August 1964 giving President Lyndon Johnson permission to defend American service personnel in South Vietnam with whatever force was necessary. Adopted overwhelmingly in both chambers of Congress, it was used as the basis for continuing large-scale American military involvement in Vietnam.

Office of Management and Budget White House agency responsible for formulating the president's annual budget and monitoring the use of funds and performance of all federal agencies.

political executive those public officials who are appointed and can be removed from office by the president.

recess appointments positions filled by the president when the Senate is not in session; unless the Senate confirms them, the appointments end on the last day of the next session of Congress.

veto ability of the president or local executive to reject a bill by returning it to the legislature without signing it.

war powers the president's personal authority to engage in war to ensure the security of the nation.

War Powers Act a law requiring the president to notify Congress and seek support for impending hostilities involving American troops; passed in 1973 in response to perceived abuses by previous presidents, particularly President Richard Nixon.

Watergate scandal a 1972 attempt by close associates of President Richard Nixon to bug the Watergate building headquarters of the national Democratic party in Washington, D.C., in order to gain the upper hand in the coming presidential race became a scandal when the administration attempted to obstruct efforts by Congress, the courts, and the news media to investigate. Ultimately, the scandal led to the resignation of the president and the criminal convictions of a number of top administration officials.

Chapter Highlights

1. Each president embodies the hopes and expectations of the American people, and much is expected of those elected to the office. Yet governing is only possible through the many staffers, advisers, and administrators appointed by the president, who comprise the political executive. The Executive Office of the President (EOP) has grown significantly in the past 50 years. Among the most important clusters of advisers are the White House Office, the Office of Management and Budget, and the National Security Council.

2. Managing the political executive is never a simple task for presidents. Since appointed officials may disagree with the president and seek different policy choices, presidents have turned to close personal staff in the White House to carry out many of their important directives. Management styles in the center of power differ with each executive, but typically follow the formalistic, competitive, or collegial models. Recent presidents have found it useful to rely heavily on their chiefs of staff to manage day-to-day affairs. The position of the vice president has also become more important in recent years.

3. The Constitution provides only brief details about the formal powers delegated to the executive branch. As a result, each president has been allowed considerable freedom to determine how he will meet the changing demands facing him. Among the formal powers of the president are those of legislative leadership, conduct of foreign policy, command of the armed forces, appointment of top public officials, and oversight of the execution of laws. As a rule, presidents have more success in managing foreign affairs; domestic policy initiatives are frequently delayed or defeated by opponents.

4. Beyond the Constitution, all presidents have relied on certain informal powers that have evolved since the days of George Washington. Those who project the symbolic authority of the office in a persuasive manner can often convince the public and Congress of the worthiness and strength of their policies. The news media play a particularly vital role in this process.

5. Presidents are not infallible, nor is their power unlimited. Each faces difficulties in attempting to accomplish objectives in a relatively brief term of office. Opposition may come from presidential appointees, large bureaucratic agencies, and rival power seekers in Congress. The most significant limitation is found in the Constitution, which gives Congress the power to remove the executive through the impeachment process.

Study Questions

1. In what ways does the public misunderstand the presidency?
2. What is the political executive, and why is it so important to the success of every president?
3. What important function does the White House Office serve?
4. What are the specific tasks and responsibilities of the Office of Management and Budget and the National Security Council?
5. Explain the circumstances surrounding the Iran-Contra affair.
6. Why is the CIA so controversial?
7. Describe the various tasks carried out by the president's top advisory staff.
8. Identify the differences among the three presidential management styles.
9. Why is the White House chief of staff so important?

10. How have recent presidents drastically altered the traditional role of the vice president?
11. Identify each of the formal powers delegated to the president under the Constitution.
12. What kinds of difficulties do presidents encounter when seeking to provide legislative leadership?
13. How does a pocket veto differ from a traditional veto?
14. What powers do presidents have in conducting foreign policy?
15. Explain how the War Powers Act was intended to limit the power of the president to commit armed forces abroad.
16. Why are presidential appointees sometimes turned down by the Senate?
17. Explain why the president's authority to issue executive orders to the bureaucracy can be controversial.
18. Identify several informal precedents set by past presidents.
19. Why is the president's persuasive power so critical to his success as chief executive?
20. What kinds of limits exist on presidential power?

Quizzes

True-False Questions

_____ 1. No president can take for granted his power to control the policy agenda.
_____ 2. The White House Office is another term for the president's cabinet.
_____ 3. The prime function of the OMB is to formulate the president's budget.
_____ 4. Cabinet members are always loyal to the president and his personal agenda.
_____ 5. Most recent presidents have relied on the formalistic style of management.
_____ 6. It is customary for the president to take the lead in launching new ideas and proposals in Congress.
_____ 7. The War Powers Act frees the president from having to consult Congress when going to war.
_____ 8. The news media contribute little to the success of the president.
_____ 9. In 1974, Richard Nixon was the first president ever to be impeached.
_____ 10. A pocket veto occurs only when Congress is out of session.

Multiple-Choice Questions

_____ 1. The president must delegate a great deal of authority to advisers and associates because:
   a. Congress may try to take over many tasks if the president cannot do them well.

b. the American people generally do not trust the president to do a good job alone.

c. one person cannot handle the many demanding responsibilities of the job alone.

d. the president needs someone to blame in case something goes wrong.

_____ 2. The Office of Management and Budget has all of the following responsibilities except:

a. taking operational control over foreign policy.

b. preparing the president's budget.

c. improving efficiency in government.

d. formulating the president's fiscal policy.

_____ 3. The Iran-Contra affair of 1986 was significant because:

a. it was the first time that any presidential adviser had ever resigned from office in disgrace.

b. it brought up the issue of how much control the OMB should have over federal agencies and departments.

c. it demonstrated that the War Powers Act was not effective in controlling the president.

d. it raised the question of what role Congress was to have in making foreign policy.

_____ 4. Presidents often find that they cannot rely on their cabinet members because:

a. many of them plan to run for president in the future and see him as a rival.

b. they become advocates for the programs and perspectives of the department they administer.

c. they prefer to seek alliances with Congress rather than with the president.

d. they spend little time in Washington and are out of touch with the president's agenda.

_____ 5. The formalistic management model is preferred by many presidents because:

a. it generates creative ideas through the stimulus of competition among advisers.

b. it conserves the president's time and energy for major decisions.

c. it tends to generate solutions that are more politically feasible.

d. it involves the president in the information network.

_____ 6. The White House chief of staff has the important job of:

a. determining foreign policy for the president.

b. issuing executive orders to the bureaucracy.

c. controlling access to the president.

d. creating the president's annual budget.

_____ 7. The phrase "the president proposes, Congress disposes" is a reference to the fact that:

a. the president plays a key role in sponsoring new initiatives, whereas Congress reacts to them.

b. Congress represents districts and states, whereas the president represents the entire country.

c. Congress always rejects the legislative initiatives of the president.

d. Congress is mostly concerned about domestic policy, while the president has a free hand in foreign policy.

_____ 8. The ability of the president to use his discretion in seeing that the law is "faithfully executed" has to do with:

a. seeking to defend himself through executive privilege in the midst of scandals.

b. evaluating and reviewing the annual budget.

c. issuing Executive Orders to the bureaucracy.

d. the appointment of politically unpopular people to top administrative posts.

_____ 9. According to Neustadt's model of presidential leadership, which type of power is most effective?

a. the power to command others

b. the power of persuasion

c. the power to impose sanctions

d. the power to bargain with others

_____ 10. The power of the president is severely limited by all of the following except:

a. opposition from personal advisers who disagree with their president.

b. the constant tug-of-war with Congress over policy.

c. bureaucratic agencies that conduct much of their activity without considering the president's goals.

d. the president's lack of influence in formulating the budget.

Matching Questions

1.

_____ executive orders

_____ executive privilege

_____ political executive

_____ executive agreements

a. international agreements reached by the president with other countries that do not require the approval of the Senate

b. presidential directives implementing provisions of a statute or treaty

c. public officials who are appointed and can be removed from office by the president

d. assertion by the president that some matters are of such national importance that information regarding them can be withheld

2.

____ White House Office
____ Office of Management and Budget
____ Executive Office of the President
____ National Security Council

a. advisers who consider policies and make recommendations to the president on questions of national security

b. group responsible for formulating the president's annual budget and monitoring the performance of all federal agencies

c. small, loosely organized group of the president's most trusted advisers

d. cluster of staff agencies that help the president in the formulation, evaluation, coordination, and monitoring of government policy

3.

____ formalistic management style
____ collegial management style
____ competitive management style
____ persuasive power

a. makes use of the conflict created by overlapping jurisdictions

b. emphasizes order and established lines of communication

c. stresses convincing others that it is in their interest to do what the president wants

d. emphasizes sharing of responsibilities

4.

____ war powers
____ veto
____ recess appointments
____ War Powers Act

a. the president's refusal to sign a bill passed by both chambers of Congress

b. positions filled by the president when the Senate is not in session

c. the president's personal authority to engage in war to ensure the security of the nation

d. requirement that the president notify Congress and seek support for impending hostilities involving American troops

5.

____ vice president
____ president
____ chief of staff
____ political executive

a. controls access to the president
b. is only a heartbeat away from the presidency
c. takes care that the laws are faithfully executed
d. serves at the pleasure of the chief executive

Answers

True-False

1. T, 2. F, 3. T, 4. F, 5. T, 6. T, 7. F, 8. F, 9. F, 10. T

Multiple Choice

1. c, 2. a, 3. d, 4. b, 5. b, 6. c, 7. a, 8. c, 9.b, 10. d

Matching

1. b, d, c, a 2. c, b, d, a 3. b, d, a, c 4. c, a, b, d 5. b, c, a, d

8 STUDY GUIDE

Bureaucracy

Key Terms

bureaucracy an ordered, hierarchical organization in which tasks are specialized. In government, bureaucracies establish rules and administer public programs to implement statutes (laws) passed by elected politicians.

bureaucrats people who hold positions in hierarchical organizations (bureaucracies). In government, these are career employees working for public agencies, departments, and commissions.

civil service a government employment system in which both selection and promotion of employees are based on merit rather than on political influence or partisan loyalty.

General Schedule the job classification system used in the federal civil service, with distinct pay grades ranging from 1 to 18.

independent agencies public organizations established outside the formal structure of the 14 cabinet departments, yet technically administered by the president. Examples include the Tennessee Valley Authority, NASA, and the Social Security Administration.

independent regulatory commissions public organizations that operate independently of any political control and serve the purpose of monitoring some important aspect of private business activities or the economy. Examples include the Federal Reserve Board, FTC, and FAA.

incrementalism the theory that decision making by public administrators (bureaucrats) consists of a regular series of small adjustments rather than major changes of direction. This phenomenon is especially apparent in the budgetary process.

patronage the practice of awarding government jobs or other material benefits to political supporters.

Schedule B position classification in the federal government comprising any job considered to be temporary. This classification does not require a civil service exam and can be filled through political appointment.

Schedule C position classification in the federal government that involves politically sensitive work and thus is eligible for presidential appointment rather than civil service selection.

Senior Executive Service top-most level of the federal civil service job classification system, occupied by career officials who are subject to reassignment, promotion, and removal by political executives.

spoils system a government employment system in which a newly elected executive (president, governor, or mayor) appoints relatives, influential friends, and campaign supporters to fill all job positions in government.

Chapter Highlights

1. The federal bureaucracy comprises of some three million public employees who work and administer government programs. In contrast to the political executive, these administrators are not appointed. Rather, they are hired, paid, and promoted on the basis of the civil service system, which emphasizes merit. The civil service system was adopted only gradually over the past century, but now comprises all but a small percentage of government workers. However, it still suffers from lingering discrimination against women and minorities and allegations of favoritism in pay and promotions.

2. The federal bureaucracy is made up of an extensive array of departments, bureaus, agencies, and commissions that were created piecemeal by Congress. These organizations vary tremendously in the extent to which the president may exercise direct control over their operations. Cabinet-level departments are under the complete guidance of the president. In addition, there exist three types of independent agencies: single-purpose organizations, government corporations, and regulatory commissions, each with its own particular characteristics. Those organizations that are not under the direct supervision of the executive branch exercise a significant degree of independence in determining their rules and procedures, implementing decisions, and adjudicating disputes.

3. Bureaucratic agencies derive their power from Congress, which traditionally has furnished only broad guidelines governing their structure, mission, and functions. The federal courts have reinforced the legitimacy of this practice. As a result, the decisions guiding the conduct of these agencies are largely up to the discretion of bureaucrats themselves. Public policy is thus greatly influenced by administrative officials and their priorities. Nowhere is this impact more greatly felt than in the formulation of the president's budget. Through the lengthy process of budget formulation, career bureaucrats attempt to assert their position with the Office of Management and Budget, warding off any changes they perceive to be threatening to their status. The push and pull of these negotiations often frustrates presidents and results in only marginal yearly adjustments to the budget and public policy, a phenomenon known as incrementalism.

4. For many years, presidents have been plagued by the tendency of the federal bureaucracy to block or otherwise resist the major policy changes they would like to make. Among the options available to presidents are upgrading the managerial responsibility of the political executive, increasing the number of political appointees, and working with Congress to bring about significant policy alterations and bureaucratic reorganization. But career bureaucrats have many political resources available to protect their domains. Principal among these are the allies in Congress and interest groups that join them in keeping programs alive and resisting changes in rules, procedures, and regulations.

5. Congress is a far more effective check on the independence of the federal bureaucracy than the president. Aside from formal control over organization and funding, lawmakers work closely with the bureaucracy in the course of casework for constituents and sponsoring government projects in their home districts and states. They can use their influence on key committees, through the appropriations process, and in many informal contacts to win concessions from individual agencies. In this reciprocal relationship, Congress and the bureaucracy are mutually dependent on each other to accomplish shared goals and objectives.

Study Questions

1. What characteristics does the government bureaucracy have?
2. What is the fundamental difference between the political executive and the bureaucracy?
3. Identify the major defects of the spoils system.
4. What are the guiding principles of the civil service system?
5. Distinguish the General Service classification from that of the Senior Executive Service.
6. What complaints have been raised about the employment practices of the federal civil service?
7. Why has Congress created independent agencies not under the direct control of the president?
8. Explain the essential differences among single-purpose organizations, government corporations, and independent regulatory commissions.
9. Why are independent regulatory commissions so powerful?
10. Why have Congress and the federal courts granted the bureaucracy so much discretion over public policy?
11. Explain the differences among formulation, implementation, and adjudication of public policy.
12. What is the most effective means held by the president for control over the bureaucracy?
13. What is incrementalism, and why might it be a problem in American government?
14. Why do presidents rarely get everything they ask for when they formulate and submit their annual budget?
15. What strategies have past presidents employed to overcome bureaucratic inertia in the federal government?
16. How do federal bureaucrats manage to successfully resist new initiatives proposed by the president?
17. What means does Congress have at hand to gain compliance and cooperation from the federal bureaucracy?
18. Why is the relationship between Congress and the bureaucracy best described as reciprocal?

Quizzes

True-False Questions

____ 1. Professional bureaucrats are not subject to presidential appointment or removal.

____ 2. The spoils system ensured the hiring and promotion of qualified people in government.

____ 3. Women and minorities now comprise a slight majority of the federal workforce.

____ 4. Regulatory commissions have more independent power than other types of agencies.

____ 5. Only the courts are granted the responsibility to act as judges in disputes over implementation.

____ 6. Most of the federal budget is uncontrollable from the perspective of the president.

____ 7. Bureaucrats are not involved in framing the president's yearly budget.

____ 8. Presidents have attempted to create more appointed positions in the bureaucracy.

____ 9. The president has the power to create and reorganize the federal bureaucracy.

____ 10. Congress and the bureaucracy are closely allied and need each other.

Multiple-Choice Questions

____ 1. The federal bureaucracy has all of the following characteristics except that:

    a. it is a pyramid-shaped hierarchy of organizations.

    b. its members are subject to presidential appointment and removal.

    c. its members make government service their careers and work their way up through the ranks.

    d. its members operate out of the limelight and seldom attract attention from the press.

____ 2. A major problem with the federal bureaucracy today is:

    a. a drastic decline in the number of women hired in recent years.

    b. the illegal use of public money for private purposes.

    c. nonadvancement of women and minorities into important jobs.

    d. a lack of patriotism and loyalty among public employees.

____ 3. Government organizations that raise their own source of revenue to support their operations are called:

    a. independent regulatory commissions.

    b. single-purpose organizations.

    c. independent agencies.

    d. government corporations.

____ 4. Independent regulatory commissions are unique in that:

    a. they are under the direct control and supervision of the president.

    b. they possess significant legislative, judicial, and executive powers.

    c. members of these commissions are appointed for staggered terms by the Senate.

    d. they do not rely upon the federal budget to derive their operating revenues.

____ 5. Which of the following is an independent regulatory commission?

    a. the Postal Service

    b. the Department of Justice

c. the Tennessee Valley Authority

d. the Food and Drug Administration

____ 6. Bureaucratic agencies are often granted considerable power in formulating policy because:

a. Congress furnishes only general guidelines, leaving the bureaucrats to fill in the specifics.

b. the president personally has neither the time nor the energy to formulate policy.

c. the Constitution stipulates that the bureaucracy "see to it that the laws are faithfully executed."

d. neither Congress nor the president has any significant role in creating the federal budget.

____ 7. The budgetary phenomenon known as incrementalism is attributable to all of the following reasons except that:

a. administrators are able to rally enough political support to keep their programs going.

b. much of the federal budget is already committed to mandatory outlays.

c. Congress is reluctant to eliminate current programs that have outlived their usefulness.

d. bureaucrats refuse to cooperate with the Office of Management and Budget in formulating the annual budget.

____ 8. The Army Corps of Engineers is continually able to obtain larger amounts of funds than the executive allocates because:

a. no member of Congress likes to endanger national security through defense cuts.

b. it does not have to submit its annual budget requests to the president and OMB for consideration.

c. it has the capacity to provide benefits for almost all congressional districts.

d. it has the unique status of being a government corporation.

____ 9. Which of the following strategies was not used by the Reagan administration to increase its influence over the bureaucracy?

a. creating more independent regulatory commissions

b. centralizing control over the appointment process

c. reclassifying government positions as Schedule C

d. giving the OMB responsibility for clearing all new regulations

____ 10. One reason that Congress exercises considerable influence over the federal bureaucracy is that:

a. it has responsibility for adjudicating disputes between private citizens and government agencies.

b. it can appoint new people to oversee the federal agencies if existing officeholders are not cooperating fully with the president.

c. it has the capability of proposing amendments to the Constitution.

d. it controls the annual appropriation of funding for all government agencies.

Matching Questions

1.

____ bureaucracy

____ civil service system

____ spoils system

____ patronage

a. employment system in which both selection and promotion of employees are based on merit

b. an ordered, hierarchical organization in which tasks are specialized

c. the practice of handing out government jobs or other material rewards to political supporters

d. employment system in which a newly elected executive (president, governor, or mayor) appoints relatives, influential friends, and campaign supporters to fill government jobs

2.

____ political executive

____ members of Congress

____ bureaucrats

____ presidents

a. have a great deal of influence with government agencies through casework, projects, and appropriations

b. have made government service their career

c. have been appointed by the president

d. have experienced frustration and resistance from government agencies

3.

____ government corporation

____ single-purpose (independent) agency

____ Senior Executive Service

____ independent regulatory commission

a. operates independently of any political control and monitors some important aspect of private business activities or the economy

b. top-most level of the federal civil service job classification system

c. is established outside the formal structure of the 14 cabinet departments, yet still administered directly by the president

d. operates independently of direct political control and generates its own source of revenue

4.

____ Ronald Reagan

____ Bill Clinton

____ Richard Nixon

____ Jimmy Carter

a. experienced difficulty in making timely appointments and withdrew a number of controversial candidates

b. found little success with the legislative strategy, so he handed all domestic policy proposals over to White House staff to direct

c. found that his appointees sometimes did not agree with his policies

d. increased the number of political appointees through the use of Schedule B and Schedule C classifications

Answers

True-False

1. T, 2. F, 3. T, 4. T, 5. F, 6. T, 7. F, 8. T, 9. F, 10. T

Multiple-Choice

1. b, 2. c, 3. d, 4. b, 5. d, 6. a, 7. d, 8. c, 9. a, 10. d

Matching

1. b, a, d, c   2. c, a, b, d   3. d, c, b, a   4. d, a, b, c

9

Supreme Court

Key Terms

amicus curiae literally, friend of the court; a legal argument or brief filed by one who has an interest in a court case but is not a party to it.

appeals attempts by litigants to get a higher court to reverse the decision rendered by a lower court.

appellate jurisdiction power of a higher court to review the actions taken by a lower court with regard to issues of fairness and justice before the law.

briefs formal written documents that state the factual and legal positions of the parties to a court case.

certification a seldom-used technique for securing a Supreme Court decision when a lower court is unable to resolve an issue.

certiorari, writ of an order from a higher court to a lower court to send up a case for review.

conference (judicial) a meeting of the justices of the Supreme Court to consider which cases to hear and to decide those that have been heard.

docket the agenda of cases to be considered by a court in a given year.

impeachment a formal accusation alleging wrongdoing on the part of a public official brought by the lower house of a legislature, the House of Representatives. Conviction requires a two-thirds vote of the higher house, the Senate.

judicial review the power of a court to consider the actions of government agencies and statutes to determine whether they are in conformity with the Constitution.

mandamus, writ of a judicial order requiring a public official, a private citizen, or a corporation to perform some official duty.

opinion (judicial) a written statement issued by a court that specifies the reasons for the judgment (decision) rendered in a particular case. Judicial opinions are closely read to see decisions might apply to similar cases.

oral argument a statement of factual and legal positions given by opposing sides in a court case before the Supreme Court. This lasts an hour for each case, and each of the judges is free to ask questions throughout the session.

original jurisdiction the authority of a court to be the first to hear a case and render a judgment.

political questions issues considered by the Supreme Court to be inappropriate for their consideration and better resolved by those in the executive and legislative branches.

stare decisis the practice in judicial rulings of upholding past precedents, thus honoring the decisions of earlier courts.

Chapter Highlights

1. The Supreme Court and other federal courts enjoy a prominence unrivaled by judiciaries in other nations. This power derives from the open-ended authority given to them in interpreting the laws of the United States. The Supreme Court is by far the most prominent and closely watched, with virtually unlimited jurisdiction over the entire legal system, including all state and local courts. It hears cases on appeal, by certification, and through its own original jurisdiction. The lower federal courts consist of state-level district courts and appeals courts at the regional level. In addition, Congress has created a number of special courts with limited jurisdictions.

2. The federal courts exercise significant political power in three important areas. Judicial review is the capacity of the courts to consider the standing of any law or official action in light of the Constitution. This impressive power was not firmly established until the landmark case of *Marbury v. Madison* (1803), and has been employed only sparingly since that time. Boundary maintenance refers to the power of the courts to act as umpires in resolving conflicts between separate institutions of federal and state government. Finally, statutory interpretation is the power of the courts to interpret or otherwise clarify the precise meaning of existing statutes or administrative rules and regulations.

3. The Supreme Court has achieved considerable success in maintaining its role as arbiter of the federal system. There are several reasons for this success. First, the Court is insulated from strong political and public pressure because of the fragmented nature of American society and political institutions. Second, the court is able to muster support for its positions because of its tendency to render rulings in line with most prevailing political sentiments and its reliance on precedent in making judgments. Third, the Court has been vigilant in protecting its public image, seeking to maintain an aura of respectability closely associated with the Constitution itself.

4. The Supreme Court is not free to rule on all controversies, nor is it capable of correcting all injustices, because of the formal and informal limitations of its power. The Constitution imbues the president with the authority to appoint new justices. Congress is given the authority to determine the organization of the courts, specify their jurisdictions, pass constitutional amendments, and impeach justices if necessary. More commonly, Congress attempts to assert its power by altering the wording of statutes as a means of changing court interpretations.

5. The Supreme Court is limited by its design and by the legal restraints it imposes upon itself. One important limit is its composition—nine judges, each of whom is encouraged to be independent of the others. Self-imposed legal restraints also restrict its ability to exercise decisive power. These include rules about the kinds of cases eligible for a hearing, the manner in which the Court must consider cases, the existence of a large and fragmented state court system, and the lack of legally binding force in its advisory opinions.

6. There are no constitutional or political provisions for forcing the Supreme Court to decide a particular issue. The Court operates far out of the public limelight and according to its own set of rather strict rules of procedure. Cases are heard on the basis of secret votes. Those selected for a hearing are given a brief public audience called the oral argument, followed by several weeks of deliberations by the justices, held in seclusion. During this time, there is much lively debate and argument among the nine justices. Eventually, their decisions are released to the public in batches and disseminated in writing to the legal community.

7. Although the federal courts are largely removed from many areas of public policy, they do have a profound impact on areas in which they choose to become involved. Most significant are cases dealing with civil liberties and civil rights, which have been aggressively pursued with regard to the actions and laws of state governments.

   The courts also have a significant impact on regulatory issues and decisions regarding the relative roles and powers of the various institutions that make up American government.

Study Questions

1. What makes the Supreme Court unique in relation to the courts of other nations?
2. What kind of jurisdictional authority does the Supreme Court have?
3. How did the Eleventh Amendment restrict the jurisdiction of the federal courts?
4. What three methods are used to bring a case before the Supreme Court?
5. Who really determines which cases will be heard by the Supreme Court?
6. Why is there competition among the federal and state courts over hearing cases?
7. Identify the differences among the federal district courts, appeals courts, and special courts.
8. What does the power of judicial review mean?
9. In what way did the *Marbury v. Madison* Supreme Court case influence the power of the federal courts?
10. What kinds of cases have been most frequently subject to judicial review by the federal courts over the past 150 years?
11. Explain how the meaning of boundary maintenance has changed in recent years.
12. Why is it often necessary for the federal courts to hear cases dealing with statutory interpretation?
13. Give three reasons why the Supreme Court has been relatively successful in maintaining its unique status in American politics.
14. How does the Supreme Court maintain its aura of constitutional authority in the eyes of the American public?
15. What kind of formal influence does the president have over the federal courts?
16. Describe the various ways that Congress can exercise its influence over the federal courts.
17. Why is the composition of the Supreme Court a kind of limitation on its ability to exercise decisive influence?
18. Identify and describe the self-imposed rules and procedures that further limit the authority of the Supreme Court.
19. How does the Supreme Court determine which cases it will hear each year?

20. To what extent do debate and deliberation among the nine justices of the Supreme Court affect their final decision?
21. What areas of public policy are largely removed from the consideration of the Supreme Court?
22. What specific areas of public policy are heavily influenced by Supreme Court intervention?

Quizzes

True-False Questions

____ 1. Federal judges in the U.S. are different from those of the rest of the world because they are directly elected by the people.

____ 2. Most cases heard by the Supreme Court come under appellate jurisdiction.

____ 3. Federal district courts hear appeals from the state court system.

____ 4. Alexander Hamilton wrote against the power of judicial review in *The Federalist* papers.

____ 5. *Marbury v. Madison* supported the idea that the Supreme Court could use the power of judicial review.

____ 6. Congress frequently passes laws (statutes) that are vague and imprecisely worded.

____ 7. The Supreme Court must abide by a host of procedural rules that limit its power and authority.

____ 8. Acceptance of a case on appeal requires an affirmative vote of a majority of Supreme Court justices.

____ 9. There is no restriction on the number of opinions that the Supreme Court can issue in a case.

____ 10. The federal courts avoid issues dealing with foreign policy.

Multiple-Choice Questions

____ 1. The Supreme Court is unique in relation to the judiciaries of other countries because:

a. the judges and the Court itself are not mentioned at all in the Constitution.

b. the judges have the ability to hear cases on appeal as well as through original jurisdiction.

c. the judges have enormous power to interpret laws and to declare some of them unconstitutional.

d. the judges are not directly elected, and they serve for life terms of office.

2. An order from the Supreme Court to a lower court to send up a case for review is called:

a. an amicus curiae.

    b. a writ of mandamus.

    c. a stare decisis.

    d. a writ of certiorari.

____ 3. The federal courts that tend to be most supportive of state and local interests are called:

    a. appeals courts.

    b. special courts.

    c. legislative courts.

    d. district courts.

____ 4. *Marbury v. Madison* was an important case because:

    a. it helped to reinforce the constitutional principle of judicial review.

    b. it clarified the set of procedures to be followed when a new president was coming into office.

    c. it firmly established the supremacy of the Supreme Court over the other two branches of government.

    d. it gave legitimacy to the practice of federal courts issuing writs of mandamus.

____ 5. Judicial review has been applied most commonly by the Supreme Court to:

    a. cases dealing with the jurisdiction of federal courts.

    b. cases involving violations of the due process clause.

    c. cases based on statutory interpretation of federal regulations.

    d. cases related to the supremacy clause and boundary maintenance.

____ 6. Cases in which the Supreme Court is called upon to give clarification to a law passed by Congress or a rule in force by executive agencies are called:

    a. boundary maintenance.

    b. judicial review.

    c. statutory interpretation.

    d. judicial self-restraint.

____ 7. The independence and power of the Supreme Court is limited by all of the following factors except:

    a. self-imposed rules that determine the kinds of cases they may hear.

    b. the composition of the court, consisting of nine separate individuals.

    c. attempts by Congress to alter the jurisdiction of the federal courts.

    d. the relative insulation of the Court from public and political pressures.

____ 8. The Supreme Court selects which cases it will hear on the basis of:

    a. a careful analysis of recent public opinion polls related to the issue at hand.

b. the extent to which the cases raise significant federal questions.

c. the degree of importance placed on the issue by the president, as expressed through executive agency appeals.

d. a consideration of recent votes passed in Congress dealing with the subject.

____ 9. At what stage of the process is the Chief Justice of the Supreme Court most influential?

a. presenting opinions and views during the period of oral argument

b. clarifying which issues in a case will be considered before a vote is taken in conference

c. deciding in conference which cases will be placed on the docket

d. writing up the majority opinion that is disseminated to the public

____ 10. The Supreme Court has generally followed a tradition of avoiding which of the following areas of policy?

a. foreign policy

b. civil liberties

c. issues dealing with state and local governments

d. regulatory policy

Matching Questions

1.

____ appellate jurisdiction
____ certification
____ judicial review
____ original jurisdiction

a. a technique for securing a Supreme Court decision when a lower court is unable to resolve an issue

b. the authority of a court to be first to hear a case and render a judgment

c. higher-court review of a lower court's actions with regard to issues of fairness and justice before the law.

d. court consideration of government agency actions to determine whether they are in conformity with the Constitution

2.

____ stare decisis
____ writ of certiorari
____ amicus curiae
____ writ of mandamus

a. a legal argument filed by one who has an interest in a court case but is not a party to it

b. the practice of upholding past precedents in judicial rulings, thus honoring past court decisions

c. an order from a judge requiring a public official, private citizen, or corporation to perform some duty

d. an order from a higher court to a lower court to send up a case for review

3.

_____ district court
_____ Supreme Court
_____ appeals court
_____ special court

    a. judges hear most of the appeals cases in the federal court system
    b. judges have original jurisdiction over all cases dealing with boundary maintenance
    c. judges tend to reflect state and local interests when interpreting federal laws
    d. judges review decisions made by other courts to relieve the burden on the Supreme Court

4.

_____ conference
_____ oral argument
_____ opinion
_____ docket

    a. a meeting of the justices to debate which cases to hear or to cast votes on those that have been heard
    b. a written statement issued by a court specifying the reasons for the judgment rendered in a particular case
    c. the agenda of cases to be considered by a court in a given year
    d. time given for statements of factual and legal positions by opposing sides in a case before the Supreme Court

Answers

True-False

1. F, 2. T, 3. F, 4. F, 5. T, 6. T, 7. T, 8. F, 9. T, 10. T

Multiple-Choice

1. c, 2. d, 3. d, 4. a, 5. b, 6. c, 7. d, 8. b, 9. b, 10. a

Matching

1. c, a, d, b 2. b, d, a, c 3. c, b, d, a 4. a, d, b, c

10 STUDY GUIDE

Political Parties

Key Terms

blanket primaries elections that are open to all voters, who vote for candidates in any party.

caucus in legislatures, a meeting of party members to select their delegates to district and state conventions. Some states use party caucuses to nominate candidates for president.

closed primary an election that permits only those registered with a particular party to vote.

converting election an election that results in changes in the underlying support for political parties, but in which the changes offset each other, leaving the same party in the majority.

critical elections elections that indicate a fundamental shift in support for political parties and that bring a new majority coalition into existence; also called a **realigning election.**

dealignment a shift of voter preference away from political parties and toward independent status.

deviating elections elections in which a prominent minority-party candidate for president wins office, while the underlying support for the major parties remains unchanged.

direct primary an election held to select a party's candidates for the upcoming general election.

gerrymandering (redistricting) the drawing of district boundaries for legislative seats with the purpose of achieving partisan advantage. The Constitution gives this power to state legislatures.

maintaining elections elections that result in no underlying shift in party support among voters.

multimember districts (MMDs) electoral districts represented by more than one person.

national party conventions meetings of political party delegates from each state to formally nominate the party's presidential and vice-presidential candidates for the general election.

office bloc ballot a ballot that lists all candidates under the name of the office for which they are running. Sometimes called the Massachusetts ballot.

open primaries elections that are open to all voters, including those registered as independents.

party column ballot a ballot that lists all candidates by party affiliation, thereby facilitating straight-ticket voting. Also referred to as the Indiana ballot.

party system the fairly stable set of issues in a given period by which people clearly distinguish between political parties.

plurality rule method of determining the winner of an election on the basis of the largest number, rather than a majority, of votes.

political parties organizations designed to formulate a platform of policy positions, select candidates, facilitate campaigns through fund-raising and other means of voter mobilization, and provide a pool of individuals suitable for appointment to government offices by elected candidates.

primary an election held before a general election for the purpose of nominating a party's candidate for office.

realigning election an election that results in a fundamental shift in popular support for the two political parties, producing a new majority coalition; also called a **critical election.**

realignment a significant and lasting change in the underlying support for political parties.

reapportionment the act of reallocating some of the 435 seats in the House of Representatives to new states on the basis of a new decennial (10-year) national census.

secular realignment a change that occurs over a number of elections in the underlying support for parties, ultimately resulting in a new majority party.

single-member districts (SMDs) electoral districts represented by only one person.

Chapter Highlights

1. Political parties emerged early in American politics, because of the need to create the majorities necessary to elect candidates and pass legislation. From the beginning, a strong two-party system appeared, characterized by distinctive ideological positions and personalities associated with each party. America has passed through five identifiable party systems in the past 200 years. These historical eras can be identified by the degree to which groups of voters consistently align themselves with a party, or shift allegiance to another in the context of a critical or realigning election. Recent trends indicate both the ongoing presence of a highly competitive two-party system and the gradual breakdown of the once-strong coalition of the Democratic Party.

2. There has been much debate as to whether American political parties are gradually losing their purpose and relevancy in the latter decades of the twentieth century. Some observers see a general trend toward dealignment among voters away from any organized party, while others find evidence that parties remain important, although their traditional standing and functions have changed. Still others suggest that we are in the midst of fundamental shift of alliances of groups between the two major parties, with Democrats still remaining in the majority. Surveys indicate that distinctive voting groups can be distinguished and readily categorized into strong or weak supporters of one or the other of the major parties.

3. In contrast to the United States, many other advanced industrial democracies have multiparty systems. The most significant reason for the strong two-party system in America is the existence of single-member electoral districts that operate on plurality rules. Second, the majority party in our two-party system tends to be overrepresented in legislative bodies, at both the state and national levels. In addition, minor or third parties experience many difficulties in raising sufficient funds and overcoming stiff ballot inclusion barriers imposed by many states. While they play a prominent role in presidential politics at times, third parties usually are reliant on the rising fortunes of a dynamic leader and the existence of a single issue for gathering support in the electorate.

4. Both major parties are essentially loose confederations of many affiliated state and local party organizations. The key role of parties in acting as conduits for political careers has been circumscribed by campaign organizations that are now heavily centered on candidates. Increasing use of direct primaries and television, as well as campaign financing laws and increasingly independent voting behavior, have all limited the parties' role. But parties still remain important as sources of fund-raising and technical support for campaigns, and as the critical means of building coalitions in legislative bodies like Congress. The major parties also play a prominent role in determining the type of ballots used in elections, which increases their strength and helps to keep out third-party competitors.

5. Candidates running for elective office are chosen in a variety of ways in American politics, depending on the rules adopted by each state. Over the past 100 years, the process has been opened up increasingly to public involvement. The number of states using the less inclusive party caucus method has declined as direct primaries have been adopted. State laws differ, however, in the extent to which these elections include independent voters or permit individuals to cross party lines. Supporters of the direct primary claim that it is the most representative of the voting public and encourages greater diversity among candidates for office. Critics argue that primaries give too much prominence to personalities rather than issues. Finally, national party conventions are still held every four years, but have been more important as a means for drafting a platform than for selecting candidates.

6. Parties also remain prominent in the process of electoral districting. State and federal laws mandate a readjustment of district lines and reapportionment of seats after each nationwide census. Redistricting almost always leads to a divisive partisan battle in state legislatures to redraw district lines so as to benefit one political party and its incumbents over the other. At the national level, dramatic population shifts from the Northeast and Midwest to the South and West have resulted in a reapportionment of seats and political clout in the House of Representatives over the past three decades.

Study Questions

1. Identify both the issues and the prominent personalities involved in America's first party system.
2. What important purposes do political parties serve?
3. What is a party system, and how many different ones has America experienced?
4. Explain the difference between maintaining and realigning elections.
5. Identify each of the groups in the Democratic Party that emerged in the New Deal era.
6. What changes led to the breakup of the Democrats' New Deal coalition?
7. Explain why some observers disagree that there is a general trend toward voter dealignment.
8. Why does a single-member, plurality-rule electoral system serve to support a two-party system?
9. Why does a multimember, proportional representation system serve to support a multiparty system?
10. Why is the majority party in a two-party system usually overrepresented in the legislature?
11. What factors usually give rise to the emergence of minor or third parties?
12. What impact do third parties generally have in American politics?

13. What accounts for the growth of candidate-centered campaign organizations?
14. What important functions do political parties continue to serve in the context of elections?
15. How do election ballots differ from one state to another?
16. Why has the balloting process proved to be such a barrier to third parties?
17. Explain the difference between a party caucus and a direct primary.
18. What different forms can party primaries take?
19. Why do some observers support the ongoing existence of primaries and others criticize them?
20. Why do national party conventions remain important for presidential elections?
21. Why is the task of electoral redistricting so politically controversial?
22. How have population trends affected the reapportionment of Congress?
23. In what way has race played a part in recent redistricting exercises?

Quizzes

True-False Questions

____ 1. The first two-party system emerged with the appearance of the Democratic and Republican Parties.

____ 2. Realigning elections result in the minority party candidate's winning the presidency and the appearance of a new majority party coalition.

____ 3. Recent trends indicate that the current party system is no longer very competitive.

____ 4. Stanley B. Greenberg feels that neither major party is attractive to many voters.

____ 5. The majority party in a two-party system tends to be overrepresented in the legislature.

____ 6. A declining proportion of members of Congress are voting consistently with their party on bills.

____ 7. Gaining registration on the ballot can be very difficult for third parties.

____ 8. Detractors of primary elections claim that they discourage popular participation.

____ 9. National party conventions mainly serve the purpose of making a presidential candidate more attractive to the voters.

____ 10. With the onset of computer-based calculations, electoral districting exercises have lost their partisan character.

Multiple-Choice Questions

____ 1. The first party system in American politics that emerged in about 1795 involved competition between:
   a. Democrats and Republicans.
   b. Democrat-Republicans and Federalists.
   c. Democrats and Whigs.
   d. Federalists and Anti-Federalists.

____ 2. An election that results in the majority party's staying in power and no shift in the underlying support for the parties is called a:
   a. realigning election.
   b. critical election.
   c. converting election.
   d. maintaining election.

____ 3. The New Deal coalition that formed the basis of the Democratic Party has recently lost support from:
   a. blacks.
   b. liberals.
   c. white Southerners.
   d. labor union members.

____ 4. In analyzing the recent voting preferences of Americans, Raymond Wolfinger claims that:
   a. support for Democrats has dropped in recent years as voters become more and more independent.
   b. the number of people voting as independents has remained constant for the past 40 years.
   c. the movement of groups of people away from the Democratic Party has been offset by a similar movement of persons away from the Republican Party.
   d. the country is undergoing a significant realignment toward the Republican party.

____ 5. The New Deal coalition supporting the Democratic Party included all of the following groups except:
   a. white Midwesterners.
   b. Intellectuals.
   c. Labor.
   d. Farmers.

____ 6. Which of the following quotes is not taken from the 1992 Democratic Party Platform?
   a. "No one who works should live in poverty."
   b. "All Americans should have universal access to quality, affordable health care—not as a privilege, but as a right."
   c. "We reaffirm our support for a human life amendment to the Constitution."
   d. "The only way to lay the foundation for renewed American prosperity is to support both public and private investment."

____ 7. The main reason that America has a strongly established two-party system is because:

    a. of a long-standing tradition of seeking to solve each of our problems by considering two workable alternative solutions.

    b. we have never believed that third parties could come up with any good ideas that the two big parties have not already considered.

    c. of the continual alignment and realignment of Americans faithfully behind either of the two major parties.

    d. an electoral system based on single-member districts and plurality rules.

____ 8. Which of the following is not a reason that campaigns have become more candidate-centered?

    a. the rise in importance of television as the primary means of mass communication

    b. the replacement of party caucuses with direct primaries

    c. the inability of party organizations to effectively sanction their members

    d. the general decline of political parties as an important source of money and fund-raising assistance

____ 9. Critics complain about the use of direct primaries to select candidates because they:

    a. discourage a diversity of candidates from running for office.

    b. focus voter attention more on personalities than on issues.

    c. generally result in less participation than party caucuses.

    d. are less representative of the voting public.

____ 10. The highly politicized nature of electoral redistricting for Congress has been encouraged by all of the following events except:

    a. the gradual decline in voter preferences for either Republicans or Democrats since the mid-1960s.

    b. a string of Supreme Court decisions calling for "one person, one vote."

    c. the 1909 decision by the House to freeze its membership at 435.

    d. a shift of our national population from the Northeast and Midwest to the Sunbelt.

Matching Questions

1.

____ Farmers
____ White Southerners
____ Immigrant groups
____ Intellectuals

a. supported the Democratic Party because they felt it used government to solve major social problems
b. supported the Democratic Party because they had been hard-hit by the Depression
c. supported the Democratic Party because they resented what Republicans had done during Reconstruction
d. supported the Democratic Party because they lived primarily in large metropolitan areas

2.

____ converting election
____ critical election
____ deviating election
____ maintaining election

a. results in a prominent presidential candidate from the minority party winning office, but with the underlying support for political parties remaining unchanged
b. results in no underlying shift in party support among the voters
c. results in a fundamental shift in support for political parties that brings a new majority coalition into existence
d. results in changes in the underlying support for political parties, but with the special distinction that changes offset each other, leaving the same party in the majority

3.

____ blanket primary
____ closed primary
____ caucus
____ open primary

a. election that is open to all voters, in which people can vote for candidates in any party
b. election that is open to all voters, including those registered as independents
c. a gathering of party members to select their delegates to district and state conventions.
d. election that permits only those registered with a particular party to vote

4.

____ Eugene V. Debs
____ Theodore Roosevelt
____ H. Ross Perot
____ Robert M. La Follette

a. was the only third-party candidate in U.S. history to win the presidency
b. was the Progressive candidate for president in 1924
c. ran for president as a Socialist in four elections
d. was the second most successful third-party presidential candidate in U.S. history

5.

____ realignment
____ gerrymandering
____ dealignment
____ reapportionment

a. a significant and lasting change in the underlying support for political parties
b. a shift of voter preference away from political parties and toward independence
c. a reallocation of some seats in the House of Representatives to new states after the a decennial (10-year) national census
d. the drawing of district boundaries for legislative seats with the purpose of achieving partisan advantage

Answers

True-False

1. F, 2. T, 3. F, 4. T, 5. T, 6. F, 7. T, 8. T, 9. F, 10. F

Multiple-Choice

1. b, 2. d, 3. c, 4. b, 5. a, 6. c, 7. d, 8. d, 9. b, 10. a

Matching

1. b, c, d, a 2. d, c, a, b 3. a, d, c, b 4. c, a, d, b 5. a, d, b, c

11 STUDY GUIDE

Electoral and Voting Systems

Key Terms

absentee voting votes cast by citizens who will not be present in their home area on election day. Voters request absentee ballots from election officials by mail and must have them completed, notarized, and returned before the election.

absolute majority in an election, situation in which 50 percent plus 1 of those eligible to vote select the same candidate or issue position.

decision rules varying methods by which elections are decided, such as simple majority, absolute majority, etc.

Electoral College U.S. system of electing a president; comprised of delegates who meet in their state capitals one month after the popular vote to cast their votes. Each state's number of electors equals its representation in Congress.

extra majorities electoral rules that call for more than 50 percent plus 1 of votes to be case for the winner; the most common is the two-thirds majority, although the Senate occasionally requires three-fifths.

franchise the right to vote.

initiative an electoral procedure in which private citizens can propose legislation by obtaining the required number of signatures on a petition.

majority rule the percentage that determines the winner in an election; in a simple majority, the

winner receives 50 percent plus 1 of the votes cast; an absolute majority requires 50 percent plus 1 of all eligible voters.

political action committee (PAC) a special committee set up by an interest group to collect and distribute funds to support political campaigns and candidates.

proportional representation rules that allocate seats in a legislature to each political party based on the proportion of the popular vote it received in an election.

recall election a popular vote to decide whether an elected official should be removed from office before the end of his or her term; used in many states, but not at the federal level, where impeachment is the only recourse.

referendum a popular vote taken on a ballot issue proposed by a legislature. Referenda provisions exist in many state constitutions.

simple majority electoral rule in which the winner must gain 50 percent plus 1 of all votes cast.

spin doctors public relations consultants retained by political candidates to help shape their media images and build popular support; so-called because they often suggest what "spin" should be placed on the candidate's statements and actions.

Chapter Highlights

1. Decision rules influence the outcome of elections and shape the type of political system that emerges in a democracy. Although these rules vary widely in the United States, most are forms of the majority rule principle. Nevertheless, plurality rules govern most elections for public office.

2. Other rules govern voting. The right to vote, or franchise, has expanded slowly over the past 200 years, limited by racial, age, gender, citizenship, and property qualifications that have been altered or abolished through a series of constitutional amendments. Registration requirements still act as a barrier in many instances, leading to calls for further reform.

3. The impact of decision rules can be illustrated in the context of selecting the president. Candidates must compete for their party nomination in primaries and caucuses, which vary from state to state by dates, method of delegate selection, and degree of commitment to candidates required of delegates. National party conventions, which follow the primaries, serve as important means of consolidating party support and generating coherent themes for the coming election. The formal rules for presidential elections are focused on the electoral college, a body of delegates in each state who are chosen by the voters to select the winner of the race. If no candidate receives an absolute majority in the electoral college, the election is decided in the House of Representatives, a circumstance that has occurred only twice in American history. Opinions differ on whether the electoral college should be abolished or reformed.

4. Although virtually any citizen in theory can choose to run for political office in America, there are social, legal and political constraints that keep out all but a few. Such social characteristics as race, gender, marital status, and religion were once critical factors but have receded in importance in recent years. Legal restraints including age and residency requirements are still in place. Far more crucial in contemporary politics are the enormous demands on individuals for time for campaigning, connections within a local party organization, and finances sufficient to defray the enormous costs of running for office.

5. In recognition of the impact of decision rules on outcomes, many reforms have been proposed to make elections a purer expression of popular preferences. One of the most important early reforms was the imposition of the secret ballot. This was followed by the adoption of direct primaries, popular initiatives, recall elections, and nonpartisan races among many state and local governments. Discussion of election reforms at the federal level today is dominated by concerns about the excessive influence of money on the process. Federal campaign finance reforms have included the adoption of public financing for presidential elections and regulation of political action committees (PACs). Yet concerns remain about the many loopholes that exist in current federal laws that continue to permit the proliferation of "soft money."

6. Despite the efforts of many state governments to change public policy through the adoption of direct democracy mechanisms such as referenda and recall elections, our political system is still dominated by indirect democratic rules, especially at the federal level. The evidence as to whether or not direct democracy leads to policy that is more reflective of the popular will is, to date, mixed. This question is complicated by the fact that the

electorate does not generally hold clear, consistent policy positions over time.

Study Questions

1. Approximately what percentage of Americans regularly turn out to vote in presidential and nonpresidential elections?
2. Clarify the difference between simple and absolute majorities.
3. Explain how proportional representation and multimember districts work.
4. Under what circumstances are plurality rules and extra majorities called for in American elections?
5. What mechanisms did the Framers put into the Constitution to ward off the influence of pure majority rule by the people?
6. How is it possible for differing sets of voting rules to lead to different winners in the same election?
7. What barriers existed on the popular franchise in early American history?
8. Identify each of the constitutional amendments that has contributed to the expansion of the franchise.
9. Why is registration a barrier to voting for many people?
10. Explain why each of the four types of nonvoters do not participate in elections.
11. How do laws and procedures regulating presidential primaries vary from state to state?
12. How does the use of a primary as opposed to a caucus influence presidential selection?
13. What factors lead to a successful run for the presidency?
14. Explain the purpose and impact of national party conventions.
15. What role does the electoral college play in electing the president?
16. Why was the Twelfth Amendment adopted in 1804?
17. Discuss why some people defend the electoral college, and why others argue that it should be eliminated.
18. What alternatives exist to the present electoral college system?
19. What kinds of social, legal, and political restraints limit the number of people who run for office?
20. Why is it that most candidates who run for prominent offices today must have substantial financial resources?
21. What factors besides money influence an election?
22. What kinds of electoral reforms were adopted in the late 1800s and early 1900s?
23. Identify the major campaign finance reforms that have been adopted into federal law.
24. What is "soft money," and why should it concern us?
25. Why do efforts to rewrite decision rules often fail to effect significant policy changes?

Quizzes

True-False Questions

____ 1. Most Americans regularly turn out to vote in elections.

____ 2. Election to the House of Representatives is determined by the plurality rule.

____ 3. The Twenty-Fourth Amendment lowered the legal voting age to 18.

____ 4. The "Motor-Voter" law forces people to register to vote if they want to obtain a driver's license.

____ 5. Caucus selections help political outsiders succeed in presidential races.

____ 6. If there is a tie in the electoral college, the presidential race must be held over again.

____ 7. Today, successful candidates for any federal office must be wealthy or have substantial financial backing.

____ 8. Electoral reforms have had the impact of weakening the political parties.

____ 9. It is very difficult for interest groups to get around current federal laws that limit campaign donations.

____ 10. Most public decisions today are made by elected representatives, not through direct democracy.

Multiple-Choice Questions

____ 1. A decision rule that requires the winner to receive 50 percent plus 1 of the total votes cast is called:

    a. an extra majority rule

    b. an absolute majority rule.

    c. a plurality rule.

    d. a simple majority rule.

____ 2. The Framers attempted to impose limits on rule by the popular majority with all of the following mechanisms except:

    a. the plurality rule for election of members of the House of Representatives.

    b. the election of senators by state legislatures.

    c. the right of federal judges to be appointed for life terms of office.

    d. the power of the president to veto bills presented by Congress.

____ 3. States are prohibited from imposing poll taxes on their citizens by which amendment to the Constitution?

    a. Twelfth

    b. Seventeenth

    c. Twenty-fourth

    d. Twenty-sixth

____ 4. Which of the following no longer represents a barrier to voters in America?

a. registration
b. residency requirements
c. citizenship
d. race

_____ 5. People who tend not to vote because they have moved or are in some other way constrained from voting are called:
a. Political Passives.
b. Contented Apathetics.
c. System Disenfranchisees.
d. Politically Alienated.

_____ 6. In contrast to party caucuses, party primaries for the nomination of presidential candidates:
a. are far less democratic.
b. provide an effective means for outsider candidates to win.
c. encourage far higher voter turnout.
d. do a better job of measuring intensity of support for a candidate.

_____ 7. Which of the following is not considered to be an election reform?
a. simple majority rule
b. direct primary
c. nonpartisan election
d. secret ballot

_____ 8. Any group that forms a political action committee is limited by federal campaign finance laws:
a. to a maximum donation of $1,000 to a candidate per election.
b. to a total of $20,000 per year to a national party committee.
c. to a total of $5,000 in matching funds from the government.
d. to a maximum donation of $5,000 to a candidate per election.

_____ 9. An important concern about the influence of money in political campaigns today is:
a. poor accounting procedures by campaign treasurers.
b. the "soft money" that does not come under the limitations imposed by federal laws.
c. the decline of unions as a source of campaign funds for candidates.
d. the concentration of political action committee (PAC) money on congressional campaigns.

_____ 10. All of the following are decision rules designed to achieve direct democracy except:
a. referenda.
b. recall elections.
c. popular election of representatives.
d. citizen initiatives.

Matching Questions

1.

____ absolute majority
____ extra majorities
____ simple majority
____ majority rule

a. requirement of more than 50 percent plus 1 of votes to win an election
b. requirement that 50 percent plus 1 of eligible voters select the same candidate or issue position
c. requirement that the winner of an election have 50 percent plus 1 of all votes cast
d. the percentage that determines the winner in an election

2.

____ Twenty-fourth Amendment
____ Twenty-third Amendment
____ Twenty-sixth Amendment
____ Twelfth Amendment

a. separated voting by the electoral college for president and vice president
b. lowered the national voting age to 18.
c. granted residents of the District of Columbia three electoral votes in presidential contests
d. prohibited the states from imposing a poll tax on voters

3.

____ at-large election
____ initiative
____ recall election
____ referendum

a. all representatives are elected from the entire jurisdiction
b. popular vote on a ballot issue proposed by a legislature
c. private citizens propose legislation by obtaining a required number of signatures on a petition
d. popular vote on whether an elected official should be removed from office before the end of his or her term

4.

____ Political Passives
____ Politically Alienated
____ Contented Apathetics
____ System Disenfranchisees

a. those who have been prevented from voting by institutional constraints
b. those who are far out of the political mainstream
c. those who feel they are unable to influence their government
d. those who are largely content and believe their lives change little regardless of who wins

5.

____ individual contributors
____ political action committees
____ all contributors
____ presidential candidates

a. limited to a donation of $1,000 per candidate each year
b. eligible to receive federal matching funds
c. must report all contributions of over $100
d. may not donate more than $15,000 per year to a party

Answers

True-False

1. F, 2. T, 3. F, 4. F, 5. T, 6. F, 7. T, 8. T, 9. F, 10. T

Multiple-Choice

1. d, 2. a, 3. c, 4. d, 5. c, 6. c, 7. a, 8. d, 9. b, 10. c

Matching

1. b, a, c, d 2. d, c, b, a 3. c, a, d, b 4. b, c, d, a 5. a, d, c, b

12 STUDY GUIDE

Interest Groups

Key Terms

access ability of those concerned about government policy to express their views directly and personally to key decision makers.

clientele groups those whose members receive a direct benefit from a government program or from the activities of a government agency.

cross-pressures conflicting demands made on an individual because of his or her membership in multiple groups.

individual membership interest groups associations comprised of people with a shared view of an issue rather than a shared employer or profession.

institutional interest groups associations organized to represent the interests and concerns of such institutions as governments, universities, professions, and corporations.

iron triangles mutually beneficial alliances among members of committees in Congress, administrators from government agencies, and interest group representatives.

issue networks informal groups of specialists who move in and out of involvement with a policy more on the basis of intellectual commitment than of self-interest goals.

lobbyists interest group representatives who try to influence government policy through face-to-face discussions with key decision makers in the executive and legislative branches.

political interest groups organizations formed for the purpose of influencing policy decisions through a party or other political means.

public interest groups organizations promoting the interests of the public or society at large rather than those of their own members.

Chapter Highlights

1. Interest groups were envisioned by the Framers and have been an integral part of American politics since the nation's beginning. Groups organized for political influence can be divided into two broad categories. Institutional groups represent businesses, governments, foundations, and professions that provide goods and services to society. Individual membership interest groups represent people who are dedicated to a shared cause or view of an issue. Public interest groups claim to serve society at large by seeking regulatory or governmental reforms. Interest groups have proliferated in American politics in order to advocate more specialized concerns than the two major political parties can accommodate.

2. Interest groups occupy a prominent place in electoral politics. They devote their members' time and resources to organizing voters, distributing literature, raising funds, and sometimes supplying candidates to the major parties. Interest groups' influence has been facilitated by legal loopholes that permit contributions beyond statutory limits and the provision of gifts, trips, and honoraria to legislators.

3. Interest groups have proliferated in the past 30 years largely in response to the increasing numbers of federal programs. While more groups have brought greater diversity of representation and more technologically sophisticated grass-roots lobbying, interests are still not represented equally. Indeed, this massive group mobilization over-represents institutional business interests and remains dominated by those with the most wealth.

4. Interest groups secure benefits from government by gaining access to top-level decision makers to persuade them of the worthiness of their position on key issues. Offers of future campaign support or promises of grass-roots voter mobilization often provide the necessary incentive for persuasion. Well-funded groups that can afford to hire professional lobbyists—often former public officials—enjoy an edge over rival groups. For lawmakers, lobbyists can also provide critical information and formal testimony to support favored legislative action. Access in American politics is considerably enhanced by the large number of officials and institutions involved in policy decisions. It is conceivable that some of the influence wielded by powerful groups in Washington would be reduced if more functions of federal government were handled by state and local authorities.

5. Some regulation is currently imposed on the activities of interest groups. All lobbyists and their expenditures must be reported for the public record, and political action committee contributions are restricted by campaign finance laws. Regulation has been largely ineffective in evening the competition among groups, however, owing to loopholes in finance laws, the informal nature of much lobbying, and constitutional protections. Perhaps the biggest check on lobbying are lawmakers who are aware that the economic and social interests of their home constituents are more important.

6. Much of the influence of interest groups is derived from close relationships that their representatives develop in government. This can come through the appointment of group members to influential positions in the executive branch and obtaining government work contracts. Even more compelling are mutually beneficial alliances, or iron triangles, that are cultivated among interest groups, lawmakers, and government bureaucrats. These serve to protect and promote favored programs that benefit each member of the triangle. Some observers feel that the triangle concept is oversimplified, and they describe alliances as issue networks that loosely bring together like-minded policy experts. Such alliances may be tested by budget constraints, political parties, or determined efforts by presidents to overcome them. Finally, many interest groups have also found their influence enhanced by pursuing litigation in the courts and by involving themselves in nomination battles in the Senate.

7. Interest groups have both positive and negative effects on democracy. From the negative viewpoint, there is evidence that some groups engage in deceptive or otherwise unethical practices, especially in funneling money and favors into the system. Competition among groups is also slanted in favor of middle- and upper-income classes and institutional establishments. On

the other hand, interest groups do contribute to democracy by providing a diverse array of ideas and information, and they often are at the center of the negotiations and compromises necessary to get legislation passed in Congress. In addition, they can be seen as more genuinely representative of Americans than either political parties or territorially defined legislative seats.

Study Questions

1. What opinion did James Madison have about interest groups?
2. Explain the difference between institutional and individual membership groups.
3. What purposes do interest groups serve better than political parties are able to do?
4. What role do interest groups play in campaigns and elections?
5. What accounts for the rise in the number of interest groups?
6. Which segments of American society are overly represented by interest groups?
7. Why is the American political system more open to interest group access than many other societies?
8. How has the nationalization of political conflict affected interest group activities?
9. How do lobbyists use information as a source of power?
10. What kinds of people are most valued as lobbyists?
11. How much of an impact have regulatory controls had on lobbying? Why?
12. Under what circumstances is lobbying members of Congress most effective? When is it largely ineffective?
13. How do interest groups obtain access within the bureaucracy?
14. Identify all participants in an iron triangle and explain why such relationships are mutually beneficial to all.
15. In what ways does an understanding of policy coalitions as issue networks alter our understanding of lobbying?
16. What kind of an impact do iron triangles have on public policies?
17. Explain how the power of iron triangles and issue networks can be overcome by decision makers on the outside.
18. How do interest groups make use of the courts to push their agendas?
19. What arguments can be made against interest groups?
20. What arguments can be made in favor of interest groups?

Quizzes

True-False Questions

_____ 1. James Madison believed that interest groups were a necessary and vital part of government.

_____ 2. The Christian Coalition is an example of a public interest group.

_____ 3. The decline in contributions to political action committees (PACs) has reduced the influence of interest groups.

_____ 4. Interest groups are overwhelmingly biased in favor of higher-income groups.

_____ 5. Most political decisions benefit some interest groups and hurt the interests of others.

_____ 6. Interest groups prefer to simply hand out money and remain anonymous in legislative policy battles.

_____ 7. Federal regulation of lobbying activities has helped to reduce the influence of the biggest and most powerful groups.

_____ 8. Members of Congress will frequently vote against their home constituency if interest groups offer them big money.

_____ 9. Iron triangles can be broken by overarching concerns about budget deficits.

_____ 10. Interest groups usually stay out of highly charged nomination battles for federal justices.

Multiple-Choice Questions

_____ 1. Which of the following did James Madison say about interest groups and American politics?

a. The existence of competing interest groups was both natural and necessary in politics.

b. Americans were remarkable for their propensity to join in groups.

c. Political parties were an effective means for overcoming the negative influence of interest groups.

d. Interest groups in America were overwhelmingly dominated by the rich and landowning groups of society.

_____ 2. Interest groups differ from political parties in that they:

a. have the important job of promoting candidates for elective office.

b. are far more pragmatic and better able to bring about compromise and consensus.

c. better represent the hopes and ideas of relatively small numbers of people.

d. are the sole source of campaign funds and grass-roots voter support for elections.

_____ 3. Which of the following is considered to be a public interest group?

    a. American Cotton Manufacturers Institute
    b. Common Cause
    c. National Organization for Women
    d. American Public Transit Association

____ 4. Which of the following changes has not affected interest groups over the past 30 years?
    a. an increase in the number of interest groups
    b. the centralization of group operations in Washington, D.C.
    c. more effective use of grass-roots voter mobilization
    d. a decline in the number of single-issue groups

____ 5. What accounts for the significant increase in the number of interest groups over the past three decades?
    a. rising levels of government intervention in American society.
    b. the emergence of an increasingly competitive two-party system.
    c. the growing dominance of wealthy individuals in funding campaigns.
    d. a succession of federal laws designed to protect and promote interest groups.

____ 6. What kind of interest group tends to be the most influential in American politics?
    a. public interest groups
    b. institutional groups
    c. clientele groups
    d. individual membership groups

____ 7. Legally, lobbyists may engage in all of the following activities except:
    a. paying a member of Congress to give a speech at one of their group's formal meetings or conventions.
    b. writing up bills for members of Congress to submit on their behalf.
    c. providing testimony at public hearings held in Congress.
    d. paying airfare and hotel expenses for members of Congress who attend their annual conventions.

____ 8. Observers are concerned about the existence of iron triangles because:
    a. they deliberately exclude the executive and legislative branches from important policy decisions.
    b. they are sources of many illegal campaign donations.
    c. they seek to suppress active scrutiny of favored programs and projects.
    d. they serve only the interests of the wealthiest interest groups, who can give the biggest campaign donations.

____ 9. Where a large number of participants move in and out of policy deliberations, they tend to create:
    a. iron triangles.
    b. revolving doors.
    c. issue networks.

d. cross-pressures.

_____ 10. Critics complain about interest groups for all of the following reasons except that:

a. they are biased toward middle- or upper-income classes in membership and political advocacy.

b. they have had the impact of funneling excessive amounts of money into the democratic system.

c. they engage in deceptive or unethical practices.

d. they represent relatively few interests and are not very competitive with one another.

Matching Questions

1.

_____ clientele groups
_____ institutional groups
_____ public interest groups
_____ individual membership groups

a. associations organized to represent the interests and concerns of established institutions

b. those who receive a direct benefit from a government program or the activities of a government agency

c. those who have come together to serve the public interest, rather than their own self-interest

d. associations comprised of citizens with a shared view on an issue

2.

_____ American Association of Retired People (AARP)
_____ Christian Coalition
_____ Common Cause
_____ American Public Transit Association

a. institutional group

b. public interest group

c. individual membership group

d. clientele group

3.

_____ interest group lobbyists
_____ bureaucrats
_____ members of Congress
_____ policy experts

a. hope to persuade government to adopt policies favorable to them

b. move in and out of the policy process based on commitment to issues

c. want power to control the distribution of benefits

d. seek new programs to administer and more funding

4.

____ cross-pressures
____ iron triangles
____ revolving doors
____ issue networks

a. informal groups of policy experts who move in and out of policy involvement on the basis of intellectual commitment
b. mutually beneficial alliances among congressional committee members, government agency administrators, and interest group representatives
c. conflicting demands faced by individuals because of membership in several different groups
d. tendency of former members of Congress and former employees of government agencies to become lobbyists

Answers

True-False

1. T, 2. F, 3. F, 4. T, 5. T, 6. F, 7. F, 8. F, 9. T, 10. F

Multiple-Choice

1. a, 2. c, 3. b, 4. d, 5. a, 6. b, 7. a, 8. c, 9. c, 10. d

Matching

1. b, a, c, d 2. d, c, b, a 3. a, d, c, b 4. c, b, d, a

13 STUDY GUIDE

Political Culture, Media, and Public Opinion

Key Terms

culture the shared beliefs, traditions, and myths of a group of people.

fairness doctrine a federal rule requiring electronic media to provide equal time for opposing views on controversial subjects.

gatekeepers individuals or groups able to decide which issues are covered by the media or included in the government agenda and which are excluded.

Iran-Contra affair scandal affecting the Reagan and Bush administrations; involved selling arms to the terrorist state of Iran in exchange for hostages and using the profits to fund the Contras in Nicaragua, for whom Congress had stopped appropriations.

media the means of publicly disseminating information; includes books, magazines, newspapers, radio, television, and computers.

political culture a broadly shared set of beliefs about the role of politics and government in society.

public opinion polling method of determining the attitudes, knowledge, or opinions of a population through questionnaires.

random samples representative groups of people who have a high probability of reflecting the views of larger groups or of the whole society.

schematic thinking a patterned way of thinking, of viewing the world, based on a cultural perspective.

Chapter Highlights

1. Political culture is a reflection of the values and beliefs that people hold about government and politics. In American society, the values of liberty, equality, democracy, and civic duty are deeply rooted in historical documents and traditions surrounding the birth of our nation. They are regularly reinforced in our current political discourse, literature, educational institutions, and news media coverage. Yet there are many differences in the way individuals understand these values. The most familiar frame of reference is that of liberal and conservative viewpoints, but this terminology is imprecise and full of contradictions. A more helpful framework divides society into four categories on the basis of perceptions of hierarchy and imposed norms: fatalism, hierarchy, individualism, and egalitarianism.

2. We acquire our political orientation in the early, formative years of life in a process called socialization. Differences among people regarding these values come through the variable influences of family, education, peers, group affiliations, and exposure to the media. Television in particular has

become a principal source of information for young people, overcoming illiteracy and language barriers that limit other means of socialization. But learning gained from the media is very selective, often merely reinforcing values that individuals already hold.

3. Firmly embedded in American political culture and reinforced by judicial precedent is a strong tradition of freedom of the press. The print media in particular enjoy many constitutional safeguards against censorship and protection from libel. The electronic media have not been extended the same degree of freedom, since air space for broadcasting is seen as a public resource. Government regulation restricts content and broadcasting procedures and requires equal time and fairness in the airing of an array of viewpoints.

4. Although lauded as promoting the free expression of ideas and a healthy public skepticism toward politicians, the media have not been without critics. In recent years, the industry has witnessed a substantial trend toward concentration of ownership, with only a few powerful corporations now dominating many key sectors. Critics contend that this concentration compromises Americans' access to alternative media perspectives.

5. Concern has been raised about the bias of news editors, producers, and other media gatekeepers in setting the political agenda and influencing popular evaluation of important public issues. Allegations of a liberal bias among reporters are counterbalanced by more compelling evidence that media coverage, rather than serving some hidden political agenda, is driven by a predilection for sensational and controversial stories. Media coverage may also be slanted by government officials and politicians who seek to promote their interests through carefully managed briefings and leaks.

   Coverage of terrorism offers another source of ethical controversy, since the perpetrators apparently benefit from media hype and sensationalism.

6. Among all media sources, television has risen to a central position of importance in politics. Politicians realize that TV is the most effective means for reaching the largest possible audience. Their heavy use of the medium has driven up the cost of political campaigns dramatically. In addition, media and marketing experts now structure entire campaigns around the image and messages conveyed by the television camera. This trend concerns analysts who believe that television promotes political passivity, false images, and a decline in public participation. Others argue that television has opened up the political process and thereby enhanced the quality of democracy.

7. Public opinion represents the thinking and values of groups of people concerning issues that affect them. Today, most polling is conducted over the phone with carefully worded questions and random samples that generate substantially accurate results. As polling has been refined, more and more policy makers have sought to find ways both to respond to it and to manipulate it for their own ends. The overall linkage between opinion polls

and public policy is not very exact. The nature of public opinion at any given time is never very clear or focused. Moreover, much of public policy results from complex processes of political bargaining and compromise that are largely insulated from public input.

Study Questions

1. What is political culture?
2. Identify the basic shared values of American political culture.
3. Distinguish between the basic political perspectives of liberals and conservatives.
4. Why are the liberal and conservative labels not very helpful in understanding American politics?
5. Identify Wildavsky's four political culture types and describe how they differ.
6. How do Americans acquire their values and beliefs about politics?
7. Contrast television and print media with regard to how they influence individual socialization.
8. What kind of perspective did Thomas Jefferson have about freedom of the press?
9. Why does the opinion of the courts differ with regard to the freedoms permitted to print and electronic media?
10. Identify the government restrictions imposed on the electronic media today.
11. Why is the concentration of ownership of the media a source of concern?
12. What influence do media gatekeepers have on politics?
13. What kind of political orientation do news reporters and producers generally have?
14. Why might the personal bias of journalists not make much difference in American politics?
15. What barriers do reporters often face regarding information released from official government sources?
16. Explain why terrorism poses many ethical dilemmas for the press.
17. What kind of impact has television had on campaigns and elections?
18. Why do some believe that television poses a threat to democracy?
19. How do politicians make use of opinion polls to push their own agendas?
20. Why is there only a tenuous link between public policy and opinion polls?

Quizzes

True-False Questions

____ 1. The notion of equality of opportunity is accepted by most Americans.

____ 2. The individualist cultural type is characterized by apathy toward society.

____ 3. Television has relatively little impact on the process of socialization.

____ 4. Most people hear and see what they want to hear and see, and filter out the rest.

____ 5. The U.S. courts generally are supportive of government efforts to impose prior restraint on the media.

____ 6. The print media tend to be far less closely regulated than the electronic media.

____ 7. The media are increasingly controlled by fewer and fewer corporate conglomerates.

____ 8. Most media reporters, producers, and editors have a conservative bias.

____ 9. Government officials frequently attempt to manipulate and control the information they release to the press.

____ 10. Americans tend to have clearer opinions about policy outcomes than about the policies themselves.

Multiple-Choice Questions

____ 1. The basic value of equality that is a part of American political culture refers to a conviction that:
   a. all persons should be free to do as they please.
   b. all persons should have the same opportunities.
   c. all persons should participate in government.
   d. all persons should have the same income.

____ 2. The use of liberal-conservative labels is not helpful for all of the following reasons except that:
   a. the number of people who consider themselves either liberal or conservative has not really changed much.
   b. many people hold contradictory opinions that defy liberal and conservative labels.
   c. both liberals and conservatives may be on the same side of a particular political issue.
   d. neither of these ideologies says anything about such fundamental issues as equality and liberty.

____ 3. The political culture type that describes individuals who have weak group attachments, self-determined norms, and highly competitive values is called:
   a. egalitarian.
   b. individualist.
   c. hierarchical.
   d. fatalist.

____ 4. Democracy benefits from a good mix of all of the political culture types except:
   a. egalitarians.
   b. individualists.

c. collectivists.

d. fatalists.

____ 5. In the process of socialization, the most important type of media today is:

a. newspapers.

b. radio.

c. television.

d. weekly newsmagazines.

____ 6. In commenting on the issue of a free press, Thomas Jefferson believed that the news media:

a. often misrepresented the facts and engaged in libel.

b. favored only the interests of the rich and powerful.

c. were a vital element in informing the people about their leaders.

d. had the important job of promoting good political candidates.

____ 7. A government restriction on the media that is *not* permitted by the Supreme Court is:

a. requirements of equal time for opposing opinions on radio and television stations.

b. the use prior restraint on newspapers.

c. the right of public officials to sue the media for slander or libel.

d. rules that prohibit intelligence service employees from publishing material about their jobs.

____ 8. The biggest concern about slanted news reporting by the media is that:

a. public officials often use reporters to try to discredit opponents or shift attention away from their mistakes through strategic leaks of information.

b. the general public will only take notice of media reports that focus on good news about their government leaders.

c. many reporters, producers, and media personalities are conservative in their political orientation.

d. the media gatekeepers are really only interested in making a profit, not in reporting accurate and balanced stories to the public.

____ 9. Those who are concerned about the impact of television in American politics complain that:

a. television has enabled the political parties to become too powerful.

b. television portrays values and beliefs that are fundamentally antidemocratic.

c. television provides information about politics to illiterate people and/or those who don't speak English.

d. television encourages people to watch but not to participate in politics.

____ 10. A real problem with many opinion polls today is that they can produce misleading results because:

    a. a large percentage of persons will deliberately lie to pollsters about their opinions.

    b. the wording of questions may lead respondents to particular answers.

    c. pollsters depend on telephone interviews and neglect critical face-to-face contact.

    d. sample sizes are frequently too small to permit accurate assessments of public opinion.

Matching Questions

1.

____ conservatives
____ fatalists
____ liberals
____ gatekeepers

a. feel apathetic about politics, believing that they are manipulated by forces outside of their control

b. are concerned with limiting the role of government, especially in business

c. decide which issues and stories are covered by the media and which are excluded

d. favor government protection of the individual, especially from corporate power

2.

____ egalitarian type
____ individualist type
____ hierarchical type
____ fatalist type

a. have self-determined norms, weak group attachments, and highly competitive values

b. have weak group attachments, favor strong, imposed norms, and feel apathetic about politics

c. have strong group attachments, favor imposed norms, and prefer well-defined relationships among groups

d. have self-determined norms, strong group attachments, and shared views of society

3.

____ electronic media
____ fairness doctrine
____ print media
____ prior restraint

a. government efforts to censor information and prevent it from being disseminated by the media

b. must be licensed to use a portion of the public's airwaves

c. requirement to provide equal time for opposing views on controversial subjects

d. do not need licenses to publish

4.

____ political culture

____ schematic thinking

____ socialization

____ culture

a. a patterned way of thinking and viewing the world based on a cultural perspective

b. a shared set of beliefs about politics and the role of government in society

c. the gradual process by which individuals acquire an understanding and personal orientation about their lives and the world they live in

d. the shared beliefs, traditions, and myths of a group of people

Answers

True-False

1. T, 2. F, 3. F, 4. T, 5. F, 6. T, 7. T, 8. F, 9. T, 10. T

Multiple-Choice

1. b, 2. d, 3. a, 4. d, 5. c, 6. c, 7. b, 8. a, 9. d, 10. b

Matching

1. b, a, d, c 2. d, a, c, b 3. b, c, d, a 4. b, a, c, d

14 STUDY GUIDE

Public Policy Making

Key Terms

feedback loop a model of policy in which the actions of government have an impact on society and create changes in the demands on government, representing feedback.

gatekeepers individuals or groups with the power to determine which issues reach the media or the government agenda and which are excluded.

General Agreement on Tariffs and Trade (GATT) an international treaty designed to promote a greater degree of free trade among countries and to remove unfair competition; extends "most favoured nation" status to members and provides mechanisms for settling disputes over trade issues.

Group of Seven (G-7) the seven major capitalist democracies (Canada, France, Germany, Italy, Japan, the United Kingdom, and the United States), whose leaders have met regularly for the past 20 years to better coordinate economic policy.

implementation bureaucratic translations of laws into the rules and procedures necessary for the application of those laws.

International Bank for Reconstruction and Development (World Bank) an international bank established in 1946 that combines loans with economic development projects to better enable Third World nations to compete in the world economy; currently has about 150 members.

International Monetary Fund (IMF) an international loan agency established in 1946 to help stabilize exchange rates and provide liquidity to countries with excessive debts. Member states, now about 150, that accept its loans must agree to domestic economy policies designed to increase liquidity.

maximal decision-making arena the group of legislative decisions reached among the upper levels of Congress, the political executive, and national media and political parties.

minimal decision-making arena the group of legislative decisions reached among the lower levels of the bureaucracy, congressional subcommittees, and affected interest groups.

OPEC Organization of Petroleum Exporting Countries an organization formed in 1960 comprised of 13 Third World oil-exporting nations. The group coordinates oil production strategies in a cartel arrangement in force up the world market price for this commodity.

political agenda a series of policy issues under consideration by political leaders.

political entrepreneurs those who invest the time, energy, and resources in projects designed to address a policy issue.

Third World countries of the world that were not aligned with either the U.S.-led Western bloc or the Soviet-led Eastern bloc. More commonly referred to as less developed nations or developing nations.

Chapter Highlights

1. Democratic systems may be evaluated on the basis of the policy outcomes that result from the process of political decision making. This policy process involves a complex series of steps through which public programs are identified, formulated, implemented, and evaluated through feedback. Ideally, this process results in solving problems in a responsive and effective manner.

2. Before any problem can be resolved by governmental action, it must be officially recognized and placed on the political agenda. Many social issues compete for attention, but only those that are given a significant push from issue entrepreneurs, powerfully organized groups, and institutional gate-keepers are addressed in a meaningful way. Issues differ in the type of response they elicit. Most items on the agenda receive only minor adjustments and remain in the minimal decision-making arena. The few that become highly visible and controversial reach the maximal decision-making arena, where fundamental changes in policy occur.

3. Implementation involves the important step of translating policy intentions into a plan of governmental action. Once implementation has occurred, the differential impact of policy rules, procedures, and programs in turn leads to demands for change through the feedback loop. Further refinement of policies then takes place in a continuous process that is not unlike a life cycle. An example of this kind of cycle is the annual budgetary process, which involves yearly adjustments and refinements to a taxing and spending plan that actually changes very little over time.

4. An understanding of the relationship between government and the economy, or economic policy, enhances our appreciation for the kinds of activities associated with policy making in America. Economic policy's major purposes are to promote growth, full employment, price stability, a more equitable distribution of income, and a positive balance of trade. The federal government uses several important instruments designed to achieve these goals. Monetary policy relates to the regulation of the money supply and is largely the responsibility of the independent Federal Reserve Bank. Fiscal policy refers to strategies that use taxing and spending mechanisms to influence the economy positively. This arena of policy is managed by Congress and the executive branch and includes a combination of adjustments to the federal tax code, business subsidies, and spending for infrastructure improvements. Finally, regulatory policy involves efforts by independent agencies and commissions to monitor and control economic activities to promote public safety and well-being.

5. The Savings and Loan scandal highlights the dilemmas faced by our society as it seeks to fulfill the laudable goals of economic policy. The scandal involves a complex series of events that began when the Reagan administration lifted many of the strict regulatory controls that had formerly governed savings and loan institutions. Although deregulation was intended to free up investments and promote economic growth, many unscrupulous industry executives took advantage of the change to engage in careless, unwise investments as well as patently illegal practices in the early 1980s. Uncollectible loans led to the failure of hundreds of thrift institutions by the middle part of the decade, along with a huge taxpayers' bill to cover federally insured deposits. The scandal grew in the late 1980s as evidence mounted that members of Congress and administration officials alike had

used their influence to block bank investigations in return for large campaign donations and other favors from industry executives.

6. The American economy is increasingly affected by foreign trade and investment activities. This interdependence has led to the growing importance of international trade negotiations through such organizations as the Group of Seven, IMF, and the World Bank. The goals of American international economic policy include opening up foreign markets for free trade and aiding in the development of emerging nations in the Third World and Eastern Europe as they seek to compete in the international economy. These issues have become even more important as many Americans grow increasingly concerned over the loss of U.S. manufacturing jobs and the rise in ethnic tensions and civil instability in many parts of the world. Foreign policy is further complicated by trade disputes over tariffs, unfair competition, and the ongoing bitterness of Third World states over the inequities of a global economy that leaves them at a distinct disadvantage.

Study Questions

1. How does the study of public policy help us to better understand American government?
2. Identify the steps involved in the policy process.
3. What is the difference between the social and political agendas?
4. What role do political entrepreneurs and gatekeepers play in the policy process?
5. Whose interests are generally reflected in the political agenda?
6. Describe the different kinds of actions that are taken in the minimal and maximal decision-making arenas.
7. What purpose is served by the feedback loop?
8. How does the formation of the budget help us to understand the fundamental problems associated with policy making in America?
9. What are the five major goals of economic policy?
10. How does government policy address the problem of unemployment?
11. Describe the goals of international economic policy.
12. What basic issues are addressed in carrying out monetary policy?
13. What organization is in charge of monetary policy?
14. Identify the major instruments used in managing fiscal policy.
15. Explain how federal agricultural policy works at cross-purposes with the goals it is intended to achieve.
16. How do governments adjust tax codes to influence the economy?
17. What groups of individuals played major roles in the savings and loan scandal?
18. What kinds of activities led to the enormous taxpayer burden caused by the savings and loan crisis?
19. Why does the United States participate in international organizations like G-7, GATT, and the World Bank?

20. What complaints do Third World nations have about the world economy, and what measures are being taken to address their concerns?

Quizzes

True-False Questions

____ 1. Public policy involves the study of whether or not government actions make people better off.

____ 2. Nondecisions occur when policy makers cannot decide how to address an important public issue in an effective manner.

____ 3. Political entrepreneurs are involved in promoting the establishment of new businesses.

____ 4. Decisions made in the maximal arena often result in fundamental policy changes.

____ 5. Efforts to reduce the federal budget are often frustrated by mandated spending.

____ 6. Increasing capacity refers to efforts by the government to train workers and promote education.

____ 7. The gap between the rich and the poor in America has widened over the past 15 years.

____ 8. Fiscal policy refers to adjustments made to the money supply.

____ 9. The federal tax code favors some kinds of businesses with tax breaks more than others.

____ 10. GATT is concerned primarily with making loans to developing nations.

Multiple-Choice Questions

____ 1. The first step that must occur in the process of policy making is that:
a. public officials must write up a new set of policy guidelines.
b. decision making has to occur at the highest levels of government.
c. a problem must be recognized and placed on the political agenda.
d. information must come to the attention of policy makers through the feedback loop.

____ 2. Political entrepreneurs are important in the policy process because:
a. they have the power to choose which problems will be given the attention of government.
b. they push an issue through the process until it is recognized by government.
c. they have responsibility over implementation of programs and policies.

d. they can affect any or all steps in the process by controlling the feedback loop.

_____ 3. Economic policy involves all of the following goals except:
   a. equal opportunity.
   b. price stability.
   c. full employment.
   d. increasing capacity.

_____ 4. When our country has a negative balance of payments, it means that:
   a. the income gap is widening between rich and poor.
   b. structural unemployment is affecting growing numbers of people.
   c. money is flowing to investments outside the country.
   d. foreign countries are closing their markets to American products.

_____ 5. Efforts by our government to use taxing and spending mechanisms to influence the economy in a positive way are called:
   a. monetary policy.
   b. regulatory policy.
   c. economic policy.
   d. fiscal policy.

_____ 6. The Federal Reserve Bank has all of the following responsibilities except:
   a. adjusting reserve requirements.
   b. determining the amount of government securities to purchase.
   c. raising and lowering the discount rate.
   d. making adjustments to the federal income tax code.

_____ 7. Government policies that give assistance and subsidies to farmers were originally designed to:
   a. create full employment.
   b. promote economic growth.
   c. achieve a positive balance of payments.
   d. regulate private industry.

_____ 8. The savings and loan crisis was triggered by all of the following factors except:
   a. the negligence and criminal complicity of federal regulators.
   b. the deregulation of the savings and loan industry.
   c. the unscrupulous activities of bank executives.
   d. the willingness of members of Congress to do favors for powerful bank executives.

_____ 9. Third World countries complain about the international economic system because:
   a. internal strife and poor government have left them destitute.
   b. they are unable to get loans from such organizations as the World Bank and the IMF.

c. development loans have many strings attached, requiring them to adopt domestic policies they may not want.

d. they are losing manufacturing jobs to the rich countries.

_____ 10. In which of the following organizations is the United States not a participating member?

a. General Agreement on Tariffs and Trade

b. Organization of Petroleum Exporting Countries

c. International Bank for Reconstruction and Development

d. Group of Seven

Matching Questions

1.

_____ deregulation
_____ monetary policy
_____ fiscal policy
_____ regulatory policy

a. designed to remove what are perceived as unnecessary government rules that increase business costs

b. designed to use taxing and spending mechanisms to influence the economy in a positive way

c. designed to ensure that society will be protected from possible harm resulting from the pursuit of private economic activity

d. Federal Reserve Board (Fed) efforts to adjust the amount of money in circulation through interest rate changes to bring about desired adjustments in the national economy

2.

_____ political agenda
_____ public policy
_____ social issues
_____ nondecisions

a. problems that concern a community and about which there is a feeling that something can be done

b. an underlying plan to deal with a political issue, from which flows a set of laws and administrative rules

c. issues that are currently under consideration by government leaders

d. ways of avoiding issues because influential people do not want them to be addressed

3.

_____ General Agreement on Tariffs and Trade
_____ International Bank for Reconstruction and Development
_____ International Monetary Fund
_____ Group of Seven

a. leaders meet regularly to better coordinate economic policy

b. seeks to ease trade between countries and remove unfair competition

c. helps countries that are experiencing difficulties with exchange rates and debt payments

d. combines loans with economic development projects to better enable Third World nations to compete in the world economy

4.

____ economic growth
____ full employment
____ balance of payments
____ stable prices

a. placing tariffs on imports and promoting free markets
b. seeking to control inflation
c. subsidizing education and job training programs
d. increasing the productive capacity of the economy

5.

____ issue entrepreneurs
____ feedback loop
____ gatekeepers
____ implementation

a. provides government leaders with guidance in adjusting public policy
b. choose from among various problems which ones will be considered by government
c. turns laws and regulations into specific rules and procedures
d. invest their time, energy, and resources in ensuring that a problem is addressed by government

Answers

True-False

1. T, 2. F, 3. F, 4. T, 5. T, 6. F, 7. T, 8. F, 9. T, 10. T

Multiple-Choice

1. c, 2. b, 3. a, 4. c, 5. d, 6. d, 7. b, 8. a, 9. c, 10. b

Matching

1. a, d, b, c   2. c, b, a, d   3. b, d, c, a   4. d, c, a, b   5. d, a, b, c

The Constitution of the United States

PREAMBLE

We the People of the United States, in Order to form a more perfect Union, establish Justice, insure domestic Tranquility, provide for the common defence, promote the general Welfare, and secure the Blessings of Liberty to ourselves and our Posterity, do ordain and establish this Constitution for the United States of America.

ARTICLE I
Congress

Section I. All legislative Powers herein granted shall be vested in a Congress of the United States, which shall consist of a Senate and House of Representatives.

House of Representatives

Section 2. The House of Representatives shall be composed of Members chosen every second Year by the People of the several States, and the Electors in each State shall have the Qualifications requisite for Electors of the most numerous Branch of the State Legislature.

No Person shall be a Representative who shall not have attained to the Age of twenty five Years, and been seven Years a Citizen of the United States, and who shall not, when elected, be an Inhabitant of that State in which he shall be chosen.

Representatives and direct Taxes shall be apportioned among the several States which may be included within this Union, according to their respective Numbers, which shall be determined by adding to the whole Number of free Persons, including those bound to Service for a Term of Years, and excluding Indians not taxed, three fifths of all other Persons. The actual Enumeration shall be made within three Years after the first Meeting of the Congress of the United States, and within every subsequent Term of ten Years, in such Manner as they shall by Law direct. The Number of Representatives shall not exceed one for every thirty Thousand, but each State shall have at Least one Representative; and until such enumeration shall be made, the State of New Hampshire shall be entitled to chuse three, Massachusetts eight, Rhode-Island and Providence Plantations one, Connecticut five, New-York six, New Jersey four, Pennsylvania eight, Delaware one, Maryland six, Virginia ten, North Carolina five, South Carolina five, and Georgia three.

When vacancies happen in the Representation from any State, the Executive Authority thereof shall issue Writs of Election to fill such Vacancies.

The House of Representatives shall chuse their Speaker and other Officers; and shall have the sole Power of Impeachment.

Senate

Section 3. The Senate of the United States shall be composed of two Senators from each State, chosen by the Legislature thereof, for six Years; and each Senator shall have one Vote.

Immediately after they shall be assembled in Consequence of the first Election, they shall be divided as equally as may be into three Classes. The Seats of the Senators of the first Class shall be vacated at the Expiration of the second Year, of the second Class at the Expiration of the fourth Year, and of the third Class at the Expiration of the sixth Year, so that one third may be chosen every second Year; and if Vacancies happen by Resignation, or otherwise, during the Recess of the Legislature of any State, the Executive thereof may make temporary Appointments until the next Meeting of the Legislature, which shall then fill such Vacancies.

No Person shall be a Senator who shall not have attained to the Age of thirty Years, and been nine Years a Citizen of the United States, and who shall not, when elected, be an Inhabitant of that State for which he shall be chosen.

The Vice President of the United States shall be President of the Senate, but shall have no Vote, unless they be equally divided.

The Senate shall chuse their other Officers, and also a President pro tempore, in the Absence of the Vice President, or when he shall exercise the Office of President of the United States.

The Senate shall have the sole Power to try all Impeachments. When sitting for that Purpose, they shall be on Oath of Affirmation. When the President of the United States is tried, the Chief Justice shall preside: And no Person shall be convicted without the Concurrence of two thirds of the Members present.

Judgment in Cases of Impeachment shall not extend further than to removal from Office, and disqualification to hold and enjoy any Office of honor, Trust or Profit under the United States: but the Party convicted shall nevertheless be liable and subject to Indictment, Trial, Judgment and Punishment, according to Law.

Congressional elections, prerogatives, and procedures

Section 4. The Times, Places and Manner of holding Elections for Senators and Representatives, shall be prescribed in each State by the Legislature thereof; but the Congress may at any time by Law make or alter such Regulations, except as to the Places of chusing Senators.

The Congress shall assemble at least once in every Year, and such Meeting shall be on the first Monday in December, unless they shall by Law appoint a different Day.

Section 5. Each House shall be the Judge of the Elections, Returns and Qualifications of its own Members, and a Majority of each shall constitute a Quorum to do Business; but a smaller Number may adjourn from day to day, and may be authorized to compel the Attendance of absent Members, in such Manner, and under such Penalties as each House may provide.

Each House may determine the Rules of its Proceedings, punish its Members for disorderly Behav-

iour, and, with the Concurrence of two thirds, expel a Member.

Each House shall keep a Journal of its Proceedings, and from time to time publish the same, excepting such Parts as may in their Judgment require Secrecy; and the Yeas and Nays of the Members of either House on any question shall, at the Desire of one fifth of those Present, be entered on the Journal.

Neither House, during the Session of Congress, shall, without the Consent of the other, adjourn for more than three days, nor to any other Place than that in which the two Houses shall be sitting.

Section 6. The Senators and Representatives shall receive a Compensation for their Services, to be ascertained by Law, and paid out of the Treasury of the United States. They shall in all Cases, except Treason, Felony and Breach of the Peace, be privileged from Arrest during their Attendance at the Session of their respective Houses, and in going to and returning from the same; and for any Speech or Debate in either House, they shall not be questioned in any other Place.

No Senator or Representative shall, during the Time for which he was elected, be appointed to any civil Office under the Authority of the United States, which shall have been created, or the Emoluments whereof shall have been encreased during such time; and no Person holding any Office under the United States, shall be a Member of either House during his Continuance in Office.

Section 7. All Bills for raising Revenue shall originate in the House of Representatives; but the Senate may propose or concur with Amendments as on other Bills.

Every Bill which shall have passed the House of Representatives and the Senate, shall, before it become a Law, be presented to the President of the United States; If he approve he shall sign it, but if not he shall return it, with his Objections to that House in which it shall have originated, who shall enter the Objections at large on their Journal, and proceed to reconsider it. If after such Reconsideration two thirds of that House shall agree to pass the Bill, it shall be sent, together with the Objections, to the other House, by which it shall likewise be reconsidered, and if approved by two thirds of that House, it shall become a Law. But in all such Cases the Votes of both Houses shall be determined by yeas and Nays, and the Names of the Persons voting for and against the Bill shall be entered on the Journal of each House respectively. If any Bill shall not be returned by the President within ten Days (Sundays excepted) after it shall have been presented to him, the Same shall be a Law, in like Manner as if he had signed it, unless the Congress by their Adjournment prevent its Return, in which Case it shall not be a Law.

Every Order, Resolution, or Vote to which the Concurrence of the Senate and House of Representatives may be necessary (except on a question of Adjournment) shall be presented to the President of the United States; and before the Same shall take Effect, shall be approved by him, or being disapproved by him, shall be repassed by two thirds of the Senate and House of Representatives, according to the Rules and Limitations prescribed in the Case of a Bill.

Congressional powers

Section 8. The Congress shall have Power To lay and collect Taxes, Duties, Imposts and Excises, to pay the Debts and provide for the common Defence and general Welfare of the United States; but all Duties, Imposts and Excises shall be uniform throughout the United States;

To borrow Money on the credit of the United States;

To regulate Commerce with foreign Nations, and among the several States, and with the Indian Tribes;

To establish an uniform Rule of Naturalization, and uniform Laws on the subject of Bankruptcies throughout the United States;

To coin Money, regulate the Value thereof, and of foreign Coin, and fix the Standard of Weights and Measures;

To provide for the Punishment of counterfeiting the Securities and current Coin of the United States;

To establish Post Offices and post Roads;

To promote the Progress of Science and useful Arts, by securing for limited Times to Authors and Inventors the exclusive Right to their respective Writings and Discoveries;

To constitute Tribunals inferior to the supreme Court;

To define and punish Piracies and Felonies committed on the high Seas, and Offences against the Law of Nations;

To declare War, grant Letters of Marque and Reprisal, and make Rules concerning Captures on Land and Water;

To raise and support Armies, but no Appropriation of Money to that Use shall be for a longer Term than two Years;

To provide and maintain a Navy;

To make Rules for the Government and Regulation of the land and naval Forces;

To provide for calling forth the Militia to execute the Laws of the Union, suppress Insurrections and repel Invasions;

To provide for organizing, arming, and disciplining, the Militia, and for governing such Part of them as may be employed in the Service of the United States, reserving to the States respectively, the Appointment of the Officers, and the Authority of training the Militia according to the discipline prescribed by Congress;

To exercise exclusive Legislation in all Cases whatsoever, over such District (not exceeding ten Miles square) as may, by Cession of particular States, and the Acceptance of Congress, become the Seat of the Government of the United States, and to exercise like Authority over all Places purchased by the Consent of the Legislature of the State in which the Same shall be, for the Erection of Forts, Magazines, Arsenals, dock-Yards, and other needful Buildings;—And

To make all Laws which shall be necessary and proper for carrying into Execution the foregoing Powers, and all other Powers vested by this Constitution in the Government of the United States, or in any Department or Officer thereof.

Limitations on congressional power

Section 9. The Migration or Importation of such Persons as any of the States now existing shall think proper to admit, shall not be prohibited by the Congress prior to the year one thousand eight hundred and eight, but a Tax or duty may be imposed on such Importation, not exceeding ten dollars for each Person.

The Privilege of the Writ of Habeas Corpus shall not be suspended, unless when in Cases of Rebellion or Invasion the public Safety may require it.

No Bill of Attainder or ex post facto Law shall be passed.

No Capitation, or other direct, Tax shall be laid, unless in Proportion to the Census or Enumeration herein before directed to be taken.

No Tax or Duty shall be laid on Articles exported from any State.

No Preference shall be given by any Regulation of Commerce or Revenue to the Ports of one State over those of another; nor shall Vessels bound to, or from, one State, be obliged to enter, clear, or pay Duties in another.

No Money shall be drawn from the Treasury, but in Consequence of Appropriations made by Law; and a regular Statement and Account of the Receipts and Expenditures of all public Money shall be published from time to time.

No Title of Nobility shall be granted by the United States: And no Person holding any Office of Profit or Trust under them, shall, without the Consent of the Congress, accept of any present, Emolument, Office, or Title, of any kind whatever, from any King, Prince, or foreign State.

Limitations on powers of state

Section 10. No State shall enter into any Treaty, Alliance, or Confederation; grant Letters of Marque and Reprisal; coin Money; emit Bills of Credit; make any Thing but gold and silver Coin a Tender in Payment of Debts; pass any Bill of Attainder, ex post facto Law, or Law impairing the Obligation of Contracts, or grant any Title of Nobility.

No State shall, without the Consent of the Congress, lay any Imposts or Duties on Imports or Exports, except what may be absolutely necessary for executing its inspection Laws: and the net Produce of all Duties and Imposts, laid by any State on Imports or Exports, shall be for the Use of the Treasury of the United States; and all such Laws shall be subject to the Revision and Controul of the Congress.

No State shall, without the Consent of Congress, lay any Duty of Tonnage, keep Troops, or

Ships of War in time of Peace, enter into any Agreement or Compact with another State, or with a foreign Power, or engage in War, unless actually invaded, or in such imminent Danger as will not admit of delay.

ARTICLE II
The President

Electing the president

Section 1. The executive Power shall be vested in a President of the United States of America. He shall hold his Office during the Term of four Years, and, together with the Vice President, chosen for the same Term, be elected, as follows:

Each State shall appoint, in such Manner as the Legislature thereof may direct, a Number of Electors, equal to the whole Number of Senators and Representatives to which the State may be entitled in the Congress: but no Senator or Representative, or Person holding an Office of Trust or Profit under the United States, shall be appointed an Elector.

The Electors shall meet in their respective States, and vote by Ballot for two Persons, of whom one at least shall not be an Inhabitant of the same State with themselves. And they shall make a List of all the Persons voted for, and of the Number of Votes for each; which List they shall sign and certify, and transmit sealed to the Seat of the Government of the United States, directed to the President of the Senate. The President of the Senate shall, in the Presence of the Senate and House of Representatives, open all the Certificates, and the Votes shall then be counted. The Person having the greatest Number of Votes shall be the President, if such Number be a Majority of the whole Number of Electors appointed; and if there be more than one who have such Majority, and have an equal Number of Votes, then the House of Representatives shall immediately chuse by Ballot one of them for President; and if no Person have a Majority, then from the five highest on the List the said House shall in like Manner chuse the President. But in chusing the President, the Votes shall be taken by States, the Representation from each State having one Vote; A Quorum for this Purpose shall consist of a Member or Members from two thirds of the States, and a Majority of all the States shall be necessary to a Choice. In every Case, after the Choice of the President, the person having the greatest Number of Votes of the Electors shall be the

Vice President. But if there should remain two or more who have equal Votes, the Senate shall chuse from them by Ballot the Vice President.

The Congress may determine the Time of chusing the Electors, and the Day on which they shall give their Votes; which Day shall be the same throughout the United States.

No Person except a natural born Citizen, or a Citizen of the United States, at the time of the Adoption of this Constitution, shall be eligible to the Office of President; neither shall any Person be eligible to that Office who shall not have attained to the Age of thirty five Years, and been fourteen Years a Resident within the United States.

In Case of the Removal of the President from Office, or of his Death, Resignation, or Inability to discharge the Powers and Duties of the said Office, the Same shall devolve on the Vice President, and the Congress may by Law provide for the Case of Removal, Death, Resignation or Inability, both of the President and Vice President, declaring what Officer shall then act as President, and such Officer shall act accordingly, until the Disability be removed, or a President shall be elected.

The President shall, at stated Times, receive for his Services, a Compensation, which shall neither be encreased nor diminished during the Period for which he shall have been elected, and he shall not receive within that Period any other Emolument from the United States, or any of them.

Before he enter on the Execution of his Office, he shall take the following Oath or Affirmation:—"I do solemnly swear (or affirm) that I will faithfully execute the Office of President of the United States, and will to the best of my Ability, preserve, protect and defend the Constitution of the United States."

Powers and duties of the president

Section 2. The President shall be Commander in Chief of the Army and Navy of the United States, and of the Militia of the several States, when called into the actual Service of the United States; he may require the Opinion, in writing, of the principal Officer in each of the executive Departments, upon any Subject relating to the Duties of their respective Offices, and he shall have Power to grant Reprieves and Pardons for Offences against the United States, except in Cases of Impeachment.

He shall have Power, by and with the Advice and Consent of the Senate, to make Treaties, provided two thirds of the Senators present concur; and he shall nominate, and by and with the Advice and Consent of the Senate, shall appoint Ambassadors, other public Ministers and Consuls, Judges of the supreme Court, and all other Officers of the United States, whose Appointments are not herein otherwise provided for, and which shall be established by Law: but the Congress may by Law vest the Appointment of such inferior Officers, as they think proper, in the President alone, in the Courts of Law, or in the Heads of Departments.

The President shall have Power to fill up all Vacancies that may happen during the Recess of the Senate, by granting Commissions which shall expire at the End of their next Session.

Section 3. He shall from time to time give to the Congress Information of the State of the Union, and recommend to their Consideration such Measures as he shall judge necessary and expedient; he may, on extraordinary Occasions, convene both Houses, or either of them, and in Case of Disagreement between them, with Respect to the Time of Adjournment, he may adjourn them to such Time as he shall think proper; he shall receive Ambassadors and other public Ministers; he shall take Care that the Laws be faithfully executed, and shall Commission all of the Officers of the United States.

Section 4. The President, Vice President and all civil Officers of the United States, shall be removed from Office on Impeachment for, and Conviction of, Treason, Bribery, or other high Crimes and Misdemeanors.

ARTICLE III
Federal Judiciary

Section 1. The judicial Power of the United States, shall be vested in one supreme Court, and in such inferior Courts as the Congress may from time to time ordain and establish. The Judges, both of the supreme and inferior Courts, shall hold their Offices during good Behaviour, and shall, at stated Times, receive for their Services, a Compensation, which shall not be diminished during their Continuance in Office.

Section 2. The judicial Power shall extend to all Cases, in Law and Equity, arising under this Constitution, the Laws of the United States, and Treaties made, or which shall be made, under their Authority;—to all Cases affecting Ambassadors, other public Ministers and Consuls; —to all Cases of admiralty and maritime Jurisdiction;—to Controversies to which the United States shall be a Party;—to Controversies between two or more States;—between a State and Citizens of another State;—between Citizens of different States,—between Citizens of the same State claiming Lands under Grants of different States, and between a State, or the Citizens thereof, and foreign States, Citizens or Subjects.

In all Cases affecting Ambassadors, other public Ministers and Consuls, and those in which a State shall be Party, the supreme Court shall have original Jurisdiction. In all the other Cases before mentioned, the supreme Court shall have appellate Jurisdiction, both as to Law and Fact, with such Exceptions, and under such Regulations as the Congress shall make.

The Trial of all Crimes, except in Cases of Impeachment, shall be by Jury; and such Trial shall be held in the State where the said Crimes shall have been committed; but when not committed within any State, the Trial shall be at such Place or Places as the Congress may by Law have directed.

Section 3. Treason against the United States, shall consist only in levying War against them, or in adhering to their enemies, giving them Aid and Comfort. No Person shall be convicted of Treason unless on the Testimony of two Witnesses to the same overt Act, or on Confession in open Court.

The Congress shall have Power to declare the Punishment of Treason, but no Attainder of Treason shall work Corruption of Blood, or Forfeiture except during the Life of the Person attainted.

ARTICLE IV
Relations among the States

Section 1. Full Faith and Credit shall be given in each State to the public Acts, Records, and judicial Proceedings of every other State. And the Congress may by general Laws prescribe the Manner in which such Acts, Records, and Proceedings shall be proved, and the Effect thereof.

Section 2 The Citizens of each State shall be entitled to all Privileges and Immunities of Citizens in the several States.

A Person charged in any State with Treason, Felony, or other Crime, who shall flee from Justice, and be found in another State, shall on Demand of the executive Authority of the State from which he fled, be delivered up, to be removed to the State having Jurisdiction of the Crime.

No Person held to Service or Labour in one State, under the Laws thereof, escaping into another, shall, in Consequence of any Law or Regulation therein, be discharged from such Service or Labour, but shall be delivered up on Claim of the Party to whom such Service or Labour may be due.

Section 3. New States may be admitted by the Congress into this Union; but no new State shall be formed or erected within the Jurisdiction of any other State; nor any State be formed by the Junction of two or more States, or Parts of States, without the Consent of the Legislatures of the States concerned as well as of the Congress.

The Congress shall have Power to dispose of and make all needful Rules and Regulations respecting the Territory or other Property belonging to the United States; and nothing in this Constitution shall be so construed as to Prejudice any Claims of the United States, or of any particular State.

Section 4. The United States shall guarantee to every State in this Union a Republican Form of Government, and shall protect each of them against Invasion; and on Application of the Legislature, or of the Executive (when the Legislature cannot be convened) against domestic Violence.

ARTICLE V
Amending Procedures

The Congress, whenever two thirds of both Houses shall deem it necessary, shall propose Amendments to this Constitution, or, on the Application of the Legislatures of two thirds of the several States, shall call a Convention for proposing Amendments, which, in either Case, shall be valid to all Intents and Purposes, as Part of this Constitution, when ratified by the Legislatures of three fourths of the several States, or by Conventions in three fourths thereof, as the one or the other Mode of Ratification may be proposed by the Congress; Provided that no Amendment which may be made prior to the Year One thousand eight hundred and eight shall in any Manner affect the first and fourth Clauses in the Ninth Section of the first Article; and that no State, without its Consent, shall be deprived of its equal Suffrage in the Senate.

ARTICLE VI
Supremacy Clause

All Debts contracted and Engagements entered into, before the Adoption of this Constitution, shall be as valid against the United States under this Constitution, as under the Confederation.

The Constitution, and the Laws of the United States which shall be made in Pursuance thereof; and all Treaties made, or which shall be made, under the Authority of the United States, shall be the supreme Law of the Land; and the Judges in every State shall be bound thereby, any Thing in the Constitution or Laws of any State to the Contrary notwithstanding.

The Senators and Representatives before mentioned, and the Members of the several State Legislatures, and all executive and judicial Officers, both of the United States and of the several States, shall be bound by Oath or Affirmation, to support this Constitution; but no religious Test shall ever be required as a Qualification to any Office or public Trust under the United States.

ARTICLE VII
Ratifying the Constitution

The Ratification of the Conventions of nine States, shall be sufficient for the Establishment of this Constitution between the States so ratifying the Same.

Done in Convention by the Unanimous Consent of the States present the Seventeenth Day of September in the Year of our Lord one thousand seven hundred and Eighty seven and of the Independence of the United States of America the TwelfthIN WITNESS whereof We have hereunto subscribed our Names,

G$^{o.}$ Washington	Presid^{t}. and deputy from Virginia.
New Hampshire	John Langdon, Nicholas Gilman.
Massachusetts	Nathaniel Gorham, Rufus King.
Connecticut	Wm. Saml. Johnson, Roger Sherman.
New York	Alexander Hamilton.
New Jersey	Wil: Livingston, David Brearley, Wm. Paterson, Jona: Dayton.
Pennsylvania	B Franklin, Thomas Mifflin, Robt Morris, Geo. Clymer, Thos. FitzSimons, Jared Ingersoll, James Wilson, Gouv Morris.
Delaware	Geo: Read, Gunning Bedford jun, John Dickinson, Richard Bassett, Jaco: Broom.
Maryland	James McHenry, Dan of St Thos. Jenifer, Danl Carroll.
Virginia	John Blair–, James Madison Jr.
North Carolina	Wm. Blount, Rich'd Dobbs Spaight, Hu Williamson.
South Carolina	J. Rutledge, Charles Cotesworth Pinckney, Charles Pinckney, Pierce Butler.
Georgia	William Few, Abr Baldwin.

Attest: William Jackson, Secretary.

AMENDMENTS

[The first 10 Amendments, known as the Bill of Rights, were ratified on December 15, 1791.]

AMENDMENT I
No Religious Establishment; Freedom of Religion, Speech, Press, and Assembly

Congress shall make no law respecting an establishment of religion, or prohibiting the free exercise thereof; or abridging the freedom of speech, or of the press, or the right of the people peaceably to assemble, and to petition the Government for a redress of grievances.

AMENDMENT II
Right to Bear Arms

A well regulated Militia, being necessary to the security of a free State, the right of the people to keep and bear Arms, shall not be infringed.

AMENDMENT III
Quartering of Soldiers

No Soldier shall in time of peace be quartered in any house, without the consent of the Owner, nor in time of war, but in a manner to be prescribed by law.

AMENDMENT IV
Searches and Seizures

The right of the people to be secure in their persons, houses, papers, and effects, against unreasonable searches and seizures, shall not be violated, and no Warrants shall issue, but upon probable cause, supported by Oath or affirmation, and particularly describing the place to be searched and the persons or things to be seized.

AMENDMENT V
Grand Jury Indictments, Double Jeopardy, Self-Incrimination, Due Process, and Just Compensation

No person shall be held to answer for a capital, or otherwise infamous crime, unless on a presentiment or indictment of a Grand Jury, except in cases arising in the land or naval forces, or in the Militia, when in actual service in time of War or public danger, nor shall any person be subject for the same offence to be twice put in jeopardy of life or limb; nor shall be compelled in any criminal case to be a witness against himself, nor be deprived of life, liberty, or property, without due process of law; nor shall private property be taken for public use without just compensation.

AMENDMENT VI
Fair Trials

In all criminal prosecutions, the accused shall enjoy the right to a speedy and public trial, by an impartial jury of the State and district wherein the crime shall have been committed, which district shall have been previously ascertained by law, and to be informed of the nature and cause of the accusation; to be confronted with the witnesses against him; to have compusory process for obtaining witnesses in his favor, and to have the Assistance of Counsel for his defence.

AMENDMENT VII
Jury Trials

In Suits at common law, where the value in controversy shall exceed twenty dollars, the right of trial by jury shall be preserved, and no fact tried by a jury, shall be otherwise re-examined in any Court of the United States, than according to the rules of the common law.

AMENDMENT VIII
No Excessive Bail or Cruel and Unusual Punishment

Excessive bail shall not be required, nor excessive fines imposed, nor cruel and unusual punishments inflicted.

AMENDMENT IX
Not an Exhaustive List of Rights

The enumeration in the Constitution, of certain rights, shall not be construed to deny or disparage others retained by the people.

AMENDMENT X
Reserved Powers

The powers not delegated to the United States by the Constitution, nor prohibited by it to the States, are reserved to the States respectively, or to the people.

AMENDMENT XI
Suits against States

[Declared ratified January 8, 1798]

The Judicial power of the United States shall not be construed to extend to any suit in law or equity, commenced or prosecuted against one of the United States by Citizens of another State, or by Citizens or Subjects of any Foreign State.

AMENDMENT XII
Separate Ballots for President and Vice President

[Declared ratified September 25, 1804]

The Electors shall meet in their respective states and vote by ballot for President and Vice-President, one of whom, at least, shall not be an inhabitant of the same state with themselves; they shall name in their ballots the person voted for as President, and in distinct ballots the person voted for as Vice-President, and they shall make distinct lists of all persons voted for as President, and of all persons voted for as Vice-president, and of the number of votes for each, which lists they shall sign and certify, and transmit sealed to the seat of the government of the United States, directed to the President of the Senate;-The President of the Senate shall, in the presence of the Senate and House of Representatives, open all the certificates and the votes shall then be counted;- The person having the greatest number of votes for President, shall be the President, if such number be a majority of the whole number of Electors appointed; and if no person have such majority, then from the persons having the highest numbers not exceeding three on the list of those voted for as President, the House of Representatives shall choose immediately, by ballot, the President. But in choosing the President, the votes shall be taken by states, the representation from each state having one vote; a quorum for this purpose shall consist of a member or members from two-thirds of the states, and a majority of all the states shall be necessary to a

choice. And if the House of Representatives shall not choose a President whenever the right of the choice shall devolve upon them, before the fourth day of March next following, then the Vice-President shall act as President, as in the case of the death or other constitutional disability of the President. The person having the greatest number of votes as Vice-President, shall be the Vice-President, if such number be a majority of the whole number of Electors appointed, and if no person have a majority, then from the two highest numbers on the list, the Senate shall choose the Vice-President; a quorum for the purpose shall consist of two-thirds of the whole number of Senators, and a majority of the whole number shall be necessary to a choice. But no person constitutionally ineligible to the office of President shall be eligible to that of Vice-President of the United States.

AMENDMENT XIII
Abolition of Slavery

[Declared ratified December 18, 1865]

Section 1. Neither slavery nor involuntary servitude, except as a punishment for crime whereof the party shall have been duly convicted, shall exist within the United States, or any place subject to their jurisdiction.

Section 2. Congress shall have power to enforce this article by appropriate legislation.

AMENDMENT XIV
Citizenship, Due Process, and Equal Protection

[Declared ratified July 28, 1868]

Section 1. All persons born or naturalized in the United States, and subject to the jurisdiction thereof, are citizens of the United States and of the State wherein they reside. No State shall make or enforce any law which shall abridge the privileges or immunities of citizens of the United States; nor shall any State deprive any person of life, liberty, or property, without due process of law; nor deny to any person within its jurisdiction the equal protection of the laws.

Section 2. Representatives shall be apportioned among the several States according to their respective numbers, counting the whole number of persons in each State, excluding Indians not taxed.

But when the right to vote at any election for the choice of electors for President and Vice president of the United States, Representatives in Congress, the Executive and Judicial Officers of a State, or the members of the Legislature thereof, is denied to any of the male inhabitants of such state, being twenty-one years of age, and citizens of the United States, or in any way abridged, except for participation in rebellion, or other crime, the basis of representation therein shall be reduced in the proportion which the number of such male citizens shall bear to the whole number of male citizens twenty-one years of age in such State.

Section 3. No person shall be a Senator or Representative in Congress, or elector of President and Vice President, or hold any office, civil or military, under the United States, or under any State, who having previously taken an oath, as member of Congress, or as an officer of the United States, or as a member of any State legislature, or as an executive or judicial officer of any State, to support the Constitution of the United States, shall have engaged in insurrection or rebellion against the same, or given aid or comfort to the enemies thereof. But Congress may by a vote of two-thirds of each House, remove such disability.

Section 4. The validity of the public debt of the United States, authorized by law, including debts incurred for payment of pensions and bounties for services in suppressing insurrection or rebellion, shall not be questioned. But neither the United States nor any State shall assume or pay any debt obligation incurred in aid of insurrection or rebellion against the United States, or any claim for the loss or emancipation of any slave; but all such debts, obligations and claims shall be held illegal and void.

Section 5. The Congress shall have power to enforce, by appropriate legislation, the provisions of this article.

AMENDMENT XV
Voting Rights

[Declared ratified March 30, 1870]

Section 1. The right of citizens of the United States to vote shall not be denied or abridged by the United States or by any State on account of race, color, or previous condition of servitude.

Section 2. The Congress shall have power to enforce this article by appropriate legislation.

AMENDMENT XVI
Income Tax

[Declared ratified February 25, 1913]

The Congress shall have power to lay and collect taxes on incomes, from whatever source derived, without apportionment among the several States, and without regard to any census or enumeration.

AMENDMENT XVII
Direct Election of Senators

[Declared ratified May 31, 1913]

The Senate of the United States shall be composed of two Senators from each State, elected by the people thereof for six years; and each Senator shall have one vote. The electors in each State shall have the qualifications requisite for electors of the most numerous branch of the State legislatures.

When vacancies happen in the representation of any State in the Senate, the executive authority of such State shall issue writs of election to fill such vacancies: Provided, That the legislature of any State may empower the executive thereof to make temporary appointments until the people fill the vacancies by election as the legislature may direct.

This amendment shall not be so construed as to affect the election of term of any Senator chosen before it becomes valid as part of the Constitution.

AMENDMENT XVIII
Prohibition

[Declared ratified January 16, 1919]

Section 1. After one year from the ratification of this article the manufacture, sale, or transportation of intoxicating liquors within, the importation thereof into, or the exportation thereof from the United States and all territory subject to the jurisdiction thereof for beverage purposes is hereby prohibited.

Section 2. The Congress and the several States shall have concurrent power to enforce this article by appropriate legislation.

Section 3. This article shall be inoperative unless it shall have been ratified as an amendment to the Constitution by the legislatures of the several States, as provided in the Constitution, within seven years from the date of the submission hereof to the States by the Congress.

AMENDMENT XIX
Women's Suffrage

[Declared ratified August 26, 1920]

The right of citizens of the United States to vote shall not be denied or abridged by the United States or by any State on account of sex. Congress shall have power to enforce this article by appropriate legislation.

AMENDMENT XX
Lame Duck Amendment

[Declared ratified February 6, 1933]

Section 1. The terms of the President and Vice President shall end at noon on the 20th day of January, and the terms of Senators and Representatives at noon on the 3d of January, of the years in which such terms would have ended if this article had not been ratified; and the terms of their successors shall then begin.

Section 2. The Congress shall assemble at least once in every year, and such meeting shall begin at noon on the 3d day of January, unless they shall be law appoint a different day.

Section 3. If, at the time fixed for the beginning of the term of the President, the President elect shall have died, the Vice President elect shall become President. If a President shall not have been chosen before the time fixed for the beginning of his term, or if the President elect shall have failed to qualify, the Vice President elect shall act as President until a President shall have qualified; and the Congress may by law provide for the case wherein neither a President elect nor a Vice President elect shall have qualified, declaring who shall then act as President, or the manner in which one who is to act shall be selected, and such person

shall act accordingly until a President or Vice President shall have qualified.

Section 4. The Congress may by law provide for the case of death of any of the persons from whom the House of Representatives may choose a President whenever the right of choice shall have devolved upon them, and for the case of the death of any of the persons from whom the Senate may choose a Vice President whenever the right of choice shall have devolved upon them.

Section 5. Sections 1 and 2 shall take effect on the 15th day of October following the ratification of this article.

Section 6. This article shall be inoperative unless it shall have been ratified as an amendment to the Constitution by the legislatures of three-fourths of the several States within seven years from the date of its submission.

AMENDMENT XXI
Repeal of Prohibition

[Declared ratified December 5, 1933]

Section 1. The eighteenth article of amendment to the Constitution of the United States is hereby repealed.

Section 2. The transportation or importation into any State, Territory, or possession of the United States for delivery or use therein of intoxicating liquors, in violation of the laws thereof, is hereby prohibited.

Section 3. This article shall be inoperative unless it shall have been ratified as an amendment to the Constitution by conventions in the several States, as provided in the Constitution, within seven years from the date of the submission hereof to the States by the Congress.

AMENDMENT XXII
Two-Term Limit on President

[Declared ratified March 1, 1951]

Section 1. No person shall be elected to the office of the President more than twice, and no person who has held the office of President, or acted as President for more than two years of a term to which some other person was elected President shall be elected to the office of the President more than once. But this Article shall not apply to any person holding the office of President when this Article was proposed by the Congress, and shall not prevent any person who may be holding the office of President, or acting as President, during the term within which this Article becomes operative from holding the office of President, or acting as President, during the remainder of such term.

Section 2. This article shall be inoperative unless it shall have been ratified as an amendment to the Constitution by the legislatures of three-fourths of the several States within seven years from the date of its submission to the States by the Congress.

AMENDMENT XXIII
Electors for the District of Columbia

[Declared ratified April 3, 1961]

Section 1. The District constituting the seat of Government of the United States shall appoint in such manner as the Congress may direct:

A number of electors of President and Vice President equal to the whole number of Senators and Representatives in Congress to which the District would be entitled if it were a State, but in no event more than the least populous State; they shall be in addition to those appointed by the States, but they shall be considered, for the purposes of the election of President and Vice President, to be electors appointed by a State; and they shall meet in the District and perform such duties as provided by the twelfth article of amendment.

Section 2. The Congress shall have power to enforce this article by appropriate legislation.

AMENDMENT XXIV
Anti-Poll Tax Amendment

[Declared ratified January 23, 1964]

Section 1. The right of citizens of the United States to vote in any primary or other election for President or Vice President, for electors for President or Vice President, or for Senator or Representative in Congress, shall not be denied or abridged by the United States or any State by reason of failure to pay any poll tax or other tax.

Section 2. The Congress shall have power to enforce this article by appropriate legislation.

AMENDMENT XXV
Presidential Disability

[Ratified February 10, 1967]

Section 1. In case of the removal of the President from office or of his death or resignation, the Vice President shall become President.

Section 2. Whenever there is a vacancy in the office of the Vice President, the President shall nominate a Vice President, who shall take office upon confirmation by a majority vote of both Houses of Congress.

Section 3. Whenever the President transmits to the President pro tempore of the Senate and the Speaker of the House of Representatives his written declaration that he is unable to discharge the powers and duties of his office, and until he transmits to them a written declaration to the contrary, such powers and duties shall be discharged by the Vice President as Acting President.

Section 4. Whenever the Vice President and a majority of either the principal officers of the executive departments or of such other body as Congress may by law provide, transmit to the president pro tempore of the Senate and the Speaker of the House of Representatives their written declaration that the President is unable to discharge the powers and duties of his office, the Vice president shall immediately assume the powers and duties of the office as Acting President.

Thereafter, when the President transmits to the President pro tempore of the Senate and the Speaker of the House of Representatives his written declaration that no inability exists, he shall resume the powers and duties of his office unless the Vice President and a majority of either the principal officers of the executive department or of such other body as Congress may by law provide, transmit within four days to the President pro tempore of the Senate and the Speaker of the House of Representatives their written declaration that the President is unable to discharge the powers and duties of his office. Thereupon Congress shall decide the issue, assembling within forty-eight hours for that purpose if not in session. If the Congress, within twenty-one days after receipt of the latter written declaration, or, if Congress is required to assemble, determines by two-thirds vote of both Houses that the President is unable to discharge the powers and duties of his office, the Vice President shall continue to discharge the same as Acting President; otherwise, the President shall resume the powers and duties of his office.

AMENDMENT XXVI
Eighteen-Year-Old Vote

[Ratified July 1, 1971]

Section 1. The right of citizens of the United States, who are eighteen years of age or older, to vote shall not be denied or abridged by the United States or by any State on account of age.

Section 2. The Congress shall have the power to enforce this article by appropriate legislation.

AMENDMENT XXVII
Congressional Pay Raise

[Ratified May 7, 1992]

No law, varying the compensation for the services of the Senators and Representatives, shall take effect until an election of Representatives shall have intervened.

The Federalist No. 47

To the People of the State of New York:

HAVING reviewed the general form of the proposed government and the general mass of power allotted to it, I proceed to examine the particular structure of this government, and the distribution of this mass of power among its constituent parts.

One of the principal objections inculcated by the more respectable adversaries to the Constitution, is its supposed violation of the political maxim, that the legislative, executive, and judiciary departments ought to be separate and distinct. In the structure of the federal government, no regard, it is said, seems to have been paid to this essential precaution in favor of liberty. The several departments of power are distributed and blended in such a manner as at once to destroy all symmetry and beauty of form, and to expose some of the essential parts of the edifice to the danger of being crushed by the disproportionate weight of other parts.

No political truth is certainly of greater intrinsic value, or is stamped with the authority of more enlightened patrons of liberty, than that on which the objection is founded. The accumulation of all powers, legislative, executive, and judiciary, in the same hands, whether of one, a few, or many, and whether hereditary, self-appointed, or elective, may justly be pronounced the very definition of tyranny. Were the federal Constitution, therefore, really chargeable with the accumulation of power, or with a mixture of powers, having a dangerous tendency to such an accumulation, no further arguments would be necessary to inspire a universal reprobation of the system. I persuade myself, however, that it will be made apparent to every one, that the charge cannot be supported, and that the maxim on which it relies has been totally misconceived and misapplied. In order to form correct ideas on this important subject, it will be proper to investigate the sense in which the preservation of liberty requires that the three great departments of power should be separate and distinct.

The oracle who is always consulted and cited on this subject is the celebrated Montesquieu. If he be not the author of this invaluable precept in the science of politics, he has the merit at least of displaying and recommending it most effectually to the attention of mankind. Let us endeavor, in the first place, to ascertain his meaning on this point.

The British Constitution was to Montesquieu what Homer has been to the didactic writers on epic poetry. As the latter have considered the work of the immortal bard as the perfect model from which the principles and rules of the epic art were to be drawn, and by which all similar works were to be judged, so this great political critic appears to have viewed the Constitution of England as the standard, or to use his own expression, as the mirror of political liberty; and to have delivered, in the form of elementary truths, the several characteristic principles of that particular system. That we may be sure, then, not to mistake his meaning in this case, let us recur to the source from which the maxim was drawn.

On the slightest view of the British Constitution, we must perceive that the legislative, executive, and judiciary departments are by no means totally separate and distinct from each other. The executive magistrate forms an integral part of the legislative authority. He alone has the prerogative of making treaties with foreign sovereigns, which, when made, have, under certain limitations, the force of legislative acts. All the members of the judiciary department are appointed by him, can be removed by him on the address of the two Houses of Parliament, and form, when he pleases to consult them, one of his constitutional councils. One branch of the legislative department forms also a great constitutional council to the executive chief, as, on another hand, it is the sole depositary of judicial power in cases of impeachment, and is invested with the supreme appellate jurisdiction in all other cases. The judges, again, are so far connected with the legislative department as often to attend and participate in its deliberations, though not admitted to a legislative vote.

From these facts, by which Montesquieu was guided, it may clearly be inferred that, in saying "There can be no liberty where the legislative and executive powers are united in the same person, or body of magistrates," or, "if the power of judging be not separated from the legislative and executive powers," he did not mean that these departments ought to have no *partial agency* in, or no *control* over, the acts of each other. His meaning, as his own words import, and still more conclusively as illustrated by the example in his eye, can amount to no more than this, that where the *whole* power of one department is exercised by the same hands which possess the *whole* power of another department, the fundamental principles of a free constitution are subverted. This would have been the case in the constitution examined by him, if the king, who is the sole executive magistrate, had possessed also the complete legislative power, or the supreme administration of justice; or if the entire legislative body had possessed the supreme judiciary, or the supreme executive authority. This, however, is not among the vices of that constitution. The magistrate in whom the whole executive power resides cannot of himself make a law, though he can put a negative on every law; nor administer justice in person, though he has the appointment of those who do administer it. The judges can exercise no executive prerogative, though they are shoots from the executive stock; nor any legislative function, though they may be advised with by the legislative councils. The entire legislature can perform no judiciary act, though by the joint act of two of its branches the judges may be removed from their offices, and though one of its branches is possessed of the judicial power in the last resort. The entire legislature, again, can exercise no executive prerogative, though one of its branches constitutes the supreme executive magistracy, and another, on the impeachment of a third, can try and condemn all the subordinate officers in the executive department.

The reasons on which Montesquieu grounds his maxim are a further demonstration of his meaning. "When the legislative and executive powers are united in the same person or body," says he, "there can be no liberty, because apprehensions may arise lest *the same* monarch or senate should *enact* tyrannical laws to *execute* them in a tyrannical manner." Again: "Were the power of judging joined with the legislative, the life and liberty of the subject would be exposed to arbitrary control, for *the judge* would then be *the legislator.* Were it joined to the executive power, *the judge* might behave with all the violence of *an oppressor.*" Some of these reasons are more fully explained in other passages; but briefly stated as they are here, they sufficiently establish the meaning which we have put on this celebrated maxim of this celebrated author.

If we look into the constitutions of the several States, we find that, notwithstanding the emphatical and, in some instances, the unqualified terms in which this axiom has been laid down, there is not a single instance in which the several departments of power have been kept absolutely separate and distinct. New Hampshire, whose constitution was the last formed, seems to have been fully aware of the impossibility and inexpediency of avoiding any mixture whatever of these departments, and has qualified the doctrine by declaring "that the legislative, executive, and judiciary powers ought to be kept as separate from, and independent of, each other *as the nature of a free government will admit; or as is consistent with that chain of connection that binds the whole fabric of the constitution in one indissoluble bond of unity and amity.*" Her constitution accordingly mixes these departments in several respects. The Senate, which is a branch of the legislative department, is also a judicial tribunal for the trial of impeachments. The President, who is the head of the executive department, is the presiding member also of the Senate; and, besides an equal vote in all cases, has a casting vote in case of a tie. The executive head is himself eventually elective every year by the legislative department, and his council is every year chosen by and from the members of the same department. Several of the officers of state are also appointed by the legislature. And the members of the judiciary department are appointed by the executive department.

The constitution of Massachusetts has observed a sufficient though less pointed caution, in expressing this fundamental article of liberty. It declares "that the legislative departments shall never exercise the executive and judicial powers, or either of them; the executive shall never exercise the legislative and judicial powers, or either of them; the judicial shall never exercise the legislative and executive powers, or either of them." This declaration corresponds precisely with the doctrine of Montesquieu, as it has been explained, and is not in a single point violated by the plan of the convention. It goes no farther than to prohibit any one of the entire departments from exercising the powers of another department. In the very Constitution to which it is prefixed, a partial mixture of powers has been admitted. The executive magistrate has a qualified negative on the legislative body, and the Senate, which is a part of the legislature, is a court of impeachment for members both of the executive and judiciary departments. The members of the judiciary department, again, are appointable by the executive department, and removable by the same authority on the address of the two legislative branches. Lastly, a number of the officers of government are annually appointed by the legislative department. As the appointment to offices, particularly executive offices, is in its nature an executive function, the compilers of the Constitution have, in this last point at least, violated the rule established by themselves.

I pass over the constitutions of Rhode Island and Connecticut, because they were formed prior to the Revolution, and even before the principle under examination had become an object of political attention.

The constitution of New York contains no declaration on this subject; but appears very clearly to have been framed with an eye to the danger of improperly blending the different departments. It gives, nevertheless, to the executive magistrate, a partial control over the legislative department; and, what is more, gives a like control to the judiciary department; and even blends the executive and judiciary departments in the exercise of this control. In its council of appointment members of the legislative are associated with the executive authority, in the appointment of officers, both executive and judiciary. And its court for the trial of impeachments and correction of errors is to consist of one branch of the legislature and the principal members of the judiciary department.

The constitution of New Jersey has blended the different powers of government more than any of the preceding. The governor, who is the executive magistrate, is appointed by the legislature; is chancellor and ordinary, or surrogate of the State; is a member of the Supreme Court of Appeals, and president, with a casting vote, of one of the legislative branches. The same legislative branch acts again as executive council of the governor, and with him constitutes the Court of Appeals. The members of the judiciary department are appointed by the legislative department and removable by one branch of it, on the impeachment of the other.

According to the constitution of Pennsylvania, the president, who is the head of the executive department, is annually elected by a vote in which the legislative department predominates. In conjunction with an executive council, he appoints the members of the judiciary department, and forms a court of impeachment for trial of all officers, judiciary as well as executive. The judges of the Supreme Court and justices of the peace seem also to be removable by the legislature; and the executive power of pardoning in certain cases, to be referred to the same department. The members of the executive council are made ex-officio justices of peace throughout the State.

In Delaware, the chief executive magistrate is annually elected by the legislative department. The speakers of the two legislative branches are vice-presidents in the executive department. The executive chief, with six others, appointed, three by each of the legislative branches, constitutes the Supreme Court of Appeals; he is joined with the legislative department in the appointment of the other judges. Throughout the States, it appears that the members of the legislature may at the same time be justices of the peace; in this State, the members of one branch of it are ex-officio justices of the peace; as are also the members of the executive council. The principal officers of the executive department are appointed by the legislative; and one branch of the latter forms a court of impeachments. All officers may be removed on address of the legislature.

Maryland has adopted the maxim in the most unqualified terms; declaring that the legislative, executive, and judicial powers of government ought to be forever separate and distinct from each other. Her constitution, notwithstanding, makes the executive magistrate appointable by the legislative department; and the members of the judiciary by the executive department.

The language of Virginia is still more pointed on this subject. Her constitution declares, "that the legislative, executive, and judiciary departments shall be separate and distinct; so that neither exercise the powers properly belonging to the other; nor shall any person exercise the powers of more than one of them at the same time, except that the justices of county courts shall be eligible to either House of Assembly." Yet we find not only this express exception, with respect to the members of the inferior courts, but that the chief magistrate, with his executive council, are appointable by the legislature; that two members of the latter are triennially displaced at the pleasure of the legislature; and that all the principal offices, both executive and judiciary, are filled by the same department. The executive prerogative of pardon, also, is in one case vested in the legislative department.

The constitution of North Carolina, which declares "that the legislative, executive, and supreme judicial powers of government ought to be forever separate and distinct from each other," refers, at the same time, to the legislative department, the appointment not only of the executive chief, but all the principal officers within both that and the judiciary department.

In South Carolina, the constitution makes the executive magistracy eligible by the legislative department. It gives to the latter, also, the appointment of the members of the judiciary department, including even justices of the peace and sheriffs; and the appointment of officers in the executive department, down to captains in the army and navy of the State.

In the constitution of Georgia, where it is declared "that the legislative, executive, and judiciary departments shall be separate and distinct, so that neither exercise the powers properly belonging to the other," we find that the executive department is to be filled by appointments of the legislature; and the executive prerogative of pardon to be finally exercised by the same authority. Even justices of the peace are to be appointed by the legislature.

In citing these cases, in which the legislative, executive, and judiciary departments have not been kept totally separate and distinct, I wish not to be regarded as an advocate for the particular organizations of the several State governments. I am fully aware that among the many excellent principles which they exemplify, they carry strong marks of the haste, and still stronger of the inexperience, under which they were framed. It is but too obvious that in some instances the fundamental principle under consideration has been violated by too great a mixture, and even an actual consolidation, of the different powers; and that in no instance has a competent provision been made for maintaining in practice the separation delineated on paper. What I have wished to evince is, that the charge brought against the proposed Constitution, of violating the sacred maxim of free government, is warranted neither by the real meaning annexed to that maxim by its author, nor by the sense in which it has hitherto been understood in America. This interesting subject will be resumed in the ensuing paper.

PUBLIUS

The Federalist No. 51

To The People Of The State Of New York:

To what expedient then shall we finally resort for maintaining in practice the necessary partition of power among the several departments, as laid down in the constitution? The only answer that can be given is, that as all these exterior provisions are found to be inadequate, the defect must be supplied, by so contriving the interior structure of the government, as that its several constituent parts may, by their mutual relations, be the means of keeping each other in their proper places. Without presuming to undertake a full development of this important idea, I will hazard a few general observations, which may perhaps place it in a clearer light, and enable us to form a more correct judgment of the principles and structure of the government planned by the convention.

In order to lay a due foundation for that separate and distinct exercise of the different powers of government, which to a certain extent, is admitted on all hands to be essential to the preservation of liberty, it is evident that each department should have a will of its own; and consequently should be so constituted, that the members of each should have as little agency as possible in the appointment of the members of the others. Were this principle rigorously adhered to, it would require that all the appointments for the supreme executive, legislative, and judiciary magistracies, should be drawn from the same fountain of authority, the people, through channels, having no communication whatever with one another. Perhaps such a plan of constructing the several departments would be less difficult in practice than it may in contemplation appear. Some difficulties however, and some additional expense, would attend the execution of it. Some deviations therefore from the principle must be admitted. In the constitution of the judiciary department in particular, it might be inexpedient to insist rigorously on the principle; first, because peculiar qualifications being essential in the members, the primary consideration ought to be to select that mode of choice, which best secures these qualifications; secondly, because the permanent tenure by which the appointments are held in that department, must soon destroy all sense of dependence on the authority conferring them.

It is equally evident that the members of each department should be as little dependent as possible on those of the others, for the emoluments annexed to their offices. Were the executive magistrate, or the judges, not independent of the legislature in this particular, their independence in every other would be merely nominal.

But the great security against a gradual concentration of the several powers in the same department, consists in giving to those who administer each department, the necessary constitutional means, and personal motives, to resist encroachments of the others. The provision for defense must in this, as in all other cases, be made commensurate to the danger of attack. Ambition must be made to counteract ambition. The interest of the man must be connected with the constitutional rights of the place. It may be a reflection on human nature, that such devices should be necessary to control the abuses of government. But what is government itself but the greatest of all reflections on human nature? If men were angels, no government would be necessary. If angels were to govern men, neither external nor internal controls on government would be necessary. In framing a government which is to be administered by men over men, the great difficulty lies in this: You must first enable the government to control the governed; and in the next place, oblige it to control itself. A dependence on the people is no doubt the primary control on the government; but experience has taught mankind the necessity of auxiliary precautions.

This policy of supplying by opposite and rival interests, the defect of better motives, might be traced through the whole system of human affairs, private as well as public. We see it particularly displayed in all the subordinate distributions of power; where the constant aim is to divide and arrange the several offices in such a manner as that each may be a check on the other; that the private interest of every individual, may be a sentinel over the public rights. These inventions of prudence cannot be less requisite in the distribution of the supreme powers of the state.

But it is not possible to give to each department an equal power of self defense. In republican government the legislative authority, necessarily, predominates. The remedy for this inconveniency is, to divide the legislature into different branches; and to render them by different modes of election, and different principles of action, as little connected with each other, as the nature of their common functions, and their common dependence on the society, will admit. It may even be necessary to guard against dangerous encroachments by still further precautions. As the weight of the legislative authority requires that it should be thus divided, the weakness of the executive may require, on the other hand, that it should be fortified. An absolute negative, on the legislature, appears at first view to be the natural defense with which the executive magistrate should be armed. But perhaps it would be neither altogether safe, nor alone sufficient. On ordinary occasions, it might not be exerted with the requisite firmness; and on extraordinary occasions, it might be perfidiously abused. May not this defect of an absolute negative be supplied, by some qualified connection between this weaker department, and the weaker branch of the stronger department, by which the latter may be led to support the constitutional rights of the former, without being too much detached from the rights of its own department?

If the principles on which these observations are founded be just, as I persuade myself they are, and they be applied as a criterion, to the several state constitutions, and to the federal constitution, it will be found, that if the latter does not perfectly correspond with them, the former are infinitely less able to bear such a test.

There are moreover two considerations particularly applicable to the federal system of America, which place that system in a very interesting point of view.

First. In a single republic, all the power surrendered by the people, is submitted to the administration of a single government; and usurpations are guarded against by a division of the government into distinct and separate departments. In the compound republic of America, the power surrendered by the people, is first divided between two distinct governments, and then the portion allotted to each, subdivided among distinct and separate departments. Hence a double security arises to the rights of the people. The different governments will control each other; at the same time that each will be controlled by itself.

Second. It is of great importance in a republic, not only to guard the society against the oppression of its rulers; but to guard one part of the society against the injustice of the other part. Different interests necessarily exist in different classes of citizens. If a majority be united by a common interest, the rights of the minority will be insecure. There are but two methods of providing against this evil: The one by creating a will in the community independent of the majority, that is, of the society itself, the other by comprehending in the society so many separate descriptions of citizens, as will render an unjust combination of a majority of the whole, very improbable, if not impracticable. The first method prevails in all governments possessing an hereditary or self-appointed authority. This at best is but a precarious security; because a power independent of the society may as well espouse the unjust views of the major, as the rightful interests, of the minor party, and may possibly be turned against both parties. The second method will be exemplified in the federal republic of the United States. While all authority in it will be derived from and dependent on the society, the society itself will be broken into so many parts, interests and classes of citizens, that the rights of individuals or of the minority, will be in little danger from interested combinations of the majority. In a free government, the security for civil rights must be the same as for religious rights. It consists in the one case in the multiplicity of interests, and in the other, in the multiplicity of sects. The degree of security in both cases will depend on the number of interests and sects; and this may be presumed to depend on the extent of country and number of people comprehended under the same government. This view of the subject must particularly recommend a proper federal system to all the sincere and considerate friends of republican government: Since it shows that in exact proportion as the territory of the union may be formed into more circumscribed confederacies or states, oppressive combinations of a majority will be facilitated, the best security under the republican form, for the rights of every class of citizens, will be diminished; and consequently, the stability and independence of some member of the government, the only other security, must be proportionally increased. Justice is the end of government. It is the end of civil society. It ever has been, and ever will be pursued, until it be obtained, or until liberty be lost in the pursuit. In a society under the forms of which the stronger faction can readily unite and oppress the weaker, anarchy may as truly be said to reign, as in a state of nature where the weaker individual is not secured against the violence of the stronger: And as in the latter state even the stronger individuals are prompted by the uncertainty of their condition, to submit to a government which may protect the weak as well as themselves: So in the former state, will the more powerful factions or parties be gradually induced by a like motive, to wish for a government which will protect all parties, the weaker as well as the more powerful. It can be little doubted, that if the state of Rhode Island was separated from the confederacy, and left to itself, the insecurity of rights under the popular form of government within such narrow limits, would be displayed by such reiterated oppressions of factious majorities, that some power altogether independent of the people would soon be called for by the voice of the very factions whose misrule had proved the necessity of it. In the extended republic of the United States, and among the great variety of interests, parties and sects which it embraces, a coalition of a majority of the whole society could seldom take place on any other principles than those of justice and the general good; and there being thus less danger to a minor from the will of the major party, there must be less pretext also, to provide for the security of the former, by iroducing into the government a will not dependent on the latter; or in other words, a will independent of the society itself. It is no less certain than it is important, notwithstanding the contrary opinions which have been entertained, that the larger the society, provided it lie within a practicable sphere, the more duly capable it will be of self government. And happily for the *republican cause,* the practicable sphere may be carried to a very great extent, by a judicious modification and mixture of the *federal principle.*

PUBLIUS

References

Abraham, Henry J. 1991. *The Judiciary.* 7th ed. Boston: Allyn & Bacon.

Abraham, Henry J. 1993. "The Bill of Rights after 200 Years: Some Unfinished Business." *Extensions,* Spring. Carl Albert Center, University of Oklahoma.

Abraham, Henry J. 1993a. *The Judicial Process.* 6th ed. New York: Oxford University Press.

Adams, Gordon. 1982. *The Iron Triangle.* Washington, DC: Council on Economic Priorities.

Advisory Commission on Intergovernmental Relations (ACIR). *Federal Grant Programs in Fiscal Year 1992: Their Numbers, Sizes, and Fragmentation Indexes in Historical Perspective.* Washington, DC: U.S. Government Printing Office.

Alexander, D. S. 1916. *History and Procedures of the House of Representatives.* Boston: Houghton Mifflin.

Alexander, Herbert E. 1983. *Financing the 1980 Election.* Lexington, MA: Lexington Books.

Alexander, Herbert E., and J. A. Schwartz. 1993. "Laboratories of Reform: The States' Experience with Public Funding of Elections." *The National Voter* 43(1): 9–11.

Ambrose, Stephen E. 1993. *Rise to Globalism: American Foreign Policy since 1938.* 7th ed. New York: Penguin Books.

Aristotle. *Politics,* Book I. 1947. Ed. Richard P. McKeon. New York: Random House Modern Library.

Arnold, R. Douglas. 1979. *Congress and the Bureaucracy.* New Haven, CT: Yale University Press.

Auletta, Ken. 1995. "Pay Per Views." *The New Yorker,* June 5.

Avery, M. J. 1988. *The Demobilization of American Voters.* Greenwood, IL: Greenwood Press.

Ayres, B. D. Jr. 1994. "Big Drop in Drunken Driving." *San Francisco Chronicle,* May 22.

Babcock, Charles R. 1994. "The Overrated Power of PACs." *Washington Post National Weekly Edition,* June 20–26.

Bach, Stanley, and Steven S. Smith. 1988. *Managing Uncertainty in the House of Representatives.* Washington, DC: Brookings Institution.

Bachrach, P., and M. Baratz. 1962. "The Two Faces of Power." *American Political Science Review* 56: 947–52.

Bailey, Thomas A., and David M. Kennedy. 1994. *The American Pageant.* 10th ed. Lexington, MA: D. C. Heath.

Baln, R. A. 1989. "A Slap at the 'Hidden-Hand' Presidency." *Washington Post,* July 6.

Bauer, Raymond A. 1968. "The Study of Policy Formation." In *The Study of Policy Formation,* eds. Raymond A. Bauer and K. I. Gergen. New York: Free Press.

Baum, Lawrence. 1992. *The Supreme Court.* 4th ed. Washington, DC: Congressional Quarterly Press.

Beeman, Richard, S. Botein, and E. C. Carter II, eds. 1987. *Beyond Confederation: Origins of the Constitution and American National Identity.* Chapel Hill: University of North Carolina Press.

Benson, Peter L., and Dorothy L. Williams. 1982. *Religion on Capitol Hill: Myths and Realities.* San Francisco: Harper & Row.

Bentley, Arthur F. 1908. *The Process of Government.* Chicago: University of Chicago Press.

Berman, D. 1964. *In Congress Assembled.* New York: Macmillan.

Bibby, John F., Cornelius Cotter, J. L. Gibson, and R. Huckshorn. 1983. "Parties in State Politics." In *Politics in the American States,* 4th ed., eds. Virginia Gray, Herbert Jacob, and Kenneth N. Vines. Boston: Little, Brown.

Bickel, Alexander M. 1962. *The Least Dangerous Branch.* Indianapolis: Bobbs-Merrill.

Biden, Joseph. 1987. *Advice and Consent: The Right and Duty of the Senate to Protect the Integrity of the Supreme Court.* Congressional Record, S10522–29, July 23.

Birnbaum, Jeffrey H. 1992. *The Lobbyists: How Influence Peddlers Get Their Way in Washington.* New York: Times Books.

Blakesley, L. 1995. *Presidential Leadership from Eisenhower to Clinton.* Chicago: Nelson-Hall.

Bonafede, D. 1978. "Carter Sounds Retreat fro 'Cabinet' Government. *National Journal* 1852–57.

Brademas, John. 1986. *Washington, D. C., to Washington Square.* New York: Weidenfeld & Nicolson.

Brady, H. E., Sidney Verba, and Kay L. Schlozman. 1995. "Beyond SES: A Resource Model of Political Participation." *American Political Science Review* 89(2): 271–94.

Brams, S. J., and P. C. Fishburn. 1982. *Approval Voting.* Cambridge, MA: Berkhausen Boston.

Bronson, Edward J. 1971. "On the Conviction Proneness and Representativeness of the Death-Qualified Jury." *University of Colorado Law Review* 42: 3–42.

Bronson, Edward J. 1979. "The Exclusion of Scrupled Jurors in Capital Cases." California State University, Chico, School of Behavioral and Social Science.

Bronson, Edward J. 1989. "The Effectiveness of 'Voir Dire' in Discovering Prejudice in High-Publicity Cases: An Archival Study of the Minimization Effect." Presented at the annual meeting of the Law and Society Association, Madison, WI.

Bronson, Edward J., and Robert S. Ross. 1991. "Justice and the High-Publicity Criminal Case: Does the Change of Venue Work?" Presented at the annual meeting of the American Political Science Association, Washington, DC.

Brown, Richard D. 1987. "Shays' Rebellion and the Ratification of the Federal Constitution in Massachusetts." In *Beyond Confederation,* eds. Richard Beeman, S. Botein, and E. C. Carter II. Chapel Hill: University of North Carolina Press.

Bullock, Charles S. III. 1982. "The Inexact Science of Congressional Redistricting." *Political Science* 15:431–38

Burns, James M. 1983. *The American Experiment: The Vineyard of Liberty.* New York: Vintage Books.

Burns, James M., Jack W. Peltason, Thomas E. Cronin, and David B. Magleby. 1993. *Government by the People.* 15th ed. Englewood Cliffs, NJ: Prentice Hall.

Cahn, R., and P. Cahn. 1987. "Disputed Territory." *tional Parks,* 28–33, May/June.

1995. "Revolving Door between Con-obbyists Spins on Yearlong Cooling-ll Street Journal,* January 24.

The Adams-Jefferson Letters. North Carolina Press.

er Broker: Robert Moses New York: Knopf.

ald Stidham. 1991. *The* Washington, DC: Con-Press.

Causey, Michael. 1991. "The Federal Diary." *Washington Post,* July 14.

Chapman, W. 1975. "Food Stamps: Too Little and Too Few." *The Progressive* 39: 24–27.

Chubb, J. M., W. H. Flanigan, and N. H. Zingale. 1990. *Partisan Realignment.* Boulder, CO: Westview Press.

Clancy, M., and Michael J. Robinson. 1985. "General Election Coverage." *Public Opinion* 7:49–54.

Clark, T. B. 1980. "The Public and the Private Sectors—The Old Distinctions Grow Fuzzy." *National Journal,* 99–104, January 19.

Clymer, Adam. 1995. "Congress Passes Bill to Disclose Lobbyists' Role." *New York Times,* November 30.

Cobb, Roger W., and Charles D. Elder. 1983. *Participation in American Politics.* 2nd ed. Boston: Allyn & Bacon.

Cohen, Richard M., and Jules Witcover. 1973. *A Heartbeat Away: The Investigation and Resignation of Vice President Spiro T. Agnew.* New York: Viking Press.

Commons, John R. 1950. *Economics of Collective Action.* New York: Macmillan.

Conlin, Joseph R. 1993. *The Morrow Book of Quotations in American History.* New York: William Morrow.

Cony, A. 1992. "Over $100 Million in Subsidies for State Grain, Cotton Growers." *Sacramento Bee,* October 10.

Cook, Terrence E. 1989. *Making Laws and Making News.* Washington, DC: Brookings Institution.

Cortner, Richard C. 1970. *The Apportionment Cases.* Knoxville: University of Tennessee Press.

Corwin, Edwin S. 1957. *The President: Office and Powers.* 4th ed. New York: New York University Press.

Crigler, A. N., M. Just, and W. Russell Neuman. 1990. "News Patterns, Public Perceptions, and Learning." Presented at the annual meeting of the American Political Science Association, San Francisco.

Cronin, Thomas E. 1970a. "Everybody Believes in Democracy until He Gets to the White House." *Law and Contemporary Problems,* Summer.

Cronin, Thomas E. 1970. "The Textbook Presidency and Political Science." Presented at the 66th annual meeting of the American Political Science Association.

Cronin, Thomas E. 1980. *The State of the Presidency.* 2nd ed. New York: Crowell.

Cushman, J. H. Jr. 1992. "$400 Million Paid by S & L Auditors, Settling U.S. Case." *New York Times,* November 24.

Cushman, R. A. 1995. "Clean Water." *New York Times.*

Dahl, Ronald A. 1981. *Democracy in the United States.* 2nd ed. Chicago: Rand McNally.

Danziger, Jeff. 1994. "No Decorations, No Perforations." *San Francisco Chronicle,* June 10, sec. A.

Davidson, Roger H. 1992. "From Monopoly to Management: Changing Patterns of Committee Deliberation." In *The Postreform Congress,* ed. Roger H. Davidson. New York: St. Martin's Press.

Davidson, Roger H., and Walter J. Oleszek. 1996. *Congress and Its Members.* 4th ed. Washington, DC: Congressional Quarterly Press.

Davis, David Brion. 1990. *Revolutions: Reflections on American Equality and Foreign Liberations.* Cambridge, MA: Harvard University Press.

Davis, R. 1992. *The Press and American Politics: The New Mediator.* New York: Longman.

Dearborn, Philip M. 1994. "The State-Local Fiscal Outlook from a Federal Perspective." *Intergovernmental Perspective* 20(2): 20–23.

Denitzer, S. 1995. "Age 51, and Ready for Change." *U.S. News and World Report,* June 19.

Dexter, Louis A. 1969. *How Organizations Are Represented in Washington.* Indianapolis: Bobbs-Merrill.

Dexter, Louis A. 1971. "The Job of the Congressman." In *Readings on Congress,* ed. Raymond E. Wolfinger. Englewood Cliffs, NJ: Prentice Hall.

Dexter, Louis A. 1972. "Some New Initiatives." In *American Business and Public Policy: The Politics of Foreign Trade,* eds. Raymond A. Bauer, Ithiel de Sola Pool, and Louis A. Dexter. 2nd ed. New York: Atherton.

Dionne, E. J. Jr. 1991. *Why Americans Hate Politics.* New York: Simon & Schuster.

Dolbeare, Kenneth M., and Linda Metcalf. 1987. "The Dark Side of the Constitution." In *The Case against the Constitution,* eds. J. F. Manley and Kenneth M. Dolbeare. Armonk, NY: M. E. Sharpe.

Drucker, Peter F. 1969. *The Age of Discontinuity.* New York: Harper & Row.

Duverger, Maurice. 1963. *Political Parties.* New York: Wiley.

Dworkin, Ronald. 1977. *Taking Rights Seriously.* Cambridge, MA: Harvard University Press.

Dworkin, Ronald. 1992. "The Center Holds!" *New York Review of Books,* August 13.

Dye, Thomas R. 1990. *American Federalism: Competition among Governments.* Lexington, MA: Lexington Books.

Dye, Thomas R. 1994. *Politics in States and Communities.* 8th ed. Englewood Cliffs, NJ: Prentice Hall.

Dye, Thomas R., and L. Harmon Zeigler. 1993. *The Irony of Democracy: An Uncommon Introduction to American Politics.* 9th ed. Belmont, CA: Wadsworth.

Easton, David. 1953. *The Political System.* New York: Knopf.

Ebeling, J. S., et al. 1988. "Political Participation in California: Final Report to the Office of Research, California State Senate." Survey Research Center, California State University, Chico.

Edelman, Jacob M. 1971. *Politics as Symbolic Action.* Chicago: Markham.

Edelman, Jacob M. 1988. *Constructing the Political Spectacle.* Chicago: University of Chicago Press.

Elazar, Daniel. 1994. *The American Mosaic.* Boulder, CO: Westview Press.

Elkins, Stanley, and Eric McKitrick. 1961. "The Founding Fathers: Young Men of the Revolution." *Political Science Quarterly* 76:181–216.

Engelberg, S. 1995. "Farm Aid to Chicago? Miami? Study Hits an Inviting Target." *New York Times,* March 16.

Epstein, Leon D. 1987. *Political Parties in the American Mold.* Madison: University of Wisconsin.

Epstein, Leon D., J. A. Segal, Harold J. Spaeth, and Thomas G. Walker. 1994. *The Supreme Court Compendium: Data, Decisions and Developments.* Washington, DC: Congressional Quarterly Press.

Eyestone, Robert. 1978. *From Social Issues to Public Policy.* New York: Wiley.

Farquharson, R. 1969. *Theory of Voting.* New Haven, CT: Yale University Press.

Fassell, P. 1990. "The Tax-Rise Question." *New York Times National Edition,* May 10, B14.

Fenno, Richard F. 1966. *The Power of the Purse: Appropriations Politics in Congress.* Boston: Little, Brown.

Fenno, Richard F. 1981. *Home Style.* Boston: Little, Brown.

Fenno, Richard F. 1994. "Senators and Citizens: A View from the Campaign Trail." *Extensions,* University of Oklahoma.

Fiorina, Morris J. 1989. *Congress: Keystone to the Washington Establishment.* 2nd ed. New Haven, CT: Yale University Press.

Fiorina, Morris J. 1992. *Divided Government.* New York: Macmillan.

Fisher, Louis. 1985. "Judicial Misjudgments about the Lawmaking Process: The Legislative Veto Case." *Public Administration Review* 45:705–12.

Fisher, Louis. 1988. *Constitutional Dialogues.* Princeton, NJ: Princeton University Press.

Fisher, Louis. 1990. "Separation of Powers: Interpretation outside the Courts." *Pepperdine Law Review* 18(1): 57–93.

Fisher, Louis. 1993. *The Politics of Shared Power.* 3rd ed. Washington, DC: Congressional Quarterly Press.

Fisher, M. 1989. "Ralph Nader's Paradise Lost." *Washington Post Magazine,* July 23.

Ford, P. L. 1892–1899. *The Writings of Thomas Jefferson* (10 vols.).

Fowler, F. C. 1994. "Basic Values Underlying the Works of Four Major Neoliberals: Implications for Federal Education Policy." Presented at the annual meeting of the American Education Research Association, April, New Orleans, LA.

Franck, Thomas M., and Edward Weisband. 1979. *Foreign Policy by Congress.* New York: Oxford University Press.

Frohlich, Norman, and Joe A. Oppenheimer. 1978. *Modern Political Economy.* Englewood Cliffs, NJ: Prentice Hall.

Froman, Lewis A. Jr. 1967. *The Congressional Process.* Boston: Little, Brown.

Fuller, Lon L. 1948. "The Case of the Speluncean Explorers." *Harvard Law Review* 62:616–45.

Galbraith, John Kenneth. 1990. "The Ultimate Scandal." *New York Review of Books,* January 18.

Gaus, John. 1947. *Reflections on Public Administration.* Tuscaloosa: University of Alabama Press.

Gerth, H., and C. Wright Mills, eds. 1946. *From Max Weber: Essays in Sociology.* New York: Oxford University Press.

Gilmour, Robert S., and A. A. Halley. 1994. *Who Makes Public Policy: The Power Struggle for Control between Congress and the Executive.* Chatham, NJ: Chatham House.

Gladwell, M. 1990. "In Voting, As in Life, There May Be No Objective Reality." *Washington Post National Weekly Edition,* June 11–17, 12.

Glennon, Michael J. 1984. "The War Powers Resolution Ten Years Later: More Politics than Law." *American Journal of International Law* 78:571–81.

Goldenberg, E. N., and M. W. Traugott. 1984. *Campaigning for Congress.* Washington, DC: Congressional Quarterly Press.

Goldman, Sheldon, and Thomas P. Jahnige. 1985. *The Federal Courts as a Political System.* New York: HarperCollins.

Goodwin, G. Jr. 1970. *The Little Legislatures: Committees of Congress.* Amherst: University of Massachusetts Press.

Gordon, George J., and M. E. Milakovich. 1995. *Public Administration in America.* 5th ed. New York: St. Martin's Press.

Goulden, Joseph C. 1970. *The Superlawyers: The Small and Powerful World of the Great Washington Law Firms.* New York: Weybright & Talley.

Gowing, Nik. 1994. "Lights, Camera, Atrocities." *Guardian Weekly,* August 14.

Graber, Doris A. 1988. *Processing the News: How People Tame the Information Tide.* 2nd ed. New York: Longman.

Graber, Doris A. 1993. *Mass Media and American Politics.* 4th ed. Washington, DC: Congressional Quarterly Press.

Graber, Doris A. 1994. *Media Power in Politics.* 3rd ed. Washington, DC: Congressional Quarterly Press.

Greenberg, S. B. 1971. *The Quality of Mercy.* New York: Atheneum.

Greenberg, Stanley B. 1995. *Middle Class Dreams: The Politics and Power of the New American Majority.* New York: Times Books.

Greve, F. 1992. "Some 'Waste' Tough to Dump." *Sacramento Bee,* November 27, sec. A.

Grosscup, Beau. 1991. *The New Politics of Terrorism.* Far Hills, NJ: New Horizons Press.

Grummand, J. A. 1989. *The Demobilization of the American Voter.* Ann Arbor: University of Michigan Press.

Gunther, R. 1989. "Electoral Laws, Party Systems, and Elites: The Case of Spain." *American Political Science Review* 83(3): 835–58.

Haldeman, H. R. 1994. *Inside the Nixon White House.* New York: Putnam.

Hall, Donald R. 1969. *Cooperative Lobbying: The Power of Pressure.* Tucson: University of Arizona Press.

Hamilton, Alexander, James Madison, and John Jay. 1961. *The Federalist* papers. New York: New American Library.

Hammond, S. W., A. G. Stevens, and D. P. Mulhollan. 1983. "Congressional Caucuses." In *Interest Group Politics,* eds. Burdett A. Loomis and Allan J. Cigler. Washington, DC: Congressional Quarterly Press.

Hardin, Garret J. 1971. "The Tragedy of the Commons." In *Introductory Readings in American Government,* eds. Robert S. Ross and W. C. Mitchell. Chicago: Markham.

Hardin, Garret J. 1974. "Lifeboat Ethics: The Case against Helping the Poor." *Psychology Today* 8: 38–43, September.

Harris, Fred R. 1993. *Deadlock of Decision.* New York: Oxford University Press.

Havemann, J. 1987. "The Government Has Been Sorely Tested and Found Wanting." *Washington Post National Weekly Edition,* March 23.

Hayes, Michael T. 1992. *Incrementalism and Public Policy.* New York: Longman.

Heclo, Hugh H. 1972. "Policy Analysis." *British Journal of Political Science* 2:84–85, January.

Heclo, Hugh H. 1990. "Issue Networks and the Executive Establishment." In *The New American Political System,* 2nd ed., ed. Anthony S. King. Washington, DC: American Enterprise Institute.

Herman, Edward S., and Noam Chomsky. 1988. *Manufacturing Consent: The Political Economy of the Mass Media.* New York: Pantheon Books.

Hero, R. E. 1989. "The U.S. Congress and American Federalism: Are 'Subnational' Governments Protected?" *Western Political Quarterly* 42:93–106.

Hill, L. B. ed. 1992. *The State of Public Bureaucracy.* Armonk, NY: M. E. Sharpe.

Hilts, Philip J. 1995. "Cigarette Makers Debated the Risks They Denied." *New York Times,* June 16.

Hinkley, B. 1988. *Stability and Change in Congress.* 4th ed. New York: Harper & Row.

Hodge, D., and S. Freeman. 1992. *The Political Tales and Truth of Mark Twain.* San Rafael, CA: New World Library.

Holcombe, Randall G. 1986. *An Economic Analysis of Democracy.* Carbondale: Illinois University Press.

Holmstrom, D. 1995. "The 'Quiet Strength' of Rosa Parks." *Christian Science Monitor,* January 13.

Huitt, Ralph K. 1965. "The Internal Distribution of Influence: The Senate." In *The Congress and America's Future,* ed. David B. Truman. Englewood Cliffs, NJ: Prentice Hall.

Huntington, Samuel P. 1965. "Congressional Responses to the Twentieth Century." In *The Congress and America's Future,* ed. David B. Truman. Englewood Cliffs, NJ: Prentice Hall.

Ignatius, D. 1990. "Speak Softly and Carry a Big Agenda." *Washington Post National Weekly Edition,* January 1–7, 24.

Irvine, W. B. 1987. "'Brutus': An Anti-Federalist Hero." *Wall Street Journal,* February 6.

Iyengar, S. 1991. *News That Matters: Television and American Opinion.* Chicago: University of Chicago Press.

Iyengar, S., and D. R. Kinder. 1991. *Is Anyone Responsible? How Television Frames Political Issues.* Chicago: University of Chicago Press.

Jackson, B. 1990. *Broken Promises: Why the Federal Election Commission Failed.* New York: Priority Press.

Jacobs, Lawrence R., et al. 1994. "Public Opinion, Institutions, and Policy Making." *PS: Political Science and Politics,* March.

Jacobson, Gary C. 1987. *The Politics of Congressional Elections.* 2nd ed. Boston: Little, Brown.

Jacobson, Gary C. 1990. *The Electoral Origins of Divided Government: Competition in U.S. House Elections, 1946–1988.* Boulder, CO: Westview Press.

Jacobson, Gary C., and Samuel Kernell. 1981. *Strategy and Choice in Congressional Elections.* New Haven, CT: Yale University Press.

Jennings, M. Kent, and Richard G. Niemi. 1975. "Continuity and Change in Political Orienta-tion: A Longitudinal Study of Two Generations." *American Political Science Review* 69:1316–35.

Johannes, John R. 1972. *Policy Innovation in Congress.* Morristown, NJ: General Learning Press.

Johnson, Richard Tanner. 1974. *Managing the White House: An Intimate Study of the Presidency.* New York: Harper & Row.

Kaufman, Herbert. 1976. *Are Government Organizations Immortal?* Washington, DC: Brookings Institution.

Kernell, Samuel. 1993. *Going Public: New Strategies of Presidential Leadership.* 2nd ed. Washington, DC: Congressional Quarterly Press.

Kernell, Samuel, and Samuel L. Popkin. 1986. *Chief of Staff: Twenty-Five Years of Managing the Presidency.* Berkeley: University of California Press.

Kerwin, Cornelius M. 1994. *Rulemaking: How Government Agencies Write Law and Make Policy.* Washington, DC: Congressional Quarterly Press.

Ketcham, R., ed. 1986. *The Anti-Federalist Papers and the Constitutional Convention Debates.* New York: New American Library.

Key, V. O. 1955. "A Theory of Critical Elections." *Journal of Politics* 17:3–18, February.

Key, V. O. 1958. *Politics, Parties, and Pressure Groups.* 4th ed. New York: Crowell.

Killian, Johnny H., and G. A. Costello. 1996. *The Constitution of the United States: Analysis and Interpretation, 1995 Supplement.* Washington, DC: U.S. Government Printing Office.

Kingdon, J. W. 1984. *Agendas, Alternatives, and Public Policies.* Boston: Little, Brown.

Kolbert, E. 1992. "A Loss Spurs Clinton to Seek Consensus." *New York Times,* September 28.

Kurland, P., and R. Lerner, eds. 1987. *The Founders' Constitution.* Chicago: University of Chicago Press.

Kurtz, Howard. 1995. "Tuning Out the News." *Washington Post National Weekly Edition,* May 29–June 4, 6–7.

Kwitny, Jonathan. 1992. "All the President's Friends." *Village Voice,* October 20.

Ladd, Everett Carll Jr. 1982. *Where Have All the Voters Gone?* 2nd ed. New York: W. W. Norton.

Ladd, Everett Carll Jr. 1986. "Alignment and Realignment: Where Are All the Voters Going?" *Ladd Report #3.* New York: W. W. Norton.

LaFraniere, S. 1992. "FBI Settles Dispute with Black Agents." *Washington Post,* March 20.

Leighley, J. E., and J. Nagler. 1992. "Socioeconomic Class Bias in Turnout, 1964–1988: The Voters Remain the Same." *American Political Science Review* 86(3): 725–49.

Levine, M. A. 1995. *Presidential Campaigns and Elections: Issues and Images in the Media Age.* 2nd ed. Itasca, IL: F. E. Peacock.

Levy, M. B. 1988. *Political Thought in America.* 2nd ed. Chicago: Dorsey.

Liebert, L. 1989. "Cranston Suffers Constituents' Wrath." *San Francisco Chronicle,* November 16.

Linsky, Martin. 1986. *Impact: How the Press Affects Federal Policy Making.* New York: W. W. Norton.

Lippmann, Walter. 1922. *Public Opinion.* New York: Harcourt Brace.

Lipset, Seymour Martin. 1990. *Continental Divide: The Values and Institutions of the United States and Canada.* London: Routledge.

Loomis, Burdett A., and Allan J. Cigler. 1983. "Introduction: The Changing Nature of Interest Group Politics." In *Interest Group Politics,* eds. Allan J. Cigler and Burdett A. Loomis. Washington, DC: Congressional Quarterly Press.

Lowi, Theodore J. 1965. *Legislative Politics U.S.A.* 2nd ed. Boston: Little, Brown.

Lowi, Theodore J. 1985. *The Personal President: Power Invested, Promise Unfulfilled.* Ithaca, NY: Cornell University Press.

Lutz, D. S. 1991. "The State Foundations of the U.S. Bill of Rights." *Intergovernmental Perspectives* 17(4): 6–16.

Magleby, David B., and Candace J. Nelson. 1990. *The Money Chase: Congressional Campaign Finance Reform.* Washington, DC: Brookings Institution.

Maisel, L. Sandy. 1990. *The Parties Respond: Changes in the American Party System.* Boulder, CO: Westview Press.

Malbin, Michael J. 1980. *Unelected Representatives: Congressional Staff and the Future of Representative Government.* New York: Basic Books.

Manheim, Jarol B. 1991. *All the People, All the Time.* Armonk, NY: M. E. Sharpe.

Manley, J. F. 1968. "Congressional Staffs and Public Policy-Making." *Journal of Politics* 30:1046–67, November.

Manning, Richard. 1995. "Vanishing Grasslands." *New York Times,* March 23.

Maraniss, David. 1983. "Back Home Again in Indiana." *Washington Post National Weekly Edition,* November 14.

Massachusetts School of Law *Journal.* 1995. "Law Clerks: The Transformation of the Judiciary." Spring.

Mayhew, David R. 1991. *Divided We Govern.* New Haven, CT: Yale University Press.

McCloskey, Robert G. 1994. *The American Supreme Court.* 2nd ed. Chicago: University of Chicago Press.

McClosky, H., and A. Brill. 1983. *Dimensions of Tolerance.* New York: Basic Books.

McCormick, J. M. 1992. *American Foreign Policy and Process.* 2nd ed. Itasca, IL: F. W. Peacock.

McKinley, Albert E. 1905. *Suffrage Franchise in the Thirteen English Colonies in America.* Philadelphia: University of Pennsylvania.

Mead, Lawrence M. 1995. "Public Policy: Vision, Potential, Limits." *Policy Currents,* February, 1–4.

Meier, Kenneth J. 1987. *Politics and the Bureaucracy.* 2nd ed. Belmont, CA: Wadsworth.

Mikva, Abner J. 1983. "How Well Does Congress Support and Defend the Constitution?" *North Carolina Law Review* 61:587–610.

Milbrath, Lester. 1982. *Political Participation.* Lanham, MD: University Press of America.

Miller, Warren E., and Donald E. Stokes. 1963. "Constituency Influence in Congress." *American Political Science Review* 57:45–56.

Mitchell, William C. 1962. *The American Polity.* New York: Free Press.

Mitchell, William C. 1971. *Public Choice in America: An Introduction to American Government.* Chicago: Markham.

Morin, Richard. 1994. "An Attitude Problem: Anti-Semitism Is Decreasing But Remains Persistent, A Study Shows." *Washington Post National Weekly Edition,* June 20–26, 37.

Morris, R. 1989. *Richard Milhous Nixon: The Rise of an American Politician.* New York: Henry Holt.

Moynihan, Daniel P. 1969. *Maximum Feasible Misunderstanding.* New York: Macmillan.

Murphy, Walter F. 1964. *Elements of Judicial Power.* Chicago: University of Chicago Press.

Nagel, J. H. 1987. *Participation.* Englewood Cliffs, NJ: Prentice Hall.

Nathan, Richard P. 1983. *The Administrative Presidency.* New York: Wiley.

Nathan, Richard P. 1975. *The Plot That Failed: Nixon and the Administrative Presidency.* New York: Wiley.

Nathan, Richard P. 1993. *Turning Promises into Performance: The Management Challenge of Implementing Workfare.* New York: Columbia University Press.

Neuman, W. Russell. 1986. *The Paradox of Mass Participation.* Cambridge, MA: Harvard University Press.

Neustadt, Richard E. 1954. "Presidency and Legislation: The Growth of Central Clearance." *American Political Science Review* 48:641–71.

Neustadt, Richard E. 1990. *Presidential Power and the Modern Presidents.* New York: Basic Books.

Newcomb, Theodore M., K. E. Koenig, R. Flack, and D. P. Warwick. 1967. *Persistence and Change: Ben-*

nington College and Its Students after 25 Years. New York: Wiley.

Nixon, Richard M. 1978. *Memoirs.* Vol. 2. New York: Warner Books.

O'Brien, David M. 1993. *Storm Center.* New York: W. W. Norton.

Oleszek, Walter J. 1992. "House-Senate Relations: A Perspective on Bicameralism." In *The Postreform Congress,* ed. Roger H. Davidson. New York: St. Martin's Press.

Oleszek, Walter J. 1996. *Congressional Procedures and the Policy Process.* 5th ed. Washington, DC: Congressional Quarterly Press.

Ornstein, Norman J., Thomas E. Mann, and Michael J. Malbin. 1994. *Vital Statistics on Congress 1993-94.* Washington, DC: Congressional Quarterly Press.

Orren, G. R., and Nelson W. Polsby. 1987. *Media and Momentum.* Chatham, NJ: Chatham House.

Osborne, David, and Ted Gaebler. 1992. *Reinventing Government.* Lexington, MA: Addison-Wesley.

Ott, D. J., and A. F. Ott. 1977. *Federal Budget Policy.* 2nd ed. Washington, DC: Brookings Institution.

Padover, Saul K. 1969. *Thomas Jefferson.* New York: Greenwood Press.

Palsey, J. L. 1987. "Green Thumbs: The PiK and Roll and Other Scams from the Farm Belt." *Washington Monthly* 19, September, 11-16.

Parenti, M. 1983. *Democracy for the Few.* 4th ed. New York: St. Martin's Press.

Parker, Glenn R., and Roger H. Davidson. 1979. "Why Do Americans Love Their Congressman So Much More Than Their Congress?" *Legislative Studies Quarterly* 4:53-62, February.

Patterson, Thomas E. 1993. *Out of Order.* New York: Knopf.

Pearlstein, S. 1995. "The Rich Get Richer and. . . ." *Washington Post National Weekly Edition,* June 12-18, 6-7.

Peirce, Neal R. 1993. *Citistates: How Urban America Can Prosper in a Competitive World.* Washington, DC: Seven Locks Press.

Persinos, J. 1994. "Has the Christian Right Taken over the Republican Party?" *Campaigns and Elections,* September.

Peters, B. Guy. 1993. *American Public Policy.* 3rd ed. Chatham, NJ: Chatham House.

Pfiffner, J. P. 1988. *The Strategic Presidency: Hitting the Ground Running.* New York: St. Martin's Press.

Pfiffner, J. P. 1994. *The Modern Presidency.* New York: St. Martin's Press.

Phillips, K. 1992. "Crashing the Money Club: The Populist Challenge to 'Borderless' Economics." *Washington Post,* July 5.

Pizzo, Steven, Mary Fricker, and Paul Muolo. 1989. *Inside Job: The Looting of the Savings and Loans.* New York: McGraw-Hill.

Platt, Suzy, ed. 1992. *Respectfully Quoted: A Dictionary of Quotations from the Library of Congress.* Washington, DC: Congressional Quarterly Press.

Pois, Joseph. 1979. *Watchdog on the Potomac.* Washington, DC: University Press of America.

Polsby, Nelson W. 1977. *Congress and the Presidency.* 3rd ed. Englewood Cliffs, NJ: Prentice Hall.

Polsby, Nelson W., and Aaron Wildavsky. 1992. *Presidential Elections.* 8th ed. New York: Free Press.

Pomper, Gerald. 1980. *Elections in America.* 2nd ed. New York: Longman.

Posner, B. G., and L. R. Rothstein. 1994. "Reinventing the Business of Government: An Interview with Change Catalyst David Osborne." *Harvard Business Review,* May-June.

Postman, Neil. 1992. *Technopoly: The Surrender of Culture to Technology.* New York: Knopf.

Price, Charles M. 1989. "Attack of the Radio Talk Show Hosts." *California Journal,* September.

Price, Charles M., and Charles G. Bell. 1996. *California Government Today: Politics of Reform.* 5th ed. Belmont, CA: Wadsworth.

Prichard, Edward F., and Archibald MacLeish, eds. 1930. *Law and Politics.* New York: Harcourt Brace.

Pusey, Merlo J. 1951. *Charles Evans Hughes.* New York: Macmillan.

Quirk, Paul J. 1992. "Structures and Performance: An Evaluation." In *The Postreform Congress,* ed. Roger H. Davidson. New York: St. Martin's Press.

Rae, Douglas W. 1967. *The Political Consequences of Election Laws.* New Haven, CT: Yale University Press.

Reagan, Michael D., and John G. Sanzone. 1981. *The New Federalism.* 2nd ed. New York: Oxford University Press.

Reedy, George E. 1970. *The Twilight of the Presidency.* New York: World Publishing.

Reid, T. R. 1980. *Congressional Odyssey.* San Francisco: W. H. Freeman.

Reisner, Marc. 1986. *Cadillac Desert.* New York: Free Press.

Reston, James. 1986. Editorial. *New York Times,* May 21.

Reuben, R. C. 1992. "The High Court Drama behind *Roe v. Wade.*" *Sacramento Bee,* August 30.

Richardson, Richard J., and Kenneth N. Vines. 1970. *The Politics of the Federal Courts.* Boston: Little, Brown.

Riker, William H. 1964. *Federalism.* Boston: Little, Brown.

Riker, William H. 1986. *The Art of Political Manipulation.* New Haven, CT: Yale University Press.

Riordan, William L. 1963. *Plunkett of Tammany Hall.* New York: E. P. Dutton.

Ripley, Randall B., and G. A. Franklin. 1991. *Congress, the Bureaucracy, and Public Policy.* 5th ed. Belmont, CA: Wadsworth.

Robinson, J. P. 1972. "Perceived Bias in the 1968 Vote: Can the Media Affect Behavior after All?" *Journalism Quarterly* 49:245–55.

Robinson, J. P., and J. A. Fleishman. 1988. "Report: Ideological Identification." *Public Opinion Quarterly* 52(1): 134–45.

Robinson, Michael J. 1986. "An Absence of Malice: Young People and the Press." *Public Opinion* 7:43–47.

Roche, John Pearson. 1961. "The Founding Fathers: A Reform Caucus in Action." *American Political Science Review* 55:799–816.

Rochefort, D. A., and Roger W. Cobb. 1994. *The Politics of Problem Definition.* Lawrence: University Press of Kansas.

Rosenheim, D. 1986. "An Army of Lobbyists Besieges Tax Reformers." *San Francisco Chronicle,* August 13.

Rosenstone, Steven J., Roy L. Behr, and Edward H. Lazarus. 1984. *Third Parties in America.* Princeton, NJ: Princeton University Press.

Rosenthal, Alan. 1993. *The Third House.* Washington, DC: Congressional Quarterly Press.

Ross, Robert S. 1987. *Perspectives on Local Government in California.* Belmont, CA: Star.

Rossiter, Clinton. 1960. *Parties and Politics in America.* Ithaca, NY: Cornell University Press.

Rourke, Francis E. 1987. *Bureaucracy, Politics and Public Policy.* 4th ed. Boston: Little, Brown.

Rourke, John T. 1996. *International Politics on the World Stage.* 5th ed. Guilford, CT: Brown & Benchmark.

Sabato, L. J. 1985. *PAC Power.* New York: W. W. Norton.

Sach, K. 1992. "New York Court Voids Searches Allowed by U.S." *New York Times,* April 3.

Saffell, David C. 1993. *State and Local Government: Politics and Public Policies.* 5th ed. New York: McGraw-Hill.

Salisbury, R. H. 1984. "Interest Representation: The Dominance of Institutions." *American Political Science Review* 78:64–76.

Sanzone, John G. 1989. "Issues in Economic Development: Regional Economic Development in the New Economy." University Center for Economic Development and Planning, California State University, Chico.

Sanzone, John G. 1994. "Regional Economic Development in the New Economy." University Center for Economic Development and Planning, California State University, Chico.

Schattschneider, E. E. 1960. *The Semisovereign People.* New York: Holt, Rinehart & Winston.

Schiller, Bradley R. 1992. "Filling in the Blanks of a Bush Tax Cut." *Washington Post National Weekly Edition,* September 7–14.

Schlesinger, Joseph A. 1985. "The New American Political Party." *American Political Science Review* 79:1152–69.

Schneider, William. 1987. "When the Candidate Must Quit." *Los Angeles Times,* September 27.

Seidman, Harold. 1970. *Politics, Position and Power.* New York: Oxford University Press.

Seligman, Lester G. 1956. "Presidential Leadership: The Inner Circle and Institutionalization." *Journal of Politics* 18:410–26.

Shannon, J. 1989. "Competitive Federalism: Three Driving Forces." Intergovernmental Perspective 15(4): 17–18.

Shuman, H. E. 1992. *Politics and the Budget: The Struggle between the President and the Congress.* 3rd ed. Englewood Cliffs, NJ: Prentice Hall.

Siegel, Beatrice. 1992. *The Year They Walked: Rosa Parks and the Montgomery Bus Boycott.* New York: Four Winds Press.

Sinclair, Barbara A. 1989. *The Transformation of the Senate.* Baltimore: Johns Hopkins Press.

Sinclair, Barbara A. 1992. "House Majority Party Leadership in an Era of Legislative Constraint." In *The Postreform Congress,* ed. Roger H. Davidson. New York: St. Martin's Press.

Smith, Steven S. 1992. "The Senate in the Postreform Era." In *The Postreform Congress,* ed. Roger H. Davidson. New York: St. Martin's Press.

Smith, Steven S., and Christopher J. Deering. 1990. *Committees in Congress.* 2nd ed. Washington, DC: Congressional Quarterly Press.

Sorensen, Theodore. 1975. *Watchmen in the Night.* Cambridge, MA: MIT Press.

Spiro, P., and D. Mirvish. 1989. "Whose No-Fault Is It Anyway?" *Washington Monthly,* October.

Stanley, Harold W., and Richard G. Niemi. 1994. *Vital Statistics on American Politics.* 4th ed. Washington, DC: Congressional Quarterly Press.

Stern, Philip M. 1992. *Still the Best Congress Money Can Buy.* Washington, DC: Regnery Gateway.

Stewart, William E. 1988. *Understanding Politics.* Novato, CA: Chandler & Sharp.

Stockman, David J. 1986. *The Triumph of Politics.* New York: Harper & Row.

Storing, Herbert J. 1981. *What the Anti-Federalists Were For.* Chicago: University of Chicago Press.

Stouffer, S. A. 1955. *Communism, Conformity and Civil Liberties.* Garden City, NY: Doubleday.

Strom, G. S., and B. S. Rundquist. 1977. "A Revised Theory of Winning in House-Senate Conferences." *American Political Science Review* 71: 448–53.

Sullivan, J. L., J. E. Pierson, and G. E. Marcus. 1979. "Political Intolerance: The Illusion of Progress." *Psychology Today* 12, February.

Sullivan, R. R. 1970. "The Role of the Presidency in Shaping Lower-Level Policymaking Processes." *Polity* 3:201–21.

Sundquist, James L. 1969. *Making Federalism Work.* Washington, DC: Brookings Institution.

Sutherland, Arthur E. 1965. *Constitutionalism in America.* New York: Blaisdell.

Szatmary, David P. 1980. *Shays' Rebellion: The Making of an Agrarian Insurrection.* Amherst: University of Massachusetts.

Thomas, Michael M. 1991. "The Greatest American Shambles." *New York Review of Books,* January 31.

Thomas, S. 1994. *How Women Legislate.* New York: Oxford University Press.

Thompson, Michael, Richard Ellis, and Aaron Wildavsky. 1990. *Cultural Theory.* Boulder, CO: Westview Press.

Thompson, R. E. 1974. *Revenue Sharing: A New Era in Federalism.* Washington, DC: U.S. Government Printing Office.

Tocqueville, Alexis de. 1956. *Democracy in America.* New York: New American Library.

Truman, David B. 1951. *The Governmental Process.* New York: Knopf.

Truman, David B. 1959. *The Congressional Party.* New York: Wiley.

Verba, Sidney, N. Nie, and J. Kim. 1978. *Participation and Political Equality.* New York: Cambridge University Press.

Vertz, S. L., J. P. Frendreis, and B. R. Weingast. 1987. "Nationalization of the Electorate in the United States." *American Political Science Review* 81: 961–72.

Viciano, F. 1995. "Berlusconi Can Keep His Media Empire, Italian Voters Decide." *San Francisco Chronicle,* June 12.

Waste, Robert J. 1989. *The Ecology of City Policymaking.* New York: Oxford University Press.

Wayne, S. J. 1992. *The Road to the White House.* 4th ed. New York: St. Martin's Press.

Weingast, B. R. 1989. "Floor Behavior in the U.S. Congress: Committee Power under the Open Rule." *American Political Science Review* 83(3): 795–815.

Westin, T. E. 1973. "The Constituent Needs Help: Casework in the House of Representatives." In *To Be a Congressman: The Promise and the Power,* eds. S. Groennings and J. P. Hawley.

Wheare, Kenneth Clinton. 1966. *Modern Constitutions.* New York: Oxford University Press.

White, Theodore H. 1982. *America in Search of Itself: The Making of the President, 1956–80.* New York: Harper & Row.

Whitesides, T. 1972. *The Investigation of Ralph Nader: General Motors v. One Determined Man.* New York: Arbor House.

Wildavsky, Aaron. 1979. "The Two Presidencies." In *Perspectives on the Presidency,* ed. Aaron Wildavsky. Boston: Little, Brown.

Wildavsky, Aaron. 1987. "Choosing Preferences by Constructing Institutions: A Cultural Theory of Preference Formation." *American Political Science Review* 81(1): 3–21.

Wills, Garry. 1992. *Lincoln at Gettysburg: The Words That Remade America.* New York: Simon & Schuster.

Wilson, Woodrow. (1885) 1956. *Congressional Government.* New York: Meridian.

Winter, W. O. 1981. *The Urban Policy.* 2nd ed. New York: McGraw-Hill.

Wittenberg, Ernest, and Elisabeth Wittenberg. 1989. *How to Win in Washington.* Cambridge, MA: Basil Blackwell.

Wolamin, T. R. 1974. "Committee Seniority and the Choice of House Subcommittee Chairman, 80th–91st Congresses." *Journal of Politics* 36: 687–702.

Wolfinger, Raymond A. 1992. "Point of View." *Chronicle of Higher Education,* October 14.

Wolfinger, Raymond A., and Steven J. Rosenstone. 1980. *Who Votes?* New Haven, CT: Yale University Press.

Wolpe, Bruce C. 1990. *Lobbying Congress: How the System Works.* Washington, DC: Congressional Quarterly Press.

Wood, Gordon S. 1990. "Americans and Revolutionaries." *New York Review of Books,* September 27.

Woodward, Bob. 1987. *Veil: The Secret Wars of the CIA, 1981–1987.* New York: Simon & Schuster.

Woodward, Bob. 1994. *The Agenda: Inside the Clinton White House.* New York: Simon & Schuster.

Woodward, Bob, and S. Armstrong. 1979. *The Brethren.* New York: Simon & Schuster.

Wright, Peter. 1987. *Spycatcher.* New York: Viking.

Zeigler, L. Harmon, and G. Wayne Peak. 1972. *Interest Groups in American Society.* 2nd ed. Englewood Cliffs, NJ: Prentice Hall.

Zeigler, L. Harmon, and G. Wayne Peak. 1974. *Governing American Schools.* North Scituate, MA: Duxbury.

Zimmerman, Joseph F. 1991. *Federal Preempt* *The Silent Revolution.* Ames: Iowa State Ur sity Press.

Supreme Court Case Index

General Index

Page numbers in boldface indicate glossary terms.